ALSO BY HOWARD SOUNES:

Down the Highway: The Life of Bob Dylan
Charles Bukowski: Locked in the Arms of a Crazy Life
Bukowski in Pictures
Seventies
Heist
Fred & Rose
The Wicked Game

To hear a playlist of music by Paul McCartney, chosen by the author
and discussed in *Fab*, please visit www.fabplaylist.co.uk

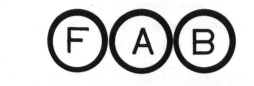

FAB

AN INTIMATE LIFE OF

Paul McCartney

HOWARD SOUNES

HarperCollins*Publishers*

Howard Sounes asserts the moral right to be
identified as the author of this work

A catalogue record of this book is
available from the British Library

ISBN 978-0-00-723706-7 (hardback)
ISBN 978-0-00-723705-0 (paperback)

Printed and bound in Great Britain by
Clays Ltd, St Ives plc

Mixed Sources
Product group from well-managed
forests and other controlled sources
www.fsc.org Cert no. SW-COC-001806
© 1996 Forest Stewardship Council
FSC

FSC is a non-profit international organisation established to promote the
responsible management of the world's forests. Products carrying the FSC
label are independently certified to assure consumers that they come
from forests that are managed to meet the social, economic and
ecological needs of present and future generations.

Find out more about HarperCollins and the environment at
www.harpercollins.co.uk/green

CONTENTS

PART ONE: WITH THE BEATLES

PART TWO: AFTER THE BEATLES

PART ONE

WITH THE BEATLES

1

A LIVERPOOL FAMILY

AT THE START OF THE ROAD

'They may not look much,' Paul would say in adult life of his Liverpool family, having been virtually everywhere and seen virtually everything there is to see in this world. 'They're just very ordinary people, but by God they've got something – common sense, in the truest sense of the word. I've met lots of people, [but] I have never met anyone as interesting, or as fascinating, or as wise, as my Liverpool family.'

Liverpool is not only the city in which Paul McCartney was born; it is the place in which he is rooted, the wellspring of the Beatles' music and everything he has done since that fabulous group disbanded. Originally a small inlet or 'pool' on the River Mersey, near its confluence with the Irish Sea, 210 miles north of London, Liverpool was founded in 1207, coming to significance in the seventeenth century as a slave trade port, because Liverpool faces the Americas. After the abolition of slavery, the city continued to thrive due to other, diverse forms of trade, with magnificent new docks constructed along its riverine waterfront, and ocean liners steaming daily to and from the United States. As money poured into Liverpool, its citizens erected a mini-Manhattan by the docks, featuring the Royal Liver Building, an exuberant skyscraper topped by outlandish copper birds that have become emblematic of this confident, slightly eccentric city.

For the best part of three hundred years men and women flocked to Liverpool for work, mostly on and around the docks. Liverpool is and has always been a predominantly white, working-class city, its people made up of and descended in large part from the working poor of surrounding Lancashire, plus Irish, Scots and Welsh incomers. Their regional accents combined in an urban melting pot to create Scouse, the distinctive Liverpool voice, with its singular, rather harsh pronunciation and its own witty argot, Scousers typically living hugger-mugger in the city's narrow terrace streets built from the local rosy-red sandstone and brick.

Red is the colour of Liverpool – the red of its buildings, its left-wing politics and Liverpool Football Club. As the city has a colour, its citizens have a distinct character: they are friendly, jokey and inquisitive, hugely proud of their city and thin-skinned when it is criticised, as it has been throughout Paul's life. For Liverpool's boom years were over before Paul was born, the population reaching a peak of 900,000 in 1931, since when Liverpool has faded, its people, Paul included, leaving to find work elsewhere as their ancestors once came to Merseyside seeking employment, the abandoned city becoming tatty and tired, with mounting social problems.

Paul's maternal grandfather, Owen Mohin, was a farmer's son from County Monaghan, south of what is now the border with Northern Ireland, and it's likely there was Irish blood on the paternal side of the family, too. McCartney is a Scottish name, but four centuries ago many Scots McCartneys settled in Ireland, returning to mainland Britain during the Potato Famine of the mid-1800s. Paul's paternal ancestors were probably among those who recrossed the Irish Sea at this time in search of food and work. Great-grandfather James McCartney was also most likely born in Ireland, but came to Liverpool to work as a house-painter, making his home with wife Elizabeth in Everton, a working-class suburb of the city. Their son, Joseph, born in 1866, Paul's paternal grandfather, worked in the tobacco trade, tobacco being one of the city's major imports. He married a local girl named Florence Clegg and had ten children, the fifth of whom was Paul's dad.

Aside from Paul's parents, his extended Liverpool family, his relatives – what Paul would call 'the relies' – have played a significant and ongoing part in his life, so it is worth becoming acquainted with his aunts and uncles. John McCartney was Joe and Flo McCartney's first-born, known as Jack. Paul's Uncle Jack was a big strong man, gassed in the First World War, with the result that after he came home – to work as a rent collector for Liverpool Corporation – he spoke in a small, husky voice. You had to lean in close to hear what Jack was saying, and often he was telling a joke. The McCartneys were wits and raconteurs, deriving endless fun from gags, word games and general silliness, all of which became apparent, for better or worse, when Paul turned to song writing. McCartney family whimsy is in 'Maxwell's Silver Hammer' and 'Rocky Raccoon', also 'Rupert and the Frog Song'.

There was a son after Jack who died in infancy; then came Edith (Edie) who married ship steward Will Stapleton, the black sheep of the family; another daughter died in infancy; after which Paul's father, James, was born on 7 July 1902, known to all as Jim. He was followed by three girls: Florence (Flo), Annie and Jane, the latter known as Gin or Ginny, after her middle name Virginia. Ginny, who married carpenter Harry Harris, was Paul's favourite relative outside his immediate family and close to her younger sister, Mildred (Milly), after whom came the youngest, Joe, known as Our Bloody Joe, a plumber who married Joan, who outlived them all. Looking back, Joan recalls a family that was 'very clannish', amiable, witty people who liked company. In appearance the men were slim, smartly dressed and moderately handsome. Paul's dad possessed delicate eyebrows which arched quizzically over kindly eyes, giving him the enquiring, innocent expression Paul has inherited. The women were of a more robust build, and in many ways the dominant personalities. None more so than the redoubtable Auntie Gin, whom Paul name-checks in his 1976 song 'Let 'em In'. 'Ginny was up for anything. She was a wonderful mad character,' says Mike Robbins, who married into the family, becoming Paul's Uncle Mike (though he was actually a cousin). 'It's a helluva family. Full of fun.'

Music played a large part in family life. Granddad Joe played in brass bands and encouraged his children to take up music. Birthdays, Christmas and New Year were all excuses for family parties, which involved everybody having a drink and a singsong around the piano, purchased from North End Music Stores (NEMS), owned by the Epstein family, and it was Jim McCartney's fingers on the keys. He taught himself piano by ear (presumably his left, being deaf in his right). He also played trumpet, 'until his teeth gave out', as Paul always says. Jim became semi-professional during the First World War, forming a dance band, the Masked Melody Makers, later Jim Mac's Band, in which his older brother Jack played trombone. Other relatives joined the merriment, giving enthusiastic recitals of 'You've Gone' and 'Stairway to Paradise' at Merseyside dance halls. Jim made up tunes as well, though he was too modest to call himself a songwriter. There were other links to show business. Younger brother Joe Mac sang in a barber-shop choir and Jack had a friend at the Pavilion Theatre who would let the brothers backstage to watch artists such as Max Wall and Tommy Trinder perform. As a young man Jim worked in the theatre briefly, selling programmes and operating lights, while a little later on Ann McCartney's daughter Bett took as her husband the aforementioned Mike Robbins, a small-time variety artiste whose every other sentence was a gag ('Variety was dying, and my act was helping to kill it'). There was a whiff of greasepaint about this family.

Jim's day job was humdrum and poorly paid. He was a salesman with the cotton merchants A. Hannay & Co., working out of an impressive mercantile building on Old Hall Street. One of Jim's colleagues was a clerk named Albert Kendall, who married Jim's sister Milly, becoming Paul's Uncle Albert (part of the inspiration for another of Paul's Seventies' hits, 'Uncle Albert/Admiral Halsey'). It was perhaps because Jim was having such a grand old time with his band and his extended family that he waited until he was almost forty before he married, by which time Britain was again at war. It was Jim's luck to have been too young to serve in the First World War, and now he was fortunate to be too old for the Second. He lost his job with Hannay's, though, working instead in an aircraft factory during the day and fire-watching at night. Liverpool's docks were a prime German target during the early part of the war, with incendiary shells falling almost nightly. It was during this desperate time, with the Luftwaffe overhead and Adolf Hitler's armies apparently poised to invade from France, that Jim McCartney met his bride-to-be, Paul's mother Mary.

Mary Mohin was the daughter of Irishman Owen Mohin, who'd left the old country to work in Glasgow, then moving south to Liverpool, where he married Mary Danher and had four children: a daughter named Agnes who died in childhood, boys Wilfred and Bill, the latter known as Bombhead, and Paul's mother, Mary, born in the Liverpool suburb of Fazakerley on 29 September 1909. Mary's mother died when she was ten. Dad went back to Ireland to take a new bride, Rose, whom he brought to Liverpool, having two more children before dying himself in 1933, having drunk and gambled away most of his money. Mary and Rose didn't get on and Mary left home when still young to train as a nurse, lodging with Harry and Ginny Harris in West Derby. One day

Ginny took Mary to meet her widowed mother Florence at her Corporation-owned ('corpy') home in Scargreen Avenue, Norris Green, whereby Mary met Gin's bachelor brother Jim. When the air-raid warning sounded, Jim and Mary were obliged to get to know each other better in the shelter. They married soon after.

Significantly, Paul McCartney is the product of a mixed marriage, in that his father was Protestant and his mother Roman Catholic, at a time when working-class Liverpool was divided along sectarian lines. There were regular clashes between Protestants and Catholics, especially on 12 July, when Orangemen marched in celebration of William III's 1690 victory over the Irish. St Patrick's Day could also degenerate into street violence, as fellow Merseysider Ringo Starr recalls: 'On 17th March, St Patrick's Day, all the Protestants beat up the Catholics because they were marching, and on 12th July, Orangeman's [sic] Day, all the Catholics beat up the Protestants. That's how it was, Liverpool being the capital of Ireland, as everybody always says.' Mild-mannered Jim McCartney was agnostic and he seemingly gave way to his wife when they married on 15 April 1941, for they were joined together at St Swithin's Roman Catholic Chapel. Jim was 38, his bride 31. There was an air raid that night on the docks, the siren sounding at 10:27 p.m., sending the newlyweds back down the shelter. Bombs fell on Garston, killing eight people before the all-clear. The Blitz on Liverpool intensified during the next few months, then stopped in January 1942. Britain had survived its darkest hour, and Mary McCartney was pregnant with one of its greatest sons.

JAMES PAUL McCARTNEY

Although the Luftwaffe had ceased its bombing raids on Liverpool by the time he was born, on Thursday 18 June 1942, James Paul McCartney, best known by his middle name, was very much a war baby. As Paul began to mewl and bawl, the newspapers carried daily reports of the world war: the British army was virtually surrounded by German troops at Tobruk in North Africa; the US Navy had just won the Battle of Midway; the Germans were pushing deep into Russian territory on the Eastern Front; while at home Prime Minister Winston Churchill's government was considering adding coal to the long list of items only available on ration. Although the Blitz had passed for Liverpool, the war had three years to run, with much suffering and deprivation for the nation.

As his parents were married in a Catholic church, Paul was baptised into the Catholic faith at St Philomena's Church, on 12 July 1942, the day the Orange Order marches. Though this may have been coincidental, one wonders whether Mary McCartney and her priest, Father Kelly, chose this day to baptise the son of a Protestant by way of claiming a soul for Rome. In any event, like his father, Paul would grow up to have a vague, non-denominational faith, attending church rarely. Two years later a second son was born, Michael, Paul's only sibling. The boys were typical brothers, close but also rubbing each other up the wrong way at times.

Paul was three and Mike one when the war ended. Dad resumed his job at the cotton exchange, though, unusually, it was Mum's work that was more important to the family. The 1945 General Election brought in the reforming Labour administration of Clement Attlee, whose government implemented the National Health Service (NHS). Mary McCartney was the NHS in action, a relatively well-paid, state-trained midwife who worked from home delivering babies for her neighbours. The family moved frequently around Merseyside, living at various times in Anfield, Everton, West Derby and over the water on the Wirral (a peninsula between Liverpool and North Wales). Sometimes they rented rooms, other times they lodged with relatives. In 1946, Mary was asked to take up duties on a new housing estate at Speke, south of the city, and so the McCartneys came to 72 Western Avenue, what four-year-old Paul came to think of as his first proper home.

Liverpool had long had a housing problem, a significant proportion of the population living in slums into the 1950s. In addition to this historic problem, thousands had been made homeless by bombing. In the aftermath of the war many Liverpool families were accommodated temporarily in pre-fabricated cottages on the outskirts of the city while Liverpool Corporation built large new estates of corporation-owned properties which were rented to local people. Much of this construction was undertaken at Speke, a flat, semi-rural area between Liverpool and its small, outlying airport, with huge industrial estates built simultaneously to create what was essentially a new town. The

McCartneys were given a new, three-bedroom corpy house on a boulevard that leads today to Liverpool John Lennon Airport. In the late 1940s this was a model estate of new 'homes fit for heroes'. Because the local primary school was oversubscribed, Paul, along with many children, was bussed to Joseph Williams Primary in nearby Childwall. Former pupils dimly recall a friendly, fat-faced lad with a lively sense of humour. A class photo shows Paul neatly dressed, apparently happy and confident, and indeed these were halcyon days for young McCartney, whose new suburban home gave him access to woods and meadows where he went exploring with the *Observer Book of Birds* and a supply of jam butties, happy adventures recalled in a Beatles' song:

Find me in my field of grass,
Mother Nature's son,
Swaying daisies sing a lazy song beneath the sun.

('Mother Nature's Son')

In the evening, Mum cooked while Dad smoked his pipe, read the newspaper or did the garden, dispensing wisdom and jokes to the boys as he went. There were games with brother Mike, and the fun of BBC radio dramas and comedy shows. Wanting to spend more time with her sons, Mary resigned from her job as a midwife in 1950, consequently losing tenure of 72 Western Avenue. The family moved one mile to 12 Ardwick Road, a slightly less salubrious address in a part of the estate not yet finished. On the plus side the new house was opposite a playing field with swings. Resourceful Mary got a job as a health visitor, using the box room as her study. One of Jim's little home improvements was to fix their house number to a wooden plaque next to the front doorbell. When Paul came by decades later with his own son, James, he was surprised and pleased to see Dad's numbers still in place. The current tenant welcomed the McCartneys back, but complained to Paul about being pestered by Beatles fans who visited her house regularly as part of what has become a Beatles pilgrimage to Liverpool, taking pictures through the front window and clippings from her privet hedge. Paul jokingly asked, with a wink to James, whether she didn't feel privileged.

'No,' the owner told him firmly. 'I've had enough!'

Her ordeal is evidence of the fact that, alongside that of Elvis Presley, the Beatles are now the object of the most obsessive cult in popular music.

THE BLACK SHEEP

As we have seen, the McCartneys were a large, close-knit family who revelled in their own company, getting together regularly for parties. Jim would typically greet his nearest and dearest with a firm hand-shake, a whimsical smile, and one of his gnomic expressions. 'Put it there,' he'd say, squeezing your hand, 'if it weighs a ton.' What this meant was not entirely clear, but it conveyed the sense that Jim was a stalwart fellow. And if the person being greeted was small, they would often take their hand away to find Jim had slipped a coin into their palm. Jim was generous. He was also honest, as the McCartneys generally were. They were not *scallies* (rough or crooked Scousers), until it came to Uncle Will.

Considering how long Paul McCartney has been famous, and how closely his life has been studied, it is surprising that the scandalous story of the black sheep of the McCartney family has remained untold until now. Here it is. In 1924 Paul's aunt Edie, Dad's sister, married a ship steward named Alexander William Stapleton, known to everybody as Will. Edie and Will took over Florence McCartney's corporation house in Scargreen Avenue after she died, and Paul saw his Uncle Will regularly at family gatherings. Everybody knew Will was 'a bent little devil', in the words of one relative. Will was notorious for pinching bottles from family parties, and for larger acts of larceny. He routinely stole from the ships he worked on. On one memorable occasion Will sent word to Edie that she and Ginny were to meet him at the Liverpool docks when his ship came in. Gin wondered why her brother-in-law required her pres- ence as well as that of his wife. She found out when Will greeted her over the fence. As Ginny told the tale, Will kissed her unexpectedly on the lips, slipping a smuggled diamond ring into her mouth with his tongue as he did so. That wasn't all. When he cleared customs, Will gave his wife a laundry bag concealing new silk underwear for her, while he presented Ginny with a sock containing – so the story goes – a chloroformed parrot.

Will boasted that one day he would pull off a scam that would set him up for life. This became a McCartney family joke. Jack McCartney was wont to stop 'relies' he met in town and whisper: 'I see Will Stapleton's back from his voyage.'

'Is he?' the relative would ask, leaning forward to hear Jack's wheezy voice.

'Yes, I've just seen the *Mauretania** halfway up Dale Street.' Joking aside, Will did pull off a colossal caper, one sensational enough to make the front page of the *Liverpool Evening News*, even *The Times* of London, to the family's enduring embarrassment.

Will was working as a baggage steward on the *SS Apapa*, working a regular voyage between Liverpool and West Africa. The outward-bound cargo in September 1949 included 70 crates of newly printed bank notes, destined for the British Bank of West Africa. The crates of money, worth many millions in today's terms, were sealed and locked in the strongroom of the ship. Will and two crewmates, pantry man Thomas Davenport and the ship's baker, Joseph Edwards, hatched a plan to steal some of this money. It was seemingly Davenport's idea, recruiting Stapleton to help file down the hinges on the strongroom door, tap out the pins and lift the door clear. They then stole the contents of one crate, containing 10,000 West African bank notes, worth exactly £10,000 sterling in 1949, a sum equal to about £250,000 in today's money (or $382,500 US[†]). The thieves replaced the stolen money with pantry paper, provided by Edwards, resealed the crate and rehung the door. When the cargo was unloaded at Takoradi on the Gold Coast, nothing seemed amiss and the *Apapa* sailed on its way. It was only when the crates were weighed at the bank that one crate was found light and the alarm was raised.

The *Apapa* had reached Lagos, where the thieves spent some of the stolen money before rejoining the ship and sailing back to England. British police boarded the *Apapa* as it returned to Liverpool, quickly arresting Davenport and Edwards, who confessed, implicating Stapleton. 'You seem to know all about it. There's no use in my denying it further,' Paul's Uncle Will was reported to have told detectives when he was arrested. The story appeared on page one of the Liverpool *Evening*

---

* One of the largest ships in the world.

† Unless indicated, sterling/dollar exchange values are as of the time of writing.

Express, meaning the whole family was appraised of the disgrace Will had brought upon them.

'Jesus, it's the bloody thing he always said he was going to have a go at!' exclaimed Aunt Ginny.

Stapleton and his crewmates pleaded guilty in court to larceny on the high seas. Stapleton indicated that his cut was only £500. He said he became nervous when he saw the ship's captain inspecting the strong room on their return voyage. 'As a result I immediately got rid of what was left of my £500 by throwing it through the porthole into the sea. I told Davenport and he called me a fool and said he would take a chance with the rest.' The judge sentenced Uncle Will to three years in prison, the same with Davenport. Edwards got 18 months.

The police only recovered a small amount of the stolen money. Maybe Davenport and Stapleton had indeed chucked the rest in the Atlantic, as they claimed, but within the McCartney family there was speculation that Will hung onto some of that missing currency. It was said that the police watched him carefully after he got out of jail, and when detectives finally tired of their surveillance Will went on a spending spree, acquiring, among other luxuries, the first television in Scargreen Avenue.

GROWING UP

Paul's parents got their first TV in 1953, as many British families did, in order to watch the Coronation of the new Queen, 27-year-old Elizabeth II, someone Paul would see a lot of in the years ahead. Master McCartney distinguished himself by being one of 60 Liverpool schoolchildren to win a Coronation essay competition. 'Coronation Day' by Paul McCartney (age: 10 years 10 months) paid patriotic tribute to a 'lovely young Queen' who, as fate would have it, would one day knight him as Sir Paul McCartney.

Winning the prize showed Paul to be an intelligent boy, which was borne out when at the end of his time at Joseph Williams Primary he passed the Eleven Plus – an exam taken by British schoolchildren aged 11–12 – which was the first significant fork in the road of their education at the time. Those who failed the exam were sent to secondary modern schools, which tended to produce boys and girls who would become manual or semi-skilled workers; while the minority who passed the

Eleven Plus typically went to grammar school, setting them on the road to a university education and professional life. What's more, Paul did well enough in the exam to be selected for Liverpool's premier grammar school, indeed one of the best state schools in England.

The Liverpool Institute, or Inny, looked down on Liverpool from an elevated position on Mount Street, next to the colossal new Anglican cathedral. Work had started on what is perhaps Liverpool's greatest building, designed by Sir Giles Gilbert Scott, in 1904. The edifice took until 1978 to finish. Although a work in progress, the cathedral was in use in the early 1950s. Paul had recently tried out for the cathedral choir. (He failed to get in, and sang instead at St Barnabas' on Penny Lane.) Standing in the shadow of this splendid cathedral, the Inny had a modest grandeur all its own. It was a handsome, late-Georgian building, the entrance flanked by elegant stone columns, with an equally fine reputation for giving the brightest boys of the city the best start in life. Many pupils went on to Oxford and Cambridge, the Inny having produced notable writers, scientists, politicians, even one or two show business stars. Before Paul, the most famous of these was the comic actor Arthur Askey, at whose desk Paul sat.

Kitted out in his new black blazer and green and black tie, Paul was impressed and daunted by this new school when he enrolled in September 1953. Going to the Inny drew him daily from the suburbs into the urban heart of Liverpool, a much more dynamic place, while any new boy felt naturally overwhelmed by the teeming life of a school that numbered around 1,000 pupils, overseen by severe-looking masters in black gowns who'd take the cane readily to an unruly lad. The pupils got their own back by awarding their overbearing teachers colourful and often satirical nicknames. J.R. Edwards, the feared headmaster, was known as the Bas, for Bastard. (Paul came to realise he was in fact 'quite a nice fella'.) Other masters were known as Cliff Edge, Sissy Smith (an effeminate English master, related to John Lennon), Squinty Morgan, Funghi Moy and Weedy Plant. 'He was weedy and his name was Plant. Poor chap,' explains Steve Norris, a schoolboy contemporary of Paul's who became a Tory cabinet minister.

The A-stream was for the brightest boys, who studied classics. A shining example and contemporary of Paul's was Peter 'Perfect' Sissons, later a BBC newsreader. The C-stream was for boys with a science bent. Paul went into the B-stream, which specialised in modern languages. He studied German and Spanish, the latter with 'Fanny' Inkley, the school's only female teacher. Paul had the luck to have an outstanding English teacher, Alan 'Dusty' Durband, author of a standard textbook on Shakespeare, who got his pupils interested in Chaucer by introducing them to the sexy passages in the *Canterbury Tales*. 'Then we got interested in the other bits, too, so he was a clever bloke.' Paul's other favourite classes were art and woodwork, both hobbies in adult life. Before music came into his life strongly, Paul was considered one of the school's best artists. Curiously, Neddy Evans's music lessons left him cold. Although Dad urged Paul to learn to read music, so he could play properly, Paul never learned what the dots meant. 'I basically never learned anything at all [about music at school].' Yet he loved the Inny, and came to recognise the head start it gave him in life. 'It gave you a great feeling of the world was out there to be conquered, that the world was a very big place, and somehow you could reach it from here.'

It was at the Inny that Paul acquired the nickname Macca, which has endured. Friends Macca made at school included John Duff Lowe, Ivan 'Ivy' Vaughan (born the same day as Paul) and Ian James, who shared his taste in radio shows, including the new and anarchic *Goon Show*. In the playground Macca was 'always telling tales or going through programmes that were on the previous night,' James recalls. 'He'd always have a crowd around him. He was good at telling tales, [and] he had quite a devilish sense of humour.' Two more schoolboys were of special significance: a clever, thin-faced lad named Neil 'Nell' Aspinall, who was in Paul's class for art and English and became the Beatles' road manager; and a skinny kid one year Paul's junior named George.

Born on 25 February 1943,* George Harrison was the youngest of a family of four, the Harrisons being a working-class family from south Liverpool. Mum and Dad were Louise and Harold 'Harry' Harrison, the family living in a corpy house at 25 Upton Green, Speke. Harry drove buses for a living. It was on the bus home from school that Paul and George first met properly, their conversation sparked by a growing mutual interest in music, Paul having recently taken up the trumpet. 'I discovered that he had a trumpet and he found out that I had a guitar, and we got together,' George recalled. 'I was about thirteen. He was

---

*It is sometimes said that Harrison was born on 24 February 1943, but his birth and his death certificate clearly state his birthday as the 25th.

probably late thirteen or fourteen. (He was always nine months older than me. Even now, after all these years, he is still nine months older!)' As this remark implies, George always felt that Paul looked down on him and, although he possessed a quick wit, and was bright enough to get into the Inny in the first place, schoolboy contemporaries recall George as being a less impressive lad than Paul. 'I remember George Harrison as being thick as a plank – and completely uninteresting,' says Steve Norris bluntly. 'I don't think anybody thought George would ever amount to anything. A bit slow, you know [adopting a working-class Scouse accent], a bit *You know what I mean, like.*'

Paul's family moved again with Mum's work, this time to a new corpy house in Allerton, a pleasant suburb closer to town. The address was 20 Forthlin Road, a compact brick-built terrace with small gardens front and back. One entered by a glass-panelled front door which opened onto a parquet hall, stairs straight ahead, lounge to your left, with a coal fire, next to which lived the TV. The McCartneys put their piano against the far wall, covered in blue chinoiserie paper. Swing doors led through to a small dining room, to the right of which was the kitchen, and a passageway back to the hall. Upstairs there were three bedrooms with a bathroom and inside loo, a convenience the family hadn't previously enjoyed. Paul bagged the back room, which over-looked the Police Training College, brother Mike the smaller box room. The light switches were Bakelite, the floors Lino, the woodwork painted 'corporation cream' (magnolia), the doorstep Liverpool red. This new home suited the McCartneys perfectly, and the first few months that the family lived here became idealised in Paul's mind as a McCartney family idyll: the boy cosy and happy with his kindly, pipe-smoking dad, his funny kid brother, and the loveliest mummy in the world, a woman who worked hard at her job bringing other children into the world, yet always had time for her own, too. Paul came to see Mum almost as a Madonna:

Lady Madonna, children at your feet,
Wonder how you manage to make ends meet.

('Lady Madonna')

What happened next is the defining event of Paul McCartney's life, a tragedy made starker because the family had only just moved into their dream home, where they expected to be happy for years to come. Mum fell ill and was diagnosed with breast cancer. It seems Mary knew the prognosis was not good and kept this a secret, at least from her children. One day, in the summer of 1956, Mike found his mother upstairs weeping. When he asked her what was wrong, she replied, 'Nothing, love.'

At the end of October 1956 Mary was admitted to the Northern Hospital, a gloomy old building on Leeds Street, where she underwent surgery. It was not successful. Paul and Mike were packed off to Everton to stay with Uncle Joe and Auntie Joan. Jim didn't own a car, so Mike Robbins, who was selling vacuum cleaners between theatrical engagements, gave Jim lifts to the hospital in his van. 'He was trying to put on a brave front. He knew his wife was dying.' Finally the boys were taken into the hospital to say goodbye to Mum. Paul noticed blood on her bed sheets. Mary remarked to a relative that she only wished she could see her boys grow up. Paul was 14, Mike 12. Mum died on 31 October 1956, Hallowe'en, aged 47.

Aunt Joan recalls that Paul didn't express overt grief when told the news. Indeed, he and his brother Mike played rambunctiously that night in her back bedroom. 'My daughter slept in a camp bed,' says Joan, 'and the boys had the double bed in the back bedroom and they were pulling arms off a teddy bear.' When he did address the fact that his mother had died, Paul did so by asking Dad gauchely how they were going to manage without her wages. Stories like this are sometimes cited as evidence of a lack of empathy on Paul's part, and it is true that he would react awkwardly in the face of death repeatedly during his life. It is also true that young people often behave in an insensitive way when faced with bereavement. They do not know what death means. Over the years, however, it became plain that Paul saw his world shattered that autumn night in 1956. The premature death of his mother was a trauma he never forgot, nor wholly got over.

JOHN

HAIL! HAIL! ROCK 'N' ROLL

A dark period of mourning and adjustment followed the death of Mary McCartney, as widower Jim came to terms with the untimely loss of his wife and tried to instigate a domestic regime at Forthlin Road whereby he could be both father and mother to his boys. This was not easy. Indeed, Paul recalls hearing his father crying at night. It was thanks to the 'relies' rallying round, especially Aunts Ginny, Milly and Joan, that Jim was able to carry on at Forthlin Road, the women taking turns to help clean and cook for this bereaved, all-male household.

Crucially, as far as the history of pop is concerned, Paul reacted to the death of his mother by taking comfort in music. He returned the trumpet his father had given him for his recent birthday to Rushworth and Dreaper, a Liverpool music store, and exchanged it for an acoustic Zenith guitar, wanting to play an instrument that would also allow him to sing, and not liking the idea of developing a horn player's callous on his lips. Learning guitar chords proved challenging because Paul was left-handed and he tried at first to play as a right-hander. It was only when he saw a picture of Slim Whitman playing guitar the other way around (Whitman having taught himself to play left-handed after losing part of a finger on his right hand) that Paul restrung his instrument accordingly and began to make progress. Schoolmate Ian James also played guitar, with greater proficiency, and gave Paul valuable lessons on his own

Rex acoustic.* As to what the boys played, there was suddenly a whole new genre of music opening up.

Until 1955, the music Paul had heard and enjoyed consisted largely of the jazz-age ballads and dance tunes Mum and Dad liked: primarily the song books of the Gershwins, Cole Porter and Rodgers and Hart; while trips to the movies had given Paul an appreciation of Fred Astaire, a fine singer as well as a great dancer who became a lifelong hero. Now bolder, more elemental rhythms filled his ears. The first real musical excitement for young people in post-war Britain was skiffle, incorporating elements of folk, jazz and blues. A large part of the genre's appeal was that you didn't need professional instruments to play it. Ordinary household objects could be used: a wooden tea chest was strung to make a crude bass, a tin washboard became a simple percussion instrument, helping define the rasping, clattering sound of the music. Despite being played on such absurd household items, skiffle could be very exciting, as Scots singer Lonnie Donegan proved in January 1956 when he scored a major hit with a skiffle cover of Leadbelly's 'Rock Island Line' (though the recording features a standard double bass). Almost overnight, thousands of British teenagers formed skiffle bands of their own, with Paul among those Liverpool skifflers who went to see Donegan perform at the local Empire theatre in November, just a few days after Mary McCartney died.

Close on the heels of skiffle came the greater revelation of rock 'n' roll. The first rumble of this powerful new music reached the UK with the 1955 movie *The Blackboard Jungle*, which made Bill Haley a fleeting sensation. In the flesh Haley proved a disappointment, a mature, heavy-set fellow, not a natural role model for teens, unlike the handsome young messiah of rock who followed him. Elvis Presley broke in Britain in May 1956 with the release of 'Heartbreak Hotel'. The singer and the song electrified Paul at the age when boys become closely interested in their appearance. Elvis was his role model, as he was for boys all over the world, and Paul tried to make himself look like his hero. Paul and Ian James went to a Liverpool tailor, who took in their trousers to create rocker-style drainpipe legs; Paul grew his hair, sweeping it back like 'El',

---

* When James approached retirement in 2006, and his pension fund wasn't as healthy as he'd hoped, he asked Paul to authenticate the Rex as the guitar he'd learned on, and with that endorsement he sold the instrument at auction for an astonishing £333,000 ($509,490).

as they referred to the star; Paul began to neglect his school work, and spent his free time practising Elvis's songs, as well as other rock 'n' roll tunes that came fading in and out over the late-night airwaves from Radio Luxembourg. This far-away European station, together with glimpses of music idols on TV and in jukebox movies at the cinema, introduced Paul to the charismatic Americans who sat at Elvis's feet in the firmament of rock: to the great black poet Chuck Berry, wild man Jerry Lee Lewis, the deceptively straight-looking Buddy Holly, crazy Little Richard and rockabilly pioneer Gene Vincent, whose insistent 'Be-Bop-A-Lula' was the first record Paul bought.

Paul started to take his guitar into school. Former head boy Billy Morton, a jazz fan with no time for this new music, recalls being appalled by Paul playing Eddie Cochran's 'Twenty-Flight Rock' in the playground at the Inny. 'There must have been 150 boys around him, ten deep, whilst he was singing … There he was, star material even then.' Paul imitated his heroes with preternatural skill. But he was more than just a copyist. Almost immediately, Paul started to write his own songs. 'He said, "I've written a tune,"' recalls Ian James. 'It was something I'd never bothered to try, and it seemed quite a feat to me. I thought, *He's written a tune!* So we went up to his bedroom and he played this tune, [and] sang it.' Created from three elementary chords (C, F and G), 'I Lost My Little Girl' was of the skiffle variety, with simple words about a girl who had Paul's head 'in a whirl'. By dint of this little tune, Paul McCartney became a singer-songwriter. Now he needed a band.

THE QUARRY MEN

The Beatles grew out of a schoolboy band founded and led by John Lennon, an older local boy, studying for his O-levels at Quarry Bank High School, someone Paul was aware of but didn't know personally. As he says: 'John was the local Ted' (meaning Lennon affected the look of the aggressive Teddy Boy youth cult). 'You saw him rather than met him.'

John Winston Lennon, named after Britain's wartime leader, was a full year and eight months older than Paul McCartney, born on 9 October 1940. Like Paul, John was Liverpool Irish by ancestry, with a touch of showbiz in the family. His paternal Irish grandfather Jack had sung with a minstrel show. More directly, and unlike Paul, John was the product of a dysfunctional home. Dad was a happy-go-lucky merchant seaman named Freddie Lennon, a man cut from the same cloth as Paul's Uncle Will. Mum, Julia, was a flighty young woman who dated various men when Fred was at sea, or in prison, as he was during part of the Second World War. All in all, the couple made a poor job of raising their only child,* whom Julia passed, at age five, into the more capable hands of her older, childless sister Mary, known as Mimi, and Mimi's dairyman husband George Smith.

The relationship between John and his Aunt Mimi is reminiscent of that between David Copperfield and his guardian aunt Betsey Trotwood, an apparently severe woman who proves kindness itself when she gives the unhappy Copperfield sanctuary in her cottage. The likewise starchy but golden-hearted Mimi brought John to live with her and Uncle George in their cosy Liverpool cottage, Mendips, on Menlove Avenue, just over the hill from Paul's house on Forthlin Road. Much has been made of the social difference between Mendips and Paul's working-class home, as if John's was a much grander household. As both houses are now open to the public, courtesy of the National Trust, anyone can see for themselves that Mendips is a standard, three-bedroom semi-detached property, the 'semi' being a type of house built by the thousands in the 1920s and '30s, cosy suburban hutches for those who could afford to take out a small mortgage but couldn't stretch to a detached property. The essential difference between Mendips and 20 Forthlin Road was that the Smiths owned their home while Jim McCartney rented from the Liverpool Corporation, by dint of which the McCartneys were defined as working-class. It is also fair to say that Menlove Avenue was considered to be a much more desirable place to live.

John's childhood was upset again when Uncle George died in 1955. Thereafter John and Aunt Mimi shared Mendips with a series of male lodgers whose rent allowed Mimi to make ends meet and who, in one case, shared her bed. One way or another, this was an eccentric start in life, and John grew to be an eccentric character. Like Paul, John was clever, with a quick wit and an intense stare that was later mistaken for a sign of wisdom – he seemed to stare into your soul – whereas in fact

* Julia later had other children by other men.

he was just short-sighted. He also had a talent for art and a liking for language. Like many solitary children who have suffered periods of loneliness, John was bookish, more so than Paul. John's voracious reading accounts in part for his lyrics being generally more interesting than Paul's. The literary influence of Edward Lear and Lewis Carroll is strongly felt in John's penchant for nonsense, for example, which first found expression in the *Daily Howl*, a delightful school magazine he wrote and drew for fun. The tone is typified by his famous weather forecast: 'Tomorrow will be Muggy, followed by Tuggy, Weggy and Thurgy and Friggy'. This is also the humour of the *Goon Show*, which Paul and John both enjoyed. Above all else, the boys shared an interest in music. John was mad for rock 'n' roll. Indeed many friends thought John more or less *completely* mad. In researching the story of Paul's life it is remarkable that people who knew both Paul and John tend to talk about John most readily, often with laughter, for Lennon said and did endless amusing things that have stuck in their memory, whereas McCartney was always more sensible, even (whisper it) slightly dull by comparison.

Like Paul, John worshipped Elvis Presley. 'Elvis Presley's all very well, John,' Aunt Mimi would lecture her nephew, 'but I don't want him for breakfast, dinner and tea.' (Her other immortal words on this subject were: 'The guitar's all very well, John, but you'll never make a living out of it.') In emulation of Elvis, John played guitar enthusiastically, but badly, using banjo chords taught him by his mum, who was living round the corner in Blomfield Road, with her current boyfriend, and saw John regularly. Playing banjo chords meant using only four of the guitar's six strings – which was slightly easier for a beginner. Having grasped the rudiments, John formed a skiffle group with his best mate at Quarry Bank High, Pete Shotton, who was assigned washboard. The band was named the Quarry Men, after their school. Another pupil, Eric Griffiths, played guitar, and Eric recruited a fourth Quarry Bank student, Rod Davis, who'd known John since they were in Sunday school together. Rod recalls: 'He was known as *that* Lennon. Mothers would say, "Now stay away from *that* Lennon."' Eric found their drummer, Colin Hanton, who'd already left (a different) school to work as an upholsterer. Finally, Liverpool Institute boy Len Garry was assigned tea chest bass. Together, the lads performed covers of John's favourite skiffle and rock 'n' roll songs at parties and youth clubs, sometimes going weeks without playing, for one of John's signal characteristics was laziness. Indeed, the

Quarry Men may well have come to nought had they not agreed to perform at a humble summer fête.

Woolton Village is a short bike ride from John's house, just east of Liverpool, its annual fête being organised by the vicar of St Peter's Church, in the graveyard of which reside the remains of one Eleanor Rigby, who as her marker states died in 1939, aged 44. Starting at 2 o'clock on Saturday 6 July 1957, a procession of children, floats and bands made its way through Woolton to the church field, the procession led by the Band of the Cheshire Yeomanry and the outgoing Rose Queen, a local girl who sat in majesty on a flatbed truck. The Quarry Men followed on another, similar truck. Around 3 o'clock the new Rose Queen was crowned on stage in the church field, after which there was a parade of local children in fancy dress, and the Quarry Men played a few songs for the amusement of the kids as the adults mooched around the stalls. Looking at photographs taken that summer afternoon one is reminded that, although John's band was named the Quarry Men, they were mere boys, gangly youths in plaid shirts, sleeves rolled up, their expressions betraying almost total inexperience as they haltingly sought to entertain an audience comprised mostly of even younger children. Typically, one little girl in a brownie uniform is captured on camera sitting on the edge of the stage looking up at John with the mildest of interest.

John, who had let his hair grow long at the front, then swept it back in a quiff, was standing at a stick microphone, strumming his guitar and singing the Dell-Vikings' 'Come Go With Me'. Unsure of the correct words, never having seen them in print, John was improvising lyrics to fit the tune, singing: 'Come and go with me, down to the penitentiary ...' Paul McCartney thought this clever. Paul had been brought along to the fête by Ivan Vaughan, who knew John and thought his two musical friends should get together. The introduction was made in the church hall where the Quarry Men were due to play a second set. A plaque on the wall now commemorates the historic moment Lennon met McCartney. John recalled: '[Ivan] said, "I think you two will get along." We talked after the show and I saw that he had talent. He was playing guitar backstage, doing "Twenty-Flight Rock".' In emulation of Little Richard, Paul also played 'Long Tall Sally' and 'Tutti-Frutti'. Not long after this meeting Pete Shotton stopped Paul in the street and asked if he'd like to join the Quarry Men. He was asking on behalf of John, of course. 'He was the leader because he was the guy who sang the songs,' explains Colin Hanton, who was surprised how quickly John made up his mind about this new boy. '[Paul] must have impressed him.'

EARLY SHOWS

That summer Rod Davis went to France on holiday and never rejoined the Quarry Men. John Lennon left Quarry Bank High, having failed his O-levels, and was lucky to get a place at Liverpool College of Art, which happened to be next door to Paul's grammar school on Hope Street. In their summer holidays, Paul and Mike McCartney attended scout camp, where Paul accidentally broke his brother's arm mucking about with a pulley, after which Jim McCartney took his sons to Butlin's in Filey, Yorkshire, where Paul and Mike performed 'Bye Bye Love' on stage as a duo.

Girls started to feature in Paul's life around this time. A pale, unsporty lad with a tendency to podginess, Paul was no teenage Adonis, but he had a pleasant, open face (with straight dark brown hair and hazel eyes) and a confidence that helped make him personable. Meeting Sir Paul today it is his winning confidence that strikes one most strongly. Initially he just buddied around with girls in a group, girls like Marjorie Wilson, whom he'd known since primary school. Likewise he knocked about with Forthlin Road neighbour Ann Ventre, despite getting into a fight with her brother Louis after Paul made a derogatory remark about the Pope (indicating that he didn't see himself as a Catholic). Paul said one interesting thing to Ann. 'I'll be famous one day,' he told her boldly.

'Oh yes. Ha! Will you now?' she replied, astounded by that confidence. Like many people who become very successful, Paul *knew* at a young age that he would do well. No doubt the fact he had come from such a happy and supportive home helped, being the apple of Mother's and Father's eyes. We must also credit him with natural musical talent, some genius even, of which he was himself already aware. If not misplaced, confidence is very attractive and by the time he was 15 Paul had his pick of girlfriends. He lost his virginity to a local girl he was babysitting with, the start of what became a full sexual life.

Being in a band was an excellent way to meet girls; it is one of the primary reasons teenage boys join bands. But early Quarry Men gigs brought the lads more commonly into the company of the men who operated and patronised the city's social clubs: the Norris Green Conservative Club and the Stanley Abattoir Social for example. Small-time though these engagements were, Paul took every gig seriously. It was he who first acquired a beige stage jacket, John following suit, and it was Paul who got the Quarry Men wearing string ties. 'I think Paul had more desire to be successful than John,' comments drummer Colin Hanton. 'Once Paul joined there was a movement to smarten us up.' Paul was also quick to advise his band mates on their musicianship. Having taught himself the rudiments of drumming, he gave Colin pointers. 'He could be a little bit pushy,' remarks Colin, a sentiment many musicians have echoed.

Of an evening and at weekends Paul would cycle over to John's house to work on material. It was a pleasant bike ride across Allerton Golf Course, up through the trees and past the greens, emerging onto Menlove Avenue, after which Paul had to cross the busy road and turn left to reach Mendips. 'John, your little friend's here,' Aunt Mimi would announce dubiously, when Master McCartney appeared at her back door. The boys practised upstairs in John's bedroom, decorated with a pin-up of Brigitte Bardot, whom they both lusted after. Sometimes they played downstairs in the lounge, a large, bright room with a cabinet of Royal Albert china. Uneasy about the boys being in with her best things, Mimi preferred them to practise in the front porch, which suited John and Paul, because the space was acoustically lively. Here, bathed in the sunlight that streamed in through the coloured glass, Lennon and McCartney taught each other to play the songs they heard on the radio, left-handed Paul forming a mirror image of his right-handed, older friend as they sat opposite each other, trying to prevent the necks of their instruments clashing, and singing in harmony. Both had good voices, John's possessing more character and authority, which Paul made up for by being an excellent mimic, particularly adept at taking off Little Richard. Apart from covering the songs of their heroes, the boys were writing songs, the words and chord changes of which Paul recorded neatly in an exercise book. He was always organised that way.

During term time, Paul and John met daily in town, which was easy now with John studying next door at the art college. Here, Lennon fell in with a group of art students who styled themselves self-consciously the Dissenters, meeting over pints of beer in the pub round the corner,

Ye Cracke. Like students the world over, the Dissenters talked earnestly of life, sex and art. Beatnik culture loomed large, the novels of Jack Kerouac and the poetry of Allen Ginsberg and Lawrence Ferlinghetti being very fashionable. The work of these American writers was of great interest to the Dissenters up to the point, significantly, where they decided they didn't have to be in thrall to American culture. 'We sat there in the Cracke and thought Liverpool is an exciting place,' remembers Bill Harry, a founder member of this student group. 'We can create things and write music about Liverpool, just as the Americans [do about their cities].' Although the Quarry Men, and later the Beatles, would play rock 'n' roll in emulation of their American heroes, importantly John and Paul would create authentic English pop songs, with lyrics that referred to English life, sung in unaffected English accents. The same is also true of George Harrison.

When Paul slipped next door to the art college to have lunch with John, his friend Georgie would often tag along. John treated Paul more or less as his equal, despite the age difference, but George Harrison was a further year back, and he seemed very young: a skinny, goofy little kid with a narrow face, snaggly teeth and eyebrows that almost met in the middle. Lennon regarded this boy with condescension. Paul did, too, but he was shrewd enough to see that George was becoming a good guitar player, telling George to show John how well he could play the riff from the song 'Raunchy'. John was sufficiently impressed to invite Harrison to join the band. George's relationship with Paul and John was thus established. Ever afterwards the two senior band members would regard George as merely their guitarist. 'The thing about George is that nobody respected him for the great [talent] he was,' says Tony Bramwell, a Liverpool friend who went on to work for the Beatles (John Lennon called Bramwell 'Measles' because he was everywhere they went). 'That's how John and Paul treated George and Ringo: George is [just] the lead guitarist, and Ringo's [only] the drummer.'

Ringo is not yet in the group. But three of the fab four are together in John's schoolboy band, Paul and George having squeezed out most of John's original sidemen. When the resolutely unmusical Pete Shotton announced his decision to quit the group, John made sure of it by breaking Pete's washboard over his head, though they stayed friends and, like Measles Bramwell, Shotton would work for the boys when they made it. Eric Griffiths was displaced by the arrival of George, while Len Garry dropped out through ill-health. Only the drummer, Colin Hanton, remained, with Paul's school friend, John Duff Lowe, sitting in as occasional pianist. Of a Sunday, the boys would sometimes rehearse at 20 Forthlin Road while Jim McCartney sat reading his paper. 'The piano was against the wall, and his father used to sit at the end of the piano facing out into the room, and if he thought we were getting too loud he'd sort of wave his hand. Because he was concerned the neighbours were gonna complain,' says Duff Lowe, noting how patient and kindly Paul's dad was. 'At four o'clock we'd break and he'd go and make [us] a cup of tea.'

Despite Paul's drive to make the Quarry Men as professional as possible, they were still rank amateurs. So much so that Duff Lowe got up from the piano and left halfway through one show in order to catch his bus home. It is also a wonder that their early experiences of the entertainment industry didn't put them all off trying to make a living as musicians. On one unforgettable occasion, auditioning for a spot at a working men's club in Anfield, the Quarry Men watched as the lad before them demonstrated an act that was nothing less than eating glass. The boy cut himself so badly in the process he had to stuff newspaper into his mouth to staunch the blood. Paul's show business dreams were not quelled. Indeed, he seemed ever more ambitious. At another audition at the Locarno Ballroom, seeing a poster appealing for vocalists, Paul told John, 'We could do that.'

'No, we're a *band*,' replied John severely. It was clear to Colin Hanton that Paul would do anything to get ahead in what he had seemingly decided would be his career; or at least as much of a career as music had been for Dad before he settled down and married Mum. It is important to remember that in going into local show business in this way Paul was following in the footsteps of his father, Jim, who had entertained the people of Merseyside between the wars with his Masked Melody Makers. The fact Dad had been down this road already also accounts for Paul's extra professionalism.

The next step was to make a record. In the spring of 1958, John, Paul, George, John Duff Lowe and Colin Hanton chipped in to record two songs with a local man named Percy Phillips, who had a recording studio in his Liverpool home. For seventeen shillings and sixpence (approximately £13 in today's money, or $19 US) they could cut a 78 rpm shellac disc with a song on each side. The chosen songs were Buddy Holly's 'That'll Be the Day' and 'In Spite of All the Danger', credited to McCartney and Harrison, but essentially Paul's song. 'It was John's band, but Paul was [already] playing a more controlling part in it,' observes Duff Lowe. 'It's not a John Lennon record [sic] that we are gonna play, it's a *Paul McCartney* record.' This original song is a lugubri-ous country-style ballad, strongly reminiscent of 'Trying to Get to You,' from Elvis's first LP, which was like the Bible to the boys. John and Paul sang the lyric, George took the guitar solo, the band striking the final chord as Mr Phillips waved his hands frantically to indicate they were almost out of time. 'When we got the record, the agreement was that we would have it for a week each,' Paul said. 'John had it a week and passed it to me. I had it a week and passed it on to George, who had it a week. Then Colin had it a week and passed it to Duff Lowe – who kept it for twenty-three years.' We shall return to this story later.

A COMMON GRIEF

Despite living with the redoubtable Aunt Mimi, John kept in close touch with his mother, who was more like a big sister to him than a mum. Julia Lennon attended Quarry Men shows, with the band sometimes rehears-ing at her house in Blomfield Road, where the boys found her to be a good sport. Paul was fond of Julia, as he was of most motherly women, feeling the want of a mother himself. John also slept the night occasion-ally at Julia's. He was at Mum's on 15 July 1958, while Julia paid a visit to sister Mimi. As Julia left Mendips that summer evening, and crossed busy Menlove Avenue to the bus stop, she was knocked down and killed by a car. The effect on John was devastating. In later years he would remark that he felt like he lost his mother twice: when Julia gave him up when he was 5; and again when he was 17 and she was killed.

In the wake of this calamity, John, always something of a handful, became wilder and more obstreperous, while his friendship with Paul strengthened. The fact that Paul had lost his mother, too, meant both boys had something profound in common, a deep if largely unspoken mutual sadness. It was at this time that they began to write together more seriously, creating significant early songs such as 'Love Me Do'. Paul would often 'sag' off school now to write with John at Forthlin

Road when Dad was at work. But Paul was not dependent on John to make music. He wrote alone as well, composing the tune of 'When I'm Sixty-Four' on the family piano around this time, 'thinking it could come in handy in a musical comedy or something'. Unlike John, whose musical horizon didn't go beyond rock 'n' roll, Paul had wider tastes and ambitions.

The Quarry Men played hardly any gigs during the remaining months of 1958, and performed only sporadically in the first half of the next year, including an audition for a bingo evening. The boys were to play two sets with a view to securing a regular engagement. The first set went well enough, even though the MC got the curtain stuck, and the management rewarded the lads with free beer. They were all soon drunk, with the result that the second set suffered. 'It was just a disaster,' laments Colin Hanton. John started taking the piss out of the audience, as he had a tendency to do, and the Quarry Men weren't asked back. John was often sarcastic and downright rude to people, picking on their weaknesses. He had a particularly nasty habit of mocking and mimicking the disabled. On the bus home that night, this same devilment got into Paul, who started impersonating the way deaf and dumb people speak. 'I had two deaf and dumb friends in the factory [where I worked] and that just got me so mad I sort of rounded on him and told him in no uncertain terms to stop that and shut up,' says Colin, who picked up his drums and left the bus, and thereby the band. Steady drummers were hard to come by – few boys could afford the equipment – and the loss of Colin was a bigger blow than they realised. John, Paul and George would struggle to find a solid replacement right up to the point when they signed with EMI as the Beatles.

WHY A SHOW SHOULD BE SHAPED LIKE A W

After George Harrison left school in the summer, without any qualifications, to become an apprentice electrician, the drummerless Quarry Men started playing the Casbah Coffee Club, a homemade youth club in the cellar of a house in Hayman's Green, east of Liverpool city centre. This was the home of Mona 'Mo' Best, who had turned her basement into a hang-out for her teenage sons Pete and Rory and their mates.

The Quarry Men played the Casbah on its opening night, in August 1959, and regular Saturday evenings into the autumn. It was at one of these rave-ups that Paul met his first serious girlfriend, Dorothy 'Dot' Rhone, a shy grammar school girl who fancied John initially, but went with Paul when she discovered John was going steady with fellow art student Cynthia Powell.

While playing in the band with Paul and George, John maintained a parallel circle of college friends, headed by art student Stuart Sutcliffe, who becomes a significant character in our story. Born in Edinburgh in 1940, Stu was the son of a Scottish merchant seaman and his teacher wife, who came to Liverpool during the war. John and Paul were both artistic, with a talent for cartooning. Paul was given a prize for his artwork at the Liverpool Institute speech day in December 1959. But Stuart Sutcliffe was *really* talented, a true artist whose figurative and abstract work made Paul's drawings look like doodles. Around the time Paul won his school prize, Stuart had a painting selected for the prestigious John Moores Exhibition at the Walker Art Gallery. What's more, the painting sold for £65 ($99), part of which John and Paul persuaded Stu to invest in a large, German-made Höfner bass guitar, which he bought on hire-purchase. So it was that Paul found himself in a band with John's older, talented and rather good-looking college friend, someone John grew closer to as he and Stu moved into student digs together in Gambier Terrace, a short walk from the Inny. There was naturally some jealousy on Paul's part.

Still, John and Paul remained friends, close enough to take a trip down south to visit Paul's Uncle Mike and Aunt Bett, who, between theatrical engagements, were managing the Fox and Hounds at Caversham in Berkshire. Mike regaled the boys with stories of his adventures in show business and suggested they perform in his taproom. The locals could do with livening up. He billed John and Paul the Nerk Twins – meaning they were nobodies – asking his young cousin what song he planned to open with. 'It's got to be a bright opening,' Mike told Paul. 'What do you know?'

'I know, "The World Is Waiting for the Sunrise",' replied Paul, citing an old song. 'Me dad used to play it on the piano.'

Uncle Mike sanctioned the choice, giving the lads some advice. 'A good act is shaped like a W,' he lectured, tracing the letter W in the air. It should start strong, at the top of the first stroke of the W, lift the set in the middle, and end high. 'Too many acts are shaped like an M,' Mike told the boys: they started quietly at the foot of the M, built to a climax in the middle, then faded at the end. With this advice fixed in their heads, the Nerk Twins did well at the Fox and Hounds, and Paul never forgot Uncle Mike's alphabetical advice. All his shows from now on would be shaped like Ws.

THE MAN WHO GAVE THE BEATLES AWAY

One of the places Paul and his friends hung out in Liverpool was the Jacaranda coffee bar on Slater Street, managed by an ebullient Welshman named Allan Williams. Born in 1930, Williams was a former encyclopaedia salesmen, who sang tenor in Gilbert & Sullivan operettas, and had recently begun to dabble in concert promotion. His first big show was to feature the American stars Eddie Cochran and Gene Vincent. Cochran died in a car crash before he could fulfil the engagement. The concert went ahead with Vincent and a cobbled-together support bill.

Williams's partner in this enterprise was the London impresario Larry Parnes, known for his stable of good-looking boy singers, one of whom nicknamed his parsimonious manager 'Parnes, Shillings and Pence'. Parnes's *modus operandi* was to take unknown singers and reinvent them as teen idols with exciting stage names: Reg Smith became Marty Wilde, a fey Liverpudlian named Ron Wycherley was transformed into Billy Fury. When he came to Liverpool for the Gene Vincent show, Parnes discovered that hundreds of local groups had formed in the city in the wake of the skiffle boom. These were mostly four- or five-piece outfits with a lead singer, typically performing American blues, rock and country records they heard in advance of other people around the country because sailors working the trans-Atlantic shipping routes brought the records directly from the USA to Merseyside. While Parnes had plenty of groups in London to back his singers on tours of the southern counties, he wasn't so well provided with backing groups in the North and Scotland. So he asked Allan Williams to line up a selection of local bands with a view to sending them out on the road with his boy singers. John Lennon had been asking if Williams could get the Quarry Men work, so Williams suggested the Quarry Men audition for Parnes.

At this juncture, John Lennon's group didn't have a fixed name, being in transition between the Quarry Men and the Beatles. Lennon's friend Bill Harry recalls a discussion with John and Stuart about wanting a name similar to Buddy Holly and the Crickets. They worked through a list of insects before selecting beetles. During the first half of 1960 the band would be known variously as the Beetles, the Silver Beetles, Silver Beets, Silver Beatles (with an *a*) and the Beatals, before finally becoming the Beatles. The precise sequence of these names and how exactly they decided on their final name has become confused over the years, with many claims and counter-claims as to how it happened. An obscure British poet named Royston Ellis, who spent an evening with John and Stuart at Gambier Terrace in June 1960, says that he suggested the spelling as a double pun on beat music and the beat generation.

> There have been several explanations advanced about how the Beatles got their name. I know, because it was my idea. The night when John told me the band wanted to call themselves 'the Beetles' I asked how he spelt it. He said, 'B – e – e – t – l – e – s' ... I said that since they played beat music and liked the beat way of life, and I was a beat poet and part of the big beat scene, [why didn't they] call themselves Beatles spelt with an a?

Yet Bill Harry says nobody used terms like 'big beat scene' on Merseyside before his started his *Mersey Beat* fanzine in 1961, and he chose the magazine's name because he saw himself as a journalist with a beat, like a policeman's beat, covering the local music scene. 'Once we'd started [publishing] *Mersey Beat*, after a while we started calling the [local bands] beat groups,' says Harry. 'That's where the 'beat group' [tag] came about, after the name *Mersey Beat*, the paper.'

However, the phrase 'big beat' had already been used: *The Big Beat* was, for example, a 1958 comedy-musical featuring Fats Domino. Paul himself says that it was John Lennon who dreamed up the final band name, with an A. It was certainly John who explained it best by turning the whole subject into a piece of nonsense for the début issue of *Mersey Beat*, published in July 1961, writing:

> Many people ask what are Beatles? Why Beatles? Ugh, Beatles, how did the name arrive? So we will tell you. It came in a vision – a man appeared on a flaming pie and said unto them 'From this day on you are Beatles with an A'. Thank you, Mister Man, they said, thanking him.

Even this explanation gives rise to debate, because Royston Ellis further claims that the night he gave John and Stuart the name Beatles he heated up a chicken pie for their supper, and the pie caught fire in the oven. Thus Ellis was the man with the flaming pie. All that can be said for sure is that John's band didn't call themselves 'the Beatles' consistently until August 1960.

Three months prior to this, at the Larry Parnes audition, they were the Silver Beetles, a band without a drummer. To enable his young friends to audition for Parnes, Allan Williams hooked them up with a part-time drummer, 26-year-old bottle-factory worker Tommy Moore. As it happened, Moore was late for the Parnes audition, so the boys borrowed Johnny Hutchinson from another auditioning band, Cass and the Casanovas. In the end the Silver Beetles were not selected by Mr Parnes to back Billy Fury on a northern tour, as they had hoped, but they were offered a chance to back one of the impresario's lesser acts, Liverpool shipwright John Askew, who, in light of the fact he sang romantic ballads, had been given the moniker Johnny Gentle. The Silver Beetles were to go with Johnny on a seven-date tour of provincial Scotland. It was not what they wanted, but it was something, and in preparation for this, their first foray into life as touring musicians, the boys chose stage names for themselves. Paul styled himself Paul Ramon. In mid-May 1960 they took the train from Liverpool Lime Street to the small town of Alloa, Clackmannanshire.

There was only a brief opportunity to rehearse before Johnny Gentle and the Silver Beetles went on stage for the first time in Alloa on Friday 20 May 1960. Johnny explained his act to the boys: he said he came on like Bobby Darin, in a white jacket, without a guitar, and stood at the mike singing covers such as 'Mack the Knife', before ending with a sing-along to Clarence Henry's 'I Don't Know Why I Love You But I Do'. Paul was the first to grasp what Johnny required from his backing band. 'He just seemed to know what I was trying to get over. He was one step ahead of John in that sense.' After Johnny's set, which went over well enough, the star signed autographs for his girl fans. The Silver Beetles played on, so everybody could have a dance. Johnny noticed that, as he signed, the girls were looking over his shoulder at his backing band, as much if not more interested in them than him.

On tour, Johnny's hotel bills were paid direct from London by Larry Parnes. The Silver Beetles were not so well looked after, and soon ran out of cash. Lennon called Parnes, demanding help. The promoter referred him to their 'manager' Allan Williams, who belatedly sent money, but not before the boys had been obliged to skip out of at least one hotel without paying their bill. Talking with Gentle, Lennon asked if Parnes would be interested in signing them permanently; he seemed more professional than Williams. Gentle asked Parnes, but he declined: 'No, they'll be fine for any gigs I get for you lads up North. But I don't want to take on any more groups. We've got enough down here [in London].'

'At the moment he's a bit tied up,' Johnny reported diplomatically.

'Never mind,' replied Lennon. 'We'll make it some other way.' It was that confidence again. Not just with Paul. The whole band possessed remarkable self-assurance. They didn't have a regular drummer 'and they had a bass player that was fairly useless', as Johnny observes of Stuart Sutcliffe, '[but] they had that belief that they were going to make it'.

Driving from Inverness to Fraserburgh on 23 May Johnny crashed their touring van into an oncoming car, causing drummer Tommy Moore to bash his face against the seat in front of him, breaking some teeth. The boys took the injured man to hospital, but Lennon soon had Moore out of bed, telling him: 'You can't lie here, we've got a gig to do!' Tommy played the Fraserburgh show with his jaw bandaged but, not surprisingly, quit the Silver Beetles when they all got home to Liverpool a few days later. He went back to his job in the bottle factory. The boys went round to Tommy's to plead with him to change his mind, but his girlfriend gave them short shrift. 'You can go and piss off!' she shouted out the window. 'He's not playing with you any more.'

Broke and drummerless, the boys asked Williams if he had any more work, and were rewarded with perhaps the lowliest gig in their history. Allan had a West Indian friend, nicknamed Lord Woodbine for his partiality to Woodbine cigarettes, who was managing a strip club on Upper Parliament Street. Lord Woodbine had a stripper coming in from

Manchester named Janice who would only work to live music. The Silver Beetles were persuaded to accompany Janice. 'She gave us a bit of Beethoven and the Spanish Fire Dance,' Paul recalled. '... we said, "We can't read music, sorry, but instead of the Spanish Fire Dance we can play the Harry Lime Cha-Cha, which we've arranged ourselves, and instead of Beethoven you can have "Moonglow" or "September Song" – take your pick ... So that's what she got.'

The boys got a little more exposure when they filled in at the Jacaranda for Williams's house band, a Caribbean steel band, who had upped-sticks and left one night, deciding they could do better elsewhere. The band eventually called Williams to tell him they'd gone to Hamburg in Germany, which was pulsating with life, the local club owners crying out for live music. Allan and Lord Woodbine went to see for themselves. In the city's red light district they met a club owner named Bruno Koschmider, a former First World War airman and circus clown with a wooden leg (some said his leg had been shot off in the war). A sinister impression was emphasised by the fact that Koschmider's staff addressed him as Führer. Herr Koschmider told Williams that his Hamburg customers were mad for rock 'n' roll music, but Germany lacked good, home-grown rock bands. He needed English bands. No agreement was reached at this meeting, but some time later Williams ran into Koschmider in London and this time Williams persuaded the German to take a young Liverpool act he nominally managed named Derry and the Seniors, featuring Howard 'Howie' Casey on saxophone. Derry and the Seniors did so well in Hamburg that Koschmider asked for an additional Liverpool act. This time Allan suggested the Silver Beetles. Howie Casey, who had seen the boys give their amateurish audition for Larry Parnes, advised Williams against sending a second-rater over in case they spoilt things. The matter would be moot, anyway, unless Allan could persuade the boys' guardians to let them go.

The Silver Beetles were all under 21, and a trip to Germany would disrupt what plans their families had for their future. Paul had started out as a promising student at the Liverpool Institute, passing O-level Spanish a year early. But music soon displaced hard study, and he did so poorly in his main O-levels he was kept back a year. Paul had just taken his A-levels, with half a hope of going to teacher-training college. It was an ambition that Jim McCartney wanted to hold him to. 'All the families were against them going,' says Allan Williams, who drew upon his experience as an encyclopaedia salesman to talk the adults round. 'I sort of described Hamburg as a holiday resort!' Jim McCartney was a particularly hard sell, knowing Mary would have wanted her son to get on with his studies and become a teacher, or something else in professional life. Still, if Paul really meant to go, his father knew it would be a mistake to try and stop him.

Before they could go anywhere the band had to find a new drummer. Mo Best's son Pete had taken up the drums, playing in a group named the Black Jacks. Approaching 19, Pete Best had been thumping the skins for the best part of two years, merely as a hobby. Like Paul, Pete was planning on going to teacher-training college. Paul and John watched Pete play at the Casbah, then Paul called the boy on the telephone. 'How'd you like to come to Hamburg with the Beatles?' he asked. Pete said he'd love to.

On Tuesday 16 August 1960, the Beatles, as they were now finally calling themselves, assembled outside the Jacaranda in Slater Street where Williams was loading his Austin van for the road trip to Germany. Into this puny vehicle would be crammed all five Beatles (John, Paul, George, Stu and now Pete), their baggage and musical equipment, plus five additional passengers: Allan and Beryl Williams, Beryl's brother Barry Chang, Lord Woodbine and an Austrian waiter friend of Bruno Koschmider's to whom they were giving a lift. As they waited for the off, the boys cut out paper letters spelling THE BEATLES and stuck them to the side of the van. When all their belongings had been stowed, the overburdened vehicle pulled away from the kerb and trundled down the road. Among the small crowd waving them off was John's sweetheart, Cynthia Powell, 'tears running down my cheeks as the van disappeared around the corner'. Further back, not wanting to embarrass her son, was Millie Sutcliffe, who had said goodbye to Stuart at home, but felt compelled to see him off in person. As the women wept, the boys were beside themselves with the excitement of what was going to be a great adventure.

HAMBURG

MACH SCHAU!

The 760-mile drive from Liverpool to Hamburg took Paul and his friends more than 24 hours, driving south through England, catching a ferry from Harwich to the Hook of Holland, then travelling east to the border of what was then the Federal Republic of West Germany, where the boys had to pretend to be students, because they didn't have work permits, before pushing on to their final destination.

Like Liverpool, Hamburg is a northern port on a river, the Elbe, which flows into the North Sea; and, like Liverpool again, Hamburg was bombed heavily during the Second World War, worse hit than Merseyside in fact, one devastating night of British bombing killing 42,000 people. Bearing in mind the history it is surprising how well treated the Beatles were in Hamburg only 15 years after the war. Equally remarkable is the fact that, despite being on the losing side in that recent war, Hamburg had been almost completely rebuilt by 1960, part of the *Wirtschaftswunder*, or economic miracle, that saw a defeated Germany rise again as the richest nation in Europe. Indeed, Hamburg already presented a more prosperous face than Liverpool.

The boys arrived after dark on Wednesday 17 August 1960, leaning out of the windows of Allan Williams's van to ask directions to the Reeperbahn, a road which everybody could point them towards. This most infamous of Hamburg streets lies a couple of miles east of the Hauptbahnhof, parallel with the docks in St Pauli, a neighbourhood renowned for uninhibited night-time entertainment. Men flocked here then as now to drink, eat and have sex, sex being treated more candidly in Germany than in England. Indeed, much that was and remains illegal in the UK, notably prostitution, was and remains legitimate in the red light district of Hamburg. Regulated and sanctioned by the authorities, whorehouses, sex cinemas, pornographic bookshops and lewd clubs lined the Reeperbahn and its tributary streets, such as Herbertstrasse, where hookers sat in brothel windows touting for trade. Amazing sights though these were for the boys, there was also a familiar vulgarity to St Pauli, putting Paul in mind of the Lancashire resort of Blackpool, 'but with strip clubs'.

Their van turned off the Reeperbahn into Grosse Freiheit, a side street the name of which translates as the Big Freedom. The street was lit up with lurid signs advertising sex, beer and music. They parked outside the Kaiserkeller, Bruno Koschmider's underground club: a big old joint fitted out with a nautical theme, like an underwater world. Derry and the Seniors were on stage, blasting out rhythm and blues to an audience of enthusiastic Germans, including Horst Fascher, a former featherweight boxer who'd served time for accidentally killing a man in a fight and now worked as a pimp. Horst spent much of his free time in the Kaiserkeller listening to rock 'n' roll. Hearing that a new group had just arrived from England, Horst rushed upstairs to greet them, finding 'five tired guys' in a van, rubbing the grime from the windows with their elbows as they peered out at this new world. Horst, or Horsti as Paul called him, became firm friends with the boys, a pal and protector in the rough-and-tumble world of St Pauli.

The reality of their engagement came home to the Beatles the next day when Koschmider informed the band that they weren't playing the Kaiserkeller, but a smaller place he owned up the street, a former strip joint named the Indra which he wanted to turn into a club catering to the new rock 'n' roll craze. The Indra had the dimensions and charm of a large shoebox, closed in by a low ceiling and fitted out with whore-house-red booths. Further disappointment came when the boys were shown their digs. Further up the same road, on the corner of Paul-Roosen-Strasse, was the Bambi Kino, a fleapit cinema also owned by Koschmider. The Beatles were to be accommodated in the windowless back rooms, without proper toilet facilities or even hooks to hang up their clothes. They might have been forgiven if they had turned around and gone home to Liverpool, but with the tolerance of youth the boys unpacked and made the best of it, beginning their Indra residency almost immediately.

The regime at the Indra was punishing, even slightly mad. The Beatles were contracted to play every night, starting in the early evening, a total of four and a half hours in the week and six on Saturdays and Sundays, which meant they worked into the early hours of the following morning. Even with 15-minute breaks between sets these were musical marathons. Essentially the Beatles were playing to attract customers who would spend money on drink, but the Indra's patrons seemed disappointed at first that the strippers had been replaced by five amateurish English boys – more or less fresh out of school – dressed in silly, lilac-coloured jackets (made by Paul's neighbour), performing a limited repertoire of songs with the tentativeness of beginners. 'When the Beatles came they knew about 15 songs,' recalls Rosi Haitmann, one of Koschmider's barmaids. It was hardly enough to fill half an hour, let alone four and a half hours, yet the Beatles somehow managed to play nightly at the Indra for the next seven weeks, during which time they enlarged their set. Then, after 48 nights of this apprenticeship, Koschmider closed the Indra, because of complaints from neighbours about noise, and moved the Beatles down to the Kaiserkeller to replace Derry and the Seniors.

In a bigger room, the Beatles' lack of experience became more apparent. Koschmider grumbled to Allan Williams, who wrote to the boys advising them to put on more of a show. Koschmider picked up on this advice, barking encouragement in German: 'Mach Schau! Mach Schau!'

Over-worked, over-tired, and now taunted by their German boss, the Beatles turned Koschmider's order into a joke, yelling 'Mach Schau!' in parody of the impresario as they threw themselves into an increasingly madcap performance at the Kaiserkeller. Paul hollered in uninhibited imitation of Little Richard, while John became a character from the *Goons*, singing comic songs, using funny voices, saying any outrageous thing that popped into his head, sometimes pretending to fight the others on stage. The crazier John became, the more the crowd liked it. Lennon went further, wearing a toilet seat round his neck, also Nazi insignia he'd bought from an antique shop, even shrieking 'Sieg Heil!' at the audience, which was forbidden in post-war Germany. The audiences loved it all, sending up beer and cheap champagne, which the boys guzzled greedily, though their favourite drink was Scotch and Coke, which remains Paul's tipple.

To stay awake during these seemingly endless gigs, the boys started taking Preludin, an over-the-counter slimming aid which had an effect similar to that of amphetamines. They consumed the pills recklessly, quickly building up a tolerance. 'I took half of one once,' says former Kaiserkeller barmaid Ruth Lallemann. 'I know they put like ten in a bottle, smashed them all up with Coke, and then they share it between them. So they were right away! That's why John Lennon got sometimes so wild.' Drunk on beer and speeding on pills, the boys played on hour after hour, taking requests from their audience, telling jokes, Lennon lying down under the piano for a nap when he became too exhausted, the others playing on with bemused smiles, pausing to smoke cigarettes, drink and even eat on stage. Pleased with the Beatles' *shau*, Koschmider extended their contract.

In the wee small hours of the morning, after most of the patrons had left, the Beatles slowed into a semi-somnolent blues jam, playing for themselves and their friends, that is musicians from other visiting bands and club workers like Rosi and Ruth, the girls coming round from behind the bar to jive. Despite being engaged to one of the waiters, and even though Paul had Dot waiting for him in Liverpool, Ruth Lallemann says she began to date Paul, and continued to do so throughout his time in Hamburg, though they never actually had sex: 'I never slept with him. Just kissing.' There were, however, other German girlfriends.

At first the barmaids struggled to communicate with the boys. Paul spoke a little German, having studied the language at the Liverpool Institute, but it was English they mostly all spoke, the girls' stilted questions met by the Beatles' outrageous cheek, which the barmaids gradually began to understand and laugh at, copying their Scouse phrases and swear-words. Soon they were bantering back and forth in cheerful obscenity. 'We were all *fucking* this, *fucking* that,' laughs Ruth. 'We asked them to write the song lyrics down, and they wrote really dirty words, and they were singing them on stage.' After work the friends sometimes shared a cab to the beach, where they spent the last days of summer together, returning to Hamburg for work in the evening. It was a happy time. Then the Beatles found a new set of German friends.

THE EXIS

There was a breath of autumn in the air when a fey young graphic artist named Klaus Voormann descended to the Kaiserkeller, taking a seat in one of the quaint half-boats arranged in front of the stage. He looked up to see the Beatles performing 'Hippy Hippy Shake'. Delighted by this exuberant music, Klaus rushed home to tell his sweetheart, Astrid, with whom he had just had a fight. They patched up their differences and returned the following evening with their friend, Jürgen Vollmer.

Klaus Voormann and Astrid Kirchherr, both 22, had known each other since art school in Hamburg, where they also met Jürgen. Klaus made exquisite line drawings in the style of Aubrey Beardsley, whose androgynous figures he and Jürgen resembled. Astrid was striking in her own way, a slim woman in black with cropped blonde hair, a wide mouth and a chilly Teutonic manner. One could imagine her barking 'Sieg Heil!' and indeed she had done so at school during the Second World War, thinking it meant something like 'How do you do?' As with many Germans who were children during the war, Astrid, Klaus and Jürgen had little understanding of the politics of the recent conflict, though it had affected all their lives profoundly: Jürgen's father was an army officer killed during the Siege of Stalingrad, for example; Astrid's brother died of dysentery as the family fled the invading Soviet army in 1945. After the madness of the war, the adult survivors rebuilt a Germany that was subdued and conservative, where everything worked efficiently, and where to say something was in *ordnung* (in proper order) was to give high praise, but where there was precious little excitement. Germany had had enough excitement. To younger people coming to adulthood, the generation of Astrid, Jürgen and Klaus, this new Germany seemed dull. 'Like every teenager, we wanted to have fun,' notes Jürgen. They looked to neighbouring France, especially Paris, where Jean-Paul Sartre and Jean Genet led the existentialist movement, and styled themselves Exis in honour of these free-living French intellectuals, though they understood little of existentialist philosophy. It was more a shorthand for dressing in black and adopting bohemian ways.

So it was that three young, self-conscious, middle-class Germans sat in a half-boat watching the crazy Englishmen at the Kaiserkeller. As Astrid recalls, Paul was the most animated that first night:

He was jumping up and down, and pulling faces when he was singing, and shook his head … The others were just standing there.
Stuart didn't move at all. John only moved a little bit, when he sang.
And George just tapped his foot … The only one who was a professional entertainer was Paul.

During a set break, Klaus introduced himself and his friends shyly in
broken English. The musicians admired their clothes. Jürgen said he
bought *all* his clothes at the Paris flea markets. Detecting pomposity,
John plucked an imaginary flea off Jürgen's coat and pretended to flick
it at Paul, who flinched.

John noted Jürgen's floppy haircut, asking if he had it done in Paris.
'No, I cut it myself.'

'Funny looking, ain't it, George?'

'It is.'

'Would look good on Paul, though,' said John, putting a comb under
Paul's nose to make a Hitler face.

Despite the bad-taste jokes and sarcasm, which was John's stock in
trade, the Exis and the Beatles liked each other immediately. Astrid,
Klaus and Jürgen were bright, arty middle-class young people of the
type John and Stu had mixed with at college in Liverpool, while grammar school boys Paul and George could also relate to them. Deep down
they also sensed a mutual insecurity here in the red light district of a
tough port city, and henceforth took comfort in each others' company,
meeting in the cafés and bars of St Pauli during the day and nightly in
the club, where the Beatles' other, more down-to-earth German friends,
Horsti the pimp and bar girls Rosi and Ruth looked askance at the
interlopers. 'We didn't like them, because they were always very posh,'
says barmaid Rosi Haitmann, though she had to admit Astrid had
charisma. When Astrid walked into the Kaiserkeller, it was like 'the
Queen came, with her entourage'. Staff buzzed around the Exis because
they had money, but mocked them behind their backs. 'I thought, "Oh
my God, you fucking cunt!"' recalls Rosi, laughing at their pretentious
conversation. Pete Best was also excluded from this new friendship,
not being quite as sophisticated as the other Beatles, while Stu stood
apart from the boys for his lack of musical ability, having failed to
improve as their bassist. This was a source of growing frustration to
Paul in particular. 'Paul and George occasionally gave Stuart an angry

look, because he must have played some wrong chord,' recalls Jürgen. 'Stuart was always an outsider, that didn't really fit in. But [we] liked Stuart a lot. He was more like us: he was not a rock 'n' roll musician, he was a talented artist.'

Klaus was the only real artist among the Germans. Astrid and Jürgen had been to art college, but now worked as assistants to a Hamburg photographer. Astrid took pictures herself and told the Beatles she wanted to conduct a photo session with them. The boys were flattered, Paul discussing with Klaus what he should wear. He chose a dark sports jacket with pinstripes, his hair combed back rocker-style. Astrid posed the five English boys against fairground machinery in the nearby park, the Heiligengeistfeld. Lacking much English, she manipulated the lads with her hands, like mannequins, tilting their heads this way and that. As she touched Stuart's face, Astrid felt a frisson of excitement. She resolved to learn English as soon as possible so she could communicate properly with this boy.

In emulation of their new Exi friends, the Beatles started to dress differently, acquiring black leather jackets and leather trousers to replace their lilac stage jackets, which they'd already worn to destruction, the leathers giving them a new, macho look. Underneath the leather the Beatles were still nicely-brought-up young men who craved home comforts, so they were all grateful when Astrid took them home to meet Mummy in the suburb of Altona. 'They loved mashed potatoes and peas and steak and things like that. So Mummy did all that for them, and a nice cup of tea, which they couldn't hardly get in Hamburg.' The Beatles were on their best behaviour during these Altona visits, not least Paul, in whom Jim and Mary McCartney had instilled good manners. 'Paul was very, very polite to my mummy.' The Beatles were slightly surprised to discover that Astrid lived in a self-contained studio flat at the top of her mother's house, her penthouse decorated mostly in black, with one wall gold and another covered in silver foil. Here she slept with Klaus, which would have been unusual for an unmarried couple in Liverpool. The Germans were so much more relaxed about sex, with the Kirchherrs sophisticated in other ways, too. They had an extensive collection of classical music albums, which Paul spent time looking through. He picked out and played Stravinsky's *The Rite of Spring*, as Astrid recalls, the first example of Paul's interest in such music. Meanwhile Astrid was falling in love with Stuart Sutcliffe. Within two weeks of their meeting, she had ended her relationship with Klaus and taken Stu as her new lover, a turn of events Klaus took with laudable maturity. Everybody remained friends.

Paul found that there were many girls in St Pauli eager to sleep with him and his band mates. 'We were kids let off the leash,' he later reminisced,

and we were used to these little Liverpool girls, but by the time you got to Hamburg if you got a girlfriend there she's likely to be a stripper* … for someone who'd not really had too much sex in their lives before, which none of us really had, to be suddenly involved in these hardcore striptease artists, who obviously knew a thing or two about sex, was quite an eye-opener.

By all accounts there was a virtual nightly orgy at the Bambi Kino, George losing his virginity in their squalid digs while the others lay in their cots nearby: '… after I'd finished they all applauded and cheered. At least they kept quiet whilst I was doing it.' In his memoirs, Pete Best boasted: 'The most memorable night of love in our dowdy billet was when eight birds gathered there to do the Beatles a favour. We managed to swap all four of us – twice!' One of the girls who supposedly slept with Paul McCartney during his first visit to Hamburg was a teenager named Erika Wohlers. 'I got to know Paul and the four others in 1960,' claims Erika.

We always sat beside the stage, me and my girlfriends. Back then I was 17 years old, and turned 18 on 22 November 1960. Thus I was still underage. During the breaks, the group would sit at our table. Paul and I got close to each other [and] had sex for the first time at some point in 1960 … We regularly had sex.

Erika later claimed that Paul made her pregnant, a story we shall come to.

The Beatles' popularity at the Kaiserkeller was making Bruno Koschmider's cash tills ring, demonstrating to other Hamburg club owners that there was money to be made from rock 'n' roll. In October a

* Ruth Lallemann wasn't.

new club, the Top Ten, opened on the Reeperbahn, showcasing a British singer named Tony Sheridan (who dated and later married Rosi Haitmann). The boys went to see Tony's show and sometimes got up on stage with him, playing together with a passion that was partly due to their belief that rock 'n' roll wouldn't last, that this was a moment to be seized and enjoyed before the public lost interest in the music.

Says Sheridan, explaining the passion with which they performed:

In those days it was, *There's going to be one more year of rock 'n' roll*. After that the real music was coming, the real songs. We all believed it. We had about six months to do it in, then forget it. This was the attitude. It was like burning houses. Do it and get out as quickly as possible.

The owner of the Top Ten, Peter Eckhorn, was so impressed by what he saw of the Beatles that he offered to hire the band after they finished at the Kaiserkeller. Koschmider was furious and banned the boys from visiting the Top Ten. They defied Koschmider, going to the Top Ten as often as they liked, which ruined their relationship with Koschmider. As the Beatles played out their contract, the Führer resolved to get his own back. The law stated that anybody under 18 had to leave St Pauli by 10:00 p.m., a rule the Beatles flouted nightly because George was under age. The police now enforced this law, presumably because of a tip-off from the vengeful Koschmider, deporting Harrison on 21 November 1960. The others carried on as best they could at the Kaiserkeller, moving their things over to the Top Ten, where Eckhorn had offered them digs. As they prepared to depart the Bambi Kino, Paul and Pete set a fire in the corridor. In a contemporaneous letter Paul stated that they set fire to 'a piece of cord nailed to the wall'. Subsequently he and Pete said it was a condom. Either way, it was a tiny fire of no consequence, but Koschmider reported them for arson. The police arrested Paul and Pete at the Top Ten the following morning – the first but not the last time Paul McCartney would have his collar felt. The lads were taken to the neighbourhood police station, the Davidwache, then to jail for a few hours, before being deported from Germany by air.

THE CAVERN

Paul arrived home at 20 Forthlin Road early on Friday 2 December 1960, full of stories of his German adventures, but Dad soon brought his eldest son down to earth. Having had his fun, Paul was now expected to get a proper job. For once in his life Jim McCartney played the stern father. 'He virtually chucked me out of the house,' Paul later remarked with surprise. Paul had had pocket-money jobs in the past: working on a coal lorry, a delivery van, and as Christmas relief at the Post Office. Now the Labour Exchange sent him to his first real job, at the electrical firm of Massey & Coggins Ltd in Edge Hill. Here he was set to work coiling electrical cables, though the personable McCartney soon caught the eye of management, who expressed interest in training him up as a junior executive. Paul was at the Edge Hill works when John Lennon and George Harrison slouched by to ask what he was doing. Paul explained what Dad had said: *Get a job or else!* John told Paul not to be so soft. He took the view that Paul was too easily cowed by his father, and persuaded him to come back to the band. Paul agreed, but held on to his job as well for the time being.

After a couple of warm-up gigs, the Beatles played a memorable Christmas dance at the Litherland Town Hall on 27 December 1960. Stu was still in Germany, so the boys got Pete Best's mate Chas Newby to play bass. It was at Litherland that the Beatles showed how much they'd learned in Hamburg. They were much better musicians now, their act honed by hundreds of hours on stage. Billed as 'Direct from Hamburg', they were assumed by many of the girls to be German. 'The girls used to say to Paul McCartney, "You speak *very* good English for a German,"' recalls Allan Williams, who was still nominally their manager. 'And of course Paul is a bit clever, he could speak a bit of German, he used to go along with it.' Not long after this triumphant hometown show, Stu returned from Germany and the re-formed Beatles gigged virtually daily in January and February 1961, building a Merseyside following. So busy did they become in this short period that Paul's old schoolmate 'Nell' Aspinall gave up an accountancy course to drive the boys around.

The Cavern, where the Beatles first performed in early February 1961, was a warehouse cellar, essentially; three barrel-vaulted storerooms under the pavement of Mathew Street, a short, cobbled lane off Whitechapel in the middle of Liverpool. The warehouses in the area were used to store fruit and vegetables, the smell of rotting fruit adding to the distinctive aroma of the club (rotten vegetables plus cheap scent, plus sweat and drains). The Cavern had first come into existence as a jazz club in 1957, its stage constructed coincidentally by Paul's carpenter Uncle Harry. The Cavern proved a popular but claustrophobic venue. Deep underground, without air conditioning or a fire exit, in an era when many people smoked, the club quickly became stuffy, while condensation caused the limewash to flake off the ceiling and fall like snow on the revellers. On the plus side, the cellar had good acoustics, and the narrow quarters engendered a sense of intimacy. One could feel the throb and thrum of the music as the jazzmen plucked, struck and blew their instruments. Bodies pressed close. One felt connected to the music and to the other patrons.

Ray McFall, the owner, started to open the Cavern at lunchtime as a place for office and shop workers to come for a snack, with the attraction of live bands on stage. The boys had already played the venue as the Quarry Men. They performed there as the Beatles first on Thursday 9 February 1961, and almost 300 times over the next two and half years, the Cavern becoming inextricably linked with their rise to fame. Here the band met their manager, finalised their line-up and tasted success; while the intimacy of the venue helped the Beatles bond with their audience. They were performing in what was virtually a tunnel face to face with their public, with whom they had to engage simply to get to the dressing room, or drezzy ('three coat hangers and a bench,' recalls 'Measles' Bramwell), standing close enough to the patrons when on stage to talk to them without raising their voices. Sometimes they plucked cigarettes from the lips of girls, took a drag, then handed the ciggies back.

The audience was not exclusively female. Boys also liked the Beatles from the start. 'Their sound was different and they looked different … they were an outrageous lot,' recalls Cavern regular Ray O'Brien.

Whereas all the other bands, like the Remo Four, were reasonably well dressed, and you knew what they were going to do next, you never knew with the Beatles. It was sort of off-the-cuff stuff they were doing at the time. There was a lot of repartee with the audience – I was attracted to that.

For girls, the Beatles were of course also objects of affection. 'I used to think Paul was the best-looking,' muses Frieda Kelly, a fellow Cavern-dweller who founded the Beatles' fan club, though Frieda changed her favourite Beatle almost as often as her socks; 'then I'd look at John – he's got like a strong face … then George was the youngest and he was sort of attractive [too].' Like most girls, Frieda relished the direct, friendly contact with the boys at the Cavern. Nobody became hysterical. The original female Cavern fans disdained the crazed girls who came later, when the Beatles became a nationwide, then worldwide sensation. 'I never screamed. Liverpool people didn't scream in the beginning,' says Frieda. 'If you start screaming, you can't hear what they're saying … I was a fan. But I wasn't a *maniac*.'

BACK TO HAMBURG

Since being deported from Germany, Paul had paid a visit to the German Consulate in Liverpool and written to the German police giving his account of the fire at the Bambi Kino, all to try and get permission for the band to return. The reply now came that the Beatles could return to Germany as long as they obtained work permits. They did so without delay. George had also turned 18, so there was no further difficulty there. Paul quit his job with Massey & Coggins, and returned to Hamburg with the Beatles in March 1961, gambling his future on the success of the band.

This time the Beatles would be playing for Peter Eckhorn at the Top Ten, sleeping in the club attic, which was a slightly better arrangement than before, though the conditions were still basic and the hours very long. Taking the view that they had secured this gig themselves, the boys wrote to Allan Williams informing him that he would not receive a commission. Williams wrote a two-page letter of reply, dated 20 April, that was by turns indignant, threatening and pleading: he claimed he had a deal pending to book Ray Charles, whom he knew the Beatles admired. 'I had thought of you going on tour with him.' The Beatles evidently didn't believe Williams, or didn't care. They had outgrown Allan, who would have to live with the fact that he had briefly had the biggest band in the world in his hands, but had let them slip away. 'And if you think I lose sleep over this, you are on the right track,' he wrote in his book *The Man Who Gave the Beatles Away*. 'I often wake in the night and stare at the wall, and I can feel my teeth grinding together …'

Paul and John's Liverpool girlfriends, Dot and Cynthia, came over to Hamburg for a visit. John was willing to bed down with Cyn in the band's communal room above the Top Ten, along with Paul and Dot, Tony Sheridan and his girlfriend Rosi, but Paul didn't want to bring Dot into this overcrowded den. 'Paul thought it's not good for Dot,' recalls Rosi. The boys were friendly with an older woman who looked after the toilets at the club, and she kindly allowed Paul and Dot to sleep together alone on her houseboat on the Elbe, a happy and romantic visit culminating in Paul giving Dot an engagement ring.

It was while Dot was in town that the problem of Stuart Sutcliffe came to a head. Paul's relationship with Stu was increasingly strained. While being an enviable young man in many ways, Stu was a useless musician who had failed to improve. Paul was now not only proficient on lead guitar, but could turn his hand to playing bass, piano and drums. Stu couldn't even master the simplest of rock instruments. The Beatles were carrying Stu, who was only in the band because he was John's mate. 'Very much later I understood that Paul sometimes was very angry with [Stuart], because he never practised. And when Paul moaned about it, John said, "It doesn't matter. He looks good." That was John's answer,' notes Stu's lover Astrid Kirchherr. 'Paul was a professional, [so] it was hard for him to [put] up with a guy who just looked cool, and his best mate John protected him all the time.'

Paul had recently dropped and broken his cheap Rosetti guitar. Having decided the guitar was a write-off, the boys enjoyed stomping it to pieces, after which Paul had little choice but to play the Top Ten piano during their set. One night when he was at the keyboard, Paul made a rude remark about Astrid. Nobody remembers exactly what he said, but it was bad enough to cause Stu to lose his temper. Slightly built though he was, Stu swung a punch at Paul. 'Don't you ever say anything about Astrid again!' he said, defending his sweetheart.

'I'll say what I like!'

This altercation is often presented as the only time Paul and Stu came to blows. In fact, 'they were always fighting,' says Ruth Lallemann, who remembers the boys regularly pushing and shoving each other. 'You didn't talk about things. You fought.' George Harrison said he had 'a lot of fist fights with Stuart' to establish a pecking order. Tony

Sheridan adds: 'Paul didn't get on with [Stu]. There was animosity. There was open fighting on stage ... Some ugly stuff went on.' This particular fight over Astrid was bad enough to signal the end of Stuart's tenure as a Beatle. He quit the band soon afterwards to live with Astrid and study art in Hamburg, remaining friendly with the boys. Indeed, as soon as Stuart left the band Paul seemed better inclined towards him. As a musician, Stu held them back; now he could just be a mate. As neither John nor George wanted to take up Stuart's bass – the least glamorous instrument in a band – this job fell to Paul, who needed a new instrument. To get him started, Stu generously leant him his expensive Höfner. Later Paul bought the smaller, cheaper Höfner violin bass, which became his signature instrument. It is a mark of Paul's talent, and strength of personality, that despite being on a backline instrument he remained an equal front man with John.

Soon after Stu's departure the boys were talent-spotted by a German music publisher, who hired them to back Tony Sheridan on a recording session for Polydor. The result was a single, 'My Bonnie', released locally in August 1961. Credited to Tony Sheridan and the Beat Brothers, the track is a lively cover of the traditional song 'My Bonnie Lies Over the Ocean', starting quietly, then breaking into a rave-up, Paul hollering with joy in the background. It made number 32 in the German singles chart that year, and remains a very engaging record.

The band returned to Liverpool before 'My Bonnie' was released, finding themselves increasingly in demand on Merseyside where there were now scores if not hundreds of similar 'beat bands'. The stock in trade of nearly all these groups was American songs, often learned from discs brought into Liverpool by sailors, becoming proprietorial about tunes they considered their own, though bands would swap songs. 'I remember swapping with George "Roll Over Beethoven"; and I let him do "Jambalaya",' recalls Gerry Marsden, leader of Gerry and the Pacemakers. Bands were rivals – for gigs, exposure and the El Dorado of a record contract – but also mates. One memorable night at Litherland Town Hall the Beatles and the Pacemakers joined forces. 'We said, "Let's have one band for tonight." And we called it the Beatmakers: the Pacemakers and the Beats [sic],' remembers Marsden. The musicians swapped instruments. Paul played the town hall piano, the Pacemakers' pianist played sax. 'We had a ball.'

THE MOP-TOP

When John turned 21 in October 1961 he received £100 ($153) as a gift from a well-to-do aunt, an act of such munificence Paul never forgot it, often remarking that nobody had ever given *him* a hundred quid. The gift highlighted a subtle but significant class difference between the friends. 'To us John was upper class,' Paul commented for the Beatles' multi-media documentary project, the *Anthology*. 'His relatives were teachers, dentists, even someone up in Edinburgh in the BBC. It's ironic, he was always very "fuck you!" and he wrote the song "Working Class Hero" – in fact he wasn't at all working-class.' Still, John generously used his birthday money to treat him and Paul to a trip to Paris which, despite having money to spend, they decided to see on the cheap, hitch-hiking from Liverpool to the French capital where they arrived dressed in rocker gear, their hair in long, greasy quiffs.

One of the first things John and Paul did when they got into Paris was look up their Exi friend Jürgen Vollmer, who was now working in the city as an assistant to the American photographer William Klein. Jürgen met the boys outside the church of St Germain-des-Prés. Having established that they had no place to stay, he took them to his digs in the nearby Hotel de Beaune. As Jürgen tried to sneak the boys up the stairs of this cheap hotel, he was discovered by his landlady, who threw the Englishmen out. 'We didn't like the service here, anyway,' Lennon told the biddy, with mocking hauteur.

'Shall we try the Ritz?' Paul asked his friend, readily falling into a double act.

Jürgen met up with John and Paul the next day, and started showing them around Paris. The English boys were full of fun and good humour, picking Jürgen up and running with him past L'Opéra singing nonsense arias, and generally behaving like a couple of Marx Brothers. Jürgen decided they should meet his girlfriend, Alice, arranging a rendezvous. But Alice was horrified by the English boys, whom Jürgen now saw, through her eyes, as scruffy, even dangerous-looking rockers. 'She didn't even sit down.' John and Paul weren't going to pull any Parisian birds the way they were dressed. So Jürgen took them to the flea market at Porte de Clignancourt, where they bought beatnik-type outfits. Next they wanted their hair cut like Jürgen's – combed forward over their eyes and cut in a fringe.

'They asked me, "We like that funny haircut, Jürgen, can you cut ours?" Because they knew that I always cut my hair myself.' Jürgen took John and Paul back to his hotel, managing to sneak them up to his room this time. He sat Paul down first in front of the mirror, draped a towel over his shoulders, and snipped away at his rocker quiff, changing it into a softer, floppy Left Bank mop-top. For years the Beatle mop-top was credited to Astrid Kirchherr, who said she first styled the boys' hair this way in Hamburg, a claim that infuriates Vollmer, who asserts he was the true originator of the hairstyle, and indeed Paul has backed him up in this. A trivial enough matter, one might have thought, but for a man to wear his hair like this in 1961 was rebellious. 'Very difficult for people to imagine that there was a time like that,' says Jürgen.

BRIAN

John and Paul were soon back in Liverpool where they now met one of the most important characters in the Beatles story. A short stroll from the Cavern, in Whitechapel, was a branch of NEMS, a local chain of family-owned electrical stores that also sold records. NEMS was origi-nally a furniture shop founded in 1901 by a Jewish-Polish immigrant named Isaac Epstein, the business carried on by his son, Harry, who lived with his wife Queenie in a large, detached house in Queens Drive, Childwall. Harry and Queenie Epstein had two sons, the elder of whom, Brian, was 'one of those out-of-sorts boys who never quite fit in', as he wrote in his memoirs, a coded acknowledgement that he was homosexual.

Born in 1934, making him only seven years Paul McCartney's senior, though he always seemed much older, Brian Epstein was expelled from his first secondary school aged 10, then passed through five more schools before 16, when he told his parents he wanted to be a dress designer. Although frank with his parents and friends about his sexual-ity, Brian was necessarily guarded with strangers, at a time when homosexuality was illegal in Britain, and sex caused him problems. He was 'very mixed up', as his mother said. 'He wasn't at all happy with it; his love affairs were disastrous.' In appearance, Brian possessed a soft, bashful face, with gappy teeth, a weak chin and a childhood squint that manifested itself when he felt under pressure. He dressed immaculately, his hair carefully styled, and affected an upper-class accent with a penchant for ornate and pompous expressions. Brian liked to think of himself as artistic. He enjoyed classical music and the theatre, giving the impression all in all of being a rather precious young man. 'I thought he was a popinjay. Narcissistic,' comments the family lawyer E. Rex Makin, who found himself called upon professionally when Brian's sex life got him into trouble.

After the ordeal of school, it was Brian's further misfortune to be called up for National Service, a duty Paul McCartney narrowly avoided when conscription ended in Britain in 1960. Brian was soon ejected from the military, classified 'emotionally and mentally unfit'. Next he attempted to become an actor, studying at the Royal Academy of Dramatic Art (RADA) in London, but he didn't do well here either. During his sojourn in the capital, Brian was arrested for importuning a policeman. Having quit RADA, he was blackmailed by another homosexual pick-up in Liverpool. Brian had developed a taste for rough trade. Makin recalls:

> Brian came to me one day … in great distress with a black eye and a broken this, that and the other. He'd picked up a lad at the Pier Head and he'd taken him to Sefton Park, where the customer, put it like that, turned rough on him and he handed over his wallet and didn't know what to do. I said, "The first thing you have to do is to tell your father. If you won't do it, I'll do it for you." And I did it, and we went to the police [who arrested and charged the blackmailer]. He was convicted and got a jail sentence.

Brian stayed in Liverpool after this episode, helping to manage the family businesses. For years there had been an annex to the original furniture store on Walton Road selling sheet music, records and pianos. This was North End Music Stores (NEMS), suppliers of the McCartneys' piano. During the consumer boom of the late 1950s, the Epsteins opened additional branches of NEMS, selling electrical goods and records. Brian managed these stores, and in doing so employed people who become significant in the Beatles' story. He hired Peter Brown for one, a former sales assistant at Lewis's, the biggest department store in Liverpool; also a young man named Alistair Taylor as his personal assistant. Both went on to work for the Beatles.

Mr Brian, as Brian Epstein liked to be known to his staff, invested a great deal of energy in the record division of NEMS, creating elaborate window displays in the Whitechapel shop to promote new releases, adopting a policy of ordering any record any customer requested. He prided himself on being attuned to the tastes of the public, but claims in his autobiography to have been ignorant of the existence of the Beatles until a young man named Raymond Jones walked into his shop asking for 'My Bonnie'. It has since become clear that Brian almost certainly knew who the Beatles were by this stage, and may well have seen them in NEMS, which they frequented to listen to new releases and chat up the shop girls. The truth may be that Brian had been watching the Beatles from afar, with a glad eye, before he summoned the courage to meet them.

In any event, Epstein placed an order for 'My Bonnie' for Jones. When a girl came in asking for the same record, he ordered 200 more, and it was as this point he decided to meet the band. Bill Harry informed him, if he didn't already know, that the Beatles were to be seen five minutes' walk away in Mathew Street, playing lunchtime sessions at the Cavern. Fearing he would be out of place in a cellar full of teenagers 'talking teenage talk', Brian went over the road with his assistant Alistair Taylor. The Beatles were performing when the two men descended the stairs to the Cavern, on 9 November 1961, the boys acting the goat on stage between bursts of energetic rock 'n' roll. The Cavern MC, Bob Wooler – 'Hello, Cavern dwellers, and welcome to the best of cellars' – promptly announced that *Mr* Epstein was in the room, as if that was a big deal, and all eyes turned to the gentleman at the entrance. Brian was only 27, but must have appeared middle-aged to the denizens of the Cavern, though many were likewise in their twenties. It was the way Brian dressed, carried himself and spoke. 'He could speak English, which none of us could,' comments Tony 'Measles' Bramwell with hyperbole. 'Brian had been elocuted [sic].'

George Harrison asked what brought Mr Brian down to see them. Epstein asked in reply about their song, 'My Bonnie', and they proceeded to banter back and forth. 'They were extremely amusing and in a rough "take it or leave it way" very attractive,' Epstein later wrote, giving the clear impression of a flirtation. 'I will never know what made me say to this eccentric group of boys that I thought a further meeting might be helpful to them and me.' Still, a meeting was scheduled at his office, which was over the NEMS shop, for 3 December. The Beatles approached the date with a mixture of hope and scepticism. After all, what could the manager of an electrical shop do for them in show business? At least they'd been to Germany, played on stage and cut a record. Brian hadn't done much except get kicked out of the army and RADA. He only had his current job because Daddy owned the store.

When the appointment came, Paul couldn't even be bothered to be punctual, which was out of character, though it wouldn't be the last time he would keep Brian waiting. Brian asked George to telephone Forthlin Road and ask what had happened to young McCartney. 'Paul's just got up and he is having a bath,' Harrison reported.

'This is disgraceful!' fulminated Epstein, who took himself far too seriously. 'He's very late.'

'And very clean,' quipped George, who though not academically bright possessed a lively wit.

When Paul finally showed up they adjourned to a milk bar to talk business. Brian asked the boys if they'd considered professional management. They talked about how this might work and agreed to meet again. In the meantime, Epstein asked around town about the group. He consulted Allan Williams, who was so bitter about the way the band had treated him that he'd banned the boys from the Jacaranda. He advised Epstein not to touch the Beatles with a barge pole. 'Then I clarified it. I said, "Look, they are good musicians. But believe me they'll walk all over you once they've used you."' Not put off, Epstein went to see Rex Makin, asking his lawyer to draw up an 'unbreakable' contract for himself and the Beatles. 'I told him there was no such thing,' said Makin, who thought Brian's latest brainwave stupid. So Brian went to another lawyer and duly presented the four Beatles – that is John, Paul, George and Pete Best – with a contract that bound them to him for five years, during which time Brian would have a hand in every part of their act, taking up to 25 per cent of their gross earnings in commission. It was a key decision. Paul was hesitant, weighing up the pros and cons. Then he said he hoped the Beatles would make it. 'But I'll tell you now, Mr Epstein, I'm going to be a star anyway.'

LONDON

EMI

The boys put their names to Brian Epstein's contract in January 1961, Paul's bold signature countersigned by his dad because he was still under 21. Epstein himself didn't get around to signing until October, but they had an agreement, one of the stated aims of which was to get the band a recording contract. The Beatles were in fact already under contract to Polydor in Germany, but Brian was determined to get them out of that deal and sign them instead to a major British company. Naturally, he went first to EMI.

'The greatest recording organisation in the world', as it liked to be known, Electrical Musical Industries (EMI) had been created in 1931 following the merger of the Gramophone Company and its rival, the Columbia Phonograph Company. EMI was part of the British Establishment, George V having recorded a message to the Empire with the company in 1923, and its subsidiary labels embraced a wide variety of music. His Master's Voice (HMV), for example – with its famous emblem of a dog listening to an old record player – was celebrated for its classical releases, but the company also remained in touch with popular trends, releasing records by American singers such as Peggy Lee and Gene Vincent, both favourites of Paul.

At the start of his working relationship with the Beatles, Brian sent 'My Bonnie' to EMI headquarters in London as a sample of the band's work, receiving a letter of reply informing him that neither HMV nor the Columbia label wanted to sign his group. It was the first of several slaps in the face, but Brian persisted. He had recently been corresponding with journalist Tony Barrow, who wrote a record review column in the *Liverpool Echo* as a sideline to composing sleeve-note copy for Britain's second biggest record company, Decca. This contact led to Brian securing an audition for the Beatles at Decca. It would be in London on New Year's Day, 1962.

Then, as now, London was more than just the capital of the United Kingdom; the city was the financial, mercantile and creative heart of the nation, to which all roads led. Paul knew that if he meant to make it in show business he had to go 'down south', even though southerners had a reputation for being unfriendly and condescending to northerners such as himself. The Beatles' first professional foray in this direction had been inauspicious. A few weeks before Christmas, Merseyside promoter Sam Leach, having tried and failed to book the band in London proper, got them a gig at the Palais Ballroom in Aldershot, 43 miles west of the capital, but nonetheless 'a gig down south'. When advertisements for the show failed to appear in the local newspaper, however, a mere 18 people attended. Seeing the funny side, Paul sang 'There's No Business Like Show Business'. At the end of this absurd evening the boys travelled into the metropolis and took a turn round the clubs of Soho, the bohemian neighbourhood north of Shaftesbury Avenue and south of Oxford Street, a place Paul liked so well he later established his private office there. Three weeks after this first sniff of London air the Beatles headed south again, driven by Neil Aspinall in the band's newly acquired van. At a time when Britain's motorway system was only just being constructed, the drive from Liverpool took up to ten hours, made more arduous that New Year's Eve by snow. The lads arrived in the capital late, checking into the Royal Hotel on Russell Square, sufficiently excited about being in London to rush over to Trafalgar Square where they helped usher in 1962. Hardly had the boys got back to the Royal Hotel than they had to be up again for their audition.

Fifteen songs from the band's live show had been selected for the Decca audition, including covers and standards such as 'Three Cool Cats' and 'The Sheik of Araby', which the boys sang with *Goon*-ish comedic asides. Also showcased were three early and rather weak Lennon-McCartney compositions, including 'Like Dreamers Do'. Epstein had the say-so in the choice of material and he forbade the boys from playing their usual, much more raucous rock 'n' roll set (though they did perform one rave-up, 'Money (That's What I Want)'), and the result was a sadly lacklustre audition, partly because the musicians were nervous and over-tired. Some weeks later Brian went back to Decca to receive the decision. 'Not to mince words, Mr Epstein, we don't like your boys' sound,' record executive Dick Rowe told Epstein, ensuring his place in history as one of those hapless souls who let the Beatles slip through his hands. Brian gave the Beatles the bad news when he met them on his return at Lime Street station. 'And Pye have turned us down,' he added gloomily.

Brian's family was starting to weary of the Beatles, Mum sighing indulgently when her son insisted that his boys would be 'bigger than Elvis', while Dad was concerned that Brian was neglecting his real job running the family's record outlets. It was therefore with a sense of having one last go that Brian returned to London in February 1962 to have the Decca auction tapes transferred to vinyl, at the HMV shop in Oxford Street, with a view to hawking the discs around town. The technician cutting the discs suggested, in light of the fact Brian's act wrote their own material, that he might speak to Sid Colman, who worked upstairs for the music publisher Ardmore & Beechwood, itself part of EMI. Brian went to see Colman, explaining that he really needed a record contract before a publishing deal, and Colman suggested Brian contact his friend George Martin at Parlophone. 'I think he might be very interested indeed.'

Above and beyond talent, timing and luck – three prerequisites in any successful career – a large part of the Beatles' success, and thereby Paul McCartney's, can be put down to the fact that the boys worked with first-rate people from the start. Naive though he was, Brian was an honest and devoted manager, while the man who was to become their record producer was an even more impressive fellow without whom the Beatles may not have achieved half of what they did. A tall, lankily handsome man with floppy blond hair, kindly blue eyes and a patient, patrician manner, George Martin was intelligent, sophisticated and cultured. He is the sort of man about whom almost no one has a bad word to say, and indeed almost everybody loves, so we can add that he was also witty, modest, hard-working and dependable, an English gentleman to his fingertips, despite his ordinary background.

Born in 1926, the son of a London carpenter, George transformed himself into 'an officer and a gentleman' during the Second World War, in which he served in the Fleet Air Arm. He married shortly after the war and used his serviceman's grant to study at the Guildhall School of Music. Already a talented pianist, and a composer in the impressionistic style of Debussy, George learned the oboe at the Guildhall. There was a dearth of professional oboists at the time and he hoped proficiency on the instrument would guarantee him a living as a session musician. Playing the oboe proved a thin living, however, and George was employed in the BBC Music Library when he went for a job at EMI in the North London suburb of St John's Wood.

Back in the 1930s, the Gramophone Company had bought a mansion on the wide residential boulevard of Abbey Road, NW8, building a warren of recording studios behind the stucco façade, the largest of which, Studio One, regularly accommodated Sir Thomas Beecham conducting the Royal Philharmonic Orchestra. In fact, countless stars of classical and popular music used the studios, including Sir Edward Elgar, perhaps the greatest British composer of recent times. George became an assistant to the head of Parlophone, originally a small German label that had become part of the EMI empire. His duties varied from producing classical music to making jazz and comedy records for the likes of Spike Milligan, writer and star of the *Goons*, who became a personal friend of George's and, later, Paul's. Martin was promoted to head of Parlophone in 1955, by which time he was known in the industry as the Comedy King. It was not a moniker he relished. Success with comedy records was all very well, but they didn't lend themselves to follow-ups, and Martin badly wanted to sign a pop act that would enjoy longevity. He put the word out to friends like Sid Colman that he was willing to listen to almost anything, which is what brought Brian Epstein to his door.

Epstein gave Martin a passionate sales pitch about his wonderful young band and the exciting musical renaissance taking place in Liverpool. 'I almost asked him in reply where Liverpool was,' Martin later noted, displaying typical London snobbery. 'The thought of anything coming out of the provinces was extraordinary at that time.' The men hit it off nonetheless. Although Martin was eight years the senior, Brian's mature manner made him appear to be of an age with the producer. Moreover both seemed to belong to an older, more formal Britain where men were seldom seen without a jacket and tie, and placed great significance on speaking properly and having good manners. Brian noted that when George Martin listened to the Beatles' demo disc he rocked gently to and fro to the beat of the music, smiling polite encouragement. Martin wasn't particularly impressed by what he heard, but he was intrigued by the fact that more than one person was singing, concluding that Paul had the 'most commercial voice', and the producer was reassuringly pleasant and polite to everyone. At the end of this cordial meeting, Martin suggested that Brian Epstein bring his group into the studio for an audition when convenient.

AUF WIEDERSEHEN, STU

Before they could audition for EMI, the Beatles had to return to Hamburg to fulfil an engagement at the newly opened Star-Club on Grosse Frei-heit. John, Paul and Pete travelled to Hamburg together by plane on 11 April 1962, George, who had been unwell, being due to follow on with Brian. Part of the fun of going back to Germany was seeing Stuart Sutcliffe and his fiancée Astrid Kirchherr again, and sure enough Astrid was at the airport when they arrived. She was not there to greet them, however, but to meet Stu's mother, Millie, who was flying in from Liverpool because the most dreadful thing had just happened – Stu had died the previous day of a brain haemorrhage.

Since leaving the band, Stuart had lived with Astrid in the penthouse flat at her mother's house in Altona, studying with the British artist Eduardo Paolozzi, then teaching in Hamburg, developing considerably as a collagist and painter in the abstract expressionist style. Latterly, he painted big, dark canvases that coincided with a severe deterioration in his health. Stuart suffered increasingly from headaches; his mood became erratic and his beautiful handwriting degenerated into a scrawl. He felt tired, and suffered seizures. Tests failed to show what was wrong. On Tuesday 10 April 1962, at Astrid's flat, Stuart shrieked with pain, collapsed and died. He was 21.

The tragic circumstances of his death have given Stu a posthumous significance he might not otherwise have enjoyed, and there has been a great deal of supposition about the cause of his death and his rela-tionship with the Beatles, some of it wild. In her book, *The Beatles' Shadow*, Stuart's sister Pauline writes that she believes her brother died as a delayed consequence of a kick in the head he'd received from John

Lennon during an altercation in Hamburg. In the same book Pauline speculates, sensationally, that John and her brother had a homosexual relationship. 'I have known in my heart for many years that Stuart and John had a sexual relationship,' she writes, though she fails to provide any firm evidence. Pauline wonders whether this 'relationship' was the real cause of the antagonism between Paul and Stu. Astrid Kirchherr, who is best placed to know the facts, dismisses both the kick in the head and gay sex theories as 'nonsense', saying Stuart had an existing physiological condition that simply caught up with him in April 1962. 'John never, ever raised his hand towards Stuart. Never ever. I can swear that. That's all Pauline [saying that],' she says with irritation. 'The doctor explained it to me that his brain was, in a way, too big for his head – one day it just went *click*.'

John became hysterical when told Stuart had died. Stu had been his best friend. Not so Paul who, when Mrs Sutcliffe arrived from Liverpool, tried to be consoling, but managed to say the wrong thing, as he had before, and would again when faced with death. 'My mother died when I was 14,' he supposedly told the grieving woman, according to Philip Norman's book *Shout!*, 'and I'd forgotten all about her in six months.' If he really did say this, it can be excused as the sort of gauche comment young people do make at times of crisis, and of course it wasn't true. Paul often thought about Mary McCartney. As the years passed it became plain that he was very deeply affected by memories of his mother.

The Beatles did not return to Liverpool for Stuart's funeral. They stayed in Hamburg to play the Star-Club, the newest, biggest rock 'n' roll venue in St Pauli, which attracted not only two-bit Liverpool bands, but such established American stars as Gene Vincent and Little Richard, heroes whom Paul now found himself rubbing shoulders with in the club's changing rooms, which like everything else about the Star-Club were superior to the facilities the Beatles had experienced previously in Germany. The Star-Club was the best club the Beatles had played, and the band was correspondingly more professional-looking now that Brian had got them out of their leathers into suits and ties, though they hadn't lost the elemental, slightly rough sound they'd developed in the clubs. There was also still a loutish element to these young men, as was demonstrated by the way they treated their new digs, an apartment opposite the club on Grosse Freiheit. Lennon, roaring at the world now that Stu had died, on top of the traumatic loss of his mother, erected a profane crucifix outside the apartment window, decorated with a condom, and urinated over nuns walking to nearby St Joseph's Church. When George threw up in the flat, the vomit was left to fester; the boys made a feature of the sick, stubbing their cigarettes out in it. The next group into the flat after the Beatles was fellow Merseysider Kingsize Taylor and his band the Dominoes. 'I just nearly threw up,' recalls Kingsize (whose tape recording of the Beatles at the Star-Club became one of the most famous of all Beatles bootlegs). The vomit wasn't the worst of it. 'There was a heap of crap behind the door where somebody would have a crap and put a newspaper over it ... the whole place was just a total shambles. It had to be fumigated.' Horst Fascher recalls another less than charming habit the Beatles had: a filthy game whereby John and Paul would hawk up against the wall to see whose phlegm slid down first.

The Beatles were rescued from their own muck by a telegram from home. Wired by Brian Epstein on Wednesday 9 May, the message read: CONGRATULATIONS BOYS. EMI REQUEST RECORDING SESSION. PLEASE REHEARSE NEW MATERIAL. Having initially suggested Brian bring the boys in to audition when convenient, George Martin had met with Brian again and was showing a keener interest in the Beatles as a Parlophone act. He agreed that a contract should be drawn up so that, if he liked what he saw and heard when he met the boys, he could sign them forthwith. This justified Brian's telegram.

CHANGES

It was love at first sight, as George Martin would write of the moment he met the Beatles at Abbey Road on 6 June 1962. He noted how well groomed they were – Brian's influence – and the unusual haircuts. 'But the most impressive thing was their engaging personalities. They were just great people to be with.' The band performed for him with gusto, Paul singing favourite numbers from their stage show, including old chestnuts such as 'Besame Mucho' and Fats Waller's 'Your Feet's Too Big'. Martin wasn't madly impressed by these covers, nor by the original songs John and Paul had written, including an early, dirge-like 'Love Me Do', sung in harmony by Paul and John, the latter interjecting a bluesy harmonica in the style of Delbert McClinton on Bruce Channel's

'Hey! Baby'. When John was blowing the harp, Paul sang on his own, and he sounded nervous. Still, the boys exuded an energy and charm that gave Martin a warm feeling. If audiences could be made to share that feeling the Beatles could be big. The producer agreed to sign the band for one year, during which time he would have the right to record six titles, with the Beatles receiving a niggardly but then standard royalty of a penny-per-disc. At least they had a deal and, surprisingly, it was with an EMI label, even though they'd previously been turned down by head office. Brian had sneaked the Beatles in through the back door of 'the greatest recording organisation in the world', which led to problems later.

A more immediate concern was that Martin didn't like the Beatles' drummer. He found Pete Best personally less engaging than the others, 'almost sullen', and didn't think he kept time well. The producer asked John and Paul if they would consider replacing him. 'We said, "No, we can't!"' Paul recalls. 'It was one of those terrible things you go through as kids. Can we betray him? No. But our career was on the line.' In truth, Pete had never fitted in. He didn't share the same history with John, Paul and George: hadn't been with them in the Quarry Men; didn't go to Scotland. He'd been hired as a stopgap for Hamburg and, despite the orgiastic evenings they shared in the Bambi Kino, he often seemed the odd man out in St Pauli, not sharing the same jokes and references. Curiously, this enhanced his image with fans on Merseyside. The lonesome persona Pete had involuntarily acquired was taken for 'mean, moody magnificence', in the oft-quoted words of Cavern MC Bob Wooler. Girls fancied Pete, more than the other Beatles, as became evident when the band went to Manchester on Whit Monday 1962 to record a radio show.

The Beatles had a fan club now, run in the first instance by Cavern dweller Roberta 'Bobbie' Brown, then Frieda Kelly, who went to work for Brian Epstein, bringing the fan club under his management. The relationship between the fan club and the band was symbiotic. The girls (and most fan club members were female) got to have a relationship with the Beatles, directly at first, when the members were virtually all Cavern-goers, then more remotely by post. In return Brian could marshal supporters whenever the boys needed a boost. When the Beatles travelled to Manchester, on 11 June 1962, to perform for the BBC Light Programme – one of their first BBC broadcasts – fan club members were invited to go on the coach with them to ensure the band had an enthusiastic audience. This worked well except that after the show the fans made much more of a fuss of Pete than the other Beatles, to the obvious displeasure of Paul's father who found himself sitting on the bus with his son waiting for Pete. 'It was Pete Best all the girls wanted,' recalls Bill Harry, who was also on the coach. 'Eventually Pete was able to extricate himself, got into the coach, and Jim McCartney started telling him off, saying he was trying to upstage them all.' While Pete argued that it wasn't his fault the girls made a fuss of him, the fact that Paul's mild-mannered father had spoken out against Pete so soon after George Martin questioned Pete's musical ability sealed the young man's fate.

Change was to come also in Paul's personal life. For two years now he'd been dating Dot Rhone, the schoolgirl he'd met at the Casbah. Dot had altered her appearance to please him, wearing a black leather skirt and growing her hair in the style of the boys' pin-up Brigitte Bardot. John had subjected Cynthia Powell to a similar, demeaning makeover. With so much in common, Dot and Cyn became friends, moving into adjacent bedsits in Garmoyle Road, comforting each other while their boyfriends were in Hamburg. Despite well-placed doubts she may have had about his fidelity, Dot wore Paul's engagement ring and looked forward to becoming his wife. Paul's family was part of the attraction. 'I think I was probably in love with Paul because I loved his family, too,' she told the *Daily Mail* years later. 'I loved his dad – he was great. At Christmas and New Year I would go [to Forthlin Road] and it was so different to my house. They had brilliant parties and they would play music together, Paul on guitar and his dad on piano.'

The relationship became serious when Dot fell pregnant in early 1962. When she told Paul about her condition, the couple took a ferry ride across the Mersey to talk it through. '[Paul] was trying to be good about it,' Dot later told author Bob Spitz, 'but he was scared. At first, he said we shouldn't get married, we were too young. I *wanted* to get married, but I couldn't tell him that.' Jim McCartney made the decision. 'His reaction was that we should get married because you either got married or you had the baby adopted. We didn't want it adopted because it was our baby, so we started to make plans to get married.' Dad made it clear that such plans would have to involve Paul getting a proper job to support his wife. Was it too late to go back to Massey &

Coggins? Jim also said Dot could come and live with them at Forthlin Road. 'He put his arm around me, made me feel looked after.' Paul told Dot he was getting the marriage licence. Aunt Ginny bustled around, as a surrogate mother-in-law-to-be, and all seemed set fair when Dot miscarried. Paul ended the relationship soon afterwards, Dot believing he was relieved not to be trapped in a marriage he didn't really want. 'He seemed upset, but deep down he was probably relieved,' she later told an interviewer. A baby might have cut short the Beatles' career. As the writer Cyril Connolly observed, 'There is no more sombre enemy of good art than the pram in the hall.'

Another very personal problem was solved around this time. Shortly after Brian Epstein had taken over management of the Beatles, he confided in Rex Makin that the boys had picked up venereal diseases in Hamburg. '[Brian] asked me could I recommend a good venereologist because all the boys had got clap,' says Makin; 'they were very promiscuous. I mean, they had women thrown at them, and they never failed to take the opportunity.' What with working in matrimonial law, Makin knew a discreet clap doctor, and the boys were sent along.

THE LUCKIEST AND UNLUCKIEST DRUMMERS IN SHOW BUSINESS

The decision having been made to fire Pete Best, the unpleasant job of telling him fell to Brian Epstein, who called Pete into his office at NEMS. 'They don't think you're a good enough drummer, Pete,' he told the boy, 'and George Martin doesn't think you're a good enough drummer.' Pete had no idea. As he tried to defend himself, the telephone rang. It was Paul calling Brian to check that he had plunged in the knife. There was no point talking further. A comment Paul had made in recent days made sense to Pete now. In the wake of the EMI deal, the drummer had been talking about buying a car. Paul cautioned him to save his money.

Having received the worst news of his life, Pete staggered downstairs to Whitechapel where Neil Aspinall was waiting, having given him a lift into town. Neil and Pete were very close. Curiously, the Beatles' roadie had recently embarked on a relationship with Pete's 38-year-old mother, with the result that Mo Best had given birth to a son, a boy they named Roag. Pete and Neil were thereby now related in blood. Neil was astounded to hear that his band had sacked his lover's son, and considered quitting their employment in protest. Pete told him there was no need, and indeed Aspinall stayed with the Beatles for the rest of his working life, ultimately becoming the head of their corporation. All that time he played an active part in Roag Best's life, while Uncle Pete suffered the daily humiliation of being a rejected Beatle. 'A very unique situation, and one that I didn't know any different from, because that was my normal life,' says Roag today. 'Pete was an ex-Beatle, and my dad worked for the Beatles. It was just the way it was.' Pete's story was a sad one. Forced to give up his show business ambitions, he worked at a series of everyday jobs in Liverpool, becoming so depressed during the height of the Beatles' success that he tried to gas himself.

Pete's replacement in the Beatles was a short, goofy-looking fellow with a skunk-like streak of white in his hair. He wore a beard to conceal a weak chin and balance a large nose, despite which he was actually quite handsome. Ringo Starr was at once the junior Beatle and the oldest member of the band, born three months prior to John in 1940. His real name was Richard Starkey – Ritchie to family and friends (and consequently referred to as such in this book) – the only child of Richard and Elsie Starkey, who met working in a Liverpool bakery. Dad deserted the family when Ritchie was three, and the Starkeys fell on hard times. They lived in a condemned house in the inner-city Dingle, with Elsie doing what work she could to make ends meet, including scrubbing floors, placing the Starkeys below the McCartneys in the working-class hierarchy. Despite their poverty, Elsie made a great fuss of Ritchie. It is worth noting that all four Beatles were blessed with such loving matriarchs – Mary McCartney and Aunt Mimi included – helping imbue their boys with confidence. When Ritchie was 13, Elsie married Harry Graves, who also became a benevolent presence in Ritchie's young life. The boy suffered two severe bouts of illness, firstly at age 6 when his appendix burst, again when he contracted pleurisy at 13. He never went back to school and was only semi-literate as a result. 'I can read, but I can't spell – I spell phonetically.' After school, Ritchie became an apprentice engineer, chucking his apprenticeship to play drums with Rory Storm and the Hurricanes, a local band fronted by an athletic blond lad whose real name was Alan Caldwell, but who went by this more exciting moniker. Rory insisted his band also adopt stage names, so Ritchie became Ringo Starr, named after the rings he wore Teddy Boy-style.

Rory Storm and the Hurricanes played the same circuit as the Beatles in Liverpool and Hamburg, and Ringo had sat in with the Beatles more than once, so was already a mate. John, Paul and George agreed that Ringo would be the ideal replacement for Pete. By nature, he was an amiable sort without much ambition, someone who would fit in and do what he was told. Ritchie was playing Butlin's at Skegness with the Hurricanes when John and Paul asked him to join the Beatles, winning Ritchie over with the offer of more money and the promise of a record deal. Cavern dwellers were indignant when Ringo took the stage with the band the first time. 'We want Pete!' they chanted, reluctant to give up on their favourite. 'Pete forever. Ringo – never!'

With the arrival of Ringo the Beatles were complete: four cheerful lookalike mop-tops who acted as one – the 'four-headed monster', as Mick Jagger described them – though they were not equals. John, Paul and George had been together for four years and had a history that Ringo had not been a part of. Joining the band was, he said, 'like joining a new class at school where everybody knew everybody but me'. Ringo would serve the others, without the talent to challenge John and Paul creatively. He was always the least important Beatle. Next up in seniority was George, never able to overcome the basic fact that he was nine months and one school-year junior to Paul, who treated him 'as though George worked for him' in the words of Tony Barrow, the Decca sleeve-note writer who would shortly come to work for the boys as their PR man. John was the boss, because the Quarry Men had been his band. Comments Barrow:

And along came this guy McCartney who could play a few chords, so he was in, but he was only in as a band member, and it meant that, from the beginning, if Paul wanted to achieve equal status or, better still, leadership of the Beatles, he had to work hard at it, and he did. Internally, he did, from the very beginning, and most of the time I don't think John noticed – in the early days at any rate – how pushy Paul was being within the group.

Paul almost leapfrogged John at the start of their recording career. In the early 1960s most pop groups were made up of a front man and his backing band: Buddy Holly and the Crickets, Cliff Richard and the Shadows, and on a much lowlier level Rory Storm and the Hurricanes. As he prepared to record his new signing, George Martin considered releasing a record by 'Paul McCartney and the Beatles'. There was also an argument for 'John Lennon and the Beatles'. It was hard to decide. 'George and I were walking up Oxford Street one day trying to work out whether it should be Paul – the good-looking one – or John, who had the big personality,' Martin's assistant Ron Richards told author Mark Lewisohn. When Martin couldn't choose, the issue drifted away. Unusually, the Beatles would have two equal front men.

George Martin was reunited with the boys at Abbey Road on 4 September 1962, when the Beatles set to work recording their first single. Smartly dressed in suits and ties – a press photographer was present – they rehearsed during the day, broke for supper, then recorded in the evening. Anxious for a hit, and not yet trusting the Beatles' own material, Martin gave the band a madly catchy tune titled 'How Do You Do It?', written by professional songwriter Mitch Murray. The boys recorded it without enthusiasm, John and Paul making it clear they would prefer to cut their own songs rather than the work of hack writers. The best they had to offer was 'Love Me Do', the slow, bluesy number written when John and Paul were boys and already demonstrated at their first meeting with Martin. They ran through it again with less than satisfactory results, Martin still detecting a weakness in the rhythm section.

When the band returned to the studio six days later to have another go at 'Love Me Do', Ritchie was dismayed to discover that Martin had hired a professional session drummer, Scotsman Andy White, to take his place. White describes the awkward moment Ringo saw him in the studio: 'When he came in I was setting up my drums. He obviously thought, *Don't tell me! It's happening to me now!*' Suspecting he was to suffer the same fate as Pete Best, Ringo went up the stairs to the control room and sat, stone-faced, with George Martin while John and Paul taught Andy their material. 'They didn't have any written music. So everything was word of mouth and trial and error,' says the Scots drummer, who found it a refreshing change to play on original songs with the writers. They then recorded 'Love Me Do'. Ringo's mood was ameliorated slightly when Martin permitted him to bang a tambourine in accompaniment on what was the Beatles' début single. Ritchie wasn't fired from the band, but he never entirely forgave George Martin for replacing him with Andy White on that first session.

Not as much of a dirge as it had been, 'Love Me Do' was still a rather ponderous number, the lyric childishly simple, though John and Paul's use of personal pronouns – 'love *me* do/*you* know I love *you* …' – was effective, making it seem as if they were singing directly to the listener. They used the same device on the slower 'PS I Love You', the lyric of which took the form of a love letter of the type Paul had written home to Dot from Hamburg. Indeed, Dot says Paul wrote the song for her before their break-up. Martin thought well enough of 'PS I Love You' to use it as the B-side of the first single.

When 'Love Me Do' was released on 5 October 1962, it meandered around the charts before reaching number 17 shortly before Christmas. While this wasn't at all bad for a début single, it fell short of being a smash hit, possibly because EMI gave the record little promotion. There was resentment in the company that Brian Epstein had got his band in through the back door after being told the Beatles weren't wanted on HMV or Columbia. Says Tony Barrow:

> I think this was part of the reason why EMI downgraded that first single so much in terms of promotion. It was given the least rating for promotion purposes, i.e. it was going to get the least number of plays on Radio Luxembourg and so on. It wasn't an important release from EMI's point of view.

Barrow had started work as a public relations man for Epstein's new management company, NEMS Enterprises, so named to indicate that it was a branch of the larger family firm. Clive Epstein, Brian's brother, was a director. One of Barrow's first jobs was to produce a profile of Paul and the other Beatles for the press. To do so he spoke to fan club secretary Frieda Kelly, who was dealing with an increasing amount of mail for the boys. Girls tended to ask about the same things in their letters: 'what colour hair they've got, what size shoes they take,' recalls Frieda, not forgetting: 'what type of girls they liked'. To save time she typed up Lifelines of each Beatle, giving the essential information.

Under 'Instruments played', Paul listed 'Bass, guitar, drums, piano, banjo'; putting 'girls, song writing [and] sleeping' as his hobbies, in that order.

Paul didn't specify in his Lifeline what sort of girls he liked, though he admitted to a soft spot for the French actresses Brigitte Bardot and Juliette Gréco. In real life he was dating Rory Storm's sister, Iris Caldwell, who caught his eye dancing at Operation Big Beat, a package show at the Tower Ballroom in New Brighton. Iris's mother was another Liverpool matriarch who supported and indulged her children, opening her door to their friends. Everybody was welcome at 54 Broad Green Road, which Vi Caldwell renamed Stormsville in honour of her rock 'n' rolling son Rory. 'We were the ones in the street that were in show business, we were like this strange family,' says Iris. The Beatles were frequent visitors at Stormsville, George Harrison the first to date Iris. 'I think George was my first kiss, when I was about 14.' This innocent affair ended around 1959, though George still carried a torch for Iris as she began work as a professional dancer, kicking up her long legs as a can-can girl in variety. She was 17 when Paul saw her jiving at the Tower Ballroom in New Brighton. 'That's when he wrote, "she was just seventeen/You know what I mean".'*

The affair was tempestuous. 'I was madly in love with [Paul] while I was going out with him, and then you're in love with the next person.' Paul could be an annoying, controlling boyfriend, as young men of his class and background typically were. He expected Iris to behave and dress to please him – 'in straight skirts below the knee, and your hair up in a bun' – and could be jealous and immature, especially when egged on by Lennon. One night when Paul and Iris and John and Cynthia went on a double date, the boys staged a mock fight in the restaurant so they would get thrown out and not have to pay; then they pulled the same trick at a second restaurant. '[Paul] was always messing about pretending he was the Hunchback of Notre Dame and doing crazy things,' sighs Iris. Another time, shortly after Paul got his first car, a green Ford Classic, they drove through the Mersey Tunnel to the Cube Coffee Bar in Birkenhead, where they had a tiff. 'I picked up this great big bowl of sugar, a big square bowl – because it was called the Cube Coffee Bar, everything was square in there – and I emptied it over his head.' Iris

* The second part of this couplet is credited to John Lennon.

then ran towards the Mersey Tunnel, 'with him driving along after me in the car trying to catch me ...'

Deciding she was finished with McCartney, Iris phoned George Harrison. 'I'm not going out with Paul any more,' she told him.

'Oh great!' exclaimed George, seeing a chance to get the advantage over Paul for once. 'Can I take you out tomorrow night?'

'Of course you can.'

As Iris was getting ready for her date, Paul turned up with tickets for the King Brothers. 'He said, "Well, I've paid for the tickets. It's a stupid waste of money, so we may as well go." I'm thinking, what am I going to do? George is going to be here in a minute.' Good as gold, Mrs Caldwell picked up the telephone and dialled George. 'Hello, is that you, Margaret?' she said, when George Harrison answered the phone, pretending she was speaking to a girlfriend of her daughter's. 'Oh listen, Margaret, Iris's boyfriend's come round and she's going out with him tonight.' George asked Mrs Caldwell what she was talking about, telling her he was *George*, not *Margaret*. ('He was a bit slow, you know,' notes Iris. 'God love him.') So Paul took Iris out. The evening ended awkwardly again when Iris attracted the attention of one of the King Brothers, who came back to Stormsville with her and Paul, the rival boys staring daggers at each other until Iris went to bed, leaving her mother to deal with the Romeos. Paul got on well with Mrs Caldwell, as he tended to with his friends' mothers. 'He used to come in from the Cavern absolutely shattered [and] he used to sit on the chair, put his feet up on the pouffe, roll his trouser legs up, and my mother used to comb the hairs on his legs for him, because he used to like that.'

Another friend was Cavern cloakroom girl Priscilla White, who signed with NEMS as singer Cilla Black, an artist second only to the Beatles in Brian's affection. Young Cilla hung out with Paul and the other Beatles, and socialised with the Caldwells at Stormsville, where one night they had a séance, Iris, Paul, Cilla and George Harrison all putting their hands on a glass on a Ouija board in the darkened living room. 'Is there anybody there?' Iris asked tremulously. The glass began to move in Paul's direction. By a system of questions and tapped answers it was established that Paul's late mother had risen from the spirit world to speak to her son. Paul became agitated. 'He was asking her all these questions, "Is that you, Mum. Where are you?"' Then

George started laughing, for he had been pushing the glass and tapping the table. Paul almost strangled his friend.

Vivacious girl that she was, Iris was also dating another young man – the Australian singer Frank Ifield, whom she'd met when they were both appearing in *Dick Whittington* in Stockton-on-Tees. Frank hit the big time in the summer of 1962 when he scored a number one with 'I Remember You', which also went top ten in the USA and was a song Paul covered in the Beatles' stage show. Anxious to win the Beatles wider exposure, and wanting to capitalise on the release of 'Love Me Do', Brian arranged for the boys to support Frank in concert in Peterborough on 2 December 1962. Frank put on what Iris called 'a proper show' in the variety tradition. Indeed she and Frank considered themselves in real show business, as opposed to Paul and George who were merely in a beat group. 'I remember them looking at me when I put my make-up on. I don't think they'd ever seen anybody putting make-up on before,' recalls Ifield of his backstage meeting with the Beatles in Peterborough. John, Paul, George and Ringo followed Frank's example, but overdid the grease paint. 'They were a bit red – like red cochineal Beatles.' They were also too loud on stage. There were boos and complaints to the management, who told the Beatles to 'Turn it down!'

Iris continued to date Frank when their schedules coincided, also seeing Paul when he was in Liverpool. Her beaus had different styles. When Frank took her out, Iris wore her hair long and put on a nice frock. They went to restaurants. Frank held the chair for her, and ordered Mateus Rosé, 'which I thought was *so* sophisticated'. With Paul it was a drink in the pub, then down the chippie. Each boy had his attractions, and she strung them both along. One night Paul surprised Iris by saying he had tickets for Frank's show at the Liverpool Empire. Iris went to the concert with Paul, trepidatious in case Frank saw them, but expecting that they would be sitting back in the cheap seats, for Paul was careful with his money. He surprised her with seats at the front of the stalls. Still, Iris figured Frank wouldn't recognise her. His eyesight wasn't brilliant, and she had her hair in a bun. As Iris tells the story, Frank *did* eventually recognise her and Paul during the course of the evening. 'I was sitting there holding hands with Paul, quite low down in me seat, and Frank did his whole piece. It was all wonderful and he never even glanced our way and I thought, *Brilliant!*' At the end of the show Frank said he'd like to sing one more song. As Iris remembers the moment, the singer rested his right foot on the footlights and pointed down at Paul. 'It's called "He'll Have to Go".' As he sang, Paul squirmed in his seat cursing the cheeky Australian bugger.

THE BREAKTHROUGH

While Paul's romantic comedy with Iris played out, the Beatles were increasingly busy playing sometimes two, even three shows a day, often starting at lunchtime at the Cavern, a venue they had nearly outgrown, then performing at theatres in the evening, big places like the Tower Ballroom and Liverpool Empire. In November the Beatles and Little Richard went to Hamburg for two weeks at the Star-Club, and then it was back to London to record with George Martin, working this time in a place that would become integral to Paul's musical life: Studio Two at EMI – a large, lofty hall with a parquet floor, cream walls and a steep staircase leading to the control room, with a banister Paul would slide down when he was in a celebratory mood. George Martin peered down at his artists from the glazed control room like God.

After the modest success of 'Love Me Do', and the Beatles' high-handed rejection of 'How Do You Do It?', Martin was anxious to see if the band had what it took to score a hit. He was sure 'How Do You Do It?' would have made number one, as indeed it later did for fellow Merseysiders Gerry and the Pacemakers, whom Brian signed to NEMS Enterprises as the second of what became a stable of local acts. The Beatles were unrepentant. 'John just said it was crap,' says singer Gerry Marsden. 'We proved [that it wasn't and] I say thank you to John every night on stage for giving me my first number one, because if they would have done it and released it we wouldn't have had that song to do.' Accepting that the Beatles really didn't want to sing this hack song, Martin asked them sternly what they had that was better, to which they suggested 'Please Please Me', a song John and Paul had had knocking around for a while. Recalls Iris Caldwell:

[Paul] sung that song in the house, 'What do you think of it?' I said, 'I've never heard of such rubbish.' *Last night I said these words to my girl, why don't you ever even try girl, come on, come on, come on, come on, please please* … 'I think it's terrible!'

As recorded, 'Please Please Me' was brighter than 'Love Me Do', the opening guitar chords creating a big, optimistic sound, while the lyric was frankly sexual in a way adolescents could identify with: trying to get your girl to do what you both wanted, but were scared of in the age before the contraceptive pill became commonplace, in case you fell pregnant like Dot, and now like Cynthia, too. Unlike Paul, John had gone ahead and married his pregnant girlfriend, though secretly. The Lennons were expecting their first child in April.

At the end of 18 takes of 'Please Please Me', George Martin pronounced from his lofty control room that the boys had cut their first number one. Before they could find out whether George's confidence was well placed, the Beatles returned to Hamburg to play a final stint at the Star-Club, a venue that had been the apex of their career only recently, but which, like the Cavern, they had now outgrown. It was December. The boys shared Christmas dinner with club friends and members of Kingsize Taylor and the Dominoes. Paul bought a pair of leather gloves to take home to Iris, and on their last night in town persuaded his long-term German girlfriend Ruth Lallemann to come to the airport and wave him off. 'He said, "Please take me to the airport, because I think it's the last time I come here, because we're going to get big."' The next time Ruth saw Paul would be in London when he was a superstar. All of a sudden, after a time when the Beatles seemed to be moving in slow motion, everything was happening very fast.

Back home, the Beatles found they had virtually no free time, as they rushed from club to theatre to recording studio, often travelling long distances to fulfil relatively minor engagements. For example, after a hectic day of promotion for 'Please Please Me' in London on Thursday 22 January 1963, recording for three different BBC radio shows, the band was driven back to Liverpool to appear at the Cavern. A new boy was behind the wheel of their van, a burly former post office worker named Mal Evans who'd joined the Beatles as a roadie, junior to Neil Aspinall who was increasingly filling the role of road manager. Schlepping up country to Liverpool on a freezing cold, foggy day, a stone shattered the van's widescreen. Mal punched out the glass, and battled on, the bitter wind blowing full in his face, as the Beatles huddled together in the back as 'a Beatle sandwich', as Paul described it.

With the release of 'Please Please Me' Paul found himself in direct rivalry with Frank Ifield, whose two previous singles had gone to number one, and who was looking for a hat trick with 'The Wayward Wind'. 'I found that they were chasing me up the charts. I thought, *Well that's fine. I give them a break on a show and now they're chasing me up the bloody chart!*' recalls the Australian star. 'I thought they were going to knock me out of the number one, but they didn't.' The Beatles' single stalled at number two.* Paul was doubly defeated when Iris finally dumped him for Frank. Surprisingly, given Paul's later well-documented love of animals, the break-up was triggered by cruelty to a dog.

One night in March 1963, shortly before Iris's birthday, Paul and Ringo called in at Stormsville after driving up from London. 'They'd got to our house really late. Me brother and I opened the door, said, "Come in, the kettle's on," you know, and they said, "Oh, we're starving. We're so tired. We've been recording."' Ringo mentioned that just before they got to the Caldwells' house, he and Paul had accidentally run over a dog. The Caldwells were great animal lovers, with a pet dog named Toby, which Paul never liked. 'Toby used to want to be stroked all the time and he used to go, "Oh, it's got fleas,"' recalls Iris. 'He didn't like dogs.' Concerned by what Ringo had said, Rory and Iris asked the boys if the dog they'd hit was all right. Ringo said they'd been too tired to stop and find out.

'Get out of the house! I never want to speak to you again!' Iris raged at the boys, appalled by such lack of feeling. She later reflected that Ringo might have simply made the story up to rile her. Still, it was enough to make her finish with Paul, who pursued her for a while, calling and visiting her house, also trying to see her when she was working summer season at Great Yarmouth, but she shunned him. 'He kept saying to me mother, "Why won't she see me?" And me mother said, "Because you've got no heart, Paul."'

---

* UK chart positions are based on the *Record Retailer* chart, used in turn for the *Guinness Book of British Hit Singles*. 'Please Please Me' went to number one in other UK charts in 1963, but the Beatles do not claim it as a number one, as is evident by its omission from the Beatles' *1* album.

5

THE MANIA

THE FIRST ALBUM

Seeking to capitalise on the success of 'Please Please Me', George Martin called the Beatles back to EMI and asked them to perform their stage show for him, thus creating in one amazing day, Monday 11 February 1963, a complete album. The Beatles recorded ten songs on the day, to which EMI later added the four numbers previously released as singles, making a 14-track LP. It opened with John and Paul singing in joyful harmony 'I Saw Her Standing There', one of eight original Lennon-McCartney compositions on the record, and ended with John alone – his voice by now in shreds – screaming 'Twist and Shout'.

This, the Beatles' début album, established the convention whereby John and Paul would write and sing most of the songs, with at least two lead vocals reserved for George and Ringo. Not yet a songwriter in his own right, George was given 'Do You Want to Know a Secret' on the first LP, while Ritchie croaked out the Dixon-Farrell number 'Boys', as he had with Rory Storm and the Hurricanes. Ringo's voice was limited, but a Ringo song was part of what became the successful recipe. Here then was essentially the sound of the Beatles on stage in 1963, as they would have sounded at the Cavern: four young men having the time of their lives, as emphasised by the album cover photo of the lads grinning from the stairs at EMI headquarters in Manchester Square. Entitled *Please Please Me*, to hook fans who'd bought the single, the LP went to number one in May 1963 and held the top spot month after month, right up until the band's second LP displaced it. This was sensational.

A careful reading of the fine print on *Please Please Me* reveals that the original songs on the LP are credited to 'McCartney/Lennon' (sic), and published by Northern Songs Ltd, details that would cause Paul more angst than almost anything in his career. The first two songs the Beatles released, 'Love Me Do' and 'PS I Love You', the A- and B-side of their début single, had been published by Ardmore & Beechwood, the firm Brian Epstein stumbled upon shopping the Beatles around London. Brian was disappointed by the way Ardmore & Beechwood promoted these songs, so when 'Please Please Me' was ready he asked George Martin to suggest a new publisher. Martin directed him to another friend, in the small world of the British music business, Dick James.

George Martin and Dick James had enjoyed a hit together in 1956 when Parlophone released a recording of James singing the theme to the television show *Robin Hood*. In mid-life, Dick settled down to work as a song-plugger and music publisher, latterly operating from an office on the Charing Cross Road near the junction of Denmark Street, where music businesses cluster. It was Dick who brought the Tin Pan Alley tune 'How Do You Do It?' to George Martin, and George assured Brian Epstein that his friend was honest and hungry for success. Like Brian, Dick was Jewish, which helped the two form a bond. Dick also knew how to charm the younger man. Forewarned that Epstein was dissatisfied with the promotion Ardmore & Beechwood had secured for 'Love Me Do', Dick telephoned a contact at BBC television while Brian was in his office and talked the Beatles onto the TV show *Thank Your Lucky Stars*. Brian was so impressed he offered Dick the rights to John and Paul's new songs. 'Please Please Me' and its B-side 'Ask Me Why' were duly published by Dick James Music, with a new company created to handle John and Paul's subsequent compositions.

The boys wanted a company. 'We said to them, "Can we have our own company?"' Paul recalled. 'They said, "Yeah."' Northern Songs was thereby created, named in honour of the fact the songwriters were from the North of England. It was not entirely Paul and John's company, though. Dick and his partner Charles Silver owned half of Northern Songs. John and Paul were assigned 20 per cent each, Brian the remaining 10 per cent. Furthermore, Northern Songs would be managed by Dick James Music, the publisher taking a 10 per cent commission off the top, which meant that James earned more money from publishing John and Paul's songs than they did themselves. Under the terms of the deal all the songs John and Paul wrote for the next three years would go into Northern Songs, with an option to extend the agreement for an additional three years. Brian wasn't experienced enough to know whether this was good or bad. He was, after all, merely a record-shop manager. He took George Martin's advice that the deal was sound, and it wasn't unfair for its day. So it was that one February morning in Liverpool, before hurrying to Manchester to do a show, John and Paul signed their songs away to Dick's company. Paul came to regret deeply the fact he hadn't taken independent legal advice before doing so, for he was agreeing to more than he realised at the time; 'we just signed this thing, not really knowing what it was all about,' as he complains now, 'and that is virtually the contract I'm still under. It's draconian!'

Paul's other eternal bugbear is song credits, the form of which was also established at this early stage in the Beatles' story. In the tradition of the great songwriting teams of the past – from Gilbert and Sullivan to Leiber and Stoller – John and Paul paired their surnames together when they became published writers, styling themselves 'McCartney and Lennon' on *Please Please Me*. This suited Paul, but his business partners didn't think McCartney and Lennon euphonious. 'You'll be Lennon and McCartney,' he was told.

'Why not McCartney and Lennon?'

'It sounds better.'

'Not to me it doesn't.' Yet Paul agreed to the change, implemented for the Beatles' third single, 'From Me to You', which went to number one in May 1963, and remaining the form for every subsequent song published in their name. This came to irk Paul when Beatles songs he had written entirely on his own, notably 'Yesterday', were credited to Lennon and McCartney, and he could do nothing to change it.

For the time being, though, there was just the pure, innocent joy of making music and seeing it successful. On one of his increasingly rare mornings home in Liverpool, in the spring of 1963, Paul awoke in his bed at 20 Forthlin Road to hear the milkman coming up the garden path whistling a familiar tune, 'From Me to You'. It was the moment that Paul felt he'd made it. And now he met the girl of his dreams.

JANE ASHER

She was a lovely-looking young woman, just as pretty as Paul had seen in the newspapers, for Jane Asher was equally if not more famous than Paul McCartney in early 1963, an actress on stage and screen since she was only five years old, recently a regular panellist on the television pop music show *Juke Box Jury*. Tonight, Thursday 18 April 1963, Asher, two weeks shy of her 17th birthday, was helping review a pop concert at the Royal Albert Hall for the BBC's listing magazine, the *Radio Times*.

The show was the Beatles' first engagement at what is perhaps the most famous concert hall in England: a colossal, oval-shaped theatre built in the 1860s to commemorate the life of the Prince Consort, Prince Albert, and a venue Paul would return to many times to perform and watch others play. The Beatles were on a bill with a host of other acts including fellow Liverpudlians Gerry and the Pacemakers and singer Shane Fenton (whom Paul's ex, Iris Caldwell, was now dating and would marry) for a show named *Swinging Sound '63*, part of which would be broadcast on BBC radio. 'Noisy' was Jane Asher's less than enthusiastic verdict of the concert until the Beatles bounded on stage. 'Now these I could scream for,' she remarked, and duly did so for the *Radio Times'* photographer, showing herself a good sport. When the Beatles met Jane backstage, they clustered around this pretty celebrity, kidding and flirting, asking – as they typically asked their female fans (even though Lennon was already married with a child, Julian, born the previous month, a fact Brian was keeping from the press) – if she would marry them. Pretty though she was, Jane looked different to what Paul had imagined. Although he had seen her many times on TV and in the papers, these were monochrome media in 1963, leading him to assume that Jane was blonde. In real life, Miss Asher was a spectacular redhead.

After the show the Beatles, Shane Fenton and Jane adjourned to the Chelsea apartment of journalist Chris Hutchins, where the boys popped pills and drank up all the wine in the flat. 'John, who could be waspish at the best of times, was in a lethal mood without the required amount of alcohol to dampen the effect of the uppers,' Hutchins recalls in his memoir, *Mr Confidential*. Falling into a contrary mood, John invited Jane to tell him and his friends how she masturbated. 'Go on, love,' he said. 'Tell us how girls play with themselves. We know what we do, tell us what you do.' Other crude and embarrassing sexual remarks followed.

Paul rescued Jane from his boorish friend, taking her into the bedroom where they talked of less provocative matters, such as the food they enjoyed. Like her mother, Jane was an excellent cook. 'It appears you're a nice girl,' Paul concluded, having realised that a person he perceived initially as a 'rave London bird' was a well-brought-up young woman of whom his mother would have approved. So began the most significant romance of Paul's young life to date.

Paul's new girlfriend was almost four years his junior, having been born in 1946 to Margaret and Richard Asher. Mrs Asher, to whom Jane owed her red hair, was a member of the aristocratic Eliot family, whose seat, Port Eliot, is a stately home at St Germans, Cornwall. The Earl of St Germans was her uncle, the poet TS Eliot a distant American cousin. Margaret Asher was a professional musician, an oboist who had taught George Martin at the Guildhall School of Music. (The story of Paul's life is filled with similar, almost Dickensian coincidences.) Jane's father was an equally interesting person: head of the psychiatric department at the Central Middlesex Hospital, an expert on blood diseases, published writer and shrink whose clients had included the Arabian adventurer T.E. Lawrence. Like Lawrence, Dr Asher was an eccentric and depressive. Shortly after Paul and Jane got together, the doc went missing for a time, causing such consternation that the story made the daily newspapers. He ultimately took his own life.

Jane was one of three children, with a younger sister, Claire, and an older brother named Peter: three personable, carrot-top kids who'd all been encouraged by their parents to go into show business from an early age. Jane's acting career had been the most notable, but Claire Asher had also made a name for herself as a regular actress in the radio drama *Mrs Dale's Diary*; while Peter Asher appeared on stage, screen and radio, and had recently formed a singing duo with his school friend Gordon Waller. The whole family was musical, Jane playing the classical guitar and Claire the violin. The Ashers often performed *en famille* at home in Wimpole Street, 'the most august of London streets', as Virginia Woolf observes in *Flush*, her book about a literary romance a few doors up. For 50 Wimpole Street was the former home of Elizabeth Barrett Browning, who famously eloped with fellow poet Robert Browning in 1846.

The Ashers lived at 57 Wimpole Street, a tall eighteenth-century townhouse with a basement music room in which Mrs Asher gave music lessons, a first-floor, book-lined drawing room in which Dr Asher kept a grand piano and, adjacent to that, his consulting room; the bedrooms arranged on the upper floors. All day, Ashers young and old dashed up and down the stairs, and across the checker-pattern threshold to pursue their interests outside the home, gathering in the evening for one of Mrs Asher's gourmet meals, and conversation, after which it was often out again to the theatre or concerts. Everything was wonderfully close at hand, with the Wigmore Hall, for example, where Jane started to take Paul to hear classical music, just around the corner. Jane was more interested in Beethoven than the Beatles when she met Paul; a cultured girl who read Honoré Balzac in bed.

Paul was welcomed into this stimulating home, which was akin to his Liverpool family in that the Ashers were another clever, energetic musical clan, but obviously socially a world apart. Paul's home life was the epitome of the northern working-class; the Ashers were an upper-middle-class London family with aristocratic connections and sophisticated interests. Sitting at their dining table, Paul began to receive the education he might have had at college, if he had turned his back on pop music. It was a world he was intellectually equal to. Paul had, after all, attended one of the best grammar schools in England. Mum would have been proud to have seen her son welcomed into this fine London home, while noticing that Paul was starting to sound different. Her son never had a strong Scouse accent, not like George Harrison, and he never lost his Liverpool twang entirely, but there was a refinement in his speech from the time he met the Ashers, teenage slang words – such as 'soft' (stupid) and 'gear' (great) – appearing less frequently in his conversation. There was, some say, an element of social-climbing in Paul's relationship with the Ashers. 'He felt it was important to be in the centre of things,' says the Beatles' PR man Tony Barrow. 'And that's where Jane Asher came in, to a great extent, being not just the girlfriend, but somebody who could lift him up that social ladder ... He felt that she would be helpful to him and useful to him in progressing his march up through London society ... there was nothing to achieve in the way of Liverpool society.'

In a deeper sense Liverpool would always be home, though, and when he turned 21 in June 1963 Paul celebrated his coming of age on Merseyside. Four days prior to his birthday, driving himself back from a Beatles' gig in New Brighton, Paul was stopped by the police for speeding. He was subsequently fined and disqualified from driving for 12 months in what was the third speeding conviction that year for a young man in a hurry. On the morning of his birthday, Tuesday 18 June, the Epsteins hosted a drinks party for Paul and Jane – suddenly very much a couple – at their house in Queens Drive, followed by a bigger, livelier party in the evening at Aunt Ginny's in Huyton, the party held here partly in order to avoid the fans who had started to find their way to Forthlin Road, and because Ginny and Harry had a big enough garden for a marquee. Paul's many relatives were invited, as were his fellow Beatles, NEMS staff and other musicians, including various Mersey Beat bands and brother Mike McCartney's new group, the Scaffold.

Having left school, Paul's lanky kid brother Mike had started work as a ladies' hairdresser in Liverpool, then formed a *Beyond the Fringe*-style comedy troupe, the Scaffold, with mates John Gorman and Roger McGough, the trio landing a TV contract in 1963 simultaneous with the Beatles' rise to fame. When Mike, now a tall, toothy 19-year-old, went into show business he took a stage name, Mike McGear, a play on the trendy teen term 'gear' (good). So long as he remained Mike McGear, Paul was relaxed about his kid brother's aspirations, and supportive. When Mike dropped the McGear mask and became a McCartney in public life, as he sometimes did, friends and associates noted a degree of tension between the brothers, though Paul never spoke about it in public. 'I think he probably got pissed off occasionally because Mike would be McCartney, occasionally, rather than McGear,' says Tony 'Measles' Bramwell, who became a Beatles roadie in 1963. 'Mike McGear was [one thing]; Mike McCartney was his brother and should not be [in show business].'

The Scaffold performed at Paul's 21st birthday party. John Lennon, in an obnoxious mood, heckled the trio, then swung a punch at fellow guest Cavern MC Bob Wooler, who had apparently teased John about a recent holiday he'd taken with Brian Epstein. Everybody knew Brian held a torch for John, so there was some surprise when, in late April 1963, John chose to leave Cynthia and baby Julian at home and go off to Torremolinos with Brian (while Paul and George spent a few days with Klaus Voormann at his parents' holiday home on Tenerife). On John's return, friends sniggered about Brian and John's 'honeymoon', a reference to the fact that John hadn't seen fit to give Cynthia a honeymoon yet. It is this wisecrack that Wooler supposedly used to John's face at the party. In another version of the story, Wooler, who was gay, propositioned John. 'Bob Wooler fancied John, and made a pass at him at Paul McCartney's 21st birthday party, and John reacted by socking him on the nose,' states Epstein's lawyer Rex Makin, who was hired to resolve the dispute. Whatever the reason, Lennon certainly attacked Wooler. Not content with this, Lennon also lunged at a girl named Rose, grabbing her breasts. Rose slapped him. 'So wonderful, save-the-Earth John Lennon turns round and chins her. Bang! Down she goes. And as she was on the floor he was going to kick her,' recalls Merseyside musician Billy Hatton, who intervened to stop John going further. Wooler went to Makin, threatening to sue the Beatle, and Makin struck a compromise whereby the MC received £200 ($306) damages and a written apology. The Beatles' new PR man was given the job of managing the story. 'It was one of the first damage limitation jobs I did,' says Tony Barrow, who gave a cleaned-up version of the fracas to Don Short of the *Daily Mirror*.

Was John gay? A question mark has been set against his sexuality. As noted, Pauline Sutcliffe has suggested John had a love affair of sorts with her brother, Stuart; while John's school friend Pete Shotton has affirmed that John told him he'd had sexual contact with Brian Epstein in Spain. Shotton says John told him Brian had made a pass at him on holiday, John's response being to drop his trousers and invite his manager to 'stick it up me fucking arse then'. Brian said this wasn't quite what he had in mind, so John masturbated him. This is only relevant in as much as what stock Paul McCartney puts in such stories about his best friend and, on balance, he rejects suggestions John was homosexual, not least because he and John spent countless nights together in hotels on the road, 'and there was never any hint that he was gay'. Certainly the suggestion has never been made about McCartney himself.

SHE LOVES YOU

John behaved loutishly at Paul's 21st, but considering the pressure the Beatles were under it is hardly surprising they let off steam occasionally. The next day the boys had to be back in London to appear on BBC radio, and hardly a day passed during the months ahead without a radio or television broadcast, personal appearance, recording session or concert. They worked like dogs and as they did so the Beatles refined their image. Paul was instrumental in this as in so many of the changes the band went through. Just before Christmas the Beatles visited Dougie Millings, a Soho tailor who dressed many celebrities, and McCartney worked with him on designs for new stage suits. 'Between my father and Paul McCartney, they started sketching, and the idea of the round-neck suit came into being,' comments Gordon Millings. This was a twist on a Pierre Cardin design, a distinctive suit with braided edges, bell cuffs and pearl buttons. Worn over shirt and tie, the suits were very light, suitable for stage work, and became an important part of the Beatles' look.

Some of the gigs the Beatles were performing during their now rapid rise to the top assume greater significance in retrospect, such as when they played the Plaza Ballroom, Old Hill, on Friday 5 July 1963, on a bill with Denny and the Diplomats. The front man, genial brummie Denny Laine, helped Paul form Wings in the 1970s. Then, in early August, the Beatles played their last show at the Cavern, two and a half years after they first got up on the stage that Paul's Uncle Harry had built. Their following had grown considerably during that time, boys and girls queuing down Mathew Street to get into the club for their last appearances.[*] 'To see people like that, with their *hur* like that, it was looking at Martians, like looking at something from another planet,' recalls schoolboy fan Willy Russell, who became a notable playwright and associate of Paul's in later years. 'You just knew the world had changed.' As ever, though, it was the girls who were most affected by the Beatles, and there was a sense of bereavement after they played their final show at the club. 'The best time really to me was the Beatles before they became famous,' says Frieda Kelly, Cavern-goer turned NEMS employee, where she was now mailing signed photos of the boys to fans across the UK, thus working, ironically, to distance the boys from original fans like herself. 'We wanted them to become famous, but as soon as they became famous you knew you'd lost them, lost the good side of them, the close contact.'

John and Paul wrote their next hit on the road, inspired by a Bobby Rydell number, 'Forget Him'. Paul: 'I'd planned an "answering" song

* The final show was a ticket-only event.

where a couple of us would sing "She loves you ..." and the other one answers, "Yeah, yeah." We decided that that was a crumby idea as it was, but at least then we had the idea for a song called "She Loves You".' The single had the energy, directness and undercurrent of sex that characterises the Beatles' early hits, the lyric referring to a triangular relationship in which a young man is telling a male friend about a girl who loves him. The refrain was banal – 'Yeah! Yeah! Yeah!' – but John and Paul's harmonising was irresistible. George Martin was initially doubtful about the song ending on a sixth, an interval in the harmony, which sounded like a musical cliché to his experienced ears.

I loved it but when they ended the phrase on a sixth, as they do with the harmonies, it was a bit like Glenn Miller, and I said [to myself], *I wonder if they are doing the right thing here.* 'Isn't this a bit unhip, laddeys?' They looked at me as though I was mad. And Paul said, 'It's great! It's great!' I said, 'I've heard it so many times before.' He said, 'We haven't, and nobody else our age has either!' So they stuck with it.

Paul was right. Released at the end of August, 'She Loves You' went directly to number one.

As their fourth single rode high in the charts the Beatles grabbed another quick holiday, Paul and Jane travelling to Greece with Ritchie and his Liverpool girlfriend, Maureen Cox. Around the same time, John finally took Cynthia on honeymoon, to Paris. Photographs from the Greek vacation show Paul and Jane, and Ritchie and Mo, behaving much as any young couple abroad might, having a laugh, getting sunburnt, snogging in the back seat of a tour coach wearing silly Greek hats. With Jane, a trip to Greece had to involve culture, so after they booked into the Acropole Palace in Athens the foursome trooped up to the Parthenon. 'I remember going around the Parthenon three times – I think to keep Jane happy – and it was really tiring,' grumbled Ringo.

When they returned to the UK, the Beatles started to live in London full time, all four men initially sharing a flat in Green St, Mayfair,* within walking distance of the night clubs, restaurants and pubs of Soho and the West End. Jane Asher's house in Wimpole Street and the EMI

---

* John soon moved out to take a flat with his wife and son in nearby Kensington.

studios were a short cab ride away. Paul soon got to know his way around Central London, often walking and using the bus and underground. If he avoided places where fans knew to congregate, and kept moving, he found that he could get about without limousines or bodyguards, though he had access to a chauffeur-driven car when he needed it.

One of the addresses Paul visited regularly was Brian's new office in Monmouth Street, Covent Garden. NEMS Enterprises had grown like Topsy in the wake of the Beatles' breakthrough as Brian signed up a roster of other Liverpool artists that included Gerry and the Pacemakers, Cilla Black and Billy J. Kramer, plus lesser names such as Tommy Quickly, a young telephone engineer who'd caught the impresario's eye. Rather like Larry Parnes, Epstein sometimes picked his boy clients by their looks. Still, he achieved a remarkable success rate. When Gerry and the Pacemakers released the Beatles' reject 'How Do You Do It?' in March 1963, it went to number one, as did the Pacemakers' next two singles. Brian was also in the fortunate position of being able to offer Lennon-McCartney compositions to his artists, some of whom (Cilla and Kramer notably) recorded them with George Martin for Parlophone, which was a neat arrangement. Black, Kramer and Quickly all released Lennon-McCartney songs in 1963, Kramer achieving number one with 'Bad to Me'. Paul was delighted. 'John and I were a songwriting team and what songwriting teams did in those days was wrote for everyone – unless you couldn't come up with something, or wanted to keep a song for yourself and it was a bit too good to give away,' he later told Mark Lewisohn. 'John and I would get together, "Oh, we gotta write one for Billy J., OK" [sings "Bad to Me"] … we just knocked them out.' Perhaps the most interesting of these Lennon and McCartney song gifts was to a new band named the Rolling Stones.

After picking up an award at the Variety Club of Great Britain luncheon at the Savoy Hotel on 10 September 1963, John and Paul found themselves mooching around the music shops on Charing Cross Road. As they did so they bumped into Andrew Loog Oldham, a young hustler who'd worked briefly in the PR department at NEMS before meeting a bunch of youthful blues aficionados who went by the name of the Rollin' Stones. Loog Oldham quit Epstein's employment to manage the group, altering their name to the Rolling Stones.

The Stones were of an age with the Beatles, both bands led by clever, ex-grammar school boys infatuated with American music. 'Although it was not exactly the same thing, partly because we were more blues-orientated, there was an awful lot of crossover,' drummer Charlie Watts observes. 'We could all meet around Little Richard and Chuck Berry, Buddy Holly, Eddie Cochran and Carl Perkins.' The musicians met while the Stones were still obscure, and became friends, Paul forming a particularly close and enduring association with Mick Jagger and Keith Richards.* It was thanks to George Harrison putting in a good word for the Stones that the London-based band got their record deal with Decca. Their début single, a cover of Chuck Berry's 'Come On', reached number 21 in the summer of 1963.

The afternoon Andrew Loog Oldham bumped into John and Paul on Charing Cross Road his band were in a jazz club on nearby Great Newport Street trying to work out what should be their next single. 'I explained I had nothing to record for the Stones' next single,' Loog Oldham recalls of his chance meeting with Lennon and McCartney. 'They smiled at me and each other, told me not to worry and our three pairs of Cuban heels turned smartly back towards the basement rehearsal.' So it was that John and Paul gave the Stones what proved to be their breakthrough second single, 'I Wanna Be Your Man', teaching the band the chords that afternoon. 'They ran through it for us and Paul, being left-handed, amazed me by playing my bass backwards,' Bill Wyman noted. The record went to number 12, from which point the Stones were in the ascendant, becoming almost as popular as the Beatles themselves. Although it is often assumed the two bands were deadly rivals, their friendship actually strengthened as they became more famous. 'They were all living that same sort of life so when they did see each other, socially, they would be some of the few individuals that they could actually sit and be completely normal with, because they were sharing the same experience,' notes record producer Glyn Johns, who worked with both bands in the Sixties. 'Mick Jagger wasn't sitting with Paul McCartney because he was Paul McCartney.'

* In the early years of his career the guitarist went by the name Richard, later reverting to his given name of Richards, which I have used throughout.

STARTIME

By now the Beatles were a youth sensation in Britain. Every teenager who listened to the radio knew about this exciting new band, which had achieved three smash-hit singles and had a number one album. The Beatles were a major concert draw; lionised on Merseyside; supported by a large and well-organised fan club, their activities chronicled in the music press and a new dedicated monthly fanzine, *The Beatles Book*. Yet the national newspapers based in and around London's Fleet Street all but ignored the band, notwithstanding the fact that the fight at Paul's 21st birthday party had made a short piece in the *Daily Mirror*. There was less entertainment news in the papers in those days, anyway, and most show business writers considered home grown pop groups of less interest than American stars. Derek Taylor, show business correspondent for the *Daily Express* in the North, felt differently. Taylor managed to review a Beatles concert in Manchester for his paper, on the basis of regional interest, and followed up with a profile of Brian Epstein, the beginning of a long and important association with the band. Taylor's interest was almost unique so far as the national print media was concerned until Sunday 13 October 1963, when the Beatles appeared on *Sunday Night at the London Palladium*.

The Palladium, a big old music hall on Argyll Street, near London's Oxford Circus, was considered the most prestigious venue in British light entertainment. A variety show was broadcast live from the theatre every Sunday night on national television, and acts from around the world made it their ambition to top the bill. 'Only the biggest acts in the world did *Sunday Night at the Palladium*. That was the ultimate career high. Lots of them would come over from America,' explains the show's presenter Bruce Forsyth, adding that when an invitation was extended to the Beatles to top the bill in 1963 it was the sign that 'they really had arrived'. Forsyth and his producer Val Parnell went to see the Beatles in concert in advance, and were troubled by the racket their fans made. It was customary for artists who topped the bill at *Sunday Night at the London Palladium* to talk to Forsyth on the show. If Beatles fans got tickets, nobody would be able to hear a word that was said.

So I hit on the idea of them doing a conversation all with idiot boards that were facing the audience. Paul would rush on and say, just written on the board, 'It's great to be here tonight.' Then John would rush on from the other side, 'Yes, what a lovely audience.' They did a whole conversation [like that] because they couldn't be heard if they'd spoken.

The fact the Beatles were topping the bill at this very important show made national newspaper editors pay full attention to the group for the first time, sending writers along to meet the Beatles at rehearsals. 'At the end of each song they bowed to an imaginary audience,' Godfrey Winn reported for the *Daily Sketch*. 'George [Harrison] went through the introduction a dozen times. "Ladies and gentlemen, we are very pleased to be here at the Palladium." The Palladium, the Palladium, they shouted out, screaming like their own fans ...' On the night, the Beatles performed briefly at the start of the programme, and again at the end, to a raucous reception from their fans, whom John mocked with his horrible spastic routine and half-jokingly told to 'Shut up!', which only made them laugh and scream more. Finally the boys joined Forsyth on the revolving stage, waving goodbye to the audience in the theatre, and the wider TV audience, to the tune of 'Startime', as every edition of the show concluded. Forsyth: 'That night we could have gone round 50 times and those young fans would have kept screaming.'

Sundays are typically quiet news days, editors struggling to find enough good stories to fill Monday's papers. On just such a quiet Sunday in October 1963 editors were only too happy to seize upon the Beatles' success at the Palladium, and the extravagant behaviour of their fans, and blow it up into front-page news. The next morning's papers thereby presented the Beatles as the stars of a new youth phenomenon, one that was not seen by journalists as dangerous and unpleasant, like the recent Teddy Boy cult which was associated with violence and vandalism, but that was approved of as part of mainstream family entertainment.

The *Daily Sketch* devoted two inside pages to an interview with the band. 'Good morning. Did you watch the Beatles on television in the *Sunday Night at the London Palladium* show?' Godfrey Winn asked his readers conversationally, going on to report that 12 million Britons had, and he was ready to reveal what these 'new kings of pop' were really like. The *Evening News* similarly reported on the 'Sweet Sound of Success', noting in a thumbnail portrait of Paul McCartney that he was 'a head in the clouds dreamer who lives for nothing but music'. Paul's egoism and personal ambition had not yet been detected, though the British press would never be keen to portray Macca, as they came to call him fondly, as anything other than a decent bloke touched by genius. Paul enjoyed good press from day one.

The Beatles' appearance at the Palladium also signalled a change in the way British newspapers covered the entertainment industry. 'Suddenly the golden years of Hollywood seemed to come to an abrupt end when the music era came in with the Beatles' music and the Rolling Stones – all the old film stars of Hollywood seemed to be of no more importance any more,' notes the *Mirror*'s Don Short, one of a coterie of Fleet Street reporters who documented the Beatles' exploits over the next few years, becoming close to the band in the process, especially Paul who cultivated writers who could help them. As an example of how accommodating he could be, Paul once picked up Don personally at the *Mirror* building in Holborn and drove him to a West End club to interview his dad; another time Paul and George came round to the Short household for dinner and Paul sang a lullaby to the journalist's six-year-old daughter. As time went by, Paul learned to manipulate his press contacts, feeding them stories that would benefit him personally, but making himself scarce when it was not to his advantage to talk. 'If it wasn't going to be helpful to Paul, he wouldn't surface,' notes Short.

It wasn't only the popular press that had become closely interested in the Beatles. At the end of 1963 William Mann, music critic with *The Times*, wrote a serious appraisal of the Beatles' music that still stands as one of the most highfalutin but perspicacious articles about the band ever published. 'The outstanding English composers of 1963 must seem to have been John Lennon and Paul McCartney,' Mann began his seminal piece, going on to explain that he was not interested in the showbiz antics of the band and their hysterical followers, but in their music, which he found fresh and authentically English.

For several decades, in fact since the decline of the music hall, England has taken her popular songs from the United States, either directly or by mimicry. But the songs of Lennon and McCartney are

distinctly indigenous in character, the most imaginative and inventive
examples of a style that has been developing on Merseyside …

It was when the writer came to analyse the songs in academic language
that he lost some of his readers, 'the major tonic sevenths and ninths
built into their tunes, and the flat submediant key switches …' Yet Mann
was clearly right when he praised 'the discreet, sometimes subtle vari-
eties of instrumentation' on the Beatles' records, and noted that their
stylised vocals had not tipped over into cliché, concluding: 'They have
brought a distinctive and exhilarating flavour to a genre of music that
was in danger of ceasing to be music at all.'

With the national press, tabloid and broadsheet, finally paying full
attention to the Beatles, the band became a nationwide phenomenon
in late 1963. The term Beatlemania started appearing in newspapers in
late October, as journalists documented the hysterical fan reaction to
the group's appearances. 'This Beatlemania' was a headline in the
Daily Mail on Monday 21 October, over a feature article by Vincent
Mulchrone, asking 'Would you let your daughter marry a Beatle?' The
same day the *Sketch* ran a profile of Ringo Starr under the heading
'Beatles Mania!' When the boys returned to Britain on 30 October 1963
from a brief Swedish expedition, hordes of fans screamed welcome at
London's Heathrow Airport. By chance, the American television
compère Ed Sullivan was passing through the airport that day, shopping for talent for his *Ed Sullivan Show*. Show business legend has it
that, seeing hundreds of girls holding up signs for Beatles, Sullivan
assumed this was an eccentric, and eccentrically spelt, British animal
act. When Sullivan was put right, he saw a booking opportunity: 'I
decided that the Beatles would be a great attraction for our TV show.'

All of which served as the build-up to the Beatles appearing, in
November 1963, on another very big show, the Royal Variety Show,
staged that year at London's Prince of Wales Theatre. As with *Sunday
Night at the London Palladium*, the Beatles were appearing on a mixed
variety bill with comics, TV stars and crooners, the show broadcast via
television to the nation. The unique aspect of this particular show was
that it was traditionally attended by senior members of the Royal Family,
this year Her Majesty the Queen Mother, her second daughter Princess
Margaret and the Princess's husband the Earl of Snowdon. The presence of Royalty always drew big stars and a large television audience,

but tended to inhibit the performers and audience on the night, making for stilted, often disappointingly bland entertainment. In being their own slightly cheeky selves, the Beatles proved a breath of fresh air.

After performing their latest hit single, 'She Loves You', Paul introduced a slower song, 'Till There Was You' from *The Music Man*, telling the audience jokingly that the song 'has also been recorded by our favourite American group – Sophie Tucker'. This safe, well-rehearsed quip – at the expense of the heavy-set Ms Tucker – earned a typically polite ripple of Royal Variety Show laughter. Then John introduced their final song, 'Twist and Shout', by asking the audience for help: 'Would the people in the cheaper seats clap your hands?' he said, adding with a nod to the Royal box, 'And the rest of you, if you just rattle your jewellery.' At a time when Royalty was treated with greater deference than today, this was considered a daring remark from young Lennon, one that fell just the right side of insolence. The audience was highly amused, with the press the next day praising the boys' naturalness and wit, further stoking the bigger story of the Beatles being a new national sensation. The *Daily Mirror* put Beatlemania on its front page, in a glowing review of the show by Don Short, who doesn't believe – as has been suggested by others – that pressmen like him *created* Beatlemania. Rather the relationship between the papers and the band was symbiotic. 'A lot of people think the press puffed it up, but in actual fact I think the Beatles used the press and the press used the Beatles as much as each other.'

MONEY, THAT'S WHAT I WANT

Two months after moving into the Mayfair flat with his fellow Beatles, Paul moved out again to lodge with the Ashers in Wimpole Street. He was spending so much time at Jane's house it made sense to stay over, though not in Jane's room. The Ashers gave him the use of a box room at the top of their house, opposite the bedroom of Jane's brother Peter, who became a great mate, while Jane and her sister Claire slept in rooms on the floor below. Paul loved his garret, where he had a piano installed so he could sit and compose new tunes in the style of a jobbing song-smith, a self-image he enjoyed, though in reality he was an increasingly wealthy and famous star.

One indication of Paul's celebrity was the fans who stood sentry outside the Ashers' front door all day, hoping to catch their idol coming or going. To help Paul avoid these pesky kids Dr Asher worked out an arrangement with his neighbours whereby Paul could climb out of his bedroom window, four storeys above the street, climb back inside the apartment of a retired colonel living next door, go down in the lift and exit the building courtesy of the people in the basement flat, whose back door brought him into the mews behind Wimpole Street. While Dr Asher deserves the credit for this ingenious escape route, it is a mark of how charming Paul was that neighbours felt sufficiently well disposed to the young man to let him use their homes in this way. It was a lesson he learned well. In years to come, when he owned many homes in Britain and abroad, Paul came to similar friendly arrangements with his neighbours whereby he could drive in and out of his properties via their land when he wanted to avoid fans and the press.

Life at Wimpole Street suited Paul so well he lodged here for the next three years, long after the other Beatles had bought houses outside the city, the sanctuary of the Ashers' home almost as important to Paul as his relationship with Jane, whom everybody in the Beatles' circle liked. 'She was lovely. She was good for him,' affirms Tony Bramwell. 'The Asher family were good for him, [too], gave him a bit of stability in London.' Margaret Asher fed Paul up between engagements and her basement music room became a cosy den for Paul and John to write in. 'We wrote a lot of stuff together, one on one, eyeball to eyeball,' John would say of these sessions.

Like in 'I Want to Hold Your Hand', I remember when we got the chord that made the song. We were in Jane Asher's house, downstairs in the cellar, playing the piano at the same time. We had 'Oh you, you got something …' and Paul hits this chord and I turned to him and said, 'That's it! Do that again.' In those days we really used to write like that.

Songwriting sessions such as these – some of the happiest and closest times John and Paul ever enjoyed – were all the more precious for being squeezed between concert engagement, the Beatles travelling considerable distances every week to play cinemas and dance halls from Cheltenham to Carlisle, a punishing regime that saw Paul succumb to flu in mid-November. The Beatles had to postpone a show in Portsmouth as a result, one of the few times Paul has ever missed a concert due to ill-health. Brian Epstein was also booking his boys onto a plethora of TV and radio shows, where they were obliged to tell jokes and act up like a comedy troupe. Before pop music became self-aware as an art form, before anybody talked of 'rock music', groups like the Beatles were considered part of mainstream show business, no different from the jugglers, ventriloquists and comics with whom they found themselves on shows like *Late Screen Extra* where, for example, they appeared on 25 November 1963 with Liverpudlian comic Ken Dodd. 'It was a way of getting [exposure],' says Dodd, who used the Beatles as a foil. 'At the time, I was hungry for publicity as well as the Beatles, and if you get a chance of being on television you go along with it.' It helped that Paul enjoyed the play-acting. As with so many members of his family, there was something of the ham about him.

With everything else that was going on, the boys still found time to record their second LP, *With the Beatles*, released in time for Christmas a mere eight months after *Please Please Me*. The cover photograph, by Robert Freeman, presented the Beatles solemn-faced in black turtleneck sweaters, a monochrome image reminiscent of the early photographs of the band taken by Astrid Kirchherr, and an indication that, while the Beatles would play the fool on TV, they had ambitions to be taken more seriously as musicians. Again the 14 tracks were a mixture of original compositions and covers. The album began with John's insistent 'It Won't Be Long' followed by an equally commanding lead vocal on 'All I've Got to Do'. As if spurred on to better his friend's performances, Paul was heard next on the explosive 'All My Loving'. The song the boys had given the Rolling Stones was also on the album, sung by Ringo, while George sang one of his own compositions for the first time, 'Don't Bother Me'. The rest of the tracks were covers, including the closer, 'Money', which had new significance now the Beatles were earning £2,000 a week ($3,060) from touring alone, a sensational sum at the time.

The new album went to number one, 'She Loves You' only relinquishing the top spot on the singles charts when the Beatles released 'I Want to Hold Your Hand'. Suddenly everybody wanted to meet the Beatles. They were invited into the EMI boardroom for lunch with the chairman, Sir Joseph Lockwood, posing with Sir Joe for a photo under the iconic painting of His Master's Voice. The band was also being inundated with requests to invest in projects or lend their name to good causes. In Liverpool, Brian Epstein introduced the boys to two beady-eyed Oxford University students, Jeffrey Archer and Nicholas Lloyd, who persuaded the boys to back a fundraising drive for the charity Oxfam. 'I thought Paul and John were very bright, though I found John a little cynical, whereas Paul was enthusiastic, and what clearly struck me – both in the case of John and Paul – was that if they'd wanted to go to Oxford themselves they so clearly had good enough brains to go,' recalls Archer, later Lord Archer, novelist and disgraced Tory peer.*

A week later the Beatles were presented with further evidence of their fame when they met 3,000 fan club members at a ballroom in Wimbledon, South London. First the Beatles greeted their excited admirers in person, the boys sheltering behind the theatre bar for their own safety as they signed autographs. 'They shook hands with all the fans,' noted Neil Aspinall, 'about 10,000 of them, actually, because they kept going back to the end of the queue and coming round again.' The band then performed in a cage for their protection, which was a first. 'It was like being in a zoo, on stage! It felt dangerous. The kids were out of hand,' commented Ringo. As if being in a cage wasn't strange enough, as they performed the boys were pelted with jelly babies. John had mentioned in an interview that he'd recently been sent a present of the sugary sweets but George had eaten them all, a casual remark that caused girls to inundate the band with what they now presumed were the Beatles' favourite treats. Unable to deliver the jelly babies personally, they threw them. George stalked off stage in protest, already irritated by 'the mania', as he pointedly described it, emphasising the real madness at the heart of what was happening to them. Paul kept on smiling, showing a greater tolerance for all aspects of their burgeoning success, as he always would.

* Jailed in 2001 for perjury.

6

AMERICA

NEW YORK, BEATLE TIME

For Christmas 1963, Beatles fan club members received the first of what became an annual yuletide gift, a giveaway record on which Paul and the boys thanked everybody for their support and sang seasonal songs in silly voices. Then came a London Christmas show in which the boys and other NEMS acts performed songs and took part in panto-mime-style skits before sold-out audiences of screaming, jelly-baby-hurling young ladies. The screaming had become ridiculous. These were not screams of anguish, but girls enjoying the catharsis of yelling until their faces went red and tears streamed down their cheeks, some screaming until they wet themselves, or fainted, or both. Girls had screamed at music acts before the Beatles, and acts contemporaneous with them, Gerry and the Pacemakers for one, but it was more pronounced and on a bigger scale with the Beatles, who entertained 100,000 fans in this hysterical fashion by mid-January 1964, when their run of London Christmas shows ended.

After the briefest of breaks, the group flew to France for a three-week residency at L'Olympia, a Parisian music hall associated with the can-can and Edith Piaf. Les Beatles shared the bill with nine acts including the Texan singer Trini Lopez, who'd scored a hit with 'If I Had a Hammer', and local 'yé-yé' chanteuse Sylvie Vartan. The Beatles fared badly. Their amplifiers failed on the first night, and audi-ence reaction was muted. The boys grumbled about the screamers back home, but at least English audiences were enthusiastic. Olympia drew an older, more laid-back crowd, who clapped politely at the end.

There were some fans at the stage door, but *sur le continent* the lads attracted the attention of effeminate boys, rather than over-excited girls. On top of which, the reviews were bad. Not that the Beatles seemed to care. 'They were not upset that the reception in Paris was a little bit cool. They were still just young kids out there having fun,' says Trini Lopez drummer Mickey Jones, who hung out with the boys at the luxurious Georges V hotel, a sign of how much money was suddenly flowing their way. 'They were having parties [with] girls from the Lido [club].'

The Lido girls were ushered away when Jane Asher visited from England, along with Paul's father and brother, Mike McCartney noting that Paul was listening to Bob Dylan's new LP, *The Freewheelin' Bob Dylan*, in his suite, having previously dismissed folk music as 'rubbish'. Dylan would become an increasingly important influence. George Martin also came to Paris to record the boys singing German-language versions of 'She Loves You' and 'I Want to Hold Your Hand', a chore they didn't want to fulfil. When they failed to make their appointment at the studio in Rue de Sèvres, Martin called the Georges V to be told by Neil Aspinall that the band had decided not to do the German record – the first time they'd defied their producer so directly, and an intimation of trouble ahead. 'You just tell them I'm coming right over to let them know exactly what I think of them!' stormed Martin. He arrived at the Georges V shortly thereafter to find a scene akin to the Mad Hatter's Tea Party in *Alice in Wonderland*.

> Around a long table sat John, Paul, George, Ringo, Neil Aspinall and Mal Evans, his assistant. In the centre, pouring tea, was Jane Asher, a beautiful Alice with long golden [sic] hair. At my appearance the whole tableau exploded. Beatles ran in all directions, hiding behind sofas, cushions, the piano – anything that gave them cover.

'You bastards,' Martin yelled at the boys, who emerged one by one to apologise to their producer and invite him to join them for tea. They did the German-language recordings on 29 January.

These high jinks were as nothing compared to the excitement in the Georges V caused by a telegram from the USA. 'One night we arrived back at the hotel from the Olympia when a telegram came through to Brian from Capitol Records of America,' Paul recalled. 'He came running into the room saying, "Hey, look. You are number one in America!" "I Want to Hold Your Hand" had gone to number one.' Ecstatic, the boys rode the obliging Mal Evans around the suite like cowboys yelling: *Ya-hoo! America, here we come!*

A few days later, on 7 February 1964, the Beatles flew to New York, with a large entourage that included Brian Epstein, Cynthia Lennon, Neil Aspinall and photographer Robert Freeman. The American record producer Phil Spector also latched onto the Beatles party, which was trailed by a contingent of Fleet Street reporters and cameramen. The mood on the long, time-cheating flight across the Atlantic was apprehensive. 'They've got everything over there, will they want us, too?' Ringo asked the pressmen rhetorically.

The drummer's gloom reflected what a struggle it had been to generate interest in the band in the USA. Despite the fact Capitol Records was owned by EMI, the American label declined repeated suggestions from George Martin that they should release the Beatles' early singles, Americans having little interest in foreign practitioners of what was, after all, their music. Martin recalls a curt message from Alan Livingston, President of Capitol: 'We don't think the Beatles will do anything in this market.' Livingston's comment was based on the historical fact that few British pop stars had enjoyed success in the US, a recent example being Cliff Richard who discovered that his considerable popularity in the UK counted for nought in Poughkeepsie. Desperate to get their music out in America in some form, Brian Epstein cut deals with two minor US labels, Vee Jay and Swan, who released 'Please Please Me', 'From Me to You' and 'She Loves You', without much initial success. Epstein also hired an American song plugger to promote the records. Radio stations proved resistant, but slowly things started to change. Curiously, the assassination of President Kennedy in November 1963 may have had some bearing on America taking the Beatles to its heart. In the depressing aftermath of the murder young Americans looked beyond their country for something new and innocent to cheer them up, and heard a fresh, joyful sound coming from England. American disc jockeys began to play imported copies of 'I Want to Hold Your Hand' prior to Christmas 1963, the popularity of the song spreading across the States and into Canada. Alan Livingston woke up to the fact that there was now US interest in the Beatles. Capitol released 'I Want to Hold Your Hand'/'I

Saw Her Standing There' on 26 December, with plans for an LP in the new year. Vee Jay re-released 'Please Please Me' in January 1964. Suddenly American airwaves were crackling with the happy English sound.

A number of other factors fell into place. A theatrical agent in New York named Sid Bernstein, who'd kept up with news from Britain since being stationed there during the war, had been reading about the Beatles with growing interest, to the point that he struck a deal with Brian Epstein to present the Beatles at Carnegie Hall in New York on 12 February 1964. Even more significantly, Ed Sullivan, who'd witnessed fan reaction to the Beatles at Heathrow Airport, arranged to have the band appear on his syndicated television show. Brian accepted a modest fee from Sullivan's people, but insisted shrewdly that his boys get top billing. Furthermore, it was agreed that the Beatles would appear on three consecutive editions of this important show – on 9, 16 and 23 February – the first two appearances live, the third pre-recorded. This was good work on Epstein's part, counterbalanced by an example of his ineptitude.

In recent months, manufacturers in Britain and North America had been approaching NEMS asking permission to produce Beatles merchandise. A small range of novelty goods had been sanctioned and were already selling strongly, not least plastic Beatles wigs, which enjoyed a popularity in Britain not seen since the 1954 craze for Davy Crockett hats (sparked by a Disney TV series). Not everything was authorised, however. When Blackpool confectioners started to manufacture Beatles rock without permission, NEMS sued. It soon became too much for Brian Epstein to deal with, on top of his other responsibilities, so he delegated merchandising to his lawyer, David Jacobs, known as the 'stars' lawyer' for his celebrity clientele. Jacobs sold the rights to merchandise any and all items under the Beatles imprimatur to a couple of young British hustlers named Nicky Byrne and John Fenton. There being little precedent for such a deal, Jacobs agreed that Byrne and Fenton could sub-license to manufacturers in Britain and abroad on a 90–10 split – in the entrepreneurs' favour. 'It was an inequitable deal. I knew that when it was done,' comments Fenton, who expected NEMS to renegotiate once they realised their blunder, but they didn't seem to see what a mistake they'd made, and for the next few months Fenton and Byrne were free to make a fortune.

The young men set up a US licensing operation named Seltaeb – Beatles spelt backwards – to capitalise on the new American interest in the band. To raise start-up capital, Fenton and Byrne went to friends in the Chelsea Set, fashionable, often wealthy young people living in and around London's King's Road. These gadabouts were the progenitors of swinging London, though many preferred jazz to pop in 1964. 'I didn't like the Beatles' music,' says Fenton, not untypically. 'The "She loves you Yeah! Yeah! Yeah!" stuff to me was like my worst nightmare. That was the only way I could justify selling Beatles toilet paper to people. I felt there was a similarity there.' An Old Etonian friend of Byrne's, Simon Miller Mundy, invested £1,000 ($1,530) in Seltaeb and got his friend, Lord Eliot, to invest the same. By coincidence, Eliot was Jane Asher's cousin. 'London in those days was very, very small,' notes His Lordship (who became Lord St Germans on the death of his father). 'Her mother's father was [an earlier] Lord St Germans.' In advance of the Beatles' visit to the USA, Nicky Byrne booked himself into a suite at the Drake Hotel in New York and began fielding offers from US manufacturers who wanted to produce Beatles products. Within days Seltaeb had signed licences for everything from Beatles golf bags to toothpaste, bringing in a revenue of $3.5 million (£2.2 m). 'It was absolutely *astonishing*,' comments St Germans.

As the Beatles' first visit to America approached, Seltaeb and their manufacturing partners became concerned that Capitol Records wasn't doing enough to promote the band. So they took independent action. 'We had every lift boy in New York saying, "The Beatles are coming – which floor do you want?"' remembers John Fenton. Disc jockeys such as B. Mitchel Reed began counting off the days, hours and minutes to the Beatles' arrival. Rival DJs, notably the irrepressible Murray 'the K' Kaufman on WINS, joined in, using Beatle as an adjective. 7 February 1964 became Beatle-Day or B-Day:

It is now 6:30 a.m., Beatle time … They left London 30 minutes ago … They're out over the Atlantic Ocean, headed for New York … The temperature is 32 Beatle degrees …

Announcements went out over the air in the New York area that any girl who made it to the newly renamed Kennedy Airport in time to greet the boys would receive a buck and Beatles T-shirt. The T-shirt manufacturer bussed girls to the airport to make sure of a success. By the time Pan Am Flight 101 landed there were thousands of fans at Kennedy screaming for the Beatles. 'Without Seltaeb the Beatles would have found it a lot harder to conquer America. We really whipped up hysteria there,' says Fenton with a touch of exaggeration. After a slow start, Capitol Records *had* started to push the Beatles, spending upwards of $50,000 on promotion [£76,500], promising to make 1964 'the year of the Beatles'. It all helped to create the day the Beatles arrived in America; the 'turning point', Brian always called it.

When the door of the Pan Am jet opened, and the Beatles emerged onto the steps, clutching Beatle bags, a heaving mob surged forward to greet them, held back by gum-chewing New York cops. The ensuing airport press conference was a bear pit. Paul, George and Ringo appeared nervous. Lennon exuded more confidence, telling the squabbling press pack to 'shut up', which made them laugh. While some reporters were evidently intent on deflating this Beatles bubble, their tricky questions served as a foil for the Beatles' wit. After a hesitant start, everyone got off a good line, including Paul. Told by a reporter that Detroit had a 'Stamp Out the Beatles' campaign, he rejoined: 'We're bringing out a "Stamp Out Detroit" campaign.'

A fleet of Cadillacs conveyed the band into Manhattan, where they booked into the venerable Plaza Hotel. Impresario Sid Bernstein watched the limousines pull up at the Fifth Avenue entrance amidst a scrimmage of fans. Paul paused on the threshold, turned and waved. 'I said, "Wow! He's a good-looking kid and he's got the smarts." The girls were screaming for Paul. There was a lot [more] screaming for him than the other boys.' A little later Brian took Bernstein through to meet the lads in their suite on the twelfth floor. 'They had the shades drawn, and they are looking out the window and waving to the kids downstairs. "Mr Bernstein, this is crazier than where we live. These kids are mad!"'

The trip could have ended in disaster right there. Brian consorted with male escorts and cruised for rough trade in Central Park during his stay at the Plaza, according to former NEMS employee Geoffrey Ellis. The Beatles' manager may even have been photographed in a compromising situation in his suite. A story that a press photographer, lowered outside the hotel in a bosun's chair to shoot pictures in through the windows, got a snap of Epstein with a rent boy was later reported in a book by Ross Benson. Unlikely though the story sounds, John Fenton says Seltaeb hushed up a scandal by buying an item that would have incriminated somebody involved with the Beatles on the trip. He won't say who, other than it wasn't a member of the band, but states: 'If it hadn't been for us there would have been no Beatles in America because they'd have been killed stoned dead by the federal rape law.' It was only because of their connections with 'Italian gentlemen' in the New York merchandising business that they managed to take the evidence out of circulation. 'It was a huge indiscretion which could have got them into a lot of trouble.'

It is hard to appreciate how unusual the Beatles looked to a mainstream American television audience when they appeared live on the *Ed Sullivan Show* on Sunday 9 February 1964. 'We came out of nowhere with funny hair, looking like marionettes or something,' Paul has reflected. 'Up until then there were jugglers and comedians like Jerry Lewis [on the show], and then suddenly, The Beatles!' When Sullivan – a grim-faced man with an awkward manner – had introduced them, the camera first found Paul, who sang lead on 'All My Loving', the first of five songs divided between two spots. The 700-strong studio audience squealed with pleasure throughout, while an estimated 73 million people across the United States watched on TV, the highest Nielsen rating yet recorded. For many young Americans this was the moment that ushered in the 1960s as we have come to perceive the decade – a time of exploration, modernity and increased personal freedom. The Beatles would become the soundtrack to their young lives, ensuring that all four band members, not least Paul, would command attention and affection in the US for the rest of their careers.

Two days later, when the Eastern Seaboard was blanketed in snow, the Beatles took a train from Penn Station to Washington DC to play a show at the Washington Coliseum. During the southbound journey the press were able to hang out with the Beatles in the Pullman car, finding the Englishmen relaxed and playful. By the time they pulled into the capital they were all friends, though Al Aronowitz of the *Saturday Evening Post* detected evidence that Paul was letting the attention go to his head. The others were calling him 'the star' sarcastically. Another journalist on the train had a ticklish question for the star. David English of London's *Daily Mail* took Paul aside and told him his office had information that a Hamburg barmaid was claiming to have given birth to his daughter. What did he have to say to that?

The woman in question was Erika Wohlers, one of the girls the Beatles apparently hung out with in Hamburg, though Paul's German barmaid friends have only a dim memory of Erika and no recollection of her dating Paul. 'Maybe he went with her one day, I don't know. But she definitely wasn't his girlfriend, because I was going out with him every day,' says Paul's regular Hamburg girlfriend Ruth Lallemann. In any event, Erika claims that she had an affair with Paul in Hamburg and that the daughter she gave birth to at Hamburg's Barmbeck Hospital in December 1962, a month shy of her 20th birthday, was Paul's.

> In July 1962 my doctor informed me that I was pregnant. There was a lot of arguing with Paul because he was of the opinion that we were still too young to have a baby. Paul and the owner of the Star-Club wanted me to have an abortion, but I refused, and on 19 December 1962 my daughter Bettina was born.

Here is the first problem with Erika's story. Working back nine months places conception in March 1962, when the Beatles were in England. Erika's explanation: 'Bettina was born prematurely, in the seventh month.' (The Beatles were in Hamburg from 13 April to 2 June 1962.) Erika claims that Paul's 'less than favourable reaction' to the pregnancy ended their relationship. After her daughter was born, she placed Bettina in care, and went to work as a barmaid. By the time of the Beatles' first US adventure Bettina was 14 months. When David English tried to confront Paul with this story on the train to Washington, McCartney avoided the reporter. When English persisted, Paul exclaimed: 'Oh fuck, why did you have to say that now?' This was less than an admission and, lacking hard evidence that Erika's story was true, the *Daily Mail* didn't publish. But that wasn't the end of the matter.

'THE BEATLES IN THEIR FIRST FULL LENGTH, HILARIOUS ACTION-PACKED FILM!'

A week after returning from the USA, the Beatles began work on their first feature film. Paul and his band mates had grown up with the cinema, and had great affection for jukebox movies such as *The Girl Can't Help It*. In their career to date there had been an element of play-acting, while their contract with Brian made explicit reference to their ambition to make pictures together. Epstein now cut a deal with the American company United Artists for the Beatles to star in a movie named after a Ringoism. 'It's been a hard day ...' the drummer sighed at the end of another gruelling day, only to notice it was already night, causing him to correct himself mid-sentence, '... day's night.' Playwright Alun Owen wrote the script, having had the benefit of spending time with the band on the road, while the director was 32-year-old American Richard Lester, who would shoot quickly in black and white on a low budget, United Artists wanting the movie in theatres before the Beatles craze passed.

A Hard Day's Night was a musical, essentially, featuring tracks George Martin had in the can, plus new songs written especially. But the *cinema-verité* style in which Lester shot the picture gave it the feel of a documentary, one in which four cheeky but nice youngsters are pitched against their own over-excited female fans (most of them mere children, as can be seen from the crowd scenes in which Lester used real fans) and adult authority figures who are depicted as comically inept, creepy, or out of touch and pompous, the latter exemplified by an advertising executive into whose office George Harrison stumbles. 'Now, you'll like these. You'll really *dig* them. They're *fab* and all the other pimply hyperboles,' the advertising executive tells the Beatle, whom he assumes has come to help them promote a new range of shirts.

'I wouldn't be seen dead in them,' replies George. 'They're dead grotty.'

'Grotty?'

'Yeah, grotesque.'

Spending time with the Beatles, Alun Owen had picked up on slang expressions like grotty and fab commonly used by and, in at least one instance, coined by the boys. The first usage of grotty in English was by George in the film, according to the *Oxford English Dictionary*; while fab – simply an abbreviation of fabulous – had been in common usage among young British people since 1961, but came to be associated primarily with the Beatles who, in their early days, were sometimes billed as 'the fabulous Beatles'. The Beatles' PR man Tony Barrow wrote about the 'fabulous foursome' in his press releases, shortening this to the 'fab four'. More than any other trendy term, fab suited them.

The Beatles acquitted themselves adequately in *A Hard Day's Night*, though Richard Lester thought Paul tried too hard:

Paul was the most theatrical of them all. He had a girlfriend who was an actress. She and her parents and her brother went to the theatre a lot and Paul went with her. He loved the theatre. He loved show business, as it were, in a way that the others didn't care. I think this was a disadvantage to him, that in a way Paul sometimes tried too hard to act … Had he been less enamoured of the trappings of cinema and the theatre he might have been a bit more relaxed.

It would be hard for Paul to be truly relaxed. He was under too much pressure. While making the movie, the Beatles were also recording an original soundtrack album, for which he and John had to come up with new songs. They rose to the challenge, with Paul largely responsible for the stand-out tracks, such as 'Things We Said Today', the lyric of which had a new maturity. Paul was also responsible for 'Can't Buy Me Love', a 12-bar blues rearranged by George Martin as the band's next single, going to number one virtually simultaneously in the UK and the USA. The success of the song in the United States was proof that American fans hadn't forsaken them after their flying visit. Indeed, plans were being finalised for a full-scale US tour. Before this took place the Beatles were committed to play shows in Denmark and Holland, after which they had to schlep halfway round the world to Hong Kong and Australia. When Ritchie fell ill with tonsillitis the day before departure, stand-in drummer Jimmy Nicol was despatched in his place, clear evidence that not all Beatles were equal. It is inconceivable that the tour could have gone ahead without Paul or John.

The mania followed the band on tour abroad, with scenes equally if not more excessive than seen in Britain and America. Young Dutchmen and women leapt into the canals of Amsterdam in a desperate attempt to reach the Beatles on a boat trip they took through the city. A girl caller got through to the Beatles' Copenhagen hotel suite saying she was dying and her last wish was to speak to a Beatle. Journalist Derek Taylor, who had recently joined the Beatles' entourage as an additional PR man, was taken in, but Paul had seen and heard enough of the mania to guess it was a ruse, taking the phone and ticking off the caller, as Taylor recalls: '"Now Mary Sue," he said, lofty, dry and mildly admonishing, "you know you shouldn't go around telling lies …"' When they got to Australia, so many people gathered around the Beatles' Melbourne hotel that the city centre was brought to a standstill, while

one fan reportedly burst a blood vessel screaming. It was at this fren-
zied stage in the tour that Ritchie rejoined the band, continuing with
them for shows in Sydney, where Paul celebrated his 22nd birthday
with a party attended, at his own suggestion, by the winners of a beauty
competition.

All these foreign concerts were triumphs. Britain, Sweden,
Denmark, Holland and Australia had fallen to the Beatles, to para-
phrase Brian Epstein. Only Paris held out, but France would fall. Two
and a half years earlier, Brian had been the manager of a provincial
record shop. Now he saw himself as the Napoleon of Pop, and his next
campaign would be his biggest: the Beatles' invasion of the United
States.

CONQUERING HEROES

Before going back to the USA there were two British premières for *A
Hard Day's Night*, the first at the Pavilion in London on 6 July 1964, Jim
McCartney bringing a delegation of 'relies' down from Liverpool to
support 'our Paul'. The film opened with the resounding first chord of
the theme song – *CHUNNNNG!* – sending John, George and Ringo
running helter-skelter towards a train station, pursued by their fans and
the press. The lads meet Paul, dressed in disguise, and board a train
where they bump into some schoolgirls (one of whom, a pretty young
model named Patricia 'Pattie' Boyd, became George's girlfriend, later
his wife). The subsequent plot was simply the process of the Beatles
coming to London to perform on a TV show, which gave them an excuse
to perform their songs. Over and above the musical sequences, which
were excellent, the Beatles came across as likeable and natural lads
with aspects of a comedy troupe, almost cartoonish in appearance,
while the picture itself was clean and sharp. As the credits rolled, you
wanted more.

Afterwards everybody repaired in a celebratory mood to the Dorchester Hotel where Paul introduced his father to Princess Margaret, a hitherto unimaginable situation for the Liverpool cotton merchant. At the
end of a long meal, with the 'relies' lounging around the table, full to
bursting, Paul presented Dad with another surprise: a picture of a racehorse. 'Thank you, son. It's very nice,' said Jim, who was to celebrate his

62nd birthday the following day. 'It's a horse,' Paul told his old man, with the exasperation of youth.

'I can see that, son.'

'It's not just a painting … I've bought you a bloody horse.' So Jim McCartney came into possession of Drake's Drum, a £1,000 gelding. The affection between father and son represented by this gift is a contrast to John Lennon's unhappy relationship with his father, the ne'er-do-well Freddie Lennon, who'd made himself known to his son recently after years of estrangement, only to be greeted with icy indifference. Later John slammed a door in his father's face.

Still, the McCartney family was not without their disagreements. At 22, Paul found himself an exceedingly rich young man in a family who'd never had much. Though careful with his money, Paul felt compelled to share his good fortune around. He handed out gifts, notably Dad's racehorse, and helped family members financially. Brother Mike told Paul he couldn't support himself on the bits of money he was earning as a member of Scaffold; at least he couldn't live the way Paul was. 'Sometimes my brother is rather slow in catching on but when eventually he does, he soon makes up for it,' Mike would write in his memoirs. 'On seeing the impossible situation I was in, being a Beatle brother with very little personal money … he arranged for me to receive a weekly tax-free "covenant" of ten pounds from his accountant till I was on my feet.' Several other family members became financially dependent on Paul, who helped them buy houses, and in some cases put them on what became known as the McCartney Pension, so they never had to work again. This didn't necessarily engender harmony.

These were mostly problems for the future, however. Four days after the London première of *A Hard Day's Night*, Paul and his fellow Beatles returned home for the northern première of their picture at the Liverpool Odeon. There was a holiday feeling on Merseyside on Friday 10 July as the Beatles' British Eagle Airways plane touched down at Liverpool Airport, where 1,500 people had gathered to greet them. The boys were driven in triumph into Liverpool City Centre, via Speke, where Paul had lived, his old neighbours standing at the kerb waving. 'Me mum, me dad, me auntie, me uncle, all the family, everybody was there,' recalls resident Frank Foy, who had typically been given the day off school for the occasion. Like many children, Frank wore a plastic

Beatles wig, which became uncomfortably hot in the sunshine. The Beatles entered the Town Hall on Dale Street to a fanfare of 'Can't Buy Me Love', played by the Liverpool Police Band. Ringo danced up the stairs in joy. They stepped out onto the balcony to a rapturous reception from 20,000 of their people. There had been many high points recently – number one records, playing for the Queen Mother, the *Ed Sullivan Show*, mobbed in London, Amsterdam, New York and Melbourne – but this was home. The boys beamed with pride.

Yet down among the crowd, trampled underfoot in Dale Street and blowing down the back alleys, were pieces of paper that threatened to blacken the name of James Paul McCartney. Just months after a *Mail* reporter confronted Paul with the story of a German barmaid who claimed to have borne his child, a Liverpool man had papered Liverpool with fliers claiming Paul had got his 'niece' pregnant. The girl in question was a typist named Anita Cochrane, who claims she met Paul just prior to her 16th birthday in 1961, going to see the Beatles play the Tower Ballroom on Friday 1 December that year.

'It was my sixteenth birthday that day,' Anita told the *Daily Mail* in 1997. (In fact, her 16th birthday was the next day, one of two factual inconsistencies in her story.) Anita claims she and Paul went to bed that night, and that she slept with him twice more over the ensuing 16 months. 'We used to go back to John Lennon's flat in Gambier Terrace …' she told the *Mail*. (Here is the second problem with Anita's story: John didn't live at Gambier Terrace at this stage.) When Anita found herself pregnant, in the summer of 1963, she decided that Paul had to be the father and told her family as much. 'When my mum and grandmother found out I was pregnant, I thought I'd write to Paul and tell him what had happened. I was that sure the baby was his.' When Anita didn't receive a reply, her mother Violet went to see Jim McCartney, who said his Paul didn't know her Anita. On 10 February 1964, Anita gave birth at Billinge Hospital, Merseyside, to a boy named Philip Paul. No father's name was entered on the birth certificate. Anita's family then took her to a lawyer, who contacted NEMS.

In truth neither Paul nor Brian Epstein had the slightest idea whether this typist, or the German barmaid, had a genuine claim. The boys had been such libertines, especially in Hamburg, that it wouldn't have been surprising if they had fathered some illegitimate children. While Paul did not, and never would, accept the paternity claims of the barmaid or the typist, the decision was made to pay off any such claimants for the sake of expediency. 'Brian Epstein, on behalf of the Beatles, took the stance that, unless they were talking vast sums, it was better to buy off people who were threatening to expose small things about the Beatles, and that included paternity [claims],' explains Tony Barrow.

> I think Brian was particularly sensitive about sex, because of his own sexuality, and at all costs wanted to avoid intrusion upon his own private life, because what he was at the time was not just gay, but doing illegal things.* And I think he realised that anything about him would brush off on the boys ... The policy was pay 'em off, get rid of them, move on.

Anita Cochrane claims to have been offered two pounds ten shillings ($3.82) a week by NEMS: 'The solicitor put in a request for more money and we got this offer of a one-off payment of £5,000 ($7,650). That was more than a house in those days.' An agreement was drawn up, dated 23 April 1964, on the basis that Anita wouldn't go public. But her 'uncle' (actually her mother's boyfriend) took issue with what had happened and distributed leaflets around Liverpool describing Paul as a 'cad'. Epstein heard about this the morning of the Liverpool première. Leaflets had been left at the Press Club in Bold Street. 'They were [also] given out in Castle Street, round the Town Hall, saying Paul give a girl a baby in Waterloo, and I think it named her,' recalls Anita's brother, Ian, who believed the story. A poem parodying 'All My Loving' was sent to newspapers:

> *My name is Philip Paul Cochrane, I'm just a little boy ...*
> *In spite of all her lovin' we got no thanks from him,*
> *It seems he loved my mother, just long enough to sin ...*

Brian Epstein asked Derek Taylor to break the news to Paul. 'He shrugged with astonishing nonchalance, said "OK" and that was that,' Taylor later wrote. The trip to Liverpool went ahead and the press – in love with the Beatles, and wary of unsubstantiated, defamatory allegations – didn't touch the story, while Anita's 'uncle' was warned by the

---

* In the sense that homosexuality itself was still illegal in the UK.

police he could face charges if he wasn't careful. Like the German claim, however, this tale had a long way to run.

NORTH COUNTRY BOYS

Paul returned to North America with the Beatles in August 1964 to give a series of concerts in the USA and Canada, starting at the Cow Palace in San Francisco, an indoor livestock pavilion. Something strange had happened in America since their first visit. The Beatles were now not only screamed at by their fans, but a focus for nutcases and extremists. 'Beatle worship is idolatry,' read a placard wielded by a picket of the ultra-religious at the San Francisco show. The boys moved on to play under equally trying circumstances in Las Vegas and Vancouver, where Republican Canadians, who wanted to sever the nation's constitutional links with Britain, protested against the Beatles as emissaries of the Queen. Even more alarmingly, Ringo received death threats in Quebec from anti-Semites who mistook him for a Jew. For their concerts at the Montral Forum, Ritchie had a bodyguard sitting beside him on stage. What with the screaming fans, the inadequate sound systems, and now the fear that there might even be assassins in the audience, the Beatles' brief set got shorter by the night. They rushed through their shows, wanting them over with as soon as possible.

It was the sound quality that bothered George Martin most when he came out to record the boys playing the Hollywood Bowl on 23 August for a live LP. The producer found the challenge of getting a decent recording insuperable. 'It was like putting a microphone at the end of a 747 jet – just a continual screaming sound.'* The following afternoon the boss of Capitol Records, Alan Livingston, completely uninterested in the Beatles just recently, hosted a garden party in their honour at his Beverly Hills home. Wherever the band went these days, hotel managers, record executives and mayors wanted to meet them and introduce their family members, especially their children, and Livingston was no different. He sat the lads under a tree in his garden so friends and associates could parade their daughters down the line, each Beatle expected to say a word to the girls, who were too young to raise more than a polite

---

* Nonetheless, *Live at the Hollywood Bowl* was finally issued in 1977.

smile from the musicians, until a rather more mature young lady thrust herself forward.

'My God, you're beautiful,' remarked Paul, as he took her hand.

'You're not so bad yourself,' replied Peggy Lipton.

At 19, Peggy was an actress under contract to Universal Studios, more or less unknown, though she later achieved celebrity in the TV show *Mod Squad*. Like many American teens, Peggy was enamoured of the Beatles, and had papered her bedroom walls with their pictures. Unlike most of her contemporaries, Peggy also had the chutzpah and contacts to engineer a meeting with her idols, her sights set firmly on Paul, whose name she had screamed at the Las Vegas Convention Center the previous week. After the show Peggy and a girlfriend inveigled themselves into a party the boys were due to attend. 'I affected the schoolgirl nymphomaniac look,' Peggy recalled in her autobiography, *Breathing Out*. Unfortunately, the Beatles didn't show. Alan Livingston's garden party was Peggy's second attempt to meet Paul, and this time she managed to speak to him and slip her phone number to a member of his entourage. Peggy was summoned that evening to the Bel Air house where the Beatles were staying.

> I arrived almost sick to my stomach with butterflies. I had lost my virginity only six months earlier and I'd been thinking about Paul day-in, day-out for a year. He greeted me sweetly and checked me out with a quick once-over. He liked what he saw. We sat downstairs. He played the piano. The next thing I knew we were on our way upstairs [where] he took me in his arms and kissed me ... I took a shower to slow things down and when I came out wrapped in a towel, he caressed me in front of the window and let the towel fall to the floor. This to me was an utterly romantic gesture. Paul was a romantic.

Afterwards Peggy left the house feeling cheap. She returned the next day, though, clear evidence of Paul's unfaithfulness to Jane Asher, who remained his steady girlfriend in London.

After shows in Denver and Cincinnati the Beatles returned to New York, where they booked into the Hotel Delmonico, the manager of the Plaza being unwilling to accommodate them after the mayhem of their first visit. The Beatles were to play two shows at Forest Hills tennis stadium. The second night they met Bob Dylan.

The meeting and subsequent relationship between the American musician and the Beatles is significant. Along with Elvis Presley, Dylan and the Beatles form the great triumvirate of rock, interconnected on different levels. Like the Beatles, Dylan was a young man in his twenties from a provincial, working-class, northern town, in his case Hibbing, Minnesota, where he was a high school rock 'n' roller before he discovered folk music, sharing Paul's passions for Buddy Holly, Little Richard and Elvis. Dylan's musical path diverged when he discovered the folk troubadour Woody Guthrie and joined the New York-based folk revival whereby emphasis was put on reconnecting with the roots of American vernacular music, singing songs with a strong narrative, often a moral or otherwise instructive story, framed with poetic language. Dylan was a folk star before the Beatles found fame, his début album released on CBS when the boys were still playing Merseyside dance halls with Pete Best. By the time CBS released Dylan's second album, the *Freewheelin' Bob Dylan*, Dylan and the Beatles were both stars, though of a different order. Girls screamed at the Beatles. Dylan's audiences listened to him in respectful silence, as to a poet with important things to say. 'He was proud of that,' notes Bob's journalist friend Al Aronowitz, who also knew the Beatles and helped effect their historic meeting.

Dylan and the Beatles were also singer-songwriters, at a time when few artists wrote and performed their own material, extremely fecund writers who were rapidly creating fat song books with ample material for themselves and other artists to perform. As Brian Epstein bestowed Lennon & McCartney songs on acts he managed, Dylan's manager Albert Grossman gave Bob's compositions to his own stable of artists, notably 'Blowin' in the Wind' to Peter, Paul and Mary, who had a big hit with it in 1963. Initially suspicious of folk music, Paul had been very impressed by *The Freewheelin'*; hard on the boot-heels of which came *The Times They Are A-Changin'*, then *Another Side of Bob Dylan*, albums that featured lyrics more sophisticated than anything John and Paul had so far written. At the same time the Beatles had something Dylan didn't have, and wanted, which was chart success. For all these reasons, Bob and the Beatles were curious about one another. A summit meeting had been on the cards for some time when John Lennon asked their mutual friend Al Aronowitz to set it up.

Bob drove down from his digs in Woodstock for the occasion, with his roadie Victor Maymudes, a tall, saturnine hipster who rarely left

Dylan's side. They picked up Aronowitz at home in New Jersey *en route* to the Delmonico in Manhattan, where Big Mal Evans escorted the Americans up to the Beatles' suite. In an anteroom, a number of celebrities were waiting to be admitted to the presence, including Peter, Paul and Mary. Dylan was ushered past them, Aronowitz making the introductions, 'a proud and happy *shadchen*, a Jewish matchmaker', as he wrote. Drinks were poured. The Beatles offered Bobby and his friends pills, which they'd been guzzling since Hamburg days. Aronowitz suggested they smoke dope, he and Bob assuming – having misheard the phrase 'I can't hide' in 'I Want to Hold Your Hand' as 'I get high' – that the Beatles were fellow pot-heads. As it turned out, the Beatles hadn't smoked pot before – at least not good pot, as Victor Maymudes was careful to qualify: 'They actually had smoked pot before, but they hadn't smoked good pot. They didn't know the power of pot.' Dylan himself rolled the first joint, which was given to John, who handed it to Ritchie, who proceeded to smoke it like a cigarette, not passing it around. More joints were rolled so every Beatle had his own herbal ciggie, with another for their normally strait-laced manager.

A few hours earlier Brian had ticked off Derek Taylor in his usual tight-ass way for drinking Courvoisier cognac in the hotel. 'You'll pay for that bottle, Derek. That is to go on your bill.' Under the influence of dope, Brian was transformed into a totally different person, reeling around the Beatles' suite like a happy child. He said he felt like he was on the ceiling and, pointing at his refection in a mirror, repeatedly said: 'Jew!' The others thought this and everything else hilarious and profound. 'I remember [Paul] saying that he was thinking for the first time,' said Aronowitz. 'He told Mal Evans to follow him around and write down everything he said.' Mal couldn't find a piece of paper, so Paul noted down his revelations. The next day when he read his notes he saw that he'd written, 'There are seven levels.'

Dylan and the Beatles bonded that night, Bob later taking the boys on a tour of New York. In turn, the Beatles entertained Dylan when he came to England. Both influenced the other. Dylan began to set his poetic songs to rock 'n' roll music, partly because of the success of the Beatles, thus 'going electric', which was a turning point in his career. Conversely, Dylan's influence was heard in the Beatles' lyrics, which became more story-based and at the same time lyrical and mysterious in Dylanesque style. Lennon and McCartney's debt to the American was deep. 'At the time they all loved Bob,' noted Victor Maymudes, pointing out, however, that his boss could be a difficult guy to love: a fast-living, egocentric loner who could be cold, even cruel, to those around him. The Beatles weren't immune from Dylan's sharp tongue. 'Bob was out of his mind in those years. I remember him screaming at Paul: "No one writes like me!"' There was an elemental truth to this. Try though he might, Paul would never equal Dylan's consistent ability to write lyrics that are poetic and seem to contain original insight into what it is to be a human being. Dylan at his best is profound. McCartney at his best is a brilliant tunesmith. In time he also became a great showman. But he is a mediocre lyricist for the most part, which makes him seem less important.

Still, that first night together in New York had been an uproarious, hilarious evening, a truly historic meeting: the night Dylan and his friends turned the Beatles on to pot. They were all pot-heads forthwith, Paul becoming a habitual grass smoker, which would get him into a lot of trouble.

YESTERDAY

HOME SWEET HOME

When Paul and the boys returned to England after their 1964 North American tour John went back to his new home, Kenwood, a 27-room mansion on the St George's Hill estate at Weybridge in Surrey, a private gated community built around a golf course. Ritchie and George, who weren't earning as much from publishing (Starr hadn't yet written any songs), remained for the time being in London, sharing a new flat in Knightsbridge, though they too would soon buy country homes. Although a fortune was piling up in his account at Coutts, the private bank patronised by the Royal Family, Paul felt no urgent need to splurge on a country mansion like John, who had a wife and child to look after, and when he did buy property McCartney always occupied less ostentatious houses.

At this stage, London life was the thing, and when Paul wasn't on the road it gave him a cosy feeling to be part of the Asher family at Wimpole Street. Jane's brother Peter was an increasingly good friend. Peter and Gordon Waller were enjoying a surprisingly successful pop career on the strength of songs given to them by Paul, including a pot-boiler entitled 'A World Without Love'. It wasn't deemed good enough for the Beatles, and had even been rejected by Billy J. Kramer, but Jane's brother took it to number one in Britain and the USA in the autumn of 1963, the first of three hits Peter and Gordon scored with Paul's cast-offs.

When he did decide to buy property, Paul looked first for a house for Dad. The Beatles' original home addresses were all well known to fans, and Jim McCartney had become used to girls knocking on his door asking to see inside 20 Forthlin Road. 'I'd usually ask the ones who'd come a long way if they'd like some tea,' Jim would say. 'When they said yes, I'd say there's the kitchen. They'd go in and start screaming and shouting because they'd recognise the kitchen from photographs.' Patient though he was, Jim had just about had enough of this carry-on and, at 62, he was ready to stop work. So Paul put Dad on the 'McCartney Pension', retiring the very first McCartney Pensioner to a detached house on the Wirral.

For working-class Liverpudlians like the McCartneys, the Wirral peninsula represented a better, gentler way of life where professional people lived in larger, often detached homes in a semi-rural setting. For £8,750 ($13,387), Paul bought such a home for Dad, a five-bedroom property named Rembrandt in the village of Gayton. The house was mock-Tudor in style, with views across the River Dee to Wales. It would primarily be a home for Jim and Mike McCartney, but also a Merseyside base for Paul when he was up north, and indeed it is a house he still uses. 'He says it's his best house, best memories,' a member of McCartney's domestic staff confides, pointing out what a big social shift it was for the family to move across from Liverpool in 1964. 'It was like coming abroad, he said, when they moved over here.'

Jim had plenty to occupy himself with at Rembrandt, which had large gardens front and back, surrounded by mature trees. He planted laurel and lavender by the front door and kept himself busy mowing the lawns and raking the leaves. Still, there was more to life than gardening. There had been no woman of significance in Jim's life since Mary died, but with the boys grown up Jim had a twinkle in his eye again. 'He was looking for a young, smart bird,' confides cousin Mike Robbins, who became match-maker when he introduced Jim to his friend Angela Williams, a former Butlin's Holiday [camp] Princess who'd lost her first husband in a car crash, leaving her a widow at 35 with a young daughter, Ruth, to look after. The child was now five. Angie was working as a secretary for Littlewood's, the football pools company, when Mike and Liz Robbins went round to her flat for dinner. 'Will you ever marry again, Ange?' Mike asked the widow.

'No. Unless it's a rich old man who loves music,' replied Angie, who was an accomplished pianist. Mike and Liz looked at each other. 'Who are you thinking of?' Angie asked them.

'Uncle Jim.'

'Who's he?'

'Have you heard of Paul McCartney? His father.'

'Ooo, really?'

Jim and Angela went on a date. Four more followed. One night at Rembrandt Jim put a proposition to Angela.

While I sat playing the piano, Jim put his hands firmly on my shoulders and said, 'You're costing me a fortune in taxis. I want to ask you something ... Do you want to get married? Do you want to be my housekeeper? Or do you just want to live with me?'

Angela replied that, for Ruth's sake, they should marry. They rang Paul immediately, and he drove up from London in his new Aston Martin sports car. The initial meeting between the star and his prospective stepmother was friendly. Always good with children, Paul bonded with Ruth, who became his stepsister when, on 24 November 1964, Jim and Angela were married by the McCartneys' clergyman relative Buddy Bevan in North Wales. However, relations between Paul and Angie would deteriorate considerably.

Three days after Jim McCartney married, the Beatles released their new single, 'I Feel Fine', which opened with a wow of feedback, the first time such a sound had been used deliberately as an effect on a pop record. 'I Feel Fine' was a John song. 'There was a little competition between Paul and me as to who got the A-side, who got the singles,' John said of this period of their partnership. 'If you notice, in the early days the majority of the singles – in the movies and everything – were mine ...' Gradually, this would change. The B-side of the new single, 'She's a Woman', was a Paul song and it's an excellent composition, into the lyrics of which he sneaked a crafty drug reference about turning on, a nod to his recent meeting with Bob Dylan. The single went to number one in the US and Britain in December, where it stayed into the new year.

A new LP, *Beatles for Sale*, was released a few days later, packaged slightly differently in the USA as *Beatles '65*. Because the Beatles' British career predated their success in the United States, Parlophone and Capitol were out of sync with album releases, the Americans releasing Beatles recordings under different titles with slightly different tracks initially. To catch up with the UK, Capitol put out no less than four Beatles albums in 1964 – *Meet the Beatles!*, *The Beatles' Second Album*, *Beatles '65* and *Something New* – without consulting the band about titles, cover art or song selection. Capitol included singles on these LPs, whereas at home a Beatles single was often released as an extra treat, with an exclusive and often equally delicious B-side, neither of which would be on the LP. The new single, 'I Feel Fine', was not on *Beatles for Sale*, for example, but did feature on *Beatles '65* in the USA.*

Beatles for Sale had been recorded by George Martin on the fly between the Beatles' engagements, and Martin rates it as one of their lesser works. 'They were rather weary during *Beatles for Sale*,' he has commented. 'One must remember they'd been battered like mad throughout 1964 …' As with previous albums, the LP was comprised of original compositions and cover songs including the rock 'n' roll warhorse 'Kansas City', but there was still much of interest. Dylan's influence is heard on John's 'I'm a Loser', while Paul's 'I'll Follow the Sun' was pretty. The inspiration for 'Eight Days a Week' came from a casual conversation Paul had with his chauffeur on the drive to Kenwood. 'How've you been?' Paul asked as they headed out of town.

'Oh, working hard,' grumbled the chauffeur, 'eight days a week.'

When Paul arrived at John's country mansion, he told his friend what the driver had said. 'John said, "Right – 'Ooh, I need your love babe …'" and we wrote it. We were always quite quick to write.' When they finished a new song like this, Lennon and McCartney would usually perform it for Cynthia Lennon, or whoever else was around, to see what sort of reaction they got, making sure to write down the chords and lyrics. 'We couldn't put it down on a cassette because there weren't cassettes then,' notes Paul. 'We'd have to remember it, which was always a good discipline, and if it was a rubbish song we'd forget it.'

The first full year of Beatlemania ended in December with *Another Beatles Christmas Show*, staged at the Hammersmith Odeon, a huge West London cinema that was becoming one of the capital's premier music venues. Once again the Beatles were obliged to act the fool as well as perform, and again there were a host of support acts, including

---

* Because the British albums were released – with the notable exception of *Let it Be* – as the Beatles intended, this book deals with the band's LPs under the British titles.

the Yardbirds, featuring Eric Clapton who became an important friend. 'Paul played the ambassador, coming out to meet us and saying hello,' recalls Clapton, who also remembers Paul playing a new tune back-stage. It had come to him in a dream at Wimpole Street, and he wasn't sure whether it was an original composition or an old melody that had lodged in his unconscious. Neither Clapton nor his band mates recog-nised it.

The Christmas show compère this year was Jimmy Savile, night-club owner and DJ. One of Jim's business interests was the Three Coins club in Manchester, which the Beatles played twice, in 1961 and 1963. 'The first time, they travelled over from Liverpool and got a fiver for the whole gig, and they went down well. So they came back [and] got £15 [$23],' recalls Savile, who was best known as a Radio Luxembourg disc jockey. As such, Jim had helped promote the Beatles' career. They rewarded the DJ with what he calls 'the greatest non-job' he ever had.

Because first of all you couldn't hear yourself *think*, at all. And the audience, when they saw me come on, knew that I was coming on to introduce the lads, and you could actually taste the noise. The noise was just quite unbelievable! And for the whole of the [20] days I never, ever uttered a word. All I did was just mime all sorts of things, and sort of dived about the stage, and suddenly I would look over to the wings and put my hands on my head as though I can't believe what I'm seeing, and then I'd run off the other side, and the Beatles would run on this side, and that was it. That's how I'd introduce [them].

The DJ also appeared in skits with the boys in Hammersmith.

I was a yeti, and what I did I appeared, having climbed up a ladder with a yeti outfit on, looking at the Beatles who were standing about down there doing bits of things, and of course all the crowd is shout-ing 'Behind you! Behind you!' It was real pantomime stuff.

After a break in which Paul took Jane to Tunisia, and Ritchie married Maureen Cox, the Beatles went back into the studio to record songs for their second United Artists movie, *Help!* Despite having had little time to prepare, John and Paul were able to write strong new material for the film and its soundtrack album, much of which has a Dylanesque quality. There is a new introspection in 'Ticket to Ride', for example, the title of which is also a punning reference to Paul's Uncle Mike and Aunt Bett, who were now running the Bow Bars pub in Ryde on the Isle of Wight. To visit Uncle Mike, Paul was obliged to buy a ferry ticket from Portsmouth – literally a ticket to Ryde.

John later claimed the title song 'Help!' was a cry of anguish at a time when he had lost direction in life, though this wasn't apparent to his band mates. The only sign John may have been unhappy was that he had put on weight, which altered his appearance markedly. One of the curious things about John was how much his looks changed over the course of a relatively short life. His original boyish face fattened and widened around the time of *Help!*, giving him the full face of Henry VIII. As he lost weight in the latter druggy stages of the Beatles' career, his face became thin, pinched and bony, making him look like a different person entirely, which was appropriate for a man of many moods. In contrast, one could always see the happy boy Paul had been in the confident man he became.

George Martin kept the tape running continuously when the band was in the studio, to capture every precious second of Beatles' sound, with John and Paul's between-songs chatter preserved for posterity as a result. The boys were working on one of John's songs, 'You've Got to Hide Your Love Away', on Thursday 18 February 1965, when Paul broke a glass in the studio. 'Paul's broken a glass, broken a glass …' Lennon chanted like a child, before asking: 'You ready … Macca?' using his friend's schoolboy nickname. They were still making music together much as they had when Paul sagged off from the Inny to hang out with John at Forthlin Road, but now the friends were partners in business, too – big business. This very day Northern Songs was floated on the London stock exchange.

The flotation of Northern Songs was tax efficient for John and Paul. High earners were taxed excessively under Harold Wilson's Labour Government of 1964–70, those earning over £20,000 a year ($30,600) suffering a 50 per cent surtax on their income, rising to 55 per cent in 1965, meaning that most of the Beatles' money went to the taxman. By floating the company in which their songs were held – 56 titles so far – Paul and John created shares that could be sold tax-free. Northern Songs was divided into five million ordinary shares, two and a quarter million of which were offered to the public at seven shillings and nine pence each in pre-decimal money (39 new pence, or 59 cents). The prospectus revealed that the Beatles were contracted to the company until 1966, with Northern Songs having an option to renew for a further three years, with John and Paul obliged to write at least six new songs per year. In reality they were writing many more, and figures showed that Northern Songs was a rapidly growing business. In its first two years, the company reported six-monthly profits rising from £17,294 ($26,459) to almost a quarter of a million pounds. The flotation was oversubscribed, giving Northern Songs an initial paper value of £1.9 million ($2.9 m). The share value then fell below offer price, as speculators took a quick profit. Thinking this might happen, the Beatles bought shares back, a shrewd move as the shares recovered and doubled in value over 12 months, during which time they added another 35 songs to the catalogue. Paul had initially been allotted one million shares in Northern Songs, to which he added bought-back shares, giving him just over a fifth of the public company, worth approximately £300,000 ($459,000), a vast sum at the time. John had the same, with Brian, George and Ritchie all holding smaller stakes. Over half the limited company was still owned by Dick James, though.

At this stage in his career, Paul left business decisions to others, more interested in making music and having fun than reading contracts. Having been introduced to marijuana, grass had become part of the Beatles' quotidian lives, creating a problem for director Richard Lester when he came to shoot *Help!* in February 1965. 'We showed up a bit stoned, smiled a lot and hoped we'd get through it,' admits Paul. 'We giggled a lot.' Like their first film, *Help!* was a musical in which the Beatles played themselves and performed their songs, while a slightly larger budget meant Lester could shoot in colour, which helped him decide to make *Help!* a Pop Art fantasy poking fun at 'the state of Britain in 1965 and Harold Wilson's white-hot, modern society'.* At the start of the picture, the Beatles are seen returning home to four adjoining terrace houses in an ordinary British street. 'Lovely lads, and so natural,' comments a neighbour approvingly. When the camera cuts to the interior we see that the Beatles actually inhabit one huge open-plan bachelor pad fitted with every mod con. There was a surprising

---

* Harold Wilson, a Labour MP representing a Liverpool constituency, had become Prime Minister in October 1964, promising to reforge Britain in 'the white heat [of] the scientific revolution'.

personal connection between this outlandish set and Paul's Liverpool family. Aunt Ginny and Uncle Harry had recently moved into a terrace house in Mersey View on the Wirral. When Ginny's widowed sister Milly moved into the house next door, Harry knocked a secret door through the partition wall so the sisters could come and go as they pleased without anybody knowing the cottages were connected. The plot of *Help!* is 'nutty', as actor Victor Spinetti has observed. Ringo owns a ring coveted by an Indian Thug sect led by the homicidal Clang, who pursues Ringo and his fellow Beatles across Britain, Austria and the Bahamas. If the boys were going to make a movie, they figured they might as well go somewhere nice, and their accountant had recently established a tax shelter for them in the Bahamas. They flew to Nassau on 23 February, staying on the island two weeks. Jim McCartney decided to surprise his son by taking Angie to the Bahamas for a belated honeymoon at the same time, which displeased Paul. 'The Beatles arrived several days before our holiday ended,' Angie later recalled. 'Jim said, "Let's go to their press conference and surprise them." But all Paul said was, "What are you doing here?" I felt that Paul was angry that we had turned up when he was there to work.'

After the Bahamas, the Beatles travelled to Austria. Neither Paul nor any of the other Beatles had skied before and there was a great deal of falling over and general mucking about in the snow, again partly due to pot-smoking. Dick Lester's patience was tested to the limit. Unlike their first film, in which the boys appeared determined to do their best, they seemed less interested in being actors now than in getting high and having a laugh. For Paul, though, the trip was memorable for John paying him a cherished, virtually unique compliment. 'I remember one time when we were making *Help!* in Austria. We'd been out skiing all day for the film and so we were all tired,' he reminisced in the 1980s. 'I usually shared a room with George. But on this particular occasion I was in with John.' The Beatles could have had a suite each, of course, but they preferred to share rooms on the road, taking comfort in each others' company. John and Paul were listening to one of their albums as they changed out of their ski clothes.

There were three of my songs and three of John's songs on the side we were listening to. And for the first time ever, he just tossed it off, without saying anything definite, 'Oh, I probably like your songs

121

better than mine.' And that was it. That was the height of praise I ever got off him … There was no one looking, so he could say it.

THE SMASH OF THE CENTURY

It was a fine time to be in London, which started to 'swing' at least a year before *Time* identified the phenomenon with its famous April 1966 cover story, 'London: The Swinging City'. The death of Sir Winston Churchill in January 1965 can be seen as a watershed, marking the end of the drab post-war period, after which the nation seemed to embrace colour and change. Most British people were much the same, of course, but a creative and cultural renaissance was taking place in the heart of the capital, one that caught the attention of the world, and Paul was at the centre of it.

The Beatles may have been the premier British pop band of the day, but they were not the only ones making exciting new music. As other Mersey Sound acts fell by the wayside, new, mostly London-based bands, such as the Stones, the Who and Pink Floyd came to the fore, remaking rock 'n' roll into a more elaborate form of popular music. Rock, as it was becoming known, would be one of Britain's great exports, something the country could do as well as America, with the success of the Beatles in the USA paving the way for these new British bands. It was also partly thanks to the success of the Beatles that talented, young, working-class people from diverse walks of life were accepted as celebrities, the likes of photographer David Bailey, actor Michael Caine and Bradford-born painter David Hockney, who along with his friend Peter Blake became a leading light in modern art. Writers grouped together as the Angry Young Men had also paved the way for this cultural change with their plays and novels. A working-class accent, which had hitherto been a disadvantage in British life, was now very much in vogue. The snobby Chelsea Set wanted to mix with such people. 'Anybody who had any sort of character or creativity or charisma was welcome,' notes Lord St Germans, one of the dandies involved in Beatles merchandising, adding that 'it helped to be good-looking'. The young started to dress differently, women wearing bright make-up and short skirts, pioneered by the designer Mary Quant; while men grew their hair and affected an eclectic mixture of modish, foppish and antique clothing. The trend-setters shopped in boutiques in the King's Road and on Carnaby Street in Soho. They met up at night in such fashionable clubs as the Ad Lib, a penthouse above Leicester Square from which one could observe the futuristic Post Office Tower – an icon of the new, white-hot Britain – being erected in Fitzrovia.

How wonderful it was to be young, good-looking and successful in London at this time, moreover to be loved and admired by people all over the world, the money absolutely pouring in. Paul was in this happy position. Despite the niggardly royalty deal the Beatles had with EMI, and the unfavourable terms of the publishing agreement with Dick James, the star was informed by his accountant in 1965 that he was a millionaire. He was earning so much he kept fat envelopes of spare cash in his sock drawer at Wimpole Street. He'd done the right thing by his nearest and dearest, buying Dad a house on the Wirral, and giving his kid brother an allowance; he'd treated himself to some boys' toys, notably his Aston Martin and Radford Mini de Ville (a souped-up Mini with a luxurious interior); and he'd given Jane some nice gifts, too, bits of jewellery and other fripperies. Now he proved how serious he was about their relationship by taking Jane shopping for a house.

Paul chose a property in Cavendish Avenue, a quiet residential street in St John's Wood, within walking distance of Lord's Cricket Ground, Regent's Park and, most importantly, the EMI studios on Abbey Road. 'He wanted to be right above the shop,' notes Tony Barrow. 'He wanted to do that for the purposes of self-achievement, further climbing up the ladder. You can't do that if you are stuck out in the country.' Paul could also get into the West End easily from St John's Wood, while his chosen neighbourhood retained a village-like atmosphere, community life focused around the shops on Circus Road, where Paul became a patron of the pub, Post Office, greengrocer, café and grocery store. To this day he pops into Panzer's for his bagels and enjoys a drink at the Star on nearby Charlbert Street.

As Tony Barrow correctly indicates, buying a house in this neighbourhood represented a further step up for Paul. Step one had been from Speke to a better class of council house on Forthlin Road; step two was lodging in Wimpole Street with the Ashers; step three saw him ensconcing himself among rich and distinguished neighbours living in grand mid-nineteenth-century houses built for the gentry. The Honourable David Astor, Editor of the *Observer* and son of Lord and Lady Astor

– whose stately home, Clivedon House, had been used for the 'Buckingham Palace' scenes in *Help!* – was one such neighbour, as were the journalist Woodrow Wyatt, Labour MP Leo Abse and the actor Harry H. Corbett, star of *Steptoe and Son*. On the west side of the avenue, behind high brick walls and double gates, stood a series of large, detached mansions with raised ground-floor drawing rooms, kitchens below and servants' quarters in the attics, very *Upstairs Downstairs*. There were stables in the back from the days when residents kept carriages. Most had since been converted into garages, and one or two neighbours ran a chauffeur-driven Rolls Royce. It was one of these properties, 7 Cavendish Avenue, that Paul bought for £40,000 ($61,200) in April 1965, then spent a small fortune having done up over the course of the next year. Paul referred to his new house simply as Cavendish. It is still his London home.

As renovations were made to his new home, Paul remained in his garret in Wimpole Street, where was born the most successful song he or virtually any songwriter of his generation wrote, a song that would be covered by more than 3,000 artists and played millions of times on the radio, what Paul refers to as 'possibly the smash of the century'. One morning in 1963 Paul awoke in his garret with a melody in his head that he assumed was a jazz standard, one of the songs his father used to play that had insinuated itself into his unconscious. Paul went straight to the piano. 'I just fell out of bed, found out what key I had dreamed it in, and it seemed near G, and I played it,' he told journalist Ray Coleman.

I said to myself: I wonder what it is, you know. I just couldn't figure it [all out], because I'd just woken up. And I got a couple of chords to it. I got the G, then I got the nice F sharp minor seventh, that was the big *waaaahhhh*. That led very naturally to the B which led very naturally to the E minor. It just kept sort of tumbling out with those chords. I thought: well this is very nice, but it's a nick … [By which he meant that the melody was so perfect he couldn't believe it had come to him in a dream.] There was no logic to it at all. And I'd never had that. And I've never had it since. This was the crazy thing about this song. It was fairly mystical when I think about it, because of the circumstances. It was the only song I ever dreamed!

Paul played the tune for friends wherever he went, at the Georges V in Paris, backstage at concerts, to the extent that it became a joke within the band, George Harrison grumbling that anybody would think Paul was Ludwig van-bloody-Beethoven the way he went on about *that tune*. Paul was canvassing as many people as possible to see if it really was an original composition, and played the tune one evening at the home of the singer Alma Cogan. At this point there were no words. Alma's mother came in and asked if anybody would like a snack of scrambled eggs. Paul began to play the tune over with new dummy lyrics, 'Scrambled eggs/Oh my baby how I love your legs/oh scrambled eggs', and this became the working title of the song: 'Scrambled Eggs'.

In May 1965 Paul and Jane took up a standing invitation from Bruce Welch of the Shadows to visit him at his holiday home in Portugal. The couple flew first to Lisbon, and were then chauffeur-driven the 160 miles south to the Algarve. Paul occupied himself during the long drive by fitting words to his new tune. The moment they got to the villa, Paul dashed for a guitar like somebody in need of the toilet. 'He said straight away, "Have you got a guitar?" I could see he had been writing the lyrics on the way down; he had the paper in his hand as he arrived,' recollects Welch. Although Paul had written reflective love songs before, notably 'Things We Said Today', the lyric to this new song was surprisingly mature for a man approaching his 23rd birthday, reflecting on a broken love affair.

Why she had to go, I don't know, she wouldn't say.
I said something wrong, now I long for yesterday.

It was a song of confusion, defeat and regret, emotions one wouldn't imagine Paul had much experience of, from what we know of his young life, and radically different to the upbeat songs that had made the Beatles popular. Here was a lachrymose ballad more suited to artists like Frank Sinatra or Ray Charles (both would cover it). Paul's innately musical mind had somehow conjured a classic – a mark of genius – to which he'd finally put words. The words are not brilliant, but the lyric does resonate. Paul has suggested that the song related to the death of his mother, showing how deep that loss ran.

When he got back to London, Paul performed 'Yesterday' for the band and George Martin at EMI where they were finishing the *Help!* soundtrack.

Ringo said, 'I can't really put any drums on – it wouldn't make sense.' And John and George said, 'There's no point in having another guitar.' So George Martin suggested, 'Why don't you just try it yourself and see how it works?' I looked at the others: 'Oops. You mean a solo record?' They said, 'Yeah, it doesn't matter, there's nothing we can add to it – do it.'

Played solo on acoustic guitar, 'Yesterday' sounded a little like a Dylan song. What made 'Yesterday' distinctively Beatlesque was George Martin's decision to orchestrate it with strings, not in the schmaltzy style of Mantovani, but using a string quartet to lend the song a classical elegance. Unable to read or write music, Paul's contribution to creating the string accompaniment was limited to listening to what George did and making comments, though his comments didn't lack perspicacity. Paul made it clear, for example, that he didn't like the way the session musicians hired for the job – two violins, cello and viola – added vibrato. Paul insisted they play the notes precisely. A little vibrato crept in, but not enough to make the recording like Muzak (though 'Yesterday' would be used as that). Arranging this record was a turning point for George Martin in his relationship with the band, after which he made an increasingly significant, creative contribution. 'It was on "Yesterday"', he said, 'that I started to score their music.' Partly as a result, Beatles' records began to become more interesting. Paul knew they had done something special. He went out clubbing that night, running into a friend at the Ad Lib. 'I just recorded this great song,' he told Terry Doran (a car dealer friend of Brian Epstein's, later referenced in 'She's Leaving Home' as the 'man from the motor trade'). 'It's so good!' he told Terry, who thought Paul impossibly conceited.

It was at the Ad Lib around this time that John and George had their first, life-changing acid trip, long before Paul tried the drug. John and Cynthia and George and his girlfriend Pattie Boyd had been to a dinner party at the home of their dentist. After dinner the dentist slipped the drug – then unrestricted and little understood – without warning into their coffee, insisting mysteriously that they stayed where they were. John and George suspected the dentist was trying to get them and the girls into an orgy. The dentist said no, admitting rather that he'd dosed them with LSD. John was furious. George didn't even know what LSD was. Although it had been in existence since the 1940s, lysergic acid diethylamide was only beginning to be used recreationally, its powers as yet little understood. It would come to have a considerable effect on the Beatles' music.

Despite his warnings, the Beatles decided they would have to leave their dentist's house. Their Hamburg friend Klaus Voormann had formed a band with Paddy Chambers and Gibson Kemp, the drummer who replaced Ringo in the Hurricanes. Paddy, Klaus and Gibson were playing the Pickwick Club, and John, George and the girls wanted to see them. George drove them all in Pattie's Mini, which seemed to be shrinking as they travelled across town. After watching Paddy, Klaus and Gibson at the Pickwick, the party moved on to the Ad Lib. 'Suddenly I felt the most incredible feeling come over me,' George recollected. 'It was something like a very concentrated version of the best feeling I'd ever had in my whole life.' To reach the Ad Lib the Beatles had to enter a door on Leicester Place, next to the Prince Charles Theatre, and take an elevator to the penthouse. There was a red light in the lift. As the lift rose, the light seemed to glow like fire. As George recalled, 'it felt as though the elevator was on fire and we were going into Hell, but at the same time we were all in hysterics and crazy. Eventually we got out at the Ad Lib, on the top floor, and sat there, probably for hours and hours.' Ritchie was there. He listened as his friends babbled about the fire in the lift. John noticed that their table was s – t – r – e – t – c – h – i – n – g. At dawn George drove Pattie, John and Cynthia home to Surrey very, very *slowly*.

The boys couldn't wait to tell Paul. John had always loved *Alice in Wonderland* and here was a drug that could send him down the rabbit hole any time he liked. He urged Paul to take LSD without delay. Paul's reaction highlights an essential difference between him and his friend, one that would become more pronounced.

I really was frightened of that kind of stuff because it's what you are taught when you're young. "Hey, watch out for them devil drugs." So when acid came round we'd heard that you're never the same. It alters your life and you never think the same again, and I think John was rather excited by that prospect. I was rather frightened by that prospect. I thought, *Just what I need! Some funny little thing where I can never get back home again.*

So Paul declined LSD, and kept declining as John and George took more acid trips, growing closer as a result. They were in the LSD club now, and Paul wasn't. It created a rift.

At the end of June the Beatles went on a European tour, after which was the London première of *Help!* 'It looks good but becomes too tiresome to entertain,' as film critic Leslie Halliwell wrote succinctly. Although not as enjoyable as *A Hard Day's Night*, *Help!* did well at the box office; the eponymous single was number one and the album, with its striking semaphore cover, would also top the charts. Buried on side two of the UK release, between 'I've Just Seen a Face' and the closing track 'Dizzy Miss Lizzy', was Paul's 'Yesterday', which was a strange way to present such a great ballad, but then again the song sounded different to everything the Beatles had previously recorded.

The stage début of 'Yesterday' took place in the unlikely setting of a TV variety show broadcast from Blackpool, the seaside resort north of Liverpool. *Blackpool Night Out* was an independent television programme presented by comedian brothers Mike and Bernie Winters, broad family entertainment featuring comics, dancers and singers. Televised live, the show was watched by millions of people across the country. So it was that the band took the stage at the Blackpool ABC on Sunday 1 August 1965 to promote *Help!* Halfway through their set, George announced that Paul was going to sing the next song alone. He made the introduction with a sarcastic reference to another popular TV show, *Opportunity Knocks*, in which neophyte acts tried to break into the big time by winning the votes of a television audience: 'And so for Paul McCartney of Liverpool,' George said, in impersonation of presenter Hughie Green, 'Opportunity Knocks!'

'Thank you, George,' muttered his friend, now alone on stage with his acoustic guitar. A spotlight focused on Paul as he mimed to the EMI recording of 'Yesterday', a song so sad that the girls in the audience momentarily ceased screaming. At the end John led the other band members back on stage, handing Paul a joke bouquet of flowers that came apart in his hand. 'Thank you, Ringo,' Lennon said snidely to McCartney. 'That was wonderful.'

SHEA STADIUM

From Blackpool to New York! The show the Beatles played two weeks later at the William A. Shea Municipal Stadium in New York City was nothing less than the first ever stadium pop concert.

Hitherto, British pop bands worked their way up from clubs to dance halls before establishing themselves on a national circuit of cinemas and theatres. Some – the Hammersmith Odeon, the London Palladium – were larger and more prestigious than others, holding around 3,000 people, and occasionally bands played the Royal Albert Hall, which seated over 5,000, but few artists ever played anything larger. The Beatles, being unique, had played to bigger audiences in North America – 18,700 at the Hollywood Bowl; 20,000 at Empire Stadium in Vancouver, big arenas by modern standards – but no music act, British or American, had ever attempted to put on a show in a sports stadium. No act had the pulling power to fill so many seats and, technically speaking, it was impossible to amplify a band adequately in such a capacious venue.

It was Sid Bernstein who had the chutzpah to make history. Having successfully booked the Beatles for two shows at Carnegie Hall on their first visit to the United States, the ebullient New York promoter realised he could have sold those seats many times over. He started talking to Brian Epstein about putting the boys on at Madison Square Garden in '65. The Garden then held 17,000 people.* When he did his sums, Sid saw that even this venue wasn't large enough to accommodate all the New Yorkers who might want to see the boys perform. 'I'm changing my mind. I'd like to do them at Shea Stadium,' Sid told Brian over the telephone, referring to the home of the New York Mets.

'How big is that?' asked Epstein.

'Fifty-five thousand seats,' replied Sid. This meant that the Beatles could play to as many people in one night as they could over three weeks at Carnegie Hall. When Brian had digested the data, he expressed cautious excitement.

'I don't want an empty seat in the house, Sid.'

'Brian, I'll give you $10 for every empty seat.'

---

* The current Madison Square Garden, built in 1968, holds 20,000.

Neither Sid nor Brian needed to worry. All 55,600 tickets – priced around $5.00, plus taxes – sold. Not only would the Beatles at Shea Stadium be the biggest show any act had played, it would be the Beatles' highest-earning single engagement at $180,000, worth about $1.2 million in today's money (or £802,352).

Sunday 15 August 1965 was a beautiful late summer day. Fans started arriving early, girls dressed in light dresses, tanned from the long holidays, many accompanied by their parents. Gradually the layers of bleacher seats filled, the noise level escalating as thousands of girls decided to start screaming early. They carried on screaming through the sunny day, through all the support acts – a peculiar selection of singers, jazz bands, disco dancers and celebrity announcers – enjoying a collective and prolonged hysterical fit. Many got so worked up they fainted. Late in the afternoon the Beatles boarded a helicopter in Manhattan and were flown out to the gig, everybody crowding the windows to peer down at the horseshoe-shaped stadium. In the sulphurous gloaming, 55,000 fans looked up at the red, white and blue chopper hovering overhead and, realising the Beatles were on board, many took flash pictures 'to create a momentary display of dazzling light that lit up the evening sky', as Tony Barrow later wrote. When they landed, the boys were transported to the stadium in a Wells Fargo armoured truck.

Around a quarter past nine, when the temperature had dropped and it was properly dark, Ed Sullivan, whose company was filming the show, sidled on stage to make the introduction. 'Here are the Beatles!' White noise. 'Here they come.' Louder noise. Unlike a modern stadium show, where the audience's first view of the act is the moment they appear on stage, the Beatles ran out of the tunnel under the stands, as if they were about to play a baseball game, sprinting across the diamond to take their places on the stage. Another way in which this seminal stadium show was arranged more like a sports event than a rock concert, as we have become accustomed to, was that fans weren't permitted to sit or stand in front of the stage. Everybody was seated back in the bleachers, though virtually the entire audience was on their feet now, screaming, many girls trying to scale the mesh fence penning them back while fatherly cops tried to persuade them to be sensible and get down.

John, Paul, George and Ringo, wearing beige, army-style tunics with black trousers and Wells Fargo badges, looked happy and excited. Ever the professional, Paul paused to thank Mr Sullivan for his introduction, then joined the others in their usual short, frantic set, a set that looks puny and amateurish in such a vast space when viewed today on DVD, especially so in comparison to the thunderous stadium concerts Paul McCartney now plays. Each short song was prefaced with a few corny words of introduction. 'We'd like to carry on with a song from *Yesterday and Today*,' said George, for example, referring to the Capitol album of that name. 'This one is a single as well, and it features Paul singing a very nice song called "Yesterday".' The sound was appalling, like listening to somebody singing down the telephone from Australia. Normally the Beatles used 30-watt Vox speakers on stage; for Shea they had special 100-watt speakers, but the music was essentially relayed via the PA system, as used for baseball announcements. Also, the acoustics in an open-air stadium are different to a theatre. Sound is blown about with the wind. And, of course, there were no Jumbo screens to help the fans see the performers. Despite all these shortcomings, almost everybody at Shea had a great time. Among the thousands straining to see and hear were Mick Jagger and Keith Richards, who went on to perfect the stadium rock tour with the Rolling Stones in the Eighties and Nineties. A bank of white lights were shining directly at Paul, making him sweat profusely on what was already a warm evening. The show was being filmed by cameramen standing directly in front of the stage. Nevertheless, all the Beatles had a ball, with John behaving much as he had back at the Kaiserkeller when he got over-excited: pulling faces, speaking in tongues and stopping short to comment on what he saw. 'Ah! Look at 'er. Ah!' he said as he watched cops chase a stray fan running across the diamond. By the time they came to the last song, John was playing the organ with his elbows and laughing his head off, George giggling along with him. Paul, 'sweating cobs' under the lights, as they say in northern England,* remained focused, as if he had done it all before, though even he had to laugh at the end.

After New York the Beatles played a series of arena concerts across North America, working their way west to California where five days had been set aside for rest and recuperation. The boys ensconced themselves in a house in the Hollywood Hills, where they hung out with

---

* Sweating 'cobs' (cobwebs) being a phrase that seems to derive from the patterns of sweat that streak the faces of pit workers, and one Paul would use in his excellent 2007 song 'That Was Me'.

actor Peter Fonda and members of the Byrds, and where John and George turned Ritchie and Nell on to LSD. 'I played pool with Neil Aspinall,' recalls Don Short, one of the friendly Fleet Street journalists invited to hang out with the band in LA. 'Neil Aspinall played like a demon genius. He potted every ball. He said later that he saw every ball as the size of a football – I was totally unaware of what they were up to.'

Though he still refrained from trying LSD, Paul did get laid in Los Angeles, according to starlet Peggy Lipton, his squeeze from his last trip to the coast. Paul invited her over to the house for dinner, to John's amusement, as the actress recalls: 'I got the idea that he thought Paul was an idiot to take a girl so seriously he'd actually invite her to dinner, when all he really needed to do was fuck her after dinner.' Again, the chief point of interest is that Paul was prepared to cheat on Jane, whom he was still with. He'd just given her a diamond pendant for her 19th birthday, and was planning to move into Cavendish with her when the decorators were finished. Considering what was on offer to the Beatles, it would of course have been amazing had Paul remained faithful on the road, and it seems he was far from that. On his return from America, Paul confided to his Uncle Mike how wild he had been out west. 'He said to me, "Have you ever tried four in the bed?" when they came back from America and [the girls] were laid on by the studios. I said, "Four in a bed?" He said, "Yes." Three gorgeous blondes and him.' To which Uncle Mike could only exclaim: 'Gor blimey!'

This was also the week the Beatles met Elvis Presley at his house in Bel Air. Expectations for the meeting were high. Elvis had been Paul's number one musical hero as a boy, likewise John, though both had a low opinion of the work Presley had done after being drafted into the army. The Elvis the boys were about to meet was now 30 years old and settled into an undemanding life of routine and mediocrity, acting in a seemingly endless series of jukebox movies, the likes of *Paradise, Hawaiian Style*, which he'd just finished shooting. In this, as in everything he did professionally, Elvis was the pawn of his manager, Colonel Tom Parker, who exploited his artist without a care for the music that originally entertained and inspired so many people. In many ways Elvis was an example of how *not* to conduct a career.

When the boys entered Elvis's home on North Perugia Way, the King was watching a mute TV, simultaneously playing electric bass to a record on the jukebox. The Memphis Mafia were gathered around him, the Beatles bringing their own gang of cronies. On this occasion the gang included Neil, Mal, Tony Barrow and *NME* journalist Chris Hutchins, who'd helped arrange the meeting. Brian and the Colonel were also present, 'watching over their stars like parents', as Hutchins observed. After some desultory conversation, the boys picked up instruments and played along with Presley, Paul sitting on the sofa next to his hero. He wasn't overwhelmed. Indeed, he joked that Brian might be able to find El a job playing bass in one of his Mersey Beat bands. They also talked of cars and touring, exchanging horror stories. 'We've had some crazy experiences,' Paul told Presley. 'One fellow rushed on stage and pulled the leads out of the amplifiers and said to me, "One move and you're dead."' The King concurred that it could be real scary out there. As they left the house after what was a relatively short and stilted meeting, John Lennon quoted from the movie *Whistle Down the Wind*, in which Alan Bates's fugitive character is mistaken briefly for Jesus Christ by a gang of children. 'That wasn't Jesus,' he told the lads, 'that was just a fella.' In later years Paul put the best perspective on the summit, saying: 'It was one of the great meetings of my life.' It was Elvis after all, the man who had inspired them, his career in decline as theirs was ascendant. 'I only met him that once, and then I think the success of our career started to push him out a little; which we were very sad about ... He was our greatest idol, but the styles were changing in favour of us.'

Elvis's highest-placed single in the *Billboard* chart that year was 'Crying in the Chapel', which reached number three in May 1965. The Beatles scored five US number ones in the same year, the fourth of which was Paul's 'Yesterday'. Never released in Britain as a single, but put out by Capitol in the USA, 'Yesterday' spent four weeks at the top of the chart that autumn. Over the years it would become the most successful Beatles song of all, the first to receive five million airplays in America and counting.

FIRST FINALE

SUMMONED TO THE PALACE

In a few short years Paul McCartney had become one of the most famous people in the Western World, the Beatles as recognisable as the President of the United States, the Queen of England, and the biggest stars of sport and film. The Beatles were moreover a living cartoon, followed daily by the public as avidly as they read the comic strips in the newspapers. The lads were a source of entertainment not only to people in Britain and North America, but throughout Western Europe, in Asia, South America, even behind the Iron Curtain, where Beatles records were banned, along with other forms of degenerate Western culture, but traded avidly on the black market. The Beatles were not the first global pop icons, Elvis had that honour, but even Elvis hadn't been fêted so lavishly so far and so wide. It had all happened in the blink of an eye.

At home perhaps only the Queen was more famous, and in 1965 the boys became the first pop stars to be honoured by Her Majesty as Members of the Order of the British Empire, another way in which the Beatles broke new ground. In the future Her Majesty would bestow chivalric awards on numerous rock and pop stars, in recognition of the export income they earned, for their charitable works and to mark their popularity. When the fab four received their MBEs on 26 October 1965, they were the first pop stars to be invited into Buckingham Palace in this way and, just as it is hard now to comprehend how famous the Beatles were all those years ago, it is difficult to comprehend the fuss caused by the Queen's decision to bestow the award upon the band, albeit that it was the lowest class available in the circumstances, a lesser honour than the humble OBE and a full five ranks below a knighthood. Some old soldiers sent their hard-won military medals back in disgust (even though the military system is separate), while a large crowd of over-excited schoolgirls gathered outside the Palace to shriek the Beatles through the iron gates, the clash of pop and pageantry broadcast on TV as national news.

While many onlookers didn't think the Beatles deserved to be honoured for essentially having fun and getting rich, others saw the pragmatic sense in what was at root a political gesture orchestrated by the nation's publicity-conscious Prime Minister. Harold Wilson saw correctly that the Beatles were good for Britain. As McCartney himself says, 'most people seemed to feel that we were a great export and ambassadors for Britain. At least people were taking notice of Britain; cars like Minis and Jaguars, and British clothes were selling … in some ways we'd become super salesmen for Britain.' George expressed this same thought more cynically, as was his way: 'After all we did for Great Britain, selling all that corduroy and making it swing, they gave us that bloody old [medal].' John sent his MBE back in 1969, 'in protest against Britain's involvement in the Nigeria-Biafra thing* … and against "Cold Turkey" slipping down the charts'. Ritchie also became disenchanted with the Royal Family, stating in 2004, after Paul had got his knighthood but he had been passed over: 'I'm really not into Her Majesty any more, I'm afraid.'

After smoking a cigarette in the toilets of Buckingham Palace (not a joint as Lennon later claimed) the Beatles were presented to the Queen in pairs to receive their MBEs. Paul and Ritchie went up together. 'How long have you been together as a band?' Her Majesty asked politely, as an equerry handed her the presentation cases. In reply the boys sang a snatch of the music hall song, 'My Old Dutch':

We've been together now for 40 years
An' it don't seem a day too much!

---

* At the time refugees were facing starvation in the former British colony of Nigeria, which was engaged in a civil war with breakaway Biafra. Lennon evidently felt Britain should do more to help. 'Cold Turkey' was his current single.

The Queen looked at the young men with amusement, the beginning of a long and surprisingly warm relationship between Paul and his Queen.

RUBBER SOUL

The Buckingham Palace investiture took place during the making of an important new album with George Martin, whose situation at EMI had changed significantly. After a long-running dispute over pay, Martin had quit as head of Parlophone that summer to start his own company, Associated Independent Recording (AIR), striking a deal with EMI whereby he would continue to produce the Beatles on a free-lance basis for a producer's royalty. It may or may not be coincidental that, with his enhanced financial stake in the band (though not an overly generous one), Martin became more involved in the creative process from this point, increasingly adding the orchestral touches that are a hallmark of the Beatles' mature work and that do so much to raise the band above the pop herd. Indeed, their next album together was the breakthrough.

Working with George, the boys had got into the habit of delivering two LPs a year to EMI, and at the end of 1965 the company wanted a Christmas release. So it was that they went into Studio Two at EMI Abbey Road on 12 October, with few songs prepared, and worked like the devil to crash out a new record against deadline. Bearing in mind the circumstances in which it was made, the LP *Rubber Soul* is hugely impressive, the best work they had yet done, musically and lyrically rich, inventive, fun and exciting to listen to, a true turning point. The album title was a twist on a self-deprecating remark Paul had made after recording his song 'I'm Down' that summer. 'Plastic soul, man. Plastic soul,' he said at the end of a take, meaning his performance wasn't soulful enough. A rubber soul would have more bounce, and *Rubber Soul* explodes with energy. Placed together with the album that followed it, *Revolver*, and the singles made at the same time, the Beatles closed the first half of their career, when they had essentially been a good little dance band, recording up-tempo love songs with adolescent lyrics, and became a far more ambitious creative unit. As has often been observed, with *Rubber Soul* and *Revolver* it was as if the Beatles stepped out of the black and white world of the early 1960s and began broadcasting in colour, with a concomitant new exuberance in their appearance and interests.

An Indian theme first insinuated itself into the Beatles sound at this stage. While shooting *Help!* George Harrison had taken time out to chat with the musicians hired to play in the movie's Indian Restaurant scene. Subsequently, he had taken up the sitar, which he now played inexpertly but effectively on John's song 'Norwegian Wood (This Bird Has Flown)'.

There are of course 'John songs' and 'Paul songs' on *Rubber Soul*, both men increasingly writing on their own as well as in partnership. How much help they gave one another is sometimes disputed. While 'Norwegian Wood' is considered very much a John song, for example, McCartney's recollection is that they finished it together. Paul also claims a significant hand in writing 'In My Life', while Lennon said McCartney only helped with the bridge. By comparison, 'Drive My Car', a motoring metaphor for sex, was a true collaboration, based on a melody by Paul, with John writing most of the lyrics. Paul's bass and piano are superb. The travel theme segued into drug references on 'Day Tripper', which would be released as a double A-side single with Paul's 'We Can Work it Out', hitting number one. The words of the latter can be read as an insight into Paul's dominant, my way or the highway personality. In the lyrical dialogue, apparently recounting a lovers' spat, Paul repeatedly implores his girl to 'Try to see it my way', warning that if she doesn't they will be finished. John Lennon wrote the middle eight, appealing counter-intuitively for reason in this fractuous relationship, life being too short to fuss and fight, making 'We Can Work it Out' even more interesting. Working together in this way, Lennon and McCartney were truly complementary writers.

Side One of *Rubber Soul* closed with 'Michelle', one of the most beautiful and commercially successful songs Paul ever wrote. It was based on a party trick of improvising a smoochy love song with cod French lyrics to a finger-picking tune *à la* Chet Atkins. Coming over all French at a party was a good way of pulling girls. When John and Paul faced the problem of filling this new album quickly, John suggested Paul develop his party trick. He turned for help to Janet Vaughan, French teacher wife of his old school friend Ivan, who was living in London and often saw Paul socially. One evening, when Ivy and Janet went round to Wimpole Street to visit Paul and Jane, Paul asked Janet to help him with a song he was writing.

I think what happened was that Paul said he'd written a song and could I think of a Christian name of a girl – I can't remember exactly how he put it – and then an adjective that went with it, and I think I thought of 'Michelle my belle'. We went through different French Christian names, and then we tried to find something that would rhyme and that would qualify that. Then he said, 'I want to say after that "These are words that go together well,"' having decided on the belle. So I just translated it: 'Sont les mots qui vont très bien ensemble.' And that's it, really.

Paul's other 'love songs' on *Rubber Soul* are almost as strong, though different. As 'Michelle' is sweet, 'You Won't See Me' and 'I'm Looking Through You' are bitter, the latter sang with anger:

I'm looking through you, where did you go?
I thought I knew you, what did I know?
You don't look different, but you have changed.
I'm looking through you, you're not the same.

Songwriters, like novelists, write from the point of view of characters that are often entirely or partly imagined, so it is rash to read a song too readily as autobiography. Yet Paul has made it clear in interviews that 'You Won't See Me' and 'I'm Looking Through You' give a contemporaneous insight into his relationship with Jane Asher. This is intriguing because Jane is one of only a handful of the Beatles' close associates who, apart from a handful of brief comments, has never told her story, a policy of discretion she adopted in the first flush of her romance with Paul and has stuck to, despite repeated requests by journalists and authors, myself included.* Her silence has inhibited the normally garrulous McCartney, who has said little about his time with Jane, but he has revealed that he wrote 'I'm Looking Through You' at Wimpole Street at a time of tension in the relationship, essentially because Jane insisted on pursuing her acting career, which took her away from London, whereas Paul wanted her to wait at home for him.

* Approached in connection with this book, Jane, now in her 60s, replied politely but firmly that she wouldn't diverge from her 'blanket rule' not to discuss Paul.

When Paul met Jane she was only 17, a former child star living at home with her parents, not sure what direction to take in adult life. In the early days Jane allowed her older, more worldly boyfriend to take the lead. Paul decided what they did, where they holidayed, even what clothes Jane wore, and she seemed happy with this. Almost three years had passed and the girl had grown into a young woman approaching 20, with her eyes set on a career as a stage actress. Paul and Jane still seemed well suited, but Jane was no longer as biddable as she had been, or as other Beatles partners were. 'I thought they were adorable together. She was wonderful. She was a very calm person and, in the middle of all this, you felt that she was a wonderful balance for him, and you felt that she was his equal, for sure,' comments artist Jann Haworth, who along with her husband Peter Blake had got to know the Beatles socially in recent months.

> It didn't ever feel to me as though Paul was the big deal and she was trembling along behind, whereas you felt that a bit with Pattie Boyd and some of the other gals. I mean Cynthia was left standing still, basically, by John. Whereas you felt Jane was an absolute equal to Paul and had a very supple mind. She wasn't a dumb girl. She was really smart.

When Paul was in London recording *Rubber Soul*, Jane was in Bristol rehearsing a play. After Christmas she went into a Bristol Old Vic production of *The Happiest Days of Your Life*, which kept her down in the West Country. One can imagine Paul calling Jane's Bristol digs, becoming suspicious if told that she was out, demanding to know where she was, who she was with, the jealous boyfriend of 'You Won't See Me'. The conflict was serious enough for the couple to separate briefly. 'It was shattering to be without her,' Paul admitted, and they soon patched it up. But Paul was not faithful.

Several women have attested to affairs with the star during his time with Jane, and when he came to work on his authorised biography in the 1990s, Paul admitted: 'I had a girlfriend and I would go with other girls, it was a perfectly open relationship.' A true open relationship would mean Paul and Jane were both free to see other people, but it seems the relationship was more open on his side than hers. Certainly Jane had more reason to be insecure about what Paul was up to. He was a member of the most famous group in the world, the best-looking Beatle to many eyes, and one of only two bachelor Beatles left. Girls threw themselves at him. 'You'd go down a club and half the girls on the dance floor would all immediately manoeuvre their partners so they were dancing right in front of Paul, and they would let their dresses ride up and everything. It was astonishing,' comments the writer Barry Miles, who became a friend at this time. 'All he would have had to do was say, you know, "Let's go" and off. The boyfriend would have been left standing!'

Miles was an enthusiast for American beat literature, who wanted to open an alternative London bookshop. One of his friends was the art critic John Dunbar, who was married to singer Marianne Faithfull (who in turn had a hit with 'Yesterday') and wanted to open an art gallery. With investment from their friend Peter Asher, who was coining it now as a pop star, Miles and Dunbar opened an art gallery cum book store named Indica (after the cannabis plant) at 6 Mason's Yard, Piccadilly, between a gentleman's toilet and the Scotch of St James nightclub. Miles's bookshop was on the ground floor, Dunbar's art gallery in the basement. Paul became friendly with the two young men via Peter Asher and started hanging out at Indica. Having completed *Rubber Soul*, and conducted a few concerts in December 1965, the last British shows the Beatles played as it turned out, Paul had the luxury of taking the first three months of 1966 as a holiday, part of which he and Jane, now reconciled, spent helping get Indica ready for its opening, painting the walls and putting up shelves. 'I remember once he and Jane arrived and there were about 50 people following them,' recalls Miles, who became both Paul's pal and cultural guide. 'It was very hard for him. He hated that really. He loved going on buses and generally being part of the city, behaving like a normal [person].'

Paul had an interest in literature and often quoted, or misquoted, Shakespeare, but he didn't have the time or inclination to read seriously. The books at Indica – modern poetry and literary fiction mostly – were therefore only of peripheral interest. Although he wasn't a great reader, Paul did have a voracious appetite for meeting new people and imbibing their ideas, and Miles and his friends were instrumental in expanding his cultural horizons. 'Through us he met all the art people, people like [the art dealer] Robert Fraser,' recalls Miles. 'He got to meet David Hockney [and] Claes Oldenburg, [when] he was over for his first show. He met Richard Hamilton through Robert Fraser.' Fraser was a hip young art dealer who accompanied Paul on a shopping spree to Paris, where he acquired two works by René Magritte. Paul later bought a third Magritte, a picture of an apple entitled *Le Jeu de mourre* that inspired the Beatles' record label. These were judicious purchases, relatively cheap in 1966 at two or three thousand pounds each, forming the basis of an extensive art collection. With Fraser's advice, Paul also commissioned art, hiring Peter Blake to paint a pop art variation on Landseer's *Monarch of the Glen*, which he hung over the fireplace at Cavendish. An Eduardo Paolozzi sculpture, *Solo*, a reminder of Paolozzi's student Stuart Sutcliffe, was given pride of place in the upstairs music room.

Although he wasn't a great reader, through Miles Paul met the American writers Allen Ginsberg and William Burroughs and became interested in the 'cut-up' technique of assembling stories from random newspaper clippings, a method popularised by Burroughs which later found its way into Beatles' lyrics. Another writer who caught Paul's imagination was the nineteenth-century French dramatist Alfred Jarry, a celebrated production of whose play *Ubu Roi*, with sets by David Hockney, Paul saw at London's Royal Court. One of Jarry's ideas was a quasi-science he named pataphysics, 'the science of imaginary solution', which later cropped up on the *Abbey Road* album. The inquisitive Miles also squired Paul to musical performances by avant-garde composers such as Luciano Berio, who presented an electronic piece in London in February 1966. Paul was furious when the press came to photograph him at the concert, spoiling the ambience. 'All you do is destroy things! Why don't you think of people, why don't you create things?' he raged at the snappers. Thankfully, there was no press present when Miles took Paul to see fellow avant-garde composer Cornelius Cardew, a follower of John Cage, who 'played' the piano by tapping the legs of the instrument or reaching inside and plucking its strings, anything but touching the keyboard. From attending oddball events like this Paul became generally aware of and interested in modern composers and their experiments, using atonality, collage, repetition, curious instrumentation and new technology to create, among other works, music made up of spliced tape recordings and tape loops. Inspired, Paul started to make tapes of his own at Cavendish Avenue.

London's avant-garde set were also a hedonistic bunch of people, and part of the pleasure of hanging out with his hip new friends was that Paul could smoke pot with them discreetly and get laid. Visiting the Dunbars in Lennox Gardens, Paul struck up a relationship with their attractive nanny, Maggie McGivern, who claims to have conducted a three-year affair with Paul behind Jane's back. 'Our relationship was a secret from day one.' She says they met surreptitiously in auction rooms, where Paul was buying antique furniture for his new house, and in Regent's Park where he walked his new pet, Martha, an Old English Sheepdog. When Jane was away from home, Maggie further says that she and Paul slipped over to Europe for illicit holidays. 'They saw each other on and off for quite a few years,' says Miles, noting that Maggie was 'only one of many'.

Another aspect of Paul's new London set was connections with the aristocracy. Marianne Faithfull was the daughter of a baroness, and the London scene was as thick with the scions of famous families as it was with the sons and daughters of the working-class. One posh mate was Tara Browne, son of Lord Oranmore, head of the Guinness brewing family, who was due to inherit a fortune when he turned 25. Until then, Tara was living recklessly on credit. Having left Eton, he married at 18, had a couple of kids, then abandoned them, more interested in running his Chelsea boutiques and roaring up and down the King's Road in his hand-painted sports car. As 1965 segued into '66, Paul found himself more and more in this moneyed, druggy, fast-paced world of aristo-crats, bohemians, writers, artists and beautiful girls, which is to say he was having a wonderful time. The sun seemed to shine every day during the summer of 1966; English music and youth style was applauded; the England soccer team won the World Cup; and the Beatles' *Revolver* was the soundtrack album of the season.

REVOLVER

In these exciting, one might say revolutionary times, Paul must have looked back on the first few years of the Beatles' existence as a distant, far less interesting age when he and the rest of the group were just learning their trade. Paul certainly seems to have placed a low value on the Beatles' early songs, judging by the fact that he signed away his rights to their first 56 tunes in the spring of 1966 for a modest one-off payment.

As we have seen, John and Paul had assigned the copyright of their compositions to Northern Songs, a company owned by them in partnership with Brian Epstein and Dick James. They had recently extended the agreement so all their compositions until 1973 would be held in this company. Royalty income from the initial 56 Lennon-McCartney songs, registered between 1963 and 1964, was paid to the boys via another company they'd formed with Brian named Lenmac Enterprises, a combination of John and Paul's surnames. In April 1966, John, Paul and Brian agreed to sell Lenmac to the now-public Northern Songs for £365,000 ($558,450) of the shareholders' money, Paul apparently judging it wise to take the cash before these early songs – numbers such as 'She Loves You', 'Can't Buy Me Love' and 'A Hard Day's Night' – became as obscure as skiffle tunes. From the start, the boys all felt, in common with most people in show business, that their type of music was ephemeral, and that they should look ahead to a longer-term career as professional songwriters in a more mature style. Interestingly, they didn't dispose of songs written after 1965 in the same way. As a result of the Lenmac sale, Paul stopped receiving royalties directly for those 56 early Beatles numbers, though he and John still owned shares in Northern Songs itself, which now included and was enriched by Lenmac. This was an extremely unwise decision as it turned out, because their early songs proved to be evergreen.

Having disposed of part of the family silver in this careless way, the Beatles returned to EMI in April 1966 to make *Revolver*, a complementary album to *Rubber Soul*, and one in which Paul's newfound interest in avant-garde music came to the fore, most notably on the track 'Tomorrow Never Knows', featuring John's spacey vocal, echoing drums, Indian tambura and tape loops which seem to make the sound of screaming seagulls or what one imagines Hieronymus Bosch's flying monsters would sound like. 'Tomorrow Never Knows' is an amazing song, a leap forward for a band that just recently had been yelling *Yeah! Yeah! Yeah!* at their fans, and Paul's tape loops are a large part of what makes it one of the Beatles' 'heaviest' tracks. So it is almost schizophrenic of Paul to have also recorded his first children's song on *Revolver*, the nonetheless delightful 'Yellow Submarine', complete with nautical sound effects. Children's songs would become an occasional, and perhaps underrated, McCartney specialty. They have proved popular with generations of children.

Another uplifting creation was Paul's 'Good Day Sunshine', which again is quite a contrast to the dark 'For No One', with its lyric about a love that should have lasted years, providing further insight into Paul's troubled relationship with Jane Asher. 'I suspect it was about another argument,' McCartney told Miles. 'I don't have an easy relationship with women, I never have. I talk too much truth.' When it came time to record 'For No One', Paul asked George Martin to get in a French horn player. George hired Alan Civil, the best available. Unable to express what he wanted in writing, or in technical language, Paul sang the horn solo he had in mind to Martin, who wrote notation for Civil, who played the part perfectly first time. It was a mark of Paul's inexperience that he asked Civil to do it again, as if he could do better, which exasperated producer and horn player. 'Of course he couldn't do it better than that,' recalls George Martin with irritation, 'and the way we'd already heard it is the way you hear it now.' Aside from sheer inexperience there was a touch of arrogance in Paul's request, not rare in young men, but nonetheless unattractive. Musician Gibson Kemp, then signed to Brian Epstein's management, puts his finger on an aspect of Paul's personality when he describes him at this point as: 'Quite serious, sarcastic [and] slightly up himself'.

If we read 'For No One' as an insight into the sporadic problems Paul and Jane were experiencing in their relationship, 'Here, There and Everywhere' suggests a love so nurturing that the singer hopes it will never die. Paul seems to be yearning for a settled, balanced life with a lover who would also be a home-maker, which with the previous caveat about being careful not to interpret songs too quickly as autobiography is another side of Paul's personality. The problem here is that perfect happiness rarely makes for great art, and lovely though 'Here, There and Everywhere' is, the song has an insipid quality that became more pronounced in Paul's songwriting as he got older, as if he determined at some stage not to dwell on the darker side of life. In 1966, however, Paul was still willing to explore all emotions.

There is certainly nothing insipid about 'Eleanor Rigby', one of the best songs Paul ever wrote, where the quality of the melody is matched by the poetry of the lyric. 'I just sat down at the piano and got the first line about Eleanor Rigby picks up the rice in a church where a wedding has been. That came out of the blue. I didn't know where that came from ...' McCartney has said of the creation. He had to work hard to explain this intriguing premise to himself, deciding the tune was about a 'lonely old lady type'. The mournful melody in E minor, with stately orchestration by George Martin, the strings arranged in the style of Bernard Herrmann, composer of the music for *Psycho*, is a revelation, the words evocative and moving. Too often in his songwriting Paul seems to have no original idea to convey, or particular story to tell. He just fits rhyming words to a melody, like a hack. For all its prettiness, 'Here, There and Everywhere' sounds like that. In 'Eleanor Rigby' he created a poignant, original narrative reminiscent of the isolated broken figures in a play by Samuel Beckett: the story of a lonely woman who dies and is buried without mourners by a priest who seems to have lost his congregation and faith. London may have been swinging in 1966, but in the midst of the Cold War, Britain was also a place where faith in the old religions was fading, and where many feared annihilation in an atomic Third World War. There is a bleak end-times feel to 'Eleanor Rigby':

> *Father McKenzie,*
> *Wiping the dirt from his hands as he walks from her grave,*
> *No one was saved.*

> *All the lonely people, where do they all come from?*
> *All the lonely people, where do they all belong?*

It is surely more than a coincidence that an Eleanor Rigby lies buried in St Peter's Church, Woolton. Paul had played in this graveyard as a child, and met John at the 1957 St Peter's Church summer fête. He must have seen this grave and remembered the unusual name. Yet the musician has always resisted the suggestion that he took the name from that headstone. 'It is possible that I saw it and subconsciously remembered it,' he says, insisting however that the primary inspiration came from seeing the name Rigby on a shop in Bristol when he was visiting Jane.

MRS MARCOS LOVES BEADLES MUSIC

As the Beatles began to make increasingly sophisticated music with George Martin in the EMI studios they wearied of the profitable but unsatisfying business of performing to live audiences who would rather scream at them than listen to their songs. The shows the boys had played in England and Scotland prior to Christmas 1965 had been typically dispiriting in this respect, and they had no desire to repeat the experience. In fact, the Beatles never toured Britain again. Neither did they have the inclination to continue appearing on every TV show that extended an invitation to them, for surely they had outgrown the likes of *Blackpool Night Out*. So the Beatles decided to cut back on their live television work and produce promotional films to be broadcast in their stead. They started by miming to 'We Can Work it Out', 'Day Tripper', 'Help!' 'Ticket to Ride' and 'I Feel Fine', early versions of the pop video.

In the spring of 1966, the band made two further films to promote singles released in advance of *Revolver*, Paul's 'Paperback Writer' and John's weird, droning 'Rain', which in its use of saturated sound and manipulation of tape speed has more than a touch of the avant-garde, showing that Paul was certainly not alone in his musical experimentation. To make these promotional films, the Beatles worked with a New York-born television director named Michael Lindsay-Hogg, who had the appearance of the average, trendy young man-about-town, but who – like many people the Beatles were mixing with now – had aristocratic roots. The great-grandson of the 1st Baronet of Rotherfield Hall, a stately pile in Sussex, Michael would eventually inherit the baronetcy, becoming Sir Michael Lindsay-Hogg. Back in 1966, he was plain Michael, 25-year-old employee of the independent television company Rediffusion, working mostly on the pop music show *Ready, Steady, Go!* One day he was summoned to meet the Beatles for lunch at Abbey Road.

Mal Evans came in and said, 'They're coming,' and then almost immediately in they came, and it was *them*. When I say it was *them*, in these days it's hard to remember how famous they were. It wasn't only that they were talented, but somehow they'd caught the temper of the times, and also they somehow inhabited their fame in a way that other people weren't able to do.

The Beatles sat down to eat, leaving their guest standing. Finally, Paul acknowledged Lindsay-Hogg, who continues the story: 'Paul was like the host. That is something he is very good at. Paul is famously charming when he wants to be [and] in my experience, my relationship with them, he was more the driver of certain projects.' Over time the film-maker would come to realise something else about Paul: 'Charm for him is like a weapon.' Beneath the charm, 'he is very, very tough'.

When Lindsay-Hogg shot the films for 'Paperback Writer' and 'Rain', at Chiswick House in London, Paul paid close attention, looking through the cameras himself before the shots were taken. The Beatles were under contract to make a third feature film for United Artists, and Paul was thinking about what they might do, and how they might have more creative control. In short, he wanted to become a film-maker himself, an ambition which threads through the ensuing years, usually with disappointing results. In thinking about what sort of picture they might make, Paul also consulted widely, taking advantage of his fame to meet diverse and interesting people.

Around this time Paul and Jane were granted a meeting with the philosopher Bertrand Russell to gain the Nobel Laureate's views on Vietnam and the Cold War, which Paul and Jane were both concerned about, half-expecting Armageddon to come by way of a nuclear strike from the East. 'I think that made us more determined to enjoy ourselves and live for the moment,' Jane has said. When Paul told the philosopher that the Beatles had a mind to make their next picture an anti-war film, Russell suggested Paul speak to his friend, the author Len Deighton, who was developing the First World War musical *Oh What a Lovely War* as a picture.

Deighton invited Paul to dinner to discuss the movie, an invitation to dine with Deighton being a great treat as the author was, among his other talents, a gourmet chef. Deighton served an elaborate Indian meal. Paul expressed an interest in the Beatles starring in *Oh What a Lovely War*, the project falling down when it came to how they would use music in the picture, as Deighton recalls:

> I couldn't use Beatle music as the whole point of *Oh What a Lovely War* was that all the dialogue, words and music, were taken from those actually sung or spoken at the time of the war 1914–18. Paul explained that they wanted to be in a film with a more direct reference to modern war.

Paul thanked the author, and continued his search for a suitable movie vehicle.

First the Beatles were contracted to play a series of concerts, their last as it turned out. What became their farewell tour began on 24 June 1966, when the band played three shows in Germany. Before they did so, Brian Epstein – intent on avoiding what his assistant Peter Brown describes as 'general embarrassment' – dealt with Hamburg barmaid Erika Wohlers' claim to have given birth to Paul's illegitimate daughter. Erika had recently married, becoming Erika Hübers, but her daughter Bettina, now three, was nevertheless still living in care. Erika claims that the German Youth Welfare Office had issued an arrest warrant for Paul that would have made his life difficult had he come back to Germany before reaching a settlement with her. 'He would have been arrested if he stepped foot on German soil again.' As a result, Erika says that in January 1966 a lawyer came to her home, explained that he represented McCartney, and made her a cash offer.

> On the instructions of the office in England, he should offer us a so-called 'hush-money' [payment] amounting to 21,000 Deutschmarks,* so that neither I nor my husband would 'go public'. The lawyer explained that the Beatles were coming to Germany in July 1966 and that my daughter Bettina would receive more money, money which would be held in trust until her eighteenth birthday.

Erika agreed to the deal, receiving 10,000 DM on signature, the balance payable when the Beatles left Germany. A further 30,000 DM was placed in trust for Bettina. No word of this story appeared in the press during the Beatles' valedictory tour of Germany.

Though the Hamburg barmaid had been mollified for now, the Beatles' progress around the world that summer was dogged with trouble. From Germany, the boys flew to Japan where they had been controversially booked to play the Nippon Budokan Hall, a Tokyo auditorium with special, spiritual status because of its association with the martial arts. Many Japanese considered it a desecration to stage a pop concert there. NEMS had received death threats in advance of the tour, and when the Beatles arrived in Tokyo there were street protests, members

* Then worth approximately £1,893 (or $2,896).

of the public holding up signs that read BEATLES GO HOME. The authorities sequestered the band inside the Tokyo Hilton prior to the show for fear they might be assassinated, stopping the boys when they tried to sneak outside. At least the Beatles had some dope to smoke. Peter Brown claims they were carrying a supply on tour, which was reckless. The Japanese took a hard line on drug use. Luckily, they weren't caught.

This difficult world tour became seriously unpleasant when the Beatles flew from Tokyo to the Philippines to play two stadium concerts in Manila. Led by President Ferdinand Marcos, a former army officer with a murky past, the Philippines was a corrupt police state bolstered by the US as a strategic Cold War ally in South East Asia. With US patronage, Marcos was shaping up to be a fully-fledged dictator, while his young wife, Imelda, lived like a queen. Imelda Marcos was 27 in 1966, her husband a relatively young despot of 48, 'so we were still attuned, we were close enough in age to be aware and sensitive and admirers of the Beadles', says the former First Lady, mispronouncing the band's name. Indeed, Mrs Marcos and her husband owned all the Beadles' records and very much wanted to meet the group when they came to their country, as did most of the government, which is to say Ferdinand's political and military cronies. An invitation had already been extended to visit the First Family at their palace. Brian received the invitation in Japan, and declined. The boys had grown to loathe civic receptions of this type. Unfortunately, nobody in the Philippines was brave enough to tell Imelda that the Beatles had turned her down.

A large number of Filipinos gathered to greet the band at Manila Airport on Sunday 3 July 1966, but the Beatles weren't permitted to meet their fans. Instead the boys were taken off the plane by police and driven to Manila Harbour, where they were put on a boat. 'We've no idea why they took us to the boat,' George Harrison said in an interview for the Beatles' *Anthology*. 'I still don't know to this day.' In her first interview about the Beatles' visit to her country, Mrs Marcos says the boat was for their protection.

Remember, '66 was at the height of the Cold War, when China, Russia and America were fighting in Vietnam. And the Philippines was in the centre of all of this, the Left was fighting the Right and the communists were very strong nearby, which was China. They had their

cultural revolution [and here in the Philippines] the rich and the poor
… So it was not a secure place. [So when the security services] saw
the mob and the hysteria that met the group they placed them in the
boat to make them secure.

When Brian threw a tantrum, and demanded they be taken ashore, the
Beatles were transferred to the Manila Hotel. Officials came to their
suite the next day to remind them they were expected at the Malacañan
Palace as honoured luncheon guests of the First Family. Mrs Marcos
had promised her friends the Beadles were coming and members of
the Cabinet, Congress and Senate had assembled in readiness, with
their wives and children, many dressed in Beatles costumes. Furthermore, the Filipino people had been informed by television that the party
was to be broadcast. 'And they were sure of course that [we] would ask
them to perform a bit,' says Mrs Marcos, revealing her real purpose:
she expected the Beatles to give her a private show at the Malacañan
Palace. Without consulting the boys, Brian Epstein waved the men
from the palace away, saying he'd already declined this invitation.

The Beatles played their two Manila shows on schedule on Monday
4 July, a matinée and evening performance. That night they started to
see news reports on television about how they had insulted the nation
by standing up the First Family. When the boys called downstairs for
breakfast the next morning, inedible and apparently tainted food was
sent to their suite. The newspapers screamed news of the snub. 'I was
a little embarrassed,' Mrs Marcos now says of the Beatles' failure to
come to the palace, insisting however that she and her husband didn't
orchestrate the censure in the press or the way the band was mistreated
as they tried to leave the country. She had no idea, for example, that
Brian Epstein was having trouble collecting money due for their
concerts, or that officials were demanding a tax on the withheld takings.
'We had nothing to do with [that],' she says, claiming that the misfor-
tunes that befell the Beatles after the shows were entirely a result of the
hurt pride of the Filipino people.

When the Beatles party reached Manila Airport that afternoon
airport staff refused to help with their luggage and switched off an
escalator to inconvenience them further. The Beatles and their entourage were jostled, kicked and punched as they made their way to the
departure gate for their KLM flight to London (via New Delhi, where

George was planning to take his first Indian holiday). They feared they would never make it. When they finally boarded the plane, Mal Evans and Tony Barrow were called back by officials, who questioned them about irregularities in the Beatles' paperwork. Brian was obliged to hand over $17,000 cash (£11,111) at the last minute, after which the jet was cleared for take-off. Mrs Marcos claims she was on her way to the airport to intervene on the Beatles' behalf. 'I was rushing to the airport, only to be told halfway that the Beatles had been to the plane already and gone.' As the KLM jet climbed into the safety of international air space, the Beatles felt relieved to have got out of the country in one piece. Then they blamed Brian. When they stopped in New Delhi, the band informed Brian they wouldn't tour again once they'd fulfilled the rest of their summer engagements. Epstein took the news badly.

'What will I do if they stop touring?' he asked Peter Brown. 'What will be left for me?'

For her part, Imelda Marcos looks back on the Beatles' now-notorious visit to Manila with regret. 'I feel sorry that it had to happen in the Philippines during our time,' she says. 'I'm sure the Beatles were not there to humiliate the President and the First Family and the government.' She and Ferdinand continued to like Beadles' music, and she has followed Paul's career with interest. 'It was a sad miscommunication. But you can be sure that the Filipinos are very sensitive to music and any great music is always appreciated by Filipinos. Even to this day they love the Beadles and I do, too.'*

THE LAST TOUR

Home again, Paul enjoyed a summer break in advance of the release of *Revolver*. The sleeve of the new LP featured artwork by Klaus Voormann: a collage of photos and Beardlseyesque drawings of the boys, John watching Paul through slit eyes. As the album was played and admired, widely considered an advance even on *Rubber Soul*, the Beatles steeled themselves for what would be their final live shows: a short, late summer tour of the United States, starting in Chicago on 12

* Overthrown in 1986, Ferdinand and Imelda Marcos fled to the USA where they were indicted for racketeering. Mrs Marcos was later acquitted and allowed to return to the Philippines where she was found guilty of corruption. Her husband died in 1989.

August 1966. The cloud of ill-fortune that had followed them from Germany to Japan to Manila now turned black.

Earlier in the year, John and Paul had given in-depth interviews to one of their pet reporters, Maureen Cleave of the London *Evening Standard*, in which they let their guard down to an unusual degree. In his profile, Paul came across as a pretentious young man bent on self-improvement. 'I don't want to sound like Jonathan Miller,' he told Maureen, referring to the polymath intellectual,

> but I'm trying to cram everything in, all the things that I've missed. People are saying things and painting things and writing things and composing things that are great, and I must *know* what people are doing ... I vaguely mind people knowing what I don't know.

Paul criticised the US for the plight of its black citizens, contrasting their struggle for Civil Rights with life in dear old England, 'O sceptred isle!' he said, misquoting Shakespeare,* as he often did. It was a habit that could make him appear pompous when reported in print, but may only have been meant playfully in conversation. 'He was a relentless tease,' recalls Cleave.

The journalist's subsequent interview with John Lennon at Kenwood resulted in one of the best-observed profiles of the musician ever published. Cleave found John in many ways unchanged since she had first met the band at the start of Beatlemania, still peering down his nose at her, 'arrogant as an eagle'. Kenwood was more a giant playpen than home: a suit of armour named Sidney in one corner, a gorilla suit in another; one room set out with model racing cars; another with blinking light boxes John had bought as Christmas gifts but forgotten to give away. Although he shared this house with a wife, son, staff, and a cat named Mimi, John lived like a millionaire teenager, staying up half the night playing with his toys, watching TV and reading *Just William* books; not knowing what day it was when he got up. 'He can sleep almost indefinitely, is probably the laziest person in England,' Maureen observed, which was not something one could say of Paul.

Like his partner, John enjoying pontificating, and religion held his interest at the moment. 'Christianity will go,' he predicted portentously.

* Correctly: 'This royal throne of kings, this sceptred isle ...' *Richard II*, Act II, Scene I.

'It will vanish and shrink. I needn't argue about that; I'm right and I will be proved right.' Paul had expressed similar irreligious sentiments to Maureen, saying he leaned towards atheism, but Paul would never have been so injudicious as to say: 'We're more popular than Jesus now,' as John did in his interview. 'I don't know which will go first – rock 'n' roll or Christianity. Jesus was all right but his disciples were thick and ordinary.'

Whereas British readers took John's comments as no more than an opinionated young man sounding off, when Maureen's interviews were reprinted in the American teen magazine *Datebook* American readers were hugely offended, the USA being a far more religious country than Britain. Alarming reports reached an already overwrought Brian Epstein that US radio stations were banning Beatles records because of what John had said, while their erstwhile fans were staging ceremonial burnings of the albums. The Ku Klux Klan was promising ominous 'surprises' for the Beatles when they came over for their tour. It was therefore in a state of high anxiety that the Beatles flew into Chicago in August.

Though they had enjoyed the United States in the past, the Beatles didn't feel entirely comfortable in America now. George was scared of flying and disliked the long continental flights they had to take in order to tour the US, while the excessive reactions of American fans were disconcerting. The prevalence of guns in everyday life also struck the Beatles as strange and unnerving, as it did all British visitors, with Americans seeming to be a more volatile, violent people, especially in light of recent race riots and assassinations. Paul was fascinated with the assassination of President Kennedy in particular, reading everything he could about the Dallas shooting, and frightening himself into thinking he might be a target for a marksman. 'Paul was always terrified of being shot,' says Peter Brown. 'So he was very nervous on stage.' As to what John had said to Maureen Cleave about Jesus, that had made everything more tense and difficult. Paul didn't blame John. None of the band members did. They took the view that John's comments had been taken out of context in America. But they all had to deal with the fallout.

John attempted to diffuse the situation as soon as they arrived in the United States by facing the media at the band's Chicago hotel. He apologised if his comments had been misconstrued, indicating that he was a Christian (which was more than Paul was prepared to say), and didn't have any 'un-Christian thoughts'. The Beatles gave their first concert the next day at Chicago's International Amphitheatre, Paul scanning the bleachers at this and every subsequent show for a sniper. Though no shots rang out, there were other more banal indications that America's love affair with the band might be waning. Most obviously there were unsold seats in Detroit the next day, also in New York where the band played a return engagement at Shea Stadium on 23 August. Sid Bernstein, who was once again the promoter, looked up from the baseball diamond to see a whole block of empty seats during the show.* Interestingly, standing in the press box shooting pictures was Paul's future wife Linda Eastman, who had just embarked on a career as a rock 'n' roll photographer.

The tour concluded in California, where the Beatles played firstly to a vast crowd at Dodger Stadium in Los Angeles on 28 August, an event that descended into a near-riot as fans swarmed over their limousine, threatening to crush it as they tried to leave the gig. The limo driver took shelter under a grandstand behind a high fence, which fans attacked, beaten back by cops with billy clubs. In return, the rioting concert-goers started hurling missiles at the police. 'Meanwhile the Beatles, virtually imprisoned beneath the grandstand by fans stampeding from one spot to another in the vast outdoor stadium, made good their escape by armoured car at the opposite end of the field,' wrote a news reporter of the warlike scene. The next day, the Beatles flew north to San Francisco for their final show.

The fact that Brian Epstein didn't accompany his boys to San Francisco, electing to stay at the Beverly Hills Hotel with his American business partner Nat Weiss, showed he wasn't his old self. Since Manila, Brian had been trying to adjust to the idea that the Beatles wouldn't tour again, wondering where this left him. A large part of his life these past four years had been occupied arranging publicity opportunities and concert bookings for the boys. He'd never been much involved in the other side of their career, making records. That was something they did with George Martin.

---

* Possibly an administrative cock-up. When he moved apartment some years later, Bernstein says he discovered a box of sold tickets which his assistant had failed to mail out.

As he pondered an empty future, Brian was joined at the Beverly Hills Hotel by a young hustler from Ohio, whom Brian had met the previous year. Their relationship had turned sour on that first occasion when the boy attempted to blackmail him. 'I think Brian gave him $3,000 [£1,960] to get rid of him,' says Weiss, dismayed to see the lad back at Brian's side at the swimming pool and hardly surprised to find that, when they returned to their respective rooms, their briefcases were missing, apparently stolen by the young man, who was nowhere to be found. Brian's case contained contracts, cash and amphetamine tablets, which he was using so heavily he was becoming addicted. Peter Brown says Epstein also had compromising personal letters and pictures in his case, and the hustler tried to blackmail Brian again with these documents. Weiss disagrees, saying there was nothing incriminating in Brian's attaché case, and doesn't recall any blackmail this time around, but concedes that Brian was very upset by the theft. 'Whenever someone steals from you, you feel diminished and ripped off, and it certainly hurts your ego, [especially] if it's someone you trusted and liked. That's what really bothered him,' says Weiss, who engaged a private detective to recover their property, which he did successfully. At the end of the day Brian wanted the affair hushed up. 'He didn't want any notoriety because of the Beatles being on tour.'

Meanwhile, the Beatles had reached San Francisco to play Candlestick Park, a baseball stadium outside the city. Although it was late summer, Monday 29 August turned out to be one of those unseasonal Bay Area days when cold air and fog rolls in from the ocean, making it feel like winter. Paul apologised for the weather from the stage, which was set up on the diamond as it had been at Shea, with the additional protection of being ringed with a wire fence, so they were effectively playing in a cage again.

Knowing it was the last show, Paul asked Tony Barrow to tape the concert. Tony did the best he could, but it was a futile exercise with the PA equipment as it was and the fans howling. The boys could just about make themselves heard when they performed boot stompers like 'Long Tall Sally', but when they attempted more subtle new songs, including 'Paperback Writer', with its harmonised intro, the nuances blew away on the wind. 'All you heard was screaming and these flash light bulbs [were] going off everywhere,' recalls Bay Area musician Marty Balin, who'd recently formed what would become an influential new band, Jefferson Airplane. 'It was bright as day, and you could not hear a note they played.' So it was, in a squall of white noise and white light, that Paul retired from his life as a touring Beatle.

LINDA

TIME FOR A NUMBER OF THINGS

After their last gruelling concert tour, the Beatles took time off to pursue independent projects. John went to Spain to act in Richard Lester's film *How I Won the War*; Ringo kept him company. George travelled to India to study the sitar with his new friend, Ravi Shankar. Says the Indian musician, who was already an established star with an international reputation:

> When I met all the four Beatles for the first time, I found young hand-some Paul very charming; Ringo very funny and warm; and John reserved and restrained. However, George and I clicked immediately. I was impressed by his genuine attraction for my music, as well as our ancient Vedic philosophy. Before meeting me, George had already heard my LP recordings and live concert and had used the sitar on 'Norwegian Wood'. Being a classical musician, it did not appeal much to me at that time, but later on I felt more comfortable with it.

With his band mates away, Paul decided to take a continental holiday, disguised as a nobody. Fooling around in the props department at Twickenham Film Studios, where the Beatles had filmed interiors for their first two movies, Paul had found that, by wearing a stick-on moustache, false glasses and an old coat, he could walk past even his fellow Beatles without being recognised. Jane was busy with her stage work – about to appear in *The Winter's Tale*, followed by playing Juliet in Bristol – so Paul took off on his own, driving his Aston Martin to Lydd Airport on the Kent coast, an area which would come to play an important part in his life, putting the Aston on a cargo plane, and hopping over to France where, looking not unlike the moustachioed Alfred Jarry, he motored off into the countryside, shooting an extended home movie as he went.

After a few days Paul reached Bordeaux, where he visited a discotheque in disguise only to be refused admission, something he had never previously experienced. 'So I thought, Sod this, I might as well go back to the hotel and come as him!' Paul later told Barry Miles. 'So I came back as a normal Beatle, and was welcomed with open arms.' The experience reminded Paul of the advantages of fame. Bob Dylan once remarked astutely that most musicians become pop stars because they want fame and money, but soon realise it's the money they really want. McCartney was unusual in that he enjoyed his wealth *and* his fame. Having posed briefly as a nobody, he never wanted to be a nobody again. 'It made me remember why we all wanted to get famous.' Paul met up with Mal Evans and drove down to Spain, intending to meet John and Ringo, but they had already gone home, so Paul flew on to Nairobi, where he enjoyed a brief safari holiday with Jane.

On the flight home to England Paul put his mind to what the Beatles might do next. Tired of touring, he thought it would be interesting to invent a persona for the band to inhabit, and make a special record in that persona that could almost serve as a substitute for live shows. In the first flush of flower power, bands with elaborate names had become commonplace: Big Brother and the Holding Company in the USA, for example, the Bonzo Dog Doo Dah Band in England. Fiddling with airline sachets of salt and pepper on the plane home from Africa, Paul came up with Sergeant Pepper's Lonely Hearts Club Band.

Before plunging into the phantasmagoria of the *Sgt. Pepper* album, Paul worked with George Martin on a score for the movie *The Family Way*. In Paul's mind there was no conflict between breaking new ground musically and making music, like this, to order. 'If you are blessed with the ability to write music, you can turn your hand to various forms. I've always admired people for whom it's a craft – the great songwriting partners of the past, such as Rodgers and Hammerstein,' Paul has said of his reason for scoring *The Family Way*. The film was a Boulting Brothers production about a cinema projectionist (played by Hywell Bennett) who cannot consummate his marriage to his virgin bride (Hayley Mills) because he feels inhibited living at home with his parents. Audiences may have imagined they were in for a challenging kitchen-sink drama when they bought tickets in 1966 for a film about sex set in the urban north, but *The Family Way* was a stilted, old-fashioned picture depicting an England seemingly aeons behind swinging London.

Thinking of his dad, and grandfather, and their love of traditional brass band music, Paul decided to create a brass band theme for the movie. As would subsequently be the case whenever Paul departed from straight pop music to 'write' for musicians who work from a score, he had to collaborate with an amanuensis, in this case George Martin, because Paul himself was unable to read or write music notation. The essential tune would always be Paul's, but what he gave his amanuensis was often very brief, a simple phrase he would hum or play on the guitar or piano. It was for the other person to develop this idea into a score, with Paul making comments as the work progressed. George Martin had to pester Paul for the briefest scrap of a tune to start *The Family Way*. 'I said, "If you don't give me one, I'm going to write one of my own." That did the trick. He gave me a sweet little fragment of a waltz tune ... and with that I was able to complete the score.' As a result Paul won an Ivor Novello Award for Best Instrumental Theme. It was his eleventh Ivor Novello, amazingly, and he was not yet 25.

SHE'S LEAVING HOME

Since setting up home together in Cavendish Avenue, a house they now inhabited as common-law husband and wife, Paul and Jane had become increasingly aware of their differences. Paul lived for his music and, after spending the afternoon writing upstairs in his music room, or round the corner at EMI on Abbey Road, he liked to go clubbing, often bringing a gang of musicians and other bohemians back to Cavendish late at night. Jane didn't like clubs. She'd only ever had a polite interest in pop, and was not into drugs. She had her own circle of theatrical friends who didn't mesh with Paul's crowd. There were awkward evenings at Cavendish when Paul and Jane tried to mix their friends. The couple were most simpatico on those rare quiet evenings when neither had an engagement, Jane would cook and they'd sit together watching telly, as they did on 16 November 1966 when the BBC broadcast the drama *Cathy Come Home*, in which unemployment leads to a young mother losing her home and ultimately her child. Soft-hearted Jane asked Paul if they couldn't do something to help people like Cathy, living as they did in their big house. They could give a girl a room. Paul said that if they took one in, they'd soon have others ringing up.

On the inauspicious date of Friday 13 January 1967, Jane flew to the United States with the Bristol Old Vic for a four-and-a-half-month theatrical tour. Paul was not at Heathrow to see her off. 'The trouble is I don't think Jane really wanted to leave me,' the star complained to a reporter from the *Daily Sketch* who called at Cavendish to ask what was going on. 'She signed for the trip about mid-year when it seemed a good idea, but when it came to the crunch it didn't seem such a good idea. Anyway she's gone and I'm sitting by myself.' Even if Paul had been a man who liked his own company, which he wasn't, there was no way he was going to spend four and a half months alone. He was going to have his mates round, pick girls up, drink, take drugs, leave his clothes where he dropped them and the dishes unwashed. He was going to enjoy the bachelor life. 'The thing is with Paul he was never a bachelor,' says Tony Bramwell, with a touch of exaggeration, for there had been Hamburg, but even then Paul was engaged to Dot. 'From when he became a Beatle he was with Jane, [so] he'd never had that existence of being free.'

With Jane away, Paul also threw himself into work with the Beatles at Abbey Road, where many elements came together to enable the band to take another leap forward in their musical journey. Without concert commitments, the Beatles had limitless time to devote to their work now; their musical and intellectual ideas had expanded greatly; and, importantly, George Martin was increasingly involved as their arranger and enabler. At a time when other artists in Britain and the US were creating increasingly sophisticated music, not least the Beach Boys with their *Pet Sounds* album, the Beatles also felt pricked to show they were still number one. It was time to transmute from a grub-like pop act into a butterfly by recording the seminal rock album, *Sgt. Pepper's Lonely Hearts Club Band*.

The band had started work before Jane's departure, in late November 1966, cutting John's 'Strawberry Fields Forever'. The John who returned from his film-making sabbatical in Spain looked radically different to the fat-faced Beatle of *Help!* Having had his hair cut short for *How I Won the War*, lost weight, and taken to wearing National Health Service 'granny' glasses, John had transformed himself into a professorial figure, one who was increasingly strung out on acid, his new song being a psychedelic look back on his Liverpool childhood, the tune named after the children's home Strawberry Field (sic) which stood in walled grounds near Aunt Mimi's Woolton house, a 'secret garden' he'd roamed around as a boy. Although Paul played the haunting keyboard introduction, on a mellotron programmed with flutes, 'Strawberry Fields Forever' was unmistakably John's song, maybe his greatest composition, his vocal sending a shiver down the spine as he sang the wise and penetrating lyric, 'Living is easy with eyes closed/Misunderstanding all you see'. Like Dylan, Lennon had the knack of writing couplets, like this, that seem to contain an essential truth. Paul was rarely such a philosopher. He glides along the surface of life in his songs, as he did to some extent on the next number the Beatles recorded, 'When I'm Sixty-Four'. Although this is one of Paul's best songs, and one that deals with a profound subject, old age, Paul sidestepped the darker issues involved – ill-health, loneliness, regret and fear of death – to create a jaunty number featuring old-age pensioners whom one could imagine throwing their sticks away and dancing to that cottage on the Isle of Wight. Like so much of Paul McCartney's work, 'When I'm Sixty-Four' is therefore an attractive song with a facile lyric. The song may ask a challenging question – 'Will you stand by me when I'm old?' – but the listener has no doubt the answer will be a cheery, 'Yes, of course I will, silly.'

'Strawberry Fields Forever' and 'When I'm Sixty-Four' both came out of the composers' Liverpool childhood, Paul creating the latter as a boy at Forthlin Road, only now putting lyrics to the tune. He looked homeward again with 'Penny Lane', a song he'd had kicking around for a year or so before the Beatles set to work on it in December 1966. Although the previous comments apply regarding lyrics, with 'Penny Lane' having a typically sunny sentiment, this time the words are better. Recalling the view from the top deck of the No. 86 bus, as he used to travel from Mather Avenue to the Liverpool Institute, past the circular bus and tram stop at the corner of Smithdown Road and Penny Lane, Paul was writing about a place he knew intimately, and already viewed nostalgically. Here was the landscape of his Liverpool childhood laid out as in a pleasant dream; the buildings, streets, shops and everyday characters he had grown up with:

Penny Lane there is a barber showing photographs
Of every head he's had the pleasure to know.
And all the people that come and go
Stop and say hello.

John used to get his hair cut in Bioletti's, which still exists, under new ownership, opposite Lloyd's Bank on the corner. Paul observed it all beautifully, a cheerfully ordinary English high street arrayed under 'blue suburban skies', a lovely, poetic phrase. As has often been observed, there is a hint of psychedelia in the banker in the rain without his mac, the fireman with a portrait of the Queen in his pocket, but these images could just as easily be explained away as everyday English eccentricity. Sex was here, too, as it is throughout the Beatles' work. The phrase 'finger pies' is a reference to heavy petting.

As with 'Strawberry Fields Forever', George Martin's arrangement of 'Penny Lane' was immaculate, the producer working long hours with the boys to create the equivalent of classical tone-poems. 'Penny Lane' was brightened with a piccolo trumpet, which Paul requested after watching a performance of Bach's second *Brandenburg Concerto* on television. George Martin hired the very trumpet player Paul had heard, David Mason, to play on 'Penny Lane'. 'Paul sat at the piano and played what he wanted on the track, *Can I play this? Can I do that?* And then George wrote it down,' says Mason.

> We went on like that for about three hours until they got what they wanted, because Paul was quite limited in his chord sequences and things. I mean he wasn't the greatest of pianists. He could play what he wanted to on the piano, and when he got what he thought it was going to sound like I played it a bit and then [he asked] *Can he play it a bit higher?* or *Can you play so and so?*

Many rock musicians attempted to combine their music with classical instrumentation in the years ahead, often sounding pretentious. With George Martin's help, the Beatles melded pop and classical forms successfully to create music that is natural, honest and enduringly pleasing, and whatever shortcomings we might identify in McCartney's *oeuvre* there is no lovelier song in the Beatles' canon than his 'Penny Lane'.

Like so many of his songs, Paul composed 'Penny Lane' on his little garret piano, which had been moved from Wimpole Street to the music room at Cavendish Avenue, and which, towards the end of 1966, was to be transformed by the trendy art group BEV. Comprising three young artists from the North of England — Douglas Binder, Dudley Edwards and David Vaughan – BEV was named from the first letters of their surnames. While sharing a London flat the men started painting their furniture in bright colours, inspired by the work of fairground artist FG Fowl. The furniture proved very popular. Macy's became a US stockist and socialite Tara Browne commissioned the group to customise his Cobra sports car. 'Tara, said: "You should meet my friend Paul. He'd probably like your work,"' recalls Dudley Edwards. A meeting was arranged and, at Paul's request, the group painted his piano with lightning bolts of red, yellow, blue and purple – creating one of the iconic musical instruments of the psychedelic era – returning the piano in time for Paul to complete *Sgt. Pepper*. McCartney paid them generously – their agreed fee plus a substantial tip – gainsaying what became an unwarranted reputation for meanness. As the story of McCartney's life continues, we shall read numerous examples of the star being very generous with his money.

When BEV broke up, Paul invited Dudley Edwards to come and stay with him at Cavendish. It was companionable having a young northern chap of his age around the house with Jane away. Also, like medieval princelings, each Beatle tended to maintain a court who served, flattered and amused them. Often these courtiers were given a small task to perform while they shared their Beatle's privileged existence. In theory Dudley was at Cavendish to help decorate the house in the emerging hippie style, which was characterised by a combination of old, new and hand-made. Paul invested in many mod cons including a state-of-the-art kitchen, hi-fi, and expensive new colour television (which lured Aunt Ginny down from Merseyside to watch Wimbledon). The curtains were drawn by an electric motor, while the master bedroom had the luxury of an *en suite* bathroom with sunken tub. Paul was also buying antiques, including a huge clock, built for the Great Exhibition of 1851, which hung in the dining room; a Victorian street lamp was erected in the front yard, contrasting with the geodesic contemplation dome in the back.

Paul set Dudley Edwards to work painting tiny creatures into the pattern of the William Morris wallpaper that covered his dining room walls, creating a vast mural. 'I started painting the mural in his dining room, but Paul didn't seem that bothered about the mural being done,' recalls Edwards.

> Paul would say, 'Put your brush down, we're going out shopping.' That would be one minute and the next minute he'd say, 'Put your brush down, we're going to a night club.' And the next thing, 'Are you coming to the recording studio?' I just accompanied him, went with him everywhere, basically enjoy[ing] ourselves.

With Jane away, Paul and Dudley entertained a parade of women at the house, including the American singer Nico, who visited Cavendish when her mentor Andy Warhol was passing through town and stayed. This was Paul's domestic scene, in early 1967, while he was recording *Sgt. Pepper.*

In mid-January, the Beatles started work on their monumental track 'A Day in the Life', the inspiration for which is often attributed to the untimely death of Tara Browne. Paul was sufficiently close to the playboy heir to have invited him to Rembrandt in recent months. One night he and Tara decided to ride over to see Uncle Mike on a couple of mopeds. Paul came off his bike, split his lip and broke one of his front teeth. He would wear a cap afterwards to cover the broken tooth, and grew a moustache while the scar healed, helping start a trend. All four Beatles soon wore little moustaches. Not long after this incident, on 18 December 1966, Tara was killed when his Lotus hit a van in London. It was reading news reports of the death – GUINNESS HEIR DIES IN CAR CRASH; A BOY WHO HAD TOO MUCH – that is often said to have prompted Lennon to begin work on 'A Day in the Life', though Paul doesn't recall a particular connection. The lyric was created in the cut-up style of William Burroughs, jumbling together scraps of newspaper articles, a compositional method John and Paul were a little sheepish about at first, according to BEV artist Douglas Binder who stumbled upon them doing a cut-up at Cavendish.

> I think it was John who said, 'If our fans knew how we composed our lyrics and music they'd have a real shock.' He was embarrassed about

it at this time because it was done in a surrealistic manner of actually tearing bits of paper from the newspapers, or headlines from the newspapers, connecting them to make some lyrics …

Although 'A Day in the Life' is primarily John's song, Paul's part was again significant. He played the evocative, dead-sounding piano and contributed the bridge:

Woke up, fell out of bed,
Dragged a comb across my head.
Found my way downstairs and drank a cup
And looking up, I noticed I was late.

While being a relatively slight thing in itself, the bridge provides a nice, breezy contrast to John's sombre verses (old boys from the Inny interpreting the line about going upstairs and having a smoke as Paul having a ciggie on the No. 86 bus to school).

Still more interesting are the twin passages of *ad libertum* orchestral music, coming before Paul's bridge, then again after the last verse, building to the climax. These bold musical passages were Paul's idea, working in the same uncompromising spirit of composition as Germany's Karlheinz Stockhausen. McCartney and Lennon were both now familiar with the leading 'serious' composers of their age – the likes of Berio, Cage and Stockhausen – some of whom they had met or had contact with in other ways (Paul struck up a correspondence with Stockhausen). These composers had stretched the boundaries of 'classical' music in the twentieth century, creating works seemingly as far removed from Beethoven, say, as rock 'n' roll would seem to differ from their own music, though of course 'music is music' as another avant-garde composer, Alban Berg, has remarked. Rock 'n' roll songs are shorter and simpler than symphonies, but they are made up of the same notes and not necessarily less affecting. In the spirit of these innovators, Paul put a radical suggestion to George Martin as to how they might fill 24 bars in the middle and end of 'A Day in the Life', though his initial instructions were impractical. 'He said, "I want a symphony orchestra to freak out,"' recalls Martin, who said the musicians wouldn't know what he was talking about. Instead, he wrote a musical shriek for 41 musicians, playing their instruments from the lowest to highest note.

The recording of this remarkable passage of music was organised as a happening, and filmed for posterity. The Beatles came to the session in what was becoming identifiable as flower power costume (whimsical, colourful and foppish), while George Martin and his orchestra were requested to wear evening dress. The studio was lit with coloured lightbulbs, the Beatles passing out masks and other items of fancy dress, which many of the session players obligingly wore. One elderly violinist performed wearing a gorilla paw; another wore what looked like a penis nose. The Beatles invited their friends, partners and fellow celebrities to take part, including the singer Donovan, a particular mate of Paul's, and members of the Rolling Stones and the Monkees, the American band recently created in emulation of the Beatles for a TV show. It showed how confident and essentially good-natured the Beatles were that they were friendly towards the absurd Monkees, then making their first visit to the UK. Monkee Mike Nesmith recalls being invited to the 'A Day in the Life' session as if they were equals: 'It was festive and crowded with people well known in the music scene and business of the time. Because it was a working session there was a certain understanding that there had to be work done, and that we were all part of it.' After Paul had conducted his apocalyptic ascending chord, the celebrities were asked to emit a final, punctuating *hummm*, later replaced by a crashing E chord, played by Paul and others simultaneously on keyboards, the sound allowed to reverberate on the record until the needle lifted. Thus Paul became a composer of serious orchestral music, at the cutting edge of what was happening in the twentieth century, decades before his more self-conscious and conservative forays into 'classical' composition with his *Liverpool Oratorio* and other works.

By the standards of the day, *Sgt. Pepper* took a long time to record: five months including mixing. Considering the exceptional quality of the work it now seems to have been achieved quickly, and Paul still found time to do other things. In January, Dudley Edwards asked if the Beatles would contribute music for a rave he was helping stage at the Roundhouse, a disused train shed in North London, an event the hippies were calling *The Million Volt Light and Sound Rave*. Working with his fellow Beatles, Paul created a 13-minute sound collage the band called *Carnival of Light*, made up of tape loops and extemporaneous screams and shouts. Paul handed the experimental tape to Dudley. The star was displeased when organisers at the rave allowed the tape to run on past the section he'd intended to be heard, with the result that the crowd was treated, in addition to *Carnival of Light*, to a demo of 'Fixing a Hole,' one of the new songs on *Pepper*, that also happened to be on the spool. 'He was quite angry about that,' recalls Dudley. 'It wasn't intentional. I was busy trying to do the light show, so was Doug[las Binder]. I don't know who was left with the responsibility of playing the tape, but anyway it got an airing – I think Paul forgave us in the end.'

Paul also continued to give thought to the Beatles' next film, one they were contracted to make. Having considered making an anti-war picture, as discussed with Bertrand Russell and Len Deighton, but which John had effectively now done as a solo project, and having turned down producer Walter Shenson's suggestion that the Beatles remake *The Three Musketeers*, the band commissioned an original script from the fashionable playwright Joe Orton, whose hit farce *Loot* Paul had enjoyed. Orton was riding high on the success of his second play, *Entertaining Mr Sloane*, in January 1967 when he was summoned to Brian Epstein's newly acquired townhouse in Chapel Street, Belgravia, a ritzy address near Buckingham Palace. The playwright found Paul in the drawing room listening to an advance pressing of 'Penny Lane'. Orton thought Paul's new moustache gave him the look of a turn-of-the-century anarchist. Over supper, McCartney said that while he generally only got 'a sore arse' from going to the theatre (a dig at Jane), *Loot* held his attention. This and the fact that Orton confessed to a fondness for smoking grass served to break the ice. 'Well, I'd like you to do the film,' Paul told the playwright. 'There's only one thing we've got to fix up.'

'You mean the bread?' asked Orton. He requested and received thrice his usual fee and shortly thereafter turned in a typically outrageous script, *Up Against It*, in which the Beatles would commit adultery and murder and be caught in drag *in flagrante*. It was rejected.

Although it seems obvious now that the double A-side 'Strawberry Fields Forever'/'Penny Lane' was a masterpiece, the best single the Beatles ever released, it was their first single since 'Please Please Me' to fail to reach number one in Britain, kept off the top spot by Engelbert Humperdinck, an old Larry Parnes act, crooning 'Release Me'.* Perhaps the new Beatles were too arty for their fans. The band was clearly drifting

* 'Penny Lane' did make number one in the USA.

away from the eager-to-please light entertainers of yore. The accompanying promotional film for the new double A-side showed the boys as hirsute hippies, John dramatically changed from mop-top to whiskery intellectual. At least Paul smiled from under his anarchist moustache; John increasingly wore the remote expression of the heavy drug user.

'Strawberry Fields Forever' and 'Penny Lane' did not feature on *Sgt. Pepper* in the UK or the USA, where Capitol Records used the same track listings for the first time. If they had included those two songs on the album, *Pepper* would have been even more impressive, and George Martin considers the failure to do so 'the biggest mistake of my professional career'. What would they have left off, though, to make room? Perhaps George's India-inspired 'Within You Without You', which was interesting, but didn't quite fit. Apart from 'She's Leaving Home' and 'Fixing a Hole', Paul's other contributions to the album were 'Getting Better' and 'Lovely Rita', the latter a slight work inspired by the experience of being given a parking ticket outside EMI Studios by a traffic warden named Meta Davis. That might have been dropped in favour of 'Penny Lane'. A reformatted *Sgt. Pepper* along these lines is very attractive.

Although a concept album of sorts, only the second track, 'With a Little Help from My Friends', sung by Ringo as Billy Shears, developed the narrative set up in the opening song, 'Sgt. Pepper's Lonely Hearts Club Band'. It was when Neil Aspinall suggested that the boys should reprise this tune on Side Two that the album became a song cycle of sorts, though never a full-blown one like the Who's *Tommy* (1969). It was really the way *Sgt. Pepper* was packaged and presented that gave the impression of a cohesive work of art.

Paul claims credit for coming up with the concept of the album sleeve, in which the Beatles stand with cut-outs of their heroes in an ornamental garden, the work realised by their artist friends Peter Blake and his wife Jann Haworth. Originally the cover was to be a design by the hippy art group the Fool, of whom more later. 'Robert [Fraser] pulled out this cover that the Fool had done – looked like a psychedelic Disney,' recalls Jann Haworth. 'He just showed it to us and said, "I don't like this, and I think Paul really isn't happy about it, I think really you should do it."' Husband and wife proceeded to build a three-dimensional stage set – something Jann's set designer father did for his living – Jann overseeing the planting of an ornamental garden in the foreground, red flowers spelling out BEATLES, while Peter concentrated on creating the crowd of heroes, using blown-up, tinted photographs of famous people, only some of whom the band suggested. 'Basically they chose about a third of the heads,' recalls Jann. 'It wasn't a big enough crowd.' So the artists came up with the rest. Paul's choices includod Fred Astaire and William Burroughs. John's wish list included Jesus and Hitler, both ruled out by EMI.

The pictures were assembled in Michael Cooper's photographic studio in Chelsea, the Beatles themselves dressing up in pseudo-military uniform, made from shiny fabrics in Day-Glo colours. Paul wore his MBE. To the band's right were arranged Madame Tussaud's waxworks of themselves at the time of Beatlemania, while in front of the band was a bass drum upon which the album title had been painted in fairground lettering. Paul later hung the drum skin on his drawing room wall. Finally, the assemblage was photographed by Michael Cooper. Produced in a full-colour gatefold sleeve with, for the first time in pop, the album lyrics printed on the reverse, and a cardboard insert of souvenirs designed by Peter and Jann, *Sgt. Pepper's Lonely Hearts Club Band* was a complete artwork, ambitious and stylishly realised. If one has a criticism of the music, *Pepper* can seem over-rich, like an over-egged cake. Individually the elements are brilliant, but other Beatles albums are, to these ears at least, more enjoyable.

Four days later Paul flew to the USA to visit Jane Asher, taking with him a tape of rough mixes of the new songs. Accompanied by Mal Evans, he stopped off in San Francisco first, where he decided to check out the local music scene. Jefferson Airplane were working on songs for their new LP *Surrealistic Pillow* at the Fillmore theatre when Mal announced that Paul wanted to say hello. 'We were sitting there playing at the old Fillmore, in comes this guy Mal, suit and tie, and we're all hippied out,' recalls Marty Balin, who'd last seen the Beatles as a member of the audience at Candlestick Park, subsequently becoming one of the leading lights of the San Francisco music scene. '"Master Paul McCartney would like to meet with you." Just like that. "Oh well, send him in!" We didn't know if this guy was real or a joke. So he went out and in comes Paul.' Part of Paul's reason for visiting San Francisco was to check out the psychedelic scene, which had started here, spreading across the States to England. It was in the Bay Area that bands such as Jefferson Airplane and the Grateful Dead first used

LSD, and other mind-altering substances, the drugs cooked up by their friends and dispensed freely at concerts. Wild new music, fashions and art resulted. To Balin's eyes, the visiting Paul McCartney looked very square. The musicians showed Paul around the trippy Haight-Ashbury district – he took pictures – then invited him back to their house. 'Well, what's new with the Beatles?' Balin asked. In reply, Paul took a tape from his pocket and played 'A Day in the Life'. Not so square. 'Holy Christ! This is amazing. I totally, literally did not know what to say, except "Fuckin' great!" I just couldn't believe it ...' Having reduced his American friend to a jibbering wreck, Paul replaced the tape nonchalantly in his pocket and sauntered on his way.

Paul and Jane were reunited in Denver, where the Bristol Old Vic company was currently on tour, Paul arriving in time to help Jane celebrate her 21st birthday. They spent the next few days together in the Rockies, walking in countryside thick with snow. Paul then left, allowing Jane to complete her tour, travelling with Mal in Frank Sinatra's private jet to LA where he met Brian Wilson, who was so overwhelmed by the *Sgt. Pepper* tape that he abandoned the new Beach Boys album *Smile*. Paul then flew home, coming up with a new movie idea as he travelled back across the Atlantic. Having looked for a suitable film for the band for months, Paul had the idea of getting the boys into a charabanc – of the type that traditionally took working-class Liverpudlians on day-trip holidays to the seaside, little jaunts described in advance as 'mystery tours', but which almost invariably turned out to be a run up to Blackpool – and make a film of the Beatles' own Magical Mystery Tour, 'a crazy roly-poly Sixties' film' as Paul would describe it. He jotted the concept down in the form of a pie chart on the plane.

LINDA EASTMAN

Paul returned to England at a time when the forces of law and order were starting to crack down on the drug culture, with one officer in particular, Detective Sergeant Norman Pilcher of Scotland Yard, targeting pop stars and their associates. In February 1967, police raided Keith Richards's country home, Redlands, in Sussex, where the Rolling Stone was hosting a weekend LSD party. Detectives found Marianne Faithfull, who'd left John Dunbar for Mick Jagger, naked and wrapped in a fur rug. She'd just taken a bath, having come down from an Acid trip, and didn't have a change of clothes. Jagger was charged with possession of speed (having said Marianne's pills were his), Richards with allowing his home to be used for the smoking of marijuana, and Fraser with possession of heroin. Marianne wasn't charged.

While the Redlands trio awaited trial, DS Pilcher raided Brian Jones's London flat, busting him and his friend Prince Stanislas Klossowski de Rola, the extravagantly named son of the French painter Balthus. Brian and Prince Stash, as he was known for short, were taken down to Kensington Police Station in a blaze of publicity and charged with possession of cocaine and cannabis, Jones charged additionally with possession of cocaine and methedrine.* They went from the police station to the new high-rise Hilton Hotel on Park Lane, where the Stones' new American manager Allen Klein was staying, but the hotel management made it clear that Jones and de Rola were not welcome, which is when Prince Stash took a call from Paul McCartney, whom he knew slightly.

Prince Stash explained to Paul that he and Brian couldn't stay at the Hilton, and couldn't go back to Brian's flat because of the press. Brian had other places he could go, but Stash, a foreigner, didn't know what to do. 'I'm sending my car and driver right now. You're packing your bags and moving into my house, and if they want to bust you again they'll have to bust me as well,' Paul said. So Prince Stash joined Paul and Dudley at Cavendish Avenue, running movies on Paul's 16mm projector, taking drugs and entertaining what Stash describes as *harems* of girls, including an Eskimo named Iggy, while Beatles fans camped outside, periodically bursting in through the gates 'like sort of cattle breaking through a fence'. They'd steal Paul's laundry and empty his ashtrays – 'Did he smoke this?' – before being ejected.

One night in May 1967 Paul, Dudley and Stash got into Paul's Radford Mini and drove to the Bag·o' Nails, a trendy club behind Liberty's department store. In years gone by the club had a seedy reputation, a place to meet working girls in an area frequented by prostitutes, but it was now a premier hangout. The Beatles patronised the Bag o' Nails partly because it stayed open late, going there after recording in the

---

* Jones was sentenced to nine months in jail, soon released on bail in light of his fragile mental state, while Prince Stash was discharged.

studio to get a drink and a steak sandwich, chat to friends and listen to live music. Georgie Fame and the Blue Flames were on stage when Paul, Dudley and Prince Stash walked in that spring evening. The club was already full of people Paul knew, including Tony Bramwell and Peter Brown from NEMS. Peter introduced Paul to an attractive young American photographer named Linda Eastman, who was in town shooting pictures of musicians for a book. When Dudley came back from the bar, he found Paul and Linda engrossed in conversation.

Paul suggested they all go round to the Speakeasy where Procol Harum were performing their trippy new song 'A Whiter Shade of Pale', Paul hearing it there for the first time. Dudley paired up with the singer Lulu and Paul asked everybody back to his place. Half an hour later Linda found herself inside the mansion home of one of the world's most eligible bachelors. Cavendish was not the biggest house in London, but it was a handsome residence with exquisite details that attracted the sharp eye. As Linda remarked: 'I was impressed to see his Magrittes.' Memories are hazy as to whether Linda stayed that night. Prince Stash and Dudley can't recall. It didn't seem important at the time. 'You just think, it's yet another girl, and yet another night. I didn't know if it was going to be just another one night stand,' says Dudley, 'although he did seem to like her a lot.'

Linda, who becomes one of the most important characters in our story, was born on 24 September 1941 in New York City, the second child of the wealthy Lee and Louise Eastman. She had an older brother, John, and two younger sisters, Laura and Louise. Dad had worked his way up from a poor immigrant background in the Bronx – where he was born Leopold Epstein in 1910, son of Russian-Jewish parents – via Harvard Law School, to establishing his own law firm. He married well, to Louise Lindner, daughter of a prominent Jewish family from Cleveland. Louise attended synagogue and was proud of being Jewish, but Lee decided it would be better for the children if they adopted gentile ways. Shortly before their first child was born, the Epsteins changed their surname to Eastman; there was no connection with the photographic firm Eastman Kodak, as is often suggested, the name being chosen simply to seem less Jewish. 'Lee's famous expression was, "Think Yiddish, look British,"' says his stepson Philip Sprayregen. 'If someone asked him flat out if he was Jewish, he would admit that he was, but he would never volunteer that information, and I would say that he was probably glad when people thought otherwise.' Judaism played little part in Linda's young life and she grew to be a tall strawberry blonde, as if inhabiting the WASP name Daddy had chosen. She was never a true beauty. Hers was a long face that could appear handsome or plain, but Linda possessed a good, full figure, and a flirtatious manner that attracted men.

Daddy grew rich by shrewd representation of high-earning show business clients including bandleader Tommy Dorsey, songwriters such as Harold 'Over the Rainbow' Arlen, as well as a who's who of abstract expressionist painters from Willem de Kooning to Mark Rothko. The Eastmans collected museum-quality modern art, which they hung in their mansion home in Scarsdale, Westchester, within commuting distance of Manhattan, later acquiring a duplex on Park Avenue. They also owned a beach house on Lily Pond Lane, East Hampton, a favourite place for the New York rich to take summer vacations. When Linda was four, one of Daddy's songwriter clients, Jack Lawrence, wrote a song for her entitled 'Linda'. It went to number one. Jan & Dean brought the song back to the charts in 1963, just before Beatlemania swept the States.

Although hers was a privileged upbringing, Linda had a difficult relationship with her father, a severe man who was quick to criticise. Lee had ambitions for his kids, especially John, who eventually took over the family firm, Eastman & Eastman, marrying a woman whose grandfather was a co-founder of Merrill Lynch. Sister Louise married a man whose family came over with the founding fathers. Thus the Eastmans assimilated into the WASP Establishment. Linda didn't fit the pattern. 'She was considered the black sheep of the family, the embarrassment of the family for a long time, because she wasn't scholarly like her siblings,' says stepbrother Philip. Linda was not academic, or intellectual. Rather, she had a dreamy interest in nature and animals, especially dogs and horses. As Paul later observed, Linda seemed to regard all animals as Disney creatures. As a girl she would collect injured birds and small animals and try to nurse them in her bedroom. Linda's school grades were low. Lee mocked and patronised his daughter, making a girl who was not academically inclined feel awkward and stupid. As she became a teenager, she added rock 'n' roll to her unsuitable interests, and started chasing pop stars, zeroing in first on the Young Rascals. Small world that it is, the Rascals were managed by Beatles promoter

Sid Bernstein, who recalls the teenaged Linda trailing his band around New York. 'She became one of my favourite kids that followed the Rascals. I let her come up to a recording session.'

One of Linda's beaus was Melville See Jr, known as Mel. Born in Albany, New York, in 1938, making him three years older than Linda, Mel's parents were living in Scarsdale when they met. A stocky, sandy-haired man with a thick beard – he modelled himself on Ernest Hemingway – Mel was a geology student. After graduating from Princeton, he moved to Tucson to take a masters degree at the University of Arizona (UAZ), where he developed a passion for anthropology. After dropping out of Sarah Lawrence College, Linda followed Mel to Tucson, enrolling at UAZ to major in Art History. She was living here in March 1962 when her mother died in a plane crash *en route* to visit brother John in California. Three months later Linda married Mel, and six months after that, on 30 December 1962, their only child, Heather Louise, was born.

Linda loved Arizona. She was never happier than when horse-riding among the saguaro cacti that give the desert landscape around Tucson the look of a cowboy film. She also started to take photographs, which became a lifelong interest. Marriage was not a success, though. Mel was an academic with corresponding intellectual interests. Linda hardly ever opened a book. She felt she'd been hasty to have a child with a man who now bored her. 'It wasn't that she didn't have a tremendous amount of affection for her daughter, but I heard her remark more than once, "Why did this happen to me?"' recalls Arizona friend Jonathan Kress. In 1964 Mel was offered a job in Africa. Linda refused to go with him, so he went alone. Linda took Heather back to New York, divorcing Mel the following year.

When her mother died, Linda came into a little money, as well as inheriting valuable artwork and stock, and was able to rent a nice apartment on the Upper East Side of Manhattan, at East 83rd and Lexington, getting a job as an editorial assistant at *Town & Country* magazine. Her work involved opening the post. One day an invitation came in for a press reception for the Rolling Stones. The function was to be on a boat, the *Sea Panther*, which was going to cruise the Hudson River. Linda grabbed the invite and her camera. 'I was the only photographer they allowed on the yacht. I just kept clicking away with the camera, and they enjoyed it and I enjoyed it, and suddenly I found that taking pictures was a great way to live and a great way to work.'

Lee Eastman was unimpressed by his daughter's new avocation, taking pictures of 'longhairs'. Linda seemed to bounce from one dumb thing to another. 'My father used to say, "If you want to be a photographer, go and work for a professional. Get trained." Well, I never had the patience for that. I had to trust my feelings. Besides I'm too lazy.' Photographing celebrities requires access, above all, and Linda's talent was her ability to flirt and make friends. One of her first contacts was Danny Fields, editor of the teen magazine *Datebook*. It was he who caused the 'bigger than Jesus' fuss in 1966 by reprinting John Lennon's interview with Maureen Cleave. Danny met Linda at the dockside after the Rolling Stones' cruise, having literally missed the boat, and asked Linda if he could buy some of her pictures for his magazine. 'She sent me [pictures] of Brian Jones sitting there with his legs open – these were the sexiest pictures I'd ever seen!' exclaims Fields, who became Linda's lifelong friend and ultimately her biographer. 'I never saw anyone get pictures of boys with their legs spread open … that's what happens when she's on the other side of the camera. Boys do that for her. They do peacock dances.' Linda also got a date with Mick Jagger off the back of the boat trip.

Over the following two years Linda notched up approximately twenty lovers, most of whom were famous, including singers Tim Buckley and Jim Morrison. One time, Danny and Linda went to interview Warren Beatty. 'She was taking pictures like a little kitty-cat, on the rug or on the sofa. All you could hear was the click of the shutter and the next day she said, "Guess who I spent the night with?"' It is because of this period in her life that Linda came to be tagged a groupie – a pejorative and one might think sexist term. After all, why shouldn't a single woman sleep with the handsome and famous men she met? Yet Linda didn't seem to date any ordinary boyfriends in New York in 1966–8. It became apparent that, apart from having fun, she was looking for a rich, groovy guy who could look after her and Heather. One of the people Linda knew in New York at this time was Brian Epstein's partner Nat Weiss, who remembers Linda telling him, even before she met Paul, that she had her sights set ultimately on McCartney. 'She said she was going to marry him.'

A couple of months after photographing the Stones in New York, Linda was commissioned to come to England to take pictures for a book, *Rock and Other Four Letter Words*. She photographed a number of bands, including Traffic and the Animals, and naturally wanted to photograph the Beatles. Linda's entrée was Brian's assistant Peter Brown. 'I used to go to New York, and hang out with a bunch of gay guys that I knew, and she was in that circle,' recalls Brown. 'When she came to London she called me up with her portfolio.' Now here she was at the Bag o' Nails. 'She was with a girlfriend, and I introduced [her to Paul].' Before she knew what was happening Linda was inside Cavendish looking at Paul's Magrittes. Art was something she knew about. That and the fact she had lost her mother early helped create a connection with Paul, who, importantly, also fancied Linda. He liked blondes. That Linda came from money was also attractive, as was the fact she was a motherly woman, actually a single mother.

The next day Linda showed up at the NEMS office. Peter Brown recalls owning up to having taken one of the pictures from her portfolio for himself.

> I said, 'I have to confess I've stolen one from the portfolio. I assume you have lots of copies.' And she said, 'The one of Brian [Jones]?' And I said, 'How would you know which one I would go for?' She said, 'Oh I guessed' ... that was why I let her come to the *Sgt. Pepper* photo session, which was a great professional breach on my part.

Brian Epstein was hosting a function at his new home in Belgravia to launch *Sgt. Pepper*. The Beatles would be there, together with journalists and photographers and a few select disc jockeys, including Jimmy Savile. Linda, normally no clothes-horse, dressed very carefully for the occasion, wearing a skirt and a trendy striped blazer. Her hair was immaculate. Indeed, she seems to have taken more care with her appearance than her equipment, forgetting to put any colour film in her camera bag (she had to borrow some from another photographer). Here was Paul again, this time with the other Beatles. All four together in a room was overpowering, like encountering the entire Royal Family. Linda joined in the photo shoot, getting one good shot of John shaking Paul's hand in an exaggeratedly congratulatory way, throwing his head back in sarcastic laughter. In the few minutes she had before the photographers were ejected, Linda made a beeline for Paul, crouching at his feet by the fireplace, looking up into his face. He regarded her in return with mild interest, chin on hand, as if not sure what to make of her, a moment captured for posterity by one of the other photographers.

That weekend Paul went home to Liverpool. Linda phoned Cavendish while he was away and spoke to Paul's houseguest Prince Stash. 'I said, "Paul's in Liverpool." She said, "But what are you doing?" I said, "I'm watching a movie," and she said, "I want to come over."' So Linda came to Cavendish Avenue and fell into bed with Stash, who didn't think he was betraying Paul, because he didn't see Paul and Linda as serious. 'He didn't take her to Liverpool, for instance.' Still, there was a strange vibe at the house that weekend. While Prince Stash and Linda were rolling around together, Paul telephoned and asked Stash to move out until he got back, not because of Linda, says Stash, but because Paul had heard people were coming over and helping themselves to his drugs. In particular, Stash's friend Brian Jones, now a hopeless junkie, was dipping into Paul's supply of legal pharmaceutical cocaine, which, according to Prince Stash, the Beatle kept at the time in a jar on the mantelpiece, as several of their friends did. Brian had promised but failed to replace what he had taken from the coke jar, and now Paul wanted everybody out. So Stash and Linda went to stay with the musician Graham Nash.

Stash's affair with Linda became common knowledge in London's rock community. 'I was teased extensively by Roger Daltrey and Hendrix and so on, because, you know, Linda had gone around,' says Stash, ungallantly.

She was not a groupie, she was somebody who loved love … In modern days, people say, "Oh, what an ungrateful bastard, he sleeps with his friend's girlfriend!" But that's not at all the way it was. You've got to put these things in context – everybody had very open relationships, and it wasn't cool to be jealous.

Yet when Linda flew back to New York her conversation was not about Prince Stash, but Paul McCartney. She returned home on the same flight as Nat Weiss, who recalls that she told him again that she was going to marry the Beatle. She seemed so determined he didn't doubt her.

HELLO, GOODBYE

THE WANDERER RETURNS

Having searched long and hard for a new movie project, the Beatles now committed to two films, both of which originated with Paul. His airplane doodle about the group going on a charabanc ride had been sanctioned by the others, who promptly recorded an introductory song similar to 'Sgt. Pepper's Lonely Hearts Club Band', with fairground huckster introduction – 'Roll up! Roll up!' – and brass fanfare. Fun though it is, 'Magical Mystery Tour' lacks the charm and polish of its forerunner – a criticism that can be levelled at the whole project – though the Beatles would record some very good songs for *Magical Mystery Tour*, not least Paul's 'The Fool on the Hill'.

The second movie was an animated feature based on Paul's children's song 'Yellow Submarine'. Starting in 1965, an animated children's TV series, *The Beatles*, had been running on American television, and syndicated internationally, each half-hour episode based on a Beatles song. The series proved popular with children, but not the band because the American producer, Al Brodax, used American actors to voice their characters. 'I couldn't have them sounding like themselves because the American kids would not understand them,' reasons Brodax, who now had the idea of spinning a feature-length movie out of 'Yellow Submarine'. It would complete the Beatles' three-picture deal with United Artists, while requiring them to do little work. 'They wanted to go to India,' remembers Brodax. 'I said, "You go to India. I'll do the picture." That's how I got the deal, really.'

The agreement was reached in May 1967, Brodax arranging to have the animation done in London by TV Cartoons (TVC), the same company that made *The Beatles* series. It was TVC executives John Coates and George Dunning who had the inspired idea of hiring German poster artist Heinz Edelmann to create a Pop Art look for the film, which was rush-produced on an 11-month schedule for release in 1968, when it was hailed as a masterpiece. Interestingly, Paul didn't like it. Although McCartney has gone out of his way in recent years to make the public aware that he was the Beatle most in tune with modern art in the 1960s, in his authorised biography *Paul McCartney: Many Years from Now*, and elsewhere, the star singularly failed to appreciate the Pop Art aesthetic of *Yellow Submarine*. 'He thought that a modern-day animation feature would [look like] a Disney production,' says TVC boss John Coates, who didn't warm to McCartney. Paul was also unhappy at being characterised as John's number two in the picture, as he had been in the cartoon series; and he didn't like the voice the film-makers gave him. Though the Beatles were voiced by British actors in the film, McCartney considered the Liverpudlian accents too broad. 'He was always worried about what impression everyone was making. That seemed to be one of his hang-ups,' says Coates. 'He seemed so wrapped up in himself.' As far as making a contribution to this film, the Beatles were contracted to record three new tunes, palming the film-makers off with their leftovers to a degree, though Paul's 'All Together Now' was another attractive children's song.

At the end of May, Brian Epstein threw a weekend house party at his new country retreat in Sussex, to which all four Beatles were invited. Epstein had a grand piano brought down from London so Paul could play. But Paul didn't show. 'Why couldn't he have come?' Brian asked his staff. The answer was that Jane Asher was due back from the USA and Paul had to get the house ready. 'He could have tried,' Brian whined. 'This was so important to me.'

Cavendish was in a heck of a state, having served as a bachelor pad for Paul and his mates for the past four and a half months. In the hours before Jane's return, on Monday 29 May, Paul dashed about cleaning, and herding waifs and strays out the door. Nico and Prince Stash had finally left, but Dudley Edwards was still painting the wallpaper. Paul hinted that it was time for Dudley to move on, too. Pausing to shave off his moustache, Paul drove to Heathrow, arriving at the airport in time to meet Jane making her way out of arrivals, a pack of pressmen closing in on the couple as they reunited. Reporters asked when they planned to marry. 'Not now,' replied Jane, travel-weary and nervous about meeting a lover who had been like a stranger to her for months, their Rocky Mountains tryst notwithstanding. After posing for a quick photo, Paul drove Jane home, which was the cue for the last house guest to leave. 'When Jane came back I think I was probably in the way,' says Dudley Edwards. 'Paul told me that Ringo actually wanted a mural painted in his place, and so I straight away went over to Weybridge to stay with Ringo.'*

Three days later, on 1 June 1967, *Sgt. Pepper's Lonely Hearts Club Band* was officially released, acclaimed by press and public as a triumph, enjoyed as a popular work of art, and taken seriously by critics. Composer Ned Rorem told *Time* that Paul's 'She's Leaving Home' was as good as any of Schubert's songs. Sir Joseph Lockwood, chairman of EMI, hoped the company would sell seven million copies of the album. 'I'm sure everyone will want one …' He was right. *Sgt. Pepper* went straight to number one, in Britain and America, selling more than 11 million copies in the United States alone. Moreover, *Pepper* has become recognised as the key transition record from pop to the more self-consciously serious form of rock music, perhaps the most significant album in the history of rock. A considerable amount of the credit goes to Paul. *Pepper* had been his idea, he contributed the largest number of songs, and he oversaw the packaging. The successful release of the LP was therefore a personal triumph, perhaps the high point of his career. Even John conceded in later years, when he usually spoke about Paul with scorn, that '*Pepper* was a peak all right', the last time he worked properly in partnership with Macca, 'especially on "A Day in the Life"'.

To celebrate the release, Paul and Jane threw a party at Cavendish Avenue that lasted all weekend. Sunday evening they went to the Saville Theatre on Shaftesbury Avenue – a building Brian was leasing – and saw Jimi Hendrix perform 'Sgt. Pepper's Lonely Hearts Club Band' as part of his act. Paul was thrilled to hear a significant fellow artist already covering the material.

* Starr had bought a house near John Lennon on the St George's Hill Estate.

IN THE HIGHLANDS

Paul and Jane then packed their bags, grabbed Martha the sheepdog, and hopped on a plane to Scotland, where Paul had recently bought a holiday home, one that was to become very important in his life. The house was on the Kintyre peninsula, a finger of land trailing in the seas off western Scotland, the Firth of Forth on one side, the Atlantic Ocean on the other. The Mull of Kintyre, which Paul later made famous in song, is the headland at the southern end of this peninsula. Just short of the mull lies the 'wee toon' of Campbeltown, home to 6,000 people, many of whom work in fishing, boat-building and on the small farms that dot the hill country. Paul had bought one of these farms, or steadings as they are known, as his holiday home.

The principal attraction of High Park Farm was its remoteness, and thereby the privacy it afforded a man who, while he enjoyed his fame, sometimes felt the need to get away from it all. High Park is only ten minutes' drive from Campbeltown, but Campbeltown itself is one of the remotest towns in the United Kingdom, 500 miles from London, the last 138 miles of road, from Glasgow, through wild and mostly empty country. Even if Paul broke his journey by stopping off to see Dad at Rembrandt, it was a seven-hour drive from Merseyside. Paul and Jane made the journey by car the first time they came up to High Park. As they headed into the Highlands they entered a seemingly more ancient land, the long and winding road leading past lochs reflecting snow-capped mountains, which gave Paul an idea. '[I] was in Scotland, there was a road sort of stretching off up into the hills, you could see it go for miles, and I thought [of], "The Long and Winding Road."' The final leg of the journey was south along the A83, beside long, empty Atlantic-facing beaches, into Campbeltown and thereby the end of the road. People don't come to Campbeltown *en route*, because there is nowhere to go from here, unless you get on a boat, so every visitor is noticed, especially a Beatle and an actress in a sports car. But once local people got over the surprise of seeing Paul about the place he found that they treated him much the same as anybody else and were in fact quietly protective of his privacy, helping make Kintyre an ideal retreat.

Like most of the neighbouring farms, High Park was originally owned by the Duke of Argyll, sublet to a tenant farmer named John Brown, who kept 60 sheep and eight dairy cows on his 183 acres. Old man

Brown was ready to retire when Paul's lawyers bought the farm, without revealing the identity of their client. The tenant farmer was tending his stock when McCartney came by for the first time. 'Christ, it's a Beatle!' the old boy exclaimed. His farmhouse proved to be a basic single-storey stone cottage, built in the nineteenth century, with one bedroom, a roughcast floor, an old cooking range, open fires and corrugated tin roof. There was no heating or running hot water. Many friends wondered why Paul bought such a place when he could afford luxury. It was the peace and quiet that appealed, also the rustic contrast to his metropolitan life, while a penchant for roughing it on holiday is often found among the moneyed English. Jane thought the cottage delightful and Paul, who had adopted some of her upper-crust ways, agreed.

The setting was beautiful. A meadow lay between the farmhouse and Ranachan Hill, which rose steeply in the near distance. Planted in the meadow between house and hill was a phallic finger of rock, 12 feet tall, one of the mysterious standing stones that are a feature of this part of Scotland, erected time out of mind by the Celts. Up on top of Ranachan Hill were the remains of an equally ancient fort, possibly built as a defence against the Vikings. These artefacts caught Paul's imagination and fuelled an interest in Celtic mythology. As Ranachan Hill guards High Park on the south, the steading is closed in to the north by woodland, the fields between bright with flowering primroses in spring, turning purple with the heather in autumn. Crystal clear water ran through the burn. Rabbits, hares and foxes scampered hither and yon, a veritable Eden, dead quiet, with fabulous starry skies. When Paul climbed Ranachan Hill he could look across the sea to Ireland, which helped him connect with his ancestry.

Paul introduced himself to the neighbours. 'He wanted to meet his neighbours, and he came to see us [with] Jane Asher,' recalls Katie Black, who welcomed the Beatle into her cosy kitchen at Tangy Farm. The Blacks were musical, Archie Black loving nothing better than a singsong around the piano, and Paul joined in, though Mrs Black's elderly mother was unimpressed when the music went past her bedtime. One night when they were all having a session downstairs, the old lady stomped on the floor. 'What is that noise?' she asked her daughter when she came upstairs to ask what she wanted.

'Mother, it's Paul McCartney.'

'I don't care if it's Winston Churchill, I'm not having it!'

Firm friendships were formed with established farming families like the Blacks, who proved loyal and discreet. When fans and members of the press started trickling up in search of Paul, the neighbours didn't say where he lived, nor did they trouble Paul for autographs, or resent the fact he wasn't a real farmer. Paul employed a local man to look after High Park, a fellow named Duncan Cairns, later Duncan's son Robert, but they didn't work the land for profit any more.

Paul also found the townsfolk agreeable. He could wander about Campbeltown doing his shopping, and using the pub and wee cinema, without being bothered, while also feeling welcomed into a small, tight-knit community with an everyday friendliness less common in more populous parts of the UK. New friendships were formed in town. One day a drummer from the Campbeltown Pipe Band – ordinary working men who came together in the evenings and at weekends to play traditional Scottish music on bagpipe and drum – introduced himself to Paul, who invited the band to High Park to make a home movie with him and Jane. 'He wanted us to go down in this park well below the farm, playing up and down, and Jane was supposed to be lost out in the hills, and she'd hear the band and come running down as we are marching up and down,' recalls drummer Jim McGeachy. 'We played there for an hour or so. He made a film of it.' Later Paul's association with the pipe band would lead to one of his most successful recordings.

When the sun shone, there seemed no better place to be than High Park, and the weather was glorious when Paul and Jane visited in June 1967, so nice they stayed a few days longer than they'd intended. And when they had to go home, they were able to fly to London. Another attraction for Paul was that, while Kintyre was very remote, private planes could use nearby RAF Machrihanish, which meant he could get back to Beatles business within two hours.

ALL YOU NEED IS LOVE

Paul had only just got home to Cavendish when a *Sunday People* reporter knocked on his door asking about a story in *Life* magazine that Paul had taken LSD. Paul asked the reporter inside, confirming that he had used LSD, four times, and had no regrets.

[It] opened my eyes to the fact there is a God. A similar experience could probably do some of our clergy some good. It is obvious that God isn't in a pill, but it explained the mystery of life [to me]. It was truly a religious experience.

He added that he hoped world leaders would try LSD, commenting, 'I believe the drug could heal the world.' The interview made the front page of the *Sunday People* on 18 June 1967, Paul's 25th birthday: BEATLE PAUL'S AMAZING CONFESSION 'Yes – I took LSD'. When a television crew came to Cavendish to follow up, Paul told them much the same, helping create a major news story, though his drug confessions were only partial.

Paul had succumbed to peer pressure to try LSD when his late friend Tara Browne offered him acid some months back, after a night at the Bag o' Nails. Paul's first trip wasn't pleasant. He became overly conscious of how dirty his shirt was, and felt too exhausted the next day to do any work. Then came a time, during the making of *Sgt. Pepper*, when John took acid by mistake. George Martin led John up to the roof of the EMI building to get some fresh air, not realising John was tripping. Paul rescued his friend from this perilous situation, taking him home to Cavendish, where he dropped acid to keep John company. Again, Paul found the experience less than pleasurable. He had a vision of John as 'a king, the absolute Emperor of Eternity', which would seem to betray an unconscious inferiority complex. Paul had taken acid once or twice since then, not nearly as often as John and George Harrison, but as he revealed in his authorised biography many years later, he had tried other, harder drugs. His art dealer Robert Fraser introduced Paul to cocaine, a legal, pharmaceutical supply of which the Beatle kept at home for a time, as we have seen. But Paul didn't like the come-down from a coke high. A normally upbeat person, he didn't see the point in making himself depressed, so he stopped using it, a demonstration of his strength of character. Paul also sniffed heroin with Fraser. 'I said afterwards, "I'm not sure about this, man. It didn't really do anything for me," and [Fraser] said, "In that case, I won't offer you again." And I didn't take it again.'

Paul didn't share his coke and smack experiences with the press in 1967; that came 30 years later. The little he said about his use of LSD at the time caused enough fuss, coming when the newspapers were full of stories about pop stars and their associates being busted for drugs. A photographer friend of the Beatles, John 'Hoppy' Hopkins, was jailed for possession of marijuana the day *Sgt. Pepper* was released. Following the police raid at Keith Richards's country house, Robert Fraser, Keith Richards and Mick Jagger were ultimately sentenced to six, 12 and three months respectively. The Stones were released on bail in a matter of days, pending an appeal, but Fraser served four months in Wormwood Scrubs (an experience he likened to being back at Eton). Although the intelligentsia took the view that unjust sentences had been handed down – the editor of *The Times* writing a celebrated leader that helped the Stones win their appeal – there was a feeling that the police, encouraged by and in cahoots with the tabloid press, were working up to the biggest prize of all – busting a Beatle. Paul's LSD confession was therefore awkward for John, George and Ritchie, who found themselves the subject of unwanted scrutiny about their own drug use, while the irony was that Paul had been the *last* among them to try acid. 'It seemed strange to me,' George Harrison commented sardonically years later for the *Anthology*, 'because we'd been trying to get him to take LSD for about 18 months – and then one day he's on the television talking about it.' George appeared to suggest by saying this that Paul craved the attention.

Paul's Liverpool family were concerned by the news of their Paul taking drugs. Aunt Ginny called a family conference to discuss what to do, with the result that Ginny came down south to have it out with Paul. 'So she goes to London to stay with Paul,' says family member Mike Robbins. 'About five days later she comes back and we all meet – I'll always remember – in her little cottage, in Mersey View, [my wife,] me, Milly.' The family asked if Ginny had been able to see Paul, whereupon the 57-year-old took a spliff out of her handbag and asked dreamily: 'Have you ever tried one of these?' The 'relies' sparked up and had a smoke of Paul's weed. 'We laffed like bloody drains,' says Mike. 'That was Ginny, see.'

As it turned out, Paul's drug confessions didn't do the Beatles' reputation any serious harm. The boys were still loved by the British press and public, deemed fit to represent the nation in a prestigious television broadcast that summer. Television stations around the world were marshalled together on Sunday 25 June 1967 for a unique TV show, *Our World*, featuring contributions from 18 countries via the new technology of a satellite link-up, the Beatles appearing on behalf of the United Kingdom briefly at the start and again at the end of the show, when they would perform a specially written song, John's 'All You Need is Love,' live from Abbey Road.

As with the orchestral climax to 'A Day in the Life,' Studio One was transformed into a Beatles happening for the broadcast, the band joined by their friends and family. Sitting at the Beatles' feet before the cameras were Mick Jagger and Keith Richards, together with Pattie Harrison (*née* Boyd, having married George the previous year), Jane Asher, Mike McCartney and other McCartney relations. During the show, audience members paraded for the cameras with 'All You Need is Love' spelled in different languages on sandwich boards. One of Paul's cousins held up a sign that read 'Come Back Milly!' intended to be read by Paul's aunt who had recently gone to Australia.

Presiding over everybody was George Martin, the picture of cool in a white linen suit, though he was having a trying week. George's father had died on Tuesday; his second wife Judy (formerly his secretary) was expecting their first daughter; and the Martins were moving house. On top of this, George was finding the Beatles increasingly wilful: George Harrison had tested his patience to the utmost in the run-up to the *Our World* broadcast by expressing the desire to play violin, even though he didn't know how. An ensemble of professional session musicians would fill that role, Martin hiring a selection of string and brass including David Mason, the trumpet-player on 'Penny Lane'. The session men would perform the introduction to the song, and a collage of background tunes that included 'La Marseillaise', to lend an international flavour to proceedings. The whole thing was so complex, it was almost bound to go wrong, yet it worked perfectly on the night, John delivering an immaculate vocal, the band playing without a hitch to speak of, all looking happy and confident as they sent their message of love to the world.* Released as a single a few days later, 'All You Need is Love' went to number one in Britain and the USA and embodies all the charm and optimism of the hippie era, as well as the intellectual vacuity of the beaded and bearded. It is the quintessential sound of the summer of love.

---

* The Beatles did play to a pre-recorded rhythm track, to cut down on the chance of a live mistake.

A FOOLISH AFFAIR

The Beatles were due a huge amount of money from EMI. The reason was technical. In 1966 the band's recording contract with EMI had lapsed. While Brian Epstein renegotiated their deal, EMI temporarily stayed payment of royalties. Then in January 1967, with the new contract in place, the company paid over a very large sum in back royalties, with much more to come thanks to new, enhanced royalty rates. If the Beatles retained this avalanche of cash as income they would suffer punitive surtax. If they invested the money in business they could legally avoid taxation. So the Beatles decided to establish a company, Apple Corps, a madcap enterprise the very name of which was a joke (a pun on apple core), and embarked on the weird, often comic final phase of their career.

Although Apple was a tax dodge, the Beatles were sincere about creating a company that had the financial clout of a major corporation, but that was run with kinder hippie ideals, creating and selling the groovy things they and their friends were interested in, at a fair price, to like-minded people – a kind of hippie socialism. From the main apple tree would hang many little apple companies, dealing in all sorts of things: records, of course, Apple would be prominent in the music business, its record label based on the Magritte picture of an apple that hung in Paul's drawing room; movie-making was also an important part of what Apple Corps would be about; but there would be many, smaller and more off-beat enterprises: Apple clothes, Apple Electronics, a spoken-word recording unit named Zapple; even an Apple school for Beatles children and the children of their friends. Paul's pal Ivy Vaughan was put in charge of this venture, which like so much that Apple tried to do, was well intentioned but hopelessly unrealistic.

Apple started life in offices at 94 Baker Street, a couple of bus stops from St John's Wood, which made it convenient for Paul. While Apple business was conducted upstairs, the ground floor became the Apple Shop, managed by former Quarry Man Pete Shotton, whose head Lennon had once crowned with a washboard, the intention being to sell hippie clothes and other items designed mostly by the Fool, an art group led by an attractive young Dutch couple, Simon Posthuma and Marijke Koger.

Having travelled around Europe together, Simon and Marijke established themselves as members of the London in-crowd in 1966, befriending Brian Epstein firstly, and through him meeting the Beatles. George Harrison invited the Fool to paint a mural over the fireplace of his new home in Esher, Surrey. Pattie Harrison and other Beatle womenfolk began wearing Fool clothing, giving them the look of gypsy fortune-tellers, while Simon and Marijke were invited to Beatles sessions and the *Our World* telecast, during which Marijke was seen shaking a tambourine.

Despite having had their design for the *Sgt. Pepper* sleeve rejected by Paul, Simon and Marijke were now commissioned to decorate the Apple boutique, inside and out, and to produce posters and affordable hippie garments for sale. 'It is wrong that only a few should be able to afford our things,' Simon told the newly launched American music magazine *Rolling Stone*. 'We want to be for everyone.' The concept was confused from the outset. 'I don't know why it was labelled a boutique as it was intended to be more of a cultural centre with books and musical instruments, art lectures, etc.,' says Marijke. 'Unfortunately the whole thing was badly managed, which was nothing to do with the Fool. We were just the creative idea[s] people.' To decorate the façade of the Apple building, Marijke painted a fabulous picture of a genie, four storeys tall, transforming an everyday London street corner into a psychedelic fantasy. It was the best thing about the shop.

Marijke regularly visited Paul at nearby Cavendish Avenue, giving the Beatle private Tarot readings (he kept drawing the Fool). One thing led to another and they ended up in bed. 'Paul's was a sympathetic and warm personality and he had a great sense of humour,' remembers Marijke. 'I saw empathy in the way he dealt with his hired help and he loved animals. As a lifelong animal-lover and vegetarian I could really relate to that.' Simon guessed something was going on between Paul and his girlfriend – 'Paul and Marijke were very good friends – they had this electricity' – and stormed into Cavendish one morning to confront Paul. He found the Beatle in his kitchen eating breakfast and reading his fan mail.

'What the fuck is going on?' Simon yelled.

Paul admitted the affair. He said he couldn't help it, and gave Simon to understand that Jane had found out, too. 'He had a problem, with Jane, of course … There was also hurt on Jane's side.' The men agreed that the affair would end, and they remained friends, just about. Not long afterwards, Simon and Marijke took LSD with Paul, a strange and disturbing trip for Simon, the drug serving to make the Dutchman intensely aware of what had transpired between Paul and his girlfriend. 'That was a tough trip.'

AUGUST BANK HOLIDAY, 1967

Simon and Marijke were not the only colourful characters to enter the Beatles court at this time. Another new face was Alex Mardas, a Greek-born TV repairman whom the clever but ever-credulous John Lennon came to believe was an electronics genius, and duly made head of Apple Electronics. Magic Alex was set up in a workshop behind Maryle-bone Station where he strove to develop such stupendous inventions as light-emitting paint and a spaceship that could be powered by the engine from George Harrison's Ferrari. Unsurprisingly these inventions didn't work. Alex also took the Beatles back to his homeland that summer, shopping for a Greek island the band could buy as a commune. After looking at several islands the boys lost interest and flew home, where they fell under the sway of another absurd character.

Born Mahesh Prasad Varma in India sometime around 1917 (nobody was sure), the self-styled Maharishi Mahesh Yogi had studied maths and physics at Allahabad University before going into the Himalayas and re-emerging as a holy man whose message for the world was that heavenly bliss could be experienced through 'transcendental medita-tion' or TM. Knowing which side of his poppadom had curry on, the Maharishi went to Los Angeles to set up his Spiritual Regeneration Movement, which, rather than helping initiates for free – in the Indian tradition – asked for a week's wages (the more you earned the more you paid). In exchange for this donation, one received a mantra – simply a phrase – to repeat endlessly until lulled into a state of oneness with the universe. Many wealthy Californians signed up.

Next the Maharishi came to London, where he recruited more rich, unhappy fools. Pattie Harrison was first in the Beatles circle to embrace the Spiritual Regeneration Movement, informing her husband that the Maharishi was giving a talk on Thursday 24 August. They had to go. Perhaps surprisingly for a Himalayan yogi, the Maharishi was meeting the people of Britain at the Hilton Hotel, the luxurious high-rise favoured by the Rolling Stones' sybaritic manager Allen Klein. George Harrison obtained the tickets – 'I needed a mantra – a password to get through into the other world' – and corralled John, Cyn, Paul, Jane Asher and Mike McCartney into joining him and Pattie at the master's feet. When all were assembled the yogi emerged from behind a curtain to greet his audience, giggling and clutching flowers. He was a funny, happy little fellow with long hair like a girl. The Beatles were amused and impressed by the yogi's shorthand route to nirvana, and acceded to an invitation to spend a few days with him at a teacher-training college in Bangor, Wales, where the holy man was to give a series of seminars starting that bank holiday weekend.

The Beatles arrived at Euston Station just in time to catch the 3:50 to Bangor on Friday 25 August, before the metropolis disgorged its workers for the weekend. The weather was warm and sunny and there was a holiday mood in the Beatles party, which included Magic Alex, Donovan, Marianne Faithfull and Mick Jagger, who trailed about after the Beatles like their kid brother these days, eager to be where the action was. In the inevitable kerfuffle at the station, Cynthia Lennon was held back by a policeman who mistook her for a fan. 'Tell them you're with us!' John yelled to his wife, but the train left without Mrs Lennon. 'It was horribly embarrassing,' Cynthia later wrote of the moment she found herself standing tearfully on the platform, watching her husband's train pull away. 'My tears were not simply because of the missed train. I was crying because the incident seemed symbolic of what was happening in our marriage. John was on the train, speeding into the future, and I was left behind.'

There were other pockets of darkness surrounding the Beatles that August week. Two days earlier, Joe Orton had been found battered to death by his lover, Kenneth Halliwell, who then committed suicide. 'A Day in the Life' was played at Orton's funeral. Then there was Brian Epstein, who had been in decline since the Beatles' last, unhappy tour, which reached its shabby conclusion in LA when Brian's boyfriend stole his briefcase. Not long after that depressing incident Brian took an overdose at Chapel Street, leaving an 'I can't take it any more' note, according to Peter Brown, who found him and took his friend's word that he wouldn't try anything so silly again. 'When I discovered him, when I found him that night, you know, when I took him to the Priory [Clinic], and they pumped his stomach and everything, obviously we had a conversation subsequent to that. The conversation was him full of remorse.'

The main problem was that Brian had become dependent on amphetamines, which made him erratic. Once so immaculate, so businesslike and well organised, Brian now slept late, missing appointments and key events, such as the Beatles' last concert in Candlestick Park. 'So that showed, you know, bad behaviour,' notes Brown. The stable of acts Brian had built up and made good money with during the heady days of the Mersey Beat looked tired. The Mersey Sound was yesterday's music, and Brian's recent signings hadn't made much impact. His new group Paddy, Klaus and Gibson had, for example, already disbanded. Then, in January 1967, Brian merged NEMS with the Robert Stigwood Organisation, allowing Stigwood, a young Australian, to take over part of his company. Brian kept the Beatles, but now that the boys had given up the road they didn't need him on a daily basis. Brian had never been welcome in the studio, and his suggestion that *Sgt. Pepper* should be packaged in a plain brown sleeve showed how out of touch he was with the lads. He had successfully renegotiated the band's contract with EMI in January, but the rumour was that when his own management contract came up in the autumn the Beatles might drop him in favour of Allen Klein, who'd impressed Paul by getting the Stones a $1.25 million (£816,993) advance from Decca.

Brian had always found Paul slightly difficult, more questioning and less biddable than the other Beatles. One Liverpool acquaintance recalls Paul 'taking the piss' out of Brian's sexuality, 'sort of mincing along after him', though McCartney's friendship with the art critic Robert Fraser, who was openly gay, is evidence against him being truly homophobic. When Paul went to Paris with Fraser to shop for pictures, some of his fellow Beatles made comments, as Paul later recalled in his authorised biography: 'Because he was gay [but] I was secure about my sexuality. I always felt this is fine, I can hang out with whoever I want and it didn't worry me.'

Above and beyond having a laugh at Brian's expense, as all the Beatles did to a degree, there is, however, evidence that Brian Epstein had problems with Paul. When Epstein was dictating his memoirs to his assistant Derek Taylor, published in 1964 as *A Cellarful of Noise*, he said critically: 'Paul can be temperamental and moody and difficult to deal with,' adding that McCartney had a tendency not to listen to what he didn't want to hear and possessed an 'angry exterior'. Yet Brian's

American business partner Nat Weiss insists that Paul and Brian were on better terms by the summer of '67, having resolved many of their issues, adding that he expected Brian to retain management of the Beatles. 'As a matter of fact I think Brian – and I can say this from a conversation I had with him – his thinking was to keep Cilla Black and the Beatles for himself and let Stigwood handle the rest of NEMS artists, and adjust the commissions down to 15 per cent.'

Still, Brian was increasingly volatile, bad-tempered and drug dependent, sleeping late at Chapel Street and losing his temper with his staff when he did get up. In May he checked back into the Priory Clinic. In July Brian's father died, which he took hard. His mother Queenie came to stay at Chapel Street. Paul saw Brian and his mother there on 24 August. Brian minded Martha while Paul and Jane went to see the Maharishi speak at the Hilton. When the Beatles told Brian they were going to Bangor to spend more time with the yogi, he said he'd join them after the weekend, which he planned to spend in the country with Peter Brown and Geoffrey Ellis from the office. Brian drove down to Sussex in his white Bentley convertible on the Friday, while the band was travelling to Bangor. He had arranged for some young men to visit over the weekend, but dinner came and went without the guests arriving. Brian tried to rustle up other companions but, being a bank holiday, his contacts were unavailable. He told Pete and Geoff that he was driving back to town, and headed off into the night.

London has an enervated feeling during bank holidays, especially the August bank holiday when the streets are empty, the shops closed, and many residents are away. Those who remain in the city are often lonely people like Brian, who returned home to Belgravia in his ghostly car in the middle of the night and went to bed. He telephoned his country guests the following afternoon, and assured them he was coming back. He also mentioned that he'd taken some sleeping pills. Sunday dawned. Brian didn't stir. His staff knocked on his bedroom door to see if he wanted anything, but there was no answer. The door was locked. Eventually they called a doctor, who forced the door and found Epstein dead, surrounded by pill bottles. Peter Brown called the Beatles in Bangor, getting Paul on the line. 'Paul was shocked and saddened but strangely sedate.' The press were on hand to cover the Beatles' weekend with the Maharishi. They clamoured for a reaction. John looked lost. George spoke twaddle about there being 'no such thing as death'.

Paul muttered that he was deeply shocked and put his arm around Jane, who looked increasingly like she was in a play she wanted her agent to get her out of.

PAUL TAKES CHARGE

ROLL UP! ROLL UP! FOR PAUL MCCARTNEY'S MYSTERY TOUR

'EPSTEIN DIES AT 32', screamed the front page of the *Daily Mirror* on Monday 28 August 1967, adding in parenthesis that Epstein was 'The Beatle-making Prince of Pop'. There was a hint in the coverage that the Prince of Pop may have taken his own life, but Brian's friends agree with the coroner that the death was accidental. Brian had been taking too many pills for too long and had finally overdone it. He left no note, which counted against self-murder. Likewise he had plans for the week ahead. Still, there was a sense that Brian had been going downhill for a while, and despair can come suddenly and overwhelmingly in the night. 'Brian's death was a tragedy,' says his lawyer Rex Makin, 'but a tragedy waiting to happen.'

When their manager had been laid to rest, the Beatles convened a series of meetings to decide how they should proceed without him. Robert Stigwood had an option to take over all of NEMS, and thereby the management of the Beatles, which the boys didn't want. Stigwood was paid off and the Beatles remained with the rump of the old company, now headed by Brian's brother Clive. At a meeting at Ringo's London flat, in Montagu Square, it was decided that the reins of the band's day-to-day management should be picked up by Brian's assistant and friend, Peter Brown, a member of the original Liverpool 'family' who'd come down to London with the boys (the others being, notably, Neil, Mal, 'Measles' Bramwell and Brian himself). Paul doubted frankly that Brown was up to the job. Who was Peter, after all, but a mate of Brian's who used to sell records in Lewis's? Peter himself felt out of sorts at the first band meeting after Brian's death. 'I was emotionally very distraught, and I wasn't sure what I could do, and I wasn't sure whether I was ready to [lead] the band.' During a break in discussions, he got up and walked to the window.

> The next thing I felt was arms being put around me and somebody hugging me and it was John – it always upsets me to tell the story – and he just looked at me and said, 'Are you alright?' And I realised that only he and I felt this enormous emotional loss of Brian.

Certainly Paul was the most businesslike this day and during the days ahead. 'Then Paul took the initiative of saying, "We've gotta do something. We'll do *Magical Mystery Tour*." Paul took the lead and everyone went along with it, disaster though it was.'

Having already recorded some material for *Magical Mystery Tour*, Paul led the Beatles back into the studio in September with a renewed sense of purpose, laying down John's mighty 'I am the Walrus', and George's typically insubstantial 'Blue Jay Way', as well as the instrumental 'Flying', all of which would feature in the forthcoming picture. The Beatles were in a hurry to get these songs down, and the film made, because they wanted to spend time with their new guru, the Maharishi, at his ashram in the Himalayas. It was Paul who decided *Magical Mystery Tour* could be shot very quickly indeed, having observed a two-man TV crew filming the Maharishi at the London Hilton. If the Beatles worked in a similar way, Paul figured they could make their film in a matter of weeks. Pre-production was therefore hurried and absurdly inadequate. The Beatles didn't even have a director, just a mate of Barry Miles's named Peter Theobald, a young film-maker who'd been hired as a 'Director/Cameraman', handed 15 pages of notes and told he had six weeks to shoot the picture. 'We never want that *Help!* scene again,' McCartney told Theobald, who noted that the band 'didn't want chalk marks to walk to, with lines to get right, or "Take for the 28th time – ACTION!"; they wanted it to be freewheeling, to pick up things as they happened, and they *did* want it to be *their* film as well as being *in* it'.

Paul's initial discussion with Theobald took place on Wednesday 6 September 1967. Madly, Paul decreed that the Beatles would start filming the following Monday. His idea was to hire a coach, put the Beatles in it, along with a diverse cast of supporting actors, to be plucked from the pages of the show business directory *Spotlight*, then motor down to the West Country, which Paul had fond holiday memories of, and film an impromptu road movie with musical interludes. Not only did Theobald have no script; no budget had been prepared, the coach hadn't been hired, and no actors had been engaged. John Lennon spent an afternoon floating in his swimming pool thinking of the sort of people he might like to have in the picture, and decided he'd quite like a music hall comic he'd once seen named Nat 'Rubber Neck' Jackley, so Nat received a call. Meanwhile, no one thought to consult the relevant trade unions, which had considerable control over how films were crewed in the United Kingdom at the time. As far as the unions were concerned, the whole production would be illegitimate, which caused problems later on.

The starting point for this misconceived adventure was Allsop Place, a quiet turning behind Madame Tussaud's museum, traditionally used as an embarkation point for provincial package tours of the type the Beatles once played with Helen Shapiro. Allsop Place was also close to Paul's London home. The auteur arrived bright and early on Monday 11 September 1967, dressed in costume (Paul's normal clothes, plus a Fair Isle sweater), to meet his hastily assembled crew and cast which, in addition to 'Rubber Neck' Jackley, included a heavy-set actress named Jessie Robbins, who would play Ringo's aunt; the eccentric Scots performer Ivor Cutler, who would play a courier named Buster Bloodvessel who lusted after the aunt; a dolly-bird guide; a dwarf photographer; and an accompanying team of friends and associates including Magic Alex, Neil Aspinall and Mal Evans.

Where was the coach? It still hadn't shown up. So Paul went for a cup of tea at the nearby London Transport canteen. By the time he came back, the coach had arrived. It was a Bedford VAL hire coach, of the type commonly used to take school kids to the swimming baths and pensioners on touring holidays, its sides freshly painted yellow and decorated with hippie decals and the words MAGICAL MYSTERY TOUR. The coachwork was so freshly painted the paint was still wet. Everybody climbed aboard and drove west out of London, pausing in Surrey to pick up the three suburban Beatles.

Filming began immediately all four stars were aboard, the starting point of the plot, such as it was, being that Ringo was taking his Aunt

Jessie on a coach trip. Along the way there would be songs and semi-improvised set pieces influenced by the Goons, the Theatre of the Absurd (which Paul was familiar with from seeing plays such as *Ubu Roi*) and recent LSD trips. Viewed afresh, it all looks strikingly like *Monty Python's Flying Circus*, which is a compliment to the Beatles because *Python* didn't come into existence until the following year. Unlike *Python*, however, *Magical Mystery Tour* wasn't funny.

The picture was a hoot to make, though. By evening, this twentieth-century ship of fools had reached picturesque Teignmouth, in Devon, where everybody checked into the Royal Hotel. One of the many aspects of film-making the Beatles hadn't put sufficient thought into was the logistics of looking after a cast and crew on location; Paul found he had to spend hours making sure everybody had a room for the night and something hot to eat – a terrible bore. After breakfast the following day they got back on the coach and drove towards Dartmoor, intending to film at Widecombe Fair. Negotiating the narrow country byways, the Beatles' coach got stuck on a hump-back bridge, causing a traffic jam of angry, honking motorists, who were themselves held up behind a convoy of press. Frustrated by the delay, John leapt out and started tearing the stickers off the side of the Beatles' coach in a rage. Then it rained, causing the still-wet paint to run down the sides of the vehicle.

The Beatles abandoned Widecombe Fair and drove instead to the seaside resort of Newquay, in Cornwall, where they checked into the Atlantic Hotel. The original idea had been to stay in a different location every night, but that was obviously impractical, so the Beatles used the Atlantic as their base for the remaining three days of the tour. Despite the chaos, Paul showed every sign of enjoying himself, riding a tandem on the beach with dwarf actor George Laydon, leading a singsong in a pub in Perranporth, and chatting up female holiday-makers, such as 17-year-old bikini-clad Catherine Osborne, who, on the final day of her summer vacation, found herself to her surprise in a Beatles movie. 'All I wanted was an autograph,' she told the man from the *Daily Express*.*

When they got back to London the boys filmed a striptease scene at the Raymond Revue Bar in Soho, hiring the absurdist Bonzo Dog Doo Dah Band, with whom the Beatles had become friendly, to perform a

---

* And indeed that's all she got – her scene was cut.

piece of nonsense titled 'Death Cab for Cutie' (a headline Bonzo member Neil Innes had spied in an American crime magazine). Innes recalls John and Ringo filming everything with their own 16mm cameras, while Paul directed the main production. 'What are you doing?' Innes asked.

'We're doing the Weybridge version,' Lennon replied laconically, revealing the (perhaps) tantalising prospect of an entirely different cut of *Magical Mystery Tour*.

To complete the picture the Beatles needed a studio. As nobody had thought to book Twickenham, they shot the requisite scenes at a disused air force base at West Malling in Kent, including a wacky car chase and the Beatles miming to John's 'I am the Walrus', the only real point of interest in the whole film, for this was weird and powerful music, performed by Lennon wearing an egg-head while his fellow Beatles donned strangely disquieting animal masks. Paul put on the head of a hippo.* The lads then moved into a hangar to shoot 'Your Mother Should Know', which gave Paul an opportunity to emulate Fred Astaire, putting on a white tuxedo and dancing down stairs with his band mates. The whole thing was truly nutty, as visitors observed. 'The day I went down, Paul was directing 40 assorted dwarfs, vicars, foot-ballers, mums and dads with prams full of babies and George and Ringo dressed as gangsters,' journalist Hunter Davies reported for the *Sunday Times*. 'As a starting rocket went off, [Paul] had them all charging across the empty airfield, then charging back again. John was asleep in his Rolls Royce.' Paul was now directing full time, Peter Theobald having left the production after a dispute blew up with the unions over the crewing of the picture.

At the end, the Beatles threw a wrap party at which the Bonzos again performed, the band's drummer 'Legs' Larry Smith doing a tap dance while wearing false breasts. ('Come on, Larry, show us yer tits!' heckled Lennon. 'We've all seen them before.') Paul then edited the picture in a Soho cutting room, which took most of October, at the end of which he popped over to France to film himself miming to 'The Fool on the Hill' as additional footage. Paul didn't bother to take his passport or money, but being a Beatle he managed to get there and back. With a little more work in the cutting room the whole bag of nonsense was tied up by

* Paul was not the walrus, contrary to what Lennon sings in 'Glass Onion'.

November, Paul capping the project by directing a promotional film for the band's lightweight but enjoyable new single, 'Hello Goodbye', featuring the boys in their *Sgt. Pepper* suits on stage at the Saville Theatre. The single and the accompanying double EP of songs from *Magical Mystery Tour* proved a great success in Britain, while a full length *Magical Mystery Tour* soundtrack was released as a regular LP in North America. Featuring all the film tunes, plus 'Strawberry Fields Forever', 'Penny Lane' and 'All You Need is Love', this is a surprisingly strong album.

It was Paul's mistaken decision to sell first rights to *Magical Mystery Tour* to the BBC, rather than open the picture theatrically at cinemas. The Corporation didn't pay much money for the rights, but its controllers agreed to broadcast the film on Boxing Day, when it would be guaranteed a massive audience. Paul, who like most British people held the BBC in affection and respect, thought the audience size the main thing. The problem was that the BBC intended to show what was a colour film in black and white at a time when the Corporation was still phasing in colour transmission, and the BBC wanted cuts to the picture before showing it to a family audience at Christmas. Scenes of Ivor Cutler canoodling with Ringo's aunt would have to go; bare breasts would be covered up.

With this unsatisfactory deal done, Paul and Jane went to Scotland for a few days' holiday at High Park, missing the opening of the Apple Shop on 5 December. During their stay in Kintyre, Paul and Jane called in on their farmer neighbours, the Blacks, whose teenage son Jamie was home from boarding school for the festive season. 'My vivid memory is that he played "Lady Madonna" on that piano in the living room, before he released it, which was just [fantastic],' recalls Jamie, whose school friends never believed his story, even though Paul gave him an autograph to endorse it. 'Lady Madonna' was a good and important new song, in the style of Fats Domino, that went to number one the following year. While the song has a rollicking tune, and the words are put over with brio, the lyric is also tender and personal, evoking the image of Mary McCartney as midwife, tending mothers and their babies in Liverpool as she had during Paul's childhood. The phrase 'Lady Madonna' also has a clear Christian meaning, of course, conflating Paul's memory of his mother with the Virgin Mary in what is a boogie-woogie hymn.

The trip to Scotland gave Paul and Jane a chance to talk about their relationship. There had been problems before Jane went to the USA with the Bristol Old Vic, and when she came back she found Paul, if anything, even more difficult to live with. 'Paul had changed so much. He was on LSD, which I hadn't shared. I was jealous of all the spiritual experiences he'd had with John. There were 15 people dropping in all day long. The house had changed and was full of stuff I didn't know about,' she confided in Hunter Davies, in one of the very few interviews she ever gave on the subject of her relationship with Paul. Davies enjoyed unparalleled access to the Beatles and their associates while researching an authorised biography of the band. Gamely, Jane tried to fit in with Paul's new world. She went along with him and the others to see the Maharishi, even though she (in common with the sensible George Martin) didn't think much of the yogi. Jane put up with the drug-taking, and got along as best she could with Paul's hippie friends. When wallpaper painter Dudley Edwards came back to Cavendish for a visit, Jane traded her Ford Popular with him for a statue of Shiva. 'At that time they seemed to be very much a couple,' comments Dudley, 'everything seemed to be fine.' Others weren't so sure. During visits to Rembrandt, Jim and Angie McCartney overheard arguments. Jim hoped the youngsters would be all right. Everybody liked Jane, and thought her a positive influence on Paul.

The Scottish break seemed to do Paul and Jane good. Afterwards, the couple invited Paul's father and Angie and her daughter Ruth to Cavendish for a family Christmas. When they were all gathered around the tree on Christmas Day, unwrapping their presents, Jane opened a special gift from Paul to reveal a diamond engagement ring. He asked her to marry him, and she said yes. The engagement was announced to the press shortly thereafter. Whatever problems they had had, the couple seemed to have reached an understanding by which Paul would stop being jealous of Jane's career. 'I always wanted to beat Jane down,' Paul admitted to Hunter Davies. A striking phrase, *beat her down*, but one that summed up the way men of his background typically treated women. John, Paul, George and Ritchie all expected their partners to stay home. Cyn, Mo and Pattie didn't work after they married into the band. Even though his own mother had worked, Paul didn't want Jane to have a career. 'I wanted her to give up work completely,' he told Davies during a joint interview with his fiancée for the book.

'I refused,' Jane interjected. 'I've been brought up to be always doing something. And I enjoy acting. I didn't want to give that up.'

'I know now I was just being silly,' admitted Paul. 'It was just a game, trying to beat you down.'

With Paul and Jane's future apparently settled, the McCartneys sat down together at 8:35 p.m. on 26 December 1967 to watch *Magical Mystery Tour* on BBC1, as did millions of people across the UK. It was a huge disappointment. The film was plotless and, although apparently meant to be amusing, failed to raise a laugh. Even though there were several good songs, and the film was less than an hour long, it dragged, and the decision to broadcast what was a colour picture in black and white robbed the flick of the modicum of visual appeal it originally possessed. Viewers called the BBC with complaints, others wrote to the newspapers to express how let down they felt. 'Everyone was looking for a plot. But purposely it wasn't there ... We did it as a series of disconnected, unconnected events. They were not meant to have any depth,' commented Paul, defending the picture to Don Short of the *Daily Mirror*. At least the Beatles had *tried* to do something different. As he said: 'We could always write and do nice things and become more and more famous. But we wanted to try something different ... It doesn't mean that we won't go on trying.' Indeed, the remaining months of the Beatles' existence as a working band would be marked by an unswerving, and laudable, commitment to innovation.

THE BEATLES IN THE HIMALAYAS

The Beatles flew to India in mid-February 1968 for what George Harrison described, with his facility for a phrase, as 'the world famous "Beatles in the Himalayas" sketch'. They travelled in two groups. John, Cynthia, George and Pattie flew first to Delhi on 15 February, with Pattie's sister Jenny and Mal Evans. Paul, Jane, Ritchie and Maureen followed four days later. They then drove 200 miles to Rishikesh in a fleet of old, British-made cars that served locally as taxis. As ever, the Beatles were trailed by a pack of reporters and photographers, who were having a fine time following the crazy Beatles around the world. The press found George difficult; he pretended to sleep all the way to India, for example, so they couldn't ask him questions. Ringo was good for a laugh. He'd brought a case of Heinz baked beans with him, claiming not to be able to stomach foreign food. John was also entertaining, but unpredictable; while Paul was the newspaperman's pet, the sensible Beatle they could usually count on to say a few words and pose for a picture, as he did on the Lakshman Jhula bridge crossing the Ganges into Rishikesh.

The Maharishi's ashram was situated on a 15-acre plot of land beside the Ganges, at a point where the river gushes out of the Himalayas, with a large and comfortable bungalow accommodating the yogi and huts for his followers, fifty or so people at this time, most of whom were Westerners. The Beatles brought a host of celebrity friends and flunkies with them, including Donovan, Magic Alex, Mike Love of the Beach Boys, and Mia Farrow with two of her siblings. The band members, who'd parted with the requisite week's wages in exchange for their stay (a huge sum in their case), moved into their huts with the intention of remaining for two months, and acclimatised as best they could. Although they were high up in the mountains, the weather was oppressively hot. Each morning began with a communal vegetarian breakfast, interrupted by apes swinging down from the trees to pinch their food. The disciples then met with the Maharishi to talk and meditate. After lunch there was more time for meditation. There was indeed a rare amount of time for the Beatles to hang out together, think and make music, which was the happiest outcome of the trip. They wrote a lot of songs in India.

George loved the atmosphere, sinking deeply into the Indian spiritual life, which became part of his quotidian existence. Ritchie and Maureen weren't so happy. The Starkeys wouldn't eat the local food; Mo disliked the flies, and they missed their kids, two-year-old Zak and Jason, born the previous summer, whom they had left at home. For her part, Cynthia Lennon hoped for a second honeymoon with John, but found her husband moody and distant, taking himself off to sleep in a separate hut and spending much of his time writing songs, numbers such as 'Yer Blues' and 'Dear Prudence', about Mia Farrow's sister, who caused concern by shutting herself away and meditating at inordinate length.

For his part, Paul wrote a ska pastiche, 'Ob-La-Di, Ob-La-Da', and a pretty tune, 'Junk', which he was never able to fit good words to, finally settling on a seemingly random jumble of images. The result is virtually meaningless:

Motor cars, handlebars, bicycles for two,
Broken-hearted jubilee.
Parachutes, army boots, sleeping bags for two,
Sentimental jamboree.

Inevitably, business interrupted this Indian idyll. George thought Apple should make a picture about transcendental meditation, and Denis O'Dell, head of Apple Films, was sent for to discuss the idea. When O'Dell arrived, he tried to talk the Beatles into committing instead to a film of J.R.R. Tolkien's *The Lord of the Rings*, which had become a cult book with the hippie generation. For a brief time the band considered the suggestion. Lennon fancied himself in the role of the wizard Gandalf. Paul might have been the plucky hobbit hero, Frodo. Stanley Kubrick had been approached to direct. The bizarre idea of the Beatles starring in Stanley Kubrick's production of *The Lord of the Rings* came to nought, like the TM film and so many putative movies. More to the point, when Paul tried to talk to George about the Beatles' next album, Harrison almost bit his head off. 'I remember talking about the next album and he would say: "We're not here to talk music – we're here to meditate." Oh yeah, all right Georgie Boy. Calm down, man ...' Ritchie and Mo returned home, fed up with the strange food, the flies, the thieving monkeys and the heat. Paul and Jane followed shortly thereafter.

After Ritchie, Mo, Paul and Jane had all left, John Lennon got it into his head that the Maharishi had made passes at some of the Western girls in the ashram, including Mia Farrow, and decided this was gross hypocrisy on the yogi's part. Lennon confronted the Maharishi in 'his very rich-looking bungalow', then left the ashram in high dudgeon, denouncing the yogi as a randy conman. This was all very odd, and probably disingenuous on Lennon's part. While he may well have been a charlatan, and the whole TM programme stuff and nonsense, didn't the yogi have as much right as the next man to try and get laid? The truth was perhaps that, by throwing his tantrum, John was creating a cover for his own imminent and far more discreditable act of sexual betrayal, which we shall come to shortly. George Harrison remained loyal to the yogi, though, and Ritchie and Paul also maintained a long-term respect for the Maharishi and transcendental meditation, which Paul continues to practise.

THIS MAN HAS TALENT ...

Back in London the Beatles decided that they wanted members of the public to come forward with their songs and other ideas, which Apple would help them produce. To promote this egalitarian initiative Paul created a print advertisement, featuring Alistair Taylor from the Apple office. Taylor was photographed as a busker under the line, 'This man has talent ...' The copy read that the busker had sent his audition tape into Apple and thereby transformed himself into a star who now drove a Bentley. The ad was placed in the music press inviting people to send in their demos. The Apple office in Baker Street was inundated with mail as a result. No great new talent was discovered this way, but Apple did begin to sign acts, some of whom proved very successful.

Jane's brother Peter Asher introduced James Taylor to the Apple record label, which Peter now helped run. Paul played on Taylor's début LP, which launched the American star on a long career. Less notably, Jackie Lomax, a former member of the Mersey Beat group the Undertakers, also joined Apple around this time. Perhaps the most surprising Apple artist was a devoutly religious classical composer named John Tavener, a doubly surprising signing because Tavener came to Apple via Ringo Starr, who'd been introduced to the composer by his builder brother Roger Tavener, who'd been working on Ringo's new house at St George's Hill. Uncommercial though his music was, John Tavener fitted into the strange world of Apple, which released his oratorio *The Whale*. 'I felt comfortable because of the enthusiasm of the Beatles,' says the composer, who discovered that Paul in particular was really quite interested in the elite world of 'serious' composition. 'Stockhausen sent him records of his, and he was listening a lot.'

Apart from the eclectic nature of the Apple artists, it was striking how often Paul's instincts proved right. Paul gave another Apple signing, the band Badfinger, a simple but nonetheless catchy song he'd written entitled 'Come and Get it', and told the group exactly how to record it. When the band did what he said, 'Come and Get It' became a top ten hit. Even more spectacular was Paul's success with Mary Hopkin, a Welsh folk singer who was drawn to his attention by the model Twiggy, a good enough friend to be invited to dinner with the McCartneys at Rembrandt. Twiggy mentioned to Paul that she had seen Hopkin on the TV talent show, *Opportunity Knocks*, the show

George Harrison invoked sarcastically when Paul first performed 'Yesterday' live on stage in Blackpool. 'Twiggy said she had seen a great girl singer on *Opportunity Knocks* and luckily as it turned out this was the time we were looking around for singers for Apple Records.' When he got back to London, and heard other people talking about Mary Hopkin, Paul invited her to London.

Mary was a shy 18-year-old with an ethereal voice reminiscent of Joan Baez. Paul didn't like the Baez sound personally, but he thought he might have the right song for Mary to sing. Alongside his interest in the avant-garde, Paul never lost his love of traditional entertainment. As often as he would attend a performance of electronic music, or see a play at the Royal Court, Paul would go to concerts by crooners and watch cabaret acts at the Blue Angel in Mayfair. He'd recently seen Gene and Francesca Raskin at the Blue Angel performing 'Those Were the Days', their own arrangement of a traditional folk song. Paul wanted Mary to record a cover. The teenager found the nostalgic, world-weary lyric hard to empathise with and sang it at first as though she didn't mean it. 'I kept showing her the way she should sing it and generally worked on it and suddenly she got it ...' said Paul, who instinctively felt he knew best. As with Badfinger, he was right. When Mary sang the song Paul's way, it went to number one in 13 countries.

LINDA AND YOKO

John and Paul flew to New York on Saturday 11 May 1968 to further promote Apple, taking Magic Alex along for the ride. Though their arrival at Kennedy Airport lacked the hysteria of their first visit to the States four years previously, there was a sizeable crowd of fans and press to greet the two Beatles and trail them to the St Regis Hotel. Not wanting to be prisoners in the hotel, as they had once been at the Plaza, the boys called Brian Epstein's former partner Nat Weiss, who invited John and Paul to use his apartment on East 73rd Street while he stayed in their suite.

On Sunday John and Paul left Nat's apartment to take an Apple board meeting on a Chinese Junk sailing around the Statue of Liberty, and to meet the press, explaining Apple and appealing for more ordinary people to come forward with their ideas. 'We really want to help people, but without doing it like charity or seeming like ordinary patrons of the arts,' Paul told reporters earnestly. Their intentions were laudable, but Paul and John appeared astonishingly, and endearingly, naive. It is almost impossible to imagine a major star today saying as Paul did in New York in 1968:

> we're in the happy position of not really needing any more money, so for the first time the bosses aren't in it for the profit. If you come and see me and say, 'I've had such and such a dream,' I will say, 'Here's so much money. Go away and do it.' We've already bought all our dreams, so now we want to share that possibility with others.

While they were in town, Lennon and McCartney also gave a press conference at the Americana Hotel. Linda Eastman, whom Paul had met in London the previous summer, showed up. 'It was at the Apple press conference that my relationship with Paul was rekindled. I managed to slip him my phone number,' she recalled. 'He rang me up later that day and told me they were leaving that evening, but he'd like it if I was able to travel out to the airport with him and John. So I went out in their limousine, sandwiched between Paul and John ...' Nat Weiss was also in the car. To his mind, this was all part of Linda's relentless campaign to make Paul her husband. 'Linda's been after him for the longest time. An unstoppable event, [but] I don't think he'd made his mind up about Linda at that point.'

As they flew home from New York, Paul and John were in fact both on the cusp of making momentous changes in their personal lives. Paul was falling in love with Linda Eastman, but hadn't yet decided to break with Jane Asher, whom he had been with for four years, and was engaged to marry. When he arrived home, the couple carried on as normal, for now. Just as Jane had stood by Paul during these manic Beatles years, Cynthia Lennon had been John's rock. Yet John's eyes were also on someone new.

There are striking similarities between Linda Eastman and Yoko Ono, two strong women who now stride into the Beatles story, elbowing aside the loyal, sweet-natured Englishwomen John and Paul had been with for so long, and taking their places as consorts. Yoko was eight years older than Linda, considerably older than all four members of the Beatles, with a complex background. Born in Japan in 1933, Yoko came to America as a girl, was educated in the USA and made the United States her permanent home, becoming almost as American as Linda herself, though Yoko never relinquished Japanese nationality. Like Linda's father, Yoko's daddy was a man of wealth, a financier who managed the Bank of Tokyo in New York after the war. The Uno family lived in Scarsdale, the same upstate town Linda grew up in. Even more remarkably, Linda and Yoko both attended, then dropped out of, Sarah Lawrence College. Both women then drifted into bohemian New York City, to the disapproval of their parents. As Linda became a Manhattan press photographer, with friends on the arts scene, Yoko became a conceptual artist in the city's Fluxus movement (artists who staged happenings, concerts and other free-form events). So Linda and Yoko were still swimming in the same pool. Furthermore, both were now divorcees with young daughters. Yoko married first a Japanese composer named Toshi Ichiyanagi; second, American film-maker Tony Cox, with whom she had a child, Kyoko, eight months younger than Linda's daughter Heather See.

In 1966 Yoko came to London and, like Linda, made a beeline for the Beatles, specifically Paul, coming to Cavendish Avenue to ask McCartney to donate Beatles sheet music as a birthday gift for her composer friend John Cage. Paul referred Yoko to John Lennon, whom she first met at the Indica Gallery in November when she staged an art show, *Unfinished Paintings and Objects*. The work consisted of absurdist and humorous works in the tradition of Marcel Duchamp, including *Ladder Piece*. John gamely climbed a ladder to peer through a magnifying glass at a sign on the ceiling. It read 'YES'. John laughed. He was also amused by an apple Yoko had on sale for the mad price of £200. 'I thought, "Fuck, I can make that. I can put an apple on a stand. I want more."' Yoko sent John an enigmatic little book she'd written entitled *Grapefruit*, in which were printed such gnomic sentences as 'Listen to the sound of the Earth turning'. John, with his weakness for twaddle, invited Yoko to lunch at Kenwood, after which she deluged him with invitations to her events, one of which he was persuaded to finance. John invited Yoko in return to a Beatles session, and made a clumsy initial pass, which she rebuffed. But when John went to Rishikesh, Yoko wrote to him regularly. Cynthia Lennon became sick of Yoko's missives and what she saw as the woman's 'determined pursuit' of her husband. Poor Cyn still loved John.

After India, Cynthia wanted to go to New York with John and Paul, but John wouldn't allow it, so she went instead on holiday to Greece with a group of friends including Pattie Harrison and Magic Alex, leaving four-year-old Julian with a babysitter. When John returned home from New York, and found he had Kenwood to himself briefly, he lost no time in asking Yoko over. So it was that Cynthia came home to find her husband and his Japanese lover sitting in bathrobes in her sunroom, having been up all night making music and making love. Shocked and confused, Cynthia blurted out that she was going for lunch. Would anybody like to join her? John and Yoko declined. 'The stupidity of that question has haunted me ever since,' says Cynthia, who fled by taxi.

A Beatle had fallen in love with a strong-minded divorcee of moneyed American background, not a classical beauty, but a tough, worldly woman who would make a formidable life partner. That describes John Lennon and Yoko Ono as it does Paul McCartney and Linda Eastman. Two men who had been like brothers since school days were falling for almost identical women.

WEIRD VIBES

THE BEATLES AT WAR

Shortly after returning home from India, in May 1968, the Beatles convened at George Harrison's home in Esher to run through 23 new songs that became the basis of their next album, *The Beatles*, better known as the *White Album* (and hereafter referred to as such) because it was packaged in a plain white sleeve. John brought the largest number of songs to the demo session including 'The Continuing Story of Bungalow Bill', 'Dear Prudence', 'Everybody's Got Something to Hide Except Me and My Monkey', 'I'm So Tired', 'Julia', 'Revolution', 'Yer Blues' and 'Sexy Sadie', the last being a swipe at the randy Maharishi. George's contributions were notably 'Piggies' and 'While My Guitar Gently Weeps', while Paul demonstrated 'Back in the USSR', 'Blackbird', 'Honey Pie', 'Junk,' 'Mother Nature's Son', 'Ob-La-Di, Ob-La-Da' and the delightfully silly 'Rocky Raccoon'.

Here then was the backbone of the only double studio album the Beatles recorded, a relative rarity in the music industry at the time, with songs to spare. Moreover, here was a wide range of musical styles, from the country sound of 'Rocky Raccoon' via Paul's Beach Boys-on-the-Volga pastiche ('Back in the USSR') to the experimentation of 'Revolution 9', together with more traditional songs of love and regret, graced by some of the best lyrics the boys ever penned.

The *White Album* is a boldly, unapologetically ambitious and arty record. Gone are the corny songs of Beatlemania. The Beatles were now men making mature, reflective music, the quantity and variety of which sets the *White Album* apart as one of their greatest achievements. This important and welcome musical variety – the variety of a box of Good News chocolates, which George references on another of his songs, 'Savoy Truffle' – is partly a result of the fact the Beatles were no longer a harmonious team. They were increasingly at war with one another, often working individually on their own songs, sniping at each other and at odds with the studio staff who'd served them for years, which had an unexpectedly positive result in that the set-up changed; old faces left, new people and new studios were used. The format was shaken up, the Beatles getting away from making the self-consciously clever albums of the mid-1960s, culminating in *Sgt. Pepper*, allowing themselves instead to spread out and do as they pleased, however wild the music sounded, and indeed the wilder the better. It is when the Beatles seem to go too far that the *White Album* is most interesting.

In a way Yoko Ono is to be thanked for this shake-up in the Beatles' working methods, even if her presence ultimately proved toxic. Having usurped Cynthia and moved into Kenwood, Yoko went everywhere with John nowadays, including attending the opening of the Beatles' new King's Road tailoring shop on 23 May. It soon became clear Yoko was not a docile Beatles partner in the mould of Cyn, Mo and Pattie. Yoko was also unlike Jane Asher, who had a career of her own but was assiduous in not getting mixed up in Paul's work. 'She was great because she didn't interfere with anything, she had her own life to lead,' Measles Bramwell says approvingly. In contrast Yoko interfered constantly.

When the band assembled in Studio Two at EMI to begin their new album, on Thursday 30 May 1968, Paul, George and Ringo were flabbergasted to find Yoko sitting with John, apparently intending to stay there while they recorded. In the past the Beatles hadn't even liked Brian in the studio. Select friends were invited to watch sessions, it was true, and occasionally guests were asked to sing a backing vocal or shake a tambourine at a special event like *Our World*, but the Beatles' day-to-day studio work was, in the union language of the day, a closed shop. Yoko broke the rules. She intruded, sitting with the boys among the mike stands and baffles, and when they began John's 'Revolution', a blues that referenced the revolutions and uprisings sweeping the world, from Mao Tse-tung's Cultural Revolution to the student protests in Paris, Yoko started contributing vocals – one couldn't say *singing* – rather she yelped, moaned and squawked along with her lover.

John then decided he might get a better vocal if he lay down on the floor to sing this strange new song, to which he devoted the following two weeks. Ultimately, there were three versions of 'Revolution', or perhaps better to say variations on the theme: a blues crawl, 'Revolution 1', with *shooby-doo-wah* backing vocals; a faster hard-rock version that would appear on the flip-side of the Beatles' next single; and the radically different 'Revolution 9', a sound collage in the *musique concrete* style; that is music created by combining a variety of recorded sounds, as Stockhausen did in 1956 with *Gesang der Jünglinge*. Although the form had been around for a decade, it was new to rock.

Then John suggested Yoko dub a backing vocal – instead of Paul. McCartney 'gave John a look of disbelief and then walked away in disgust', recalls studio engineer Geoff Emerick, who'd worked on every Beatles album since *Revolver*, but wasn't enjoying this one. Before long, Yoko was in the control room, venting her opinion on what they'd recorded so far. 'Well, it's pretty good,' she told George Martin of one take of 'Revolution', 'but I think it should be played a bit faster.' A line had been crossed. John was allowing this strange little woman, with whom he'd become infatuated, to enter into and meddle with a band that, aside from small disagreements, had hitherto been four friends united against the world. It was a shocking breach of etiquette. 'It just spoiled everything,' laments Tony Bramwell, who blames Yoko ultimately for the break-up of the band. 'Yoko was the acerbation (sic) in the studio that caused the split between all of them. George called her the witch; Ringo hated her; Paul couldn't understand why somebody would bring their wife to work.'* There was some sexism in the attitude to Yoko, even a touch of xenophobia. Unkind remarks were made about 'the Jap'. But one can see why Paul, George and Ringo were irritated. Yoko wasn't a musician, at least not as they were, but the latest flaky character to have taken John's fancy. At the same time, she was a catalyst for change.

When the Beatles were recording, they normally started with a John song, then a Paul song. This time they went straight from 'Revolution' (not that it was finished) to a Ringo song, 'Don't Pass Me By', which showed how strange things had become. Stranger followed. It was unheard of for band members to leave London while an album was in

---

* Though Paul did exactly this later.

production. Yet Paul, George and Ringo now left John and Yoko to fiddle with 'Revolution', and amused themselves elsewhere: George travelling to California to take part in a documentary about Ravi Shankar, Ringo going with him for company; while Paul went up north to be best man at his brother's wedding.

Mike McCartney married his fiancée Angela Fishwick on Saturday 7 June 1968 in North Wales, the service conducted by Buddy Bevan, the relation who'd married Jim and Ange four years earlier. Mike's show business career had taken off in recent months, the Scaffold scoring a novelty hit with 'Thank U Very Much', making Paul's brother a celebrity in his own right under the stage name of Mike McGear. Mike deported himself like an archetypal Sixties' dandy, coming to his wedding in a flamboyant white suit, black shirt and groovy white neckerchief. In contrast, Paul wore a conservative suit and tie to the wedding. Jane was also simply dressed. The couple posed obligingly for pictures with the bride and groom after the service, then everybody went back to Rembrandt to celebrate the union, Paul reading out the congratulatory telegrams. He and Jane seemed happy. 'They could not have been more lovey-dovey and it was in very private circumstances where they didn't have to put anything on for the press,' recalls Tony Barrow, who was present. Yet as soon as he got back to London, Paul took another woman to bed.

When Paul went on American television asking the public to send Apple their ideas, Francie Schwartz was one of those viewers who took the star at his word. A 24-year-old advertising agency worker from New York, Francie bought a plane ticket to London and presented herself at the Apple office with a movie script she wanted produced. She persuaded Tony Bramwell to let her see Paul. 'I only introduced them because she had this strange film idea which I thought would appeal to him,' recalls Bramwell. It wasn't actually that difficult to meet Paul in this way. Unlike his fellow Beatles, Paul came into the Apple office most days, and made the time to listen to at least some of the new ideas that came in. Anybody who was personable and persistent had a chance of having a word with the star. It helped if you were an attractive young woman. In fact, Francie was a rather plain woman, with prematurely grey hair. Yet Paul found her pretty enough. 'Am I impressing you now, with my feet up on this big desk?' he asked, as they flirted in his office.

Nothing happened between them until after Mike's wedding, when Jane had gone back to the Bristol Old Vic. With Jane out of the way, Paul came over to Francie's Chelsea flat, with Martha the dog, and jumped into bed. 'The sheepdog followed us into the bedroom to watch,' Francie wrote In her candid memoir, *Body Count*. She called Paul Mr Plump, for reasons unexplained. Likewise, he called her Clancy. It was clear to Clancy that, despite being engaged to be married, and putting on such a good show at his brother's wedding, Mr Plump and his fiancée were not getting along. Paul seemed to think Jane had a boyfriend in Bristol, and rather than try and win her back he chose to get even with her, allowing Francie to move into Cavendish with him while Jane was away, also getting his new girlfriend a job in the Apple press office. He even invited Francie along to EMI recording sessions – surely a touch of tit for tat. While John and Yoko worked together on 'Revolution 9' in Studio Three at Abbey Road, Paul took Francie next door to watch him record 'Blackbird' in Studio Two. A greater contrast to 'Revolution 9' is hard to imagine than this pretty, guitar-picking tune, the melody based on a Bach bourrée, while the lyric, recorded shortly after the assassination of Dr Martin Luther King Jr, was meant as a metaphor for the American Civil Rights struggle. 'As is often the case with my things, a veiling took place, so, rather than say "Black woman living in Little Rock" and be very specific, she became a bird, became symbolic …'

Paul then left Francie and the difficult *White Album* sessions to go on a business trip to Los Angeles with Apple staff men Ron Kass and Tony Bramwell, plus his school friend Ivan Vaughan. The threesome flew to LA via New York where, in the transit lounge at JFK, Paul called and left a message with Linda Eastman's answering service, saying he was on his way to the West Coast and could be reached at the Beverly Hills Hotel. Arriving in LA several hours later, Paul checked into the pink hotel on Sunset Boulevard, taking Bungalow Number Five, which was favoured by Howard Hughes, then hit the clubs. Word soon got around that Paul was in town. 'He pulled a few slappers [and] by the time we got back to the Beverly Hills Hotel there was queues around the block of girls trying to get in,' says Bramwell.

The next day, after fooling about by the pool with the girls he'd met, Paul went to see Capitol Records chief Alan Livingston, then came back to change before his next engagement. 'And there was Linda!'

recalls Bramwell. 'Sitting on the doorstep.' Having received Paul's message, Linda had taken the first available flight from New York to LA. 'So immediately Paul got me to clear away all the birds, and just locked himself in the room with her.' That night Paul attended to the main bit of business he had come to California for, which was making a personal appearance at a Capitol Records sales convention, screening a promotional movie about Apple, and telling the executives that future Beatles records would appear under the Apple label (though the band still remained tied to EMI). Having played the businessman, Paul returned to Linda at the Beverly Hills Hotel.

At this stage another girlfriend showed up. One of the local calls Paul had made when he arrived in Los Angeles was to actress Peggy Lipton, his bedfellow on two previous trips to LA. Seemingly, he was ringing around to see who was available. Despite the fact Peggy was now living with the record producer Lou Adler, she hopped in her car and sped over to the Beverly Hills Hotel, where she found a number of young women already waiting outside Bungalow Five. Measles told Peggy that Paul was sleeping – it was 4 o'clock in the morning – and that when he got up they were going out on a boat with the film director Mike Nichols. Peggy decided to wait. When Paul emerged from his room at 8:00 a.m., Peggy figured she was on for the boat trip. 'As I gathered my things, preparing to join him, I spotted a woman coming out of the bedroom in Paul's bungalow,' Peggy later wrote. 'Apparently, she had shown up before I arrived, and Paul, in his altered state, had forgotten I was on the way.' Peggy watched tearfully as Paul and Linda Eastman ran for a limousine that took them to the harbour. This was the end of Peggy and Paul.

Paul and Linda spent the day together on Mike Nichols's motorboat, the *Quest*, drinking champagne, eating bacon sandwiches and canoodling like love birds. 'They were absolutely inseparable. It was like instant,' notes Bramwell. 'She was perfect for him: motherly …' (Tony figured Paul had been looking for a mother substitute) '… big-breasted, and she had a *je ne sais quoi*.' Like Paul, Linda was also a dedicated pothead. She'd brought a bag of grass with her, which they dipped into, becoming closer as they got stoned, really close in the way John and Yoko were. 'We were all conscious of – and somewhat amazed by – the depth of feeling Paul obviously had for Linda,' adds Bramwell, noting that when they checked out of the Beverly Hills Hotel the next day Paul and Linda were 'like Siamese twins, holding hands and gazing into each other's eyes all the way to the airport'.

Paul was flying to London, Linda to New York. Before her domestic flight, Linda waited with her lover in the international VIP lounge at LAX. The couple were startled by the sudden arrival of FBI agents. 'We're investigating a bomb scare on the flight to London; do you know anybody who might want to blow up the plane?' an agent asked McCartney.

'It might be a Rolling Stones fan,' Paul joked. More likely a jealous boyfriend or husband. The Beatles always left a trail of cuckolds behind them. The FBI wanted to search their luggage, at which point Linda had the foresight to kick her bag, in which she had her marijuana, under a chair, then sauntered off to the domestic terminal to catch her own flight at the end of what she would later refer to nostalgically as their first 'dirty weekend' together.

When McCartney got home to Cavendish Avenue, he continued his affair with Francie Schwartz, who didn't rate him as a lover. Opining that Paul was basically lonely without Jane, whom he hadn't told about Francie, she wrote in her memoirs:

He had his hang-ups, and I think he felt sometimes that he wasn't manly enough. His body was sweet, and beautiful … one could be happy if one didn't demand too much, or even want too much. The relationship had begun on the "save me" lament, not on a rush of sexual flashes … He hadn't formally dumped Jane and so at first I was a secret. I stayed in the house for weeks, cleaning, reading, calling the dope dealer. I was to score for my old man. You'd think he could have taken care of it, but he didn't.

When Jane telephoned from Bristol 'he would get very uptight, very awkward and phony'. Apart from the sheepdog Martha, there was now a puppy in the house, Eddie, whom Paul had bought for Jane, plus five cats, the beginning of what became a menagerie of domestic animals, few of which seemed house-trained. 'I was constantly cleaning up shit.'

While his domestic life descended into farce, Paul retained enough discipline to go into the EMI studios and Apple office most days, working on the new band album and diverse Apple projects. He liked to be busy. One side-project was creating a theme tune for a television series named *Thingumybob*. Having dreamt up the tune, Paul decided it needed a brass band, so he called upon the Black Dyke Mills Band, the most famous band of its kind in the world, originally comprised of employees of a Yorkshire worsted mill. The band's conductor, Geoffrey Brand, came into Apple to see Paul, whom he found sitting under a Liverpool Institute school photo. Paul pointed out the little boys who were George Harrison, Neil Aspinall, brother Mike McCartney and himself. This trip down memory lane was interrupted by the telephone ringing. 'As soon as he started to talk the phone rang and it was someone from New York who'd been waiting to get to him for days and so he said, "I have to talk to this chap," and we started off again,' recalls Brand, 'and then it was somebody from Tokyo, you know.' Finally, Paul silenced the calls, picked up a guitar and played the tune to *Thingumybob*, humming it as well. Brand made a note on manuscript paper. Paul told him to take the little bit he'd demonstrated and extend it to fill three minutes as a score for the Black Dyke Mills Band. Apple would probably put it out as a record, which meant he needed a B-side. 'I'll tell you what, and this is going to be a hit, we're doing a film called *Yellow Submarine*,' Paul told the conductor. 'Do an arrangement for "Yellow Submarine" as well. We'll put that on the back.'

A recording date for *Thingumybob* was arranged at the Victoria Hall, Saltaire, on Sunday 30 June 1968. Geoffrey Brand checked into the Victoria Hotel in nearby Bradford for the session, and Paul asked him to book an extra room. 'Paul came down to breakfast on the Sunday morning with his dog,' recalls the conductor. 'Martha sat next to Paul at the breakfast table and Paul ordered two cooked breakfasts, one of which he ate and the other he fed to Martha.' To get the sound he wanted on the recording Paul had the brass band perform outside the Victoria Hall, drawing a crowd of children whom he amused by playing a trumpet. When a cornet player asked to check a note, Paul said, 'It's no use asking me, I can't read music.' Paul was at his best at times like this, allowing ordinary people to share in and enjoy his celebrity, whilst his decision to make a record with a brass band, in the middle of the *White Album* sessions, showed how rooted he remained in northern working-class culture.

Back in London, the Beatles were seriously getting on each others' nerves. When he finished 'Revolution 9', John asked Paul's opinion of the record, which is without doubt the most radical piece of music the

Beatles ever released: an uncompromising musical collage, without coherent tune or intelligible lyric. 'Not bad,' replied Paul unenthusiastically.

'Not bad?' snapped Lennon. 'You have no idea what you're talking about … This is the direction the Beatles should be going in from now on!'

Just as John had taken an inordinate amount of time on the various versions of 'Revolution', Paul was now driving everybody spare with 'Ob-La-Di, Ob-La-Da', not one of his best works, and one that John only reluctantly played along with, complaining that it was 'granny music shit'. When, after several days' work, Paul announced that he wanted to start all over again, Lennon walked out of the studio, reappearing at the top of the stairs screaming: 'I AM FUCKING STONED!' He descended, ranting that he fucking knew how the fucking song should fucking well go, sat at the piano and bashed out the now-familiar intro. Still Paul wasn't satisfied, and he decided, when Ritchie was out of the studio, to re-record the drums, which didn't do anything for Ritchie's ego. He was already feeling left out. George Harrison wasn't much happier, and the EMI staff felt demoralised working for bickering, demanding Beatles. Geoff Emerick woke up one morning and realised that, far from being a joy, as it had been, working as the Beatles' engineer was making him depressed. A few nights before, he'd been in the studio very late when the band came back from a club, intending to play through the night, as they liked to do, expecting EMI staff simply to be on hand to accommodate them. Rather than face the Beatles, Emerick hid behind a cupboard.

Now the usually unflappable George Martin got into an argument with Paul over 'Ob-La-Di, Ob-La-Da', as Emerick recalls in his memoir *Here, There and Everywhere*. 'Paul, can you try rephrasing the last line of each verse?' Martin asked from the lofty control room.

'If you think you can do it any better, why don't you fucking come down here and sing it yourself?' Paul retorted.

Gentleman George finally lost his temper. 'Then bloody sing it again!' he shouted down at McCartney. 'I give up. I just don't know any better how to help you.'

The next day Emerick resigned as the Beatles' engineer, refusing to work one more day with them. He was replaced by Ken Scott. George Martin went on three weeks' holiday, leaving his young assistant Chris

Thomas to deal with *the impossible bastards*, as the great producer sometimes called the Beatles under his breath.* On the first day after George's departure, Paul walked into the studio and asked Thomas abruptly what he was doing there, as though nobody had told him Martin was going away. 'George told me to come down, didn't you know?' Thomas asked.

'Oh well, if you want to produce us, fine, and if you don't, we'll just tell you to fuck off,' McCartney replied unpleasantly. Then he strode out. Despite this unpromising start, Chris Thomas stuck with the sessions and made an important contribution to the album, forging a good enough relationship with Paul to work with him deep into his solo career.

The pressure was starting to tell on Paul, who let his frustrations out at Cavendish. 'If he wasn't in a good mood, he'd drink hideous Scotch–Coke combinations, throw food at the dogs and cats, drop his clothes in a path to the bed, and ignore me completely,' Francie Schwartz would write, further claiming that there was a wild, rough-house element to their love-making. Sometimes Paul would grab Francie and pull her into the bath with him; they made love in the open at night on Primrose Hill; and she went down on Paul while he was driving around London, possibly the inspiration for Paul's 'Why Don't We Do It in the Road?' One night, Paul took Francie to a new club, Revolution, then stopped on the way home to pay a house call on another girlfriend, possibly Maggie McGivern, who says she was still seeing Paul at this time. Francie suffered the humiliation of waiting for Mr Plump while he did what he had to do. 'When he returned, about 15 minutes later, I was burning. "Why did you do that? Why the hell couldn't you take me home first?" "I don't know," he answered, and I could tell he was a little sick inside about it, too.'

One morning, Paul and Francie were in bed together at Cavendish when there was a knock at the bedroom door. 'Who is it?' asked Paul, for there were always friends floating around the house.

'Jane,' replied his fiancée, who had returned to London to appear in a play.

Paul leapt out of bed, put on some clothes, and led Jane downstairs and into the garden. Francie came to the window to watch them. Paul

---

* Martin once told NEMS employee Geoffrey Ellis: 'Sometimes when a reporter asks me for a quote on what the Beatles are really like, I'm tempted to answer: "they're the same stupid, arrogant bastards they always were".'

Top. Born in 1942, Paul (left) around the age of seven, with his mother Mary and younger brother Michael, born in 1944.

Bottom (right). In the mid-1950s the McCartneys moved to 20 Forthlin Road in the Liverpool suburb of Allerton, a council or 'corpy' house where the family was very happy until Paul's mother fell ill with cancer.

Bottom (left). Paul was nine when he posed for this school picture. He remains recognisable as the confident, happy child he was at Joseph Williams Primary School in Liverpool.

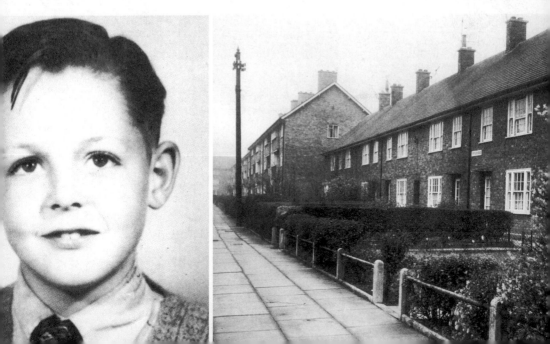

Top. John Lennon (centre) aged 16 with his school skiffle band, the Quarry Men, playing at St Peter's Church Fête, Woolton, on 6 July 1957, the day he met Paul McCartney.

Bottom (left). This fascinating 1959 picture shows Paul and John as teenagers performing together at the Casbah, a youth club set up by Liverpool housewife Mona Best in the basement of her home. Her son Pete became the Beatles' drummer.

Bottom (right). In 1960 the Beatles went to Hamburg, Germany, where they met new friends including Astrid Kirchherr, who took this iconic photograph of the band's first line-up. Left to right are Pete Best, George Harrison, John Lennon, Paul McCartney and Stuart Sutcliffe.

Top. The Beatles playing the Cavern, Liverpool, February 1961, between their first and second trip to Hamburg.

Bottom (left). Although he had a girlfriend at home, Paul spent much of his time in Hamburg with German barmaid Ruth Lallemann.

Bottom (right). A fussy young man with little experience of show business, Brian Epstein was running the family record shop in Liverpool when he became the Beatles' manager.

Top (left). In 1962 the Beatles, with their new drummer Ringo Starr, began recording with George Martin at EMI in London. Paul learned to trust the producer, whom he remained close to into his solo career.

Top (right). In the early days the Beatles were part of mainstream light entertainment, obliged to act the fool on TV and on stage. Here they are dressed up for the first of two runs of Beatles Christmas shows, London, December 1963.

Bottom. The Beatles' first visit to the United States was a sensation. Here they are on the *Ed Sullivan Show*, February 1964.

Top (left). The Beatles' first feature film, *A Hard Day's Night* (1964), was their best, with all the band members acquitting themselves reasonably well on screen. Here McCartney is seen with actor Wilfrid Brambell, who played his grandfather.

Top (right). Paul met the teenage actress Jane Asher in 1963. By 1965, when this picture was taken, he was lodging with her wealthy and sophisticated family in London's Wimpole Street.

Bottom. The Beatles at Shea Stadium, New York, on 15 August 1965. The band was playing the first ever stadium rock concert to an audience of 55,600 people.

Top (left). Paul and Jane Asher had an open relationship, with Paul seeing other women, including Maggie McGivern, who worked as a nanny for Marianne Faithfull. Paul is seen here in 1966 with Maggie as he accepts a light from mutual friend Barry Miles.

Top (right). Another attractive young woman linked with Paul was Marijke Koger of the hippie art group the Fool, which created the genie mural for the Apple shop.

Bottom (left). Paul is seen here with his father Jim outside the star's new London home, 7 Cavendish Avenue, a short walk from EMI's Abbey Road studios.

Bottom (right). Paul and Linda Eastman gaze into each other's eyes at a press reception for *Sgt. Pepper's Lonely Hearts Club Band* at Brian Epstein's London home, May 1967.

Top. The Beatles' concert on the roof of the Apple building on 30 January 1969 was their last public performance. Apple executive Peter Brown is seen (with beard) between Paul and John.

Bottom (left). Paul married Linda Eastman at Marylebone Register Office, London, on 12 March 1969, just before the Beatles recorded their last LP. It was to be a very successful marriage.

Bottom (right). As the Beatles fell apart, Paul and Linda retreated to their remote Scottish farm, High Park. They are seen here on the property in 1971, with their pet dog Martha.

Top. Visitors to Paul and Linda's Scottish farm were often surprised by how small and basic it was – just a little stone house with an iron roof. The location was, however, private and beautiful, with an ancient standing stone directly in front of the cottage.

Bottom (left). In 1971, Paul launched his new band, Wings, featuring (clockwise from top) guitarists Denny Laine and Henry McCullough, Paul and Linda and drummer Denny Seiwell.

Bottom (right). Paul and Linda bought Waterfall, a rotunda hidden in woodland near the village of Peasmarsh, East Sussex, as a second country retreat in 1973. They subsequently made the house their principal home.

yelled at Francie to get back inside. Then Jane left. A little later, Margaret Asher came to Cavendish and boxed up her daughter's belongings, leaving a note for Paul. The boy she had given a home to when he came down from Liverpool, fed and looked after as a mother would, had let her daughter down.

A couple of days after this the Beatles attended the London première of the *Yellow Submarine* film, which had turned out better than expected. Although the Beatles had little to do with the project, Heinz Edelmann and the TVC animators had captured the character of the band, their style and wit, as well as the feel of swinging London in exuberant Pop Art images that were attractive and amusing. The film was capped by a brief personal appearance by the boys introducing the final number, Paul's 'All Together Now', which proved a perfect ending. The première audience laughed and clapped and sang along, endorsing *Yellow Submarine* as an instant classic.

Beatles partners accompanied the boys to the *Yellow Submarine* première, including Yoko Ono, but there was no sign of Jane Asher on the red carpet. The reason emerged a few days later when, on Saturday 21 July, the actress appeared on Simon Dee's BBC television show and told the presenter her engagement was off. 'Did you break it off?' Dee asked.

'I haven't broken it off, but it's finished,' Jane replied firmly, which was all she had to say on the matter, then and ever more.

The announcement caught almost everybody by surprise. 'It just seemed such a mistake!' laments Jann Haworth. 'What little I knew of them, it looked right, and they were really cut out to be together, and it seemed a real shame.' Taking a more masculine view, Tony Bramwell figured Paul simply got caught out. 'He was caught with his pants down with the horrible Francie. *Brrr*,' he shudders at the memory of the American, whom he did not like. 'She was horrible.' For his part, Paul seemed surprised by Jane's public announcement, which made him look foolish. He and Francie drove to Rembrandt, where he was obliged to face the press before retreating inside Dad's house in what his girlfriend terms 'a poisonous mood'.

Having vacated Kenwood in favour of Cynthia and Julian, John and Yoko moved into Cavendish with Paul and Francie. By Francie's account, she, John and Yoko got into the habit of watching TV in the evening while they ate opium cookies. Meanwhile, Paul continued to race between home, office, recording studio and night clubs, attending to band business and Apple projects. One morning, when John was going through his mail at Cavendish, he found a postcard addressed to him with the message, 'You and your Jap tart think you're hot shit.' Paul admitted he'd sent the card for a joke. He had a strange habit of sending anonymous postcards, another of his victims being Derek Taylor, who ran the Apple press office with more profligacy than Paul liked. The card to John and Yoko may have been meant as a joke, but it made for an awkward atmosphere in the house. 'It was embarrassing. The three of us swivelled around, staring at him. You could feel the pain in John,' Schwartz wrote of the moment Paul admitted to sending it. Not long afterwards, John and Yoko moved out of the house and into Ritchie's flat in Montagu Square, both drifting into heavier drug use, ultimately heroin, which further altered John's mood and appearance. Behind his pebbled spectacles, Lennon's face paled and seemingly attenuated, making his bony nose more prominent. The chameleon Beatle started to resemble Yoko's twin brother.

At this stage, Francie was given her marching orders from Cavendish. Her relationship with Paul had never been smooth. Friends recall McCartney throwing her out at least once before the final split, literally throwing her bag out the door on one occasion. Finally, she gave up and booked a ticket home to the United States. 'Don't cry. I'm a cunt,' McCartney told her, in their not-so-romantic farewell. At least one member of the Beatles organisation believes Paul used Francie as an excuse to end his relationship with Jane.

'I think [Schwartz] thought there was a lot of love on his side for her, and there was none whatsoever that I could detect. He used her entirely. I'm not saying that he didn't get on with her physically, that it was a good extended one-night stand, but I don't think in Paul's mind it was ever more than that,' says Tony Barrow, who is also of the opinion that Jane took her break-up with Paul in her stride. 'I think she had realised by then that he was not going to marry her, simply because she was determined not to give up the theatre, and he was determined that she should.'

While this is an interesting hypothesis it is hard to believe that a relationship that had lasted more than five years, one both partners expected to lead to marriage, should have come undone without hurt and regret on both sides. Also, Jane's subsequent studied silence on the matter can be interpreted as an indication of how bruised she was by the ending of her engagement to Paul, messy and public as it had been.

HEY JUDE

Having taken up with Yoko Ono, John Lennon now demanded as expeditious a divorce as possible from his wife, relegating Cynthia and their son Julian to his past. He would see little of the boy in the years ahead.

Although Cyn had been part of the Beatles' inner circle since the beginning of their great adventure – on the scene before Paul met Jane, Ritchie married Maureen, or George wed Pattie – she now fell into a state of purdah. Beatles people were scared of talking to Cyn lest it offend John. In fact, virtually the only member of the Beatles family who bothered to contact her after the break-up was Paul. To his credit, McCartney drove over to Kenwood to tell Cyn how sorry he was about the way John had treated her. Paul had hardly behaved better with Jane, and Cynthia believes Paul felt bad about that. 'Paul blamed himself and was heartbroken,' she later wrote, contradicting Tony Barrow's impression that Paul wasn't unduly bothered by the recent break-up with his fiancée. Paul may well have been more honest with an old friend like Cynthia than a male employee.

It was Paul's habit to dream up songs on the drive to Kenwood, for this is where he and John met to write in the old days, and although the circumstances were very different as he drove to console Cyn, the act of making the journey engendered a song, intended to cheer up five-year-old Julian Lennon. 'I started with the idea "Hey Jules", which was Julian, "don't make it bad, take a sad song and make it better." Hey, try and deal with this terrible thing. I knew it was not going to be easy for him,' Paul explained. 'I always feel sorry for kids in divorces ... their little brain spinning round in confusion, going "Did *I* do this? Was it me?"' He later changed the title to 'Hey Jude' because it was more euphonious. Paul perfected the song at Cavendish while John and Yoko were visiting, John interpreting the lyric egocentrically to mean that Paul *approved* of his relationship with Yoko, that 'go and get her' meant he should leave Cyn for Yoko. Paul muttered that the words weren't right yet. He needed to fix the dummy line, 'The movement you need is on your shoulder'. John insisted he keep it and, though it doesn't make sense, it has become so familiar we don't question it.

The Beatles recorded 'Hey Jude' at Trident, a small Soho studio the band was using, partly because it had an eight-track system, whereas EMI was behind the times with four-track. 'Hey Jude' was meant from the outset to be a single, rather than a *White Album* track, and it was an unusual single in several ways, not least because it was over seven minutes long at a time when most pop songs were under three. The song started quietly. Paul sang the first word 'Hey …' before a note had been struck, hitting the first F chord on the grand piano on the 'Jude', then accompanied himself through the first verse, joined by the others – George strumming guitar and harmonising with John; Ringo tapping a tambourine – from the middle of the second verse, after which Ringo's drums came in and the song began to build. 'Remember to let her under your skin/Then you begin to make it better,' Paul sang, reaching the point where most singles end. Instead, he repeated the last word with increasing excitement, Little Richard-style: 'Better, better, better, better BETTER, BETTER, BETTER …' Finally screaming: '*WHAAARRRR!*' This began the impassioned four-minute coda, the Beatles rocking out over a 36-piece orchestra as John and George repeated the Zen-like *Na na na na-na-na nas*. Seldom has such a simple refrain sounded so powerful.

While they were recording the song, the Apple Shop shut. It had failed to live up to the Beatles' vision, the freeholder doing little to help by insisting they paint over the Fool's genie mural, which was a grievous loss to Baker Street. 'The Beatles are tired of being shopkeepers,' Paul told the press. The band took away what items of stock they wanted, then let the public grab what was left for free. Before Francie Schwartz went home to the USA, she and Paul daubed 'REVOLUTION' and 'HEY JUDE' on the whitewashed windows of the abandoned building, as publicity for the new single. Unfortunately, this read like anti-Semitic graffiti to local Jewish residents (Jude being German for Jew), who reacted furiously, one man throwing a soda siphon at the shop.

More professionally, the Beatles hired Michael Lindsay-Hogg to shoot a promotional film for 'Hey Jude' at Twickenham. Talking with Paul, the director came up with the idea of surrounding the band with a small audience, who would sing along with the Beatles miming their own song. 'We probably did, I think, five or six takes on "Hey Jude" and between the takes [the] Beatles were sort of standing on their rostrum and they were surrounded by 100 people and they did what they knew how to do when they had people round them,' says Lindsay-Hogg. 'This was the first time they'd ever played to any kind of audience since they'd stopped touring in 1966, and at first they were doing it rather listlessly because they thought they had to do something … then they sort of got into it, and they kind of liked it.' The promo was first shown in the UK on David Frost's Sunday night television show, then around the world, helping launch what became the Beatles' biggest-selling single: number one in the UK for two weeks and number one in the USA for an astounding nine weeks, sales soon topping five million copies. This was all the more impressive when one remembers that the Beatles weren't touring in support of the record and had only recently suffered a major critical failure with *Magical Mystery Tour*.

'Hey Jude' was the first Beatles record released by Apple, though it was actually still a Parlophone disc in the UK, Capitol in the US, with the Apple logo attached. The corporation had new offices now, an eighteenth-century townhouse at 3 Savile Row, on the border of Mayfair and Piccadilly, next door to the tailors Gieves & Hawkes. This was a fine address in a classy part of Central London, showing how high the boys had risen in the world in the few years since Neil transported them from Liverpool in a van. It was typical of the Beatles to be so public about their place of business, very much putting themselves on show at Savile Row. Press and fans gathered daily outside No. 3, taking pictures and asking questions. There was only one main entrance (together with steps down to the basement, below the front door) so the Beatles couldn't dodge their visitors. If they hated the attention, they bought the wrong house, and indeed one can only conclude that the boys liked being on display in this way. Paul in particular seemed to enjoy being recognised.

The Beatles brought a large entourage with them to Savile Row: employees, mates, and weird and wonderful hangers-on. Along with the ridiculous Magic Alex, there was Caleb the I-Ching thrower, whose prognostications could make or break an Apple deal; and a House Hippie, American Richard DiLello, who actually had a fairly responsible job in the press office. One of the House Hippie's tasks was to deliver presentation sets of the first four Apple releases – 'Hey Jude', 'Those Were the Days', 'Thingumybob', and a Jackie Lomax song – to 10 Downing Street, Buckingham Palace and the Queen Mother's residence.

Everybody was delighted when the Queen Mum's lady-in-waiting wrote back thanking the Beatles for the gift, saying how much HRH had enjoyed their discs. What the Queen herself made of this gift might be surmised from a remark Her Majesty made to EMI chairman Sir Joseph Lockwood around this time: 'The Beatles are turning awfully funny, aren't they?' It was hard for Sir Joe to gainsay Her Majesty, grappling as he was with a request from John that EMI distribute an album he and Yoko had made named *Unfinished Music Number 1: Two Virgins*. As a record, it was almost unlistenable to, but what was most shocking was that Lennon wanted EMI to distribute the disc in a sleeve that featured full-length nude photos of himself and Yoko – cock, tits, bum, pubic hair and all. 'What on Earth do you want to do it for?' Sir Joe asked.

'It's art,' replied Yoko.

'In that case,' said the chairman, 'why not show Paul in the nude? He's so much better looking.'

Meanwhile, the Beatles were causing chaos in the hallowed EMI Studios, where Sir Thomas Beecham and Sir Edward Elgar had made beautiful music, John screaming that he was suicidal and wanted to die on 'Yer Blues'; Paul shrieking back at him on 'Helter Skelter'; George singing about pigs, complete with porcine noises. There was, as George himself would say, 'a weird vibe'. Then Ritchie quit.

'Now Ringo's gone, what are we gonna do?' John Lennon's cartoon character asks in *Yellow Submarine* after Ringo ejects himself from the sub.

'Learn to sing trios,' suggests Old Fred.

'No, let's save the poor devil,' says Paul's character.

In reality, Paul had been partly responsible for driving their drummer to resignation. Dating back to Quarry Men days, Paul had an unfortunate habit of telling his drummers what to play, and he was quite capable of having a bash himself if they didn't oblige, which pissed Ritchie off. 'Every time I went for a cup of tea, he was on the drums!'

Ritchie went round the band telling his friends individually that he was leaving, because he didn't feel he was playing well, and he felt out of things, whereas 'you three are really close'. John replied that he thought it was the other three who were close. Paul said the same, while George had always been justified in feeling ignored by Paul and John. In short, all four Beatles now felt isolated and miserable. It didn't stop them continuing work on the *White Album* in Ringo's absence, Paul playing the drums again on 'Back in the USSR', on the version we hear to this day. Ringo returned shortly thereafter, welcomed back warmly, with flowers arranged around his kit, but the Rubicon had been crossed: a Beatle had left the band.

When Paul came home from these fraught sessions he found Cavendish in chaos. His beautiful green velvet sofa was covered in dog hair; there was dog crap on the carpets; rancid milk and a rind of cheese were all that was to be found in the fridge; unwashed wine glasses, plates and dirty ashtrays littered the living room; his dope stash had been plundered; his expensive gadgets were nearly all broken, his colour TV, the hi-fi and electric curtains were on the fritz; ligger friends camped out his spare rooms; women fought like cats for a place in his grubby bed. When Barry Miles visited, he found several semi-clad chicks in residence. It was all too much, and yet not enough. So Paul reached out to the one woman who had made sense to him in recent months.

Linda Eastman was in California on assignment with her journalist friend Danny Fields when Paul called and invited her to London. She couldn't come to England immediately. Work commitments took her to San Francisco first, where she photographed the Grateful Dead and Jefferson Airplane. As in the past, Linda ended up in bed with one of the musicians, this time Paul's acquaintance Marty Balin, only she wouldn't put out. He recalls:

> She was a foxy chick, and all of us were trying to make it with her and get close to her and everything. Somehow she ended up with me sleeping the night where I was, at my pad, but she left her bra and her panties on, you know, and I was making my moves, and she just turned me down. She says, 'I'm going to be with the biggest guy in the world.' And then later she married Paul McCartney. She knew what she was headed for … She told me flat out – she had her sights set on somebody and that was that.

From Lee Eastman's point of view, his daughter was now all but a lost cause. First Linda left Mel See to set up in New York as a rock photographer, a course of action Daddy disapproved of. In recent months she had at least managed to get her daughter into Dalton, a good private school in Manhattan, yet no sooner was this arranged than Linda was running off to London after another long-haired boyfriend. With maturity, Linda came to see Daddy's point of view. 'I remember Heather was just going to start Dalton and my [father was] so furious with me. She got into Dalton. It would have been great. It was really good for Heather; I wish she had had that kind of life, instead of this crazy life,' Linda reflected with some sadness towards the end of her own life. 'But I had no feeling of responsibility, I must have been quite irresponsible to think that a five-year-old kid is starting school for the first time, and I'm buzzing off leaving her.' Finding somebody to look after Heather in New York, Linda came to London to discover her number one rock star boyfriend living in bachelor squalor at 7 Cavendish Avenue. Paul was not home when she arrived at the house. He was round the corner at EMI with the boys recording 'Happiness is a Warm Gun'. Linda went over to Abbey Road and took pictures of the band working. It was late September 1968, almost the end of the Beatles, but the beginning of Paul and Linda's life together.

WEDDING BELLS

PAUL, LINDA AND HEATHER

The Beatles finished the *White Album* with a marathon 24-hour recording session in mid-October 1968. Despite all the problems, there had been a degree of cooperation on the album between John and Paul, both of whom had gone against type in some of the music they had made. Both had contributed challenging songs to the LP (Paul's 'Helter Skelter' for example) as well as gentler, introspective work (John's 'Julia'), but probably only Paul could have come up with 'Honey Pie', a pastiche of the tea dance tunes Jim Mac's Jazz Band played in the Twenties; and a love song to his dog, 'Martha My Dear'. Both are clever and funny, as well as being in keeping with the chocolate assortment nature of the *White Album*. However, 'I Will' exemplified Paul's weakness for the soft-centred love song. The melody was catchy, but the lyric, about loving his beloved forever and ever, etc., was the sickliest cliché, a taste of what was to come.

After the record was finished, John and Yoko were busted for cannabis possession at Montagu Square by the relentless DS Pilcher and his sniffer dog Yogi.* Charges against Yoko were dropped when John pleaded guilty, receiving a fine. Meanwhile, Paul travelled to New York with Linda to meet her daughter.

One night before the New York trip, when Linda was speaking on the phone to Heather, she passed the receiver to Paul, who suggested

---

* Not, alas, a witty policeman's reference to the Maharishi, but to Hanna-Barbera's cartoon bear. A companion dog was named Boo Boo.

to the little girl (now coming up for six) that he might marry Mummy. Asking girls to marry them was something the Beatles had always done as a chat-up line, but this time Paul was sincere. He had enjoyed spending time with Linda in Beverly Hills and London. The couple formed a tight unit that mirrored John and Yoko. Apart from being his lover, Linda also had the makings of a steadfast lieutenant in the Beatles Wars. 'She watched his back,' Peter Brown comments. 'She was very, very vigilant in watching his back, totally and utterly loyal, and looked after his needs domestically and in every other way ...' Another quality Paul appreciated was that, having come from money, Linda didn't seem interested in his wealth. She preferred a simple life, as he did to a degree. So when Paul and Linda came to New York they didn't check into a deluxe hotel, but stayed at Linda's apartment on East 83rd Street, exploring the city by walking around and riding the subways like any other couple.

To help him get about unrecognised, Paul bought an old coat from a thrift shop and let his beard grow, giving him a Fenian look. Thus disguised, he went to Harlem with Linda to see shows at the Apollo Theater and generally mooched about the city, an experience very different from his previous visits to New York. Anything Paul wanted to do seemed possible with Linda, or Lin as he called her affectionately. She had bucket-loads of American confidence, which he liked. Both were relaxed and open about sex. They told each other everything about their past (and there was a lot to tell!). Lin dug rock 'n' roll in a way Jane never had, and unlike Jane this American girl wasn't uptight about drugs. Although a modern, liberated woman in some ways, Lin wasn't a committed careerist. She was already tired of scratching a living as a rock 'n' roll photographer, more than ready to settle down with a man who could look after her and Heather. She would happily allow Paul to take the traditional masculine role, which seemed like the natural order to a young man who, despite his sophisticated life, was a product of England's conservative northern working-class. Conversely, there was a hippie chick, go-with-the-flow looseness about Lin that Paul dug, exemplified when they were out walking with Heather and Lin said she had to do an errand on her own, but Heather could lead Paul back to the apartment if he got her to the 86th Street subway. So Paul let the little girl take him home. It was such a relaxed and pleasant journey – so different to his normal life – that he found himself singing a happy tune as he walked with the child to the apartment, a tune that became 'You Never Give Me Your Money'.

When Linda took Paul to meet her father at his apartment on Park Avenue, Lee Eastman didn't go out of his way to make friends with the new boyfriend. It was his method to challenge new people, to see what they were made of, and Paul seemed intimidated at first. 'Paul was scared to death of him,' states Linda's stepbrother Philip Sprayregen, whose mother Monique had become Lee's second wife. 'When my father got mad, his face would turn red … It was very intimidating to behold.' When Lee spoke condescendingly to Lin at dinner, however, Paul defended his girlfriend stoutly, took her by the hand and led her out of the apartment. It was a demonstration that he wasn't to be pushed any further, and he and Lee got along better after this.

Aside from her family and her rock 'n' roll contacts, Linda's New York circle was mostly comprised of journalists like Danny Fields, now a publicist at Elektra Records. Her other closest pals were Lillian Roxon, New York correspondent for the *Sydney Morning Herald*, and Blair Sabol, who wrote for the *Village Voice*. Although Linda had told Danny she was going to London to see Paul, now they were back in New York as a couple Paul and Linda didn't call her friends. It seems they had decided that Lin would have to drop the journalists, for fear they might write about them. It was 18 months before Blair, Danny and Lillian heard from Linda again, at which point Danny and Linda did resume their friendship, but Linda never smoothed over the rift with Blair and Lillian, who were terribly offended at being dropped in this way. Lillian died, still embittered against Linda, in 1973. Fields: 'Linda said to me the biggest regret of her life was not making up with Lillian.'

Clearly Paul and Linda were a couple heading for marriage. Passing a door in New York's Chinatown Paul saw a sign advertising that Buddhist weddings were conducted within. 'C'mon, let's go and get married,' he said. Linda declined, explaining that her failed marriage to Mel See was too recent for her to want to marry again in a hurry. This would seem to contradict stories told by the likes of Nat Weiss that Linda was set on marrying Paul from the start, and it has been used by Paul and Linda as such a defence. But perhaps she was just too canny to rush into a 'Buddhist wedding' of dubious legality; better to bide her time and do it properly. If Paul had asked her once to marry him, he would ask again. In any event, Paul and Linda were solid enough to take

Heather with them when they returned to England at the end of October 1968.

Adjusting to life in the UK did not prove easy for Linda's daughter. Having suffered the break-up of her parents when she was a toddler, and had the disorientating experience of being taken to live in New York, where Mom had an ever-changing cast of boyfriends, Heather was now relocated to a foreign country where the people, contrary to the reputation the British enjoy for good manners, were beastly towards her. The big girls who stood outside Paul's house were the worst, giving Heather and her Mommy filthy looks when they passed and writing words on the gate that Heather, thankfully, couldn't read. Children her own age weren't much nicer. Placed in Robinsfield Infants, a private school in St John's Wood, Heather was picked on for being different, that is to say American. Nobody wanted to be her friend. Paul suggested Heather sit quietly reading a book, and kids would come over to her out of curiosity. She told Paul sadly that she'd tried that and it didn't work. 'I don't think she made too many friends there,' Paul has said. 'She wasn't desperate or anything, she was just a little sad because [she's] very friendly.'

At the same time, Heather's new 'Daddy' received all this attention. 'It was so extreme. A [six]-year-old can't comprehend fame and I had no concept of Paul's world,' she would say in adult life. After the period when kids shunned Heather came a second phase when schoolmates took an interest in her because of who 'Daddy' was. 'From a child's point of view it was hard to understand.' Indeed, being brought up in Paul's shadow would blight Heather's life, which proved a troubled one with a *leitmotif* of pathos. There was a good side to having Paul as Dad; Paul liked children and was a thoughtful, attentive, funny and energetic father-figure. He lived in a cool house, what appeared to an American child as a beautiful English doll's house, for 7 Cavendish Avenue had that classic, symmetrical look. It was full of interesting things, with a large walled garden, and plenty of pets to play with. Heather was as soppy about animals as Mommy was. In addition, there was the farm in Scotland.

Paul took Linda and Heather to Kintyre as soon as possible, and mother and daughter fell in love with the place. Different though it was from Arizona, here was another wild empty landscape in which Linda could ride for miles. Paul and Heather both took up horse-riding and rode with her, developing a good seat. Linda found the light conducive for taking photographs; while, perhaps best of all, she and Paul and Heather could be alone together away from the press, the fans and the other Beatles. Admittedly, the steading was in a poor condition. Paul liked High Park tumbledown. Linda persuaded him to make some elementary home improvements: they bought bits of furniture in Campbeltown; Paul made a sofa from old packing crates, naming it *Sharp's Express* after wording stencilled on the side; they laid a new floor; and Linda ran up simple plaid curtains. The cottage was suddenly much more welcoming. After a long walk through the heather, or along nearby Westport Beach, there were long, deliciously quiet family evenings in front of the log fire. When Linda mentioned that she wanted to stop using the Pill, Paul agreed and she fell pregnant. Marriage was inevitable now, and Paul felt ready. One day Lin said, 'You know, I could make you a great home.' It was exactly what he wanted to hear.

THE BEATLES' WINTER OF DISCONTENT

One of the important points to make about the Beatles' mature period is that their albums were complete works of art, what Richard Wagner called *Gesamtkunstwerk*, music and lyrics complemented by visual presentation. Since *Sgt. Pepper*, Paul had come up with the essential concept for the album covers, working with first-class people to realise his ideas. Having employed Peter Blake and his wife Jann on *Sgt. Pepper*, Paul now turned to another significant British artist, Richard Hamilton, considered the founder of Pop Art, which he defined in 1957 as being popular, transient, expendable, low-cost, mass produced, young, witty, sexy, gimmicky, glamorous and big business. Which summed up album-cover design perfectly.

Paul's art dealer Robert Fraser brought Hamilton and the Beatles together, setting up a meeting at Savile Row. Inevitably Paul kept his visitor waiting, and as Hamilton sat watching the beautiful people flounce by he became bored and irritated. By the time he was admitted to Paul's presence, Hamilton was really disgruntled. 'So when he said that they wanted me to do the cover of this album they were working on,

I said, "Why don't you do it yourself?"' Hamilton recalled to the author Michael Bracewell.

'Come on, haven't you got any ideas?' Paul asked.

'Well, my best idea is to leave a white cover,' replied Hamilton. He hadn't intended to do a white cover when he came to the meeting. The notion occurred to him on the spur of the moment, almost as a put-down to Paul in response to being kept waiting and all the nonsense he saw surrounding the Beatles. To Hamilton's surprise, Paul agreed.

As to an album title, the band had debated several names, including *A Doll's House*, after Ibsen. Hamilton said that if they were going for simplicity they should call it *The Beatles*. Surprisingly, neither EMI nor Capitol had released an LP under that most elementary of titles, so *The Beatles* it was, and Hamilton set to work on his now-famous, absolutely simple, white gatefold sleeve, stamped with a blind impression of the title and initially a number. Like a limited edition art print, every copy of the album would in theory be numbered, the Beatles themselves getting numbers one to four. To give their fans something to look at, colour headshots of each band member would be slipped inside the sleeve together with a fold-out lyric sheet on the reverse of which was a collage poster. In response to a request from Hamilton, Paul collected snapshots from John, George, Ritchie and Linda – including a picture of Paul in his bath at Cavendish – then watched the artist assemble the items for the poster.

The album was a nightmare as far as sales reps were concerned. Shoppers searching through the shop racks for the new Beatles LP would not see the band's picture on the cover, nor could they easily make out the band name, while the idea of naming the Beatles' ninth (regular UK) album *The Beatles*, as if it were their first, was absurd. The music was also challenging in places. George Martin was of the opinion that the boys should have distilled one album from the 30 songs they recorded, instead of releasing a double album, but for once he was surely wrong. The capaciousness of the *White Album* is one of its strengths, allowing the Beatles to demonstrate their range. If 'Revolution 9' wasn't to your taste, there were plenty of other accessible and pretty tunes to listen to: the likes of 'Back in the USSR', 'Blackbird' and 'Julia'. In any event, despite its arty look, double album price and difficult tracks, the *White Album* sold sensationally well, going to number one in the UK and US, becoming an album that is rediscov-ered generation after generation, one of their best-selling albums ever in the USA.*

In some ways the often spiky and confrontational *White Album* seems more of a John album that a Paul record. Yet without Paul's major contributions – the top three being 'Back in the USSR', 'Blackbird' and 'Helter Skelter' – it would not have become the classic it is. Paul clearly still possessed a Midas touch, with the Beatles and outside projects, such as when he helped the Bonzo Dog Doo Dah Band.

'Viv [Stanshall] was down the Speakeasy with Paul. I think they used to drop into the personas of country gents, sort of thing, "Another one, dear boy?" "I don't mind if I do",' recalls Bonzo member Neil Innes, explaining how Paul came to help the band record their one top ten hit. 'Viv was saying, "We've got to do this bloody single, but the producer won't give us time to do anything." So Paul said, "Well, I'll come and produce it."' The Bonzos were working at Chappell Studio in Bond Street on a song titled 'I'm the Urban Spaceman', which Paul effort-lessly transformed into *Top of the Pops* material in one session. 'I'd like to go on record as saying the record would have been nothing like [as successful] without Paul's touch,' says Innes.

Larry was sort of doing on the drums *a-boom-chick, boom-chick, boom-chick*, and Paul said, 'Yeah, that's all right, we'll do it like that, but give it a *boom-dat-boom boom bap* with the *boom-chick, boom-chick*,' which gave it a feel. Then he snatches up Viv's ukulele and starts leaning into the microphone, Nashville-style, to fade it, live fade and fade out, *rinky-dinky-dinky-dinky-dinky-dink*, and the whole thing is taking off. And it's totally down to Paul.

As they were working, the wife of the band's manager sidled up to Paul and asked, 'What's that you've got there – a poor man's violin?'

'No, it's a rich man's ukulele,' McCartney rejoined, showing his quick wit.

* The Recording Industry Association of America (RIAA) lists the *White Album* offi-cially as the band's best-selling US album with 19 million sales, but the RIAA counts each disc as a sale, meaning this double album has actually sold 9.5 million units in the USA. *Abbey Road* and *Sgt. Pepper* have both sold more.

'I'm the Urban Spaceman', produced by Apollo C. Vermouth (contrarily, the Bonzos didn't want to advertise the fact Paul had produced it), went to number five in the UK in November 1968. Paul's brother Mike, and his mates in the Scaffold, were at number one at the time with another nonsense song, 'Lily the Pink'. It was the Christmas number one.

Before celebrating the holidays, Paul flew to Portugal with Linda and Heather to visit Hunter Davies, whose authorised Beatles biography had recently been published. Davies owned a holiday villa on the Algarve, where Paul and Linda and Heather stayed for ten days, during which time, despite some 'frosty moments' between them, as Davies observed, the couple decided to marry. Lin was after all carrying Paul's child, which meant wedding bells where he came from, and once Paul had made up his mind he enjoyed the ritual of phoning Lee Eastman in New York to formally ask his permission, which the patriarch granted, having adjusted his view of Paul for the better in the short time he'd known him. His daughter's marriage to the Beatle would become a business union between McCartney and Eastman & Eastman, which would advise and guide Paul to their lasting mutual benefit. As a result, Lee's relationship with Linda was transformed. 'She became the star of the family,' says Philip Sprayregen.

Despite Paul and Linda's happy news, Christmas 1968 wore a grim aspect. On 15 December, the Beatles' lawyer David Jacobs, who'd suffered a nervous breakdown in recent weeks, apparently caused by financial worries, hanged himself at his Sussex home. The death and inquest generated lurid publicity. Then the Hell's Angels roared into town. George Harrison was to blame. Having met members of the San Francisco chapter of the biker gang in California, he had foolishly invited them to look in at Apple if they were passing through London, never thinking they would. Now came news that they were on their way. George sent a memo to staff. 'They may look as though they are going to do you in,' he wrote worryingly, 'but are very straight and do good things, so don't fear and up-tight them.' Shortly thereafter two terrifying characters, Billy Tumbleweed and Frisco Pete, rumbled down Savile Row on their Harleys, having had the hogs flown to London at great expense (to the Beatles), and proceeded to occupy the band's elegant townhouse for the holidays.

The Angels were in time for the Apple Christmas party, a lavish affair arranged primarily for the benefit of Beatles' children. The highlight was a luncheon featuring what was claimed to be the Largest Turkey in England. This monster took a very long time to cook, testing Frisco Pete's patience. When the bird was finally borne into the dining room the famished Angel fell on it, tearing the carcass apart with his bare hands, appalling the Beatles people gathered. In years gone by, the Beatles had sent out fun Christmas records wishing their fans a Merry Crimbo (sic) and a Happy New Year. This year Mr and Mrs Christmas – as John and Yoko were at the Xmas party – had attempted to put out an avant-garde recording that incorporated the dying heartbeat of their baby, which John had recorded in the womb using a stethoscope just before Yoko miscarried in October.* While all this madness was going on, a thief managed to slip into the building and strip the lead off the roof.

The Beatles' winter of discontent, as George Harrison described it, began in earnest two days into the new year when the band, plus Yoko and a recording team, assembled on a sound stage at Twickenham to realise Paul's new *grand projet*. The Beatles were to 'get back' to their roots by rehearsing, then performing a new set of songs live on stage, possibly a Roman amphitheatre in Africa, which they hoped would be warm this time of the year, the process of rehearsing for and then giving the show filmed by Michael Lindsay-Hogg as a movie/TV special to promote the album. It was a typically high-concept McCartney idea, a good one, too, with great commercial potential, except the others weren't keen.

Assembling his production team, Paul called Glyn Johns, a freelance record producer who'd been working regularly with the Rolling Stones.

It was quite amusing, actually. I remember very distinctly taking the call and him saying, 'This is Paul McCartney,' and I thought it was Mick Jagger taking the piss, talking to me in a Liverpudlian accent … I said something like, 'Stop fucking about, what do you want?' Because I worked with [Mick] all the time at the time. But it was Paul. So that was a bit embarrassing.

Despite this awkward start, Johns was hired as recording engineer on the project, becoming the Beatles' *de facto* producer, which leads to the pertinent question: *Where was George Martin?*

---

* There was still a normal Christmas record for Beatles fans.

Having fallen out to some extent with their producer during the making of the *White Album* the Beatles had decided they didn't want George Martin working with them closely this time, Lennon telling Martin rudely that they didn't want any of his 'production shit' on this new album. 'We want this to be an honest album,' he said, a slap in the face Martin took as gracefully as was possible. He dropped into the sessions, but did not produce as he had done previously, which surprised Glyn Johns. 'I was shocked to find that George wasn't there, and I was equally shocked to find they were asking me about ideas for arrangements, or whatever else, which I didn't think I was there for at all,' says Johns, who hadn't been properly briefed by Paul – one of McCartney's failings. He liked to wing it, and expected others to do the same.

No one ever said, 'Oh, George isn't doing this, you are.' The word 'producer' was never used. I found it a little bit awkward when George did come. George actually did take me to one side and very kindly said, you know, you're not to worry; don't be concerned or feel awkward about this. It's perfectly all right. So he made me feel OK about it, which was very, very nice of him, because I did feel a bit sort of awkward.

Apart from when they were in their own homes, or in hotel rooms, the most privacy the Beatles ever enjoyed was when they were working with George Martin at Abbey Road. Now they were expected to make music with a virtual stranger while being filmed by a large crew of other strangers on a charmless sound stage outside London, and it was all Paul's idea. 'You had the slight sense that Paul was the driver of the bus, but that some of the others might want to get off at the next stop,' observes Michael Lindsay-Hogg diplomatically.

Paul tends to be what we call these days 'proactive'. He goes out and if something's not working he tried to make it work, he's a very force-ful character, forceful and, in his own way, quite a dominating charac-ter to do with what he wants, [and] one of his great qualities is a kind of enthusiasm. He said, 'Yeah, let's do this. Let's not do nothing. Let's do something. Let's do this.'

It wasn't long before the driven McCartney clashed with his less committed band mates. This happened most seriously with George Harrison when, on 10 January 1969, Paul tried to tell his friend how to play guitar on 'Two of Us', a song often interpreted as being about Paul and John, but which McCartney says referred to him and Linda. After repeated attempts to get it right, Paul told George wearily: 'We've just gone around like for an hour with nothin' … the riffs …'

'There's no riffs,' replied Harrison.

'But it's not together, so it's not sounding together.'

'So we go on playing until we …'

'Or we can stop and say, "It's not together …"' Sounding like a school teacher addressing a recalcitrant child, the teacher Paul may have become if he'd followed the career his mother envisaged, McCartney told Harrison: 'See, if we can get it simpler and *then* complicate it where it needs complication. But it's complicated in the bit …' George bristled, saying he was just playing the chords, and muttered about Paul being unreasonable. 'You know I'm not saying that,' Paul defended himself. 'I'm trying to help, you know, but I always hear myself annoying you, and I'm trying to …'

'You're not annoying me …'

'But you know what I mean …'

'You take it the wrong way …'

'I'm not trying to say that. I'm not trying to say that. You're doing it again as though I'm trying to say that. [Like] we said the other day, you know, I'm not trying to get ya,' said Paul, referring to the 'Hey Jude' sessions during which he'd asked George not to play so much guitar, which still rankled with Harrison. 'I really am trying to just say, Look lads, the band, you know, shall we try it like this?'

'Well, I don't mind. I'll play whatever you want me to play, or I won't play at all if you don't want to me to play,' George replied with the patience of a yogi. 'Whatever it is that'll please you, I'll do it …'

All this was captured on film. 'That particular day's rehearsal was slightly fractious anyway, and when you see [the film] you'll notice that the shot of Paul is down on him from above, and the shot of George is over Paul's shoulder,' explains Michael Lindsay-Hogg, who continued shooting knowing the Beatles had final say on what was used, but being careful to keep his distance. 'It's a fairly fuzzy camera look, and that's because I felt [a] row was going to break out amongst some of them, and I wanted to pull the cameras away from them so they wouldn't be inhibited.'

Michael and his crew were eventually asked to leave, so the Beatles could continue their argument in private. The upshot was that George walked out of the sessions, going home to write his song 'Wah Wah'. He had been unhappy at work for some time, 'bringing home bad vibes', as Pattie Harrison says. Now he'd followed Ritchie's lead. The roots of this particular problem were deep in George's relationship with Paul and John, dating back to when Georgie carried the older boys' guitar cases, always condescended to because he was that bit younger. Stupid. Despite all the time that had passed, and all they had done together, things hadn't changed. 'He didn't like the feeling that John and Paul were more dominating. They were older. They'd been older all the time,' observes Lindsay-Hogg. 'I think he felt under the thumb of the other two and I think the other two saw him the way they'd seen him when he was 15 years old. He was talented but he had to be – I always felt – kept down a bit.' John, Paul and Ritchie held a crisis meeting, whereby John suggested they might hire Eric Clapton to replace George. Paul assumed John was joking. Then they all went over to Esher to tell George they loved him and needed him, and he agreed to come back on the understanding they leave Twickenham, which he hated, give up the idea of a live performance, and continue their work at Savile Row.

For the past few months Magic Alex had been working on a new recording studio for the basement of the Apple building, an advanced multi-track facility that would make EMI's Abbey Road look antique. When the Beatles came back from Twickenham, this bespoke studio facility proved useless. Alex's idea of a 16-track system was, ridiculously, to equip the studio with 16 individual speakers, whereas any junior engineer could have told him only two were needed for stereo; he'd also built the studio in a room where the boiler was located, meaning the Beatles had to turn the heating off to avoid it being heard on their recordings; and they couldn't use the control room anyway because Alex had neglected to cut holes through the wall for the cables; while the recording console looked to Glyn Johns's eyes like something from *Buck Rogers*. 'It was just hysterical,' says Johns.

Unfortunately, George Harrison, who I think was probably the main team leader as far as the studio was concerned, George was rather upset that I refused to have anything to do with this load of shit. It was just like the king without his clothes, they'd just been taken – completely and utterly. It was just a joke! An absolute joke. And George wouldn't let go of the fact that he thought Alex was a good guy. Anyway, George wasn't best pleased when I threw it all out. So we borrowed a bunch of gear from Abbey Road and carried on.

Once these technical difficulties were resolved, everybody relaxed. The new basement studio was at least cosy, with a fireplace and thick apple-green carpets extending throughout the building. There was a staffed kitchen next door to serve them with snacks, and four floors of mates upstairs to hang out with. George suggested that keyboard player Billy Preston sit in with them, Billy being an old pal from Hamburg, when he'd played in Little Richard's band, and the presence of a guest had a civilising influence on the band, as did a visit from Linda and Heather See, a blonde moppet of a child wearing a fringy Western jacket. 'Hello Heather!' John called out with avuncular gruffness when she entered the room. Uncle Ringo let Heather have a bash on his drums, clutching his ears in alarm as she did so, which made her laugh. As Daddy led the boys through covers of old favourites, including 'Besame Mucho' and 'Lawdy Miss Clawdy', Heather danced around and around until she fell over giddy, the Beatles smiling at each other over their instruments, everybody now in a much better mood.

In playing these old songs, and in their conversation between numbers, the Beatles showed themselves already nostalgic for their past. One of the songs they were working on, 'One After 909', had been dredged up from the cache of 100 or so tunes John and Paul wrote as kids, but had thought too simple to bother with.

More significantly as far as Paul was concerned were two substantial new ballads he had composed, 'Let it Be' and 'The Long and Winding Road', both similar in structure to 'Hey Jude' in that they were piano-based numbers, starting with Paul at the keyboard, the band coming in behind him, building to a climax. 'Let it Be' was inspired by memories of Mary McCartney, specifically by a dream Paul had of his mother, while the hymn-like lyrics had the ability to evoke personal nostalgic feelings in others. 'The Long and Winding Road', with its theme of returning home, also had this nostalgic quality, while reflecting the journey the boys had been on since they were teenagers. It was also a song about Scotland, and the search for true love. Like many successful songs it can be read in multiple ways. Paul had started work on 'The Long and Winding Road' in the autumn of 1968, and in that context it could also be seen as addressing the chaos of his personal life at that time, having just split with Jane, not sure who he wanted to spend his life with. This is a reading given corroboration by Paul in *Paul McCartney: Many Years from Now*, where he says the song was written when, 'I was a bit flipped out and tripped out ...'

Many times I've been alone,
And many times I've cried,
Anyway, you'll never know
The many ways I've tried.

And still they lead me back
To the long, winding road.

It was Paul who also contributed the theme song to this new movie project, the country blues 'Get Back', evolved from a satire he had written entitled 'Commonwealth Song', lampooning Britons who were saying that immigrants from the nation's former colonies should 'get back' to where they came from. This was a common sentiment in the UK at the time, given dramatic expression by Enoch Powell in his 1967 'rivers of blood' speech, predicting that mass immigration would result in civil war. Paul had subsequently changed the words to make the song about a character named Jojo in Tucson, Arizona.

Jojo was a man who thought he was a loner,
But he knew it couldn't last.
Jojo left his home in Tucson, Arizona,
For some California grass.

Get back, get back,
Get back to where you once belonged.

Although Paul has stated firmly that Jojo is a fictional character, neither man nor woman in his mind, fans have long wondered whether the words were a veiled reference to Linda's ex-husband, Mel See, whose given first name was Joseph, and who lived in Tucson. In an interview for this book, Mel's partner during the last years of his life reveals that Mel himself felt that 'Get Back' referred to him. Specifically, the song seemed to Mel to be about Linda and Paul pushing him away when he tried to have contact with Heather during the early part of her time with Paul. 'I guess at one time they really wanted to avoid him,' says Mel's former partner Beverly Wilk, adding that Mel didn't blame Linda for not coming to Africa with him in 1964; rather he felt he had been selfish and, when he returned to the USA, he regretted the fact that his action had led to losing contact with his daughter, who was now living in England with another man, although he believed Paul would make a good father. When 'Get Back' was released in the spring of 1969 it was a US number one for five weeks, so Mel could not avoid hearing the song, and the lyrics seemed to relate to his attempts to reconnect with Heather. 'People said they thought that [it was about him]. He thought sometimes it was,' says Beverly. 'Well, they didn't want him around. So, Get back. Go home, go back to where you belong.' When Mel tried to contact Heather, Beverly says, 'it was all excuses' as to why he couldn't see his daughter. 'They weren't really nice to him in the earlier years.'

THE ROBIN HOOD OF POP

During the making of *Get Back*, John Lennon gave an interview to journalist Ray Coleman of *Disc* magazine complaining that Apple was a financial mess and he was down to his last £50,000 ($76,500). 'If it carries on like this, we'll be broke in six months,' he said. The remarks were picked up by newspapers and magazines around the world, read with particular interest by the Rolling Stones' manager Allen Klein, who set out to persuade Lennon that he could rescue the Beatles.

Klein was born in Newark, New Jersey, in 1931, son of a kosher butcher. At the age of two, following the death of his mother, he was placed in an orphanage, later raised by an aunt. He became an account-ant who built a reputation as the 'Robin Hood of Pop' by recovering royalties owed to his pop star clients, in return for a commission. Before long he was representing a number of well-known artists including Sam Cooke, whom he once offered to Brian Epstein as a support act for the Beatles. At the same time Klein suggested he might take a look at the Beatles' books. This impertinent offer was rebuffed, but over the years Klein edged closer to the biggest act on Earth, signing Paul's friend Donovan, then the Stones, for whom Klein negotiated that thumping $1.25 million advance from Decca. Paul was impressed, but Klein made no real headway with the Beatles until John's 'six-months-from-bankruptcy' interview.

Paul was furious when he read John's comments in print, berating Ray Coleman for reporting Lennon's loose talk: 'You know John shoots his mouth off and doesn't mean it!' The quote was misleading. John may have been down to his last £50,000 'in readies', as Paul would say, but that was a lot of money in 1969, and in reality they were all rich men. John and Yoko lived like royalty, chauffeur-driven to the studio in a white Rolls Royce, dining on caviar, soon to move into Tittenhurst Park, a mansion near Ascot set in 72 acres of grounds. John wasn't alone in living extravagantly. George and Pattie Harrison were about to move into a similarly vast pad, a gothic mansion at Henley-on-Thames named Friar Park; it featured 25 bedrooms and two lakes, one of which extended under the house. Ritchie was also acquiring expensive tastes. Only Paul lived modestly, owning one substantial but not ostentatious London home, a Scottish hideaway, some judiciously purchased works of art, and a couple of nice cars.

Paul was losing money, too, of course, because of Apple's crazy schemes, lack of business discipline and day-to-day expenses. Derek Taylor's press office operated as a free all-day bar for Derek's journalist mates while Peter Brown enjoyed *cordon bleu* luncheons in his office. Nevertheless, Brown insists that the core business, Apple Records, made money. 'I will always [maintain] that Apple was a very successful company,' he says trenchantly.

All this about people ripping us off and all that kind of thing – of course there was some latitude. It was marginal in the big picture, and also part of our image was that we had to be nice people – cool people and nice people – it was the culture of the time. You didn't do nasty things. You're not cruel. We were artists, and we were treating people with more respect than maybe the rest of the business world. So I always feel that Apple, the reputation it got for being misman-aged or out of [hand], was unfair.

Allen Klein was very different to the cool, nice people at Apple. A small, squat American with a pugnacious face, slicked-back hair and a fat belly, Klein looked like a truck driver and had a calculator brain. He also had the ability to charm the credulous, which for all his wit and clever-ness Lennon was. When he met Klein at the Dorchester Hotel, John warmed to a man who told him that he, too, had had a tough upbring-ing, being an orphan and all; Klein exhibited a wide knowledge of John's music, which was nice to hear; and, cleverly, Klein was attentive and respectful to Yoko, whose influence he discerned. The meeting went so well that John drafted an immediate memo to Sir Joseph Lock-wood, informing the EMI chairman that Klein was authorised to repre-sent John's interests forthwith. With the issuing of this missive, the Beatles' end-game began.

WHY DON'T WE DO IT ON THE ROOF?

Despite George Harrison's declared opposition to Paul's movie/TV special, and John's complete lack of interest, Michael Lindsay-Hogg had continued filming the Beatles at Savile Row, while Paul tried to persuade his band mates that they needed to return to live perform-ance, to end this film project, and for the long-term health of the group. But the others seemed to have developed stage fright in the two and a half years since they'd bowed out at Candlestick Park. When Paul argued that once they were on stage again it would be fine, John looked very doubtful.

Many novel venues were suggested for the show, including the Sahara Desert and a concert on a boat. 'It'll have to be a bloody big boat,' George observed, thinking of the space needed to accommodate the band, film crew and audience. 'It'll have to be bigger than the Royal Iris,' he added, in reference to the dances they'd once played on the Mersey ferries. As the boys bantered back and forth, Paul tried to pull them into line. 'All right, we can't go on like this … can we? We can't go on like this indefinitely,' he said, sounding like teacher again.

'We seem to be,' said Ritchie.

Lindsay-Hogg claims credit for suggesting the Beatles do the concert on the roof of the Apple building. The date was set for Thursday 30 January 1969, Glyn Johns running cables down through the stairwell to the basement so he could record the show, though the whole thing remained unconfirmed until the last minute. 'We were going to go up at 12:30, to get the lunch-time crowd, and they were still sort of batting it around amongst themselves – were they going to do it, were they not going to do it?' recalls Lindsay-Hogg.

George didn't want to do it. And Paul was saying, 'Please, why not? What's wrong with it? We're just going to go up there. If it doesn't work out, we'll just drop it in the ocean.' And they didn't decide. George was sort of a no; Ringo was on the fence; Paul was, 'This is going to be fun.' And then John said, 'Fuck it, let's do it!' Then they went up on the roof … That was the last time they played together.

It was a cold, grey day. The Beatles wore warm clothes accordingly. John had on his ex-wife's fur jacket. George wore a black jacket with lime green trousers, Ritchie a red waterproof. Paul, still with a full beard, wore a buttoned-up three-piece suit. With Billy Preston on the organ, the Beatles played for just under three-quarters of an hour that Thursday afternoon, performing all new songs including 'Don't Let Me Down' and 'Get Back', which they started and ended with. Although the concert, if indeed it could be so called, was intended as a public event, people on the street five storeys below couldn't see the Beatles on the roof, while their music blew about on the wind. Still, a sizeable crowd gathered below and the police were eventually summoned, by complaints about the noise, from the station at the top of Savile Row, as the Beatles guessed they would be. Lindsay-Hogg had a camera set up in the hall to film the officers when they arrived to shut down the gig. By the time Mr Plod emerged on the roof to ask the Beatles to desist, the boys were ready to oblige, having played until their fingers were cold. They ran through 'Get Back' one last time, Paul and John exchanging happy, comradely looks, Lennon coming up with the perfect ad-lib ending: 'I'd like to say thank you on behalf of the group and ourselves and I hope we passed the audition.' Maureen Starkey and Peter Brown led a smattering of applause.

WEDDING BELLS ARE BREAKING UP THAT OLD GANG OF MINE

Glyn Johns attempted to make an album out of the tapes he'd amassed over the past few weeks, including the rooftop concert.

> The whole reason why I came up with the idea for my version of [the record that became] *Let it Be* to be the way it was because I had sat and witnessed them having a laugh, basically, and being hysterically funny, and just behaving like normal musicians, and they had at this point made the most stunning 'produced' records you could possibly conceive of in popular music, they'd broken all the barriers, they'd reinvented the recording process, all kinds of things, and I'd seen them sitting round playing live and singing together and behaving like normal people, basically. [So] I just thought how fantastic it would be to have an album not only of them playing live with new material, but actually to show that they were human beings, that they could have a laugh ... I went to Olympic Studios one evening and I mixed, very roughly, a bunch of rehearsals of the day. I left false starts in, and I left them taking the piss out of each other or whatever in, and I had acetates cut for each of them. [I] said I thought this was a good idea that they might like to consider for the record, and they all came back the next day and said no – It wasn't what they wanted.

Meanwhile, Lindsay-Hogg worked on a rough cut of the film that, like the album, came to be known as *Let it Be*. Work was hampered by the fact that nobody had kept a record of continuity, which took months to sort out. 'I was very keen to try and get what became *Let it Be* in shape as quickly as we could, so it was in motion and nothing would happen to it.' The director was right to be fearful. Almost as soon as they came down from the roof of the Apple building, the Beatles lost interest in the whole project, and started work instead on a new set of songs at Olympic that would constitute their final album, *Abbey Road*. Before they got too deeply into this, however, Paul took time out to get married.

On the evening of Tuesday 11 March 1969, Paul called his brother Mike, on tour with the Scaffold in Birmingham, inviting him to be best man at his wedding the next day. Paul had bought the ring and booked

Marylebone Register Office, a short drive from Cavendish Avenue. All Mike had to do was show up for 10:00 a.m. *And don't be late!*

News that Paul and Linda were to marry wasn't altogether surprising. They had been a couple now for seven months, had known each other longer, and Lin was four months pregnant with Paul's baby. At the same time, theirs wasn't an entirely harmonious courtship. 'We had a row the day before we got married – and nearly called off the wedding,' Paul later revealed. 'I'd characterise our relationship as rather volatile.'

Paul had come a long way from his days as a pin-up, yet many girls still harboured an adolescent dream that they would be the one he chose to marry, and when diehard fans found out he was getting married to somebody else they almost lost their reason. One such fan was a hairdresser named Jill, who was shampooing a client in Birmingham when news came over the radio that Paul was getting married in London later that morning. Jill put down her shampoo bottle, grabbed her coat and hurried to New Street station, where she caught the first train to the capital, intent on getting to Paul before he made his mistake.

Rain was falling as Jill arrived at Marylebone Register Office, a splendid Victorian edifice flanked by stone lions. A mob of 300 fans were milling about the entrance, with press photographers and reporters standing on the steps of the building. A limousine was at the kerb, and uniformed police were trying to keep order as traffic swished past on the busy Marylebone Road. Many of the girls present were superfans like Jill, females in their late teens or early twenties who'd never outgrown their crush on Paul. The real hardcore fans – the girls who spent much of their time standing outside the Apple building – had been named the Apple Scruffs by George Harrison. The Scruffs also kept watch outside the EMI Studios on Abbey Road and the Beatles' homes, mostly Paul's house because he was the one in London. Among these Scruffs was American Carol Bedford, who later wrote a fascinating memoir about her experiences, explaining that she'd first screamed at the Beatles when they came through her home state of Texas in 1964. As soon as she left school, Carol came to England to join the girls who waited for the band outside their various addresses, along with Italian Lucy, who was obsessed with George; Chris who loved Paul; Sue, known as Sue-John, because of her obsession with Lennon; and Margo, a babysitter, who often brought her young charge, whom she called Bam Bam, to wait with her outside Paul's house. When the girls became really annoying, Paul would call the police, but as time passed he learned to live with the Scruffs, striking up friendly relationships with the regulars, whom he termed the 'Eyes and Ears of the World', in recognition of the fact that they knew what the Beatles were doing before anybody else. He sometimes entrusted the girls to take Martha to the park.

True to their reputation as the Eyes and Ears of the World, the Scruffs found out the night before the wedding that Paul was getting married, and started sending up such a lamentation outside 7 Cavendish Avenue that Paul had to come out and give them a talking to: 'You know I had to get married some time.' Now the dread morning had come, the Scruffs were standing outside the register office in the rain singing a mournful medley of Beatles songs. It was enough to drive you crackers. Belatedly, Mike McCartney pulled up in a car, his train having broken down, and ran into the building to find Paul, Lin, Heather, Mal Evans, Peter Brown and Don Short of the *Daily Mirror* waiting impatiently. 'Where the bloody hell have you been, you're an hour late!' said Paul, who was dressed in a grey suit and yellow tie. Lin wore a yellow coat. There was no sign of John and Yoko, the Harrisons or the Starkeys. George was at Savile Row, while John and Yoko were being driven to Poole in Dorset to visit Aunt Mimi, whom John had moved to the seaside after the attentions of fans had driven her out of Mendips. He heard about Paul's nuptials on the car radio.

Joe Jevans, the registrar, did his work and Paul and Linda signed the marriage certificate, Mike and Mal countersigning as witnesses. Then they stepped outside to find that the sun was shining in their honour. The girls reacted to the appearance of bride and groom with a mixture of cheers and wails of despair, press photographers mobbing the couple for pictures. Fans surged forward at the same time, causing a quick-witted policeman to gather Heather up in his arms and stride ahead of Paul, who shouted that Linda and the kid were with him. Then he saw Margo with Bam Bam. 'Is he all right, Margo?' Paul asked, concerned for the baby in the crush. Finally, the wedding party was bundled into the waiting limousine, which took them back up to St John's Wood for a blessing at the local church, then press pictures at Cavendish (Paul carried Lin over the threshold, obligingly, for the *Daily Mirror*). Later there was a reception at the Ritz Hotel. George and Pattie Harrison showed up late, explaining that DS Pilcher had chosen this of all days to raid their house in Esher, recovering a small amount of cannabis resin. George was incensed by the intrusion, exacerbated by the press, who had hopped over his garden wall to take pictures of the raid. Paraphrasing Scripture, he reminded the hacks with righteous indignation that foxes have holes, birds the sanctuary of nests, but Beatles seemingly had nowhere private to lay their heads.* He and Pattie would later plead guilty to possession and receive a fine.

What with George being busted and Paul getting married, the press had two major Beatles stories on the same day. Paul got the good press on the front page, George the bad press inside. By marrying Paul, Linda also became a public figure that day, as she would remain for the rest of her life. Her relationship with the British media was complex from the start. As noted, Fleet Street always liked Paul, but journalists never warmed to his wife. Almost everybody interviewed for this book who knew Linda personally spoke well of her, yet people in the media who met her over the years, myself included, found Linda a gauche, abrasive woman lacking charm. Paul would explain this by saying Lin was shy. Members of the family maintain she never wanted to be in the public eye. Yet that was the life she chose, and the couple manipulated and exploited the press from the start. In her first interview as Mrs McCartney, Linda told Don Short that she wanted to scotch the rumour she was connected to the Eastman-Kodak firm, as *The Times* had reported that morning. 'I don't know how that mistake came about except through the name and the fact that I am a photographer ...' Linda's friend Danny Fields says the truth is that Linda started the rumour herself to impress people she wanted to photograph. Now she was married to a Beatle she had a better way to impress the world.

When he saw that Paul had married Linda, John decided to marry Yoko. On his way to see Aunt Mimi, John told his chauffeur to take them to Portsmouth and book him and Yoko onto a ship; they'd get the captain to marry them. John figured that would be quieter and more dignified than the way Paul had behaved, playing up to the press as he had in London. When a shipboard wedding proved logistically impossible, John and Yoko flew to Paris, thence to the British dependency of Gibraltar, where a British subject could be married instantly. They did so on 20 March 1969.

* Paraphrasing Luke 9:58.

Having gone to such lengths to avoid the press, John and Yoko then made sure they garnered maximum publicity for themselves by staging the first of their so-called bed-ins during a honeymoon in Amsterdam. This was a conceptual happening with a positive if infantile message: at a time of international political tension it was better to go to bed and think peaceful thoughts than make war. In practice it involved John and Yoko tucking themselves up in the Amsterdam Hilton under signs that read BED PEACE and HAIR PEACE, the latter a reference to their own extreme hirsuteness – John was now wearing a full beard, with hair down to his shoulders; Yoko's grew halfway down her back – as well as being a Lennon pun (hair piece). When they'd arranged themselves, Derek Taylor invited the press in to photograph and interview the couple. Paul and Linda watched news coverage of this wacky event on television from their honeymoon suite in New York. It looked for all the world like John and Yoko were trying to upstage them, and in the months and years to come this rivalry became a pronounced feature of their lives, with John and Yoko pitted relentlessly against Paul and Linda. It was true, as Paul always said, in reference to an old song the Beatles once performed as part of their stage show, that wedding bells broke up the old gang.

CREATIVE DIFFERENCES

YOU NEVER GIVE ME YOUR MONEY

Returning to London from his honeymoon in the spring of 1969, Paul saw Apple on the brink of disaster. In recent months there had been discussions about bringing in a manager to sort out the financial and administrative mess at Savile Row. Paul suggested his new American in-laws, the Eastmans, for the job. When that was rejected by the other Beatles as nepotism, he floated the idea that they might hire Lord Beeching, the peer charged with rationalising the nation's railways. Beeching recommended swingeing closures of railway lines and stations. Fed up with the excess at Apple, Paul apparently wanted Beeching-style cuts here, too. This send-for-Beeching suggestion didn't go down well. Grumbled Peter Brown:

I mean it was just ludicrous. Beeching knew *nothing* about this business. Just because Beeching could fix the railways didn't mean to say he could fix Apple, but that was all part of Paul's stupidity – 'We've got to get somebody who is important, because you and Neil, you came with us, how good can you be?'

According to Brown, Paul had a habit of pontificating about matters he didn't understand. 'One of the things I personally used to get irritated with is just, if you know him, and you work with him, he is opinionated about everything, including things he knows nothing about.' And Paul's lectures were rarely short.

Also, the four Beatles were now pulling in different directions. 'For seven years there was this little unit of a jolly band just trooping around doing things,' says Tony Bramwell nostalgically. 'After Brian died it was a big change – John was going through his madness, George was going through his Indian stuff, [but] Paul was [still] pretty responsible about it. He hadn't overdosed on acid, and he hadn't ruined his life.' Paul had tried to lead the band after Brian's death, and the others had let him do so to a degree, with the result that much of what had been set up at Apple was in fact Paul's idea. As Peter Brown notes:

It was only later when John came back out of his haze of LSD and heroin, or whatever else he was on, with Yoko, and wanted to be more proactive in what we were doing [that he would say], 'Why are we doing this? Why is this like it is?' 'It's because this is what we put in place when you were out of your mind … It happened because Neil and I put it together with Paul's approval …'

Now John was more involved in the business, and he and Paul were at odds, which made for a miserable atmosphere at Savile Row. Bramwell again:

You just don't know how horrible it was at Apple in that period. It was like being in the middle of a gigantic divorce … On one phone you'd have John asking you to do this, on the other phone you'd have Paul asking you to do [something else]. By then George and Ringo had washed their hands of it, [but] John and Paul were 'Can you do this, but don't tell any of the others?' … John is like 'Can you make a film of my cock?' And Paul is like, 'Do a big billboard in Trafalgar Square.' It was just like being in a divorce.

As in any divorce, the correspondents had their antagonistic representatives. At the start of February 1969 John sent his man, Allen Klein, into Apple to conduct an audit. At the same time Paul persuaded the band to hire his father-in-law's law firm as general counsel, with the result that Linda's lawyer brother John Eastman started going through the Beatles' paperwork. Inevitably Klein and Eastman clashed, Eastman's Ivy League manner rubbing orphanage boy Klein up the wrong way. A crisis came when the Beatles had to deal with the issue of the Epstein family wanting to sell Nemperor Holdings Ltd (a new name for the rump of NEMS Enterprises). Clive Epstein had been caretaking the firm since his brother's demise, and didn't have much enthusiasm for the business. The Eastmans urged the Beatles to buy Nemperor from the Epsteins, using an advance on EMI royalties, a deal Clive and his mother were inclined to accept. But Klein was against it, saying at a meeting at the Dorchester Hotel that the deal was an expensive 'piece of crap', and John Eastman a 'shithead', according to Peter Brown, who notes that Paul and his brother-in-law then left the room in a huff. With the enemy out of the way, Klein dripped poisonous words into the ears of John, George and Ringo, saying that if he managed the group there would be a more equitable balance of power, and they would all have more money. The alternative was to let themselves be run by Paul and his in-laws. Lennon, Harrison and Starkey were easily persuaded.

Lee Eastman flew into London to support his son and son-in-law, a second meeting being convened in Peter Brown's office at Apple. Proceedings got off to a roaring start when Klein informed everybody that Lee Eastman wasn't the man they thought he was, but a Jew named Leopold Epstein. Klein wasn't making an anti-Semitic remark – he was himself Jewish – but seeking to show that Eastman was a phony. 'Klein had done some research on Lee Eastman and had turned up the information that his name had [been changed from] Epstein,' recalls Brown. 'Klein had also armed John with this intelligence, and throughout the meeting the two of them referred to the Eastmans as "Epstein".' Lee could put up with that, but when Klein began interrupting him and swearing, the lawyer lost his temper, bawled Klein out, then stormed from the meeting, taking Paul with him. This was becoming a habit. John Eastman then wrote to the Epsteins, a letter that apparently recommended they should have a meeting to discuss 'the propriety of the negotiations surrounding the nine-year agreement between EMI and the Beatles and [NEMS/Nemperor]'. According to Brown, the tone of the letter infuriated the Epsteins, who reacted by selling Nemperor to a City investment firm, Triumph. Apple responded by asking EMI to pay Beatles royalties directly to them, with the sad result that Brian's family ended up suing the Beatles.

On top of this, Dick James sold his share of Northern Songs to Sir Lew Grade's Associated Television Corporation (ATV). Sir Lew had been after Northern Songs for years and James, ignored and increasingly scorned by the Beatles, agreed a deal with his partner, Charles Silver, to sell their shares to Sir Lew, adding to a stake he already owned. The mogul now went shopping for additional shares to gain control of the company. Apple resisted this takeover, urging minority shareholders to sell to them instead of ATV, coming up with a counter-bid, underwritten by Lennon and Klein. Unwilling to get involved in any business deal with Klein, Paul withheld his support, partly as a result of which the counter-bid failed and Sir Lew acquired an additional 15 per cent of Northern Songs, thereby gaining control of all the songs John and Paul had written since 1962, plus the songs they would write under contract until 1973.

As calamity followed calamity, the Beatles continued to argue over who should lead them forward, pitching Paul and the Eastmans against John, George and Ritchie, who wanted Allen Klein. The row boiled over on Friday 9 May 1969, when the group was working with Glyn Johns at the Olympic Sound Studio in south-west London. John, George and Ringo cornered Paul, telling him they'd all signed with Klein and needed Paul's signature there and then to complete the deal. Paul prevaricated, arguing that the 20 per cent commission Klein wanted was too high. 'He'll take 15 per cent,' he told his partners, reminding them: 'We're a big act!' He certainly didn't see the need to sign anything immediately. The others insisted Paul had to sign now because Klein was on his way back to New York for a meeting with his board. The meeting was scheduled for the next day. 'I said, "It's Friday night. He doesn't work on a Saturday, and anyway Allen Klein is a law unto himself. He hasn't got a board he has to report to'," Paul recalled. "'You're not going to push me into this."' Klein, who had been on his way to the airport, was so enraged when he heard Paul was refusing to cooperate that he turned around and came to the studio. '[Klein] had this incredible row with Paul in the studio with me in the control room,' remembers Glyn Johns. 'I turned all the mikes off, because it was none of my business, but they were shouting so loudly at each other I could hear their conversation through the glass.' Around this time Paul recorded a track at Olympic named, appropriately, 'My Dark Hour', with musician Steve Miller, who recalls that Paul worked off some of his frustration playing drums on the song: '[He] really beat the hell out of those drums.'

Although Paul had not signed with Klein (he never did), the other three Beatles now out-voted McCartney, hiring the American account- ant, who instigated a reign of terror at Apple. Many of the pampered denizens of Savile Row were sent, figuratively speaking, to the guillo- tine. While this caused anguish, the office *was* over-staffed, Apple employees living royally on the Beatles' money. Derek Taylor's press office was particularly profligate. As mentioned, Taylor believed Paul was the sender of anonymous postcards the PR man received at home, some weird and 'some outright nasty ones' as Taylor recalled, with stamps torn in half and cryptic messages, one of which, addressed to Derek's wife, read: 'Tell your boy to obey the schoolmasters.' Derek was in no doubt these were from Paul, though the star didn't admit sending them. By Taylor's account, Apple staff feared the Beatle. Returning to their desks from a long lunch, the message they most dreaded was 'Paul called'. One day McCartney organised a staff meeting, to complain about the extravagant way Apple employees were conducting them- selves at the Beatles' expense, telling them bluntly, 'Don't forget, you're not very good, any of you, you know that, don't you?'

Derek survived the terror, protected as he was by his friend George Harrison, but many others went. Alex Mardas was given the chop, as was Apple Electronics. The Beatles finally got rid of 'Measles'. Denis O'Dell, head of Apple Films, left. Zapple was shut, leaving Barry Miles stranded in New York where he was recording a spoken-word LP with Allen Ginsberg. 'We'd done two tracks, and suddenly the recording studio said, "We've been told that's the end of it." I said, "What? It's news to me." I tried of course to call the Beatles. No way. You know. They just mysteriously disappear.' It fell to Peter Brown to tell Alistair Taylor that his employment with the Beatles was also over. Alistair was one of the original gang who'd come down from Liverpool with the boys, part of the 'family', and he took his sacking badly, breaking down in tears. He tried to call Paul. 'But Paul refused to come to the phone,' Taylor later told Bob Spitz. 'Nothing in my life ever hurt as much as that.' Another Apple employee who'd been close to Paul was Peter Asher who, despite Paul's split with Jane, had been running Apple Records with Ron Kass, who was now fired. Reading the writing on the wall, Peter quit. The Ashers were mourning a shocking death at the time. Jane and Peter's father had been found dead in the coal cellar of their Wimpole Street house on 2 May. The coroner found that Dr Asher, always an eccentric character, had killed himself with an overdose of barbiturates.

THEIR LAST AND GREATEST ALBUM

Paul and Lin took Heather on holiday to Corfu in May, then returned home to continue the Apple battle. The McCartneys invited Ritchie and Mo Starkey to dinner at Cavendish in the hope of talking the drummer round. Such an invitation was a treat; Linda was a superb cook. In the days before she turned vegetarian she did wonders with a chicken. After giving the Starkeys a feed, the McCartneys tried to persuade Ritchie to join them in the fight against Klein. When the drummer demurred, saying Klein didn't seem that bad to him, Linda started crying. 'They've got you, too!' she sobbed, as though Ritchie had been taken over by zombies.

John Ono Lennon, as he was now known, having changed his middle name from Winston, was also beyond reason. He and Yoko were in a world of their own, looking and behaving like members of a religious cult. Doped up and dressed in white, they floated about London conducting bizarre happenings that were part art events, part sincere peace campaigning and also clearly a grab for attention. One of their nuttiest ideas was that Apple should send an acorn to every world leader to plant for peace. Apple Staff were despatched to the royal parks to gather the acorns, only to find that it was the wrong time of year. The squirrels had already eaten their stores. Then John and Yoko flew to Canada to conduct their second bed-in for peace, at the Queen Elizabeth Hotel in Montreal, demonstrating in the process that, despite his whacked-out appearance, John still possessed a genius for music-making. He made a compelling *in situ* recording of 'Give Peace a Chance'. With overdubbed drums by Ringo, the song was released on 4 July as a single, not by the Beatles, but by a new entity, the Plastic Ono Band, a clear indication that John wanted out of the Beatles.

It therefore came as a considerable surprise to George Martin when Paul telephoned to say that the Beatles wanted to make one more album with their old producer. With no sign of the recently recorded *Let It Be* tapes being released, and with John so strange, distant and unpleasant recently, Martin had assumed his working days with the boys were over.

> My immediate response was, 'Only if you let me produce it the way we used to.' [Paul] said, 'We will, we want to.' 'John included?' 'Yes, honestly.' So I said, 'Well, if you really want to, let's do it. Let's get together again.' It was a very happy record. I guess it was happy because everybody thought it was going to be the last.

Geoff Emerick would again be their engineer. Having had the courage to walk out on the Beatles during the *White Album* sessions, when they had behaved so badly, the engineer had won the musicians' respect and trust. They rewarded Geoff with a job at Apple, and he would work with Paul on various projects for years to come.

So the old team was reunited in Studio Two at EMI seven years after the Beatles started their recording career with George Martin in this same lofty room. Remarkably, the boys' last hurrah would prove for many listeners to be their best LP. In common with the *White Album*, the record that would be named *Abbey Road* had a variety of music, ranging from loose, blues-based rock 'n' roll to sophisticated song suites, yet it was assembled more selectively, creating one immaculate disc that can be played endlessly without sounding stale.

The record didn't get off to a promising start. When the band assembled at EMI on Tuesday 1 July there was no sign of John. Their founding member had recently gone on holiday to Scotland with Yoko, Julian and Yoko's daughter Kyoko, with the intention of visiting John's Scottish relatives. With poor eyesight, and limited experience as a motorist, Lennon crashed the Austin Maxi he was driving into a ditch the day the Beatles were due to start work in London, with the result that the family were taken to hospital in the Highlands town of Golspie. All save Julian needed stitches, John requiring 17 to his face. Yoko had injured her back.

As the Lennons convalesced in Scotland, the other three Beatles started work at EMI, Paul beginning proceedings with 'You Never Give Me Your Money', the tune dreamt up on that carefree day with Lin and Heather in New York, while the lyric was seemingly inspired by his acrimonious dealings with Allen Klein. Paul also recorded the cheeky ditty 'Her Majesty', which would close the album with a flirtatious wink at the

Queen. More substantial was the song suite 'Golden Slumbers'/'Carry That Weight', the lyrics to the first part adapted from an Elizabethan verse:

Golden slumbers kisse your eyes,
Smiles awake you when you rise:
Sleepe pretty wantons doe not cry,
And I will sing a lullabie ...

These are the words of English poet Thomas Dekker (1572–1632), which Paul had seen on sheet music, at his father's house on the Wirral, set to a lullaby that Paul's stepsister Ruth had been learning to play on the piano. Although the words were originally meant to rock a baby to sleep, Paul reinterpreted the 400-year-old rhyme in a radically different way, creating music that starts sweetly, then plunges dramatically, with Paul roaring out Dekker's words. Seguing from this brief piece of music into 'Carry That Weight' was a trick Paul and John used repeatedly on this their last album, using up scraps of music and general leftovers. That this worked so well is a tribute to the superb musicianship throughout, not least Paul's bass-playing and Ringo's drumming, which had never sounded better. George Harrison's guitar parts were also judicious, while Harrison finally came into his own as a songwriter on *Abbey Road* with 'Something' and 'Here Comes the Sun', respectively the best and second best songs he ever composed. Ringo's 'Octopus' Garden' was also enjoyable in the tradition of the Beatles' children's songs, while Paul's 'Maxwell's Silver Hammer' introduced one of several creepy characters to *Abbey Road*, the maniac medical student Maxwell Edison. Paul explained Maxwell's hammer to Barry Miles as 'an analogy for when something goes wrong out of the blue', though it might also be interpreted as wishful thinking on his part. How Paul must have longed for a hammer to come crashing down on Allen Klein's head. Or John's. Or Yoko's.

Without Lennon, the early *Abbey Road* sessions were happy and harmonious, with Paul sliding joyfully down the banister from George Martin's control room like a carefree young Beatle. There was one spat with Harrison, but it blew over. Then John and Yoko appeared, dressed in matching black, a tow truck following with the smashed-up remains of their touring car, a memento of their brush with death. Men from

Harrods also came with a bed, which they erected in the studio so that the injured Yoko could lie there watching the boys work. 'I thought I'd seen it all,' Geoff Emerick noted in his memoirs of this supremely strange moment in the Beatles story, 'but this took the cake.' John asked for a microphone to be suspended over the bed so Yoko could make comments on what she heard, and she didn't hold back. 'Beatles will do this, Beatles will do that,' she'd say, omitting the definite article.

'Actually, it's *the* Beatles, luv,' Paul corrected her, just about controlling his temper. This bizarre scene became stranger still when Yoko put on a tiara.

Before continuing, the Beatles and their partners watched a rough cut of *Let It Be*. 'There was a lot more of John and Yoko than was in the final cut,' says the director Michael Lindsay-Hogg, who went out to dinner afterwards with the McCartneys and Lennons. Everybody seemed to be getting along fine, John and Paul reminiscing about old times, which was safe territory. 'Talking about their time in Liverpool when they were kids and what it was like growing up – a nice kind of cosy evening.' Lindsay-Hogg went home from the restaurant with a good feeling about the project, to watch Neil Armstrong walking on the moon. A day or two later, Peter Brown called to say there was too much John and Yoko in the first cut of *Let It Be*. Brown had received three phone calls. 'So I think it was the others, and of course the central voice will always be Paul,' says Lindsay-Hogg. 'The others thought it maybe had slanted too much to John and Yoko.'

As the director returned to his cutting room, the Beatles completed *Abbey Road*. Following in the footsteps of Maxwell Edison, John introduced two more sinister characters to the record: Mean Mr Mustard, a dirty old man, and the androgynous Polythene Pam. The latter was seemingly inspired by a long-past conversation of John's with poet Royston Ellis, whom the boys met in Liverpool, then hooked up with again on tour in the Channel Islands in 1963. While they were on Guernsey, Ellis introduced John to a girlfriend named Stephanie, whereupon they all dressed up in oilskins and polythene for a sex romp, though Ellis can't recall the exact nature of the couplings. 'There was some sexual encounter, put it like that, with John and Stephanie and myself. But I can't remember [the details].'

'Pam' was paired as another song suite with Paul's 'She Came in Through the Bathroom Window', inspired by a recent break-in at

Cavendish Avenue. Having scaled Paul's garden wall, Chris the Apple Scruff had opened Paul's gate and ushered in Little Sue, Big Sue, Emma, Di and Carol Bedford. The girls then put a ladder up against the back of Paul's house, sending Di up first, because she was smallest.

'I'm in the bathroom!' she called down.

Carol went up the ladder next and made it through the bathroom window just before the ladder fell over, as she describes in *Waiting for the Beatles*. The two girls then ran downstairs and opened the front door to let the others in. They rootled through Paul and Linda's things, marvelling at Ringo's stage drums, seizing armfuls of Paul's clothes, Di swiping a framed photo, another girl scooping up photographic slides.

The following day Margo called at Cavendish with Bam Bam, having prearranged to take Martha for a walk. Some of the other girls were with her. Rose 'Rosie' Martin, a Cockney cleaner who'd recently started working for Paul, and would remain in his employ for the rest of her working life, told the girls that Paul wanted a word with them. He came outside with Linda, both looking serious. 'It seems someone broke into my house on Sunday afternoon,' Paul told the Scruffs. 'I hate to say it, but I think it was some of the girls.'

'What makes you think that?' asked Margo.

'By what they took. Pictures mostly. Anyone else – a real burglar – would have taken more expensive things.' Paul said the slides were Linda's, pictures she'd shot of the band, while the framed photo was of sentimental value to Paul, being a picture of him and his dad. He asked the girls to put the word around that he'd like the pictures back. They could keep the clothes. The girls returned the framed photo, and some slides, but many pictures were never recovered. This was just one of a number of burglaries Paul suffered at Cavendish over the years, in the course of which he lost a lot of memorabilia, including his home movies. 'Everything was stolen by fans, this is the sad thing,' says Barry Miles. 'He owns hardly anything. This is why he occasionally buys stuff from Sotheby's.'

A few days after the bathroom break-in Paul told the Scruffs he'd written a song about the girls who broke into his home.

'A tribute, huh?' asked Carol Bedford, missing the point. 'What's it called?'

'"She Came in Through the Bathroom Window."'

This tune forms the centrepiece of the long medley of song suites that takes up most of what was, in the days of long-playing records, Side Two of *Abbey Road*, the long medley being one of the most glorious achievements of the Beatles' recording career, beginning quietly with Paul singing his lament, 'You Never Give Me Your Money', and concluding with the aptly named 'The End', in which the Beatles seem to ascend to Heaven on a cloud of raucous rock 'n' roll, John, Paul and George locked in a three-way guitar duel as Ritchie drums furiously, the patron saints of pop dispensing groovy benedictions to the world as they depart: *love you; love you* ... The sky clears, a simple piano motif plays, and the words of Paul ring out:

And in the end,
The love you take
Is equal to the love you make.

Fab. The best lyric Paul McCartney ever wrote was the perfect ending to the Beatles' last and greatest album, emphasising that, ultimately, their message had been one of love.

Having considered naming the LP *Everest*, indicating that they had reached their peak, also incidentally a brand of cigarettes smoked by Geoff Emerick, the boys decided instead to title the album *Abbey Road*. It made sense to name the record after the London street where they had made so much wonderful music (and as a result of which the studio was later officially renamed Abbey Road Studios, hereafter referred to as such). Again Paul came up with the cover concept, sketching a drawing of the Beatles walking across the zebra crossing in front of the EMI buildings. They did so on the morning of Friday 8 August 1969, one of those glorious mid-summer days when London basks in sunshine, the trees in leaf, the red geraniums seeming to smile cheerfully from their window boxes at the red phone boxes and red pillar boxes, which stand to attention like guardsmen under forget-me-not skies.

How different the Beatles themselves looked to the four boys signed by George Martin in 1962! Seven years on, John resembled an Old Testament prophet as he strode across the zebra crossing, dressed in white with a bushy beard. George Harrison's long hair and beard emphasised his serious, cadaverous features, making him look much older than 26.

Ringo had started to take on the flamboyance of a playboy millionaire. Paul was the least changed. Having shaved off his Fenian beard, he wore a crisp white shirt and a blue suit for the photo session, kicking off his sandals on what was a very warm day, presenting a handsome, mature version of his younger self. A week later he became a dad for the first time (setting aside the paternity claims against him) when, on 28 August 1969, Linda gave birth at the Avenue Hospital, around the corner, to a daughter they named Mary after Paul's mum.

'THE BEATLES THING IS OVER'

Before *Abbey Road* was released John went to Toronto, with Yoko, Eric Clapton and Klaus Voormann, to perform as the Plastic Ono Band. During the Canadian trip Lennon told Allen Klein that he intended to leave the Beatles. Klein begged John not to say anything to the others, because he was renegotiating their contract with Capitol Records. But when the Beatles met in London on 20 September, John blurted out his news.

Paul was talking about the band going back on the road, playing small venues at first to regain their confidence. He was certain this was the right thing to do, reminding John that whenever the Beatles played live *they played good*. It was touching the way he spoke about the band; Paul loved the Beatles. 'Well, I think you're daft,' Lennon interrupted. 'I wasn't going to tell you until we signed the Capitol deal, but I'm leaving the group.'

'What do you mean?'

'I mean the group is over. I'm leaving ... I want a divorce,' said John, thrilled to be cutting free of the band, as he had cut himself loose from Cyn.

Because Klein didn't want Lennon's decision made public, and thinking perhaps that John was just shooting his mouth off, as he liked to do, no official announcement was made, and the Beatles bumbled on almost like before. Things had changed, though. *Abbey Road* was released the following week, without a single to herald it, uniquely, but went to number one all the same. Then the Beatles whimsically put out 'Something'/'Come Together' as a single; it made number four in Britain, number one in the USA. There was a new promotional film for

'Something', showing the Beatles with their partners. Paul and Linda were filmed at High Park, where they had retired after the birth of Mary. Paul, who had let his beard grow again, took to carrying Mary about in his fur-lined leather jacket, the epitome of a proud father.

The McCartneys were at their farm when the Apple press office started to receive enquiries from the United States asking if Paul had died. Weird though this sounds, a similar macabre rumour had gone around more than once before, usually as a result of Beatles fans – in order to try and deduce his actual whereabouts – ringing the newspapers with spurious enquiries about Paul being in car accidents. Tony Barrow explains: 'If they rang up and said, "We hear he's been in a car accident, hasn't he, down in Surrey?" they were hoping for the answer, "No, of course not, he's in [London]."' This time, however, the rumour started in the USA, where fans had begun to see 'hidden signs' that Paul was dead on Beatles albums. There were apparently a host of clues on the *Abbey Road* sleeve, including the fact Paul was walking barefoot across the zebra crossing with a car number plate behind him, the last four characters of which were 28IF. Supposedly this meant he would have been 28 *if* he'd survived a fatal accident that the Beatles had hushed up, replacing Paul with a double so they could continue as a band. This was preposterous, not least because Paul appeared the least changed of all the Beatles. Anyway, the death of a musician does not automatically mean the end of a band. Brian Jones had died earlier that summer. The Rolling Stones simply replaced him. Nevertheless, the Paul is Dead story grew, fuelled by the fact Paul had been out of the public eye recently, spending time in Scotland with Linda and Heather and the baby. When Paul didn't show his face, a student at Hofstra University in New York started a society: Is Paul McCartney Dead? Disc jockeys began playing Beatles records backwards to reveal hidden audio clues as to what had happened. Finally, *Life* magazine despatched a reporter and photographer to Scotland to get to the bottom of the story.

When the *Life* team knocked on Paul's farmhouse door he reacted with fury at what he saw as an intrusion into his privacy, telling the journalists to fuck off, throwing a bucket of water at them, and swinging at the snapper, Terence Spencer, who had already banged off a picture of the enraged musician, proving he was alive and kicking, or rather punching. A few minutes later Paul realised that a picture of him swinging his fists might be bad PR, so he went after the journalists and made a deal with them. In exchange for Spencer's roll of film, Paul and Linda would pose for another, nicer picture, and he would say a few words. What Paul said in this brief interview was interesting.

'Perhaps the rumour [that I was dead] started because I haven't been much in the press lately. I have done enough press for a lifetime and I don't have anything to say these days,' he told the journalists, in what was a frank insight into his state of mind, adding:

> ... the Beatle [sic] thing is over. It has been exploded, partly by what we have done and partly by other people. We are individuals, all different. John married Yoko, I married Linda. We didn't marry the same girl ... Can you spread it around that I am just an ordinary person and I want to live in peace?

The Beatle thing is over! Paul had effectively made the announcement. Yet his comment went almost unnoticed amidst the nonsense of his supposed demise.

Over the following months at Kintyre, Paul experienced something close to a nervous breakdown as he faced the fact that the band which had been almost his whole life since school was defunct, its members as redundant as Liverpool dockers. His best friend and partner didn't want to work with him any more. Hurtfully, John would rather play with mutual acquaintances of theirs like Eric and Klaus. George and Ritchie didn't seem to need him either. Paul had effectively shut himself out of Apple, because of his refusal to work with Allen Klein. There were no plans to make another album or film, or to tour. The only project on the blocks was *Let It Be*, which was his own failed attempt to unite the band. Who knew when that would be released? It was, in any event, old material now. All in all, a very sad state of affairs. 'Paul was a Beatle. He was the most Beatley Beatle of them all,' comments Tony Bramwell.

> He tried [to keep them, going] with *Mystery Tour*, and then with Apple, and got them all doing things other than sitting round doped, and then they all sort of left him on his own again. All he wanted to do was keep the Beatles together. He tried very hard at it. And when it got post-*Abbey Road* ... there was nothing left to hold together any more.

Paul stayed at High Park, sinking into depression. 'I nearly had a break-down,' he admitted to his daughter Mary years later for a documentary. 'I suppose the hurt of it all, and the disappointment, and the sorrow of losing this great band, these great friends … I was going crazy. I wouldn't get up in the morning; and when I did get up I wouldn't shave or bother with anything; and I'd reach for the whisky …' This was grim for Linda. She had a seven-year-old and a baby to look after, with a husband who was depressed and drunk. She later told friends it was one of the most difficult times in her life, while Paul reflected that he might have become a rock 'n' roll casualty at this point in his career. He had, after all, experimented with a range of drugs up to and including heroin. He liked a drink. It would have been easy to booze and drug himself into oblivion.

Linda told Paul there was a way forward. He could make music without the Beatles. She would help, if he liked. With his wife's support and encouragement, Paul began to think about a post-Beatles career, relying on Linda's advice, and in the process developing an even deeper devotion to her. They became one of those couples who are so close they are like twins, and though their relationship had its ups and downs, it proved adamantine until death.

Shortly before Christmas the McCartneys returned to Cavendish Avenue, where Paul had a four-track recording machine installed. The first scrap of a song he recorded, as a test of the machine, would open what became his first solo LP. This test song, 'The Lovely Linda', is an insubstantial, even annoying track, ending with the unattractive sound of Paul sniggering. He also recorded two Beatles leftovers, 'Junk' and 'Teddy Boy', as well as an experimental percussion track, 'Kreen-Akrore'. Some of the melodies were strong. Paul could always conjure a compelling riff – 'That Would be Something' and 'Every Night', for example – but he seemed bereft of meaningful words, with the result that nearly all the tracks he laid down are minor works. The sole exception was 'Maybe I'm Amazed', a powerful expression of his uxorious love for the woman who'd saved him from a situation that, as he sang, he didn't understand. Paul worked on this homemade album, in the kitchen of his London home, at EMI and at Morgan Studios in West London, into the new year of 1970. Not only did he write and sing all the songs, he also played all the instruments and produced the tracks, the only other contributor being Linda, who sang shaky backing vocals in the manner of a schoolgirl thrust reluctantly onto stage at her end-of-term concert. Paul's blind spot for his wife's lack of musicality, a symptom of his devotion to her, would characterise and mar his subsequent career.

As the McCartneys made their homemade record, John Lennon continued to work with Yoko in the Plastic Ono Band to greater effect. 'Instant Karma', recorded at EMI in late January, with George Harrison playing guitar and Phil Spector producing, had a big, rocking sound and challenging lyrics that outclassed Paul's efforts.

With Paul shutting himself off from the band, the other Beatles made decisions without him, giving the *Let It Be* tapes to Phil Spector to remix. Starting on 3 March, the American recast the songs in his Wall of Sound style, adding orchestra and choir to Paul's keynote ballads 'Let it Be' and 'The Long and Winding Road'. In doing so he over-egged the hymnal quality of 'Let It Be', and prefaced it with a sarcastic comment by John: 'Now we'd like to do "'ark the Angels Come".' The Spectorisation of 'The Long and Winding Road' was even more egregious, giving the song a middle-of-the road sound rarely heard in the Beatles, though it would ironically be characteristic of Paul's solo career. Was it a coincidence that Spector wrought his damage on 1 April, April Fool's Day, when pranks are traditionally played on the unsuspecting? Paul certainly had no idea what was being done to his songs.

A point of crisis was inevitable, and it came shortly after the Beatles realised that Ringo's first solo album, *Sentimental Journey*, *Let It Be* and Paul's solo LP were all due to hit the shops around the same time. John, George and Ringo decided that *McCartney* would have to be pushed back, and wrote to Paul informing him that they'd given EMI instructions to delay the release of his record until June. Ritchie was given the task of delivering the note personally to Paul, who was so incensed that he threw Ritchie out of his house, screaming: 'I'll finish you now. You'll pay!' Paul then went ahead with plans to release *McCartney* on schedule.

To launch his new record and thereby his solo career Paul worked with Derek Taylor and Peter Brown on a question-and-answer interview to be given to the press in advance of the release, as well as being included with initial pressings of the LP itself. Over the course of four pages Paul explained how he'd made *McCartney*, working essentially on his own with Linda harmonising, 'so it's really a double act … she believes in me – constantly'. Asked to describe the theme of the album, he said, 'Home, Family, Love'. As if to bear this out, the LP was packaged with family photos by Linda, including a charming picture of Heather with Martha, Heather's nose blacked like the dog's; a shot of baby Mary in Paul's jacket in Kintyre; another of their standing stone. The crux of the questionnaire came when Paul spelt out his future *vis-à-vis* the Beatles. Asked if Allen Klein would have anything to do with his album, McCartney replied sharply: 'Not if I can help it.'

'Have you any plans to set up an independent production company?'

'McCartney Productions,' replied Paul, who had already taken steps to establish his own version of Apple. During the Beatles' winter of discontent, Paul bought a company named Adagrose Ltd, changing its name to McCartney Productions Ltd, later MPL Communications, the umbrella organisation under which he would conduct all his post-Beatles business. Initially, McCartney Productions was a small affair, run by Paul and one other director, Brian Brolly, the registered office being a firm of City of London accountants. McCartney Productions registered a loss for its first few years, but the company was cash rich from the start, with assets of £82,530 ($126,270) recorded on its first return, and it grew substantially. Importantly, Paul was the sole shareholder. In this new company nobody would be in a position where they could tell him what to do.

To get back to the questionnaire, asked if he missed working with the other Beatles Paul replied, 'No'. Ditto for 'Are you planning a new album or single with the Beatles?' He held back from saying the Beatles were finished, suggesting rather that he was giving the band a rest, while having no immediate plans to perform with them or write with John. Asked about the reasons for his break with the band, Paul cited what has become a music business cliché: 'Personal differences, business differences, musical differences …'

This Q&A was released to the press on Friday 10 April 1970, with Don Short given a heads up. As a result the *Daily Mirror* splashed the story: 'Paul is Quitting the Beatles'. Although Peter Brown had helped Paul compile the questionnaire, he didn't approve of what the boss had done. 'It was sort of Paul giving the finger to the other three. You know, "I can do this without you, and I am. And here it is." Which was sort of arrogant.'

The Beatles story doesn't end here. The band would never truly cease to exist so long as there was money to be made from exploiting its back-catalogue, and everything that Paul was and would do for the rest of his life related to what he had created with the Beatles. But John, Paul, George and Ritchie couldn't continue making music together. The Sixties were over. The boys had become men, and Paul had to start a new life.

PART TWO

AFTER THE BEATLES

15

'HE'S NOT A BEATLE
ANY MORE!'

GOING ON AND ON TO GET HIS
OWN WAY

When Paul McCartney heard what Phil Spector had done to his *Let It Be* songs – to 'The Long and Winding Road' in particular – he dictated a stern memo to Allen Klein, copied to his brother-in-law[yer] John Eastman, making it clear that he disliked Spector's embellishments; explaining that he'd already considered orchestrating 'The Long and Winding Road' and chosen not to, so he wanted the strings, horns and choir reduced, the harp removed, his vocal brought up, and the original piano reinstated. McCartney ended his note with the cold authority of somebody used to getting his own way, ordering: 'Don't ever do it again.' Klein paid not a blind bit of notice, and the Spector-produced *Let It Be* was readied for release. George Martin and Glyn Johns were as dismayed as Paul by what they heard. 'It's revolting, the Spector thing. It's just like puke,' says Johns, still sounding angry.

McCartney's mood wasn't ameliorated by the critical reception of the *McCartney* LP, released in a sleeve featuring a singularly uninteresting photo, by Linda, of cherries. The record sold very well, going to number one in America and number two in the UK, but the reviews were poor. 'For most of the trip it's just a man alone in a small recording studio fiddling around with a few half-written songs and a load of instrumentals,' opined *Melody Maker*, then the Bible of British pop. 'With this record, his debt to George Martin becomes increasingly clear,' the critic went on, suggesting that without the producer's input Paul's work sounded thin. Most listeners agreed then as now that 'Maybe I'm Amazed' was *almost* a classic, but *Melody Maker* found 'sheer banality' elsewhere on the album. An irritated Paul responded with a note to the letters page of the music paper, in which he appeared to misunderstand the reference to George Martin. 'It's obvious George Martin had a lot to do with it,' Paul wrote sarcastically. 'In fact if you listen carefully to the end of the third track played backwards, you can almost hear him whistling.'

Next came the movie *Let It Be*, which had been bowdlerised by Paul, George and Ritchie inasmuch as they insisted Michael Lindsay-Hogg reduce the screen time given to John and Yoko. Other sequences that Lindsay-Hogg had expected the band to veto were left in, including the Twickenham confrontation between Paul and George, as well as Paul's attempt at Savile Row to persuade John to get the Beatles back on the road. 'I was surprised that the thing between Paul and George got in, and I'm surprised that Paul talking to John stayed in, [because] they didn't want any kind of washing of dirty laundry in public,' comments the director. Over time George Harrison at least came to regret passing the movie for release. It was Harrison who blocked Apple from reissuing the movie on DVD, which is why it is now virtually impossible to obtain other than as a bootleg. The glimpses into the fraught relationships within the band were in fact the chief interest of *Let It Be*; that and the rooftop concert, which was a joy to behold, helping make the film and album a success in 1970, the LP going to number one on both sides of the Atlantic, Spector's embellished version of 'The Long and Winding Road' becoming the Beatles' 27th and last number one single.*

McCartney would never be happy with the single or the LP, and 33 years later he contrived to have the album remixed as *Let It Be ... Naked*. There were losses and gains, with changes to the running order that reinstated a welcome 'Don't Let Me Down' from the rooftop concert, yet dispensed with John's celebrated 'I hope we passed the audition' comment. By 2003 the whole matter of what was the best version of this album was moot because the world had long got used to the Spectorised *Let It Be*; while the producer himself had bigger problems to deal with, notably a murder charge.† As he said, '[Paul] gets me mixed up with someone who gives a shit.'

---

* In the British and US markets, 1962–70.

† In 2003 Spector was charged with murdering his girlfriend, Lana Clarkson. He was convicted in 2009.

Paul turned 28 in June 1970. When the schools broke for the summer holidays, he and Linda took Heather and baby Mary to Kintyre where Paul had the brainwave of making an animated musical of the *Rupert the Bear* cartoon. The drawings had been running in the *Daily Express* newspaper since the 1920s, the Rupert Christmas annual being one of the delights of Paul's childhood. Paul wrote to Derek Taylor at Apple to ask him to investigate optioning the rights to Rupert, emphasising that he didn't want the other Beatles to know. This was one of the first bits of business McCartney Productions did, with Paul taking over a decade to bring Rupert to the screen. More immediately, he wanted to make another solo album, and in October he and Linda took the kids to New York to start work on the project, staying at Linda's old apartment.

Session musicians were called to blind auditions at a basement studio a couple of blocks west of Times Square, none told the identity of the artist who wanted to hear them play. One such was 27-year-old Denny Seiwell, a tall, lantern-jawed ex-Navy drummer who was active on the local session scene. Seiwell was amazed to encounter Paul McCartney in a West Side basement. 'I went right into my Ringo impersonation,' says Seiwell, figuring he'd play what Paul knew. Paul duly booked Seiwell and a guitarist to work with him and Linda at the CBS studios in Midtown. Having got used to recording in big rooms at EMI, Paul had asked for and got a similarly commodious studio, one usually reserved for artists like Tony Bennett, who recorded with a full orchestra.

Beatles fans soon heard about the McCartney sessions and gathered at the studio door. They included 16-year-old Linda Magno, a Brooklyn schoolgirl proud to call herself a 'first generation fan' in that she caught the Beatles bug when the boys came to the USA in 1964. 'They don't sing about violence really, it's all love, peace,' she says, explaining her attraction to the group. 'And if you're down in the dumps – this is what I'll tell anybody – if you are having a bad day just turn on a Beatle album.' Linda started following Paul during his 1970 visit to Manhattan, and continued to do so for years afterwards, becoming perhaps his most devoted American fan. She learned at the outset that Paul had his 'rules', about where and when he didn't mind signing autographs and having his picture taken, and when he definitely didn't welcome such attention, and if you wanted to have 'a good experience' with Paul you paid attention to his rules. In return he would be friendly and cooperative, saying 'Hi!', giving the thumbs up, posing for photos and signing memorabilia.

During the New York sessions, one of Paul's rules was that he didn't want fans coming round the studio in the morning when he and Linda had Mary with them, because he didn't want Mary photographed. As soon as he started to have children Paul became mindful that his family might be the target of a kidnap gang, such as the one that infamously snatched the son of the aviator Charles Lindbergh in 1932. Even though a ransom was paid, the kidnap gang murdered the child. '[Paul's] always had [this fear] of some bugger snatching [his kids],' reveals his cousin Mike Robbins.

Thank you very much, I've got Paul McCartney's baby, I've run off with it, and that will cost you four million to get it back. And there are nutters around. His own children, when they were very small, he was watching them like a bloody hawk ... He's always a little bit edgy with strangers round him.

If fans came to the studio in the afternoon, when Mary was with a nanny, he would pose for pictures. So long as fans complied with rules like this they found Paul and Linda reasonably affable, though Linda could be a little short with them sometimes. 'He's not a Beatle any more!' she snapped at fans one day.

In the studio, Paul began to record what became the *Ram* album, working with Denny Seiwell and session guitarist Dave Spinoza. Linda was there, too, but she spent most of her time minding the kids in the control room. As we have seen, Paul's début solo album had been a homemade record of fragmentary songs that, upon release, didn't find favour with the critics. As a result, Paul was determined to make his second solo record more professional, putting more work into the songs, some of which seemed to express his feelings about the break-up of the Beatles, notably 'Oh Woman, Oh Why' and 'Too Many People', which could be read as an attack on John and Yoko. 'I really think that *Ram* was all the angst coming out,' comments Seiwell. 'A lot of these tunes were written at the end of the Beatles period and there was a lot of emotion in all of the writing, and the preparation for the tunes, and I think he was getting a lot off his chest.' There were other musical textures. 'Uncle Albert/Admiral Halsey' was a song suite with sound effects, strings, comical voices and a tempo change, all features reminiscent of the Beatles. Other songs celebrated family life ('Eat at Home'). 'Ram On' punningly recalled Paul's stage name for the Scottish tour with Johnny Gentle (Paul Ramon), with Linda singing backing vocals. 'She wasn't spot on a lot of the time. But we would just work with what we could, and she did improve over the years,' says Seiwell, who didn't view Paul's wife as a fellow musician, but nonetheless admired her 'spirit' in pitching in with them. Paul had originally intended to play with Seiwell for a week, then try out a different drummer, but they were getting on so well they kept recording together, starting work each day around 10:30 a.m., playing until 2:30, then breaking for lunch before continuing into the late afternoon.

Working with the Beatles at EMI, where the band had been cosseted and indulged to a rare degree, Paul was used to having everything and everybody at his disposal when he wanted to record. He didn't seem to understand that the new people he was working with in America might have other things to do as well. When Dave Spinoza excused himself once or twice to fulfil other commitments, Paul was not pleased, and replaced Spinoza with guitarist Hugh McCracken. McCartney, McCracken and Seiwell worked together until 20 November, by which date Paul had the bulk of *Ram*, plus an additional catchy love song, 'Another Day', which would be his first post-Beatles single.

The McCartneys then returned to Scotland where, as 1970 drew to a close, Paul put his mind to resolving his relationship with the Beatles, telling a reporter:

> I think the other three are the most honest, sincere men I have ever met. I love them, I really do. I don't mind being bound to them as a friend – I like that idea. I don't mind being bound to them musically, because I like the others as musical partners. I like being in their band. But for my own sanity we must change the business arrangements we have. Only by being completely free of each other financially will we ever have any chance of coming back together as friends …

John Eastman came to Kintyre to discuss the options. The brothers-in-law went for a walk, climbing a hill near the farm, at the top of which Paul reached a momentous decision. 'We were standing on this big hill which overlooked a loch – it was quite a nice day, a bit chilly – and we'd been searching our souls. Was there any other way? And we eventually said, "Oh, we've got to do it."' They would go to court to ask a judge to dissolve the Beatles partnership and appoint a receiver to run Apple until a new manager could be agreed. Allen Klein would oppose this, and John, George and Ritchie would line up behind Klein. So Paul would have to sue his band mates.

At the time it looked to many people as if Paul was acting selfishly, motivated by pique. Paul had never liked Klein. He was bitter about *Let It Be* and the way the release of *McCartney* had been handled. His character was such that he would never tolerate being told when he could release his records. So in order to win his creative and financial freedom he took his friends to court. In years to come he would argue that the court case was in fact to the ultimate benefit of all four Beatles; by going to court he rescued the band from Allen Klein. 'I single-handedly saved the Beatles empire! Ha! Ha! He said modestly. I can laugh about it now; it was not so funny at the time,' McCartney told Barry Miles for his authorised biography, going so far as to comment in *Rolling Stone*, in 2007, that the court case was the 'worst moment of my life'. This was surely an exaggeration, bearing in mind the traumatic loss of his mother, and his calamitous second marriage, but the court case was, nevertheless, 'a horrific thing to go through'.

John, George and Ritchie received letters from Paul's lawyers informing them that they were being sued by the guy they'd worked with like brothers for years, by their own Macca. It came as a profound shock. 'I just couldn't believe it,' said Ritchie.

The writ was issued on the last day of 1970 in the Chancery Division of the High Court at the Royal Courts of Justice in London, a fantastical Victorian-Gothic building on the Strand. In a preliminary court hearing, McCartney's barrister, David Hirst QC,* informed the judge, Mr Justice Stamp, that the Beatles' finances were in a mess. With the group earning vast sums by the standards of the day, between four and five million pounds sterling in 1970, the Beatles now faced an income tax bill of £678,000 ($1.03m) plus surtax and corporation tax. 'The latest accounts suggest there is probably not enough in the kitty to meet even the individual Beatles' income and surtax liability,' Hirst warned His Lordship.

---

* Queen's Counsel, a senior barrister.

Moreover, the company books were in a lamentable state – McCartney had never been given audited accounts – and Allen Klein was 'a man of bad commercial reputation'. The matter was adjourned, with Klein issuing a statement that the Beatles' accounts were not in bad shape, and there *was* enough money to pay the taxman.

Paul was in Scotland when the initial legal skirmish took place, his attention diverted by the latest issue of *Rolling Stone* which carried the first sensational instalment of a two-part interview with John Lennon conducted by the magazine's Editor, Jann Wenner. Under the influence of the new Primal Scream therapy, pioneered by American psychologist Arthur Janov, which encouraged one to let it all hang out, Lennon had given Wenner the unexpurgated scoop on the Beatles. McCartney read with horrified fascination how he'd taken over the leadership of the Beatles after Brian Epstein died, only to lead the band 'round in circles' while John, George and Ringo had been made to feel like his sidemen. McCartney 'thought he was the fuckin' Beatles, and he never fucking was … none of us were the Beatles, four of us were,' John growled. Lennon complained about *Let It Be*. 'When Paul was feeling kindly he would give me a solo,' he said of his guitar part on 'Get Back', while he asserted that the movie was edited to Paul's advantage, with scenes involving him and Yoko cut 'for no other reason than the people were orientated towards Engelbert Humperdinck …' It was this comparison, to the middle-of-the-road balladeer of 'Release Me', that cut McCartney most deeply; that and John's assessment of his first solo album: 'I thought Paul's was rubbish,' opined Lennon, saying that he (like most people) preferred George's *All Things Must Pass*. McCartney studied the article with the morbid fascination of a jilted lover receiving a kiss-off letter. 'I sat down and pored over every little paragraph, every sentence. "Does he really think that of me?"' Paul said a couple of years later in 1974. 'And at the time I thought, "It's me …That's just what I'm like. He's captured me so well; I'm a turd …" [Then] Linda said, "Now, you know that's not true …"'

Paul came down to London to attend the opening of his court case on 19 February, the first part being an application to appoint a receiver to manage the Beatles' affairs. Heavily bearded and wearing the same suit he'd worn for the *Abbey Road* cover, Paul was accompanied by a protective Linda, who clutched his arm as they entered Court 16 of the Royal Courts of Justice. Inside McCartney's QC listed reasons –

including tax offences in the USA – why Klein was not a man to be trusted, and told the judge Paul had never agreed that Klein should represent him. In reply Klein said he was appealing against convictions of having failed to file tax returns, and McCartney hadn't complained about the enhanced royalties he'd negotiated for the band. The Beatles' income had increased to £4.3 million a year during his tenure ($6.5m). Now McCartney was trying to extricate himself from the partnership so that he could benefit from his solo career.

The court heard from Lennon, Harrison and Starkey in the form of written affidavits, read aloud by barristers. In his statement, Lennon revealed the chaotic manner in which Apple Corps operated. He had only recently discovered that two company cars Apple had bought had 'completely disappeared, and that we owned a house which no one can remember buying'. Lennon described fractious business meetings with Klein and the Eastmans, describing Paul's brother-in-law as 'excitable and easily confused. Lee Eastman was more impressive at first sight, but after five minutes' conversation he lost his temper and became quite hysterical, screaming and shouting abuse at Klein'. In his affidavit, George Harrison contrasted a happy, relaxed time he'd spent recently with Bob Dylan in upstate New York with working with Paul, who, he said, had always shown a 'superior attitude' to him. George believed, however, that the showdown at Twickenham had cleared the air. 'Since the row Paul has treated me more as a musical equal ...' In perhaps the most revealing affidavit, Ritchie said: 'Paul is the greatest bass player in the world. He is also very determined. He goes on and on to see if he can get his own way. While that may be a virtue, it did mean that musical disagreements inevitably arose from time to time.' On Friday 26 February, as 'Another Day' went to number two in the UK charts, Paul went into the witness box to answer these affidavits, telling the court, among other things, of a conversation he'd had with Allen Klein in which Klein blamed Yoko for the discord within the band, saying, 'The real trouble is Yoko. She is the one with ambition.' Paul wondered aloud what John would have said if he'd heard that basic truth. He had now.

Leaving the lawyers to get on with the case, Paul and Linda flew to Los Angeles to complete *Ram*. Despite the good work done in New York, Paul had become bogged down in indecision, unable to select between the 20 or so songs he had recorded. To try and help his brother-in-law finish the record, John Eastman introduced Paul to the fashionable producer Jim Guercio, a fellow Eastman & Eastman client who'd won a Grammy for his work with Blood, Sweat and Tears. Guercio was so keen to produce Paul that he cancelled his honeymoon to help out with *Ram*, laying down a new track, 'Dear Boy', and working to make a final selection from the songs Paul already had in the bag. It was clear McCartney felt under pressure to do better than his début album, partly in answer to Lennon's criticism of *McCartney* as Engelbert Humperdinck music. Yet the pressure had a paralysing effect on the star. Instead of finishing *Ram* in LA, Paul kept fiddling with it, block-booking a Hollywood studio and insisting Guercio was there every day from 10:00 a.m. so they could record, though Paul rarely showed up before mid-afternoon. Then he'd smoke a joint and jam. Guercio tried to assert some discipline, but could not guide or control his star: 'Paul is not an artist you can direct or collaborate with. You kind of have [to] support his ideas.' As weeks passed, and the album was no nearer completion, Guercio gave Paul a suggested track listing and told him the engineers could do what was necessary. He had to go. 'I think he took offence. I said, "No, no, this isn't personal, Paul, you don't need me. I can't come in here every day. We've got to finish … I have other obligations … I gave up my damn honeymoon here!'

The McCartneys were still in LA when, on 12 March 1971, Justice Stamp ruled in Paul's favour at the High Court in London. 'The appointment of Abkco [Klein's company], without the concurrence of Paul, was in my judgement a breach of the terms of the partnership deed,' said the judge. There was no evidence Klein had stolen money from the Beatles, but he had received excessive commission, and McCartney had grounds to distrust the American, whose statements read 'like the irresponsible patter of a second-rate salesman'. Under the terms of the Partnership Act, the judge appointed an accountant, James Douglas Spooner, to manage the Beatles' affairs until a full hearing on the issue of dissolving the partnership, which was McCartney's ultimate goal. The judge expected Paul to be successful, saying: 'The Beatles have long since ceased to perform as a group.' McCartney had conducted his case well, with the help of a first-class legal team, showing himself to be a formidable courtroom adversary, one whom judges tended to side with in the future, appreciating his sensible, civil responses to difficult situations. When he went to law, McCartney usually got what he wanted. That evening a thwarted John Lennon threw bricks through the windows of Paul's London home in a childish attempt to get even with him.

James Spooner therefore became the Beatles' new, court-appointed manager, though his role was strictly that of a disinterested professional, rather than pop Svengali. He didn't move into the Apple Building, but undertook his duties from his usual desk in the City of London. Spooner (later Sir James Spooner) got on well with Paul, the little he saw of him, and tended to agree with McCartney's view that Allen Klein was a crook, while the accountant considered John Lennon simply impossible. 'John Lennon was a popular hero, a brilliant man, but terribly tiresome,' he observed, likewise declaring McCartney was correct to sue his band mates. 'They'd have been bust otherwise. The [others] foolishly took on this crook called Klein as a manager and Klein firstly ripped them off something shocking, by taking a percentage off the *gross*, rather than off the net, after expenses.'

Sir James alleges that when McCartney failed to sign with Klein in 1969, his signature was actually forged. 'They wrote some document which they claimed Paul had signed as a partnership deed, or new partnership deed, or new partnership agreement. In fact he wasn't in the room when it was signed … it was a very crooked piece of paper, as far as I recall.' Sir James concedes that Klein negotiated an advantageous royalty deal with EMI, 'the percentage that the Beatles were getting out of EMI was *far* higher than *any*body had ever achieved before, but the trouble was that Klein, as I say, took his cut before any expenses of any sort, or tried to do so'. If Paul hadn't sued the Beatles, Sir James believes the band would have drowned in debt.

If they hadn't been a success they'd all have been bankrupt because they had huge tax liabilities on previous years, which nobody had ever helped them [with], or told them how to meet or reserve for. But happily they were earning a million a year each even then, and going upwards, so they were able to pay past tax liabilities out of the current income and future income.

Having won the first round of his legal battle, Paul retreated with Linda to High Park, where he atavistically enjoyed the rural life his Irish forebears had led before Owen Mohin crossed the Irish Sea. Unlike his ancestors Paul was a millionaire smallholder, one who commuted to his steading in a convertible Rolls Royce, or private jet, depending on how much time he had, shearing a few sheep for recreation before leaving the farm in the hands of his estate manager Duncan Cairns, disappearing back down to London or abroad. Neighbours were amazed at the way Paul and Linda flitted about the world. Alec McLean, who farmed adjacent High Ranachan Farm with his brother Duncan, was cutting thistles one afternoon in May 1971 when he saw Paul and Linda driving down to the main road. The McCartneys stopped to say hello, and mentioned that they were on their way to a wedding. Alec wished them well, imagining this was a local wedding. When he turned on the television that night, he discovered that in the few hours since he'd seen Paul and Linda they'd flown to France to attend Mick Jagger's nuptials.

Despite the remoteness of High Park, fans increasingly found their way to the farm. One morning the McLeans were getting their cows in when their dog started sniffing round the sheds. Duncan discovered five hippies inside. They wanted to practise their yoga near a Beatle. The hippies turned out to be nice people, but other fans could be worrying. 'I've been working at the sink and looked around and somebody was peeking in the window, thinking this was maybe [Paul's house],' says Alice McLean. One Christmas Day a man came to the door asking where Paul lived, saying he *had* to see him. 'He said he wrote songs and the more I engaged him in conversation the more I realised he was quite cracked – he was a musician, and he was victimised.' When the McCartneys became aware that such people were in the area, or if they knew the press were up, Linda would ring round and apologise for any inconvenience, reminding her neighbours to please not tell strangers where they lived. Linda proved adept at befriending local people, fitting surprisingly snugly into Kintyre life. The American particularly enjoyed hailing Scottish neighbours with the local cry of 'Hoots happenin' in the wee toon?',* which sounded very amusing coming from a foreigner.

One of the most bothersome fans was a Mormon girl from Utah. She camped with a friend on the edge of a wood within 100 yards of Paul's farmhouse, watching the McCartneys from the trees. 'And they couldn't move them,' recalls neighbour Rory Colville, 'as long as they didn't

---

* Translates as 'What's happening in the little town?' – the 'wee toon' being Campbeltown.

intrude they could sit there all day with their binoculars and watch Paul.' In the summer of 1971, the Mormon complained to the local police that Paul had assaulted her: 'Paul came out of the house and drove up in his Land Rover. He jumped out and began shouting and swearing. I don't remember much about what happened, but my nose was bleed-ing.' Paul confirmed that he had confronted the girl, but denied assault. 'For three years now I have been asking her politely – pleading with her – to leave me and my family alone. She refuses to recognise that I am married with a family.' Nothing came of the complaint and Paul ulti-mately solved the problem by buying the wood in which the girls had camped. This was the start of a process of purchasing adjacent tracts of land, indeed whole farms, as they came on the market, to gain privacy. When Archie Revie at Low Ranachan retired, Paul bought his 304 acres, plus his farmhouse, which the star began to use as a rehearsal space and accommodation for visiting musicians. Next he bought Low Park Farm from the McDougals, by which time it was diffi-cult to gain a glimpse of Paul's cottage without straying onto his land.

Despite the occasional intruder, Paul and his family continued to enjoy High Park, and their happy life there is commemorated on *Ram*, particularly the song 'Heart of the Country', while the album cover features a photo Linda took of Paul shearing their Black Face sheep. Inside, the album was illustrated with a collage of snapshots, many of which were also taken by Linda on the property, emphasising the fact that, although they had employed session musicians and indeed an orchestra to make *Ram*, this was another homemade McCartney production, one in which all the songs were credited to Paul and Linda McCartney. This may have been a ruse. Under the terms of the contracts he had signed as a Beatle, any songs Paul wrote until 1973 were owned by Northern Songs and an entity named Maclen Music. By crediting new songs to Paul and Linda McCartney, he clawed back half the royal-ties. How much writing Linda actually did is questionable, and indeed Paul's publishers took the view that his wife wasn't capable of being his co-writer, suing him on that basis (the dispute was later settled out of court). Paul said in their defence (making one feel somewhat sorry for Linda):

You know — suddenly she marries him and suddenly she's writing songs. 'Oh sure (wink, wink). Oh, sure, she's writing songs.' But actually one day I just said to her, 'I'm going to teach you how to write if I have to strap you to the piano bench.' ... I like to collaborate on songs [and] if I can have Linda working with me, then it becomes like a game. It's fun. So we wrote about ten songs [together].

For many people, *Ram* is one of Paul's best solo albums, with a Beatles sparkle, notably on 'Uncle Albert/Admiral Halsey', which became a hit single, as indeed *Ram* was a very successful album, reaching number one in the UK, number two in the US charts. *Ram* is certainly more highly finished than *McCartney* and it has an abundance of catchy tunes. Despite all the prevarication over the final song selection there was, however, a sense that Paul had released a record that still needed work. The lyrics are so-so, ranging from veiled sarcasm ('Too Many People') to simplistic celebrations of love ('Long Haired Lady') via novelty ('Uncle Albert/Admiral Halsey'). Taken as a whole, there is a lack of discipline and focus as there was on *McCartney*, as well as a sense that, without a strong collaborator like John Lennon, or an authoritative producer like George Martin, Paul struggled to distinguish between what was good enough to release and what would be better cut.

Although frequently derided, the rock music of the early 1970s was often superb. Recent months had yielded *Bridge Over Troubled Water* (Simon and Garfunkel), *Hot Rats* (Frank Zappa), *All Things Must Pass* (George Harrison), *Tapestry* (Carole King) and *Blue* (Joni Mitchell); with *Who's Next* (The Who), Led Zeppelin's untitled fourth album, and David Bowie's *Hunky Dory* soon to follow. All these records had a musical and/or intellectual weight that made them great in their day, and marks them as classics now. *Ram* is not and never was in the same class, which is concerning because there was much more of this sort of music to come from Paul McCartney. All such judgements are, of course, subjective. Many fans loved *Ram*. Other listeners wondered what had happened to the man who had been a prime mover in the world's greatest pop band. While it had been ridiculous to suggest in 1969 that Paul McCartney was dead, one might wonder if he'd undergone a lobotomy before leaving the Beatles.

Whimsy had always been one of Paul's musical moods, as it was one of John's. In the context of the Beatles it was charming – Paul's

'Yellow Submarine', for example, John's 'I am the Walrus' – but in Paul's solo career whimsy too often became annoying. There is a surfeit on *McCartney* and *Ram*, and in June 1971 Paul indulged this side of himself to the full by hiring session musicians to record light orchestral versions of the *Ram* songs. One of the musicians hired for the gig was Clem Cattini, who'd known Paul when the Beatles were playing the ABC Blackpool and Clem was drumming with the Tornados on the North Pier. 'I crapped myself a bit when I walked in[to Abbey Road] and I'm doing a session for Paul McCartney.' Paul wasn't going to play on this new record himself, just direct. To play bass, he hired Brian 'Herbie' Flowers. Also on the sessions were the Mike Sammes Singers, a vocal group who sang on 'I am the Walrus', but more typically emitted the *oohs* and *aahs* on television commercials. Partly as a result, the record they made at Abbey Road sounds like incidental television music, with a *soupçon* of the tea dance. Jim Mac's Band must have sounded similar. While Paul naturally enjoyed hearing his tunes orchestrated, with the help of the arranger Richard Hewson, one suspects he may have made these curious recordings primarily to please his father. In short, this was an indulgence. It was also an anachronism in the context of his career and it wasn't released for six years. When Paul did finally put this odd record out, he did so as quietly as possible under a pseudonym, titling the album *Thrillington* after an invented character named Percy 'Thrills' Thrillington 'Born in Coventry Cathedral in 1939'. Somehow this wasn't as amusing as Paul obviously thought it was.

More importantly, in the week of the *Thrillington* session, Paul formally adopted eight-year-old Heather See as his daughter. Although a couple of hippies in many respects, there was a traditional parental firmness to Paul and Linda McCartney. 'We explain to Heather that she can't have too much ice-cream or that sweets will ruin her teeth – that sort of thing,' Paul said. 'She's going to get the lot when she's 21 and I want her to have learned how to cope when that time comes. I don't want her to be a spoilt little brat. We're really quite strict with her in some ways.' Indeed some observers felt Paul was stricter with Heather than his own natural children. As yet, Heather could only be measured against Mary McCartney, who was coming up for two, but Lin was pregnant again.

ANOTHER BAND

Having begun to extricate himself from the Beatles, and having released two exploratory solo albums, Paul's next move was to form a band. He intended to develop the group slowly, as the Beatles had been able to grow naturally, enjoying the process of playing small shows again, and making records in a relaxed collaborative atmosphere.

When it came to choosing the members, Paul first telephoned the New York session men he had been working with on *Ram*, Denny Seiwell and Hugh McCracken, inviting the guys and their wives over to Scotland. 'I thought he meant take a vacation,' says Seiwell, who arrived in the UK with his wife Monique on 23 June 1971. 'That's when he says, "Yeah, I've invited Hugh up here as well. I'm thinking of putting together a band."' Seiwell hadn't been to the UK before, and its Scottish extremities were a culture shock. 'It wasn't as much fun as I thought it was going to be.' He and Monique, and Hugh and Holly McCracken, were put up at the Argyle Arms Hotel in Campbeltown, where they found the food disappointing while the nights were so cold they had to go to bed with hot water bottles. And this was supposed to be summer!

Although it was only a short drive from the Argyle Arms to Paul's farm, High Park seemed incredibly remote and basic to the New Yorkers, who wondered, as many others would, why such a rich man chose to rough it like this, not appreciating that Paul and Linda enjoyed a rustic contrast to their metropolitan life. 'Two bedrooms and a kitchen, a cement floor. The walls were finished in unpainted pine. It was very, very bare,' says Seiwell, ticking off the primitive features. Recording equipment was set up in an adjacent lean-to shed, which Paul named Rude Studios: a nod to reggae influences (Paul and Lin had recently started to holiday in the Caribbean and loved reggae music). The McCartneys showed their American friends over the farm, and had a few drinks with them in the evening. Relaxed and convivial though Paul was, one subject was obviously out of bounds. Paul did not mention the Beatles, and without anything being said the American visitors understood that they shouldn't ask him about the band.

Music-making started awkwardly. 'As we were leaving, Linda said, "Would you mind coming back tomorrow and maybe leaving your wives at home? We're going to spend the day playing some music,"' Seiwell recalls. This didn't go down well with Monique and Holly. Having come

to Scotland with their husbands for what they thought was to be a vacation, the American women were obliged to entertain themselves at the
Argyle Arms while their menfolk made music with the McCartneys up
at High Park. After a few days of this, Hugh McCracken told Paul that
he and his wife had to go back to New York. Hugh didn't want to be in
Paul's band. The Seiwells were also going back to New York, but Denny
told Paul he would return if he wanted him.

The nucleus of the new group therefore became Paul, Linda and
Denny Seiwell. As yet Linda didn't play an instrument. Paul was sure
she could pick up keyboards, so when they got back to London Lin went
for lessons with an elderly Cavendish Avenue neighbour named Mrs
Matthews. The lessons didn't go well. 'Mrs Matthews gave up. She
said, "I can't teach you any more!"' recalls Evelyn Grumi, whose family
occupied the apartment over Mrs Matthews's basement flat in Cavendish Avenue, across from Paul, and were thereby obliged to listen to
Linda plonking about on the piano. 'Mrs Matthews said, "I've had
enough of her, she's stupid, she doesn't even know her right hand from
her left."' So it was that Paul found himself in a band with a woman who
could neither sing nor play. As George Martin remarked drily, 'I don't
think Linda is a substitute for John Lennon.'

To be fair, Linda never pretended to be Paul's musical peer. She
didn't really want to be in the band at all. It was Paul's fancy that his wife
should work with him. He found it 'comforting'. Professional sidemen
would cover Linda's bum notes. Her value was the moral support she
gave Paul. More than a wife and band member, he saw Linda as his
career partner now, using her as his link with the world, which is to say
that Mrs McCartney was the one who made calls on Paul's behalf,
getting information he wanted, screening out people he didn't want to
speak to, making the peace with those he'd upset, and dispensing hard
news. It was of course Paul who wanted Monique Seiwell and Holly
McCracken out of the way so he, Denny, Hugh and Lin could jam
together at High Park, but he delegated the ticklish task of telling the
women they were surplus to requirements to Lin, a tough broad who
grew tougher during their long marriage.

Still, Paul also felt the need of a more experienced musician in the
band, someone he could write with, play with and sing harmony with,
as he had with Lennon. He chose Denny Laine, a musician he'd known
since the early 1960s when Denny had fronted the Midlands band the

Diplomats. The musician's given name was Brian Hines, born in Birmingham of Romany Gypsy descent in 1944. He took the stage name of Laine in honour of Cleo Laine and Frankie Laine, two singers he admired. Denny was a childhood nickname. A friendly, easy-going guy with a broad Birmingham accent and a wide love of music, particularly jazz and blues, in 1964 Denny co-founded the Moody Blues, who supported the Beatles on tour and went to number one with 'Go Now'. Denny knew the Beatles well by this stage. 'All the boys were friends of mine … I used to go to the clubs with Paul and Jane Asher, and we used to talk forever about music … I used to go-to the parties, I went to Abbey Road to some of their *Sgt. Pepper* sessions.' As a result, Denny was relaxed around Paul, not somebody who would ask a lot of star-struck questions about the Beatles. 'I think that's why Paul wanted me in the band – because he knew I wouldn't bring up all that stuff. That's kind of boring for him.' In 1966 Denny left the Moodies to form the Electric String Band, after which he played briefly with Ginger Baker's Air Force. Always bad with money, Denny was unemployed, broke, and sleeping in his manager's office when Paul called offering him a gig. 'Hey man, how's it going? Long time no see. Fancy putting a band together?' McCartney asked, as Denny recalls their perfunctory conversation.

'Yeah, great. That's perfect timing. I'm doing nothing … I'll see you tomorrow.' Denny flew to Scotland the next day, meeting Linda McCartney and Denny Seiwell at the farm.

Confusingly, this meant there were now two men named Denny in the band, both hired on a salary basis and initially paid a retainer of £70 a week ($107). This was a reasonable wage in 1971, when you could rent a house for £5 a week ($7.65), but certainly not riches, especially not for Seiwell who had the additional expense of relocating from New York to the UK. He and Monique rented a farm near the McCartneys initially, Laine staying as their house guest. Money soon became an issue with Seiwell, whereas happy-go-lucky Laine was more relaxed about it. 'I wasn't looking for anything more than that to start with, because I knew there would be a deal along the line, that it was just a retainer so we wouldn't go off and do something else.'

Not long after the formation of the band, the McCartneys returned to London so that Lin could give birth to her third child, Paul's second. She went into labour at King's College Hospital and it was a long and complicated labour, Linda finally giving birth on 13 September 1971 to a daughter the couple named Stella Nina McCartney. So anxious had Paul been about the difficult pregnancy, and so thankful was he that mother and daughter had come through OK, that he imagined a guardian angel with wings standing over the family. It was this image that gave him the name for the new band. They would be Wings.

THE NEW BAND

'TAKE IT, TONY!'

Wings began recording their first album in London, working quickly and using up leftovers from Paul's LA sessions. The record was *Wild Life*, named after one of Paul's new compositions – an inchoate song about animal welfare the lyrics of which were sketchy to the point of meaninglessness. 'Man, you've gotta care' was the considered message. Musically, this and several other tracks on Wings' début album sound like stoned jams; the very first track, 'Mumbo', most obviously *was* a jam, over which Paul could be heard yelling excitedly to his engineer. As with his two previous albums, Paul was the producer, and again, without a strong hand to rein him in, he was content to release tracks that should never have left the studio, including folderol like 'Bip Bop'.

The whole album was recorded and released with reckless speed. 'Five of the eight tracks* were first takes,' notes the drummer, Denny Seiwell.

> Whatever we did as a band was going to be compared to the last thing they heard of the Beatles, so what we were trying to do was give an honest representation of this new band, and we didn't want to use every studio trick in the world … it's gonna be a little raggedy, but that is what we are … that record was done in a heartbeat. I mean

---

* Eight tracks were listed on the original LP, plus two instrumental interludes listed as additional tracks when the album was re-released on CD.

'Mumbo', we were just jamming, fooling around in the studio and you can hear him screaming at the engineer, cos it was getting good: 'Take it, Tony!'*

The band had a rocking sound, which was partly Denny Laine's influence. The guitarist says he envisaged Wings as 'a rough and tumble rock/blues-type' band. But there were no shortage of good-time rock 'n' roll bands in the early 1970s, and in the cold light of day there were only two interesting songs on *Wild Life*: 'Tomorrow' and 'Dear Friend'. Recorded in LA during the West Coast sessions for *Ram*, the latter is sometimes read as a message from Paul to John Lennon, but in truth it could mean almost anything, so insubstantial are the words, and by the time Paul had made *Wild Life* John had addressed their broken friendship much more eloquently on his *Imagine* album, which he made with help from George Harrison and Klaus Voormann, under the direction of Phil Spector, demonstrating in the process what a difference a professional producer can make. Paul's record sounded amateurish and thin; *Imagine* sounded big as a mountain, Lennon touching profundity with the title song, 'Imagine'; delivering a powerful anti-war message in 'I Don't Wanna be a Soldier Mama I Don't Wanna Die'; and writing a love song as tender as any Paul had penned with 'Jealous Guy'.

Lennon was still sufficiently irked with Paul to mock him with *Imagine*, having himself photographed wrangling a pig for a souvenir postcard included with the LP, in parody of Paul shearing sheep on the cover of *Ram*, and including two songs that expressed contempt for his former partner. 'Crippled Inside', a country-and-western pastiche, described a man who was emotionally dead, while 'How Do You Sleep?' was direct character assassination, suggesting that Paul didn't know what the Beatles had on their hands when they made *Sgt. Pepper*, noting nastily that 'those freaks' were right when they said Paul was dead; criticising Paul for living with 'straights' while being bossed about by his 'Mamma' (Linda). Most hurtfully, Lennon stated in 'How Do You Sleep?' that the only song of consequence Paul had written was 'Yesterday', since when his music had been typified by the sugary 'Another Day', and soon everybody would realise his music was actually just Muzak – a disparaging reference to the American company that

* Tony Clark, one of the engineers.

created muted versions of pop hits for public places, a use Paul's tunes were suited to. In summary, Lennon asked his old mate how he slept at night, the implication being that Macca was such a complete bastard his conscience – if he had one – should keep him awake. Was Lennon speaking the truth, seeing McCartney through the clear eyes of someone who had known him as man and boy, or was he merely trying to get even after his defeat in court? There is probably truth in both hypotheses. It should be remembered also that Lennon was abetted at this stage in his career by Phil Spector, whom Paul had crossed on *Let It Be*. Spector now seemed to encourage Lennon in his feud, as an exchange between the two while they were working in New York on a new Christmas song illustrates: 'Have you heard Paul's new album?' Spector asked Lennon, referring to *Wild Life*.

'No.'

'It's really bad,' replied the producer spitefully, 'it's awful.'

'Don't talk about it. It depresses me.'

'Don't worry, John. *Imagine* is number one, and this will be number one, too. That's all that matters.'*

These comments were reported in *Melody Maker* the week Paul launched Wings with a party at the Empire Ballroom in London's Leicester Square. Although security was tight, and many famous faces were among the guests, there was a relaxed, homely feel to the event that typified Wings, from the hand-made invitation cards to the McCartneys' own party clothes. Paul showed up in a baggy tartan suit, like a Caledonian clown. Lin wore a maternity dress. Paul had cut a sharp figure during the Sixties, never more so than when he strode across the Abbey Road zebra crossing in a beautifully tailored Savile Row suit. Now he had mislaid his style compass. It would be years until he found it again. Not all Seventies fashion was bad, but it is fair to say that Paul McCartney dressed appallingly throughout that decade and much of the Eighties, wearing vulgar and ill-chosen clothes and sporting a trendy yet hideous mullet haircut.

There was a conscious turning away from the Sixties in other areas of his life. Despite the size of the Wings launch party, none of the other Beatles attended, and there were hardly any old faces from

* 'Happy Xmas (War is Over)' never charted in the US. It reached number 4 in the UK in 1972.

Apple at the function. It was as if Paul wanted to forget his illustrious past. 'This was a fresh start, clean slate,' says Denny Seiwell, 'and we did not discuss the Beatles. Every once in a great while he might make a reference to an old story or something, but very, very seldom.'

The exception came when interviewers drew Paul on the ongoing legal fight over the break-up of the Beatles. 'I just want the four of us to get together somewhere and sign a piece of paper saying it's all over, and we want to divide the money four ways,' Paul told *Melody Maker* that month. Paul's personal assistant Shelley Turner, together with Laine and Seiwell, sat and listened uneasily as Paul went on about the Beatles break-up in what was meant to be a band interview. ('He's talking about money now. That's one of his pet points. He'll never stop,' Turner told the reporter in a worried aside. 'Please get him on to talking about Wings.') Still, Paul had more to say on the rift, responding to John's dig in 'How Do You Sleep?': 'So what if I live with straights?' he asked. 'It doesn't affect *him*. He says the only thing I did was "Yesterday" and he knows that's wrong.'

Mild though this and Paul's other remarks were, Lennon retaliated with an open letter to *Melody Maker*, which had become a forum for the ex-Beatles to snipe at each other. 'Dear Paul, Linda, et all [sic] the wee McCartneys,' Lennon began, before resuming the old arguments about who owed what to whom, and challenging Paul's version of events in his recent interview. He mocked his former friend mercilessly through-out, referring to 'my obsessive old pal', and saying Paul took 'How Do You Sleep?' way too literally. One of the bones of contention between the men was Maclen Music. Lennon wanted Paul to sell his share to the other three, but according to Lennon Paul had refused. '… two weeks ago,' Lennon harangued his ex-friend,

> I asked you on the phone, 'Please let's meet without advisors etc., and decide what we want,' and I especially emphasised 'Maclen' which is mainly your concern, but you refused — right? You said under no condition would you sell to us, and if we didn't do what you wanted, you'd sue us again … If *you're not* the aggressor (as you claim) who the hell took us to court and [shit] all over us in public?

Paul chose not to respond publicly to these allegations.

BACK ON STAGE

The McCartneys went to the United States for Thanksgiving, leaving their pets – Eddie, Martha, a Dalmatian named Lucky and several cats – in the care of their housekeeper Rose Martin. The McCartney menagerie was a source of disquiet in Cavendish Avenue where, despite his fame and wealth, Paul was not altogether popular. Some neighbours snobbishly looked down on Paul as *nouveau riche*, considering the press and fans he attracted a damn nuisance. Then there was the time the McCartneys painted their listed house in bright colours, which led to complaints to the council, who made Paul change back to an authorised scheme; while one particular neighbour, Alice Griswold, an elderly woman whose wealth and class were established by the fact she ran a chauffeur-driven Rolls Royce, seemed to have it in for the family. Mrs Griswold got it into her head that the McCartneys were neglecting their dogs, leaving them locked in the house while they were in America, and made a complaint to the Royal Society for the Prevention of Cruelty to Animals (RSPCA). When the McCartneys returned home, Paul went over the road and had 'a right row' with Mrs G. He told her sharply he'd never harm his dogs; he and Lin were animal-mad, and Rosie had been in every day to make sure the animals were all right. The man from the RSPCA agreed. Lin remarked that, 'Mrs Griswold gives me a pain in the you-know-what.'

After Christmas, Paul hired an additional guitarist for Wings. Born in Northern Ireland in 1943, Henry McCullough had been a professional musician since the age of 17, playing notably with Joe Cocker's Grease Band, and was an old friend of Denny Laine's. 'I wanted to bring more of a blues element into the band,' explains Laine. 'I didn't want to be in a pop group, and Henry was the epitome of a blues player.' So Henry joined Wings on the standard £70-a-week deal, rehearsing initially with the group in rooms off the Mall. It soon became clear that Henry didn't quite fit into Wings, which was poppier than both he and Laine wished, with a distinct weakness in the keyboard department. Henry suggested to Paul that they hire a professional keyboardist to strengthen their sound. Paul admitted that his wife was 'absolute rubbish' on keyboards, but there was no prospect of replacing her. 'Once that was accepted by meself and everybody else, that was it. Linda was 100 per cent a part of the band and that's the way we worked,' says Henry, who developed a respect for Mrs McCartney, as most Wings members did, not for her musical ability, but for her pluck and charm.

On Sunday 30 January 1972, what became known as Bloody Sunday, news came from Northern Ireland that the British Army had opened fire on a Republican demonstration, killing 13 people: In the wake of this appalling incident, Paul did something that was for him very rare indeed: he wrote a protest song, not only condemning the shootings, which most people lamented, but calling for the British to get out of Ireland, which was more problematic because the Protestant Loyalist population feared they would be murdered by their Catholic neighbours if the British Army withdrew. In writing this song, Paul put himself on the side of the Republican movement and its terrorist group, the IRA, which was engaged in a murderous campaign against the British. Paul's maternal grandfather had been Irish, which gave him a personal connection to Ireland, but one wonders if his decision to write a Republican marching song had more to do with wanting to match John Lennon, who projected a trendy image of political engagement these days and had written two songs of his own about Bloody Sunday, both of which shared the simplistic sentiment expressed by Paul in his self-describing 'Give Ireland Back to the Irish'. It is also possible that Paul wanted to reach out to John again by aligning himself with one of his old friend's pet causes. Certainly Paul tried hard to remake their friendship in the Seventies.

A slow song, with incongruously jaunty hand-claps, 'Give Ireland Back to the Irish' was released as a single in February 1972. It was the first major Wings project for Henry McCullough, an Ulster Protestant who says he didn't discuss the song with Paul and had been on the road too long to feel personally connected to Irish politics. 'I knew it would cause a little bit of a fuss,' is as far as he will go, diplomatically. It is hard to believe Henry was truly indifferent to a song that commented directly on the delicate politics of his homeland, and he certainly looked uncomfortable when Paul invited a US television crew into Cavendish Avenue to film Wings rehearsing the number. Paul gave the Americans a short interview, in which he said he didn't intend to become a political singer, but 'on this one occasion I think the British government overstepped the mark and showed themselves to be more of a sort of oppressive regime than I ever believed them to be'.

As the song was rush-released, Paul led his fledgling band out on the road for the first time. On the morning of Tuesday 8 February 1972, an Avis truck and green van pulled up outside 7 Cavendish Avenue. The McCartneys, together with their children, the band and the family dogs, climbed aboard the van; roadies Trevor Jones and Ian Horn loaded the truck with equipment, and the two vehicles headed north on the M1, whither no one knew. Paul was realising the ambition he'd harboured in the latter years of the Beatles to go back on the road and play small provincial shows, but he'd taken the concept to the extreme, setting off without any theatres booked.

After driving 130 miles north, Wings reached Nottingham University, where the roadies informed the students' union that they had Paul McCartney outside. Could Wings put on a show? Strange though this now seems, British rock bands such as the Who and Led Zeppelin did play universities at this time, building up their fan base, but acts didn't turn up at universities unannounced in the hope of a chance booking, and Paul McCartney's status as an ex-Beatle elevated him above and beyond everyday rock musicians. Then, as now, McCartney was one of the most famous entertainers in the world, and the students didn't believe he had come to play for them until they saw him for themselves sitting in the van with Lin and the kids, at which point the booking was made. The McCartneys went off to find a guest house, leaving their roadies to make the necessary arrangements. Fliers were posted around the campus advertising a surprise show the next day. The entrance fee would be just 40 new pence (61 cents).

So it was that the following lunchtime Paul McCartney got back on stage in Nottingham University Hall to play for a live paying audience for the first time since Candlestick Park. In a clear return to the start of his professional career he opened with a Little Richard cover, 'Lucille', after which it was mostly unknown territory. For Paul wasn't going to play any Beatles songs, and Wings were a new band without much of a repertoire. 'We haven't got too many numbers yet,' McCartney told the students, much as he and John must have apologised to the patrons of the Indra when the jejune Beatles first went to Hamburg. 'We're just checking things out.' The kids yelled that they didn't mind. Even so Wings could only play four original songs, including 'Wild Life'. The show was padded with Elvis covers, some jamming and more Little Richard, Paul closing with 'Long Tall Sally'.

Back in the van, Wings divvied up the takings, mostly in coins and one pound notes. 'Paul would go, "Here we go, one for you, one for you, one for you ..."' recalls Seiwell, adding with some bitterness: 'It was probably the most money I ever made touring with Paul and it was nothing, you know.'

The next night they played Goodridge College in York, followed by a string of university towns including Hull, Newcastle and Leeds. At each show, Wings performed 'Give Ireland Back to the Irish', which usually went down well with the students, but was banned by the BBC from its radio network for being too political, with Paul roundly criticised in the normally pro-McCartney national press for taking a simplistic stance on Northern Ireland. In response, he took out an advertisement in the *Sun* newspaper urging the public to buy the record and make up their own mind. While many did purchase the single, the radio ban hindered sales, and 'Give Ireland Back to the Irish' rose no higher than number 16 in the UK charts. When Wings passed through the university town of Lancaster, Linda aired her views on the issue for *Melody Maker*, saying: 'Look, in Ireland the IRA was forced into existence by the fact that Britain took over the country more than 800 years ago, or whenever it was. Therefore if the British got out of Ireland there'd be no need for the IRA ...' In response, a reader from Ulster wrote to the paper asking, if the McCartneys were so committed to the province, why didn't they come over and play in Ulster? Over the next few years Wings played all over the world, but they never gave a show in Northern Ireland. Perhaps Paul considered the province to be too dangerous.

Linda's musicianship proved as feeble as her political history. On one occasion, when Paul counted the band into 'Wild Life', he was met by silence from his left. Looking over, he saw his keyboardist wife mouthing back that she'd forgotten the chords! The audience didn't care, and neither did Paul. He was having a ball, while the guys in the band learned to accept Linda as an enthusiastic amateur, appreciating the family vibe a husband and wife playing together engendered.

Despite what Denny Laine hoped for, Wings was not 'a rough and tumble rock/blues-type' band. It was a Mom and Pop act. Backstage you were liable to find Mary and Heather McCartney drawing pictures while baby sister Stella (known as Stelly in the family) slept in a makeshift cot in a drawer. When Paul and Linda decided they needed a Wings fan club, they devised the jokey Wings Fun Club, seemingly pitched at children Heather's age rather than adults. Most significantly, the band's next single – despite the fact Paul was always talking about wanting to shake off his soft-centred image – was an arrangement of the children's nursery rhyme 'Mary Had a Little Lamb', because Mary McCartney had a pet lamb in Kintyre. Wings put the record out in May, as big a contrast to 'Give Ireland Back to the Irish' as could be imagined. Some commentators suggested it was meant sarcastically, as if Paul was telling the BBC: 'You won't play serious music, so we'll give you nursery rhymes.' But it was really about indulging the kids. Denny Laine felt very uncomfortable. 'If it was going to be going in that direction, and no other direction, I would not have liked it at all.' One can imagine how Laine felt when Paul had Wings mime to the song on the *Basil Brush Show*.

Most rock stars would be too concerned with their image to contemplate singing a nursery rhyme on a kids' TV show hosted by a fox glove puppet, but Paul had been so successful for so long that he seemed immured from such considerations. It was as if he believed the public would like him whatever he did, and if they didn't, so what? He was rich enough to do as he pleased. It was in this spirit that the McCartneys indulged their interests, however whimsical or childish. Linda was soppy about animals and, under her influence, Paul became animal-mad too, the couple and their children looking upon the entire animal kingdom as if it were of a piece with *The Wonderful World of Disney*. Apart from working on the putative *Rupert the Bear* cartoon, and performing on the *Basil Brush Show*, the McCartneys now decided they should make an anthropomorphic Disney-type film about 'a family of cartoon mice living underneath the stage when we were performing', as Denny Seiwell recalls. Wings did some work on this at Elstree Film Studios, though the picture never saw the light of day. 'There was a lot of that kind of stuff going on.'

Being a parent had evidently changed Paul. Family life was now all important, and when he took Wings out on a European tour in the summer of 1972 there was a strong family feel to the enterprise. The band travelled in a brightly coloured double-decker bus, painted with the legend WINGS OVER EUROPE, the open top deck laid out with bean bags and mattresses for the McCartneys, their band and the kids to lounge about on. While the bus was no doubt huge fun for the wee McCartneys, it was a slow and inefficient way to navigate the continent.

'It only went 35 mph, so people would go whizzing by us on the motorways and see this gang of hippies in this bus. It was quite nice, but it didn't make a lot of sense,' remembers Seiwell, who also recalls that Linda suffered a severe attack of stage fright prior to their first-night show at Châteauvallon, a cultural centre near Marseille in the South of France. 'She was crying on my shoulder, she was scared.' Audiences were so thrilled to see a Beatle they hardly paid any attention to Paul's wife, and McCartney's confidence carried the night, as it always would.

The idea of this European tour was to play small venues in mostly out-of-the-way places to get the band some road experience before they attempted anything more ambitious. So the Wings double-decker trundled up through France into Germany, then into Switzerland where, fatefully, Denny Laine met Joanne 'Jo Jo' Patrie. Jo Jo was a vivacious American model turned groupie whom Linda McCartney suspected of having her true sights set on Paul, which turned out to be correct. 'She was basically trying to go through me to get to Paul,' concedes Laine, who discovered Jo Jo had sent Paul love letters as a teenage Beatles fan. 'I didn't know this to start with. I found out later.' Paul and Linda treated Denny's new girlfriend disdainfully, which offended both Denny and Jo Jo as they grew closer together, becoming a regular couple, having children and ultimately getting married. 'I find it insulting that Linda looked on Jo Jo as a groupie. Linda was one of the biggest groupies on the face of the Earth if you want to put labels on people,' Denny said in an angry interview in the 1980s. 'Jo Jo was a groupie – nobody is denying that. But what is a groupie? Just a chick that likes musicians.' These days Laine sees things slightly differently. 'They tried to get on with Jo Jo,' he says of Paul and Lin, 'but she was a lot of work. What can I say?'

Almost all the adults on the Wings double-decker smoked grass, Paul having been an avid pot smoker since meeting Bob Dylan in 1964. For a long tour they needed a regular supply. Rather than risk taking drugs through customs, the band had dope posted to them from England. One parcel was addressed to Denny Seiwell care of the Gothenburg Park Hotel, where Wings arrived on 10 August to play a show at the nearby Scandinavian Hall. While the roadies set up their equipment, the McCartneys took a limousine to the hotel to collect Denny's parcel, which contained five and a half ounces of prime marijuana. Unbeknownst to the McCartneys, the Swedish police had been alerted and were watching the drop. As the band came off stage that night, Paul, Linda and Denny Seiwell were seized by Swedish detectives. 'It was just me at first – then I hear Paul and Linda ... They were being brought in, too, screaming bloody murder,' says Seiwell, who was arrested because his name was on the package; Paul and Linda were nicked because they picked it up. Also dragged down to the station was Paul's secretary.

The McCartneys initially denied the drugs were theirs, then admitted it, according to the police: 'They said they had made arrangements to have drugs posted to them each day they played in different countries ...' Paul, Linda and Denny Seiwell were ordered to pay a fine/good behaviour bond totalling £1,000 ($1,530), and allowed to go on their way. 'They said, "Tell your rock 'n' roll friends not to bring marijuana into Sweden, because we'll find it and they'll be arrested,"' says Seiwell. 'It was lame. It was really no big deal. If I remember correctly we had some marijuana a day later!' It *was* a big deal, though. The drug conviction meant Paul was now unable to take Wings to the United States and Japan, as he had planned. The Gothenburg bust also seemed to show the McCartneys to have an arrogant attitude towards the law, while there was really no need to get into this sort of trouble. Many rock stars use drugs routinely on tour, but do so with enough discretion to avoid arrest. Paul had blundered into this situation through his cack-handed arrangements, and would make similar mistakes again and again during the course of his career.

Another chronic problem with post-Beatles Paul was the way he paid his musicians. When the Wings Over Europe tour concluded in Berlin on 24 August 1972 his sidemen found themselves more or less broke. During the tour the band had been booked into the same luxury hotels as the McCartneys. Bed and breakfast was paid for, but room service and bar bills were not covered, and the boys ended up spending most of their wages on extras. 'When the whole thing was over,' complains Seiwell, who was increasingly concerned about the way the band was being treated, 'it cost us money. Sold out every concert and when it was all over the band got paid nothing for 28 cities and two and a half months of a European tour. We got nothing. Because the expenses were so high.' The money was only part of the problem. As bad was the superior attitude Paul and Lin showed on occasion. Seiwell again:

There were times when we were a family. We really bonded as a family, the five of us, musically and socially with the wives and the kids. Everybody was a family. And then there were times when it was – this is really hard to say – but there were times when it just was about them, and we did not matter whatsoever.

The McCartneys were back in London when news reached Cavendish Avenue that Paul was in trouble again with the police, this time in Scotland. In the aftermath of the Gothenburg bust, Detective Constable Norman McPhee of the Campbeltown police had found marijuana growing in a greenhouse at High Park Farm. The story given to the press was that DC McPhee had been on a routine crime prevention tour of the area when he spotted the plants, recognising the leaf shape he had been taught to look out for on a recent drug-awareness course. The truth was that the police had been tipped off, according to Paul's Scottish lawyer Len Murray, meaning Paul wasn't as popular in Kintyre as he thought he was. In any event, Paul was summoned to appear before the sheriff's court in Campbeltown to face charges under the Misuse of Drugs Act. 'And of course that was really quite serious. Growing cannabis was viewed a great deal more seriously in those days,' says Murray, who organised Paul's defence when the case came to court in the spring of 1973.

Paul's reaction to these busts remained one of defiance, so much so that Wings released what might loosely be termed their second protest song, 'Hi, Hi, Hi', only loosely because while it could be interpreted as a celebration of getting high on grass the song was also a paean to sexual intercourse. The man who had written so eloquently of blue suburban skies and the love you make being equal to the love you take was now singing of giving his baby his 'sweet banana' and doing it to her 'like a rabbit' all night long! Released at the end of the year as a single, with a reggae number, 'C Moon', on the flip side, this truly stupid song was promptly banned by the BBC for its sexual content. It reached number five in the UK charts, anyway, number ten in the USA. On the grounds of taste, it shouldn't have been released at all. 'What it was supposed to be getting at was a "Why Don't We Do It in the Road?" kind of thing, trying to be sexual, but I thought it was a bit kind of lightweight,' says Laine. 'You know what, I think Paul's always had a bit of a problem of wanting to be a little bit tougher than he is, and sometimes he'll write a song to try and show that side of him.'

The following spring Paul and Lin flew by private plane to RAF Machrihanish in Kintyre, where they met their lawyer Len Murray and John McCluskey QC, the advocate hired to represent them in court on drugs charges. For once, the McCartneys didn't have their children with them and, freed from parental responsibility for the day, Linda had seemingly enjoyed a joint on the flight. 'She was stoned out of her mind,' notes an unimpressed Murray, '*stoned out of her mind*.' A giggling Linda borrowed John McCluskey's bowler hat and wore it throughout the day, as though laughing at the proceedings. Paul was in a more sober frame of mind, knowing the problems a drugs conviction could cause him. There was immediate good news, though. Before leaving the airport, Paul's legal team explained to the star that they had persuaded the Prosecutor to drop two charges of possession, owing to a technical problem with the way the case had been brought, agreeing in return that Paul would plead guilty to the lesser charge of cultivation. This was good for Paul, who had been set to plead guilty to all three charges. The legal conference at an end, the lawyers drove Paul and Linda to Campbeltown's court house, which was surrounded by journalists and cameramen. 'We had to fight our way through, saying nothing,' says Murray. 'Linda enjoyed it all. She was obviously in her element having all this attention.'

Inside the court, John McCluskey told the sheriff that his client had grown the marijuana plants at High Park from seeds sent to him by a fan. With his 'genuine interest in horticulture' Mr McCartney had planted and watered the seeds, though his horticultural interest didn't extend to a knowledge of what it was he was growing. The matter was dealt with as a first offence (Paul's spot of bother in Sweden couldn't be used against him in a Scottish court). The sheriff fined Paul a nominal £100 ($153), at which point Linda tossed her hat in the air for joy. Outside the court, Paul told the press: 'I still think cannabis should be legal for use among consenting adults. It is no more dangerous than drink.' Linda was evidently still as high as kite as they got back in their plane. 'I was quite impressed with the way he conducted himself throughout that morning,' Len Murray says of McCartney. 'He was quite respectful and conscious of the responsibility of it all, and the importance of it all ... He certainly never gave the impression of not caring ...' The same could not be said about his wife.

Paul and Linda were as one, however, Paul's devotion to his wife expressed in Wings' new single, 'My Love', recorded at AIR Studios, George Martin's new facility above what had been Peter Robinson's Oxford Street department store, overlooking Oxford Circus. Paul had come to AIR because he wanted to record with an orchestra, and George was the best man for that job. One of the most uxorious of Paul's 'I-love-you-Linda' songs, 'My Love' was lifted by a stirring guitar solo by Henry McCullough, who, when it came to the recording date, bucked against Paul's regimented way of making music – 'in blocks', as he characterises McCartney's method. 'I was in there with a fifty-piece orchestra, just meself and guitar and I wanted to change the solo.'

'What are you going to play?' Paul asked his guitarist.

'I have no idea,' replied Henry, who wanted to extemporise.

'Oh Jesus, Henry!'

As the orchestra played, McCullough tore off the solo of his life. 'It wasn't a confrontation, [but] it had got to the point where I *achingly* wanted to be the guitar player in the band, instead of learning parts,' says the guitarist, 'and Paul, I think, found that way of working a little risky, which it is, but it hit the mark and it was left there.' The song was released as Wings' next single, becoming a number one hit in the USA. This success was followed by the new album, *Red Rose Speedway*, which Paul asked another old friend to produce.

To try and create a collaborative atmosphere in Wings, Paul was experimenting with becoming just another member of the group, on a par with Lin, Laine, McCullough and Seiwell. 'The first session he came into the control room and he said, "Now I don't want you to think of me as Paul McCartney, I want you to think of me as the bass player in the band,"' recalls Glyn Johns, grimacing as he tells the story. 'Well, you can imagine how long that lasted! The minute I started talking to him like the bass player in the band it was, you know, "Who the bloody hell do you think you're talking to?"'

Following the *Let It Be* fiasco, Johns had gone on to become one of the foremost producers in rock, working successfully with Eric Clapton, the Eagles, Led Zeppelin and the Who. To his mind, Wings were not in the same league as these acts, couldn't really be considered a band at all. 'It's called Wings, [but] it's Paul McCartney. It doesn't really make

any difference who's in the band. They are all very competent, professional musicians, but they're not a band in my view – it's Paul McCartney [with] a bunch of guys.'

The essential problem to Glyn's mind was that, despite the presence
of Denny Laine, Paul lacked a musical equal in Wings. 'I think that while
the Beatles existed Paul had John Lennon keeping a beady eye on him,
and he wouldn't let him get away with anything too syrupy, if you like.
He'd take the piss out of him, he'd sit on him, he'd squash him,' says
Johns. Glyn had come to see Paul as an insecure person in some ways.
'You've only got to look at his body language.' Paul clearly needed
people around him, like Linda, but Linda 'just wasn't a musician. Period.'
The result was that Wings smoked dope and jammed in the studio to
little effect. Johns didn't even bother to run tape. He sat in the control
room and read the newspaper. One evening Laine and Seiwell remon-
strated with him.

> They said, you know, 'We're not happy with you as a producer. You're
> not taking any interest in what we are doing.' I said, 'When you do
> something that's interesting, I'm there. But if you think because you
> are playing with Paul McCartney that everything you do is a gem of
> marvellous music, you're wrong. It isn't. It's shite. And if you want to
> sit and play shite and get stoned for a few hours that's your preroga-
> tive, but don't expect me to record everything you're doing, because
> frankly it's a waste of tape and it's a waste of my energy.'

Paul joined the discussion, the band sitting in a semi-circle around the
producer, who felt as though he was on trial. He didn't appreciate it, or
the sycophantic atmosphere around Paul (despite the conceit of Paul
just being the bass player in Wings). 'The fact is that they were all obviously really thrilled to be in a band with Paul McCartney … they all were
up his bottom.' So Johns quit *Red Rose Speedway*, describing the album
Wings went on to make without him as 'a load of rubbish', which is
harsh, but in a record review one couldn't award it more than three out
of five stars.

More mediocrity followed when Paul agreed to take part in a music
special for the television arm of Sir Lew Grade's media empire. Grade,
the owner of Northern Songs, had been suing Paul over registering his
new songs to Paul and Linda McCartney, thereby depriving Grade of

royalties he would receive if titles such as 'Another Day' were credited to Paul alone. To settle the dispute, Paul agreed that Wings would appear in a 55-minute television special for Grade's Associated Television company (ATV). Broadcast on 10 May 1973, *James Paul McCartney* consisted of a series of musical performances by Wings and Paul, including Beatles songs such as 'Blackbird' and 'Michelle' (a sign of what a hard bargain Grade had driven). Many numbers were presented in the form of short, video-like films. For 'Mary Had a Little Lamb', Wings mimed along to a backing track while surrounded by a flock of sheep. The most interesting part of the show was footage of Paul hosting a family party in a Merseyside pub. Jim McCartney was present, a smartly dressed gent of 70; also, the aunts. Paul was evidently delighted when Ginny hoved into view, a stout old lady with a fag on the go. 'All right, darling, how are you?' Paul hailed his favourite aunt. 'Get yourself parked, Ginny.' The McCartneys then enjoyed a singsong, rattling through 'Pack Up Your Troubles' and 'You Are My Sunshine' as the cigarette smoke thickened and the bar till rang.

The other highlight of the ATV film was a performance of a dramatic new song titled 'Live and Let Die', which Paul had written for the new James Bond film of the same name, having read the Ian Fleming novel over a weekend. He cut the record with George Martin at AIR, Martin having written an arrangement for orchestra. Despite the fact that the producers didn't like the song at first, thinking Paul had merely recorded a demo, 'Live and Let Die' was a perfect Bond theme, capturing all the excitement of the secret agent character; it was a top ten hit on both sides of the Atlantic, and became a mainstay of Paul's stage show. It is in fact one of the best half-dozen songs of his post-Beatles career, not coincidentally because McCartney was working again with the old pro himself, George Martin, one of the few people in the music business whom he respected enough to be guided by. 'Live and Let Die' was also a very modern-sounding song, tailored for the bombastic, pyrotechnically enhanced stadium rock shows of the 1970s, which were just around the corner for Wings.

IN THE HEART OF THE COUNTRY

HOME AGAIN

Paul led Wings out on a UK tour in the spring of 1973, playing to their largest audiences yet, including a show at the Liverpool Empire on 18 May. Liverpool had declined since Beatlemania briefly revived the city's profile. The docks closed in 1972, primarily due to competition from more modern ports, the waterways soon silting up and the warehouses falling into desuetude, exacerbating unemployment. At the same time, the city centre was radically modernised, with the demolition of St John's Market, through which Paul had wandered many a time to and from Lime Street Station. In its place was erected a monolithic shopping plaza, car park and hotel complex, surmounted by a 450ft ventilation tower known as St John's Beacon. At the top of this concrete tower was a modish revolving restaurant. This monstrosity now faced the visitor stepping forth from Lime Street Station, and if one went looking for Mathew Street another rude shock awaited.

The Cavern had continued to operate into the early 1970s, with many good new acts gracing the stage, but the heyday of the Mersey Sound was gone, and nostalgic Beatles fans were not yet coming to Liverpool in great numbers to visit the places associated with the band, while the boys themselves were reluctant to dwell on their past lest it detract from what they were doing now. While he was in Liverpool in May, Paul didn't even take the time to say farewell to the Cavern, which was about to be demolished to allow construction of an underground railway ventilation shaft. Liverpool Corporation could have saved the club, but Liverpool's civic leaders lacked the foresight to see the importance of the Cavern in rock 'n' roll tourism. Absurdly, the ventilation shaft was never actually needed. The last club night was 27 May 1973, shortly after which workmen bulldozed the buildings above ground, and destroyed the caverns below. 'They should never have pulled it down. It was the most maniacal move possible,' said Paul ten years later, when the magnitude of the vandalism had sunk in. 'I think there was a bit of an attitude going around at the time which was, "Well, the Beatles left us. They hate Liverpool anyway." We used to get an awful lot of that. If someone's got to live somewhere else, it doesn't mean he hates Liverpool.'

On the contrary, Paul remained deeply attached to his home town, visiting Merseyside frequently to see his relatives and take nostalgic drives around his old haunts. When Jim McCartney found the stairs at Rembrandt too tiring, Paul bought the house from Dad and moved Jim, Angie and Ruth into a bungalow in nearby Gayton. Paul kept Rembrandt as his own Merseyside base, though most of his time was necessarily spent in London, his main residence being 7 Cavendish Avenue, with High Park the principal family getaway. What with Scotland being so far from London, it made sense to acquire a second weekend retreat nearer the capital, and this is what Paul did in June 1973.

For some years Paul and Linda had been in the habit of driving out of London on impromptu mystery tours of the Home Counties, to get away from the pressures of their metropolitan life and enjoy the countryside. One such mystery tour took them 60 miles south of the capital to the village of Peasmarsh in East Sussex, not far from the historic town of Rye. Along Peasmarsh's main road were arranged the village school, post office, the Flackley Ash Hotel, Jempson's food store and a couple of pubs. The unmarked lanes that led off the A268 wound away through a green landscape of undulating farm- and woodland that had hardly changed in centuries. The primary sounds were still those of animals – bird song, the clip-clop of horses in the lanes, deer flitting through the trees, badgers rustling in the undergrowth – together with the grumble of farm machinery, the buzz of chainsaws and the distant popping of shotguns as farmers hunted for the pot. Tucked away in the woods off Starvecrow Lane, an eccentric circular house was for sale, built in the 1930s from oddments of older buildings. At the centre of this round house was a living room with a fireplace, off which radiated triangular rooms, with two bedrooms upstairs. A stream running through the wood led to a nearby waterfall, hence the house's name: Waterfall. The property was only accessible via a private, 300-yard track, and completely hidden by the trees. At the same time London was only an hour away by car, with a convenient aerodrome at nearby Lydd, which Paul had used in 1966 to hop over to France. In a break in Wings' 1973 UK tour, the McCartneys bought Waterfall as a weekender, soon expanding their landholding by buying additional neighbouring tracts and farms, creating an extensive country estate that eventually became their main home.

Waterfall cost £42,500 ($65,025) at a time when McCartney Productions was recording an annual loss of £110,742 ($169,435), but Paul's company had assets of a quarter of a million pounds, in addition to the star's personal fortune: that is to say the money he had tucked away in Coutts Bank and elsewhere; plus his property interests and his all-important stake in the Beatles. In fact Paul had so much money washing around that he was looking for investment opportunities. It was his father-in-law Lee Eastman who suggested Paul invest in song-publishing, which was one of Lee's specialist areas.

Linda's dad is a great business brain. He said originally, 'If you are going to invest, do it in something you know. If you invest in building computers or something, you can lose a fortune. Wouldn't you rather be in music? Stay in music.' I said, 'Yeah, I'd much rather do that.' So he asked me what kind of music I liked. And the first name I said was Buddy Holly.

That spring the Eastmans bought the Nor Va Jak publishing company, in which were held US rights to Buddy Holly's biggest hits, making Paul the proud owner of 'Maybe Baby', 'Not Fade Away' and 'Peggy Sue' among other classics. The Eastmans went on to acquire more song catalogues for Paul, building a substantial publishing business that provided the star with steady additional income, though the songs he most wanted to own, those he'd written with John Lennon, remained stubbornly beyond his reach, either because they weren't for sale or, when they were, they were priced too high.

Aside from publishing, cash and property, Paul owned a valuable and growing art collection, several luxury cars, including a Rolls Royce and a Lamborghini, and he gave Linda magnificent gifts, including an emerald and diamond necklace for her 30th birthday. The financial circumstances of the other members of Wings were in complete contrast to this lifestyle. Henry McCullough, Denny Laine and Denny Seiwell were all still being paid a paltry £70-a-week, with occasional bonuses (receiving £1,000 each [$1,530], for example, at the end of the recent UK tour). The musicians were all under the impression they would be cut in on the band royalties eventually. 'That just never happened,' says Seiwell,* who had to get a bank loan when he wanted to buy a car, which was not the lifestyle the American envisaged when he and Monique came to the UK at Paul's behest. 'There was very, very little money that came down to the band. Yet we were working on a gentleman's agreement that we would all be part-owners of [Wings].' By the time the band convened at Paul's Scottish estate to work on what became the next and most celebrated Wings album, *Band on the Run*, these financial complaints were starting to have a negative effect on morale, particularly on the spirits of Denny Seiwell and Henry McCullough.

Paul had written some good new songs which he wanted to work up as demos in Kintyre before cutting the new album abroad. The idea was to get inspiration from a different setting and culture, as Denny Laine recalls, though Laine also believes there may have been a tax advantage to recording abroad. Paul had discovered that EMI operated recording studios in countries as far-flung as Brazil, China, India and Nigeria. It would be a different experience to make a record in Africa, so Paul booked Wings into the EMI facility in the Nigerian port city of Lagos for September 1973. In preparation for the trip, Wings worked on Paul's new songs in the barn on Low Ranachan Farm, just over the hill from Paul and Linda's High Park cottage, and part of McCartney's enlarged Scottish estate. Denny Laine and his pregnant girlfriend Jo Jo Patrie were staying in another cottage on the estate.

When Wings played at Low Ranachan, cows drifted over from neighbouring farms to listen; 'they'd be craning their necks to this music,' notes farmer Duncan McLean. Despite the charming rural setting there were fractious words in the barn. Money had become a critical issue with Seiwell and McCullough, while Paul seemed fed up

---

* At least it didn't happen to Seiwell. Laine was put on such a deal later, as we shall see.

with his musicians. 'On occasions he would maybe go home early from rehearsals or something because maybe he was tired or something wasn't working out,' notes Henry McCullough, whose loose, improvisational style didn't mesh with Paul's systematic way of working. The men came to an impasse on 14 July when Paul told Henry once too often what he should play. Just as happened with George Harrison during *Let It Be*, this led to Paul's guitarist walking out. Without saying anything to Paul, at the end of the day Henry put his guitar case in his car and drove home to London. He didn't return. 'I just had to move. If I hadn't of moved at that time I think eventually I may have been sacked.' Money was certainly part of the problem. 'It's all very well getting into a bloody Lear Jet and flying off to [Lagos], but at the end of the day when you get home you still have to [eat].' When Paul came to the barn the next day to continue work, and was told by the others that Henry had gone, he continued as if nothing had happened, never discussing the matter with Seiwell or Laine, who defends Paul in this instance. 'It's not a matter of being told [by Paul] what to play,' he says of Henry's reason for quitting; 'it's just [Paul's] personality. If you don't come up with something, then he'll suggest something, and he can be a bit overpowering like that. But at the same time if Henry had been a little bit more enthusiastic [then] maybe it would have been different.'

The next day Denny Seiwell returned to his London home to prepare for the Africa trip. Denny Laine and Jo Jo were packing up ready for their own departure to the capital, where Jo Jo was expecting to give birth to their first child, when Jo Jo realised she was about to go into labour. The couple dropped everything and rushed to the local Kintyre hospital, where they had a son (who they named Laine, rather absurdly). Oblivious to this family drama Paul and Linda rode over the hill on horseback to find Denny and Jo Jo's belongings strewn about outside their cottage, like the remnants of a gypsy encampment. 'What the Hell's going on with this mess?' they asked the farm-hands angrily, as Laine later heard it, not knowing about Jo Jo's emergency. The way Denny Seiwell heard the story second hand the McCartneys were totally unsupportive to Denny and Jo Jo during the birth of their son, not visiting the hospital or even sending flowers when they found out about the birth. Laine himself doesn't remember this being an issue, but Seiwell got it into his head that Paul and Lin had let his friends down and, even though he may have had the facts wrong, he added this perception to a list of grievances.

The band were due to fly to Lagos on 30 August. In the last few days before departure Seiwell talked to Paul on the phone about his concerns. Recalls the drummer:

> I said, 'Listen, can't we just postpone this trip and break in a new guitar player, so we can rehearse a new guitar player, teach him Henry's parts, teach him the songs, so we can go into this project and play it as a band kind of live and then embellish it?'
>
> He said, 'No, no, no, we're just going to continue. EMI have set up the studio for us. We'll do it like *Ram*. It'll all be over-dubbed, but we'll make it good.' I thought, *I don't want to do that again*. We had just spent all this time and effort becoming a real rock 'n' roll band, and it was becoming very good. So between Henry leaving, the bad news of Denny and Jo Jo, no contract one more time, I just took it upon myself to say, 'That's it!'

Seiwell quit.

Paul was 'very angry and very upset'. He swore at his drummer, then slammed down the phone.

> Linda called us back immediately and said, 'How dare you inconvenience us?' I replied, 'I can't even talk about the inconvenience. I've been inconvenienced for three years here. This just isn't right!' So that was it. There was no more. It was totally harsh, and then we didn't speak for years.

Paul had lost two band members in a matter of a few days, but he carried on regardless, flying to Lagos at the end of August to make the new record with Linda, Laine, and Paul's favourite engineer, Geoff Emerick. Like Paul, Laine was able to shrug off the desertions. 'It didn't bother me. When you've been through what we've been through with different bands, and different members, you just get on with it. It's not like, "Hey! It's the end of the world."'

The actual recording sessions for *Band on the Run* were no less fraught than the build-up to the record. Paul discovered that Lagos was not a paradise resort where he and Linda could swing on hammocks under coconut trees, but a dirty, dangerous, disease-ridden city, stickily hot in the monsoon season. Villas had been hired to accommodate the McCartneys, Laine and Emerick, the latter alarmed to discover that his lodgings were alive with spiders, insects and lizards. The EMI studio was situated down the road in the port of Apapa, which had given its name to the SS *Apapa*, the ship Paul's nefarious uncle Will Stapleton stole from in 1949, bringing disgrace on the family. Uncle Will had come ashore at Apapa to spend some of his ill-gotten gains. Odd to think Paul was retracing his uncle's steps so exactly.

The EMI facility in Apapa turned out to be little more than a shed attached to a pressing plant. 'When you opened [the back door] you saw a couple of dozen shirtless guys standing ankle deep in water pressing records in this small, steaming-hot room,' Emerick remembered in his memoirs. The studio lacked basic equipment; Emerick had to hire a carpenter to knock up some acoustic screens before they could start. Then local Nigerian musicians made it known that they didn't appreciate Paul coming to their country, believing the star was there to steal their music. The next thing Paul knew he was being mugged during an evening walk with Linda. As Lin screamed at the muggers not to hurt her husband, the men made off with his valuables, including the *Band on the Run* demo tapes.

When a writer loses his manuscript and is obliged to write a work over again from memory, as sometimes happens, the writing often comes more cleanly the second time. This seems to have been the case with *Band on the Run*. Forced to remember his songs after muggers stole his demo tapes, Paul laid down a series of minor classics, playing the drums himself and dividing up the guitar parts with Laine. '[We] made the album as though we weren't in a band, as though we were just two producers/musicians,' recalls his band mate, emphasising that Paul still made no allusion to the loss of McCullough and Seiwell, preferring to keep his own counsel on this as on other matters. Laine always found Paul a self-contained man. 'Paul's personality is that he likes to be positive, he likes to be up – and there's a strength there somehow – he doesn't like to share his down-time with other people. He likes to cope with it himself in private.' The strain of it all got to the star, though. Halfway through the work he collapsed in the Apapa studio. Linda screamed that Paul was having a heart attack. It turned out to be a panic attack.

When Paul returned to London seven weeks later, he had the basis of the best studio album Wings ever made. Lyrically *Band on the Run* is slightly weak, as usual, but musically it has an energy and cohesiveness lacking from *McCartney*, *Ram*, *Wild Life* and *Red Rose Speedway*. Apart from the fact that the underlying melodies were good, it seems that Paul's desire to show Seiwell and McCullough he could do without them made him raise his game. Highlights included 'Let Me Roll It', an immensely exciting yet very simple song built around a hot guitar riff. The lyrics are of no consequence, other than to form the hub around which the musical wheel turns, yet the song works brilliantly, destined to become a staple of Paul's live show. It must be galling, therefore, when Lennon fans observe that 'Let Me Roll It' sounds like a John rip-off. The title track 'Band on the Run', has a hokey but enjoyable desperado feel, also making one think of the band members who ran out on Wings; while other songs had diverse and often homely references. 'Jet' was the name of a black Labrador the McCartneys owned; 'Helen Wheels' was the family nickname for the Land Rover they used on Kintyre; 'Mamunia' was inspired by a recent holiday to the La Mamounia (sic) hotel in Morocco; while a Caribbean holiday gave Paul 'Picasso's Last Words (Drink to Me)'. The McCartneys were in Jamaica when they met Dustin Hoffman, who was in the islands filming *Papillon*. The actor challenged Paul to write an impromptu song based on a random magazine article, using a copy of *Time*. Pablo Picasso had just died, aged 91. In his *Time* obituary it was reported that the artist had been forbidden from drinking in his final days, telling his friends to drink for him. Paul made an instant song from the story.

Denny Laine contributed one song to *Band on the Run*, 'No Words', which Paul helped him finish. Paul was eager for Laine to share the burden of writing, and Laine says they increasingly wrote together from this point on, as Paul had written with John, citing the example of 'Getting Better' from *Sgt. Pepper*.

There's a great line he says about John Lennon, you know, 'I wrote "[I've] got to admit it's getting better," and John Lennon said, "It can't get no worse."' There's the two personalities coming out there. The cynical John Lennon line and then there's the real positive, almost overly enthusiastic Paul line. That's the way a lot of our lyrics went.

Laine found working creatively with Paul a pleasure. 'The thing about Paul is, being such a famous person as he was, such a recognisable guy, that it was difficult to be his equal if you like as far as the public was concerned, but in the studio we were pretty much on an equal par.' Paul was also very fair with song credits and the split of publishing income.

That autumn Paul went into AIR in London to add strings and horns to *Band on the Run*, hiring Howie Casey, whom he had known back in the days of Derry and the Seniors, to play sax on several tracks, most winningly on 'Bluebird'. Paul then staged an elaborate *Pepper*-like photo shoot for the album, inviting a disparate bunch of celebrities to pose with him, Lin and Laine in a jail-break pose. The models included club singer Kenny Lynch, whom Paul had known in the 1960s, Liverpool boxer John Conteh, and the actors James Coburn and Christopher Lee. The resultant cover was fun to look at, while the music was good. Here at last was the old McCartney panache, proof that Paul hadn't been lobotomised after leaving the Beatles, but had just lost focus. *Band on the Run* was a deserved number one album in the US and UK at the end of 1973, yielding several hit singles.

A BEATLES *RAPPROCHEMENT*

An element of routine creeps into most lives, especially when children are involved, and what might be termed the McCartney Year begins to evolve around the mid-1970s. The family (and Paul did most things with Lin and the kids) generally spent the working week in London, the kids in local schools and Paul in the studio much of the time. At the weekend they usually drove down to Waterfall, their new cottage in the Sussex woods. They went north in the school holidays, invariably visiting their relatives on Merseyside for Christmas and New Year, then spent a couple of weeks each summer in Kintyre in time for the annual agricultural show, properly named the June Show, but actually held in August when the weather was better, and consequently known as 'the June Show in August'. Heather McCartney rode in the gymkhana while Paul and Linda had fun entering their livestock in competition. Paul would attend the judging, to see what rosettes they'd won, slipping away when the crowds arrived, though few locals bothered him. As noted, the McCartneys had made many friends on the peninsula, especially the Blacks at Tangy Farm, where Heather went riding with Lorna Black; and the Colvilles, whose property the McCartneys rode across to Westport Beach where Paul and Linda would often swim in defiance of the undertow and freezing Atlantic temperatures. When they looked out over the surf they could imagine Linda's family in Long Island, on the other side of the ocean.

Apart from their horses and ponies, the McCartneys shared their Scottish holiday home with a pack of hounds led by the Old English Sheepdog Martha (My Dear), who was still going strong, and including Lucky the Dalmatian, Jet the black Labrador and a Golden Lab named Poppy. A canine romance in Kintyre led to Martha having a litter of mongrel pups, one of whom Heather named Captain Midnight, her special pet. One day the McCartneys rushed into their vet's surgery in town cradling one of these mongrel pups. The pooch had been kicked by a horse, breaking its leg. 'At that time it was beyond our capabilities to do any pinning, so it was arranged that it would go up to Glasgow Veterinary Hospital by taxi,' says the vet Alastair Cousin. The injured pup was chauffeur-driven to Glasgow, where it was treated, returning to Campbeltown again by taxi, a 280-mile round trip, by which time the McCartneys had gone home to London, so the dog was flown down to the capital to join them, at considerable additional expense. 'Only somebody like Paul could and would do that sort of thing,' notes the vet, who recalls another memorable occasion when he was called to High Park to tend a duck with a broken leg. That's right – a duck. 'It was crazy stuff, but that was what they did – they were a bit sentimental about their animals.'

For some time now Paul had only been able to look out across the Atlantic towards the Americas, unable to visit because he'd been denied a US visa due to his drug convictions. In the spring of 1974 this visa problem was solved and Paul and Linda began going to the States again. Paul immediately took the opportunity to call on John Lennon, who was himself stranded in America.

After making the *Imagine* album in England, John and Yoko had moved to New York in 1971, living originally in the St Regis Hotel, then in a Greenwich Village apartment before moving into the Dakota, a grand old apartment building on Central Park West with fabulous views across the park, but a sinister aspect for anybody familiar with the horror movie *Rosemary's Baby*, which Roman Polanski shot there. Because of John's UK conviction for possession of marijuana, the US authorities wanted Lennon out of the country. John's lawyers advised him to apply for US residency. While his application was in the pipeline, John was permitted to remain in the United States, but warned that he might not be let back in if he left the country, which meant he was marooned.

A degree of staleness had crept into the Lennon marriage, and in the autumn of 1973 John had left Yoko for their assistant May Pang (who was a childhood friend of Linda McCartney's; they were both fans of the Young Rascals). With Yoko's blessing, John and May conducted a 14-month affair, a period John later referred to as his 'lost weekend' in recognition of the fact he was drinking heavily. His drinking companion was the dipsomaniac singer Harry Nilsson, with whom he was also working. By March 1974, Lennon and May Pang were living in Santa Monica, California, while John produced Nilsson's album *Pussy Cats* at Burbank Studios. One night, the McCartneys called by to say hi.

Considering all John had said about Paul over the past few years, the meeting was surprisingly cordial, the ex-Beatles feeling comfortable enough in each other's presence to jam together. The time was right for a *rapprochement*. John and Paul's contract with Northern Songs had expired, allowing them to benefit from their new songs via their respective publishing companies; both had enjoyed solo success; and John had come round to the view that Paul had been right about Allen Klein. In fact, all the Beatles had turned their backs on Klein and were now suing him. The boys had also agreed sensibly that their faithful retainer, Neil Aspinall, should head up Apple Corps, which he ran successfully until his retirement in 2007. Furthermore, John, Paul and George had contributed individually to Ritchie's recent *Ringo* album, Paul giving his friend the hit, 'You're Sixteen'. In short, they were almost back to being mates. The day after the studio visit, the McCartneys paid a house call on John in Santa Monica, and this also went well. Before he left, Paul gave John some brotherly advice. He told him Yoko missed him and, if he felt the same, he should try and win her back, which is what Lennon did.

Making full use of his new visa, Paul decided to take the family and Wings to Tennessee for a working holiday. It was musical associations that drew Paul to the Nashville area, the family's love of horse-riding leading the McCartneys to rent a ranch from songwriter Claude 'Curly' Putman Jr. Success with the tune 'Green, Green Grass of Home' had enabled Putman to buy a 130-acre property outside Nashville, which the McCartneys rented for six weeks, arriving with a newly configured version of Wings. Denny Laine was still in the band, but there was a new British drummer, Geoff Britton, and a new lead guitarist, a diminutive 20-year-old Glaswegian named Jimmy McCulloch, who'd already experienced success with Thunderclap Newman. Talented but highly strung, Jimmy had a tendency to become obstreperous when drunk. 'He had a London accent, normally,' recalls Howie Casey, who worked regularly with Wings at this time. 'Soon as he had a drink he became Scottish. *I'll see you.* It was all that.'

The Putmans went on holiday to Hawaii, leaving their ranch to Paul, who enjoyed playing at being a cowboy. He and Linda rode horses most days, while Paul also enjoyed riding a trail bike belonging to Curly's son, Troy. They had a barbecue for Paul's 32nd birthday, and invited Roy Orbison over for supper, rekindling an old friendship. Paul rehearsed Wings in the garage next to the ranch house and recorded with the band in a Nashville studio, laying down 'Walking in the Park with Eloise', a dance tune created by Paul's dad, later released under the *nom de plume* of the 'Country Hams'.* Wings also recorded 'Junior's Farm', inspired by their stay on the ranch, and this became a top ten hit in the USA.

Paul enjoyed riding Troy Putman's motorbike so much he bought a bike of the same sort for himself and, at the end of his Nashville vacation, put it on a trailer and hauled it up to New York, where the McCartneys called in on Linda's family. The visit was so successful that a new element was added to the McCartney Year. Each summer Paul and Lin would bring the kids to spend a couple of weeks with the Eastmans on Lily Pond Lane, East Hampton, where Lee and John Eastman both maintained summer homes. The McCartneys usually stayed with John and his wife Jody, partly so that their children could play together.

---

* When McCartney told his father he'd recorded a song he wrote, Dad replied that he'd never written any music. 'When I sang "Walking in the Park with Eloise" to him,' said Paul, 'he said, "Oh, that one. Oh I made it up, but I didn't write it."'

VENUS AND MARS

One of the early signs of a second, nostalgic wave of interest in the Beatles came in 1974 with the staging of *John, Paul, George, Ringo ... & Bert* at the Liverpool Everyman. The author was Willy Russell, a local playwright who'd developed a love of the Beatles while watching them on stage at the Cavern as a schoolboy. The premise of his play was that a former member of the Quarry Men, an invented character named Bert, attends a Wings show and is prompted to reflect upon the history of the Beatles, which is told with music in flashback. The play benefited from a superb cast, including Trevor Eve as McCartney, and transferred successfully to London.

When excerpts from *John, Paul, George, Ringo ... & Bert* were broadcast on BBC television around Christmas 1974, Paul was infuriated because the sequence he watched seemed to portray him as the one who broke up the band. '[The BBC] substantially showed the scene in which there's the ultimate spat between John and Paul, and the scene was very specifically written to take account of the fact that – as history now acknowledges – the first person to announce he was leaving the Beatles was John Lennon,' explains Russell, 'but the way they edited the scene it pandered to the perception, as is still now the case, that Paul McCartney was responsible for the break-up of the Beatles ... apparently Paul saw this and was incensed.' As a result, McCartney blocked an attempt to produce a movie of *John, Paul, George, Ringo and ... & Bert*. The success of the musical, though, and the interest in making it into a movie, showed how potent the Beatles story remained; while Paul's strong reaction to the play demonstrated how deeply he felt about the way his part in history was represented, something that would become a veritable obsession. The affair also led to a meeting between McCartney and Russell, whom Paul would call on when he decided to make a film himself.

In real life, the Beatles partnership was finally dissolved in London's High Court in January 1975, a quiet end to a long and public war, with Paul the clear victor. He had achieved everything he wanted, plus the satisfaction of knowing that the others had come to the conclusion that he had been right about Klein. And Apple was now in Neil's safe hands.

A few weeks after the ruling, Paul and Linda took the children and Wings to New Orleans for Mardi Gras. The McCartneys had themselves made up as clowns so they could mingle with the crowd during the carnival. They also recorded tracks for their next album, *Venus and Mars*, the two dramatic opening tunes of which, 'Venus and Mars' and 'Rock Show', were created with a view to playing American arena shows in the near future. Taken together, the songs on the new album were much weaker than *Band on the Run*, with more than the usual amount of whimsy and silliness, including an arrangement of the theme to the television soap *Crossroads*. Apparently meant as a joke, choices such as this served to debase McCartney's currency. He either didn't realise this, or didn't care. Probably the latter, judging by his decision to also have Wings record a commercial for a brand of white, sliced bread, as recalled by a friend from the swinging Sixties, Prince Stanislas Klossowski 'Stash' de Rola: 'After a long time not seeing him, I went back to Cavendish Avenue once and Paul proudly said, "I've got something to play you," and I was horrified because he had proudly played me *Sgt. Pepper* acetates [in the Sixties, and now] he played me a Mother's Pride commercial that he'd composed!'*

Venus and Mars, however, yielded one good single, 'Listen to What the Man Said', with at least one other worthwhile song, though not written by Paul. 'Medicine Jar' was written and sung by Jimmy McCulloch, a young man of considerable talent, but challenging personality. 'I liked Jimmy, but he was a lot of trouble,' recalls Denny Laine. 'He and Paul clashed quite a lot.' Jimmy reduced Linda to tears with sharp remarks about her musicianship. One might think that crossing Linda in this way was a sure way to get fired from Wings, but Paul levelled similar criticisms at his wife. 'I did once say to her in a row I could have had Billy Preston [on keyboards],' Paul remarked in 1976 (Preston being one of the best keyboard players in the business as well as being a former Beatles sideman). 'It just came out.' Meanwhile, the new drummer, Geoff Britton, wasn't fitting in. He was let go midway through *Venus and Mars*.

From New Orleans, the McCartneys flew to Los Angeles, renting an apartment in Coldwater Canyon as Paul put the finishing touches to *Venus and Mars*. On Saturday 1 March 1975, Paul and Linda attended the Grammy Awards, in which Wings were nominated for *Band on the Run*, winning two awards on the night, one for Best Pop Vocal Perform-

* Never used.

ance by a Group, and another for Geoff Emerick's engineering – a worthy winner considering the trying circumstances under which the record had been made. John Lennon showed up at the ceremony, pale and thin, to present the award for Record of the Year to Olivia Newton-John singing 'I Honestly Love You'.

Forty-eight hours later Paul and Linda were driving back to their rented home in Coldwater Canyon when they were stopped by police for jumping a red light on Santa Monica Boulevard. As the officer wrote a ticket he smelt marijuana and ordered the family out of their Lincoln Continental (it was late and the kids were sleeping in the back). Sixteen ounces of grass were found in Linda's purse. She was taken away for questioning, her bail set at $500. Like many very famous people, Paul didn't tend to carry much if any cash, and certainly didn't have enough in his wallet to make bail. Ringing round his contacts, he located former Apple executive Peter Brown at the Beverly Hills Hotel, drove over and got a loan. 'Linda took the rap because she was an American citizen,' explains Brown, who talked the matter over with Paul. 'Therefore it wasn't onerous to her … we got him the money, and he went back and got her out.' Although the matter was quickly resolved, this was the McCartneys' third drug conviction in two and a half years.

The next day Linda called one of her old journalist pals, Blair Sabol, whom she hadn't spoken to since 1969, being one of the media friends Linda dropped when she and Paul got together. Linda's former best girlfriend, the reporter Lillian Roxon, had never forgiven her for this slight, getting her own back on Linda by writing a catty review of Paul's 1973 TV special, shortly after which Lillian died. No chance of reconciliation there. Linda had long ago made her peace with journalist Danny Fields, but Blair hadn't heard from Linda until now, and like Lillian she got her own back on Linda in print, writing a caustic article about their reunion in the *Village Voice*. 'Now you must understand the last time I knew Linda was in her groping groupie days [when] Linda was into photographing stars with little or no film in her camera,' Blair later wrote.

> I remember how impressed I was with her come-on talents as she sat in front of [Warren Beatty] in a mini-skirt and her legs in full wide-angle split for at least six rolls of Ectachrome. Warren ended up ushering me out of his Delmonico's suite within 30 minutes and kept

Linda for two days. Her pictures turned out to be mediocre to poor, but we became fast friends.

When Linda invited Blair to the LA studio where Paul was finishing *Venus and Mars*, Blair encountered a woman who seemed to have become totally false since her celebrated marriage, speaking in a *faux* English accent, also affecting a lazy rock 'n' roll manner. 'I mean Mahh-hhhhn, I cahn't stand this town,' she said of LA. Linda shrugged off the latest drug bust: 'Well, you know it happens to everybody and it's time-consuming with the lawyers, but we'll get it taken care of.' Then Paul came in, wearing a hideous black satin smoking jacket with a dragon stitched on the back. 'Linda's told me so much about you. Really glad to meet you,' he said politely. Whether he meant it, he made the effort. Blair warmed to Paul, but found Linda a complete phoney whose 'manipulation of Paul' was 'obnoxious'; as if she was using him to make herself a star, which Blair seemed to think Linda had always wanted to be, though most people don't see Linda that way. The prevailing view, rather, is that Lin was humouring Paul in trying to play the part of a band member.

Evidently, the journalist kept her thoughts to herself at the time, because she received an invitation to a party the McCartneys were giving to celebrate the completion of their album. 'It's gonna be *verrrrrry* private,' Linda assured Blair, affectedly. 'No press and just our immediate good friends. You know, nice and quiet.' This intimate party turned out to be a blow-out for 350 people on the Queen Mary, the retired ocean liner docked at Long Beach. Some of the most famous names in show business attended including Bob Dylan, who treated everybody to a rare display of his disco dancing. George Harrison also showed up, looking a little drawn after a difficult period personally and professionally. In recent times George had scandalised the Beatles family, and enraged Ritchie, by having a fling with his wife Mo. Pattie then left George for his friend Eric Clapton, after which George embarked on a poorly received US tour. On top of everything, he'd developed a cocaine habit. George's presence at Paul's party, however, underlined the Beatles *rapprochement*.

In commercial terms, Paul had done considerably better than John, George and Ritchie since the break-up of the band. After a strong start with *All Things Must Pass*, Harrison's career had fallen flat. Lennon had enjoyed chart success, but he'd also released flop albums, and he didn't tour. After he returned to Yoko from his lost weekend, and they had their son, Sean, John essentially retired from public life, no further rival to Paul. And Ritchie was never going to be anything but a novelty act. Paul was leaving the boys in his dust. He had always been the most hard-working Beatle, the most prolific and focused. He was also the one who really enjoyed live performance, and he had the happy knack of being able to write hits whenever he pleased. His long-playing records were uneven, *Venus and Mars* typically patchy, with some tracks that are virtually unlistenable to today (try 'Magneto and Titanium Man'), but this sort of soft rock was what the market wanted. The LP went to number one in the USA and Britain, with 'Listen to What the Man Said' a US number one. Sometimes an artist is in tune with his times. Paul had enjoyed that experience in the Sixties, spectacularly so, and his luck was holding into the Seventies. He capitalised on the success of his new records by taking Wings out on the road in the UK in the autumn of 1975, followed by an Australian tour, all part of the build-up to a major tour of the USA, where Wings songs were a staple of FM radio playlists. John Lennon might have scorned Paul's material with some justification as Muzak, but millions of Americans happily tapped their steering wheels to the sound of Wings as they drove to and from their jobs in 1975.

That Christmas, John and Yoko were home in the Dakota with two-month-old Sean, and their photographer friend Bob Gruen, when the doorbell rang. They were startled. People didn't just come knocking on the front door within the Dakota. Security was too tight. Anybody paying a visit reported first to the security man in a gilded sentry box at the West 72nd Street entrance, then went to reception where staff would ring up to check before allowing anybody into the elevator. For a moment, John thought they might be being busted. He asked Gruen to see who it was. As the photographer cautiously approached the front door of the apartment he heard somebody singing 'We Wish You a Merry Christmas' outside. 'So I called back to John and Yoko, "Don't worry, it's some kids from the building singing carols."' Gruen then looked through the spy hole and saw Paul and Linda McCartney on the doorstep. The photographer opened the door and took the McCartneys through to John and Yoko, who were in their white bedroom, where they spent much of their time. Here, the two chief Beatles had another reunion which, according to Gruen, was a happy occasion: 'they all seemed like giddy old school chums. Hugging, patting each other on the back … like high-school buddies who hadn't seen each other in a long time and really liked each other.'

In the new year, John and Paul received the shocking news that Mal Evans had died, killed in bizarre circumstances at the age of 40. Along with Neil Aspinall, Mal had been a faithful Beatles courtier from the beginning. He had also been underappreciated. On one hand Mal was made to feel part of the Beatles family, yet the boys were always quick to put him in his place, with Paul being cold towards Mal when the Beatles fell apart, getting the roadie to fetch and carry for him while making his first solo album, but telling him curtly that he didn't want him in the studio, because he was with Linda now. Mal became a lost soul after the Beatles disbanded. He separated from his wife, Lily, moved to Los Angeles, where he shared an apartment with a woman named Fran Hughes, and tried to write his memoirs. He was due to deliver his manuscript on 12 January 1976. Eight days before the deadline, Mal became stoned and depressed. His girlfriend called his collaborator on the book, who came over. When they tried to talk to Mal he picked up a rifle. The police were summoned. When Mal pointed his gun at the cops, they shot him dead. In many ways his death seems like a suicide. Mal must have known the Beatles wouldn't want him to publish that book, and that the choice he faced was dropping the project, and losing money, or further estranging himself from the boys. Better perhaps to die.

Closer to home, Paul's father was in failing health. For the last few years, Jim McCartney had lived as an invalid in his Gayton bungalow, nursed by Angie. 'She was very nice, Angie … My God she looked after Jim!' comments their neighbour Doug Mackenzie – a tribute worth bearing in mind given that Angie's reputation would be blackened in the months to come. The other member of the household was Angie's daughter, Ruth, now a teenager, with ambitions to go into show business. In 1975 Ruth auditioned successfully for a spot as a dancer on a TV show with Paul's brother Mike, going round to Paul's house to tell him the good news. According to a press interview Ruth later gave a Sunday newspaper, Paul was far from being pleased. In fact, he was furious. Ruth alleged that her stepbrother pinned her against a wall, with his left hand above her, and used his right to wag a finger as he delivered a lecture about people in the business only wanting to hire Ruth because she was *his* sister. Although she asserted in her interview that Paul had yelled at her, Ruth concluded that 'he meant it for the best'.

Jim McCartney rarely left home now. When the weather was fine, he sat in his front garden watching the world go by. But most of the time he stayed inside, huddled by the fire, crippled by arthritis. A lifelong smoker, Jim also suffered from bronchitis. As his health deteriorated in February and March of 1976, there was tension between Paul and Angie over what should be done. On visits to the Wirral, Paul urged his father to be more active, as if Dad could will himself back into health. Then Jim developed bronchopneumonia, often a prelude to death in the elderly. Paul wanted Dad in hospital; Angie insisted she look after her husband at home. 'We had a falling out as the rest of the family wanted Jim to die in hospital, where his life would have been prolonged by a few painful weeks. But Jim wanted to die in his own bed,' Angie said, 'so I kept him at home. It caused a lot of bad feeling at the time.'

Having lost Mum traumatically at a young age, Paul seemed unable to face the fact Dad was now going to die as well and carried on with his work as normal. Wings were about to embark on a European tour, starting in Copenhagen on Saturday 20 March 1976. Two days before the first show, Jim McCartney died at home at Gayton, aged 73, his demise attributed to pneumonia and heart failure, with bronchitis and arthritis underlying factors. Paul went ahead with a scheduled Wings press conference in London the next day, then flew to Copenhagen to open the tour on Saturday as if nothing had happened. He didn't tell the band his father had died and, remarkably, he didn't return home for the cremation at Landican Cemetery on the Wirral on Monday 22 March. Paul could easily have done so; Wings didn't have a show that day, being between engagements in Denmark and Germany, so he could have hopped over by private plane. But Paul wasn't at the cemetery, and he was in Berlin the next day when Jim's ashes were scattered over the rose garden in front of the chapel. The spot, as with his mother's grave, remains unmarked, which seems odd considering how very sentimental Paul is about his parents. It is possible he deliberately left these places unmarked to avoid fans finding them.

Members of the Beatles had chosen not to attend funerals in the past, such as that of Brian Epstein, for fear their celebrity would attract a mob of press and fans and detract from the occasion, which was a fair point. But to deliberately miss one's father's funeral – especially when, as in this case, father and son had been so close – is strange. Mike McCartney has written in explanation that 'Paul would never face that sort of thing'. Denny Laine says he only found out that Jim had died when he was on a French TV show with Paul and the teen idol David Cassidy later that month. When the interviewer asked Paul about his parents, he said simply they were both dead. Says Laine:

> I was physically shocked, on camera. David Cassidy said, 'You should have seen your face when he said that.' He didn't tell me, and I wasn't that close to his dad, but I knew him quite well. I suppose Paul felt, *I'm not going to get into that*. This is one thing you've got to remember about Paul: he's a very, very private guy. He doesn't like to be talking about his family, or anything to do with anything other than music, if he can possibly help it, in public. He doesn't like to share certain things. He takes them on his own shoulders. And this may be part of his personality: he likes to stay positive, because if he gets negative he gets really negative, and he knows it, so he tries to rise above these things, and not have other people reminding him of too many negative things, or hurtful things, because of who he is. He has to be out there looking like he's Paul McCartney, happy-go-lucky, and not bothering the world with his problems. You can understand that. [So] he probably thought, 'Jesus, I can't handle all that!'

Nevertheless, Laine was surprised Paul didn't return home for the funeral. 'I'm sure in his position he could have just jumped on a private plane and done it, but maybe he just couldn't face the emotional thing of it right in the middle of having to go out and do a gig the next night, and pretend that everything's fine.'

In the aftermath of Jim's death, Paul's relationship with Angie McCartney deteriorated. His stepmother went on holiday after the funeral, with what seemed to the 'relies' indecent haste. 'She and Ruth had their suitcases packed going off on holiday to Spain, a plane to catch from Manchester Airport at half past nine, and the family hated her by then. God she's upset everybody!' remarks Mike Robbins, who'd introduced Angie to Jim. When Angie subsequently decided to go into theatrical management, and Ruth continued to pursue her show business dreams, there were further clashes with Paul, culminating in a blazing telephone row over money, according to an interview Angie gave the *Sun* newspaper. Ruth McCartney has alleged in a separate interview that Paul then stopped the £7,000-a-year pension ($10,710) that had formerly been paid by McCartney Productions Ltd* to Jim. Increasingly hard up, mother and daughter moved out of their bungalow into a flat. A deep rift was opening up between Paul and his stepmother and stepsister.

* In April 1976, Paul changed his company's name to MPL Communications.

THE GOOD LIFE

LAST MEETINGS WITH JOHN

Despite a shaky economy, optimism, even a sense of celebration, returned to the United States in 1976. The Vietnam War was over, Watergate had forced Richard Nixon from office, with a benign young farmer from Georgia promising a brighter future. Many people wanted to believe in Jimmy Carter in the nation's bicentennial year. In the two centuries since the Declaration of Independence, US relations with Britain had improved considerably, of course, a few Britons becoming as popular in the USA as they were at home. Dickens, Chaplin and Churchill spring to mind. The Beatles were in that same august company, Paul's status in the USA remaining sky high, even higher than at home, having achieved four number one singles and four number one albums in America since 1970. Interestingly, he was yet to score a single number one in Britain, where, despite the generally good press Paul enjoyed, critics and audiences were more circumspect about his songs, often considering them overly sentimental, even vacuous. In April 1976, Wings released a single that answered such criticism in audacious style. In 'Silly Love Songs' Paul made his case plain. He liked writing love songs. If people had a problem with that, it was tough. He would continue to write them. The strength of the melody made 'Silly Love Songs' Paul's fifth US number one, holding the top spot for five weeks, but again it failed to reach the top of the British charts, and was in fact mocked at home.

'Silly Love Songs' heralded a new album, *Wings at the Speed of Sound*, which showcased songs sung not only by Paul, but also by his fellow band members including the third Wings drummer, Joe English, a big, bearded fellow with a surprisingly sweet voice. This was the strongest line-up of Wings yet, but many of the tracks on *Wings at the Speed of Sound* were mediocre. No amount of production could disguise the fact that Linda's 'Cook of the House', a nod to her culinary skills, was a weak song which she sang badly. The best track, 'Let 'em In' was a very different proposition, a catchy tune with a good, semi-autobiographical lyric delivered in one of Paul's most persuasive vocal performances: insinuatingly dreamy, a touch melancholy, a whisper of past magic. It was another US hit, helping drive *Wings at the Speed of Sound* to the top of the American album charts.

Paul was in New York. Buoyed up by chart success, he and Linda dropped by the Dakota on the evening of Saturday 24 April 1976 to see the Lennons. John was home watching *Saturday Night Live* (*SNL*) and Paul sat and watched TV with him. So it was that the two ex-Beatles saw Lorne Michaels, the executive producer of *SNL*, and a personal friend of Paul's from the Hamptons, jokingly offer to effect a Beatles reunion, something that was increasingly rumoured in the press, with wild stories going about as to how many millions such a gig would earn for the boys. Michaels announced that NBC could offer the Beatles the union rate of $3,000 for the performance of three songs. He held up a cheque, made out to the Beatles. 'You divide it any way you want; if you want to give Ringo less, that's up to you.' John and Paul discussed going down to NBC there and then for a *laff*, but in the end it was too late.

The next night Paul dropped by the Dakota again. This time he met a less positive reception. As is often the way with men who have known each other as boys, then drifted apart, picking up an old friendship can be difficult. The initial, part-instinctive, part-merely polite warmth of 'Well, hello, how *are* you?' is replaced by an irritation that somebody from the past has come blundering in on the present as if nothing has changed, whereas everything has. At least John seemed to feel that way. He may also have been a tad jealous of Wings' success. John had read that Paul was now worth $25 million (£16.3m), and complained to Yoko that they'd never be as rich as that. Yoko made a deal with her husband. If he stayed and home and looked after Sean, she would manage and build their fortune. Yoko proved a successful business-woman, though it is doubtful she ever caught up with Paul.

'That was a period when Paul just kept turning up at our door with a guitar. I would let him in,' Lennon later said of Paul's 1976 visits to the Dakota, 'but finally I said to him, "Please call before you come over. It's not 1956, and turning up at the door isn't the same any more. You know, just give me a ring." That upset him, but I didn't mean it badly.'

John's friend, the broadcaster and PR man Elliott Mintz, believes the friendship had simply run its course. Mintz recalls another night with John and Paul at the Dakota (he can't remember the date) when the Beatles apparently had nothing more to say to each other:

> Think of yourself sitting in a theatre as audience, and the film stock that's moving through the projector ran out, and instead of the lights coming on in the theatre and the curtains closing as they usually would, you just saw the white projection light on the screen, as if it had run out of film. It felt like that – they didn't really have anything more to talk about.

Had history been otherwise, though, Mintz believes that John and Paul would have seen more of each other in the years ahead. 'Today they would be men pushing 70 years old. Would they be sitting around bickering and sending nasty emails to each other over some infraction of their relationship that was conceived [decades] earlier?' he asks rhetorically. 'I don't think so.' As it was, John and Paul never saw each other in the flesh again after these last Dakota visits.

ROCK SHOW

As John settled back into his quiet domestic life in New York, Paul began his Wings Over America tour in Fort Worth, Texas, on 3 May 1976. It was to be the most successful tour Wings ever gave. The first the audience saw of the star of the evening was when Paul stood spotlit on stage, in swirling dry ice, singing 'Venus and Mars', the lyrics of which begin with the narrator standing just so, waiting for his show to begin, red and green spotlights appearing on cue as McCartney sang. He segued from this introductory number into the faster 'Rockshow', also designed specifically for the arena stage.

As the lights came up, Paul appeared clean-shaven and fresh-faced, his hair cut short in a fringe over his eyes, worn long at the back. He smiled broadly, with frequent glances at Linda, sitting prettily at her keyboards on a riser, the base of which changed colour during the show. Lin looked happy and relaxed, not the nervous wreck of early Wings tours. Denny Laine stood to Paul's left, wielding a fashionable double-neck guitar; young Jimmy McCulloch stood beside Denny, agape with concentration as he peeled off his solos; behind them Joe English thrashed his drums like Animal in the *Muppet Show*. Alongside Joe stood four horn players, featuring Paul's old friend Howie Casey on saxophone, the brass section adding punch to Wings' sound. This was a long way from the university tour of 1972. It was a big, expensive, state-of-the-art rock show with a laser light display during 'Live and Let Die'. Most importantly, Wings was now tight. 'It was the first time we'd really spent enough time on the road to get really good as a band,' says Laine. And the sound quality was good. The last time Paul played the States was with the Beatles, when their inadequately amplified sound was drowned out by fans. The technology of the rock show had improved sufficiently in the ten years since Candlestick Park to enable everybody in the Fort Worth arena to hear the nuances of Wings' sound. The show could be loud, as in 'Rockshow' and 'Live and Let Die', but it also featured effective quiet moments such as Paul's acoustic set, when he played 'Bluebird'.

Wings' repertoire was impressive considering the band had been together less than five years. 'Jet', 'Let Me Roll It', 'Maybe I'm Amazed', 'Listen to What the Man Said', 'Let 'em In' and 'Band on the Run' all worked well in concert, better than on record where one tended to notice the paucity of the lyrics. Live rock music is as much theatre as a listening experience and the songs delivered drama. The undoubted highlight of the show came, however, when Paul sat at the piano and played 'Lady Madonna', the first of four Beatles songs in the set, having moved on from his original position of ignoring his past. Paul only performed Beatles songs he had written alone, and just a handful – 'Lady Madonna', 'The Long and Winding Road', 'Blackbird' and 'Yesterday'– but each held his audience spellbound.

To transport Wings around the USA, McCartney hired a BAC 1-11 passenger jet, the Wings logo stuck to its fuselage, the interior transformed into an open-plan rock star lounge. There was a discotheque in the back for the McCartney children, who'd once again been taken out of school to be with their parents: 13-year-old Heather; Mary, almost seven; and four-year-old Stella. To cut back on travel as much as possible, and retain a semblance of normal family life, the McCartneys rented three regional homes for the tour: a house in New York for the East Coast leg; a home in Dallas for the Midwestern shows; and a third property in LA. When their jet landed, a limousine took the McCartneys to the relevant regional home. Driving to the Dallas house one day Linda spotted an appaloosa stallion (a type of horse distinguished by its spotted markings), stopped and bought it, having the animal shipped home to England. Lucky Spot became a beloved family pet.

Although the McCartneys commuted to concerts from their rented homes, there were still long hours in the air with the band and its entourage. Among others, the tour party included the McCartneys' Cockney housekeeper Rose Martin, who minded the kids when Paul and Lin were on stage; an ex-FBI man who looked out for potential assassins and kidnappers; and a new road manager, 27-year-old Londoner John Hammel, who'd previously worked for Humble Pie. The term 'road manager' is a vague one under which somebody like Hammel acts as driver, bodyguard and all-round gofer. Hammel proved so satisfactory in the role that he has stayed by Paul's side ever since Wings Over America, his job description evolving into Personal Assistant.

During the long intercontinental flights the horn players fell into an extended game of Ten Card Brag, betting nickels, partly because they were not well paid. After watching the game for a while, Paul sat in with the lads, borrowing his stake. The pot of money grew into a large pile of change. 'Here you are, boys – four of a kind,' Howie Casey announced one day, laying down his winning hand. 'Thank you very much.' As Howie gathered in his coins, McCartney went berserk, as if he'd been cheated out of a fortune, to the amusement of his sidemen. 'I think it's the winning. It's not the money,' says Howie, who notes that when he and others grumbled about the wages they were paid, Paul gave them a generous end-of-tour bonus. 'He said, "Give them all $10,000 each [£6,535]." OK, that's great. He did that sort of thing, but it would have been much better for all concerned if we'd have had a decent [salary in the first place].'

Howie asked for and received a bottle of Scotch in the dressing room before each show. Yet there was a predominantly family vibe during

Wings Over America, as there had been on the double-decker tour of Europe. To unwind after the show, Paul and Lin screened a movie, and they liked the band to watch the film with them. Then Paul and Lin went to their rented home, where Rosie had already put the kids to bed. There was an official ban on drugs backstage, also on groupies. That way Linda kept Paul away from temptation, though he showed no signs of straying. 'I never saw [Paul with another woman] and I never sensed any of it,' says Denny Laine, who knew Paul as well as anyone during the decade. Indeed, Denny hardly ever saw Paul without Linda. If Paul walked into a room, you could bet Lin would follow. 'He wanted somebody he could rely on,' says Denny, explaining the attraction Paul felt for his wife. 'She came from money, too, so he could trust she wasn't after his money, [and] they had kids. The kids went everywhere with them. This was a life he hadn't had much of and really loved.'

THE SUMMER OF 1976

After returning home from this hugely successful US tour Paul decided to celebrate the life of one of his musical heroes, Buddy Holly, with a luncheon party on what would have been Buddy's birthday, thus also celebrating his ownership of a slice of Buddy's publishing. The party was held at the Orangery in London's Kensington Gardens on 7 September 1976, attended by MPL staff, Wings members, and musicians from other bands including Queen and 10cc, whose co-founder Eric Stewart had known Paul since Cavern days and would soon come to play a significant part in Paul's career.

The lunch proved so enjoyable that Paul decided to celebrate Buddy's life and music every September with Buddy Holly Week, featuring a lunch or party that Paul would attend, plus public events for fans – creating an additional fixture on the McCartney Calendar. The McCartney Year now invariably started with a family party in Liverpool, followed by a sunshine break in the Caribbean, with a two-week family holiday in Scotland in August, closely followed by another fortnight in East Hampton with the Eastmans, then back to London for Buddy Holly Week in September, followed by Hallowe'en and Thanksgiving, which the family tended to celebrate in London. Linda was largely responsible for introducing the American tradition of trick or treat to St John's Wood and, before the McCartneys turned vegetarian, she cooked a scrumptious Thanksgiving turkey. Band members and friends were always grateful for an invitation to this annual feast, especially homesick Americans. In the days before cranberries were widely available in the UK, Linda cleverly made an ersatz cranberry sauce from English jam. At Christmas Paul hosted a jolly office party at MPL – one year hiring the actor Andrew Sachs to serve the drinks in character as Manuel from the TV show *Fawlty Towers* – before going back to Liverpool for New Year and starting over again. Recording and concerts were fitted in around this family-orientated calendar, and virtually everywhere Paul and Lin went the kids came, too. The McCartneys were a remarkably close family.

A couple of weeks after the first Buddy Holly luncheon, Paul and Linda took Wings to Venice to play a charity concert and celebrate Lin's 35th birthday with a family party (naturally the kids came), after which Paul didn't play live for three years. While he loved performing, Linda only did so to please him, so this was a welcome break for her, and of course the McCartneys didn't need the money. Wings Over America had filled the coffers; MPL turned over more than £3 million ($4.5m) in 1976–7, out of which Paul paid himself a chairman's salary of £96,500 (or $147,645) at a time when national average earnings in the UK were less than £4,000 ($6,120), and the company still cleared a £1.1 m profit ($1.68). 'In the last two years I have earned more money that I have ever earned in all the so-called boom years [of the Beatles] put together,' the star revealed in a 1977 interview. 'I was sick with companies. But Lee [Eastman] told me that if I got an office and a couple of good people to pay out of my own pocket I could own my own material.' Lee's advice had proved sound. Some Beatles-related income is included in these MPL figures, which are a matter of public record, but the main royalty stream from the Beatles' back catalogue does not appear in the registered company accounts, meaning that Paul had substantial additional earnings accruing elsewhere. The full picture of his personal wealth would emerge many years later, as we shall see.

After operating out of rented rooms in Greek Street, Soho, for the past couple of years, in 1977 MPL moved around the corner to Soho Square, at the centre of which is a small park popular with office and shop workers. Soho Square is in the middle of a very busy area of Central London, the large clothes shops of Oxford Street a few strides away to the north, Charing Cross Road to the east, with its book and music shops, the bustling life of Soho – with its bars, restaurants and clubs – all around. Paul had bought 1 Soho Square, a five-storey Edwardian townhouse, the ground floor of which resembles a shop, with large, curved, plate-glass windows. Stairs lead up from the reception to four floors of offices, Paul taking as his private study the front office on the second floor. Sitting at his desk, speaking on the phone, he could watch people in the park below, an interesting view for a man always on the look-out for song ideas. Before MPL moved into 1 Soho Square, Paul had the building gutted and redecorated Art Deco-style by the people who designed the celebrated Biba shop in Kensington, commissioning expensive blue carpets, curtains and upholstery, all woven with a music note motif, which was repeated in the hand-carved oak door handles and as a stencil pattern around the windows. Other bespoke features included an antique Wurlitzer loaded with Paul's favourite records, valuable art works and a restored pipe organ on the first-floor landing. There was a penthouse flat at the top of the building, and space in the basement for a recording studio.

A small team of people worked full time for Paul at 1 Soho Square. The most senior role was personal manager to Paul. It is a reflection of how demanding Paul can be that there was a high turnover of people in this position. First came Vincent Romeo, then Brian Brolly, followed by an Australian named Stephen Shrimpton. Brolly stayed with MPL throughout the changes, looking after Paul's money alongside accountant Paul Winn, both stalwart members of the MPL team. So too was the ebullient Alan 'the Crowd' Crowder, who served as office factotum. In addition there was a changing cast of receptionists and secretaries. Sue Cavanaugh ran the Wings Fun Club and oversaw its magazine, *Club Sandwich*, launched in February 1977 to 'narrow the gap between the band and its audience'. Initially, *Club Sandwich* consisted of a single folded sheet of newspaper, printed in black and white like the music papers of the day, though it was less like *Melody Maker* in tone than a kids' magazine, apparently designed principally for the amusement of the wee McCartneys, benevolent, informal and jokey, with room for fan drawings, a letters page (Sue's Lettuce [sic]), and a crossword puzzle drawn by Paul's cousin, Bert Danher, a professional crossword compiler.

The MPL building was Paul's own, better-organised version of the Apple operation at 3 Savile Row, another handsome townhouse building, and one which Apple finally got around to selling in 1976. Looking back from a time when stars, for security reasons, are usually concerned that the public *don't* know where they live and do business, the Beatles had always been refreshingly public about their place of work. They put themselves on the high street with Apple in the Sixties, and Paul did the same with MPL now. Anybody who was interested could find his new office easily, and even if fans couldn't get past the girls on reception they could sit in Soho Square watching the building for Paul who was often to be seen walking about the area, using local restaurants and popping into the Nellie Dean pub. He still uses 1 Soho Square as his business headquarters and can be seen occasionally in the neighbourhood.

Likewise, Paul's Cavendish Avenue address has always been well known to his fans, though the house has changed over the years. After his marriage to Linda, especially since they had children, Cavendish transformed from 1960s bachelor pad into family home, with a scruffy, lived-in feel, the kids hurtling about followed by their dogs, none of whom seemed house-trained, hand prints and crayon marks on the walls, often under valuable artwork, paw prints and dog mess on the rugs, while the McCartneys' large back garden put the neighbours in mind of the TV sit-com *The Good Life*. In this popular Seventies' comedy a middle-class couple turn their suburban garden into a small-holding complete with livestock. Similarly Linda had taken to growing vegetables in her back garden, which also included a small zoo of animals featuring rabbits, ducks and chickens, the latter roosting in Paul's Rolls Royce after he carelessly left a window open. It cost £6,000 ($9,180) to have the Rolls re-upholstered.

The McCartney cockerel woke the whole avenue at dawn. 'It wouldn't just crow, it would escape, and you would see all the kids running down the street after [it],' laughs Adrian Grumi, who grew up in Cavendish Avenue with the McCartney children. Adrian's mother was less than impressed when Paul and Linda stabled four horses in their garden. Granted, the houses had been built with stables, to pull the carriages of the Victorian gentry who originally lived here, but it was an incongruous sight in 1976/77 to see the McCartneys clip-clopping out of their gate on Sunday mornings, under the mistaken belief they could go riding in Regent's Park. 'They had their helmets and all sorts of things, and the jodhpurs, just to go along the bottom of the street to the top of the street. They used to poo, the horses, and the neighbours went mad,' says Mrs Grumi.

The McCartneys were in fact less often in St John's Wood nowadays, spending more time at their Sussex bolthole, Waterfall, even though the house was too small for a family of five. As in Scotland, it was the privacy and simplicity of country life that appealed. 'It was great [for Paul] to get away from being a superstar to being just a family man,' notes Denny Laine. In September 1976, Paul began improving and expanding his Sussex property, making a planning application for the erection of a stable block and, unusually, for a 70ft observation tower, both of which were granted. The tower attracted a great deal of media attention, not least because it looked like something from a prisoner-of-war camp. Newspapers published pictures of the tower as part of fanciful stories about the high security at Paul's Sussex home, which the neighbours were apparently calling Paulditz, a pun on another popular TV show of the day, the POW drama *Colditz*. In fact, Paul had little personal security and, rather than erecting the tower to watch for intruders, he wanted to be able to look out over the tree canopy. 'You see, when you are right in the forest, there's no views, no outlook, you were just in the trees,' explains his neighbour Veronica Languish. 'So when he had that tower built he could see further around.' The Languishes were among the local farming families who had watched the arrival of the McCartneys with curiosity in the late Sixties, but grew to like the family. 'He fits in. He is just like everybody else really to us now, he's been here long enough,' says Mrs Languish, having known Paul over 30 years. Like so many people, Mrs Languish was particularly fond of Linda, who made the biggest effort to meet and befriend local people. 'She was a nice girl, Linda, she was a very friendly girl.' And the McCartneys' marriage was evidently solid. That Christmas, Linda bought Paul one of his best presents: the double bass Bill Black played on Elvis Presley's Sun sessions, while there was further good news when a live triple album of their US tour, *Wings Over America*, went to number one in the United States.

ALL ABOARD

In the first week of December 1976, the Sex Pistols had burst upon the consciousness of the British public with an outrageous appearance on tea-time television, the band members cursing and baiting the presenter on the show to the extent that they made front-page news the next day. Punk rock had arrived, and many young Britons took it to their hearts, feeling themselves to have more in common with scruffs like Johnny Rotten and Sid Vicious than a millionaire rock star like Paul McCartney. Even Paul's daughter Heather, now 14, had turned punk. Paul tried to write a punk-style song to entertain her, named, hilariously, 'Boil Crisis', but at the age of 34 he was too long in the tooth to empathise with rebellious teens.

In March, Paul had allowed the orchestral *Thrillington* album to be released, six years after he had recorded the curiosity, with a jokey promotional campaign that involved placing short, enigmatic items in the personal column of London's *Evening Standard*, supposedly written by the fictional band leader, Percy 'Thrills' Thrillington. Releasing an album of tea-dance instrumentals the same month as the Sex Pistols' 'God Save the Queen' showed how out of step with youth culture Paul had become. But did it matter? He and Linda were rich and happy. They were expecting another baby – Paul hoped for a boy – and plans were being laid to make the next Wings album in the Caribbean. No wonder punks resented him.

Ten years on from the summer of love, Great Britain was a much less attractive and confident place to be than in the mid-Sixties. As 1976 segued into '77 high interest rates, strikes and mounting unemployment were all symptoms of an ailing economy, while the euphemistically termed 'troubles' of Northern Ireland continued to result in bloody murder both in the province and on mainland Britain, with bomb scares and actual blasts commonplace in the capital. In the music industry the talk was all about the Sex Pistols, the band having been sacked from EMI by its new chairman Sir John Read as too controversial for a firm that had built its reputation on making recordings of such great British composers as Vaughan Williams, Sir Edward Elgar and, well, Lennon & McCartney. Paul was a favourite son at EMI HQ, and continued to patronise Abbey Road Studios, which had become the most famous recording facility in the world thanks to the

Beatles. The zebra crossing outside the studios had become a major tourist attraction in the few years since *Abbey Road* was released, fans coming from all over the world to have their picture taken walking across, to the annoyance of cab and bus drivers who were obliged to stop for them.

In the grey days of February 1977, Paul took Wings back into the EMI studios on Abbey Road to work on their new *London Town* album, named after the title song, which sought to express the feel of the capital in winter. While there is a definite gloomy charm to London at this time of year, Paul soon tired of the dark, damp days of winter. He announced to his band that, after a break in proceedings, Wings would resume recording *London Town* in the Caribbean (again probably partly for tax reasons). What's more they would do so on a boat.

The McCartneys flew to Jamaica in April for a family holiday, before travelling to the US Virgin Islands where Wings' advance party had hired three vessels, including the motor launch the *Fair Carol*, into the stern of which Geoff Emerick and Mark Vigars fitted a 24-track recording machine. Captain Tony Garton feared his vessel would sink under the weight. A trimaran, *El Toro*, was hired for the McCartney family, that is Paul and Linda, heavily pregnant with her fourth child, and the girls Heather, Mary and Stella; while a third vessel, *Samala*, accommodated Wings, the roadies and the engineers. The McCartney family came aboard at St Thomas, then sailed to St John to collect Denny, Jimmy and Joe.

This eccentric Caribbean adventure began well, with the band and crew diving into the water to swim from one boat to another, delighting in the coral and brightly coloured fish. Fun was had shouting 'Shark!' when friends were bathing. One day a dolphin rose to the surface, cocking its head as if to listen to Paul playing guitar. As the sessions continued, however, there were numerous shipboard mishaps. Alan Crowder slipped and broke his foot, returning from hospital on crutches like Long John Silver; Denny Laine got sunstroke; Jimmy McCulloch temporarily lost his hearing; and Geoff Emerick electrocuted himself. At night, with the three boats moored together, everybody would meet for a long communal supper under the stars. One night, Paul entertained everybody with a production of a story called *The Two Little Fairies*, narrating and playing piano, while his daughters Mary and Stella acted out the parts of the fairies. Too old for this sort of childish nonsense, Heather was to be found skulking in a corner listening to the Damned.

Drink and weed were part of the nightlife, and when the boats were moored in Watermelon Bay two US Park Rangers came aboard to remonstrate with Paul about the noise. The following day the Rangers delivered a letter, warning that if they came back and found drugs onboard arrests would follow. Spooked, Captain Garton tried to impose order on his rock star client, who told him he didn't need the aggravation and hired a new boat, the *Wanderlust*. Later, a song of that name appeared on the *Tug of War* album, the lyrics making it clear that Paul considered hassles with the authorities over dope a petty matter.

When summer came, the McCartneys headed back to Scotland. Denny Laine and his partner Jo Jo were living at the time in a cottage on Paul's estate so that he and Paul could write together. One afternoon Paul came over to the house with an idea for a song about their holiday home. 'He had the chorus. He already had the "Mull of Kintyre" title,' remembers Laine, referring to the tip of the Kintyre peninsula. 'He wanted to write a song that reminded him of the area.' The men had a couple of glasses of whisky, then sat outside Laine's cottage and finished the song, looking at the scenery: 'that was the way that song came about, looking around and seeing what was there. You didn't have to come up with anything. It was just in front of you.' The finished song was a waltz with good, poetic lyrics. The words are in fact noticeably superior to all Paul's solo work to date, which is explained by the fact that McCartney didn't write them. At least not all of them. While Paul wrote the chorus, and already had the title, Laine says he wrote 'quite a lot' of the rest of 'Mull of Kintyre', meaning that Paul has to share the credit for what may be his best post-Beatles lyric. Laine says his input is strongly felt, for example, in the following romantic verse:

Far have I travelled and much have I seen
Dark distant mountains with valleys of green
Past painted deserts, the sunsets on fire
As he carries me home to the Mull of Kintyre

The recording of the song was highly unusual, using the services of the Campbeltown Pipe Band, one member of which was Jimmy McGeachy, teenaged son of a piper of the same name. Aged 15 when 'Mull of Kintyre' was recorded, Jimmy was in his final year at Campbeltown Grammar School, after which he would become an apprentice fitter in the shipyard. In his spare time he played in the pipe band. The band members met at Castle Hill Church two evenings a week to practise, and when summer came they sallied forth in Royal Stewart tartan kilts, sporrans and feathered bonnets to perform in the streets of the town and at regional competitions. As with the Black Dyke Mills Band, there was considerable community pride in the band, with youngsters always eager to join. Jimmy saw no conflict between playing drums in the pipe band and drumming in his school punk band.

The Pipe Major was a former Scots Guardsman named Tony Wilson, a larger-than-life character often to be found in the pub. One day Paul invited Wilson up to High Park to play him his new waltz, asking if the pipe band, whom he'd last had up to High Park when he was with Jane Asher, would like to play on a recording. Wilson put the idea to his colleagues at their next meeting at Castle Hill. 'We thought it was a wind-up, obviously,' notes Ian McKerral, then a young piper. 'We knew Paul had a farm in Kintyre and we used to see him around the town, he was quite regular, but Tony was a bit of a character and we thought he was having us on.' Tony was in earnest, however. He chalked Paul's tune on the blackboard, and they started rehearsing it.

On the evening of Tuesday 9 August 1977, Wilson took seven pipers and seven drummers, all dressed in tartan, to Low Ranachan Farm. Geoff Emerick and Mark Vigars were there to make the recording. 'All of a sudden the dogs come on down, there's the sheepdog Martha, and then the McCartneys. He's there in front of us. "Hi, how are you going?" His family is all there, who were just kids at the time, Mary, Stella, and Heather was my age,' recalls Jimmy McGeachy, who got to know Heather a little. 'She was quite clingy, she was always at mother's side ...' Denny Laine and Joe English were also present, but not Jimmy McCulloch. The volatile guitarist had parted company with Wings after a silly incident at the farm when, no doubt drunk, he'd thrown eggs against a wall. The eggs came from Linda's pet chickens and she was upset. As a result, Jimmy left to join the Small Faces.

Wings had already recorded the basics of 'Mull of Kintyre'. Now the pipers recorded their part, priming their pipes by inflating the sheepskin bags, then unleashing the fierce, weird, almost mechanical noise of the instruments. Paul counted them in, for the pipes aren't heard until after the third verse. When this was done to his satisfaction, he went outside and recorded the drums, yelling 'Whoo-hooo!' at the end, as can be heard on the record. With the work done, Paul went away and reappeared with a wheelbarrow loaded with cans of McEwan's Export beer, which the pipe band members drank while Paul tried on John McGeachy's tartan and attempted to squeeze a tune out of the pipes, which was harder than it looked. Linda made sandwiches for the men. 'She was a lovely woman,' says John McGeachy, the town mechanic. 'You could meet her in the streets of Campbeltown – I met her quite a bit – and she would always stop to chat ...' Young Jimmy McGeachy (no relation) wandered inside the barn and had a go on Joe English's drums, Linda coming to join him for a jam session. 'She makes you feel really welcome, you know. There [was] a warmth about her.' Although eight months pregnant, Linda sneaked a cigarette from young Jimmy. 'Don't tell Paul,' she whispered.

Although Joe English seemed on good terms with the McCartneys during the 'Mull of Kintyre' session, he left Wings soon afterwards, grumbling about money. Once more, Wings were the irreducible trio of Paul, Linda and Denny Laine, again putting a question mark against Paul's relationship with his musicians. 'Paul is wonderful but he can be pretty ruthless to people around him,' comments former Apple man Tony 'Measles' Bramwell, who was doing PR for Wings nowadays. Band members came and went 'without any sort of acknowledgement'. To be fair, Paul had more important things happening in his life. His dream of having a son was fulfilled the following month when, on 12 September 1977, Linda gave birth to a boy. They named the child James Louis, after Paul's father and Linda's grandfather respectively. In registering the birth Paul was obliged to provide Linda's previous married name. He gave Lerch, though he knew full well that Heather's father was Mel See; probably an intentional dig, the McCartneys not being on good terms with Mel at the time. So proud was Paul at having a son, he had his PR put out a press release. 'I'm over the moon!' Paul was quoted as saying. 'When I knew the baby was a boy I really flipped.'

Paul had originally intended 'Mull of Kintyre' as an album track, but he had such a good feeling about the song he made it a double A-side single with 'Girls' School', the salacious lyrics of which, concerning schoolgirls and their sexy teachers, sounded out of place coming from a father of three girls. 'Girls' School' was, however, a conventional rock 'n' roll song that might play well in North America, whereas 'Mull of Kintyre' was a Scottish folk song with bagpipes that almost certainly wouldn't. Paul decided, nevertheless, to release it in the UK, shooting a promotional video with the pipe band on Kintyre. At the start of this video Paul is seen strumming his guitar outside a cottage, with Linda walking down to meet him babe in arms. The impression given is that we are looking at Paul's Scottish home. In fact, he travelled several miles up the coast to Saddle Beach to make the video and the house is nothing to do with the family. Again, the pipe band members were charmed by the McCartneys, and happily signed away their rights to royalties for a modest one-off payment. By agreement with Tony Wilson, each man got £30 cash ($46) in a brown envelope on the night of the recording, and another £300 ($460) or so for the video, which they thought generous. Nobody expected what happened next.

Released in mid-November 1977, 'Mull of Kintyre' went quickly to number one in the British charts – the first and only Wings song to be a UK number one – then stayed there for what seemed forever. Paul, who was in the habit of calling MPL to ask about weekly sales, was given astonishing figures: up to 145,000 copies a day were being sold in Britain at a time when a good daily sale was 20,000. 'Mull of Kintyre' soon sold a million, and kept selling. Not since the Beatles had Paul shifted so much vinyl. He brought the Campbeltown Pipe Band to London, where they made a second video to give the viewers of the BBC TV show *Top of the Pops* something different to look at. All told, 'Mull of Kintyre' stayed at number one for nine weeks, selling over two million copies in the UK, the biggest-selling single in British history up to that time.

The song also did well in countries with a sizeable ex-patriate Scottish community, such as Canada and New Zealand, stirring feelings of nostalgia. As expected, it sold far fewer copies in the United States, as did its flipside 'Girls' School', which Paul had hoped would do well in the USA. This disappointment contributed to Paul's decision to end his long association with Capitol Records. A light, peppy synthesiser-based tune from the new album, 'With a Little Luck', did however make number one in the United States, after which Paul launched *London Town*.

The album cover, showing Paul, Linda and Denny posed by Tower Bridge on a cold day, was at odds with the fact that much of this record had been cut in the Caribbean, while the tracks were the usual mixture of catchy ballads – with one or two stand-outs – surrounded by make-weights and songs that sounded half-finished, such as 'Backwards Traveller'. The words of 'Children Children', referring to a secret water-fall in a forest where children play, surely relates to the family home in Sussex; while it wasn't clear whether Paul was being ironical or not when he sang in mockery of rock stars and their groupie girlfriends in 'Famous Groupies'. After all, he'd married a groupie (Linda), and Denny was about to marry another one (Jo Jo). *London Town* also sounded distinctly old-fashioned in a year when most of the young record-buying public were either into disco or punk in Britain.

When Paul asked 'Measles' Bramwell what he thought of *London Town*, he didn't like the answer he received. 'I said, "Well, it'll be all right when it's finished." He did one of his prodding things. You know, he prods,' says Measles, explaining that if Paul was in a good mood he gave you his famous thumbs-up gesture, but if he was displeased with someone in private he would prod them in the chest while he told them off. 'It was just Macca being Macca: thumbs up Macca or prodding Macca.' As he poked Measles in the chest, Paul asked: 'What the fuck do you know? I fucking brought you down from Liverpool.' It was what he used to say in the old days at Apple, to Peter Brown and others, when he was pissed off. Bramwell was not given the job of promoting *London Town* and the men didn't speak for more than ten years.

Although Paul was out of step with young Britons, he continued to command a large, older audience, and *London Town* went top five in the UK and USA. It may have done even better had its release not coin-cided with a classic spoof. The story of the greatest of all Beatles trib-ute bands, the Rutles, goes back a couple of years to when former *Monty Python* member Eric Idle and Bonzo Dog songwriter Neil Innes, both great friends of George Harrison's, made a comedy series for the BBC named *Rutland Weekend Television*, satirising the conventions of television and spoofing *Hard Day's Night*-era Beatles, because, as Innes explains, 'it was a cheap visual gag – black and white, four guys in wigs and pointy shoes running around a field. It would do!' When Idle presented *Saturday Night Live* in 1976, he showed a clip of the Rutles, receiving such a favourable response from American viewers that *SNL* commissioned a full-length film of the 'the prefab four'. *All You Need is Cash* is a documentary parody presented by Idle in the character of a humourless TV journalist whose cockeyed comments poke fun at both the Beatles story and the way journalists carelessly repeat the common-place. The viewer is shown the Cavern and the Reeperbahn, 'the world's naughtiest street where the Rutles found themselves far from home and far from talented'; the Rutles making their first album 'in 20 minutes; the second took even longer'; then falling into the clutches of a Klein-like manager whose 'only weak spot was his dishonesty'. The Paul character was named Dirk McQuickly, played by Idle as a peppy Mr Showbiz always willing to talk to the press or write a quick song for another band. 'Any old slag he'd sell a song to,' sneers Mick Jagger in a delicious cameo, all the funnier because Paul gave the Stones their first hit.

NBC broadcast *All You Need is Cash* the day Paul was launching *London Town*, the parody airing on the BBC five days later, shortly after which a Rutles LP was released. As Paul tried to sell his own record, journalists asked him constantly about Rutlemania, a gag the media took to with alacrity even though it was partly at their expense. Paul was not amused. 'I don't think he liked Eric's portrayal of him,' says Neil Innes, laughing despite feeling bad about the Rutles clashing with *London Town*. When he met Paul at a party at George Harrison's house he tried to apologise to the star. 'I did take him to one side and said, "Look, old bean, I'm really sorry about [the] Rutles." He said, "Oh no, I know it's affectionate."' Still, Innes got the impression Paul was offended. 'He suddenly started to look a bit edgy.'

BACK TO THE EGG

Paul attended the London première of *Annie* in May 1978, taking not only Lin and the kids to the theatre but 37 members of his extended family, partly to celebrate the fact that the Eastmans had bought the rights to the musical to add to MPL's growing music publishing division. The show became a major hit, further enriching the star. The Eastmans were also in the process of renegotiating Paul's record deal with EMI and Capitol, with the result that McCartney signed with CBS in America for a $22.5 million advance (then £10m). The size of the deal reflected his track record in the United States. The Beatles had been the most successful act of the Sixties, and it could be argued, on the strength of US singles, that Paul was one of the most successful acts of the Seventies. There were high expectations that he would continue to deliver hits for CBS with Wings.

First, Paul had to re-form the band. This time he delegated the job to Denny Laine, who picked two Englishmen in their twenties to replace Joe English and Jimmy McCulloch: drummer Steve Holley and guitarist Laurence Juber. The auditions were perfunctory. 'We played some Chuck Berry tunes and some reggae grooves and they offered me the job on the spot,' recalls Juber. Holley believes the almost careless choice was an indication that Paul was losing interest in Wings. 'I don't think they particularly wanted a long, drawn-out audition process, which I think Paul was bored with. I think Paul was probably getting bored in general anyway, to be absolutely truthful … Perhaps the responsibility of having a band was becoming a little tiresome for him.'

Previous versions of Wings failed partly because the musicians felt they were underpaid sidemen rather than full band members. Holley and Juber were essentially hired on the same basis, but the pay was better, and the terms of unemployment were explained more clearly during a business meeting with Paul's father-in-law. Over iced tea on the lawn of his summer home in East Hampton, Lee Eastman spelt out the deal. 'Basically there was an annual amount and it was paid on a monthly basis and there was a percentage of tour revenue,' says Juber. 'It was certainly a reasonable deal.' As Paul's lieutenant, Denny Laine had a different, enhanced deal, having finally been given a share in the band's royalties – what Denny Seiwell had always hankered after, but didn't stick around long enough to get. The Eastmans were also beginning to manage Laine's financial affairs, alongside Paul's, within MPL. Unfortunately, Laine had already got into the position of owing the tax man more money than he could pay. This became a serious problem for the guitarist.

That summer Wings convened in Scotland to start work on the new album, *Back to the Egg*, produced by Paul with Chris Thomas, who'd become a well-known producer since stepping into George Martin's shoes on the *White Album*, producing Procol Harum, Roxy Music and, most recently, the Sex Pistols' *Never Mind the Bollocks*. There was an attempt to introduce something of the energy of punk and new wave music – which was essentially the rediscovery of rock 'n' roll – to *Back to the Egg*, the title indicating a return to basics. This is heard most clearly on 'Spin It On', with echoes of the Clash audible in 'Again and Again and Again'. As always with Paul there were also plenty of catchy love songs, some filler, and forays into different musical styles, including the jazzy closing track, 'Baby's Request', which his father would have loved.

Steve Holley realised that Paul missed working with John Lennon.

Actually it was the morning that we recorded 'Arrow Through Me'. The night before had been a particularly long one, it was the only time he ever spoke about it, nothing about his relationship, it was just more of a feeling that I had than anything, that he just missed that closeness … just a perception, *My God, he misses John* – that it was a huge hole in his life.

Denny Laine suggests Paul was actually bored dealing with young musicians who didn't know the ropes. Some of the elementary rock band stuff that went without being said between Laine and McCartney had to be spelt out to the new boys; 'they were more like younger fans than old-school road warriors'. Yet Paul was talking about making a movie with them.

The movie project, which ultimately morphed into the execrable *Give My Regards to Broad Street*, began when Paul invited playwright Willy Russell to Scotland to hang out with the group to see if the experience might inspire a screenplay. There was inevitably a great deal of waiting around in what passed for a green room at Low Ranachan Farm, leaving Willy alone with the musicians and roadies. As others had before, the playwright noticed a sycophantic atmosphere around Paul:

Paul's fame is such [that] everybody around him is affected in some way and the truth is not told. People would come out and moan about hanging around all day. People would come out and say privately, 'Why is he re-doing that bass part when it was brilliant four days ago?' And I'd go, 'Why don't you fucking say it to Paul?' It's not Paul who doesn't want to hear those things. Paul would probably be the first person to accept that his life would be richer and better if the people around him would have that kind of dialogue with him, but this kind of deference infects *everybody*.

To kill time the boys played *Scrabble*. Denny's game was let down by poor spelling. '[Denny] said to me one day when we were playing, he said [affecting a Midlands accent], "I've got a good one here. Do you owl think that, er, obscenity is allowed?" I said, "Yeah, it's all right." And he put down T-E-R-D.'

Willy had written a play, *Stags and Hens*, about a successful Liverpool musician who returns to Merseyside to take up with an old girlfriend. He thought this might serve as a basis for Paul's movie, supplying a challenging but manageable part for him and a role for Linda. 'What there wasn't, really, was roles for the rest of the band and [the] brief was I had to keep the Wings thing intact so there had to be a role for Steve and Laurence and Denny ...' After a week in Kintyre, Willy went home to think about it further.

Shortly after Russell left the farm, Paul transferred the recording of *Back to the Egg* to Abbey Road Studios, then to Lympne Castle, a medieval mansion not far from his Sussex home. 'Mostly we were there for convenience, because Paul and Linda were spending a lot of time down at Peasmarsh, and they didn't want to have to be driving up to London quite so much,' says Juber. Then Paul had the brainwave of cutting a track with a large number of rock musicians as an orchestra, a 'Rockestra'. Superstar friends including Dave Gilmour and Pete Townshend agreed to play guitar on the session, while Gary Brooker of Procol Harum and John Bonham and John Paul Jones of Led Zeppelin also said they'd take part. As Paul was preparing for the session, Buddy Holly Week rolled around. This year Paul celebrated with a party at a London club, followed by the première of the movie *The Buddy Holly Story*. Many stars attended, including Who drummer Keith Moon, who told Paul he'd be happy to play drums with the other celebrities on the 'Rockestra' session. Unfortunately, Moon died in the early hours of the following morning, having swallowed what his girlfriend describes as 'a bucket of pills'. Kenny Jones stepped into Keith's place at Abbey Road on 3 October, Paul conducting everybody in a monster jam recorded as the 'Rockestra Theme', whooping with excitement throughout what must have seemed like a really cool idea at the time, but now sounds like bombast.

Along with the misjudgement of Rockestra, there were worrying signs of Paul wanting to rush into his new movie. He summoned Willy Russell and his collaborator Mike Ockrent to Abbey Road to tell them he needed a script post-haste. What with him and Mike being busy people, and Christmas approaching, Willy suggested that the only way they could do a rush job for Paul was to go away somewhere quiet with their families. 'Paul said something like, "What, like you mean France?" Mike went, "Far too cold this time of year. I'm thinking of the West Indies,"' recalls Russell with a chuckle. 'And I can see Paul going, *You cheeky twat!*' Still, MPL booked the writers onto a plane to Jamaica, where a villa was put at their disposal. They returned with a screenplay titled *Band on the Run*, in which Paul would play a music star named Jet who, weary with his career, takes up with a scruffy young rock 'n' roll band featuring Linda, Denny, Steve and Laurence, leading them to the brink of success, before going back to his old life. There was a read-through at Waterfall. 'And Paul was, I think, very excited by the possibility,' says Russell, who got the impression McCartney intended to make the film as soon as he'd finished *Back to the Egg*.

'I've cleared the slate for two months' time,' he told the playwright, with a sense of purpose.

'But there's been no pre-production,' protested Willy, who knew a movie couldn't be made like this, unless Paul wanted a disaster. 'Look, you can't do this like *Magical Mystery Tour*,' he warned, realising he was sounding like 'a suit', as Paul and Linda termed company men. 'Paul and Linda used to talk very disparagingly about *the suits*, you know. I started to sound like a suit.' Still, there wasn't even a budget. 'How it was going to get made, I don't know. I think the idea was, *Look, when I turn my attention to it, it will get made*. If you are that powerful, people will say, "Yes, we can do it. We've got two weeks, yeah we can do it ..."'

Meanwhile, there were signs that, after eight years together, McCartney and Laine weren't getting along. 'I noticed that there were disagreements that sometimes became quite verbal,' observes Steve Holley.

I suspect Denny felt that he should have more of a partnership than he actually had, and I think Paul was upset about his demeanour and the way he was carrying on. I also think there were personality clashes

between the two of them, and certainly between Denny's wife Jo Jo*
and Linda. They were poles apart. Jo Jo was a high-spirited party girl,
and just loved the glitz and the rock 'n' roll lifestyle, and Linda was
much more down to earth.

Paul called a band meeting to decide what to do. The decision was that
they needed a new single. The younger band members asked Paul
what the Beatles did in situations like this. Less guarded about the
Beatles now than he had been at the start of Wings, Paul replied: 'Well,
if we needed a single, we'd just write one over the weekend and record
it on the Monday.' So that's what Paul did, writing 'Daytime Nightime
Suffering', also completing a song titled 'Goodnight Tonight'. The two
tracks were intended as a double A-side. Written and recorded quickly,
the songs have an immediacy and energy lacking from *Back to the Egg*,
which was now so overworked it might more aptly have been titled
Over-Egged. In April 1979, Paul brought the entire Black Dyke Mills Band
down from Yorkshire to play on one track at Abbey Road.

Work on the album had been going on for so long that EMI told Paul
they needed Studio Two back for other artists. So McCartney had a
replica built in the basement of the MPL office on Soho Square. Replica
Studio was an exact copy of the control room at Studio Two at Abbey
Road, with a photo of the studio on the wall so that it felt like being in
the control room at EMI. This was a great extravagance, on top of his
new movie project, but Paul was richer than ever. In signing with CBS,
he had recently been given a sweetener, the Frank Music Catalogue,
making Paul the owner of the works of Frank Loesser, American author
of *Guys and Dolls*, and adding to a publishing portfolio that included the
Buddy Holly song book, and rights to a raft of hit shows including *Annie*,
Hello, Dolly! and *A Chorus Line*, which were all earning him big money.
Sometimes Paul wondered at his own good fortune. 'Crazy, isn't it?' he
remarked that year, 'as well as gold at the bottom of the garden, he has
oil running off the roof.' But Paul's luck was about to run out.

* Denny and Jo Jo married in November 1978.

GO TO JAIL

DOWN ON THE FARM

Ever since she had been brought to England by her mother, Heather McCartney had experienced problems. At first the primary school kids in St John's Wood made fun of Heather's American accent (which she dropped); then Paul and Linda took Heather out of school to tour with them, which disrupted her education. When she turned 11, Heather went to a private secondary school in London where she mixed with the children of other wealthy people, her classmates apparently obsessed with status and fame. During an argument with her parents, Heather revealed that her school friends had given her advice about dealing with her famous father. 'They'd said to her, "You've no need to worry about your dad ... if he gives you any more trouble you can tell the papers."' So concerned were Paul and Lin that Heather was mixing with such children that they took her out of the school and moved virtually overnight to their country home in Sussex. They kept Cavendish as their London base, but the McCartneys' primary home now became Waterfall, their round house in the woods outside Peasmarsh.

Linda put Mary and Stella into the village primary school, sending Heather to the state comprehensive in Rye. Many parents tried to avoid sending their children to such schools in the 1970s, believing 'bog standard' comprehensives produced children of limited achievement and ambition. Those who could afford to do so often chose to have their children educated privately, but Paul and Linda's decision proved a wise one. It was Linda who initially met with the headmaster, Ray Fooks, at Thomas Peacock School, explaining that she and Paul had decided it would be nice for the family to live permanently in the country; she didn't allude to the problems Heather had experienced in London. Says Fooks, who subsequently also admitted Paul and Linda's three younger children to his school, finding the McCartneys model parents – caring without becoming meddlesome:

> I think in a way that [it's] a great compliment to Linda and Paul, because they made sure that their children were treated like everybody else, and their children came to the school, fitted in perfectly, were very cooperative, very pleasant people, and made the best of their education and moved on.

It was around the time of the move to Peasmarsh that the McCartney family made another life-changing decision. They all became vegetarian, a diet Paul and his fellow Beatles had dabbled with in the Sixties, but which now became a way of life and something of an obsession for the family. The epiphany occurred at High Park when the McCartneys were about to sit down to a Sunday lunch of roast lamb. They looked out of their windows at the sheep, grazing around their standing stone, and decided that eating the peaceful creatures that shared their home was wrong. Recalling the moment, Linda said,

> we just looked at the leg of lamb I was cooking and realised where it came from and we couldn't eat it any more. It was a couple of months before I figured out what to do about the gaps on our dinner plates where the chops used to be.

Linda was the driving force in the change to vegetarianism, with an ally in vegetarian guitarist Laurence Juber. His memory is that Paul wasn't keen at first on the new menu. 'I remember one occasion Linda wasn't there so I gave Paul a bag of bean sprouts and veggie stuff, and he just left it in the back of the Rolls Royce and forgot all about it. A week later Linda finds this bag of goo in the back.'

As the McCartneys settled into life in Sussex, it became clear that Waterfall wasn't large enough to be a permanent home for the family. Paul bought neighbouring Lower Gate Farm to remedy this problem, a 159-acre property costing £250,000 ($382,500) in 1979. The farm was bordered on the west by the same forest that surrounded Waterfall, and was served by the same unmarked and little-used public road, Starvecrow Lane. A 500-yard track led from the lane to a semi-derelict house on a hill. The elevated position gave the house commanding views across the countryside, which the McCartneys didn't have at Waterfall, while the trees, and the distance from the lane, meant the house was also very private. Originally the farm had been known as Blossom Wood Farm, a name the McCartneys reinstated. Paul planned to knock down the derelict farmhouse and build a substantial new home in its place. As we forge ahead with Paul's story, Blossom Farm becomes the focal point of his domestic life.

COMING UP

There was a Beatles reunion that spring in the neighbouring county of Surrey, where Eric Clapton was celebrating his marriage to George Harrison's ex-wife. After being married to George for eight years, Pattie had left the former Beatle in 1974 for his close friend, three years after which George married his secretary Olivia Arias. Eric married Pattie on tour in March 1979. Two months later, a marquee was erected in the garden of the Claptons' Surrey mansion, Hurtwood Edge, and 800 people attended a belated wedding reception. The guests included the cuckold Harrison, whose friendship with Eric and Pattie had survived the changing of the guard, a testimony to the freewheeling spirit of the decade in which they'd all come to maturity. Also present were Paul and Ritchie.

The three Beatles got up on stage in the marquee and performed 'Sgt. Pepper's Lonely Hearts Club Band', the first time they'd played together since *Abbey Road*, all looking happy and comfortable in each other's company, even though George had recently conducted an affair with Ritchie's wife.* John Lennon telephoned to tell Eric that he would have been there, too, had he known about the party, creating the tantalising thought that all four Beatles might have played together in the tent. Perhaps a Beatles reunion wasn't so unlikely after all.

* Ringo divorced Maureen Starkey in 1975, and took up with the American actress Barbara Bach, who later became his second wife.

Certainly Paul was sick of Wings. The new album *Back to the Egg* had finally been laid, with a silly, egg-theme press reception in the summer of 1979, but it was not the smash EMI and CBS had been banking on. It proved a curate's egg, good in parts, with token attempts at sounding contemporary. The disc was presented in an elaborate sleeve created by the design group Hipgnosis, a company associated primarily with progressive rock bands, thus putting off many young record buyers to whom this sort of music was now unfashionable. Paul simply moved on. Doing exactly what he had at the end of the Beatles he went home and made a DIY solo album, taking the tapes with him when the family went to Scotland for their summer holidays.

In September came news that former Wings guitarist Jimmy McCulloch had died in his London apartment at the age of 26, succumbing to heart failure brought about by over-indulgence. Though Jimmy had always been difficult, upsetting Paul and Linda with his comments and bad behaviour, Paul had come to see the Laine–McCulloch–English incarnation of Wings as the best version of the band, after which the group seemed increasingly tired. Nevertheless, McCartney went ahead with a series of Wings concerts to promote *Back to the Egg*, starting with warm-up shows at the Royal Court Theatre in Liverpool, to which Paul also pledged a charitable donation.

Before the first Liverpool show, Paul called Willy Russell, asking him to attend a press conference at the theatre. 'Get down to the Court,' McCartney told the playwright enthusiastically.

'Why?'

'I'm having this press conference this afternoon, and we're going to talk about the movie.' Willy Russell was amazed. After the initial read-through of the *Band on the Run* screenplay, the movie project had fallen flat as far as he was concerned. Paul started changing things. Then came a very tedious day when Paul summoned Willy and Mike Ockrent to Sussex, and kept them waiting hours. 'It wasn't a good day. He was terribly preoccupied with something … I think we sat around for seven or eight hours before finally we got to see Paul and it was a perfunctory [conversation],' says Russell, who'd dreaded days like this. Then Paul introduced Russell to his friend, the movie producer David Puttnam, who criticised the *Band on the Run* screenplay so comprehensively that Russell concluded Puttnam actually wanted to squeeze him out and work with Paul himself (Puttnam admits he had an ambition to film the

Beatles story). 'He patronised the fuck out of us.' On top of which, Paul wouldn't engage in discussions about pre-production, or budgets, or any of the other details to do with making a motion picture. Yet he now intended to announce *Band on the Run* to the press! Considering this 'mental', Russell sat uneasily next to Paul at the Royal Court, only to find the film was never mentioned. 'No one asks a question about the movie, so Paul doesn't say anything about the movie. It is the usual press conference, "Isn't it great to be back in Liverpool?"' McCartney assured Russell afterwards that they would make the movie. They would do it after he'd toured with Wings, giving the playwright the thumbs up as they parted company. It was at least preferable to a prod in the chest.

While he was on Merseyside, McCartney revisited the Liverpool Institute, renewing his acquaintance with his geography teacher B.L. 'Blip' Parker, now the headmaster. Paul invited Parker and the school's entire complement of boys, plus the girls from the school across the road, to a free first-night show at the Royal Court, a typically generous and sentimental gesture from a man who looked back on his school days with affection, as opposed to George Harrison who made it clear in his autobiography, *I Me Mine*, that he'd had a miserable time at the Inny. Naturally, Paul's relatives also got tickets to the Royal Court, a considerable contingent of 'relies' showing up on the first night headed by the elderly but still redoubtable aunts. Paul was always nervous before a concert – a healthy sign – but with all those eager and familiar faces out front he was more jittery than normal on Friday 23 November 1979. 'Before we went on Paul was quite nervous and he said, "Oh Jeez, I don't know if this is gonna go,"' recalls Howie Casey. 'I said, "Paul, this is going to be like the second coming … You just walk on there, and they're gonna go nuts." And they did.' It helped that Paul treated his audience to some Beatles songs, including 'Fool on the Hill' and 'Got to Get You into My Life', which gave Howie's horn section a chance to shine. 'For a long time after I started this group, I was embarrassed to do Beatles songs because it seemed like a cop-out,' Paul said afterwards. 'But that's long gone now. I wrote the songs after all …'

Wings proceeded to tour the United Kingdom until Christmas, playing relatively small theatres, like London's Lewisham Odeon, which the Beatles visited in the Sixties, the shows helping shift more copies of *Back to the Egg*, and pushing a Christmas single up the charts, 'Wonderful Christmastime', which was no worse than most songs of its ilk, though it sounds tinsel-thin compared with Lennon's 'Happy Xmas (War is Over)'. The new members of Wings enjoyed the tour, their first chance to play live with Paul, but the boss seemed unenthusiastic. Notes Steve Holley:

> I remember one show that I particularly enjoyed for whatever reason and bouncing into the dressing room and saying something [like], 'Ah, great show, great show!' His reaction was, 'Yeah, it was OK.' As I left the room I thought, Of course it was just OK. I mean, look at some of the places he's been, look at some of the concerts and experiences he's had … That was one of the first times it dawned on me – is there any way to top what playing a concert with the Beatles must have been like? And I can't imagine there was. It was almost like that was omnipresent.

Eight days before Christmas, Wings played the Glasgow Apollo, a fine old theatre with a famously rambunctious audience. To give the Glaswegians a treat, Paul closed with 'Mull of Kintyre' accompanied by the Campbeltown Pipe Band who were bussed in from Kintyre especially. To keep this a surprise, Paul had the pipe band wait outside the theatre until the last minute. Then they entered via the fire escape in full regalia. 'We come out the fire door, which is right at the front of the stage, up the steps and then formed a semi-circle behind him [on stage],' recalls pipe band drummer Ian Campbell.

> We rehearsed it during the day. He said, 'Don't just leave the stage [at the end]. Enjoy the adulation, because this song has been amazing.' So we come out, he started 'Mull of Kintyre', which drove the crowd a wee bit [mad], and then when we came out I thought the roof was going to come off. Honestly, they went insane.

This concert yielded a live recording of an excellent new song from Paul's solo project, the ebullient 'Coming Up', which became a US number one.

Less successful was a post-Christmas charity show at the Hammersmith Odeon in London. The Concerts for Kampuchea were three nights of music featuring a host of acts ranging from young artists such as Alison Moyet to old stagers like the Who, all intended to raise money for the former Cambodia, devastated during Pol Pot's regime. Paul helped organise the shows and Wings headlined the last night, 29 December 1979, by which time there was widespread expectation of a Beatles reunion on the stage where they'd once given their Christmas shows. Rumours that the Beatles were re-forming circulated almost constantly these days, but this time a sense that it really might happen was created by the Secretary General of the United Nations, Kurt Wald-heim, who publicly urged John Lennon to join his band mates at Hammersmith for charity's sake. Even if John didn't show up, it was noted in the press that his 16-year-old son Julian was scheduled to perform. Perhaps Julian might sit in with his Beatle uncles.

So much interest was generated by this rumour that when Wings arrived at the Odeon for the sound check that afternoon they found the theatre besieged by ticket touts, fans and press, and were consequently unable to leave the building until after the show, spending what seemed like an eternity cooped up backstage with their fellow artists. A good deal of drinking was consequently done – it being Christmas – and by the time Wings took the stage some musicians were the worse for wear. 'It was a pretty messed-up deal,' recollects Steve Holley. 'I don't think that performance was particularly good.' And there was no Beatles reunion. John never left the USA. He didn't want to play with Paul, and Julian Lennon was so discombobulated by speculation that he might help the Beatles re-form that he pulled out of the show altogether. Instead, Wings delivered its usual set, spiced up with a few Beatles tunes and a Rockestra finale featuring Paul's superstar mates in silver stage suits and top hats, looking for all the world like Gary Glitter's Glitter Band. 'Thank you, Pete! The only lousy sod who wouldn't wear a silver suit,' Paul remarked sharply, as Pete Townshend sauntered on in his normal, scruffy attire.

PAUL McCARTNEY'S *ANNUS HORRIBILIS*

A major Japanese tour was scheduled to begin in January 1980, with tentative plans for more shows around the world if it went well. A return to the US was certainly overdue. Yet none of this was to be, the year becoming instead Paul's *annus horribilis*. It started badly when Paul was criticised as mean by Liverpool councillors for only giving £5,000

($7,650) to the Royal Court Theatre during his recent trip to Merseyside, a small matter, but the first in what became 12 months of almost unremitting bad publicity for McCartney, who now flew to New York with Linda in advance of the Japanese tour.

The McCartneys booked into the Stanhope Hotel, just across Central Park from the Dakota, Paul calling John Lennon's private number to ask if he could come over. Yoko took the call, telling Paul it wasn't convenient, which was a slap in the face. Paul then told Yoko that he and Linda were *en route* to Tokyo, where they would be staying in the presidential suite at the Okura Hotel, which seemed to offend the Lennons because it was the suite they used when *they* were in Tokyo. Guitarist Laurence Juber joined the McCartneys at the Stanhope and, after a couple of days, during which time they socialised with other friends, including the model Twiggy, the party flew on to Tokyo, where Wings were due to start their tour at the Budokan on 21 January.

Paul hadn't played Japan since the Beatles visited in 1966. He had tried to get a visa to take Wings to Japan, but had been denied permission because of his and Denny Laine's drug convictions. 'I was looking forward to working Japan because five years earlier we were supposed to have gone there and we got our visas revoked,' explains Laine. 'He'd been busted in the past, and I'd been busted [for marijuana], or at least Jo Jo had and I'd taken the rap for it.' The problems of drug use and associated crimes were not yet as pronounced in Japan as in Western countries, and the authorities were naturally keen to discourage any growth in the drug culture. As a result, foreigners with drug convictions were usually precluded from entering Japan for seven years. With Paul having been busted most recently in Scotland in 1973, and Linda in LA in 1975, on top of Laine's conviction, the Eastmans had to work hard to get visas for the band in 1980, and it was made abundantly clear that the authorities wouldn't tolerate any drug use on the tour. MPL staffer Alan Crowder reminded the tour party before departure to be extra careful. Everybody knew it was in their interest to heed Alan's warning. In the first place, nobody wanted to end up in a Japanese jail; and, second, they didn't want to miss out on what was set to be the most lucrative Wings tour yet, with everybody finally on a good wage. Even the guys in the horn section were, to their joy, getting $1,000 a night (£653) for the gig, and the longer the tour went on the richer they would get. 'We knew that this was something that everybody had to be very responsible about,' says Laurence Juber, adding with a hollow laugh: 'or nearly everybody.'

Denny Laine and Steve Holley flew to Japan from London, arriving at Narita Airport ahead of the McCartneys on Wednesday 16 January 1980, travelling first class on TWA. The band members had all been furnished with multiple-use, first-class tickets good for any TWA flight anywhere in the world for 12 months. Recalls Steve Holley:

I remember Denny saying, 'This happened before and probably what will happen is if the Japanese tour goes well he'll say something like, "Take a vacation anywhere you want for a couple of weeks and we'll regroup for rehearsals in Australia." or whatever, which will hopefully turn into another world tour.' So in the back of my mind I'm thinking I'm embarking on the beginning of a journey of a lifetime.

Holley and Laine were processed through immigration before the McCartneys arrived, the officials taking five hours to deal with Laine because of his drug history. Then they went and waited on the tour bus for Paul.

When Paul's flight landed at Narita Airport, his party was also processed slowly through customs and immigration. 'There was a lot of time spent with bureaucrats dealing with paperwork,' remembers Laurence Juber, who was standing next to Paul as they walked through the customs hall. The McCartneys had a lot of luggage and a customs man was opening bags seemingly at random, 'not pulling *everything* out,' says Juber.

But he opened one of the suitcases and patted something, and then he got a quizzical look on his face, and he reached inside and pulled out a bag of marijuana. At that point Paul kind of turns white, and alarms started going off, and people came out from behind hidden doors and escorted him back, and me too. Because I was with him. And Linda and the kids as well. They took him off into a room and started questioning him.

In among Paul's shirts the customs official had found a clear plastic bag containing just under eight ounces of marijuana, worth about £1,000 ($1,530). Having made this discovery the Japanese went through all the luggage again, even taking musical instruments apart in case there were more drugs hidden inside. There weren't. Laurence, Linda and the kids were allowed to leave.

Tired of waiting for Paul, Laine and Holley had gone ahead to the Okura, where they checked into their rooms expecting to meet Paul, Lin and Laurence later in the hotel restaurant. Steve took a nap, woken by the bedside telephone. It was Linda calling to say that Paul had been arrested at the airport for possession.

> I thought she was joking. I said, 'Yeah, good one. I'll see you down in the restaurant,' and my wife and I went downstairs. As soon as the elevator doors opened on the main floor, and the press greeted us with a million flashbulbs, I realised that something had happened.

As almost the whole world now knew, Paul had been taken in hand-cuffs from Narita Airport to Kojimachi Police Station, where he was locked in a cell for the second time in his life (his first experience behind bars being in Hamburg in 1960 after the Bambi Kino fire). And of course it wasn't the first time he'd been fingered for drugs. It was, though, the most serious. Paul's tour managers hired an English-speaking Japanese lawyer and contacted Eastman & Eastman in New York. Lee Eastman threw a fit. 'When Paul got busted in Tokyo for pot – I was around – my father was *furious*. Furious! He went nuts. He was ballistic,' recalls Philip Sprayregen, who explains that his stepfather's rage was partly due to his fear that the bust would jeop-ardise Paul's chance of a knighthood. 'He said, "My God, my daugh-ter could have been a [lady], and he blew it!" He was very upset because he thought his daughter would be Lady Linda [sic].'* John Eastman was despatched to Tokyo to try and rescue his brother-in-law. Less reassuringly, Kenneth Lambert, a deranged American, tried to set off from Miami Airport on a self-appointed mission of mercy. When he started waving a gun about at Miami, demanding to be flown to Paul's side, Lambert was shot dead by cops. Meanwhile, Paul went to sleep in his Tokyo cell with his back against the wall, fearing he might be raped.

* If Paul were to be knighted, which he eventually was, Linda would properly be addressed as Lady McCartney.

Things always look brighter in the morning, and so it was in the land of the rising sun when Paul woke to news that he had a visitor. McCartney was shown into an interview room, partitioned by a glass screen, on the other side of which stood the reassuringly urbane figure of Britain's consul to Japan, Donald Warren-Knott, whose embassy was located next door. The Warren-Knotts had been getting ready for bed the previous evening when they received a courtesy call from the police to inform them that a distinguished British citizen, Mr *Pori Macatnee*, as the Japanese tend to pronounce his name, had been taken into custody. The consul was told that marijuana had been found in amongst Mr Macatnee's shirts, and he'd admitted the drugs were his, saying they'd been packed accidentally. Now the star and the consul met. 'He sat down, I sat down, and we began to talk – to my pleasant surprise he was very relaxed,' says Warren-Knott, who'd feared that such a celebrity might try and demand special treatment, which would have been a mistake.

Nothing of the sort. He took it quite calmly. Yes, OK, he knew the packet had been found. Yes, it was his. And it shouldn't have been there. I didn't press too closely, because it's not my business to enquire into those sort of details. I suspect – personal view – that a package was slipped in while they were packing. I don't know whether he fully intended to use it while he was in Japan. If he did, he'd be very foolish, given the circumstances of his previous arrests.

Paul said the Japanese were treating him well, and he was reassured to hear that his family were safe at the hotel, with his brother-in-law on his way from the States. He would wait to see what happened. Paul had one request. 'He said he was a vegetarian and he would be grateful if we could give any help in making sure that he did get a reasonably vegetarian diet, including fruit.' Apples, oranges, pears, and bananas would all be acceptable. The consul said he would ask the guards.

It was clear that the tour couldn't go ahead. The shows were cancelled and Wings' equipment was shipped back to the UK. The musicians were told to go home, or anywhere they liked on their round-the-world tickets. Despite the prospect of a free holiday, and the fact that they were all paid what they would have got had the Japanese shows gone ahead, the band members were upset. Says Denny Laine, who flew to France:

> I wasn't cross with him, but I was disappointed, I must say. It meant now we wouldn't be able to go to Japan and tour, we wouldn't be able to go a lot of places and tour, because once you get busted it's hard to get visas and stuff, so it was all that kind of thing. It was a let-down.

Laine later discovered that Paul was angry with him for leaving Tokyo. 'He was a bit upset because we left early, but we were told by his office to leave, because security people were watching us all the time.'

There was much debate within the tour party as to how and why Paul had got himself in this mess. Steve Holley wondered, as others have, whether Paul *meant* to get busted: 'He may not have wanted to go and do that tour in the first place ... [that's] my guess.' Although Paul had shown signs of weariness with Wings, this surely cannot be true. Paul enjoyed performing and was, in any case, somebody who could be relied upon to fulfil his commitments. Denny Laine dismisses as 'ridiculous' the notion Paul would get arrested deliberately. Howie Casey believes that Paul may have taken the rap for Linda, who'd been careless before with drugs. Some reports stated the marijuana was found in Lin's make-up bag, but the British consul recalls being told the drugs were with Paul's shirts. Later came the absurd conspiracy theory that Yoko Ono spitefully tipped off her contacts in Tokyo that the McCartneys had drugs with them, because Paul and Linda intended to use what she and John considered their hotel suite. Perhaps the most likely explanation is that Paul had taken a chance. 'I believe it was just something he thought he could get away with,' says Laine.

There was consternation in the penthouse suite of the Okura Hotel when Linda McCartney was informed that, if tried and found guilty of possession, her husband could face a prison sentence. She and the kids were virtual prisoners themselves, unable to go downstairs for fear of the press, scared to turn on the TV in case they saw distressing coverage of the case. The children were upset. 'The only one unaware of the situation was little Dee Dee,' Linda said, using the family name for toddler James McCartney, and even Dee Dee kept asking where Daddy was.

Over at Kojimachi, Daddy was getting used to prison life. He was obliged to sleep on the floor on a thin mattress, Japanese-style; rising at six a.m. with other prisoners, sitting cross-legged while he was interrogated; given half an hour to exercise and – until his fruit was delivered – eating a bowl of rice for supper. Sitting on the floor, watched by Japanese men in uniform, Paul felt like a character in a POW movie. He picked pieces of plaster off the wall and used the flakes to tally his days inside, almost starting to enjoy the experience. By the specks of plaster on the floor Paul calculated that his incarceration had exceeded a week. He was starting to smell. The police said he could have a bath, in private if he wished. Paul chose instead to bathe with his fellow detainees, a tough-looking crew whom he charmed by leading them in a bath-time sing-along, including a rendition of 'Yellow Submarine'. Donald Warren-Knott popped in regularly to ask if Paul was OK, also asking the guards if they had been able to supply Mr McCartney's vegetarian diet, with apples and oranges and so on. Yes, they nodded. And bananas? The mention of bananas was met by silence. 'My questions had been embarrassing. I couldn't think why. This was a very Japanese response to embarrassing questions. A sort of shutter comes down while they try to work out just what they are going to say, but they are obviously embarrassed. So why bananas?' It turned out that regulations forbade detainees from having bananas. 'It seems remarkably silly, but I was told that a man might peel his banana, throw the skin on the floor and a prison officer might slip and fall!' When the consul relayed this information to Paul, he roared with laughter. 'He promised that he wouldn't demand bananas. They were perfectly free never to give him a banana.'

When Linda was given permission to see her husband for half an hour, she took him a welcome cheese sandwich. Although they tried to joke about the situation, this was the longest period Paul and Lin had ever been apart; virtually the only time they had slept apart in their 10-year marriage, and it was not certain what the outcome of this situation would be. The offence was serious. After John Eastman arrived in town and started talking with the local lawyer and the presiding magistrate, it became clear that the Japanese didn't want a trial any more than Paul did. The authorities were primarily concerned that the local promoters, and the Japanese people who'd bought tickets for Wings' concerts, wouldn't be out of pocket. Refunds were swiftly arranged. 'With that little financial problem out of the way, they wanted to get rid of him as quickly as possible,' comments Donald Warren-Knott, who sat in on the legal conferences.

> I think they all realised very shortly, on the basis of their advice from the Japanese lawyer, and the presiding magistrate and so on, that provided there was a full confession and a full admittance of guilt the [Japanese] would like to get rid of Mr McCartney and the Wings group, [and] please don't come back again [for] seven years. I think they wanted to tidy it up, as was feasible under Japanese law.

So it was that after nine nights in a Tokyo cell Paul was taken under escort to the airport and put on a flight to Amsterdam, reunited with his family in the airliner's cabin, and thereby deported from Japan. The McCartneys disembarked in Holland, where Paul spoke briefly to the press, still arguing that marijuana should be decriminalised. 'I have been in jail for ten days, but I didn't go crazy because I wasn't able to have marijuana. I can take it or leave it.' Paul and his family were then flown by private plane to Lydd Airport in England, finally driven down the familiar country lanes to their house in the Sussex woods. Seldom had Paul felt so glad to be home as he did when he stepped inside his own front door and found himself surrounded by his things again, greeted by their dogs, the horses whinnying hello from the nearby stables. It was the end of a draining, expensive and embarrassing experience, one that had damaged Paul's image. Blip Parker, headmaster of the Liverpool Institute, made public his personal regret that Paul had let his fans down, so soon after treating the schoolboys to a show: 'It is hard enough nowadays trying to keep youngsters away from drugs without having people they look up to involved in something like this,' Parker told the *Daily Telegraph*. Paul's young cousins also looked at Uncle Paul askance. 'You take drugs, don't you?' one asked, the next time Paul was on Merseyside. Paul found himself struggling to explain.

'IT'S A DRAG'

Because of the phenomenal international success of the Beatles, and the success Paul had continued to enjoy since the fab four split up, together with the way he conducted himself, for the most part, Paul McCartney had come to hold a special position in British public life. In an era when rock stars were typically excessive and often vulgar in their behaviour, Paul McCartney MBE was an intelligent, polite, civilised family man, whose devotion to Linda and their children was plain to see. He was a phenomenal earner for Great Britain, a cultural ambassador, and figurehead for the nation's recording industry. Lee Eastman was right in foreseeing that his son-in-law would one day be knighted. Ultimately, Paul might even be granted a peerage in recognition of the status he enjoyed. Yet McCartney had also got himself into a remarkable amount of trouble.

Twice Macca had been banged up in a police cell, twice deported from a foreign land. He had been refused visas, been convicted of drug possession in a UK court, fined for drugs in Sweden, and narrowly escaped a prison sentence in Japan. Taken together, this was a record that put Paul in the rackety company of such bad boys of rock as Keith Richards. The Bambi Kino incident aside, Paul's basic problem was that he liked to smoke grass and was too pig-headed to moderate his behaviour. The Japanese bust didn't change him. He came out of the experience with the same cocky attitude. He never explained, let alone apologised to his band members for the inconvenience he had caused them in Japan, showing the lads instead a prison diary he wrote and had privately printed. *Japanese Jailbird* by Paul McCartney didn't reveal a man chastened. 'There wasn't a great deal of soul-searching involved,' says Laurence Juber, who read the little book. 'It was more of a narrative of his experience in jail.' And a couple of months later, when Paul's new solo album appeared in the shops, he appeared to make fun of the Japanese. The cover of *McCartney II* featured a grainy image of Paul by Linda in the style of a prison mug shot, while inside the album were photos of Paul pulling faces in impersonation of Japanese officials, with an instrumental track titled 'Frozen Jap'.

These puerile details aside, *McCartney II* was an improvement on recent Wings albums. Paul sounded contemporary again on synthesiser-based songs such as 'Coming Up' and 'Temporary Secretary', a witty, sexy number about asking Mr Marks for a secretary to sit on his knee (at a time when Alfred Marks was a well-known temping agency). 'On the Way' had an attractive wistfulness, while a lovely melody underpinned 'Waterfall', the lyrics of which appear to refer to the family home of that name in Sussex. The song can be read as Paul's advice to his children not to play in the waterfall at the head of the deep-cut stream in the forest, across which the young McCartneys had no doubt tried to leap. The warning in the song about not getting into strangers' cars seems to express another parental fear, that of the kids being kidnapped. Other good songs included 'Bogey Music', written for a proposed film of Raymond Briggs's children's book, *Fungus the Bogeyman*. A generally strong album, with less filler than one had become used to, *McCartney II* was a deserved UK number one.

It wasn't of course a Wings album, and Wings was now all but defunct. Denny Laine badly needed income to pay his back taxes. Unable to tour with Wings, he went out on the road that summer with Steve Holley. This small tour did little to alleviate Denny's problems. It looked like he would have to start living abroad as a tax exile. Paul, whose own financial affairs had been run with exemplary efficiency since he left the Beatles, had no such problems, and stayed in London, working with George Martin on 'We All Stand Together' and other songs intended for the long-planned *Rupert the Bear* movie. Paul had commissioned a succession of artists to create drawings for this picture over the past few years, but none had yet captured the snug family life depicted by Alfred Bestall in the *Rupert* stories Paul had grown up with, and remembered with particular fondness from the *Rupert* annuals published at Christmas. Bestall's ursine characters were the image of a contented, traditional British family of the day, 'mother baking, always rolling out something, father always reading the newspaper,' as Paul described the world of Rupert, relating the bear's family to the McCartney idyll at Forthlin Road before Mum died. 'It's a fantasy from the past. Very secure and cosy, which I think is nice.' The film project only began to take shape when Paul met animator Geoff Dunbar, who shared his vision for a Rupert film. 'I remember he asked me to write one paragraph of how I saw Rupert, and I said, "Well, it should stay in the 1940s, you shouldn't change it, every endeavour should be made to keep it sacrosanct to Alfred Bestall's world,"' says Dunbar, who thereby became Paul's collaborator on this and other animation projects.

Just as Paul took comfort in the Rupert project after his Tokyo humiliation, it was soothing to work again with George Martin and Ritchie. In July, Paul went to the South of France to contribute to Ringo's *Stop and*

Smell the Roses album, bringing Laurence Juber and Howie Casey with him, also Howie's fiancée Sheila McKinlay, who had sung on the same bill as the Beatles in the Sixties. Sheila would sing backing vocals on Ritchie's new album. A couple of months later, Howie and Sheila married, which leads to a nice story showing how generous Paul can be, despite his reputation for being tight with a buck. Around this time Howie asked Paul if he could help him and Sheila buy a house. McCartney agreed to lend the Caseys £10,000 ($15,300). A couple of years later, Paul Winn from MPL rang Howie to point out that he hadn't repaid any of the loan. Howie said that he was broke. The only way he could repay Paul was to sell the house. McCartney then called Howie personally and told him to consider the loan a gift. 'He said, "Look, it's a wedding present." Thank you very much!'

In the autumn of 1980, Paul gathered Wings together to rehearse again after a long lay-off, playing in a barn belonging to a friend in Tenterden, a small town near Peasmarsh. Wings then went into a local studio to work on a compilation album for CBS, which was still counting the cost of the failure of *Back to the Egg*. CBS wanted a Wings greatest hits album to recoup some of the millions they had advanced Paul. The star suggested instead that he revisit his archive of Wings demos and finish off songs that had not quite made it onto previous albums, releasing these, together with a selection of Wings hits, as a double album titled *Hot Hilz and Kold Kutz*. One of the songs that emerged from this process was the single 'Goodnight Tonight', which made number five in the US. CBS didn't share Paul's enthusiasm for the *Hot Hitz and Kold Kutz* album, however, which was never released.

Paul segued from this aborted project into making what would become his new studio album, *Tug of War*. George Martin had agreed to produce, the plan being to make the record at George's AIR studio in London and his new AIR facility on the Caribbean island of Montserrat. The album proved the death knell for Wings. 'So what happens then is we do a bunch of rehearsals for *Tug of War* and the material just didn't necessarily lend itself to Wings,' says Laurence Juber. 'Paul called one day and said, you know, "George is going to produce this and he doesn't want to do it as a Wings album, so thanks but we don't need you right now ... "At that point I saw that the writing was on the wall.' Paul was breaking Wings up, though Denny Laine stayed with him for a little while yet.

Around this time an unwelcome ghost from the past emerged in the form of Erika Hübers (*née* Wohlers), the Hamburg barmaid who had claimed back in the Sixties to have given birth to Paul's child. Although Paul had never admitted paternity, a lump sum had been paid by Brian Epstein to Erika plus maintenance for her child, Bettina, until she was 18, on the basis the family wouldn't go public. Bettina was due to turn 18 on 19 December 1980. A couple of weeks before her birthday, the *Sunday People* newspaper splashed with 'I AM BEATLE PAUL'S SECRET CHILD', naming Erika and Bettina for the first time. Looking at the published picture of Erika – a plain, heavy-set burger-bar worker – it was hard to believe Paul had ever had a fling with her, while Erika's contention that her daughter looked like the star stretched credulity. The girl had already started cashing in on her supposed link with McCartney by singing in clubs as 'Bettina McCartney, the daughter of a Beatle'. Now she seemed to see a chance for a big pay day. Paul didn't comment, but the matter refused to go away, adding to what had been a difficult year all round. It was about to get worse.

Another echo of the past came from across the Atlantic in the form of John Lennon's new studio album, *Double Fantasy*, his first for five years, and a solid collection of simple, muscular rock songs as far as his half of the record went. (Yoko had an equal number of tracks, and hers were less impressive.) The first single, the rockabilly-influenced '(Just Like) Starting Over', was released in October 1980, and did reasonable business. It was still bumping along in the lower reaches of the charts when Paul began work on *Tug of War* at AIR in London that December. Once again, John's distinctive voice was on the car radio as Paul was driven up to town from the Sussex farm each day by John Hammel, punching through the years with lyrics that had an emotional weight and a sense of personal honesty – qualities too often lacking in Paul's work. That didn't necessarily translate into sensational sales. *Double Fantasy* sold modestly in the run-up to Christmas, and received some negative reviews. Still, Paul knew there was good work here. It was the first time for years that John had made a real effort with his music, challenging Paul as he used to.

McCartney was at home at Waterfall on the morning of Tuesday 9 December 1980 when the telephone rang. It was his manager Stephen Shrimpton calling to inform him that John had been shot dead in New York, gunned down overnight outside the Dakota building by a man who'd previously asked for his autograph. Neil Aspinall had been on the telephone disseminating the news, it being his unenviable task to inform 74-year-old Aunt Mimi that she would never see her nephew again. Neil always got the dirty jobs. Paul was in the house alone when he took the call; Linda was out doing the school run. When he saw Lin's car coming back up the drive Paul walked outside to meet her. 'I could tell by looking at him that there was something absolutely wrong. I'd never seen him like that before. Desperate, you know, tears ...'

Paul had a session booked at AIR in London, with Paddy Moloney of the Chieftains flying in from Ireland to play on a track. Denny Laine was also going to be in the studio. George Martin telephoned Waterfall to ask Paul if he wanted to cancel. He said he would rather come in to work. With the press gathering outside his gates, the London studio looked like a convenient bolthole.*

Paul arrived at AIR at the same time as his record plugger Joe Reddington. As the men walked through the lobby to the lift, a journalist tried to follow them in and had to be ejected before they could ascend to the fifth-floor recording studio. Paul then attempted to do a day's work. 'He was just very, very quiet, and upset, as we all were,' recalls Denny Laine. 'He said to me, "I'm never going to fall out with anybody again in my life," which is impossible to do, but that's the way he felt. I knew he felt that maybe they didn't make up like they should have done, so therefore he felt a bit guilty ...' As the musicians stood looking out of the window, they saw a furniture van below on Oxford Street with the name Lennon's on the side, a type of van neither man had seen in London before. 'We looked at each other and went, "Uh-ho! That was an omen."'

The phone rang. Joe Reddington picked up. 'Can I speak to Paul McCartney?' asked a woman.

'He's busy at the moment. Who's calling?'

'It's Yoko.' Joe knew instinctively it really was John's widow, rather than a hoax. He told everybody to clear the room. 'And [Paul] took the call. I just closed the door and he was crying – he'd lost his best friend.'

---

* While making music on such a day might seem strange, it is worth remembering that George Harrison did exactly the same, working on a new album in his home studio at Friar Park.

Throughout that short winter day, journalists besieged AIR Studios. There were photographers waiting for Paul down at the entrance on Oxford Street, with snappers clambering over the rooftops to try for pictures through the windows. In these extraordinary circumstances, Paul's office arranged for a private security firm to help Paul when he was ready to leave the building, employing a driver in a blocker car to get between the press and Paul's Mercedes estate, which was brought round to the front door on Oxford Street. As always, Oxford Street was thick with traffic. It being nearly Christmas, the pavement was also crowded with shoppers.

It was dark when Paul came down in the lift, surrounded by employees including Joe Reddington. As McCartney stepped out of the lobby onto the pavement, journalists clustered around him. Paul stopped obligingly so they could take pictures and ask him questions. Television crews were also present. Technicians switched on their special lights. 'I was very shocked, you know, it's terrible news,' Paul said, when asked for his reaction to John's death. He was usually relaxed with journalists, having dealt with them all his adult life, but this evening Paul was distinctly edgy, his hazel eyes darting about, a touch of Scouse truculence creeping into his voice. He was also chewing gum, which gave the unfortunate impression that he wasn't taking the matter as seriously as he might. Passing shoppers stared, a few members of the public stopping to watch and listen from behind the scrum of journalists. One of the TV reporters asked Paul when he'd heard the news John had been killed. 'I got a phone call this morning,' Paul replied, giving clipped answers.

'From whom?'

'From a friend of mine.'

'Are you planning to go over for the funeral?'

'I don't know yet.'

'What were you recording today?'

'I was just listening to some stuff, you know. I just didn't want to sit at home.'

'Why?'

Bridling at the impertinence, Paul replied: 'I didn't feel like it.' When the reporters began repeating their questions, Paul concluded the interview with an offhand rhetorical question. 'It's a drag, isn't it?' he asked the newsmen, still chewing. 'OK, cheers, goodbye …' – after which he got in his red Mercedes and was driven away.

The clip was used prominently in news broadcasts around the world that night, including Britain's *News at Ten*. '"A drag" isn't how the world will see it,' commented the ITN newscaster sternly, highlighting the crassness of Paul's remark. Just as when his mother and his father had died, and when Stuart Sutcliffe passed away, Paul had reacted awkwardly to death, saying and doing the wrong thing. Whatever he really felt – and of course he was shocked, and in time would feel genuine grief – he gave the impression on the day of not caring, which was very unfortunate because in death John Lennon was transfigured into a tragic hero, seen by many as a much greater man than Paul. On top of the Japanese bust, this was a dreadful end to a horrible year, as well as being one of the defining moments of Paul's life. His partner in the Beatles, his best friend, with whom he'd fallen out and never been fully reconciled, was gone, and Paul had sent him on his way with a stupid comment. Perhaps it was true what people said of Paul, as he himself thought when the Beatles broke up, perhaps he really was a shit.

INTO THE EIGHTIES

THE MEAN SIDE OF PAUL McCARTNEY

Reportage of John Lennon's murder was the most excessive coverage of the death of a pop star since Elvis Presley died three years previously, a sensation that lasted weeks. Yoko had her husband cremated privately on 10 December 1980. Mass public memorials were held in New York and Liverpool four days later, while John's songs played seemingly constantly on the radio into the new year, the singles '(Just Like) Starting Over' and 'Woman' both posthumously going to number one in the USA, as did *Double Fantasy*. John's death also created a huge revival of interest in the Beatles, selling truckloads of the band's albums on a wave of nostalgia that hasn't abated. 'It was John's death that reignited the whole thing,' notes Lennon's college friend Bill Harry, who points out that the civic leaders of Liverpool had hitherto ignored the Beatles.

> Liverpool refused to do a Beatles statue. They refused to have Beatles streets named after them. Liverpool councillors [said], 'The Beatles, we don't want to know them, they were drug addicts ... they brought shame to the city. We don't want to have anything to do with the Beatles.' [This attitude] was transformed after John's death.

All the surviving Beatles benefited from renewed sales of their back catalogue, leading to an ongoing, lucrative programme of repackaging and reissuing their records and films. While John's death helped make Paul even richer, it also served to elevate his friend into the company of James Dean and Marilyn Monroe, show business idols who died young and were revered as a result like secular saints. This was absurd, and over the ensuing years McCartney tried to persuade the public that John wasn't a saint, and that it was unfair to label Paul as a platitudinous balladeer in comparison to Lennon the intellectual and musical heavyweight. But if John wasn't a saint, there was a grain of truth in this characterisation of their respective roles in the Beatles, and Paul's attempts to adjust the public's perception tended to make him look insecure.

Having uttered his regrettable 'It's a drag' comment the day the world heard John had died, Paul kept a low profile during the mourning period. He and Linda visited Yoko at the Dakota briefly, then returned to England where Paul resumed work with George Martin on the *Tug of War* album. Another old friend joined the team at AIR. Paul had known Eric Stewart since the Beatles and Eric's first band, Wayne Fontana and the Mindbenders, were playing the clubs. 'It was always Paul who would come out and say "Hi, how are you doing? How's it going?" So we sort of kept in touch in that way, just crossing paths on gigs and things like that, for a long, long time.' In the 1970s Eric enjoyed success with 10cc, creating such distinctive hits as 'I'm Not in Love', which he co-wrote, sang and produced at his Lancashire studio, named Strawberry in honour of 'Strawberry Fields Forever'.

Eric owned a second Strawberry studio not far from Paul's estate in the south-east of England. Driving home from this studio one winter evening in 1979, Eric's car came off the road and hit a tree. The musician was lying semi-comatose in Redhill General Hospital when Paul rang and asked the nurse to put the phone next to his friend's ear.

> She said, 'There's somebody on the phone to speak to you. It's Paul. Paul wants to speak to you.' I said, 'Who? What?' I was full of drugs, a drip, not really caring much about anything, but completely oblivious, amnesic. 'It's Paul McCartney. He wants to say hello to you.' And she put the phone next to my ear, and I said, 'Hello?' He said, 'Hi, Eric, it's Paul.' And I said, 'How are you? How are you doing?' He said, 'Fuck me! How are *you*? What have you been doing? It's Paul.' I said, 'Paul? Paul! Right, Paul. Great. How are you? Fantastic. Yeah, I'm in … I'm in a hospital. Oh my God, how are you?' It just woke me up … I don't think I'd have been a cabbage, but it certainly did take me out of whatever state I was in at that point in time.

In fact, Eric came to feel that his friend's call helped save his life.

When Paul began recording *Tug of War* he invited Eric to sing and play guitar on the record, beginning a five-year collaboration. Eric celebrated his 36th birthday as they started the project and Paul got their working relationship off to a nice start by giving his friend a drum machine as a present. 'He's incredibly generous, always has been,' says Eric, who went on to play on many of the tracks on the new LP, including the title song, a ballad with a metaphorical lyric about the struggle of life, lifted enormously by George Martin's production, as was the whole album. The record purred like a Rolls Royce under the hands of the master after years when Paul had been turning out old bangers that coughed and spluttered.

Having started *Tug of War* in London, Paul transferred the work to Montserrat where George had built a studio complex on a farm overlooking the sea. Apart from the pleasant Caribbean climate, part of the attraction of AIR Montserrat was that everybody could be accommodated in private villas within a secure compound. Security seemed important after John's death. Paul had worried in the 1960s about being shot by a maniac, when such fears had seemed like the paranoia of a young man who'd read too much about Lee Harvey Oswald. After all, who'd want to kill a pop star? When Mark Chapman murdered John Lennon, apparently to achieve fame, it became painfully obvious to Paul and other leading rock stars that there was a real danger of being targeted by a copy-cat killer. (Bob Dylan gave a member of his road band a bulletproof vest in case he took a bullet for his boss on stage.) The fact that Ringo Starr was coming down to Montserrat to play on *Tug of War* made it doubly important to have good security at the studio, which was fenced and guarded, members of the press buzzing around the perimeter in hire cars trying to get pictures of the Beatles together. One day when Paul was driving his children around in a Mini Moke he had a run-in with two such photographers. 'The man is definitely scared,' commented the *Daily Express* snapper afterwards, claiming Paul rammed their car with his jeep.

Part of George Martin's strategy for *Tug of War* was to surround Paul with new and more notable musicians than he had used in Wings, complementing a brilliant talent as a jeweller selects emeralds and rubies to set off a diamond to its best advantage. Although Denny Laine came to Montserrat, George Martin recruited new players to work alongside Paul, such as the bass guitarist Stanley Clarke and drummer Steve Gadd, two of the best session musicians in the business, as well as being close associates of Ringo's.

John's death cast a shadow over Paul and Ritchie's reunion on Montserrat. 'It was a little bit heavy,' recalls Steve Gadd. 'If they wanted to get back together again they couldn't now.' Paul had a song he'd originally intended to give Ritchie for his new album, titled 'Take It Away'. Now the guys recorded the song as a *Tug of War* track. Ringo and Steve Gadd both played drums, helping to create a swinging hit sound. When Ritchie, Steve and Stanley left Montserrat, Carl Perkins flew in to play with Paul on the likeable 'Get It'. Then a still bigger star arrived in the form of Stevie Wonder, who'd agreed to sing with Paul on a song McCartney had written inspired by the black and white keys on a piano keyboard, from which he'd created a musical metaphor for racial harmony. Many listeners find 'Ebony and Ivory' annoyingly simplistic, but it possesses the ineluctable power of McCartney's best tunes and became a massive hit. As much a musical genius as McCartney, and even more of a perfectionist, Wonder admonished Paul during the recording for being out of time with his handclaps. His claps were not 'in the pocket'. 'And you better believe I got it in the pocket,' recalled McCartney. 'He gets results and he knows what he's doing.'

McCartney and Wonder continued their collaboration in England, going into Eric Stewart's Strawberry South Studios to work on a co-written song, 'What's That You're Doing?' During the session Paul fell into a lugubrious mood. Recalls Stewart:

> He said, 'I've just realised that John has gone. John's gone. He's dead and he's not coming back.' And he looked completely dismayed, like shocked at something that had just suddenly hit [him]. I said, 'Well, it's been a few weeks now.' He said, 'I know, Eric, but I've just *realised*.' It was one of those things maybe he wanted to say something to him, but it was too late to say it then. I think personally that Paul seriously missed John's input, even when the songs were written by one or the other … You didn't have John saying, 'That's not good enough,' and I think on a lot of tracks Paul has lacked that brutal honesty.

Paul had written a new song with John in mind, 'Here Today', in which he sang about no longer holding back the tears. George Martin graced the number with a Beatlesque string arrangement.

A few weeks later, in April 1981, Ritchie married Barbara Bach at Marylebone Register Office, where Paul and Linda had married in 1969. The McCartneys were surprised to see that the registrar was the same Joe Jevans who'd married them. Anybody watching Paul and Linda at the ceremony would have to say they looked as happy together as they did on their wedding day 12 years before.

The wedding reception was at Rags, a West End nightclub, with George and Olivia Harrison joining the Starkeys and McCartneys in a Beatles reunion. Other guests included Neil Aspinall and their former press officer Derek Taylor. The musicians gathered around the piano, Paul leading the company in a singsong. Everybody was having a great time, the kids digging into the star-shaped wedding cake. Paul's four children had Beatle cousins to run around with in Ringo's kids, Zak, Jason and Lee, aged 15, 13 and 10; while George's son, Dhani, was still only two.

Despite the warm family atmosphere at the reception, this proved a particularly challenging afternoon for Paul. Denny Laine chose the day to announce he was leaving Wings, which was not much of a surprise, but ended a chapter in Paul's career on a not entirely happy note. Denny had been grumbling about tax problems that Paul's office couldn't seem to sort out for him, despite having offered to manage his affairs, and moaning about the tour revenue he'd lost because of Paul's Japanese bust. He went off to concentrate on his solo career, which soon petered away into negligible record sales and melancholy guest appearances at Beatles conventions.

More upsetting than Denny's departure, Paul heard some home truths about himself at Ritchie's wedding reception. He said some disagreeable things, too. Talking with his fellow guests Paul gave the impression he was unhappy about a memoir his brother Mike had recently published, the book *Thank U Very Much*. It included a lot of family history and many personal photographs that Paul apparently felt would have been best kept private. Looking at Derek Taylor, Paul made a critical comment equating Mike's new book with Derek trading on his friendship with the Beatles for a radio interview back in the Sixties. 'It's always a bit funny when someone you know well does something like that,' Paul remarked sharply, censuring Derek and Mike. Then Neil told Paul that Aunt Mimi was upset Paul hadn't called her since John's death. It hadn't crossed Paul's mind to do so. He had only known Mimi briefly when he was a kid, and she hadn't been particularly welcoming towards him. It surprised Paul that Mimi wanted to hear from him now.

Paul was also thrown into confusion by a conversation he had with Cilla Black, a friend since Cavern days who had gone on to have a successful career as a television personality. Paul told Cilla how much he liked her husband, Bobby Willis, who'd managed her since Brian died. 'Bobby's a nice bloke,' he told Cilla.

'Ah, but what do you really think, Paul? You don't mean that, do you, you're getting at something?' replied Cilla quizzically. It was as if everybody believed Paul spoke with forked tongue.

The weirdest conversation of the day took place in the gents' toilet at Rags, when Paul found himself standing at the urinals next to Ritchie himself.

He said there were two times in his life in which I had done him in. Then he said that he'd done himself in *three* times. I happened to be spitting something out, and by chance the spit fell on his jacket. I said, 'There you go, now I've done you three times. We're equal.' I laughed it off. It was affectionate. It wasn't a row … But *now*, I keep thinking all the time, what are the two times that Ringo thinks I put him down …?

Paul asked this question in a peevish telephone call to the writer Hunter Davies shortly after Ritchie's wedding reception. He also complained to Davies about Philip Norman's new book, *Shout!*, a lively history of the Beatles which left the reader with the impression that Paul was a shallow young man compared to the more substantial figure of Lennon. This was all part of the problem of how the public perceived Paul *vis-à-vis* John. Paul reminded Hunter grumpily that John had hurt his feelings many times, noting that Lennon could be a 'manoeuvring swine, which no one seemed to realise. Now, since his death, he's become Martin Luther Lennon.' When Hunter put these injudicious comments into print, they served to do Paul's image further damage. The mainstream press in Britain still liked Macca – they always would – but there was a sizeable minority of the nation's media and public that had an increasingly low opinion of Paul.

There was more bad publicity for the star that summer when Angie McCartney sold the story of her relationship with her stepson to the *Sun* – a three-part serial headlined 'The mean side of Paul McCartney'. Angie described how she tried to make a living as a theatrical agent after Jim died, but soon got into debt. When she wrote to Paul to say she would have to sell her home in Gayton and her possessions to clear the debts, he showed little sympathy, and when she tried to get him involved in a charity concert she was promoting in 1978 they had a heck of a row, Paul accusing her of using his name and interfering in his career, a conversation that ended with Angie putting the phone down on him. As she sank deeper into financial difficulties there were further unpleasant conversations with Paul, who advised Angie, then almost 50, to pull herself together and make a fresh start. 'I was tempted to remind Paul that Jim McCartney had told me in the past that Ruth and I would be looked after for the rest of our lives.' When Angie sold Paul's birth certificate to a Beatles collector some years later, Paul washed his hands of his stepmother. 'I consider that she married my dad for money. There are some people you just don't bother with,' he said coldly.

Many friends knew a different Paul to the controlling, penny-pinch-ing character described by Angie, someone capable of spontaneous acts of generosity – helping Howie Casey buy his house, for example, giving Eric Stewart an expensive drum machine for his birthday – and indeed Paul had been generous with Angie and Ruth McCartney, as he continued to be with other family members. If he suspected he was being taken advantage of, however, he could become implacable. An instance came in the summer of 1981 when a former member of the Quarry Men tried to sell the first record Paul ever made.

The reader will recall that back in 1958 Paul, John and George, together with their drummer Colin Hanton and occasional pianist John Duff Lowe, chipped in their pocket money to cut a 78 rpm shellac disc, making a recording of Buddy Holly's 'That'll Be the Day' and Paul's 'In Spite of All the Danger'. This disc was passed between the boys so each had a chance to play and enjoy it at home. As Paul recalled for the Beatles' *Anthology*, John had the disc for one week. 'I had it for a week, and passed it on to George, who had it for a week. Then Colin had it for a week and passed it to Duff Lowe – who kept it for twenty-three years.'

As John Duff Lowe moved from job to job, got married, divorced and married again, he took the shellac disc with him. For almost a quarter of a century the record languished in a succession of drawers. In 1981 John contacted Sotheby's, who offered to put 'his' shellac disc into an auction of rock 'n' roll memorabilia. In advance of the sale, a story about the disc appeared in the *Sunday Times*, upon which Paul telephoned John Duff Lowe's mum, who still lived in Liverpool, asking John to ring him. Guessing what McCartney wanted, Duff Lowe didn't respond immediately. The next thing he knew he received a hand-delivered letter from the London law firm Clintons to inform him that Paul could take legal action to prevent the sale of the disc, urging him instead to contact Paul personally 'so that the matter can be discussed and settled in a friendly way'. Duff Lowe called the Sussex number he'd been given. 'I ring and Linda's there. She says, "He's not in. He'll be in about 7:30." So then Paul rings me and we have a long discussion about the record, and about old times ...' Paul said John would probably receive letters from his lawyers, but he should ignore them. 'It's just the way these guys write. It's not me!' John took this with a grain of salt, gaining the impression Paul was trying to charm him into giving him the disc for free, asking if he'd like to come to London and go out on the town. No. The disc was for sale, and John wanted to know what Paul was willing to pay for it.

The former friends negotiated over the shellac disc, the price soon reaching into the thousands. John Duff Lowe could hear McCartney becoming annoyed at the other end of the line. At one point it sounded like he'd snapped his pencil in frustration. Finally they agreed a price. Duff Lowe won't say how much; he promised Paul he wouldn't, but it seems to have been in the low five figures, which is to say the price of an average family home in 1981. A couple of days later, Stephen Shrimpton of MPL, accompanied by a lawyer from Clintons, came to meet John Duff Lowe in Worcester. He took the men to his bank, where he had the disc in a briefcase in a safe deposit box. 'I opened the case, showed them the record, and obviously they saw it was in one piece. It was all that it was expected to be. The deal was done and they went off to London.' The next day John rang Paul to ask what he thought of the record. 'But the phone had been cut off.' Having got what he wanted, Paul clearly didn't want his old friend to contact him again.

That summer Paul applied for planning permission to knock down the derelict farmhouse he'd acquired in Sussex, and build a new five-bedroom family home. At present the McCartneys were squeezed into a two-bedroom cottage, which was far from ideal considering they had four children, aged between three and 18, a slightly mad arrangement bearing in mind how rich Paul was, but illustrative of his desire to maintain a tight family unit away from public life. Paul had tried as far as possible to bring the kids up in the way that Jim and Mary McCartney had raised him and Mike. In fact, he'd modelled the new house on 20 Forthlin Road: drawing up plans for a much larger but nonetheless modestly proportioned brick dwelling, the hub of which was the kitchen. Paul then handed his drawings to a firm of architects to create detailed plans. The proposed house was by no means extravagant, and notably lacking in rock star accoutrements. It included a master bedroom and sundeck upstairs for Paul and Lin, behind which were four bedrooms for the children. Downstairs there would be a series of interconnecting living rooms, leading to a large kitchen, with a semi-circular wall of windows overlooking the fields. There were no guest rooms, interestingly. Although a sociable man, outside of family and work Paul and Linda didn't have many close friends, and in any event there were other properties on the estate where guests could be accommodated. Built in red brick, with a steep-pitched tile roof and two tall chimneys, the house was slightly ugly, especially from the back, which most resembled a corpy house. In this sense the new home was an expression of Paul's nostalgia for his Liverpool childhood, a time that had become golden in his mind. It was therefore especially disturbing for him to see news coverage of riots in Liverpool in 1981.

Urban riots occurred across England that summer, during a period of industrial unrest and rising unemployment, with the young and disaffected attacking property and the police in London, Bristol, Birmingham and Chester. Some of the worst scenes were in the Toxteth district of Liverpool, not far from Paul's old school. Long-term unemployment and racial tensions in the inner city contributed to two intense weeks of trouble resulting in many injuries, one fatality, and £11 million worth of damage ($16.8m). In the aftermath, Paul resolved to do something to help the regeneration of the city, though he was not sure what. In time his philanthropy was channelled into the Liverpool Institute for Performing Arts (LIPA), an institution that would cater to talented young people, such as Paul and John had been, who wanted to make a career in show business.

At the same time the old issue of who owned the songs Paul and John had written together re-emerged, with McCartney given a rare opportunity to regain control of the Beatles' catalogue. For the past few years Northern Songs had been in the hands of the mogul Lew Grade, who'd struck up a friendly rapport with Paul, giving him to understand that he would have first refusal if Grade ever wanted to sell. In the autumn of 1981, the recently ennobled Lord Grade offered Northern Songs to Paul for £20 million ($30.6m). Paul suggested to Yoko Ono that they put up half the money each. John's widow thought the price too high and tried to get the company for £5 million ($7.6m). Lord Grade considered the offer insufficient and decided to include Northern Songs in the sale of his much larger organisation, Associated Communications Corps (ACC), which made acquiring the songs much more expensive. Even at this stage, Paul would have been wise to enter the bidding for ACC. Instead he conflated business with justice and complained publicly about the unfairness of what was happening. '[Lord Grade] should not screw me for what he could get from somebody else,' Paul moaned to *The Times*. 'I'm not interested in buying his whole company. I just want my songs. Give me back my babies, Lew!' Grade subsequently sold ACC to the Australian businessman Robert Holmes A'Court for £45 million ($68.8m), making him the owner of ATV Music in which Northern Songs was held. In the years to come the value of the song catalogue would multiply, making even £45 million look a bargain. It was a missed opportunity.

This problem was on Paul's mind when, on Christmas Day 1981, as he was unwrapping presents at home with the family, the telephone rang. An unfamiliar, high-pitched voice asked for Paul. 'Who is this?' asked McCartney gruffly, suspecting a female fan had got his number.

'It's Michael Jackson.'

'Come on, who is it really?'

'Oh, you don't believe me?'

Although Michael Jackson and Paul McCartney were 15 years apart in age, and totally different in almost every respect, the artists stood shoulder-to-shoulder in their careers in 1981–2. Both were prodigiously talented stars who'd enjoyed huge success in their youth. Both were now working with favourite producers on solo albums: Jackson with Quincy Jones on *Off the Wall*; McCartney with George Martin on the soon-to-be released *Tug of War*; and they intended to repeat the formula with their next albums, Jackson working with Jones again on *Thriller*, McCartney with Martin on *Pipes of Peace*. It made sense for the musicians to do one another a good turn by co-writing and duetting on songs for their respective LPs, creating the funky 'Say Say Say' (and less significantly 'The Man') for *Pipes of Peace*, while 'The Girl is Mine' would find a home on *Thriller*, the most successful album in pop history. By associating himself with a hip young star, Paul also hoped to reach a younger audience, while working with an ex-Beatle flattered the American's vanity.

Jackson came to England in the spring of 1981 to meet Paul, checking into a fancy Central London hotel. Paul invited his young friend to the country for the weekend, asking Michael if he would like to go riding with him and Linda in the Sussex woods. The American said he couldn't.

'Why not?'

'I'm not allowed to get dirty,' replied Jackson, a peculiar reply which rang alarm bells with the McCartneys. Jackson was clearly strange. Paul did get Michael down to Sussex, and delivered him back to his hotel after the weekend safe and sound, save some Sussex mud on his shoes, the American proclaiming that he'd had a great time. During his visit, Michael asked Paul disingenuously if he had any career advice for him. Paul suggested Jackson might invest in song publishing, as he had done so successfully. 'I'm going to buy your songs one day,' Michael told the older man cheekily.

'Great, good joke,' Paul replied, little thinking this might actually happen.

Paul brought Jackson into AIR Studios in London, telling Eric Stewart and his other sidemen that they would have to clear out while Michael recorded. Jacko didn't want to see or talk to anybody bar Paul and Lin and their four-year-old son James. Between takes Jackson played on the floor with Dee Dee. The guy was weird, but he sang like an angel.

Paul's other collaboration with an American star, the Stevie Wonder duet 'Ebony and Ivory', proved a massive hit in the spring of 1982, reaching number one in both the UK and USA where it held the top spot for seven weeks, partly thanks to a well-produced video in what was now the video age, MTV having been launched the previous year. *Tug of War* proceeded to the top of the album charts in both territories. This was in fact the high-water mark in Paul's post-Beatles career. Though he had enjoyed simultaneous number ones in the UK and US many times, *Tug of War* was his last post-Beatles album (to date) to achieve the double. All successful show business careers have a golden period, and Paul had been doubly fortunate in reaching the top with the Beatles in the Sixties and again with Wings in the Seventies. Paul would remain a great star during the decades ahead, but he would never sell as many new albums again.

With clear evidence that a duet with a major American artist was a winning formula Paul and Linda went to LA to work further with Michael Jackson on 'The Girl is Mine', which led to a reunion with Peggy Lipton, the actress who'd set her cap at Paul in the Sixties. Peggy ultimately lost out to Linda McCartney at the Beverly Hills Hotel. Fourteen years on, Peggy was married by coincidence to Michael Jackson's producer Quincy Jones who, knowing of his wife's history, insisted they all meet to show no hard feelings. McCartney was relaxed about it, greeting 'Mrs Jones' with a friendly peck on the cheek, Linda saying how nice it was to see her again, all of which Peggy found so overwhelming she went home and cried.

Over the next few days Peggy adjusted to the idea of the McCartneys being around, even babysitting Mary, Stella and James, now aged 12, 11 and four. The eldest, Heather, was now a young woman of 19 and something of a worry to her parents.

After leaving Thomas Peacock, Heather McCartney had taken a photographic course at the London College of Printing and started an apprenticeship as a photographic printer, winning an award in 1981 for a picture she'd taken of Steve Gadd in Montserrat. Mum's career as a photographer had been revived in recent years, with photo shows and the publication of a book, *Linda's Pictures*, but Heather, after initial enthusiasm, drifted away from photography; her sister Mary would be the photographer. For Heather, taking and printing pictures was only one of several phases.

Heather's teenage years were difficult. 'I was the most chaotic, clumsy teenager,' she admitted. Her appearance changed with the fashions, dressing by turn as a Punk, New Romantic and ordinary, middle-class young woman, maturing into a hippie throwback. Heather dated a number of boys, including the punk singer Billy Idol briefly, to Paul's dismay, and seemed to want to be independent of her famous family, while being too timid to stray far from Mum, who was very protective. 'Linda used to keep her sort of separate from the madness,' notes Tony Bramwell. The other McCartney kids were more robust and outgoing, especially Stelly, who was a real livewire. Heather seemed to clash with Dad sometimes. She confided in Cavendish Avenue neighbour Evelyn Grumi that she wanted a flat of her own, asking if she could rent the Grumis' basement, giving Mrs Grumi the impression that Heather and Paul didn't get along. Then, in an unfortunate and unrelated incident in May 1982, when she was riding in the Sussex woods, Heather was thrown from her mount, suffering a broken leg and collarbone. After visiting Heather in the Royal East Sussex Hospital, Paul spoke to the press in a strikingly sombre way about his adoptive daughter. 'The family has been struck down by bad luck,' he said. 'It's our personal tragedy, a family matter, and I'm not going into details about how the accident happened.'

BACK IN THE PICTURE

Paul turned 40 in June 1982 and made some changes to his life. To help stave off middle-age spread, exacerbated by Linda's cooking, he took to jogging around the country lanes in Sussex, and he quit smoking cigarettes (but not dope). He also took up painting. As a boy, Paul showed considerable artistic talent, winning an art prize at school. The only A-level he received was for art. When John Lennon entered his life, and especially when John's artist friend Stuart Sutcliffe joined the Beatles, Paul's artistic ambitions were overshadowed. Thereafter his talent was mostly expressed in sketching ideas for stage suits and album covers, and doodling on postcards. Now he bought canvases, paint and brushes and turned one of the old farmhouses on his Sussex estate into an art studio, spending hours creating large colourful abstract pictures that gave him a sense of fulfilment and helped him relax. 'I discovered that I really enjoyed it … what painting gives me is very similar to what music gives me.'

Now he'd reached middle life, Paul also determined to make the movies he'd been talking about for years, commissioning his animator friend Geoff Dunbar to go ahead with a pilot for the *Rupert the Bear* movie, the pilot based on a 1958 story in which Rupert visits a grotto inhabited by frogs. *Rupert and the Frog Song* would start with a scene showing Rupert at home with his mother and father in what Dunbar – mindful of Paul's sentimental feelings about his childhood – drew as a cosy post-war domestic setting, reminiscent of Alfred Bestall's illustrations; 'there is a thing of Mum being this central figure,' says Geoff, who was similarly sentimental. For the underwater sequence Dunbar took additional inspiration from a series of Matisse paper cuts Paul and Linda were in the process of buying.

Rupert and the Frog Song would take two years to make, and would feature a new song, 'We All Stand Together', which Paul had already recorded with George Martin. Apart from authorising the money for the film, which he was financing entirely, the project didn't require much of Paul's time. So while Geoff got on with the slow work of animation, Paul pursued his other movie-making ambition: that of bringing a live action musical adventure to the screen, the project which had begun life as Willy Russell's *Band on the Run*.

The last Russell had heard from Paul on the subject of the film was just before the star went on his ill-fated trip to Japan in 1980: he assured the playwright that they'd make their picture when he got back. After the drug bust Paul fell silent. 'Occasionally Linda would ring and we'd have a blather and she'd say, "Oh God, I wish he'd do that movie,"' says Russell. 'Next thing we heard he was making a movie called *Give My Regards to Broad Street*.' This was an almost totally different film, borrowing only one or two ideas from Russell's script. Part of the thinking was that Paul would, for the first time, try serious acting, in the sense of being a leading man. One of the first people he consulted was David Puttnam, now Britain's leading film producer, having enjoyed success with *Midnight Express* (1978) and *Chariots of Fire* (1981), for which he collected the Oscar for Best Picture. Like many of Paul's acquaintances, Puttnam was used to McCartney tapping him for advice. Linda would typically make such calls on Paul's behalf, to the point where David's wife would groan when Linda called. As the film-maker, ennobled in 1997 as Lord Puttnam, recalls: 'She said to me one day, "Why don't you pick up the phone and say, 'Yes, Linda what do you want?'"' So it was no surprise when the McCartneys called for advice on making their new movie.

Paul explained his vision for *Give My Regards to Broad Street* to Puttnam over supper with their wives at the Savoy Grill. The film was to be a 'musical fantasy drama in the classical [sic] tradition of *The Wizard of Oz*', the title being Paul's laboured pun on the George M. Cohan song 'Give My Regards to Broadway' and the fact that the dénouement would be shot at Broad Street train station in the City of London.* The plot – completely different to Willy Russell's script – had come to Paul while sitting in his chauffeur-driven car in a London traffic jam: what would happen if the master tapes of his new album were stolen? He had written the screenplay himself, and what he had written bore little relation to a professional script; it was too short, just 22 pages, and brief though it was the script was fatally flawed, as Puttnam saw from the first page:

> The script started with Paul in the back of a Rolls Royce complaining bitterly about the emptiness of his life. I said, 'Look, let me tell you on page one you've already got a problem. People see you, see a Roller, and you're *moaning*? … They might eventually, by the end of the film, come to understand some of the pressures and problems you are under. Not on reel one! They're going to hate you. You've got every-thing they want, and you're moaning about it.'

Paul disagreed and, worryingly, he seriously underestimated how much time this project would take.

> My impression was he thought it was something he could do in three months, a bit like an album. I remember saying to him, 'This is not an album. This is a *massive* commitment. Time, effort, energy and maybe money.' So, yes, I did forewarn him.

As in so many aspects of his career, having flirted with working with professionals, Paul decided to do everything himself, or as much as he could, asking Puttnam to recommend a director who'd be a cinema-graphic amanuensis, enabling him to make his own film. This was just like the approach he had taken in the Sixties with Peter Theobald on *Magical Mystery Tour*. 'He was asking me to introduce him to a director who would basically be prepared to do what he, Paul, wanted to do,' says Lord Puttnam, who suggested Peter Webb, a 40-year-old photog-

---

* Closed in 1984, to make way for the Broadgate office development.

rapher who ran an advertising agency. Webb had made a series of popular adverts for John Smith beer and won a BAFTA for a short film. He was ambitious to get into movies, though Webb's memory of his early meetings with Paul is that the star didn't say he wanted to make a movie at first, rather a 'one-hour TV special based on *Tug of War*'. Paul put up the equivalent of half a million dollars of his own money and, with this financing, Webb started shooting sequences, including Paul driving through London at night.

Along with Paul's 22-page outline there was a note that the project would feature music. Peter Webb called Stephen Shrimpton and asked what music this would be. 'Anything you want, mate,' replied Paul's Aussie manager. So they decided to film Paul singing a version of 'Eleanor Rigby', while dressed in the style of a Victorian costume drama for reasons unclear. When Lee Eastman saw how much money his son-in-law was spending he decided Paul needed a major studio behind him. Footage was shown to the American producer Harvey Weinstein, whom Paul had known for some years, with the result that 20th Century Fox bought into a 'Hollywood musical with happy ending'. Peter Webb claims he only discovered he was shooting such a picture when he came home from work one day, around Christmas 1982, to be told by his babysitter that Paul had called and left a message that he and Peter were 'going to the Fox'. The babysitter assumed this was the name of a pub.

Suddenly, Webb found himself nominally the director of a $6.8m (£4.4m) Hollywood movie, starring Paul McCartney. 'I think he got overexcited,' says Webb. 'Once he was in a movie with a Hollywood studio, then he was a Hollywood movie star.' So, apparently, was Mrs McCartney, though what Linda was doing in the picture, other than filling the role she did in Paul's daily life, Peter never understood. Likewise, parts were found for other members of the McCartney circle: studio engineer Geoff Emerick, roadie John Hammel, George Martin, Ritchie Starkey and Eric Stewart were all called upon to play themselves. Ritchie's wife Barbara came along for the ride. A professional actress, Barbara played a press photographer, a character so poorly realised as to be risible. Having acted in a flick or two himself, her husband noticed something elementary was missing from the production. 'Ringo came up to me once,' recalls Peter Webb. 'He said, "So where is the bloody script?"' There wasn't one.

As the shooting progressed, a cast of professional actors were also hired, including Bryan Brown, who played a character obviously based on Paul's Australian manager; Tracey Ullman played the girlfriend of a roadie who disappears with Paul's master tape, the McGuffin around which the action revolved; while the elderly Sir Ralph Richardson concluded his illustrious career with an absurd cameo as a publican. Sir Ralph died shortly thereafter. 'I hope it wasn't his last film because it was my film,' muses Webb.

The warning signs that should have prevented the project going further were ignored because Paul McCartney was involved. 'The Three Mile Island or the Chernobyl safety net to prevent a film going into production was side-stepped,' says Webb, comparing his picture tellingly to the worst nuclear disasters in peace-time history. 'You must have a screenplay.' They didn't. 'It must be read by the cast.' It wasn't. Having fallen flat on his face with *Magical Mystery Tour*, Paul was heading for another cinematic pratfall.

TRIVIAL PURSUITS

THAT EXTRA 15 PER CENT

The new year started badly for Paul when, on 28 January 1983, the *Sun* splashed the story of a Liverpool typist who claimed the former Beatle was the father of her son. This was ancient history as far as Paul was concerned, dating back to 1964 when Brian Epstein paid off the girl in advance of the Beatles returning to Liverpool for the première of *A Hard Day's Night*, though Paul never admitted paternity. The press had known about the story at the time, but hadn't touched it for want of corroboration. Eighteen years later, the *Sun* ran with the tale thanks to one of Paul's former employees, Peter Brown, who revealed it in his new memoir, *The Love You Make*.

Although Brown cloaked the girl in the anonymity of a false name, journalists soon found the real people concerned. The mother was now a married woman of 37 named Anita Howarth; her son, Philip, was about to turn 19. Both still lived on Merseyside. 'I would have given anything in the world for this to have stayed a secret,' Anita was quoted as telling reporters, adding that she never wanted to embarrass Paul and had hoped the story wouldn't come out for the sake of her son, though she had told Philip 'the truth about his father', mother and son both giving journalists the impression they considered Paul to be the father. The story was common knowledge among their friends and neighbours, many of whom believed it, too. Anita and Philip said they didn't want any money from Paul, who made no comment. Privately, however, he and Linda were furious at Peter Brown. When Brown sent them a copy of his book they burnt it ritually, Linda taking photographs as it went up in flames.

At the same time Paul's other supposed love-child, the German Bettina Hübers, continued to pursue her paternity claim. Now 20, Bettina came before a judge in Berlin to plead her case, letting it be known to reporters that she intended to visit London to record a song entitled 'Let it Be Me'. Bettina had also agreed to pose for a nude photo shoot for *High Society* magazine. Her lawyers apparently thought she was entitled to a pay-off of £1.75 million ($2.6m), a serious enough claim for Paul and Bettina to both undergo blood tests, Paul in London, Bettina in Berlin. The results cleared McCartney of being the father, but Bettina and her mother were not satisfied. They asserted that the test had been fixed – believing Paul had used a stand-in – and requested a second test, which the German judge ordered, telling Paul to pay Bettina £185 a month maintenance ($283) until the matter was resolved.

This unseemly court battle came as Paul lost a 14-year legal battle for additional back royalties from Northern Songs, rejected at London's High Court in February 1983. On top of which the *Sunday People* published an exclusive look 'Inside the Strange World of Paul McCartney', based on interviews with Jo Jo Laine, who had never got on with the McCartneys. Jo Jo made much of the couple's rustic domestic life, described Linda's love of dope, and Paul's dependence on his wife. 'He enjoys Big Mamma Linda running the show.' These were not particularly revelatory or hurtful claims, but Paul probably saw such tales as a betrayal and an intrusion into his privacy. In later life Jo Jo lived in a flat just around the corner from Paul's London home in St John's Wood and, according to her son Boston, Paul blanked his mother when he saw her. Where Paul's private life started and ended was hard to say, for a man who included his family in his public life, working with Linda and often posing with the kids for photos, as well as talking in interviews about the phases the children were going though, such as Heather's punk period, which one doubts Heather thanked him for. While inviting the press into his life in this way, Paul also wanted to deny the media access to his family when he wasn't in the mood for publicity.

It was this craving for time away from public scrutiny that led Paul and Linda to buy another holiday home in 1983, their most remote and private getaway. This time they went to Arizona, where Linda had lived with her first husband Mel See. Marriage to Mel had been a failure, but it had left Linda with a love of the desert country around Tucson, where she and Mel had lived briefly, and which Mel had returned to since his African sojourn. After a period when the McCartneys had little to do with Mel, they re-established friendly contact for Heather's sake, and started to visit Tucson regularly, staying initially at the Tanque Verde guest ranch, which lies 45 minutes east of Tucson in a desert land-scape studded with cacti. This area is named after the Tanque Verde wash, a small river that floods during the summer monsoons, when the afternoon sky turns black and crackles with electrical storms, drying to a trickle in the remaining months of the year. Just across the wash from the guest ranch stood an isolated tin-roof house used by a Tucson banker as his weekender. The McCartneys bought the house, and the surrounding 107 acres, having the buildings painted pink and turquoise, and installing a heart-shaped swimming pool in the yard. Like their country retreats in England and Scotland, the ranch was a modest, even Spartan abode, but one off the beaten track in an area of great natural beauty.

As in Scotland and Sussex, the McCartneys conducted themselves in a friendly, low-key manner in Arizona, pottering around in an old car, Paul often neglecting to shave. 'You can't recognise him if he's unshaven,' notes neighbour Bob Bass. 'When he's on camera he puts on a face like he's Paul! But if he looks normal, you'd never even recog-nise him.' The McCartneys continued their habit of making friends of their neighbours and buying adjacent plots of land as they came on the market, gradually extending their Arizona property up to the top of the nearby ridge, where an abandoned school house became a special hideaway for Paul and Linda, who'd ride up there together like a couple of cowboys. Eventually the McCartneys came to own 1,000 desert acres, so much land that one elderly neighbour, whom the star did not bother to befriend, found himself marooned. 'We're enclosed here by Paul McCartney,' notes retired forester Eldon Erwin, whose only access to his home became a road across Paul's land. Mr Erwin discovered he was no longer at liberty to hike up to the old school house on the ridge for recreation as he once did. Paul's caretakers told the old man the boss had said, '*nobody* goes up there'.

The Arizona ranch cost approximately $100,000 (£65,359), a price Paul could well afford. That autumn his duet with Michael Jackson,

'Say Say Say', went to number one in the United States, number two at home, earning a rich man more money. The album *Pipes of Peace* got no higher than fourth place in UK album charts, peaking at 15 in the US, which was slightly disappointing, considering the quality of the work. Made side by side with *Tug of War*, with the help of George Martin, the two albums share a sophisticated, mature sound, abounding with well-crafted tunes that came close to the high quality Paul achieved with the Beatles. Yet *Tug of War* and *Pipes of Peace* must also be marked down for a surfeit of love ballads with lamentable lyrics. 'I always think I am not that good with words,' Paul admitted in an interview around this time, and who would doubt him with rhymes like this:

I know I was a crazy fool
For treating you the way I did
But something took hold of me
and I acted like a dustbin lid

('The Other Me')

One wonders why Paul didn't abandon this, and similar weak songs, or make the effort to rework them – a thought that has troubled his friends. Film-maker David Puttnam asks whether there may be a fundamental shortcoming in Paul as an artist.

I feel about Paul the way I feel about Ridley Scott: both men of immense, immense, immense talent who on their death bed are likely to look back on their career with some satisfaction, but with some dissatisfaction, in that I'm not sure that either of them – Ridley and Paul, both very wealthy and everything – I'm not sure either of them have absolutely delivered what was in them.

Lord Puttnam believes that, in the years since the Beatles, Paul has not been able to summon the crucial extra effort – he quantifies this as an additional 15 per cent – required to transform good work into something exceptional.

Was it that it was too hard, was it that it was too challenging? Or was it that he was a reasonably contented guy and he didn't think it was worth putting himself through that amount of pain? But the difference between good and great is that last 15 per cent, and the really great artists aren't artists who have one bright, brilliant moment in their lives.

In Lord Puttnam's film analogy, Ridley Scott made at least one classic, *Blade Runner*, but directors like Akira Kurosawa are a class apart because they found it within themselves to make many important films over a long period.

Frank Capra is more like Paul – he didn't ever really make a decent film by the time he reached 40, [and] if he's the artist I think he is, if he's as sensitive as I think he is, [Paul] will be absolutely aware [of this] and he will be troubled by the question. He won't have any answer for it.

THE WORST MUSICAL EVER MADE?

The year George Orwell chose for his dystopian prophecy started well for Paul McCartney, then turned sour. After ringing in 1984 on Merseyside, Paul and Linda flew to Barbados for some winter sunshine, renting a beach house from friends in the Guinness family. Eric and Gloria Stewart were staying in a nearby house, so they spent time with the McCartneys. Paul received good news from home when he was informed that the Berlin judge had thrown out Bettina Hübers' paternity claim, after Paul had passed both blood tests. He was *not* the father after all. Paul was magnanimous in victory, remarkably so considering how bothersome Bettina and her mother had been over the years, paying not only his own legal costs but also their £60,000 costs ($91,800), on the basis that mother and daughter would be ruined financially otherwise, and hoping they would now have the good grace to fall silent. On the contrary, Bettina took the view that Paul's generosity proved his guilt, and continued to assert that he was her dad. 'McCartney paid for everything, the tests, [his] legal costs, also my legal costs. No person does such a thing out of kindness,' protests the woman who continues to argue to this day that Paul tricked the doctors.

A few nights after hearing he'd won the German paternity case, Paul and Linda were sitting on the veranda of their rented beach house in

Barbados, chatting with Eric and Gloria Stewart, when they heard a tap at the door. Linda went to see who it was. 'Christ, it's the police!' she exclaimed. There was marijuana on the coffee table. 'My wife grabbed the bag, stuffed it up her skirt,' recalls Eric. Paul asked Gloria to give him the bag back, not wanting her to get into trouble for his sake. Then the police came in. 'They said, "We believe you have some marijuana here." Paul said, "Yeah, I'm having a smoke. I buy it on the beach here. What are you talking about? You must know about this."' He showed the police the grass, as a result of which the McCartneys were taken to the police station. It transpired that their butler had informed on them. When Paul and Linda were released on bail, they didn't feel comfortable returning to the Guinness villa, taking sanctuary instead with the Stewarts. The following Monday, Paul and Linda appeared before a magistrate in Holetown, pleaded guilty to possession, and were fined a nominal $100 each. But Paul was furious: furious at the butler for going to the police in the first place, and angry with the police for busting him for something sold openly on the island, complaining to his friends that he and Linda had become targets for harassment. 'We're going back. This holiday is over,' he told Eric, booking the next flight to London.

The McCartneys arrived at Heathrow on Tuesday 17 January 1984, disembarking to go through customs before boarding a second, private plane. In the process, an item of luggage was held back. Linda was waiting for it on their private jet when a customs official came aboard.

'Have you found my luggage?' she asked.

'Yes, and that's not all we found,' came the reply. Linda was under arrest for bringing cannabis into the UK.

Despite what had happened in Barbados, Linda had carelessly brought some grass back home, a tiny amount, less than 0.2 of an ounce, but enough to be charged. The following week Linda appeared before magistrates in Uxbridge to plead guilty to importing cannabis. It was explained in court that Linda assumed the Barbadian police cleaned out her stash when they searched her belongings, and didn't realise she had a scraping of weed left in her bag. She accepted a £75 fine ($114), telling the press: 'I am glad it is all over with. It is much ado about nothing … It is horrible to feel like a criminal when you know you are not.' Be that as it may, the McCartneys had now been in trouble for drugs on six occasions in six countries, a record that casts doubt on their judgement and the example set to their children. Paul admitted this was a concern, saying he and Lin never smoked dope in front of the kids, or took hard drugs like heroin or cocaine,* and that they had explained to the children their view that marijuana was less harmful than alcohol. British tabloid newspapers, staffed as they then were by journalists who drank heavily but took a moralistic view of other drugs, mocked the McCartneys with headlines such as THE PIPES OF POT (a pun on Paul's new album *Pipes of Peace*). Then, much more damaging allegations were made by their old friend Denny Laine.

In an unremittingly negative series of articles headlined 'The Real McCartney', Laine told *Sun* readers that Paul and Lin habitually smoked two ounces of grass a day when he knew them in Wings and routinely smuggled their stash through customs. Laine said that Paul and Linda got a thrill out of cheating authority like this, laughing at the police who escorted them. He further alleged that the McCartneys, in their same thrill-seeking way, routinely stole small items from hotels. Habitual dope smoking, he suggests, had a detrimental effect on Paul's music. 'That's why Paul's albums take ages and ages to make. He just cannot be decisive about anything.' He also described Paul as a tight-fisted, inscrutable man, with few friends, who liked the sound of his own voice and patronised those around him, including his brother; while some MPL staff lived in fear of their boss. Finally, Denny mocked Paul's complex about his mother. 'He's a mummy's boy who didn't have a mummy after his mother died when he was 14. He would be lost without Linda now.'

These stories, published over four days in January/February 1984, constituted the most personal attack on Paul since John Lennon had savaged him in *Rolling Stone* in 1971. Like Lennon, Laine had been close enough to McCartney to speak with authority. Paul was furious, though he didn't sue.

All of this trouble and bad publicity forms the backdrop to the completion of *Give My Regards to Broad Street*, the project that had ballooned from a TV special into a multi-million dollar movie. In the early part of 1984 Paul was shuttling between his home in Sussex, the MPL office in Soho, and Elstree film studios, where Peter Webb was

---

* Jo Jo Laine claimed Linda used cocaine on tour with Wings in the 1970s, and later in his career Paul admitted to having experimented with cocaine and heroin before his marriage.

directing production numbers on three sound stages.* As a release date approached, executives from 20th Century Fox jetted in for meetings with McCartney and Webb, who had found directing a non-acting leading man 'a problem'. Further complications were caused by the fact that Paul was simultaneously working on a soundtrack album, with covers of Beatles songs, new versions of recent solo material, such as 'Ballroom Dancing' and 'Wanderlust', and a terrific new theme song, 'No More Lonely Nights', which he'd written over a weekend in response to Webb telling him they needed an extra song to end the picture. Celebrity mates were roped in to play on these tracks, including Dave Gilmour, Ritchie and Eric Stewart, with the A-team of George Martin and Geoff Emerick in the control room. Such a gathering of talent created a soundtrack album far superior to the movie it rode piggy-back on.

Peter Webb flew to Los Angeles to screen a rough cut of *Broad Street* for Fox. 'They had paid $6.8 million for a Hollywood musical and they got Paul McCartney's home movie, albeit nicely shot,' says the director, who recalls Harvey Weinstein leaning over his shoulder at the end of the screening and saying, 'Next time show me the script.' Editing was done in London, Webb commuting to Sussex to show Paul and Linda the result. 'Linda was quite involved in giving it quality control … we'd meet at this secret recording studio. It was a bit too secret because we could never find it.'

The secret venue was Hog Hill Mill, a windmill Paul had bought a couple of years back, near the village of Icklesham, itself not far from Peasmarsh, subsequently having the mill restored and a recording studio, offices and living quarters built under its sails. The complex was surrounded by a dry moat so passers-by using the public footpaths over the hill could not see into the windows, and included a private museum of Beatles memorabilia, including the boys' old Vox amps, Paul's Höfner violin bass, the mellotron he played on 'Strawberry Fields Forever' and other pieces of vintage Abbey Road equipment, displayed behind sliding glass doors.

There was friction between the McCartneys and Webb at this late stage in the movie-making process. The director didn't always feel his

---

* As Paul travelled between his office and Elstree, it is interesting to think he may well have passed his future wife, Heather Mills, then a 16-year-old waitress in a Soho wine bar.

work was respected, 'let alone appreciated', by Paul, gaining the impression that the star wished he'd hired a name director; 'we were in the big time, but we were the pub team [and I was] the pub director. I'm sure McCartney would have loved to have a Dick Lester.'* Webb then suffered a serious personal setback. He says he was 'hospitalised', refusing to clarify whether this was for a mental or a physical problem, only going so far as to say guardedly that he was 'removed from the frame' and 'hospitalised for a lengthy period' towards the end of the production, with the result that Paul had to direct a final sequence of the picture himself. 'I think he was concerned about "my health". He must have been because there were [so many] flowers in my house,' says Webb. 'I thought somebody had died.'

This unhappy episode was a precursor to the premières of *Give My Regards to Broad Street* in October 1984. There were four major premières, Paul and Linda travelling first to the USA to open the picture in New York and LA, followed by a Liverpool screening. Before the première at the Liverpool Odeon, Paul was honoured with the Freedom of the City, a ceremony in the Picton Library – where he'd received his Coronation prize in 1953 – and a civic luncheon, during which Paul was reunited with Ann Ventre, the Forthlin Road neighbour he'd taken to the pictures as a lad. Nowadays Ann worked as catering manager for Liverpool City Council (a new name for the old Corporation). Although they hadn't seen each other since he left home, Paul recognised Ann instantly, and asked after their old neighbours. The première that evening went better than in New York and LA. 'The [audience] were polite. There was applause at the end,' recalls BBC Radio Merseyside broadcaster Spencer Leigh. 'It was evident there wasn't much story, but you hadn't seen the musical sequences before and they were OK.'

The London première was more important, drawing the national newspaper critics to the Empire Theatre, Leicester Square. The day started with a macabre ill omen when one of Paul's Cavendish Avenue neighbours, a fellow musician named Wells Kelly, the drummer with the band Meatloaf, came home from a party, put his key in the front door of a house across the road from Paul's, and choked to death on his own vomit before he could get inside. Neighbours passed by the house

---

* Webb believes Paul may have talked to Lester about the film, but the director declined to get involved.

for hours the next day before anybody realised that the man standing rigidly at the front door was a corpse. That evening, the audience in the Empire watched another theatrical death.

Broad Street featured Paul McCartney playing himself in an old-fashioned jukebox musical, the scenes strung together by the thinnest thread of a story. Unless he got the master tapes of his new record back by midnight, Paul stood to lose his company. The songs were strong, the musical sequences attractively filmed, and Paul was adequate as a leading man, but the dialogue was witless, the supporting characters ill-defined, the story bereft of interest. Eric Stewart sat aghast in the audience with fellow members of 10cc.

> I remember Kevin Godley turning round to me [at the end] and saying, 'How could they spend that much money on a pile of crap like this? And why have they let it out?' 'Yes, well, are you going to tell Paul that?' … There was a very embarrassing silence at the end.

Paul had committed to an intensive publicity campaign for this turkey, speaking earnestly in the picture's defence to anybody who would listen while critics gave him a unanimous thumbs down. On top of a sheaf of bad reviews in the USA, Quentin Falk told readers of the *Daily Mail*: 'this is a truly terrible movie', the blame for which had to rest with Paul. 'His screenplay is relentlessly banal, formless and, most unforgivingly, humourless.' Met with scorn and mockery, Paul became defensive, then gave up the film as a lost cause. For his director, Peter Webb, making the picture was 'a damaging experience in every way'. After getting out of hospital, he went back to making commercials.

There was a financial cost. Paul had struck deals with 20th Century Fox to the effect that the studio would lend MPL $5 million (£3.2m) to make the picture, secured on rights to the film. MPL was now obliged to pay this money back, as well as meeting a $1.8 million (£1.1m) shortfall. Consequently, MPL profits were significantly down for a couple of years. Some of the financial damage was offset by the success of the soundtrack album, *Give My Regards to Broad Street*, the rights to which Paul had wisely withheld. The album made number one in the UK, while the single 'No More Lonely Nights' was a top five hit in the USA and UK. The single might have done better still – it is one of his best post-Beatles songs – had it not been associated with such a bad film.

All told, this celluloid adventure had been a calamitous mistake, one which Paul would excise from his CV, hardly ever referring to it, and, according to Webb, refusing permission for its DVD release in the UK. When Paul came to look back on the picture, he noted that Steven Spielberg required five drafts of every movie script. Paul acknowledged that he should have worked as hard: 'you've got to have that fifth draft'. Unfortunately, as David Puttnam observed, Paul didn't possess the will to make that extra effort, preferring to get by on talent. It is a character flaw that has marred his career.

There was some consolation in the animation short that accompanied *Broad Street* on its theatrical release. Paired with the picture was *Rupert and the Frog Song*, co-written and executive produced by Paul, and directed by Geoff Dunbar, as a pilot for their *Rupert Bear* movie. It was well received, winning a BAFTA. The theme song 'We All Stand Together', though often mocked as an example of McCartney at his most lightweight, should be heard as a children's song, in the same tradition as 'Yellow Submarine', in which context it is perfectly charming. Released as a single in November 1984, the song made number three in the UK charts and won Paul his 18th Ivor Novello.

Paul felt encouraged to press on with the feature-length *Rupert* film. Then Geoff Dunbar received a call from the star. 'I've got a bit of news,' Paul told his animator. 'We can't do Rupert ... He's been stolen away from us.' Having identified Paul's interest in making a *Rupert* movie, another producer had acquired the option, informing Paul that he couldn't proceed without his cooperation. So Paul pulled out. He and Linda had the animation bug, though, and continued to work with Dunbar on other short films, including one inspired by the squirrels they put food out for in their Sussex garden. To amuse his children, Paul made up stories about these engaging creatures, one of whom he named Squiggle, later becoming Wirral the Squirrel, in honour of Paul's Merseyside home. We shall return to him later.

PRESSING ON

Having worked with George Martin since the Tokyo bust, Paul felt the need of a change of producer as he approached his next studio album. George wanted a rest from the demanding Paul, too. When everybody was sitting down at the annual Buddy Holly Week lunch in September 1984, George asked Eric Stewart if he would take the helm on the new record.

> George said to me at this Buddy Holly Day dinner, 'I think you should help Paul with his next album. I've got other things to do. I need a break and I think Paul needs a break as well. We've got two great albums there, *Tug of War/Pipes of Peace*, but I think some new blood should come in.' I said, 'He's not asked me.' He said, 'Would you be interested?' I said, 'Yeah.'

Having established that Eric would accept the challenge, Paul invited his friend to Sussex to co-write some songs. It was a winter's day when Eric drove to Peasmarsh, the snow thick on the ground. Although Paul and Linda were now living in their new farmhouse, Paul had arranged to meet Eric at Waterfall, the little round house in the trees which he still owned. The house was looking pretty as a picture when Eric came up the drive.

> So I got there in the snow and I said, 'It's beautiful outside, it's so beautiful, the sun's out.' He said, 'That's great, OK, [starts singing] *It's beautiful outside* … Right, get it down, write it down.' And we wrote the whole song within [minutes]. Simple as that.

This was 'Footprints' on what would be the album *Press to Play*. Another song, 'Angry', came with similar ease a few days later in response to Paul reading an unflattering article about himself in a newspaper. Stewart can't recall what the story was, but it may well have been a negative article about the *Broad Street* débâcle.

> I walked in another morning and I said, 'You look a bit tense,' and he said, 'Yeah, I'm fucking angry.' I said, 'What's the problem?' He said, 'The Press – look at this. [Holds up a paper]. What the Hell gives them the right to tell me what to do with my life?' I said, 'What? Hold it. Write it down,' *What the hell gives you the right to tell me what to do with my life?* … And we've got 'Angry' started.

Eric and Paul swiftly completed eight songs in this way, then went into Hog Hill Mill to record them.

Although Eric had gained the impression Paul wanted him to produce the new album, McCartney had also hired the fashionable young producer Hugh Padgham, who'd enjoyed recent success with Phil Collins and the Police. Tensions soon developed between Padgham and Stewart, who seemed to be competing for the same job, with both men finding they had an even greater problem with McCartney himself.

At first, Eric had been delighted with the songs he and Paul had written at Waterfall, songs which came easily and sounded fresh to his ears. Then he started to have misgivings about the quality of the tunes. 'I thought, Are they really good enough. Are they finished? I always thought when we get them in the studio we'll finish them, but as we got in the studio and we started to record, I said, "This is not good."' One day Eric clicked the talk-back button and said: 'Paul, that vocal's not right.'

Paul asked Hugh Padgham his opinion. 'Well, it's OK, but I'm a sound man, Eric's the musician.'

'But what do you think?'

Hugh agreed with Eric. Privately, Hugh had been worried that the material was on the weak side, but assumed an artist of Paul's stature, working in tandem with someone as experienced as Eric, would improve the songs in the studio. Unfortunately, this wasn't happening. 'I don't think it's good enough,' he said, suggesting some more writing might be required. Paul's response shocked both Hugh and Eric.

'Hugh, when did you write your last number one?' McCartney asked, nastily.

As Padgham says, 'That one was a real kick in the balls, which you don't forget.' Eric switched off the talk-back and groaned, *Oh shit! This is going wrong.* 'And it really did start to go wrong. There was this conflict there. And that was something that Paul could do. He could actually wither you with a sentence if he didn't like what you've said.' Eric later realised that he should have stood up to Paul at this point, and thrashed out whatever the problem was. But it was hard to argue with the man. 'It's difficult to tell Paul McCartney, isn't it? He's a great singer, he's written the greatest songs of all time and you're saying, "That's not good enough".' John Lennon had been able to have those candid conversations; George Martin could tell Paul when he was wrong.

'Could I do it? No.' Despite the fact they had known each other since the Cavern, and had worked closely for five years, Eric was tongue-tied.

> We never discussed it afterwards. But after about another week of this, I said, 'Hold it, this is not working for me.' I said, 'You carry on with it. I'm just going to come down and pick my guitars up … I'm not really adding anything here but conflict, because it's not good enough.' Let Padgham carry on with it.

So Eric left, and Hugh found himself alone with Paul, renting a nearby beach house where he lived an increasingly miserable existence as work on this difficult album dragged on for an amazing 18 months, the producer becoming thoroughly fed up with Paul McCartney in the process.

At first it felt like a great honour to be asked to produce Paul's new album, and Padgham had hoped that, after *Give My Regards to Broad Street* and *Rupert and the Frog Song*, he could give Paul back some 'cred' (credibility), 'cred' being a vogue Eighties term people like him were using. As work on *Press to Play* stretched on month after month, Hugh discovered what other producers had before him: he couldn't tell Paul anything. Also, Paul's charm wore off. Years ago Paul hardly talked about the Beatles. Nowadays he told the same old Beatles stories again and again, until they were frankly boring, and nobody had the courage to tell him he was repeating himself. Also, he seemed obsessed with what the public thought of him in relation to John Lennon. Outside of music, Paul's conversation was banal, often about what he'd seen on TV, as Padgham recalls:

> It was like he'd been up all night watching television, because he was like a walking version of the *Radio Times*. I think he would have literally gone home at six or seven o'clock and probably stayed up till one o'clock watching TV with a spliff, and a drink, and he probably didn't really think anything of the album. He was just watching telly. He'd come in the mornings, 'Did you see this last night?'

The producer was invited up to Paul and Lin's new house, Blossom Farm. Says Hugh:

To start with I really thought he was this guy who was really normal, sent his children to the local comprehensive school, and lived in a pretty modest house, and seemed one of the lads, but by the end of 18 months I didn't feel like that at all … It was either a façade, or he's got many faces of which the charming one is maybe turned on when you're new to the fold and impressionable. All the people who work for him, if he said jump they'd go, 'From what floor?' … I've worked in this business for 30-something years with a lot of people just as famous as him and some are really nice and some are affected by it, and if you think that McCartney probably hasn't been able to walk down a street without somebody wanting to kiss his arse from the age of 17, I imagine it would affect you, possibly in an insidious way as well where you don't realise. But if he doesn't get his own way, then he throws his toys out of the pram.

Paul sometimes showed his bad temper in public, too. One day, before driving to Hog Hill Mill to work with Hugh, he and Linda took seven-year-old James to the village school in Peasmarsh. They arrived to find that teachers on strike over low pay were protesting at the school gates. One of the teachers, Brian Moses, offered Paul a leaflet explaining their action. 'Are you striking teachers?' Paul asked Moses, clearly unimpressed.

'Well, yes, we are at the moment, because our pay isn't enough for us to live on.'

'Take a good look,' Paul told his son, as if showing James particularly wicked people. 'They are striking teachers.'

When he had taken James into school, Paul came outside and tore up the teachers' leaflet ostentatiously, throwing the pieces in the road. 'I just thought, You sod! If Lennon had been there, he would have been on the picket line with us!' says Moses, who described the incident in a letter to his union newspaper, the *Teacher*, making the point that if Paul McCartney tried to support his four children on a teacher's salary he'd be eligible for supplementary benefit. At the time an average teacher's salary was £5,442 a year ($8,296). McCartney drew a basic salary from MPL of £200,000 a year ($306,000), which he used to cover his expenses. He received other, Beatles income above and beyond this, of course. Despite portraying himself as a normal bloke, Paul was therefore far removed from the lives of everyday people like Moses, whose school-gate confrontation with the star became national news. 'I had always admired him for sending his children to state schools,' the teacher told the *Daily Mirror*. 'I expected more support.'

Back at Hog Hill Mill, Paul's relationship with Hugh Padgham hit rock bottom. When Paul's 43rd birthday rolled around in June, the producer gave Paul the music edition of the popular board game *Trivial Pursuit*. Over the weekend, Paul evidently had the game out at home. When he came back into work on Monday he complained bitterly that one of the questions in the game was about the death of his own mother, something he took amiss.

> He really had a go at me as if it was my fault that it was in there, or my fault that I gave him this box of *Trivial Pursuit* questions that had this, as far as he was concerned, insensitive [question]. It was like, *Fuckin' hell, you know, it's not my fault. Sorry!* Ha!

As the two men struggled to complete this unhappy album, Paul was asked to support a charity concert at Wembley Stadium. Towards the end of 1984, Bob Geldof, leader of the new-wave band the Boomtown Rats, had been shocked by news coverage of a famine in Ethiopia into corralling pop stars together to record a charity single, 'Do They Know It's Christmas?', which surpassed 'Mull of Kintyre' as the best-selling single in the history of the British charts. A US version followed in the spring of 1985, after which Geldof organised twin concerts to aid Africa, a British show at Wembley Stadium and a sister show at the JFK Stadium in Philadelphia, with an integrated live telecast. Geldof felt he had to have McCartney headline in London, and wrote to the star asking him to perform 'Let It Be', explaining that 'Beatles' music for some reason evokes more emotional response than any other'. Although he hadn't performed live since 1979, Paul agreed to do the gig, letting Geldof know that he didn't mind if George and Ritchie were invited to join him on stage. Geldof called George Harrison at his holiday home in Hawaii, asking if he would play 'Let It Be' with Paul. 'He didn't ask me to sing on it [16] years ago, so why does he want me now?' Harrison retorted, his own relationship with Paul at a new low ebb. The men had recently had a ratty telephone conversation during which George accused Paul of boasting to the press about how much money he made, though the reported £20 million a year ($30.6m) figure was an exaggeration.

The twin Live Aid concerts held on Saturday 13 July 1985 were the most significant live events in popular music since the Sixties. Not since the Woodstock Festival had so many first-class rock acts been assembled, the international telecast adding an extra dimension to what was a truly memorable day. David Bowie, Elton John, Queen, U2 and the Who all performed in London, highlights of the American show including performances by a re-formed Led Zeppelin, Madonna and Mick Jagger singing with Tina Turner. The weather in Philadelphia was muggy. In England it was cloudy with sunny spells and a short, hard shower in the evening before McCartney came on stage alone.

It was obvious that there was a serious sound problem as soon as Paul began performing 'Let It Be' on a white grand piano on the Wembley stage. His voice was heard briefly at first, then disappeared for eight verses. Only the piano and intermittent shrieks of feedback were audible. Paul struggled on, hoping everything would work out, apparently willing the audience to help him. Although the stadium audience was made up of predominantly young people, a generation younger than those who'd followed the Beatles originally, the concert-goers recognised the tune Paul was playing and began singing the lyric in his place. When Paul's voice finally came through loud and clear the crowd gave a huge cheer, and sang along with 'Let It Be' enthusiastically until the end, David Bowie, Bob Geldof, Alison Moyet and Pete Townshend adding ragged backing vocals on stage. It was a shambolic performance, not helped by an overwrought Geldof shouting at the audience, 'Come on!', but the moment was undoubtedly moving, the strong audience reaction demonstrating the enduring power of the Beatles' songs, and showing that Paul – despite his advancing years and recent failures – was by common consensus the figurehead of British rock, which with Live Aid, attended by the Prince and Princess of Wales, was beginning to be assimilated into the Establishment. From now on, Paul's presence would be requested at virtually every large, set-piece music event of the kind, and many such concerts followed.

MIND THE GAP

A few weeks after Live Aid there was another difficult scene at Hog Hill Mill when Paul heard that someone he had considered a friend, Michael Jackson, had invested $47.5 million (£31m) of his *Thriller* fortune in ATV Music, making him the new owner of Northern Songs. When Michael had mentioned that he might buy Paul's songs, McCartney had dismissed the comment as a joke, still thinking that he might somehow buy the company back for himself one day. Now Jacko had beaten him to it. '*He was absolutely furious*,' recalls Hugh Padgham, speaking in italics. 'Oh my God, the air was blue.'

The making of *Press to Play* dragged on into 1986, to the misery of the producer, who found that the lack of any financial concern about the cost of studio time (now Paul owned his own studio), twinned with Paul's penchant for smoking dope, meant that recording a McCartney album could drift on almost indefinitely.

Sometimes it would be really tedious, like McCartney would put his bass on one of the songs and he'd get himself in a tizz about it. Then we'd stop for lunch and we'd have sandwiches, and he would go upstairs and smoke a joint up there, and he thought that we didn't know what was going on, then he'd come down and sit there for hours trying to play the bass and you could cut the air with a knife with the tension sometimes. And the *tedium*. Oh!

To put the best gloss on weak material, Hugh called in crack session men and guest stars, including the New York guitarist Carlos Alomar, Phil Collins and Pete Townshend. Recalls Alomar, who is perhaps most famous for his work with David Bowie: 'We sat down and talked, "How was your trip?" Then he says, '"Let's go upstairs." We went upstairs. He rolled a joint. We smoked a nice big spliff, and then we started talking [music].' The American stayed a week at the mill, eating with Paul, Linda and the kids, and visiting the local pub in the evening. One blustery day, he and Paul flew a kite on the hill. 'It's a simpler life than you would think of an ex-Beatle [living],' says the musician, who felt like he was spending time with a farmer and his family, whereby the farmer's daughter, Stella, would call for 'Mr Alomar' when Mum had dinner ready. 'It's like having a regular country dinner and then going to the local pub for a brew and coming back. It's not a compli-cated life.' Paul seemed confident he was making a good record. Indeed, he was so proud of the project he drew diagrammatic plans for the CD booklet to help the listener identify the musicians. 'That's pretty meticulous and it requires a certain amount of dedication and commit-ment,' comments Alomar. 'I've looked at a lot of his albums and heard a lot of his music and I've never really [seen] things like that – I thought [he believed the album] was fantastic.'

The day finally came in the spring of 1986 when work stopped. The record was finished, for better or worse. Hugh Padgham was just relieved it was all over. Up in London, Paul's manager Stephen Shrimpton was concerned that he couldn't hear a hit on *Press to Play*. It may not be a coincidence that Shrimpton left MPL around this time. In April, Paul appointed Robert Mercer as his new managing director. He lasted just six weeks, leaving the company before *Press to Play* was released in the September, indicating turmoil within McCartney's office. For want of anything better, Paul finally chose 'Press' as the single to launch this troublesome album. Like so many of Paul's songs, it is catchy – with the light, electronic sound fashionable in the Eighties – but, in common with the rest of the album, the number also sounds overworked.

When he came to make the promotional video, Paul went for simplic-ity, taking a camera crew onto London's Underground to film him miming to 'Press' as he rode the Jubilee Line. Looking happy and relaxed in light summer clothes, the star's spontaneous interactions with the public had a natural, unforced charm that showed him at his best: shaking hands with an elderly lady, receiving a kiss from a girl, encouraging normally dour commuters to smile. At one stage a young man approached Paul on a platform. McCartney made wary eye contact, circumspect about people who came up on his blind side, even more so since John had been shot, only to realise the guy just wanted directions. Paul nodded him onto the right train with a Londoner's insouciance. After all, the capital had been Paul's home now for half his life. He knew the city as well as he did Liverpool. As he waved goodbye to his crew, and the audience, at St John's Wood station, you had to like the man.

A strong video wasn't enough to save 'Press' from bombing, while a second single, 'Only Love Remains', did even less well, *Press to Play* itself selling fewer copies than any of McCartney's previous studio albums. When Eric Stewart received a copy, he felt he knew why it had failed. Fragments of their original collaboration were audible, in songs like 'Angry' and 'Footprints', but the simplicity of the demos was buried under 18 months of overdubs, with the result that 'the album became meaningless'. Eric wished he'd been strong enough to stand up to Paul when he'd snapped at Hugh Padgham in the studio: 'When did you write your last number one?' That was the key moment. John Lennon would have challenged Paul and resolved the problem; George Martin could have stood up to the star; but Eric had been cowed by Paul's status as a former Beatle, a legacy so enormous it inhibited both the star and those around him. 'Where do you go from there?' asks Eric rhetorically. 'What can you achieve from there?' Paul's answer, as we shall see next, was to celebrate that legacy.

THE NEXT BEST THING

LINDA'S PEOPLE

When *Press to Play* sold fewer than a million copies worldwide, poor by Paul's standards, he hired a new manager to help revive his career, choosing a straight-talking former Polydor executive named Richard Ogden, who set out a three-year plan to get Paul back in the charts and back on the road, after almost a decade in which McCartney hadn't toured.

Part of Ogden's job was managing Linda's career, too, which meant enabling Mrs McCartney to realise her pet projects, mostly to do with photography or vegetarianism, for which she had become a zealot. Having given up eating meat and fish, and wearing leather, Linda expected everybody else to do the same. She even had the temerity to ask the Duke of Edinburgh how he, as the figurehead for the World Wildlife Fund, could defend shooting birds for sport. The Duke muttered in reply that his eldest son was almost a bloody veggie.

Linda's vegetarianism was not so much to do with health as a horror of the slaughterhouse. In this regard, Linda found a like-minded friend in Pretenders singer Chrissie Hynde, another American in the British rock industry. Although the two women became close, Linda was capable of telling off even Chrissie if she felt her friend was insufficiently committed to the animal cause, as happened at a gathering of celebrities at Chrissie's London home. 'We're here because we are going to talk about what we can do for animals,' Hynde told her guests, 'because we have some influence.'

'Well, if I were you I'd start by not wearing a leather skirt,' Linda replied sharply.

It was at this gathering that Linda met the television writer Carla Lane, who became another ally in the cause of animal rights. Carla was a Liverpudlian, slightly older than Paul. She'd been to the Cavern in her youth, but was never a Beatles fan, being more interested in the beetles she could scoop up in her hands and put in her animal hospital. Carla made her name and fortune in the 1970s as the creator of the *Liver Birds*, a popular television sit-com about two young female Liverpool flat-mates, following this with the equally successful Eighties sit-com *Bread*, about a working-class Liverpool family. It was Carla's devotion to animals, though, rather than her Merseyside links, that endeared her to Linda, making two women who were not especially sociable close. 'We were each lonely people, really,' observes Carla, noting that although Linda was friendly with Chrissie Hynde and Twiggy, and one or two other women, she was not over-endowed with friends. Similarly, Paul didn't have many pals. 'I never saw Paul with mates. He was always surrounded by people, but he was usually in charge of them.'

Though not as rich as the McCartneys, Carla had made very good money in television, investing her wealth in an animal sanctuary at her large country home, Broadhurst Manor, 60 miles from the McCartney estate in West Sussex. Broadhurst Manor was a veritable Noah's Ark of rescue animals, with Carla always grateful to Paul and Linda for taking on the care of some of her surplus stock. They had the space at Blossom Farm, and already maintained a considerable menagerie of their own. The McCartneys kept approximately nine horses these days, including Linda's beloved appaloosa stallion Blankit (sired by Lucky Spot, the horse she'd brought back from Texas in 1976); there were numerous cats and dogs, including sheepdog descendants of the late Martha, who'd died in the early 1980s. They also had sheep, a herd of deer, and a pet bullock named Ferdinand that Paul had found loose in the lanes one day, having escaped from its farmer. When Paul discovered the bullock was on its way to slaughter he bought the animal and made a pet of it. The McCartneys also kept numerous small creatures, including rabbits, fish, a turtle that lived in a spacious aquarium adjacent to Linda's kitchen, and a parrot named Sparky, which resided in an outdoor aviary, saying repeatedly, 'Ello Sparky. Come 'ere and say somethink,' mimicking the passing farmhands.

In addition, Carla gave the McCartneys chickens, a blue-grey kitten (upon request from the children) and numerous additional deer, which she frequently found injured in lanes, having been hit by vehicles. Carla would pick the creatures up in her animal ambulance and nurse them back to health, where possible, before releasing them into the wild. On one memorably happy occasion, Carla and Linda both had rescue deer ready to release at the same time, so they arranged to meet on a track that led into the forest on Paul's Sussex estate (which he expanded considerably in the Eighties, buying two adjacent farms and a 50-acre wood, created a contiguous landholding of nearly 1,000 acres – an area three times the size of London's Hyde Park).

> The deer was in the back of our ambulance and Paul had one at the back of [his vehicle] and we did a one, two, three, let them go. And we watched the two deer that we'd nursed better gallop side by side the length of this lane. There were a lot of people there, staff, and Paul and Linda and I, and what a moment it was! Beautiful … It was just one of the nice things that we used to do that nobody knew about.

Though she meant well, Linda's concern for animals could lead to muddled thinking. She fed her animals a vegetarian diet whenever possible, even to those creatures that were naturally carnivores. She disapproved of the more pragmatic Carla feeding dead chicks to her rescue foxes, for example, and refused to countenance the idea that when her own domestic cats slipped out of the house at night they might be hunting for rodents. 'She really was against meat being consumed by [any creature],' says Carla, who believes Linda would have found a way to feed porridge to a T. Rex if she had one in her care. Linda grudgingly accepted wild animals hunted for survival, but she and Paul were implacably opposed to people hunting for sport, becoming terribly upset if they heard a hunt riding through the area or guns going off. One time, when shooting was taking place within earshot, farmer Bob Languish met Paul storming down the lane. 'Where are those people shooting those poor little bunnies?' the musician demanded of his neighbour, who informed Paul mildly that the men were only clay-pigeon shooting.

Animals at Blossom Farm lived until they died of old age, even though some local farmers thought this cruel, pointing out that sheep wear their teeth down with grazing and can starve to death if they become very old. The McCartneys took little notice, choosing to spend whatever it cost on vets to keep their ageing animal friends alive. 'I remember they were devastated when a cow of theirs died, and they had specialists from all over the place coming to this cow. They were heartbroken,' says Carla, who admits that most people would think Linda and herself eccentric. 'We are cranks, let's face it. We don't mind being called that.' And Linda drew Paul and the children into this well-intentioned but slightly cranky way of thinking, the whole family becoming evangelical about animal rights. Slaughterhouses, hunting, vivisection and the wearing of fur were their *bêtes noires*, with the young McCartneys feeling as strongly as their parents. James McCartney got up in school and gave his fellow pupils a passionate speech about why eating animals was wrong. 'All [of us] had in common this disbelief in what people do to animals, a complete horror of the abattoir and how anyone can be a part of it,' explains Carla, who also found time to collaborate on animal rights songs with Linda, a couple of which, 'Cow' and 'The White Coated Man', Paul helped the women record at Hog Hill Mill. 'He said, "Come on, our Carla," and he'd got all the music ready. I used to love it the way he called me "Our Carla". It was so Liverpudlian.' Unfortunately, Carla was no more a singer than Linda was.

It was the horror of animals being driven to their deaths for food that gave Linda the impetus to create a cookbook that didn't use as an ingredient 'dead animals', as she pointedly described meat; a book in which she would set down her recipes for the kind of hearty meals Paul liked and that she urged her women readers to serve to 'your man' – hardly the sort of language one would expect of a woman who'd been at the heart of the Sixties counter-culture, but there was an old-fashioned side to Linda. Away from the public stage, she played the role of a traditional post-war housewife-mother to Paul and their kids, what Paul had been looking for ever since his own mother died, and Paul and Linda seemed to think this was how other people still lived.

In order to create vegetarian versions of the traditional, meat-based meals Paul had been brought up on, Linda used Textured Vegetable Protein (TVP) products, such as Protoveg, in her versions of such English staples as Sunday roast and shepherd's pie. Linda created realistic-looking sausage rolls from soya, even a veggie steak Diane. Carla Lane couldn't understand why her friend felt the need to mimic the look

Top (left). Some of the music Wings made in the 1970s wasn't as good as Paul's earlier work. Some of the outfits and hair styles Paul and Linda wore were very much of that era.

Top (right). In the late 1970s, Paul moved his company, McCartney Productions Ltd (MPL), to this handsome townhouse in London's Soho Square.

Bottom. This charming family picture shows the McCartneys with some of their pets in the garden of their London home, April 1976, just before the Wings Over America tour. From left to right are 13-year-old Heather, Paul, 4-year-old Stella, Linda and 6-year-old Mary.

Top (left). Paul poses with the final line-up of Wings in front of the Royal Liver Building, Liverpool, 1979. From left to right are guitarist Laurence Juber, Linda, Paul, drummer Stev Holley and guitarist Denny Laine.

Top (right). When Paul took Wings to Japan in January 1980 he foolishly brought marijuana with him in his luggage. Arrested at Narita Airport, McCartney is seen in handcuffs being taken to Kojimachi Police Station where he spent nine nights in a cell.

Bottom (left). John Lennon was murdered in New York on the evening of 8 December 1980. The next day Paul went to work at AIR Studios in London. He is seen speaking to journalists about the death of his friend as he leaves AIR. 'It's a drag, isn't it?' he asked newsmen.

Bottom (right). In the early 1980s Paul bought Blossom Farm adjacent to his original Sussex retreat, Waterfall, and had a new family home built. The house (bottom of picture) is now the centre of a vast, 1,000-acre private estate.

Top (left).
To enable him to
spend time at home
with the family in
Sussex, Paul bought
a nearby windmill,
Hog Hill Mill, and
had it converted into
a recording studio.

Top (right). The
1984 movie *Give My
Regards to Broad
Street* proved one of
the biggest blunders
of Paul's career. any
friends were given
parts in the picture.
Here Paul and Linda
are seen in costume
with Ringo Starr
and his second wife
Barbara Bach.

Bottom. After ten
years off the road,
McCartney returned
to touring in 1989,
aged 47, with a show
that was 50 per cent
Beatles material.

Top (left). Paul branched out into orchestral composition in 1991 with his *Liverpool Oratorio*. Here he is celebrating the success of the première at Liverpool's Anglican Cathedral with his co-composer Carl Davis and soloist Dame Kiri Te Kanawa (far left).

Top (right). In the mid-1990s, the three surviving Beatles reunited for the *Anthology* project, recounting the story of the band for a TV series and book, and recording two 'new' Beatles songs, the disappointing 'Free as a Bird' and 'Real Love'.

Bottom. In March 1998, Paul and Linda went to Paris with their children Heather, James and Mary (seen left to right with their parents) to support their youngest, Stella, at her latest fashion show. Linda's cropped hair was a sign of the treatment she had been receiving for breast cancer. A month later she was dead.

Top (left). Linda McCartney died here at the McCartneys' ranch outside Tucson, Arizona, on 17 April 1998. She was 56.

Top (right). Stella McCartney makes it plain that, in her opinion, it's about time Dad was inducted into the Rock 'n' Roll Hall of Fame as a solo artist. New York, March 1999.

Bottom. Sir Paul McCartney (knighted 1997) organised two memorial services for his late wife. Here he leads children Stella, James and Mary out of St Martin's-in-the-Fields, London, on 8 June 1998.

Top (left). While still mourning the death of Linda, Sir Paul attended an awards ceremony in London in May 1999, where 31-year-old Heather Mills caught his eye. Here is Heather during her earlier career as a 'glamour' model.

Top (right). Sir Paul and Heather Mills announced their engagement in July 2001, posing for photographers outside the musician's London home. Despite a rocky courtship, they married the following June. Heather was 34; Paul was a week shy of 60.

Bottom. Over the course of his career Sir Paul has had many occasions to meet his monarch Queen Elizabeth II, developing a warm relationship with Her Majesty. Here he shows the Queen around the Walker Art Gallery, Liverpool, May 2002.

op (left). The divorce of Sir Paul and Heather Mills McCartney was acrimonious. At he culmination of the case, Heather tipped a jug of water over Sir Paul's solicitor Fiona hackleton, who is seen leaving the Royal Courts of Justice with her client on 17 March 008, her hair still wet.

op (right). Immediately after the divorce judgment, Heather Mills addressed the media : the entrance to the Royal Courts of Justice. She said she was satisfied with her £24.3 illion settlement, but she had asked for much more.

ottom. In June 2008 Sir Paul returned to Liverpool to help the city celebrate its year as uropean Capital of Culture. He is seen here at a fashion show at LIPA, his old school, ow a performing arts institute, with son James and Beatles widows Yoko Ono and livia Harrison.

Top. Since his divorce from Heath[e]
Mills McCartney, Sir Paul has spen[t]
much of his time in the company of
the American Nancy Shevell. Here
they are in Paris, October 2009.

Bottom. With John Lennon and
George Harrison gone, it has fallen
to Sir Paul McCartney to carry the
Beatles torch. The spectacular
shows he gives around the world ar[e]
emotional celebrations of the greate[st]
band in the history of popular musi[c]

and taste of meat, serving an elaborate soya turkey at Thanksgiving, for instance, and going to the expense of having 'non-meat bacon' imported from the United States so that she and Paul could snack on *faux* bacon sarnies. It didn't make sense intellectually to reject meat as part of your diet, yet eat pretend meat. 'I used to say to her, "What, you like bacon so much?" She said, "I've got to confess, Carla, I do like the taste, but you know I would never eat the real stuff."'

To help Linda spread this passionately held but confused veggie message, the McCartneys' business manager struck a publishing deal with Bloomsbury, whose office was conveniently located next door to MPL on Soho Square, with a vegetarian writer engaged to help Linda turn her veggie menus into a cookbook. For the next two years, Linda worked with Peter Cox on *Linda McCartney's Home Cooking*, which put her in the same business as Paul's former fiancée, Jane Asher. After breaking up with Paul in 1968, Jane had married and had a family with the artist Gerald Scarfe, still pursuing her acting, but also creating a successful second career as a celebrity cake-maker, appearing on television and publishing a series of best-selling recipe books such as *Jane Asher's Party Cakes*. Now Linda also thrust herself into the cook-book business. She devised most of her recipes in her kitchen at Blossom Farm which, as she explained in her book, was the heart of the McCartney home and the place she felt happiest. 'I spend a lot of time in our kitchen. I find it the cosiest, friendliest place in the house,' she wrote in the introduction to her book. 'It's a great place to nurture a happy harmonious family and to spend time with friends, chatting over a cup of tea.' Yet one of her best friends and most frequent kitchen visitors, Carla Lane, recalls that Paul and Linda were not always a harmonious couple at home in Sussex. 'They had normal quarrels,' Carla says. '[But] they were never violent. It was, "Oh, alright!" The slam of the door.'

Although Paul enjoyed the country, friends gained the impression he sometimes felt bored at Blossom Farm, hankering for the road and his old life in London, where he had been part of a community of musicians. Although Paul kept the house in Cavendish Avenue, he wasn't there much, and didn't tend to use London studios as he once had. Now that Paul owned his own recording facility at Hog Hill he had no need to be at Abbey Road Studios or AIR, where in the past he'd hang out with old friends and meet up-and-coming musicians, getting energy and ideas from what other artists were doing. Everybody who came to work at Hog Hill Mill came at Paul's invitation, resulting in a slightly stale environment.

In the summer of 1987 Paul started playing with new musicians at Hog Hill, recording demos and auditioning for a band he would ultimately take out on the road. Paul ran down favourite rock 'n' roll songs with these musicians, numbers including 'Kansas City', 'Lucille' and 'That's All Right (Mama)', which he sang with the pleasure of a middle-aged man reconnecting with his youth. His engineer recorded the sessions, and when Paul played the tapes back he decided he wanted to put them out as an album.

Richard Ogden was concerned that the time was not right for such a record. Paul's next major release had to be a strong studio album, one that would make up for *Press to Play*. Ogden also feared an album of rock 'n' roll covers might be reviewed critically in comparison to John Lennon's 1975 *Rock 'n' Roll* album. When Paul insisted, Ogden had the novel idea of allowing a Russian company to release a Paul McCartney 'bootleg'. Despite being banned in the USSR during the Cold War, the Beatles' music had been and remained hugely popular behind the Iron Curtain, with Soviet fans trading bootleg recordings of their songs. With the rise of the reformist Soviet leader, Mikhail Gorbachev, it was becoming easier to get genuine Western records in the USSR, and it seemed a fun idea to allow a Russian label to sell an apparently pirated McCartney record in traditional Soviet style. EMI licensed the Russian label Melodya to manufacture 400,000 copies of Paul's rock 'n' roll LP, guessing they would print more and that fans who wanted it in the West could buy Soviet imports, which is what happened when *CHOBA B CCCP* (Russian for 'Again in the USSR'), was released the following year.

Around the same time, the star agreed that EMI should issue a new 'best-of' LP. Although covering some of the same ground as *Wings Greatest*, released in 1978, *Paul McCartney: All the Best* sold strongly in the build-up to Christmas 1987, with Paul appearing on British chat shows to promote it. It was on occasions like this that the Wings Fun Club and *Club Sandwich* magazine came into their own, Paul's fan club secretary mobilising members to pack TV show audiences just as Brian Epstein used to do. As a result, Paul got a rousing reception when he walked out on stage at the *Wogan* show, the *Roxy*, and Jonathan Ross's

Last Resort, three programmes he graced that winter. With typical professionalism, McCartney invited the *Last Resort* house band down to Sussex to rehearse with him in advance of the Ross show, giving the boys a guided tour of his Beatles museum. Band leader Steve Nieve introduced Paul briefly to his wife Muriel. The couple were impressed a few years later when they ran into Paul again and he immediately greeted Muriel by name, demonstrating a phenomenal memory. 'I've seen him do this many times,' says Nieve. 'He has this ability to put people so at ease around him – remarkable how he keeps names and faces.'

Going round the TV studios helped *All the Best* turn double platinum, a success tempered by the death in December of Paul's beloved Aunt Ginny. She died of heart failure at 77. Ginny had been among the last of Jim McCartney's siblings. Only brother Joe and his wife Joan were left now from that generation, enjoying a comfortable old age thanks to the McCartney Pension. 'Paul was looking after everybody, he always has done. But always very quiet, you see. That's why I get bloody mad when I hear people say, "Er, he's got all that money, you'd think he'd do so and so,"' says family member Mike Robbins. 'He's been giving money to charity quietly, and looking after people quietly, for many, many years.' Several relatives had received substantial cash amounts, with Paul helping relations buy homes, but the more he gave the more some of them wanted. 'They did used to moan at Christmas,' reveals Paul's record plugger and MPL gofer Joe Reddington. '[They'd] phone Alan Crowder up, "What's the present this year? Oh Christ, haven't you got anything better?" … Just unbelievable, these people.'

While he might write five-figure cheques for relations, and he had given Linda some high-price jewellery over the years, Paul usually bought inexpensive gifts for the family at Christmas, typically popping into Hamley's on Regent Street – a short walk from his office – to get the kids the colouring pencils they liked. Recalls Joe Reddington:

> I remember one year we are standing in the queue [at Hamley's] and I'm standing behind Paul, and this guy behind me, he was an American, he said, 'Excuse me, who's that in front of you? That's not Paul McCartney, is it?' 'I don't know actually,' and then Paul turned round and said, 'Yes it is,' and he signed all this stuff this guy was getting for his kids to take back to America.

NEW BEGINNINGS

After the twin flops of *Give My Regards to Broad Street* and *Press to Play* Paul needed what was in effect a comeback record to remain an active headline star into the 1990s. He wasn't prepared to step off the merry-go-round as John Lennon had done. To help Paul achieve his ambitions, MPL got the star together with Elvis Costello, a talented singer-songwriter with whom Paul could write, sing and record, also a young man – Elvis turned 33 in 1988 – of strong character whom everybody hoped would be able to stand up to Paul in the studio, pushing him to do better than his usual 'I love you Linda' material.

Costello found McCartney a disciplined, regimented writer. Elvis tended to write his lyrics first, then make the music fit.

> If the words demanded it, I wouldn't develop the melodic line, I'd just add a couple of bars. He [Paul] thought that sounded messy. He likes logic in the lyrics, too. I might throw in ambiguous things, because I like the effect that has on the imagination. But he doesn't like anyone to walk into the song with green shoes on, unless they were wearing them in the first verse.

To record these new songs, the basis of the album *Flowers in the Dirt*, Paul assembled a band around the Scots guitarist Hamish Stuart, 38-year-old founder of the Average White Band, whose life was changed by hearing the Beatles' 'From Me to You' as a boy. 'It was the moment for me when things went from black and white to colour. It's amazing the number of people who describe it that way.'

Although the original idea was that Elvis Costello would co-write and co-produce *Flowers in the Dirt*, the old problems soon re-emerged. Paul wanted to do things his way, and Elvis was pulling in a different direction. 'It was pretty obvious pretty quickly that it wasn't going to work as a co-production, so things changed and it moved on and some stuff got discarded,' comments Hamish Stuart. 'They were kind of banging heads a little bit. Elvis had one way of working, and Paul was more about embracing technology at that time and it just didn't work, so Elvis kind of left the building.' The Costello sessions yielded several album tracks, though, including the poppy 'My Brave Face' and 'You Want Her Too', sung as a duet in the way Paul harmonised with John on 'Getting

Better', McCartney's sweet voice undercut by Costello's caustic interjections.

The drummer in Paul's new band was Chris Whitten, who'd also worked on the *CHOBA B CCCP* sessions. Enlarging the group, Paul hired guitarist Robbie McIntosh from the Pretenders. These three musicians helped Paul complete *Flowers in the Dirt* and formed the basis of his new road band, adding 32-year-old keyboard player Paul 'Wix' Wickens, whom Paul and Linda were encouraged to learn was 'almost a veggie'. Increasingly, the McCartneys had little time for anybody who wasn't vegetarian. Paul was paying good wages, the new band members getting £1,000 a week as a retainer ($1,530), £3,000 a week ($4,590) for when they were rehearsing and recording, rising to £5,000 a week ($7,650) on the road, generous by industry standards. Paul had learned the lesson of Wings. He made it clear that he'd been hurt by the stories Denny Laine sold to the *Sun* after the old band broke up, and wouldn't appreciate it if anybody in the new group did anything like that.

Meanwhile, Paul's other, more famous former band was about to be inducted into the Rock 'n' Roll Hall of Fame, an institution co-founded in 1983 by *Rolling Stone* publisher Jann Wenner that had already gained prestige in the music community. Stars were falling over themselves to be inducted into the Hall of Fame at the annual ceremony in New York, and it was expected that Paul would join George, Ringo and Yoko at the Waldorf-Astoria Hotel on 20 January 1988, when the Beatles' fellow inductees would include the Beach Boys and Bob Dylan, who counted among Paul's musical heroes. But Paul didn't show. He boycotted the event because George, Ritchie and Yoko were suing him over a deal the Eastmans had struck when he signed back with Capitol Records after a brief spell with CBS, winning him an extra per cent royalty on the Beatles' back catalogue. When the other three found out Paul was getting more than them they demanded parity, the dispute settled when Capitol gave all four partners an extra per cent on CDs, which were replacing vinyl. As of January 1988, however, the Beatles partners were in deadlock over the issue.

Paul had his publicist release a statement explaining his absence from the Hall of Fame function: 'After 20 years, the Beatles still have some business differences which I had hoped would have been settled by now. Unfortunately, they haven't been, so I would feel like a complete hypocrite waving and smiling with them at a fake reunion.' After Mick

Jagger introduced the Beatles at the Waldorf-Astoria, it fell to George Harrison to say how honoured the band felt to be inducted into the Hall of Fame, joking, 'I don't have too much to say because I'm the quiet Beatle.' Then it was Yoko's turn to speak.

Despite not attending the dinner, Paul and Linda had a keen interest in events in New York and early the next day Linda called her friend Danny Fields at his Manhattan apartment to ask what had happened. Danny, who'd helped discover Iggy Pop and managed the Ramones during his career, aside from his work as a journalist, had a seat on the Rock 'n' Roll Hall of Fame nominating committee. 'Did you go last night?' Linda asked her friend, calling from her country kitchen at Blossom Farm.

'Yeah. You would have had such a good time,' Danny drawled in his camp manner, 'you would have heard Yoko's speech.'

Knowing the McCartneys would want to hear what Yoko said, Danny had recorded her speech, and he had his tape machine cued up in anticipation of Linda's call. He asked coolly whether she and Paul would care to listen to what Yoko said, and heard Linda telling Paul to pick up the extension. 'He picks up the phone and I press the tape.' All three listened as Yoko told the Waldorf that if *her* husband had been alive, he would have attended the induction, which was as neat a put-down of the McCartneys as she'd ever made. Danny listened for a reaction. 'Paul said, "Fucking cunt, makes me want to puke."'

Paul continued working on *Flowers in the Dirt* at Hog Hill Mill throughout that summer, taking a break in August to visit Liverpool, where he was shocked to discover his old school had fallen into dereliction. Despite its long and illustrious history, the Liverpool Institute had been closed in 1985 by Liverpool City Council, when the council was under the sway of the militant socialist Derek Hatton, who was himself an old boy. The closure was not so much to do with Hatton's socialist principles as with Liverpool's declining population. Apparently there weren't enough clever boys in the shrinking city to fill such an elite school. Four years on from its closure, Paul was dismayed to see that the Inny had become a ruin. The roof was letting in so much rain the classrooms were flooded and rats scurried along corridors that had once resounded to cries of 'Walk, don't run!' Paul had a film made of himself on a nostalgic tour of this sad old place, later released as the documentary *Echoes*, during which he remembered himself and cheeky school mates and eccentric masters in happier times. Privately, he ruminated on how he might rescue the school.

Since the Toxteth riots, Paul had been looking for a way to give something back to Liverpool. Following his visit to the Inny he decided the school should be the focus for his philanthropy. But what was one to do with the place? Initially, McCartney thought he might simply put a new roof on the Institute, to save it from total ruin, but as he looked into the problem more deeply he saw that the only way to save the building in the longer term was to give it a use and, because of its history, that had to be an educational one.

George Martin, one of the few people in whom Paul placed unswerving trust, mentioned that he'd been helping an entrepreneur named Mark Featherstone-Witty raise money for a school for performing arts in London, based on the New York School of the Performing Arts depicted in the movie *Fame*. A *Fame* school for Liverpool might be a use for the Inny. Paul was circumspect. Traditionally, show business is an industry where people learn by experience. He hadn't gone to a school for performing arts. The idea was anathema, rock 'n' roll being about self-expression and rebellion. George Martin, a graduate of the Guildhall School of Music, took a different view. He believed there was a place for a formal musical education, and a need to teach young people the essentials of the music business – if future Lennons and McCartneys weren't to be ripped off, as Paul felt he'd been with Northern Songs. Sensible George went some way to persuade Paul that a *Fame*-type school for Liverpool was therefore a worthwhile project. McCartney's primary motivation remained saving the Inny, though, and, canny as ever with money, he didn't propose to buy the place. The hope was that Liverpool City Council, and the charitable trust in which the building was held, would give the premises to Paul if he devised a regeneration plan.

In April 1989, Paul wrote an open letter to the *Liverpool Echo* asking his fellow Merseysiders if they wanted a *Fame* school: 'I got a great start in life courtesy of Liverpool Institute and would love to see other local people being given the same chance.' Readers phoned in 1,745 votes in favour, 48 against. The following month, Paul invited George Martin's friend to MPL to talk about beginning the process.

Mark Featherstone-Witty proved to be an ebullient, jokey fellow of 42, with a theatrical and slightly posh manner (Paul worried that his double-barrelled name would raise hackles on Merseyside) and a varied CV ranging from acting to journalism to teaching, the last of which led him to create a number of private educational institutions. 'Then the key moment occurred, *the key moment*, whereas I was sitting in the Empire Leicester Square and saw Alan Parker's film *Fame*, and I thought, "That's what I'm going to do next."' In emulation of what he had seen at the pictures that day in 1980, Featherstone-Witty worked to create the British Record Industry Trust (BRIT) School in Croydon, which was established with the help of George Martin and others. Now he wanted a new project.

Although Mark had met many famous people working on the BRIT School, when Paul walked through the door at MPL the entrepreneur was overwhelmed.

> You are trying to carry on a reasonable conversation, but one half of your mind is saying, *I don't bloody believe it. I just don't believe it. I'm actually talking to Paul McCartney!* Over years of course that's completely gone, but at the time I was just amazed … I've seen the same reaction with other people.

Despite Mark's being star-struck, the meeting went well. It was agreed that the entrepreneur would approach Liverpool City Council with Paul's backing to see if it was feasible to turn the Inny into what Paul wanted to call the Liverpool Institute for Performing Arts (LIPA). To show he was serious, Paul pledged £1 million ($1.53m) of his own money, but, shrewd as ever, he didn't hand it over all at once. He advanced Featherstone-Witty small sums initially. 'It was £30,000 [$45,900]. *Let's see what you can do with it.* So it was to some extent payment by achievement really. Also the payment needed to be matched with a payment, not simply from him, but from other people. He was never going to be the sole funder.' Still, having started the process, Paul committed himself to a project that would take up a lot of his time, and require much more of his money, over the next few years, while Mark discovered that the charming superstar he met on day one could also be 'a right bastard'.

BACK ON THE ROAD

The first single from *Flowers in the Dirt* was released in May 1989, the catchy but unfulfilling 'My Brave Face'. Though it wasn't a hit, the LP was greeted as a return to form featuring several strong songs such as 'Rough Ride' and 'We Got Married', which seemed to document Paul's early relationship with Linda, *vis-à-vis* John and Yoko, 'the other team'. The LP went to number one in the UK, with Paul appearing on TV shows to promote it prior to his first tour since 1979.

Ticket prices were to be modest. Paul was less interested in enlarging his fortune than in playing to as many people as possible, partly because he and Lin wanted to use the concerts to proselytise vegetarianism and ecology. The tour schedule was arranged to coincide with the publication of Linda's new vegetarian cookbook, with the 81-strong tour party served a meat-free diet backstage. Remarkably, audiences front of house wouldn't be able to buy meaty snacks, not even hot dogs at Madison Square Garden. MPL banned such concessions, licensing instead the sale of veggie burgers. To accompany the tour, MPL commissioned a 100-page programme that included information about acid rain and deforestation, and exhortations to turn veggie. Unusually, the programme was given away free.

Alongside didactic articles about vegetarianism in the tour programme, Paul took the opportunity to tell his audiences his life story. A series of long interview features saw him correcting what he viewed as misinterpretations about the Beatles' history. He made the point strongly that *he*, rather than John, was the Beatle most into the avant-garde in the Sixties. Paul was checking out the new music and meeting new writers along with his friend Barry Miles, 'when [John] was living out in the suburbs by the golf club with Cynthia'. This was a foretaste of an authorised, putting-the-record straight biography Paul had started work on with Miles, who'd become a biographer of distinction in recent years, writing lives of his friend Allen Ginsberg and other counter-culture figures. Miles had come up with the idea of the book, *Paul McCartney: Many Years from Now*, agreeing to let Paul vet the manuscript and, perhaps surprisingly, retain 75 per cent of the royalties, meaning it was really going to be Paul's book.

Other old friends found themselves back in Paul's orbit as the world tour kicked off. Richard Lester had been hired to make a montage film introduction to the concerts, and to direct a full-length concert feature, the pedestrian *Get Back*. Linda's artist friend Brian Clarke was commissioned to create the stage set, as he had the *Flowers in the Dirt* album cover. To publicise the tour, Paul hired a significant new associate, a likeable former tabloid newspaper journalist named Geoff Baker, whose qualifications for the job included boundless enthusiasm for Paul's music, as well as sharing Paul and Linda's fondness for dope and their zeal for vegetarianism.

Richard Ogden asked Paul what songs he was going to play on stage, urging him to perform his greatest hits, which meant Beatles songs as well as the likes of 'Live and Let Die'. Up until now, Paul had never performed more than a handful of Beatles' numbers in concert, but feeling the need to come back strongly after ten years away from the stage he drew up a set list that featured 14 Beatles tunes, approximately half the show. He had to learn to play many live for the first time, the Beatles never having performed them on stage, though paradoxically his sidemen had in other bands, Beatles songs having become common to all musicians. As Hamish Stuart observes, 'some of them we knew better than Paul did'.

After warm-up shows in London and New York, the tour opened in Oslo on 26 September 1989, the first of a run of European arena concerts, after which Paul took his band to North America, returning to England in January 1990 to play Birmingham and London. To interject a brief personal note, the first Paul McCartney show I ever saw was on this tour, at London's Wembley Arena in January 1990. McCartney's solo career had made little impression on me so far. What I'd heard on the radio of his work with Wings and afterwards seemed lightweight, and I didn't own any of his records. The Beatles were another matter. Although they were stars before I was born, the energy and creative brilliance of the band had captured my imagination, as with millions of others. The Beatles cross generations. I therefore attended my first McCartney show with mixed feelings, as I'm sure many others did during that tour. One was coming primarily because of the Beatles, rather than the music Paul had made since 1970, and hoping not to hear too much of the latter.

McCartney bounded on stage, chubby and grey at 47, but evidently eager to entertain us. His band seemed up for the challenge, too, though Linda appeared less engaged than Hamish, Robbie, Chris and

Wix, sitting awkwardly at her keyboard, a Union flag draped next to her, periodically making V-signs as if impersonating Winston Churchill. When the show opened with 'Figure of Eight', one's spirits sank. Were we to be subjected to a series of mediocre new songs? Thankfully, the friendly opening bars of 'Got to Get You into My Life' followed, the start of a sparkling stream of Beatles songs. To see and hear Paul McCartney perform these iconic songs was genuinely thrilling, and unlike his contemporary Bob Dylan who deliberately changes his songs live to keep the work fresh for himself and his audience, McCartney and his band were playing these classics like they sounded on the records, which is the way you want to hear them, at least the first time. 'You owe something to the music to present it in as authentic a way as possible,' comments Hamish Stuart. 'I remember "Can't Buy Me Love". Robbie basically played the solo note for note, because that's part of what was written.' Although London audiences have a reputation in the rock industry for being reserved and undemonstrative, compared to elsewhere in the UK, and abroad, people were weeping with emotion, couples were embracing. 'Sometimes it was hard to watch,' says Hamish. 'Look away or you get drawn in and forget what you're doing.'

To perform 'Fool on the Hill' Paul brought an artefact of swinging London on stage, the multi-coloured piano that Binder, Edwards and Vaughan had painted for him in 1966. Paul played this fabulous Joanna on a platform that elevated and rotated as he sang, causing him to rename the instrument his Magic Piano. The crowning moment of the show came, however, in the encore when McCartney picked out the plangent opening chords of 'Golden Slumbers' on a Roland keyboard, going on to perform the complete *Abbey Road* medley, the Beatles' final exaltation proving enduringly powerful:

And in the end
The love you take
Is equal to the love you make

This spine-tingling moment was the closest one could get in 1990 to experiencing the magic of the Beatles live, and it was perhaps better than seeing the boys in the Sixties, in that Paul was performing a complex album piece the Beatles never staged, with state-of-the-art sound equipment and amplification, so it sounded great. I walked away from the show a convert to Paul McCartney as a live performer, and urged everybody I met who hadn't seen McCartney in concert to do so.

Off stage, Paul and Linda were coping with a difficult family situation. As noted, Heather McCartney had long found the McCartney name a burden. If she was introduced simply as Heather, people showed little interest in her. 'Then somebody would say McCartney and really emphasise it and I'd just watch their face change.' For a fairly simple person who didn't have a strong idea of herself, or what she meant to do in life, this turned into an identity crisis, and in 1988 the 25-year-old admitted herself to a private clinic in Sussex.

After her treatment, Heather went to the United States to spend time with her natural father, Mel See, whom she called Papa, and his girlfriend Beverly Wilk, who lived with Mel in an adobe on the opposite side of Tucson to the McCartney ranch. Mel continued to pursue his interest in anthropology, and he and Beverly took Heather with them to Mexico to visit native Hoichol Indians, who made a big impression on the young woman. Heather admired the Indians' uncompromising way of life, living on the periphery of the modern world, and picked up design ideas for her new hobby of pottery. Back home in Rye, pottery was a long-established industry, with five potteries in the town at one time. Heather had gone to school with the son of one of the most eminent Rye potters, David Sharp, and worked for a time with another local potter.

During her visit to Arizona, Heather seemed a fragile, mixed-up girl to Mel and Beverly, who says: 'I think she just needed to get away and find herself.' Despite the effort Paul and Linda had put into parenting, and the public image they projected of a happy and successful family, it seemed Heather had been left emotionally scarred by her upbringing, first in an unhappy marriage, then with a stepfather who happened to be one of the most famous people in the world. 'I guess if you had a dad who let someone else adopt you [that would be an issue], and then being in a family where you're the odd girl out,' comments Beverly. As a self-made man, Paul was ambitious for his children to build careers of their own, but Heather was a dreamy type, not academically bright, a girl who was content to potter about at home with her roll-ups and pets. She also seemed scared of being identified as a McCartney by members of the public, travelling in America under a *nom de plume*. One day, when Beverly took Heather to the bank in Tucson, the young woman emerged in an unsettled state saying that she'd signed for her money in the wrong name. 'I don't think she sometimes knew who she was – I thought, *Wow, what a way of living!*'

Although she enjoyed visiting Arizona, Heather soon returned to the family estate in Sussex, which she considered her real home, and here her emotional problems returned. During the early part of Paul's world tour, the press reported that Heather had again been admitted to a clinic. 'I think she has identity problems. It's a lot of pressure on a child to have to live in the limelight all the time,' Mel told a journalist; 'she finds it difficult to be a member of such a famous family.' Fortunately, Paul and Linda had arranged the European stage of their tour in such a way that they flew home most nights, meaning they could see Heather almost daily. As Heather got better, her parents felt confident enough to continue the tour further afield.

Paul took his band back to North America in February 1990, after which they played Japan, almost exactly ten years after Paul had been deported from the country. Then it was back to the USA, where MPL had cut an advantageous sponsorship deal with Visa. This involved the credit card company paying MPL $8.5 million (£5.5m), which covered most of the tour expenses, further agreeing to run nationwide television ads featuring Paul. The ads used snatches of his Wings and solo career songs, urging Visa card members to use their card to buy tickets for his concerts. (MPL had tried to get permission from Apple to use Beatles songs in the ads, but Apple refused, meaning George, Ritchie and Yoko wanted to limit the extent to which Paul could benefit from Beatles material.) The TV ads caused Paul's ticket sales to rocket. From selling 20,000 tickets for an average city, there was demand for 100,000 tickets per stop, transforming an arena tour into a stadium tour, which Paul capped on 21 April 1990 by playing a record-breaking show before 184,000 people in Rio de Janeiro.

After South America, Paul returned to the UK to perform in Scotland and Liverpool, the latter show staged in the disused King's Dock as a fundraiser for LIPA. Backstage, Paul was reunited with several old boys from the Inny, including Ian James who'd helped teach him how to play guitar when they were teenagers. When Paul became a star, Ian didn't get in touch 'because I didn't feel it was right somehow, like taking advantage'. He hadn't seen his mate for 30-odd years when Paul and Linda walked into the marquee. 'It was like the King and Queen's arrived,' he recalls. Emphasising this quasi-regal feel, which became increasingly pronounced over the next few years, guests were invited up one at a time to be received by McCartney. Ian hung back, falling into conversation with Paul's brother Mike. Then Paul saw Ian and all formality was forgotten: 'as soon as he saw me he came over. We just hugged.' Three decades had passed, the schoolboys had become middle-aged men, but their friendship was somehow unchanged. 'So from that point onwards we've stayed in touch, and I've been to a few things like his office Christmas party … Linda would always invite the wife and me. She was a lovely woman.' It is worth emphasising again the paradox that almost everybody who knew Linda liked her, talking of a warm, unpretentious, friendly person, yet her public image was of a pushy opportunist who'd cheated Jane Asher out of her destiny. Part of the problem was that Linda didn't come across well with the press, journalists finding her gauche and abrasive. She appeared that way on stage, too.

Two weeks after Ian James met the McCartneys backstage at the King's Dock, Paul played a charity show at Knebworth, a country estate in Hertfordshire. The concert yielded a notorious tape of Linda singing backing vocals. As we have seen, it was never Linda's desire to perform live with Paul; she did so to please him. As she became older, she felt less inclined to leave her home – where she was happy with the children and her animals – to perform, and she had to be cajoled into going on the road in 1989–91. She was particularly reluctant this time because Paul would be performing Beatles songs, which Linda had no part in creating, as opposed to her role in Wings. Comments Hamish Stuart:

> I think she felt more at home back in the Wings incarnation because she was really a part of that thing. With this band it was a little broader in scope, because of the fact we were doing Beatles tunes and things like that and I think maybe she didn't feel quite as comfortable. But everybody tried to make her feel comfortable, and Wix was very good at finding good [keyboard] parts for her that fit with what everybody else was doing … Sometimes she had it tough on the road when she wanted to be home.

Inevitably, Linda was criticised for touring with Paul, and it seems she was not held in universally high regard backstage. When they played the Knebworth Festival on 30 June 1990, a technician isolated Linda's vocal and made a bootleg recording, *Linda McCartney Live at Knebworth*, that elicited hoots of laughter from almost everybody who heard it. Singing backing vocals to 'Hey Jude', Linda was heard droning the *na na na na-na-na nas* in the manner of somebody getting up in a pub on karaoke night. Band members defend Linda, saying anybody can sound rotten if you isolate them on stage, especially at an open-air gig like Knebworth, but the evidence is clear. Linda was a flat note in the band, slogging her way joylessly through these shows to keep Paul happy, and there was much more of this to come before she could go home to Sparky, Blankit and her other pets.

The success of the Visa ad campaign led to Paul returning to the US to play an additional series of stadium shows during the summer of 1990. The band rehearsed 'Birthday' from the *White Album* so that Paul could treat his Washington DC audience to the song on 4 July. The tour finally concluded in Chicago at the end of that month, by which time Paul had played to 2.8 million people in 13 countries – the longest and most successful tour of his career to date. By getting back to a Beatles-heavy set list he had recaptured the attention of a vast international audience, who remained bewitched by the fab four. It was a lesson he didn't forget, repeating the formula for every subsequent tour he undertook, gradually increasing the Beatles content until he became a veritable Beatles jukebox, which was great for audiences. The situation was now clear. With John Lennon dead, and Paul, George and Ringo locked in almost constant disagreements over money, the next best thing to experiencing the magic of the Beatles was to see Paul McCartney live. It has been true ever since.

MUSIC IS MUSIC

THE LIVERPOOL ORATORIO

Back in 1988, Carla Lane had persuaded the McCartneys to make a guest appearance in an episode of her television show, *Bread*. The storyline was that Linda was opening an animal rescue centre in Liverpool. During filming Paul and Lin met the actress Jean Boht, who played the matriarch Nellie Boswell in the series and was married in real life to the composer Carl Davis. When Carl, Carla and Jean subsequently collaborated on a short orchestral work, *The Pigeon's Progress*, staged at the Royal Liverpool Philharmonic Hall, Paul and Linda sent a telegram of support – 'Here's to you and all the pigeons in the world' – which caused Carl to think about writing music with Paul. During a visit to the McCartneys' farm in Sussex, the composer asked if Paul would like to collaborate on an orchestral piece for the Royal Liverpool Philharmonic, for whom he was guest conductor, and which was due to celebrate its 150th anniversary. The idea of creating music with a Liverpool theme appealed to Paul, who began telling Carl his life story, starting with how he'd been born in Liverpool during the Second World War. 'That's good!' remarked Davis brightly, seeing the beginning of an oratorio – a word Paul wasn't familiar with.

'Is this a symphony we're writing?'

'No, that's slightly different.'

'Is is a concerto then?'

'No, it's not,' said Davis, explaining that an oratorio is a piece of music based on a religious story, sung by soloists and chorus; Elgar's *The Dream of Gerontius* for example. The outcome of Davis's and

McCartney's collaboration – the *Liverpool Oratorio* – was indeed to contain an element of pluralistic religiosity, but had much more to do with Paul's life.

The story starts with a character named Shanty, like Paul born in Liverpool during the last war, and having the same good fortune to attend the Liverpool Institute, which is evoked fondly in the second movement, with a reference to Paul's Spanish teacher Miss Inkley teaching the boys a rhyme about three rabbits. The story then veers off into a confusing section about Shanty meeting a ghost named Mary, who assumes corporeal form and becomes Shanty's wife in the fifth movement, their marriage reaching a crisis when Mary falls pregnant and Shanty takes to drink (wouldn't *you* if you married a ghost named after your mum!), their problems resolved in the final movement when husband and wife praise the overarching importance of family life. With a movement devoted to Shanty's father, and references to a kindly nurse, the oratorio gathered together the talismans of Paul's early life in a typically sentimental 90-minute work.

To take on such a project showed ambition, some might say hubris, on Paul's part, and was a surprising departure from rock. In his childhood, the McCartneys turned off the wireless when classical music came on the air. In the Sixties, Paul dipped into Berio and Stockhausen, as we have seen, becoming sufficiently enthused by their experimental compositions to create avant-garde music of his own. He also became friendly with Stockhausen and Tavener. He'd never shown much interest in mainstream 'classical' music, though. On the contrary, Paul and Linda walked out of a New York production of *La Bohème* when they were courting because they were bored. When the journalist Ray Connolly interviewed Wings at the time of *Back to the Egg*, he asked if anyone in the band liked classical music; Denny Laine nodded vigorously, which as Coleman noted 'contrasted strongly with Paul's bemused frown'. Yet an appreciation of classical music often develops with maturity – Paul chose Benjamin Britten's *Country Dances* as one of his records on the BBC radio show *Desert Island Discs* a couple of years later in 1982 – and there is no reason why an innately musical person shouldn't like, understand and indeed make orchestral music as well as pop, which is not necessarily a lesser form. Music is music, as Alban Berg observed, while another modernist composer, Gunther Schuller, called for a blending of traditional and pop, 'in a beautiful brotherhood/

sisterhood of musics that complement and fructify each other'. This is what Paul proceeded to do.

There was a problem, however. When Paul needed to create music for players who went by notes on a page, he had to employ an amanuensis to orchestrate his music. George Martin had filled that role in the Beatles and afterwards. It was George who scored 'Yesterday', *The Family Way* and the 'Eleanor Rigby' sequence in *Give My Regards to Broad Street*, among other pieces with Paul's name attached, raising the question of how much credit is actually due to McCartney on such projects. Modest man that he is, Martin has always been content to stand in the background. Carl Davis was a different personality. An American, born in New York in 1936, one like Linda who'd made his home in England, Carl had enjoyed a long and successful career, best known for his 1980 score for the revived silent movie *Napoleon*, and he was used to getting due credit. He assumed he would at least *share* co-credit with Paul on their oratorio, which he had suggested and would essentially write, because Paul couldn't. 'I naturally assumed it would be *The Liverpool Oratorio* by McCartney and Davis.' So Carl was 'very taken aback when he [Paul] said, quite emphatically, that he wanted it to be called *Paul McCartney's Liverpool Oratorio*'.

Work on the oratorio started around the time of Paul's 1989/90 world tour, after which the star had a live album to oversee, the serviceable *Tripping the Live Fantastic*, and other projects to attend to, including campaigning with Linda to save their local cottage hospital in Sussex. He also helped Lin launch a range of frozen veggie food; and sat for interviews with Barry Miles for their forthcoming book, *Paul McCartney: Many Years from Now*. In addition to these and other commitments, Paul found time to meet Carl Davis regularly, supplying him with the essential story of the oratorio, humming and playing tunes for it on the piano. It was Carl's task to transcribe these tunes, and do the detailed work of scoring the piece, Paul coming back with comments.

By January 1991, the composers had been working together in this way for two years, with the première of the oratorio scheduled for June. During final preparations, a documentary camera team followed Paul, the footage revealing tensions between McCartney and Davis, with Paul overruling his partner in a polite but firm way that must have been difficult for Davis to take, being so much more knowledgeable about the world that he, like Virgil with Dante, was leading Paul into. At the same time, Paul was capable of rolling out melodies on the piano that sounded so delightful Davis was scrabbling around for a pencil to note them down before Paul moved on to something else. Davis, who already had the look of a Mad Professor, appeared increasingly frazzled by the experience of working with a man who didn't technically know what he was doing, but knew exactly what he wanted, and wasn't to be brooked in argument. After all, Paul was paying for everything, giving him a crushing financial grip on proceedings. Paul's unassailable economic strength, by dint of which almost everybody working with him is in his pocket, becomes ever more pronounced as we move into the latter part of his career.

Even more than when he was a young man, the mature McCartney was also characterised by his habit of doing many things at once, which is why the MPL logo depicts a juggler. While working with Carl Davis on the oratorio, Paul was involved in various campaigns; working with Mark Featherstone-Witty on establishing LIPA; discussing animation projects – mostly films about little furry animals – with Geoff Dunbar; attending to Apple and MPL business; and working with his rock band on a new album in advance of another world tour. The band remained much as it was during the last tour, featuring Hamish Stuart, Robbie McIntosh and Wix Wickens, with a new (vegetarian) drummer named Blair Cunningham. One of the first projects they undertook together was the MTV show *Unplugged*.

. MTV had become a significant force in the entertainment industry in the past few years, with Paul embracing the concept of video films to promote his songs, often commissioning lavish productions, such as the 1983 video for his single 'Pipes of Peace', in which Paul played both a British and German soldier in the trenches of the First World War, the video shot to feature-film standard with 100 extras. Recently, MTV had pioneered a spin-off concert series, whereby rock acts who normally used amplified equipment played live in front of small audiences using only acoustic instruments. Previous MTV *Unplugged* guests hadn't adhered strictly to the format, using electric pick-ups, even some fully amplified instruments. 'Paul decided this was cheating and [we] would do it absolutely straight, which was technically very challenging,' says Robbie McIntosh; 'there were no pick-ups, everything was done on microphone.' Hamish Stuart recalls: 'I had an acoustic bass. I had to be very static – if you move *that* much away from the [mike] the bottom would drop out of the band.' Paul rehearsed with his band for three weeks in advance of the recording in London on 25 January 1991, and the show turned out to be one of the most enjoyable he'd played in a long time. McCartney helped make it special by choosing to début the very first song he wrote, 'I Lost My Little Girl', all one minute thirteen seconds of it. Rock 'n' roll favourites and selections from his solo career and the Beatles also featured. By dint of being forced to put over old songs in a new format, the likes of 'And I Love Her' were rejuvenated. Paul was so pleased with the result that he asked for a recording of the event to be put out as an *Unplugged* album, the first of what became a very successful series of such records, with contemporaries including Eric Clapton and Bob Dylan following. So successful was the MTV experience that Paul took his band out on the road that summer to play a series of small gigs, in such out of the way places as St Austell in Cornwall, which included an 'unplugged', that is to say acoustic, set.

Linda continued to play with the band, though she was very much in the background during *Unplugged*, where mistakes would have been glaringly obvious. With the kids growing up (the youngest, James, was now 13), Linda's energies outside the home were concentrated on her relentless 'go veggie' crusade, which had taken on a surprising commercial dimension. On the back of the success of *Linda McCartney's Home Cooking*, reportedly the best-selling veggie cookbook ever, Linda had, as touched upon, linked up with Ross Young, a division of United Biscuits, to market a line of Linda McCartney frozen dinners, which she launched at the Savoy Hotel in April 1991. Consequently, Linda spent a great deal of time in her kitchen creating and testing new veggie recipes, giving samples of her meals to friends, family and neighbours to gain their reaction and, hopefully, convert them to a non-meat diet. Reactions were muted. On a trip to Kintyre, Linda gave the McCartneys' vet, Alastair Cousin, samples of her veggie sausages. 'I didn't like them at all to be honest, but I didn't say as much.' Mike Robbins recalls an evening when Paul and Lin visited him and his wife Bett on the Wirral, then walked down the lane with them to visit Joe and Joan McCartney.

[Paul] linked arms with [Bett] in the dark walking down the pavement, down the village, and I walked behind with Linda and she said, because she was always plugging, 'When you going to go veggie,

Mike?' I said, 'Oh, I've never tried it. I'm always open to [the idea].' 'Oh you've gotta try veggie.' A week went by, a bloody big van arrived at the front door with a box *that* big. It was all her products that she did, Linda McCartney products, *every* one, and we lived off it for about a week. As [Bett] said, 'It's all very nice but you're still bloody hungry after veggie food.' ... So we ate it all and never went veggie, couldn't be bothered.

Despite apathy from friends and family, Linda's veggie food proved surprisingly successful with the British public, becoming a multi-million-pound business that made a rich woman even wealthier over the next few years. There were hiccups, notably when traces of meat were discovered in her pies in 1992, apparently an act of sabotage, while Ross Young found that Linda could be a demanding business partner. One day when Carla Lane was visiting Blossom Farm, she mentioned to Linda that a friend of hers had tried the veggie sausages and found them 'a bit greasy'. Linda picked up the phone immediately.

She said, 'Hi, is that Richard? OK. I want the sausages *off*.' And he must have said, 'What?' 'Yeah, OFF – O, double F!' Then he must have said 'Why?' 'Never mind why.' Then a pause. 'No, now. Not tomorrow. Now. Off the shelves. OK? I'll be back with you. OK. Bye.' And that was it. That's how fast she moved when there was anything she was keen about. Off they came and they came back with less grease, apparently. It's amazing how she did it [laughs] – she gave that man the Devil.

It was a different woman who sat in Liverpool's Anglican Cathedral listening to a rehearsal of Paul's oratorio in the spring of 1991, tears coursing down her handsome face as she allowed herself to be swept up in the music, causing daughter Mary (now an attractive young woman of 21, working for Dad at MPL) to look at Mum in surprise. Linda shrugged unapologetically.

The family were attending a full-scale run-through of Paul's *Liverpool Oratorio* three months in advance of its première, Paul having decreed that he had to hear a performance because he couldn't get the music from the score. This way he could change anything he didn't like. Aunt Joan was one of the Liverpool 'relies' invited to the demo. 'Who would ever have thought it would come to this? A McCartney in the cathedral!' she was heard to exclaim approvingly, looking around at the great building. Paul beamed back. Having achieved so much, he still felt the need to prove himself in front of his family. He was clever. He *was* talented. Look, he'd even written a *noratorio*, as he deliberately mispronounced the word in a self-mocking reference to his initial ignorance.

The première itself was held on a soft summer evening in late June, not at the Philharmonic Hall, though the Phil commissioned the work, but again in Sir Giles Gilbert Scott's Anglican Cathedral. Since its completion in 1978, the cathedral had become the dominant landmark on Merseyside, the grandest possible local venue for the première of Paul's work, which was performed by the Royal Philharmonic Orchestra and Choir, conducted by Carl Davis, the featured soloists including two of the most famous singers in the classical world: soprano Dame Kiri Te Kanawa and bass Willard White.

Beforehand, Paul found time to meet Michael Portillo MP, minister with responsibility for Merseyside in John Major's Conservative Government, showing the minister around the Liverpool Institute. LIPA needed public sector backing, so it was important that politicians were onside. Paul showed the minister the class where Fanny Inkley had tried to teach him Spanish, reciting her rhyme about the 'tres conejos [three rabbits]', which caused Portillo to reply in fluent Spanish, evidently enjoying Paul's company. Few were immune from the charms of a Beatle, from being *Beatled* as it were, especially those now in middle life who'd grown up with the fab four. Paul's ability to attract and win over influential figures in this way helped LIPA considerably. Several other eminent people had been lured to Liverpool for the première of the oratorio, including Labour Party leader Neil Kinnock, and Paul didn't waste the opportunity to promote his vision for LIPA with one and all.

Paul sat behind his celebrity guests for the actual performance, flanked by Linda and the kids. George Martin and Paul's faithful roadie John Hammel sat nearby, John keeping an eye open for anybody making an uninvited approach to the boss. The first impression of the piece itself – which opens with ethereal strings and percussion – was that, despite Paul's interest in the avant-garde, his *Liverpool Oratorio* was a traditional work, conventionally arranged and performed by orchestra, choir and soloists. As the story developed, one heard echoes of Edward Elgar as well as the Beatles. The music was varied, the playing and singing excellent, the second ('School') movement bright and engaging, with the same natural use of Liverpool vernacular language that characterised the Beatles' lyrics: 'The most important thing I found was/sagging off!' There was humour here, and pathos, with a demanding violin part for Malcolm Stewart in the sixth movement, after which the 'Crisis' section seemed attenuated and melodramatic; then a big, warm-hearted ending, the ultimate message of which was:

> ... people still want a family life,
> Nothing replaces the love and affection.

Hurrah! Applause. Paul bounded onto the rostrum to hug Carl Davis, congratulate the singers, and accept the acclaim of his audience, as he would at a rock concert. The oratorio was a success. Like 'Penny Lane' and 'Eleanor Rigby', two of his best songs, the work was rooted in the place Paul knew and loved, with a concomitant authenticity in music and libretto, though it was hard to know how much credit was due to Carl Davis, how much to Paul himself. Paul had foreseen that critics would mock him for his classical pretensions, but the reviews weren't at all bad. 'The orchestral writing is too much like background music,' wrote Michael John White in the *Independent on Sunday*, noting that the pace was slow and the texture thin. Yet White enjoyed the 'honest innocence' of the oratorio. Plans were made for further performances, in London and elsewhere, with a CD release on EMI Classics, by dint of which Paul crossed the Rubicon from pop to the classical division of the old firm, the management of which commissioned him to write a new orchestral piece for its 1997 centenary. Classical music would be part of Paul's music-making for years to come.

TRYING TO GET OFF THE GROUND

Shortly after the *Liverpool Oratorio* première, Lee Eastman died of a stroke in New York aged 81. Eastman had enriched himself and his English son-in-law greatly during the past 21 years, not least by establishing the highly successful music-publishing side of MPL. The company now owned no fewer than 25,000 original compositions, songs as diverse and famous as 'Unchained Melody', 'The Christmas Song',

'Your Feet's Too Big' and 'The Ugly Duckling', in addition to the Buddy Holly catalogue and a portfolio of hit musicals including *Grease*, which alone made McCartney millions when it became a movie in 1978. Over the years, Paul had developed a high regard for his father-in-law's acumen, marking his debt by giving the old man a Rolls Royce on one occasion, which was just about the most extravagant present Paul ever gave anyone.

Paul and Linda came to New York for the funeral, staying in Long Island into August when the area was hit by Hurricane Bob. (During the ensuing power cut Paul composed the song 'Calico Skies', which was put to one side for several years.) There were financial ramifications for Linda now her father had died. Lee had been an extremely rich man, his wealth mostly in publishing rights and art. Philip Sprayregen estimates the value of his stepfather's estate in the hundreds of millions. So long as Lee's widow survived him, most of this wealth was held in trust for Lee's children and grandchildren, Linda standing to inherit her share as and when Monique Eastman predeceased her. In the meantime, John Eastman was a trustee of the estate, also taking over control of Eastman & Eastman, from the Manhattan office of which he continued to advise Paul. The men were close. Apart from being brothers-in-law, they had worked together since Apple days, and spent their summer holidays together, watching their children grow up. Paul's partner in LIPA, Mark Featherstone-Witty, remarks that he found out early on in his dealings with Paul that, along with George Martin, John Eastman was 'one of the relatively few people Paul wholly respected and would listen to'. Unfortunately, Mark's own relationship with Paul was not nearly so good.

As we have seen, Paul promised £1 million to LIPA ($1.53m), but more than ten times that amount was needed to complete the project, and finding the money proved difficult, with Paul quickly becoming impatient. That November, Richard Ogden urged Mark to give Paul some good news soon. Under pressure, Featherstone-Witty sent out over 600 letters in Paul's name asking the great and the good for donations, including, at Paul's suggestion, Her Majesty the Queen. 'It was like one of those wonderful English exercises, because I used to be an English teacher, *Write in the style of* … I tried to write in the style of Paul McCartney to the Queen. What an exercise. It was for real, too.' Paul also wrote personally to select friends and public figures, including the Prince of Wales. As he noted in his letter to Charles, he felt some reluctance soliciting favours from well-known people, as he received such letters himself and knew how difficult they were to reply to. Also he didn't often have cause to write personally to people in the normal course of his career, so he was out of practice. Composing the letter made him feel like he was back at school. His two-page, handwritten missive did have something of the schoolboy about it – the tone familiar and jokey to start with, but also businesslike in the detail – signed with an elaborate autograph and a smiley face, as if His Royal Highness would appreciate a Beatle's signature. Or maybe not. The prince didn't return any money.

The Queen did send a personal donation, however, not a huge amount, but a gesture that encouraged others to follow her. Celebrities ranging from Chevy Chase to David Hockney also gave to LIPA. George and Olivia Harrison gave an undisclosed donation, via their charitable foundation, but Mark Featherstone-Witty had no direct contact with George who, despite being a Liverpool Institute old boy, showed precious little interest in LIPA. Meanwhile many ordinary people sent in money, including fans who paid to have their name inscribed on an auditorium chair. Paul agreed to attend three fundraising lunches in London and Brussels in 1992 to drum up more money, leading EMI to donate £100,000 ($153,000), the biggest cheque yet. At a fundraising lunch at the Groucho Club in London Paul found himself sitting opposite a familiar-looking gentleman who turned out to be Donald Warren-Knott, formerly British consul to Japan, now running an Anglo-Japanese foundation. They'd last seen each other through a glass screen in Kojimachi Police Station. It was one of those Dickensian recrossings of paths that happen so often in Paul's life. 'We both thought it rather [funny],' says Warren-Knott, regretting that his organisation wasn't able to make LIPA a grant. Indeed, at the end of this fundraising drive Mark Featherstone-Witty had only collected £500,000 ($765,000) in addition to Paul's £1 million pledge, which led to some awkward moments with his Lead Patron and staff.

One of the strangest of these incidents came at the end of 1992 when Mark Featherstone-Witty attended the MPL Christmas lunch. Mark took an accountant friend to the meal, a McCartney fan he'd known for years, which led to a strange and unpleasant row. By Mark's recollection, Paul's manager Richard Ogden summoned him into the MPL office the next day where he read him the riot act for bringing an unwelcome guest to Paul's party. 'What do you mean by bringing someone who was so obviously gay to Paul's Christmas party? Have you any idea about the responsibility you carry in this project?' he allegedly asked.

'What are you talking about?' replied Featherstone-Witty, explaining who his friend was.

'But he was gay, you stupid fucker!'

'No, he isn't.'

'You've got to be careful. You can't do anything that would embarrass Paul ...'

That Mark would be admonished for bringing a gay friend to Paul's party is extremely strange. Richard Ogden says Mark has the story wrong: he didn't berate him for bringing a 'gay' friend to the party, just for bringing somebody who hadn't been invited, and the conversation was not in his office, but at the party itself. He stoutly denies any homophobia on his or, for that matter, Paul's part. But Mark stands by his story. He says he has no idea what motivated the outburst. Maybe Richard was over-reaching himself in an attempt to protect his boss at a time when their own relationship was becoming rocky. Whatever the reason, it was disconcerting. 'I thought it was odd, but I never got to the bottom of it,' says the LIPA chief, adding that it would be surprising if Paul was homophobic, 'because he can't be completely blind to the fact that so many people around him were gay, and lesbian for that matter ...' Yet Linda's gay friend Danny Fields believes Paul *did* have such an antipathy, when he knew the star (though, as we have seen, Paul was good friends with the gay art dealer Robert Fraser for many years). 'One of the reasons Paul didn't like me, he didn't like gay. Didn't like gay near him,' states Fields. 'He knew that his wife would babble to the gay like a girlfriend and he didn't want her to have girlfriends. He didn't want her to have *any* friends, and they had no friends.'

Paul had started to think about doing something for Liverpool around the time he became 40. In the summer of '92, he turned 50, and LIPA still seemed far from being a reality. As his chief fundraiser continued to try and raise the money required, Paul returned to what he knew and liked best, making rock 'n' roll records. In advance of a new world tour, McCartney took his road band into Hog Hill Mill to make *Off the Ground*, a serviceable, tuneful, well-made CD that, like so many releases from the back end of Paul's career, made little impact on any but his diehard fans, of whom, luckily, there were still many. Paul's idea with *Off the Ground* was to make a band album, his first since *Back to the Egg*, recorded quickly with Hamish, Robbie, Wix, Blair and Linda, using a couple of songs left over from his collaboration with Elvis Costello, and getting Carl Davis to help with arrangements. The result is bland. 'I think *Flowers in the Dirt* [is] a better album,' opines Robbie McIntosh. '*Off the Ground* we recorded all in one place and it's kind of got a slightly monochromatic feel to it, everything sort of sounds the same, one track after another.' Yet the guitarist enjoyed working closely with Paul on the stand-out 'Hope of Deliverance', a call-and-response folk-style number that was released as a single in Britain and the US to little effect, but became a big hit in Germany, where Paul commands a considerable following. 'Biker like an Icon' benefited from an intriguing lyric, while the words of 'Looking for Changes' constitute an uncompromising attack on vivisectionists, the song sparked by a grotesque photograph of a cat with a scientific device implanted in its head. At a time when activists allied to the underground Animal Liberation Front were taking direct, sometimes violent action against British vivisectionists, Paul's song seemed to encourage retribution:

I saw a rabbit with its eyes full of tears
The lab that owned her had
Been doing it for years
Why don't we make them pay for every last eye ...

There was a political dimension to another song, released as a single with 'Hope of Deliverance'. The number 'Big Boys Bickering' admonished world leaders for *fucking up* the planet and became notable because the BBC and other broadcasters refused to play it on air because of the bad language. There was a sense that Paul was courting publicity in an increasingly desperate attempt to sell records in the numbers he once had. When *Off the Ground* was completed the star decided he wanted dance mixes of a couple of the songs for release as 12-inch vinyl singles, hoping to reach a younger audience this way. To undertake the work he hired Martin Glover, founder member of the band Killing Joke, who, despite being 31 years old, went by the name Youth. Youth quickly established a rapport with McCartney, the two musicians sharing a similar hippyish mindset and manner of speaking. Paul was of

course one of the original hippies. Youth was part of a second generation who found inspiration in the same values, his conversation refer-
encing bardic and pagan English traditions, talking about 'the wheel of
the year' and other such new age stuff that Paul empathised with.

> [So I] went down there [to Hog Hill Mill] and I started sampling ... I
> said, 'What would be great if you could just add a couple of other
> things to the loops I've taken off the multi-tracks and just take it a bit
> further,' and he was happy to do that. I got him jamming, got him on
> his guitar, and all these other [instruments]. He's got such a great
> collection.

One of the instruments Paul played on this very modern record was Bill
Black's double bass, a relic from the creation of rock 'n' roll.

Youth took the tapes to his home studio where he assembled alter-
nate versions of what he expected to be one final track. Then Paul came
over with the family to listen.

> He and Linda and some of the kids would come down and just sit in
> on the sessions until three or four, and got a real buzz out of some of
> the alternative mixes I was doing for the ambient ones and really,
> really loved it, and then he came back and he said, 'I want to put *all*
> these mixes out' [laughs]. I said, 'They're actually for editing into one
> mix.' 'No, no.' He's often like this [laughs]. So the first album was
> really all the different mixes from that one session.

By the 'first album' Youth means the collaborative CD *strawberries
oceans ships forest*. 'It's basically a magical reference in the English
folk tradition,' Youth says of the curious unpunctuated title, declining
to elucidate. Paul decided to put this enigmatic recording out under a
pseudonym, as he had with the Thrillington album in 1977. This time
he chose the moniker the Fireman, in honour of the fact that his father
had fire-watched in Liverpool during the Blitz. 'This was supposed to
be an antidote to him doing commercial releases or songs with record
company pressure,' comments Youth. 'It doesn't take a lot of imagination to imagine how much of a box being Paul McCartney could be,
and the idea of wanting to do things outside of that box, with no previous association, anonymously, can be very attractive.' There was no

reference to Youth in the plain packaging of the CD, no clue who had made the music apart from the fact the album was copyright Juggler Records, Inc., a subsidiary of MPL Communications. Paul's involvement became public only gradually. The album, comprising repetitive music without tunes or lyrics, the spacey voices fading in and out of an electronic sea of sound, was never going to command a big audience or make much money. 'It is a dance record, but it's also ambient, and it's a little esoteric [with elements of] electronica,' explains Youth. 'But it's also none of those things, cos it's stuff he's all played, and it's all originally recorded and that makes it different.'

While Youth continued to work on the Fireman album, Paul embarked on his New World Tour, so named because he was visiting Australia and New Zealand, places he'd missed in 1989–91, as well as playing shows in Europe and North America. Having learned how well a Beatles-loaded show went down with modern audiences, Paul drew up a set list that was 50 per cent Beatles material, a slightly different selection than last time, opening with the perky 'Drive My Car', which got the crowd on its feet, incorporating 'We Can Work It Out', 'Magical Mystery Tour', 'Paperback Writer' and 'Penny Lane' in the main set, along with songs from Wings and his solo career, including several selections from *Off the Ground*. As in 1989–91, playing Beatles songs with Paul on stage was a thrill for the band members who, in common with their audiences, had grown up with this music. 'In the '93 tour we did "Fixing a Hole" and that was always one of my favourite Beatles songs,' says Robbie McIntosh. 'Me and Hamish used to play the solo together to make it sound like the record, because it's doubled on the record.'

One element of the New World Tour was to raise funds for LIPA and, just when he was starting to feel under enormous pressure to find sponsors, Mark Featherstone-Witty got lucky with Grundig. The German electronics company offered LIPA £2 million over five years ($3.06m) for 'title sponsorship', which meant the Grundig name would have to be used over LIPA on its literature. Featherstone-Witty's excitement at the deal was quelled when Paul told him he didn't want to endorse Grundig. He'd always rejected offers to advertise products, personally or with his songs, thinking it cheap, which was why he was so angry that Michael Jackson had licensed Beatles songs to advertise cookies and sneakers in the United States. In particular, Paul disliked the idea that Grundig would have its name over the institute. 'I remem-ber him saying, "I'm not having that. I don't have my name on it, I don't see why their name should be on it. You've got to find another way, it's all too commercial."'

Although Paul didn't like endorsing products, it had become commonplace to have a corporate sponsor offset some of the costs of a rock tour, as Visa had in 1990. For this tour MPL had lined up a similar agreement with Volkswagen. It was all but signed when Linda scuppered this deal, too, saying the McCartneys couldn't associate themselves with the car industry for ecological reasons. This left Richard Ogden scratching around for an eleventh-hour replacement sponsor Linda would approve of. 'The story-boards had been done, everything had been done. You can imagine the cost,' recalls Featherstone-Witty, who benefited indirectly when MPL remembered that another German firm wanted to link its name with Paul's. 'Ah, Grundig! They seem all right, it's a tape recorder, no pollutants. Let's do Grundig! And all of a sudden Grundig were good news ...' With Grundig now able to associate its name directly with Paul, a deal was struck whereby the company paid MPL to be the tour sponsor, which he accepted as part of how a modern tour was organised, as well as giving a smaller donation to LIPA, without having its name too prominently on the institute, the agreement formalised backstage at the Frankfurt Festhalle on 23 February 1993. Mark signed with an executive from Grundig, then waited with him outside Paul's dressing room, shuffled fractionally closer to the presence by Paul's minders as show time approached. With moments remaining, Paul emerged, shook hands quickly with the man whose company was giving him so much cash, posed for a thumbs-up photo, and went on stage.

When Paul reached Australia, his tour changed from an arena to a stadium concert, with the visuals and effects correspondingly enlarged. This included the huge montage screens on which a disturbing animal rights film was shown to audiences before the gig; also the pyrotech-nics during 'Live and Let Die'. Not everything worked properly at first. Says Hamish Stuart:

The most difficult time, I think, was when we hit Australia, because we were up-scaling the production at that point and there were a lot of visuals that were a little out of sync at the beginning of that and

Paul got a little upset … But it all got sorted out. It was part of getting
it right. Musically, there [was] never a problem.

There were other irritants, though. Paul had agreed that a special LIPA
ticket could be sold at the concerts. Costing the equivalent of $1,000
US, this was a very expensive seat, and many fans who dug deep for the
money assumed that a backstage meeting with Paul was included.
Though this was never explicitly promised, McCartney did meet some
LIPA ticketholders in Australia. When LIPA tickets were subsequently
sold in the USA, promoters gave enquirers the impression they definitely would meet the star. When this didn't automatically happen, ticketholders became angry, infuriated when they saw Paul on television
meeting other, ordinary concert-goers as the whim took him. When
Paul looked out from the stage during his set, he routinely saw banners
declaring 'WE LOVE YOU PAUL' and so forth. Now there was a banner
complaining about a '$1,000 LIPA SCAM'. One American fan wrote to
Mark Featherstone-Witty in bitter complaint, explaining that she was
part of a hardcore group who had supported Paul throughout his
career, even when his records weren't first rate. 'Who do you think is
buying *Off the Ground*?' she asked pointedly, as if doing so was an act
of charity. 'It isn't selling, but everyone who had a LIPA ticket knew all
the words to all the songs.'

Even worse, not enough LIPA tickets were sold in America, part of a
wider problem of selling out the North American shows. Following the
tremendous success of the 1989–91 US tour, when Paul had been
backed by Visa's television campaign, the New World Tour had been
planned and budgeted on selling out the same vast venues, the likes of
the Houston Astrodome and Giants Stadium. But there was no national
TV campaign in 1993, and there were no takers for the last few blocks
of seats in towns like Boulder and Toronto. These empty seats often
meant the difference between profit and loss. While his motivation
wasn't purely financial, Paul didn't want to work for peanuts (as he
sang every night in 'Drive My Car'). He blamed Richard Ogden, and
Ogden resigned accordingly from MPL. Looking back on his six years
managing the star, Ogden concludes that Paul

wanted to be *successful*. He wanted to be the toppermost of the poppermost. The Beatles thing. He wanted to be number one. He never lost that desire. Lost maybe the understanding of how to get that sometimes, but was prepared to listen to someone who could tell him, 'Hey, let's do this!' 'Oh, that seems like a good idea, man, let's do that.' … I had a wonderful time managing him.

He also discovered that if you made a mistake with Paul you were up shit creek.

To balance the books, Paul extended the tour into the winter of 1993. 'Not that I need the money, but I still feel that if we bother to get out there then, like everyday working people, we'll see some sort of reward.' When Mark Featherstone-Witty came to visit Paul in Oslo in September, he found the musician in a lousy mood. Standing together at the backstage bar, Paul started berating the man from LIPA, demanding that he perform some Shakespeare on the spot to prove he'd been an actor as he claimed. 'Come on, man, you say you were an actor, do something now.' When Mark failed to rise to the challenge, Paul told him brusquely to go away. Mark was still with the tour the following week when Paul played Frankfurt again, just seven months after he'd last performed in the city, a testament to the size of his German fan base. Paul was still in a contrary mood, insisting that the Grundig sponsorship banners were hung in the Festhalle in such a way that he wouldn't see them from the stage, apparently never having reconciled himself to the sponsorship deal, and summoning Mark to his dressing room before the show to give him a lecture.

From the start, Paul's interest in the Liverpool Institute had been more to do with saving his old school than founding an educational establishment, with underlying doubts about the validity of teaching show business. On a recent trip to Liverpool Paul had met the band the Christians, a member of which asked McCartney why he was putting money into teaching middle-class kids what musicians from working-class backgrounds, like himself, had picked up by experience. Paul brooded on this conversation, venting his concerns in Frankfurt. 'He was very angry,' says Featherstone-Witty, who discovered that his Lead Patron was also contemptuous of some of the proposed LIPA courses, one of which, titled 'Image and Style', 'infuriated and worried him' because he thought it trivial. Unless

Mark did better, Paul warned he might withdraw his support altogether.

Mark stumbled from Paul's dressing room at the end of this harangue not knowing what to do. 'I was so shaken that, putting my hand out to steady myself on the wall outside the dressing room door, I mistakenly placed it on Mary McCartney ... who was standing outside waiting to go in,' he wrote in his memoir *Optimistic, Even Then*. To his horror, Mark realised that his hand was on Mary McCartney's breasts. 'Aghast at the ramifications, I sprang back, white with apology.'

So the tour rolled on, Paul releasing a spin-off live LP, *Paul is Live*, that seemed redundant only three years after *Tripping the Live Fantastic*. On this new live album, 'Let Me Roll It' held its own especially well beside the Beatles material, while Paul showed his sense of humour by including a sound-check version of 'I Wanna Be Your Man' sung in the style of Mick Jagger, whose career the song kick-started. The album got most attention for its cover, which saw Paul posing with one of his Old English sheepdogs on the Abbey Road crossing, the artwork and album title a riposte to the Sixties rumour that Paul was dead and a double had taken his place on the original *Abbey Road* sleeve.

That summer Paul's school friend Ivan Vaughan died of heart failure aged 51. Although the news was not unexpected, in that Ivy had suffered from Parkinson's disease for years, the death of a contemporary always comes as a shock. 'They had the same birthday. They'd known each other from school. They'd gone their different ways, but they had a lot of respect for each other,' says Ivy's widow Janet, who received a copy of a poem Paul wrote in response to his friend's death. In 'Ivan' Paul describes how two doors opened in Liverpool on 18 June 1942 when he and Ivy were born; how they went on to become mates, playing music together, Ivy being 'the ace on the bass'; before Ivan introduced him to a couple of other pals, a reference to the fact that Ivan had taken Paul along to the Woolton fête where John Lennon was playing with the Quarry Men. Now:

Cranlock naval
Cranlock pie
A tear is rolling
Down my eye
On the sixteenth of August

Nineteen ninety-three
One door closed
Bye-bye Ivy

The Cranlock rhyme is attractive and intriguing. 'It was like a sort of jingle that they often used to say when they were together,' explains Janet Vaughan. 'I mean, it's nonsense speak, but it's something that was very familiar to them … I recognised it immediately [in the poem] as a familiar thing that they said to each other … If they were having a conversation, occasionally they would say it, and then burst out laughing. Haha! … It's a lovely poem.' There is indeed a simple, charming warmth to 'Ivan', a fitting and evidently heartfelt lament for a long and largely private friendship that had continued in the background of Paul's public life.

Ivan's death was followed by a scare closer to home on 13 September 1993, Stella McCartney's 22nd birthday. Stella, studying in London for a career in fashion design, was home in Sussex with the family when the McCartneys received news that James, who'd celebrated his 16th birthday the previous day, had gone missing surfing off Camber Sands. A lifeboat was launched and an RAF helicopter sent up as Paul drove to the scene. 'It's a three-mile drive and all sorts of thoughts were going through my head,' Paul later said. Fortunately, James was found alive and well, though it wouldn't be the last time he frightened his parents.

In November Paul took his band to Japan, then South America, by which time everybody was road-weary. Playing with Paul had been a joy for his musicians, and the New World Tour had been brightened by the introduction of an acoustic set, yet the main show was the same every night, with Paul sticking to faithful recreations of the Beatles songs as heard on record. While this is initially thrilling, such rigid renditions become dull with repetition, for audience and band, pointing out the wisdom of Bob Dylan's policy of remaking his songs constantly, even if audiences complain that the songs don't sound like the records. Dylan says this doesn't matter. The recording is just how the song sounded that particular day. Good songs can stand being altered. This was not Paul's way. He presented his and the Beatles' greatest hits like museum pieces, even making the same comments from the stage, such as encouraging his audience to sing along to 'Hey Jude', which they did eagerly and loudly every single night, first the girls, then the boys, the left side of the stadium, then the right, harmonising on the *na na na na-na-na nas*, an apparently delighted Paul complimenting every-body for singing so sweetly as though he'd never had this reaction before. As Hamish says, 'When he knows that something works he sticks to it, which is true of [other artists]. It's mainly a different audi-ence every night, so I think you can get away with it.'

By the time they reached Santiago, Chile, for the final show, it was, in Hamish's words, 'a little tired'. They had played to 1.7 million people on five continents, with Paul transforming what looked like a loss-making tour into an earner. MPL turned over £14 million in the 12 months to December 1993 ($21.42m), squeezing a profit of £2.6 million on the year ($3.97m). Paul then said goodbye to his band, whom he'd been working with for almost six years, explaining that he was committed to a major new project that would keep him at home in 1994. 'I'm off to be a Beatle now,' he said.

A THREE-QUARTERS REUNION

THE ANTHOLOGY

For years the press had speculated about a Beatles reunion. The boys themselves said it would never happen, and indeed how could it with John dead? Yet the impossible now came to pass, in a partial sense at least, thanks to the band's old friend and servant, Neil 'Nell' Aspinall, who ran Apple on their behalf.

Since the Sixties, Nell had been collecting footage of the Beatles for a documentary film. He first edited the clips together after the band's break-up, creating a 16mm flick he called *The Long and Winding Road*. 'But then the Beatles' manager, Allen Klein, wanted to take it to America. He wanted his own in-house people to expand it into a social commentary of the Sixties. So I took it all to pieces again,' Aspinall recalled. 'I remember him coming into the editing suite in Savile Row and saying, "Where is it?" I pointed to the whole library, and said, "It's all those cans." Was he furious? Yeah.' After the Beatles parted company with Klein, Aspinall remade the film and sent copies to the individual band members for old time's sake. Nothing more was done on the project for two decades, during much of which the Beatles were arguing between themselves over money, most recently the extra one per cent royalty Paul was being paid by Capitol Records.

When all lawsuits were resolved, around 1990, Aspinall raised the idea of a definitive television history of the Beatles using the old footage he had collected. The unique selling point would be that the Beatles would tell their own story. 'I said to the guys, "Well, we're going to have to interview you,"' notes Aspinall. 'There were varying degrees of enthusiasm for that suggestion.' The three surviving Beatles were like brothers who have grown up and left home, still seeing their siblings occasionally, feeling affection for their brothers naturally, but quick to be irritated by them. Relations between Paul and George were particularly prickly, George being the least inclined to look back on 'the mania'. The excessive devotion of the fans in the Sixties had genuinely freaked him out, and he had never forgotten Paul's condescension towards him. Although the men still saw each other socially, George had a tendency to snipe at Macca in interviews, complaining about him to others, and ignoring Paul's calls and letters. Nevertheless, Harrison now had a compelling reason to work with Paul.

Although he'd made millions, George Harrison never earned as much from the Beatles as the two principal songwriters, and while his solo career got off to a promising start in 1970 with the acclaimed triple album *All Things Must Pass*, flop records followed, with George suffering the indignity of being sued successfully over his biggest solo hit, 'My Sweet Lord', which infringed the copyright of the Chiffons' 'He's So Fine'. The latter song belonged to Allen Klein, to whom Harrison had to pay a humiliating $587,000 compensation (£383,660). Harrison's one major tour, his 1974 jaunt across North America, had been a failure, after which he retreated behind the high walls of his Oxfordshire mansion, becoming a hermit gardener. In addition to the upkeep of Friar Park, George had expensive tastes for cocaine, motor racing and movie-making. In 1978, he bailed out his friends in the Monty Python troupe when EMI withdrew financial support from the heretical comedy *Monty Python's Life of Brian*. Harrison advanced the Pythons the money to make the picture, which proved a commercial and critical hit, encouraging George to invest in more movies via his company HandMade Films. He enjoyed further success with *The Long Good Friday* (1980) and *Withnail and I* (1986), but lost big money on *Water* (1984) and *Shanghai Surprise* (1986), with the result that HandMade Films was mired in debt by 1989, undermining George's financial security and leading to an expensive legal battle with his business advisor. A Japanese tour with Eric Clapton raised some needed cash, but George's best chance of a substantial pay day lay in the Beatles.

Ritchie could always do with a little extra. He'd earned far less in royalties than John, Paul and George, and had the least successful solo career, yet he pursued a relentlessly expensive jet-set life, moving so frequently even he found it difficult to keep track of his homes. Cautious, hard-working, consistently successful Paul was far richer than George and Ritchie combined, and those close to Paul talk of him agreeing to a three-quarters Beatles reunion partly to give the other two some of what he already had: 'serious money'. Despite being the Beatle who most needed the favour, George's old niggles about Paul resurfaced almost immediately. Harrison vetoed *The Long and Winding Road* as a title for the documentary project, because it was a Paul song, with the result that the reunion gained the unimaginative umbrella name of the *Anthology*.

After considering a range of directors for the documentary, the Beatles selected a big, bearded Geordie named Geoff Wonfor, who had worked with all three previously, most recently with Paul on a film of his *Liverpool Oratorio*. A production office was established, with the band's old PR man Derek Taylor (now white of hair and reedy of voice) brought in to advise the film-makers; another old friend, Klaus Voormann, was commissioned to create artwork for the packaging; while the musician and broadcaster Jools Holland was engaged to interview the Beatles. The interviews would also form the basis of an *Anthology* book. It was decided almost as an afterthought to compile a series of complementary CDs containing rare and unreleased Beatles recordings, out-takes, rehearsals, live performances and demos, starting with what George Harrison described as 'the most ancient Beatles music possible', which was the shellac disc Paul had recently bought back from John Duff Lowe. The ageing George Martin – now in his late 60s – would take charge of this aspect of the project, listening to the significant takes of every Beatles track recorded, 600 items in all, with Geoff Emerick at his side.

Work on the *Anthology* began in earnest in 1991, with Paul, George and Ritchie interviewed multiple times over the next few years, with the result that their appearance varies considerably during the series. Hair changes colour and length. Beards come and go. The men age before our eyes. Paul proved the most consistently entertaining interviewee, whether reminiscing at sound checks, in the studio, sitting at a camp fire on his Sussex estate or piloting his boat, the *Barnaby Rudge*, on the water near Rye. He enjoyed indulging in nostalgia, especially about the early days on Merseyside, and though he had told his stories until they were worn smooth as river pebbles, they were still good to hear. George was less inclined to look back and was more sardonic in his comments, but exhibited a wry sense of humour and had a knack for a good phrase, while Ringo unfortunately felt the need to hide behind dark glasses and suffered memory lapses. They all forgot things to a degree. Moreover, as Jools Holland questioned the men, it became apparent that each Beatle remembered their story differently, not necessarily because drugs had addled their minds, or they were dissembling, but in the same way that any group of people interviewed after an event will give contradictory accounts of what they did, said and heard.

Work on the *Anthology* reached a peak in 1994, which Paul began by inducting John Lennon into the Rock 'n' Roll Hall of Fame, making Lennon one of the first artists to be inducted as both a band member and a solo artist, which the McCartneys' friend and nominating committee member Danny Fields considered a mistake as it set a precedent for other multiple inductees.* Paul's induction speech was in the form of an open letter to his old pal: 'Dear John, I remember when we first met, in Woolton, at the village fête,' he began, telling the audience how John had made up words to 'Come Go with Me'. Later they sagged off school to write new songs together. George joined the band, they played the Cavern, went to Hamburg, and became stars in Britain and the USA, where they met Elvis, 'the first person I ever saw with a remote control on a TV. Boy!' Paul recalled the excitement of that LA visit. Then came drugs. 'I remember writing "A Day in the Life" with you, and the little look we gave each other as we wrote the line, "I'd love to turn you on."' John met Yoko, the Beatles went through 'all our business shit', eventually reaching a point, in the late 1970s, where 'we were actually getting back together and communicating once again ...' That gave Paul 'something to hold onto' when John was killed in 1980. 'So now, years later, here we are ... John Lennon, you've made it. Tonight you are in the Rock 'n' Roll Hall of Fame. God bless you.'

Yoko came on stage and Paul hugged her, as if they were great friends. Apart from honouring John, Paul may have had one or two other motives for helping his former partner into the Rock 'n' Roll Hall of Fame. Almost immediately the McCartneys got back to England, Danny Fields started receiving calls from Linda asking when Paul was going to

---

* Eric Clapton was eventually inducted three times: as a member of the Yardbirds, Cream and as a solo artist.

be brought into the Hall of Fame as a solo artist to gain parity with John. 'All the time she was saying, "What do you think Paul's chances are this year?" They were asking Jann Wenner the same thing.'

There was another reason for Paul doing John's memory a good service: he, long with George and Ritchie, wanted Yoko to give the Beatles some music. In working on the *Anthology*, the three surviving Beatles decided it might be fun to record some incidental music, but it didn't seem right without John. 'If we were to do something, the three of us, as interesting as it may be, and as nice as we could make it, to have John in it is the obvious thing,' George said. So Yoko was asked if she had any recordings of songs John had been working on which the other three could complete as a 'new' Beatles record. When they met in New York, she gave Paul a demo tape of 'Free as a Bird', an unfinished song from the late 1970s. The following month the surviving Beatles reunited discreetly at Hog Hill Mill to complete it. The men who met at Hog Hill almost a quarter of a century on from the break-up of the Beatles were naturally changed. George Harrison, the youngest, turned 51 during the reunion and looked the oldest of them all, having allowed himself to gain a few pounds in a life spent mostly away from the spotlight, and his hair having grown long and grey. Scruffily dressed, he looked like what he was these days: a gardener. Paul had also gone grey in the 1980s, but had cheated time by having the grey dyed out of his hair, with the result that four months before his 52nd birthday he possessed a thick mane of light brown locks. Still, the lines around his eyes gave his age away. At 53, Ritchie continued to hide behind dark glasses, longish hair and a beard, which he too must have had coloured, for he'd had a streak of white as wide as a skunk's when the Beatles met him, and yet there was no trace of it now. To help deal with the fact that they were making music without John, the trio told themselves that Lennon had already recorded his part of 'Free as a Bird' and then popped out of the studio. 'And once we had agreed to take that attitude it gave us a lot of freedom, because it meant that we didn't have any sacred view of John as a martyr, it was John the Beatle, John the crazy guy we remember,' Paul commented. 'So we could laugh and say, "Wouldn't you just know it? It's completely out of time!"'

Building the song up from John's scanty demo tape was a production challenge, not one that was overseen by George Martin, surprisingly, even though George was in overall charge of the *Anthology* CDs.

The Beatles turned instead to Jeff Lynne, Birmingham-born leader of the Electric Light Orchestra (ELO) who co-produced Harrison's 1987 album *Cloud Nine*, and its hit 'When We Was Fab', going on to join George in the *Traveling Wilburys*, whose records the musicians co-produced, achieving a smooth, commercial sound. 'I think George Harrison wanted Jeff Lynne to do it … because he had been working with Jeff in the Wilburys,' ventures Geoff Emerick. Martin insisted he was not unhappy about being passed over in this way, saying in polite explanation: 'I'm now quite old.'*

When Lynne had fixed the underlying tape, Paul and George added acoustic guitar to 'Free as a Bird', Paul doubling John's piano part and adding the bass, Ritchie playing drums, naturally, and George slide guitar. Paul risked another *Let It Be*-style row by saying he didn't want George's guitar to sound like 'My Sweet Lord'. It had to be Beatley, so Harrison was prevailed upon to play a simpler blues lick. In return, Paul allowed George to cut some of the words he had written to pad out the unfinished middle-eight. At times it all 'got a little difficult', as McCartney later conceded.

On a gorgeous summer's day two months later, Paul and Ritchie came to Friar Park to talk with George on camera about the old days, McCartney clearly being careful not to say anything that would upset his touchy friend. Footage was shot by George's lake and in his home studio, the boys trying to recreate the repartee of their early days, but appearing awkward in each other's company, and again forgetful. Stories were begun, then trailed off into silence. As with *Let It Be*, it was when the men started playing old tunes, like 'Raunchy' and 'Thinking of Linking', that they looked happiest, smiling at each other in enjoyment of their musical youth.

BACK AT THE FARM

Hardly a year had passed since Paul signed with EMI that he hadn't put out a record, with multiple releases some years. Now came a sabbatical. Following the release of *Paul is Live* and the first Fireman album in 1993, Paul didn't release a new record for three and a half years, partly

* Martin turned 68 in 1994.

to avoid competing with the *Anthology*. Yet once Paul had recorded 'Free as a Bird' and filmed his interviews for the documentary, there wasn't a great deal for him to do on the *Anthology* except wait and see what Geoff Wonfor and George Martin came up with. Along with the other Beatles, Paul viewed early cuts of the documentary programmes, sending the production office meticulous, typewritten notes of comments and changes. If any Beatle was unhappy with any detail, it was excised. There were inevitable clashes with the programme-makers, who found it virtually impossible to win an argument with a Beatle, and the Beatles themselves clearly still had unresolved issues. Recalls series director Bob Smeaton, who admits he found the project so frustrating at times he almost quit:

> Paul and George sat in the editing suite with Ringo looking at the last programme. George was on the screen, talking about the split, and Paul turned to George sitting next to him and said, 'I didn't know you felt like that. Is that really how you felt?' George said, 'Of course it was.'

Watching the *Anthology* footage proved emotional for Paul. 'I get to see my dad again. I get to see my mum again, I get to remember what she did again,' McCartney explained to readers of his fan magazine, *Club Sandwich*, still hyper-sensitive about anything to do with his parents. Listening to the tracks selected for the *Anthology* CDs also brought back memories, not always pleasant ones.

> In volume one there are a few songs that I would have preferred not being there, like 'Besame Mucho' which portrays me as a cabaret artist, whereas in my soul I am a rock and roller … But because the others wanted it in, because George Martin wanted it, I could put down my slight reservation and say, 'Cool. If you guys like it, then it's got to be alright.' And it's a very nice feeling to be on a team like that. The minute a thing is done and it's the Beatles, I'm happy with it.

With no touring commitments in 1994, and no new solo album to worry about, Paul used his free time to enjoy life with Linda at Blossom Farm, the couple celebrating their 25th wedding anniversary in March. He wrote some new songs and composed some more orchestral music, sat for interviews with Barry Miles for their forthcoming book, and did lots of painting, a hobby Paul had become increasingly passionate about, spending many afternoons in his Sussex studio and working on pictures when he was in the United States on holiday. During his annual summer break in the Hamptons, Paul took inspiration from visiting the elderly artist Willem De Kooning, a Long Island resident and fellow client of Eastman & Eastman. Fired up with enthusiasm after his meetings with 'Bill', Paul bought art materials from the same local store De Kooning used, then went home to paint. His pictures were often inspired by objects he picked up on the beach.

Stories about Paul's painting got into the press and in response he was contacted by a German curator, Wolfgang Suttner, who said he wanted to show Paul's pictures at the municipal gallery he ran in Siegen, the birthplace of Rubens. McCartney invited Suttner to Sussex to discuss the idea, meeting him in the estate house he used as his art studio. The German found room after room of the farmhouse filled with Paul's pictures, stacked up and hung on the walls. Paul explained that he'd always drawn and painted pictures, from when he was a boy, that he had won prizes for his artwork at school, but he suppressed this side of himself when he met John because John was the art student. After the Beatles broke up he had made one or two pictures. Paul showed Wolfgang a 1971 drawing, *Hooray for Stella*, which he made to celebrate the birth of his youngest daughter. He also revealed that he'd covered the kitchen door at High Park in Scotland with pictures. But it was only after John had died, and Paul himself had turned 40, that he began to explore this side of himself properly, painting large, colourful semi-abstract portraits and landscapes. Paul was wary of showing these in public in case he was mocked. To make him feel more relaxed about the idea of putting on a show, Suttner invented a fiction whereby Paul was a young artist named Paul Miller whom Suttner had discovered and was going to introduce to the German public via his provincial gallery. That way there was less pressure. McCartney fell in with the idea and began to talk with enthusiasm to Wolfy, as he addressed his new friend, about staging their exhibition, though, as with many of Paul's projects, there would be a time-lag before he got around to mounting the show.

Linda, who regularly staged exhibitions of her photographs these days, as well as publishing books of her pictures, was increasingly busy with her vegetarian food empire in 1994, opening a dedicated veggie factory in the UK, and going to the USA with Paul to try and sell veggie meals to Americans, who proved more resistant than British consumers.

Paul's parallel pet project continued to be the Liverpool Institute for Performing Arts, which was at last under construction, Mark Featherstone-Witty having lined up the necessary £12 million ($18.3m) funds. Roughly a third of the money was coming from the European Union, a third from the British public sector, the final third, including Paul's £1 million, from private donations. 'And then we discovered we got the figures wrong,' groans Mark. 'It was a very sticky moment.' The problem was that putting a new roof on the Inny proved more expensive than expected, prompting a lecture from Paul about financial prudence, not long after which Mark had another in a series of angry confrontations with his Lead Patron.

The conversation took place before a luncheon in London in October 1994. 'At some point I'd mentioned my mother was Jewish, probably to try and cement some sort of solidarity with Linda, mistakenly,' says Mark Featherstone-Witty, who says he then listened with bewilderment as Paul told him that his late father had once advised him that Jews made good businessmen, but he hadn't found it invariably true. 'He went on to note a line of Jews who had failed him in his business life, notably Brian Epstein and Allen Klein,' Mark recalled, 'and rounded the list off by saying, "And now I've got you." I wondered what had prompted this reflection and concluded that it was probably the overspend on the building, which was clearly worrying him more than I had anticipated.' Paul's comment was odd, especially so considering he'd married into a Jewish family and benefited from the Eastmans' advice all these years. His comments also seemed to echo the time Paul's manager had apparently harangued Mark for bringing a 'gay' friend to an MPL party.

Reflecting on the luncheon conversation about Jews, Mark says he hasn't 'got the foggiest' idea whether Paul is anti-Semitic, noting that it would be remarkable if he was. If one took Jews, and gays, out of show business the industry would be seriously depleted. Thinking over what Paul had said, Mark could only conclude that his Lead Patron was just looking for ways in which to vent his doubts about LIPA, and about Mark himself, while Mark had no choice other than to take the abuse. 'I'm always conscious you're not nasty to people who can't answer back [and] I couldn't risk him backing off from it. It was a sort of nightmare really if he did decide that [he wanted to pull out].' Mark got his own back in a small way when he published a little-read 2008 memoir, *Optimistic, Even Then*, in which he recapped these awkward moments with Paul and his staff. He sent Paul a copy. In reply, McCartney acknowledged that he could be 'a right bastard' sometimes, which Mark interprets as an apology. 'That doesn't stop him being a right bastard, of course.' Despite awkward moments like this, Paul continued to help Mark raise money for LIPA, bending his own rules to accept a £25,000 cheque ($38,250) from the Hard Rock Café, something he fretted about because the restaurant serves meat. Fortunately, veggie burgers were also on the menu. Paul agreed to receive the presentation cheque when the words 'in recognition of the sale of Linda McCartney's veggie burgers' were added.

Paul would have to re-open his own cheque book to make LIPA a reality. Although he was keen to raise as much money from others first, his underlying commitment to LIPA shows a generous side to his character that is often overlooked or underplayed by his critics. Paul is tight-fisted, they say. There are in fact numerous examples of the star being very generous, such as when a call came through to Hog Hill Mill in 1994 from Horst Fascher, the German pugilist the Beatles had knocked about with in Hamburg. In recent years Horst had taken up with a Hungarian girl, who had given birth to their daughter, Marie-Sophie, that February. German doctors warned Horst that Marie-Sophie would not live long because of a heart defect. Horst had already suffered the death of one child. 'So in my angst that I lose a second child I called Paul. I thought Paul has better doctors in England,' says Horst, who wept on the phone to one of Paul's assistants, saying he had to speak to the star. 'Then after 20 minutes he called me back. And he said, "What's happened?" I said, "Paul, can you help me?" He was saying, "Horst, whatever I can do for you, I do for you."' True to his word, Paul arranged to have the Faschers flown from Hamburg to London in January 1995, and accommodated in the capital while 11-month Marie-Sophie was admitted to Great Ormond Street Hospital. A team of American surgeons were then flown in to operate on the child. Despite the best treatment, she died 13 days later. 'Then it came to the payment. Paul said, "I take care of everything. You don't have to [worry],"' says Fascher. 'And he flew us back and all of that.' Horst believed the whole thing cost about $190,000. 'I said, "Paul, how can I pay you back?" He said, "Horst, forget it. Only don't tell anybody, because I don't want the big *Can you help us?*"'

This wasn't an isolated example of Paul's philanthropy. For some time Paul and Linda had backed a campaign to re-open their local NHS cottage hospital in Rye, which had closed in 1990 when a new district hospital opened in Hastings. Local people thought Hastings too far to travel and, after Paul and Linda had marched with their neighbours, and donated almost a million pounds to the cause, a new 19-bed cottage hospital and care centre was opened in Rye, with a 'Strawberry Fields' day room. In a quieter way, Paul and Lin helped out with many local charitable causes, in Sussex and Kintyre, earning respect and affection in the communities.

A year on from recording 'Free as a Bird', Paul invited George and Ritchie back to Hog Hill Mill in 1995 to record another 'new' Beatles song, based on a second demo tape Yoko Ono had supplied, Jeff Lynne again producing. 'Real Love' was another slow love song, this time with all the words in place, which made it less of a challenge and thereby less fun for Paul, who nonetheless wanted to continue with this reunion project, eager to complete a third Lennon track. George Harrison said no. He wasn't even sure 'Real Love' was good enough to release (he was right, but it was nonetheless in 1996) and he didn't want to make any more records with Paul and Ritchie, which Paul thought odd considering the *Anthology* had been created partly to help George. So the three-quarters Beatles reunion was over. But now that the grave had been exhumed, the ghosts of the past were not easily put back to rest.

James McCartney had reached an age when he was asking his father about the Sixties. A discussion about the song 'My Dark Hour', which Paul had made with Steve Miller during the rancorous end days of the Beatles, led McCartney to hook up with Miller again, at his home studio in Sun Valley, Idaho, to record a song titled 'Young Boy', the lyrics of which express the sort of conversation Paul and Lin may have had about their son as he approached adulthood. The track worked well. Later in the year, Miller came to Hog Hill to record a second song with Paul, a sloppy blues they named 'Used to Be Bad'. This also turned out successfully. Paul brought Jeff Lynne in to produce a series of other new songs he'd been working on recently, including 'The Song We

Were Singing', which described Paul's working relationship with John, and 'The World Tonight', which also referred to their past. These were some of the best songs Paul had written in years, though it would be some time before the public heard them.

At the same time, Paul was continuing to compose orchestral music, no longer with Carl Davis, but with a friend and colleague of Davis's, the English composer and arranger David Matthews. 'I know after *Liverpool Oratorio* Paul felt he'd like to do more things himself,' says Matthews. 'Carl felt perhaps [he] wasn't sufficiently acknowledged as a co-composer ... they did have a slight falling out.' As a young man, David worked as an assistant to Benjamin Britten, whose music Paul enjoyed, Matthews becoming a prolific and well-regarded composer in his own right, publishing a number of symphonies and concertos, and working on a celebrated arrangement of Mahler's Tenth Symphony, which Mahler left unfinished at his death. Matthews strove to make his additions to the score sound like Mahler, rather than his own work. This was also true of his collaboration with McCartney.

Their first meeting, at Hog Hill Mill on 17 January 1995, was very pleasant. Says Matthews, who was a year younger than Paul and had developed an appreciation and respect for the Beatles' music in his youth, as many serious composers did in the Sixties:

> Well, certainly he's very nice and very friendly, and very easy to talk to and very modest. I remember him saying, 'I'm Paul McCartney.' I thought, *Well, yes, I do know that!* [laughs] He would say things like, 'We did an album called *Sgt. Pepper.*' 'Oh yes!' ... I learned he was writing a symphonic piece of some kind, which at this stage he was quite vague about.

It gradually emerged that Paul was working on a piece titled *Spiral*, inspired by his interest in Celtic mythology, a subject he also explored in painting; the history fascinated Paul because it was the story of his own ancestry. Paul had recorded a demo on piano, getting an assistant to transcribe the music. He now wanted to develop the score with Matthews. Creating orchestral music in this way was slow work. And what exactly was McCartney trying to achieve?

'When I met him I thought, *What does he really want to be?* He wants to be a composer. OK. See if I can try to get him to do it all himself ...

My business was writing the score down and suggesting things that he wouldn't necessarily think of,' explains Matthews.

I had to make him aware of the whole range of dynamics, how a [piece of music] can be phrased. Take this, [hums a piece of orchestral music they made together] *da-da-dar*, how is that to be phrased? Should it be *da-da-dar* [staccato] or should it be *dar-larrrr*, and if it's *da-da-dar* you put staccato dots over the notes and if it's *dar-larrrr* you put a line over it, and you see that's not something he would know from playing music by ear.

Paul was also using other arrangers. The result of a collaboration with the American composer Jonathan Tunick resulted in a piano prelude titled *A Leaf*, premièred in March 1995 as part of An Evening with Paul McCartney and Friends in front of the Prince of Wales at St James' Palace. The event was in aid of the Royal College of Music. In a varied programme, Paul also performed 'One After 909' with Elvis Costello, and new arrangements of 'For No One', 'Eleanor Rigby' and 'Yesterday' with the Brodsky Quartet. At the end, Prince Charles awarded McCartney an Honorary Fellowship of the Royal College of Music, further assimilating him into the English Establishment and the classical world Paul clearly aspired to join. 'Unlike most people in the rock world he's ambitious to do new things all the time,' says David Matthews, comparing McCartney approvingly to rock stars who 'are content with recycling their early stuff ...'

Paul didn't confine himself to conventional orchestral music. Reminiscing with Barry Miles had re-awakened his interest in the avant-garde, with the result that he accompanied their mutual friend Allen Ginsberg on guitar at a poetry reading at the Albert Hall in the autumn of 1995. Ginsberg came down to see Paul at Blossom Farm first. During their rehearsals for the show Paul asked Allen if he could recommend someone who might help him polish up an epic poem he had written on a Celtic theme, a work titled 'Standing Stone'. Ginsberg referred McCartney to the British poet Tom Pickard, who took on the job, which would form the basis of Paul's next major orchestral work.

More in the mainstream, Paul found time to record a charity cover of 'Come Together' at Abbey Road Studios with Paul Weller and Noel Gallagher of Oasis. The record did well, reminding Paul that working with John at Abbey Road had been his peak. 'I think he always realised that the really great days [were with] the Beatles – he's always talking about the Beatles – [and] it's never been quite the same since he stopped collaborating with John,' observes David Matthews, who was spending a lot of time with McCartney now. 'That produced all their really great work and I think he must know that really. Nothing's quite been the same, has it?' There was another reminder of that career-defining partnership in the spring of 1995 when two Liverpool brothers, Charlie and Reg Hodgson, were clearing out their mother's house in Allerton, just around the corner from where Paul used to live in Forthlin Road, and found an old Grundig tape recorder. Many years ago Paul had borrowed the machine from the Hodgsons to make home recordings with John, George and Stuart Sutcliffe. There was an ancient tape with the machine. When the brothers played the spool, they heard McCartney singing 'The World is Waiting for the Sunrise' and other songs. After making contact with MPL, Reg's son Peter was invited to Hog Hill Mill with the tape so Paul could listen to it. 'I still remember him standing there singing to the [songs],' says Peter of the moment McCartney heard his teenage self again. 'He remembered the words to songs he hadn't sung in years [like] "I'll Follow the Sun".' There was a banging in the background. 'That's Our Mike banging [his] drum,' explained McCartney, who bought the tape from the Hodgsons for £260,000 ($397,800).

Making orchestral music became easier for Paul in May 1995 when he acquired a computer that generated sheet music from notes played on a keyboard. Paul gave reams of print-out to David Matthews, who dutifully transcribed them. Paul's compositions became increasingly ambitious and eccentric from this point, as if he wanted to reach back beyond the conventional orchestral music he'd made with Carl Davis to his more experimental Sixties self. One of the first works McCartney and Matthews produced with the aid of the computer was what David describes as 'a crazy piece' Paul titled *Pissed*, possibly because 'he was pissed when he did it', then renamed *Inebriation*. It is challenging music, sounding like discordant Erik Satie. 'Not your normal McCartney, is it?' asks Matthews, playing a section on the piano at his London home. 'That's the most extreme he got, I think.'

As they worked together, Matthews found himself drawn deeper into Paul's world. One night he and his wife were invited for supper to Blossom Farm, where they got to know Linda a little: a strong woman 'obsessed with her vegetarian ideas'. That said, it was a delightful evening, Linda serving dinner at the kitchen table in what was a remarkably unostentatious family home. The McCartneys were almost like any other middle-class, middle-aged couple, if one forgot their fame and their wealth, and the thousand private acres outside the window with estate workers watching for the determined, sometimes crazed Beatles fans who regularly came down the lane from Peasmarsh looking for Paul.

The kids were growing up and becoming more independent of Mum and Dad. Heather had moved into a cottage on the southern border of the Sussex estate, with an outhouse in which she did her pottery. She established a company, Heather McCartney Designs, in 1995. Sister Mary was still working for Dad at MPL in London, while Stelly graduated from St Martin's College with a degree in fashion design in 1995, her clothes modelled at her graduation show by celebrity friends Naomi Campbell and Kate Moss. Paul and Lin came to support their daughter along with the rest of the family and the veteran model Twiggy, one of their oldest and closest friends. Paul created a celebratory piece of music, 'Stella May Day', helping launch his youngest daughter on what became a very successful career in the fashion industry.

Their youngest, James, was still living full time at home. A quiet boy of 17, with Paul's cherubic features and his mother's straw-blond hair and pale complexion, James frightened his parents again in 1995 when he overturned a Land Rover on the Sussex estate. He got trapped underneath and had to be rescued by the Fire Brigade. In other words it was normal family life at Blossom Farm, the kids both a source of delight and worry to Mum and Dad. Above all the McCartneys were a close family. 'To see them together with [their] kids, I've never seen such a loving family,' comments Barry Miles, recalling his visits to Blossom Farm around this time.

They would all hug each other and stuff. It was a very touchy-feely kind of family. They were always telling each other they loved each other. When the girls left to drive back to town or something they would all [wave them off]. It seemed pretty good actually. Obviously tempestuous, you know, four kids and that rock 'n' roll lifestyle, so obviously there were problems from time to time, but I would have thought a very happy marriage.

The Beatles' *Anthology* premièred on ABC television in the United States on 19 November 1995, and five days later in the UK, then in 100 countries around the world. The original TV series ran to approximately five hours, long by normal standards, but nevertheless perfunctory for such an epic story with so many fascinating characters and incidents. The story was better told in subsequent, expanded video and DVD releases, the final version stretching to more than 11 hours. Well received at the time, the series remains the definitive televisual history of the Beatles, as Neil Aspinall had set out to make it, even if sensitive parts of the story were soft-pedalled to appease the protagonists. Paul didn't want to go into the whys and wherefores of who broke up the band, for instance, so there wasn't a word about his High Court action to dissolve the partnership. As with any 'authorised' biographical project, including Paul's forthcoming book with Miles, the *Anthology* was a glossing over of the truth, with key areas of the story ignored. But to hear Paul, George and Ringo talk directly at length about the amazing experiences they had shared was compensation.

A couple of days after the show was broadcast, the first of three double CDs of hitherto officially unreleased Beatles music went on sale. This included what George Martin termed a 'rather grotty' home recording of 'Hallelujah, I Love Her So', 'You'll be Mine' and 'Cayenne', all featuring Stuart Sutcliffe. These were the tapes found recently in a Liverpool attic. Beautifully produced, with excellent liner notes by Mark Lewisohn, *Anthology Vol. 1* quickly sold more than two million units in the USA alone. One of those who benefited from the runaway success was Pete Best who, like Stuart Sutcliffe, appeared for the very first time on an official Beatles record. Pete was on tracks recorded in Hamburg in 1961, at the Decca audition in London on New Year's Day 1962, and at EMI that June. As a result, Pete – who had worked in a Liverpool unemployment office in recent years, as well as playing his drums for Beatles fans – received his first substantial pay day from the band who sacked him, making him a rich man finally at 54. There was, however, a last indignity. The cover of the first volume of the *Anthology* features an early band picture of the Beatles. Pete's face had been deliberately torn out, replaced by that of Ringo Starr.

The opening track on this double CD was not an old recording, or at least not in the same way these museum pieces were old. It was the 'new' Beatles song 'Free as a Bird', released as a single in December

1995. 'It sounds like them now,' said George Harrison enthusiastically, but in truth 'Free as a Bird' was a disappointing dirge. Jeff Lynne's production was part of the problem. It gave the Beatles the same smooth sound as ELO. Also, the basic song wasn't very good. Even though EMI gave 'Free as a Bird' a massive launch it failed to hit number one in the UK, kept off the top spot by Michael Jackson's overblown 'Earth Song', to McCartney's chagrin. The *Anthology* project as a whole generated a mountain of money, though. MPL turned over £6.4 million ($9.7m) in what had otherwise been a quiet year, with Paul paying himself £1.9 million ($2.9m), including pension contributions, with the *Anthology* continuing to earn the boys millions for years to come. Two further CD sets were to be released in 1995/96, with a VHS box set of the documentaries retailing at £99 in the UK, and an expensive *Anthology* book in the works. All of this, however, was of little account to Paul, for he now faced the terrifying news that Linda had cancer, the same cancer that had killed his mother.

PASSING THROUGH THE DREAM OF LOVE

LINDA HAS CANCER

When Linda McCartney found a lump under her arm she went to see her general practitioner, who told her it was nothing to worry about and prescribed antibiotics. Still feeling unwell, Linda sought a second opinion, receiving the results by telephone at Blossom Farm in December 1995. Linda rang Paul to tell him she had a cancerous tumour in her left breast. Before going into hospital to have the lump removed, Linda also confided in Danny Fields and Carla Lane. 'She said, "Look, I want to talk to you, come on in the house,"' recalls Carla.

> We sat in the kitchen and she just looked at me. She said, 'I have cancer,' and I went to open my mouth, and she put her finger up and she said, 'Shush! Nothing. Don't think about it. I want you as my friend to know, *but we're not going to talk about it*.' I said, 'OK.'

Then Linda changed the subject, and rarely spoke of it again.

On Monday 11 December 1995 Linda underwent a lumpectomy – the removal of the cancerous tumour and surrounding tissue, rather than a whole breast – at the private Princess Grace Hospital in London, not far from the McCartneys' St John's Wood home. Paul and Linda then retired to their Sussex estate to allow Linda to recuperate. When the story broke in the press, as it inevitably did, immediately becoming a major story, Paul came up from the house to talk to the reporters gathered outside his gate in Starvecrow Lane. 'The operation was 100 per

463

cent successful, thank God,' he told the media, 'and the doctors have told her now just to get some rest.'

As he watched his wife, Paul was reminded of his mother's terminal illness. Linda was enervated like Mum had been. It was a mark of how poorly Linda felt that she wasn't with her husband on 30 January 1996 when he stood on stage in his old school assembly hall, now the Paul McCartney Auditorium, to open the Liverpool Institute for Performing Arts.

To give Liverpool its *Fame*-type school had taken longer and cost more than anticipated, almost £6 million more than the original £12 million budget ($18.36m), with Paul loaning LIPA £1.5 million ($2.2m) to help bridge the gap, a loan that became £2 million ($3.06m) with tax relief when he declared the money as a gift, bringing his total contribution to £3 million ($4.5m). Despite such munificence, some Merseysiders grumbled that Paul could have paid for the whole thing himself, part of a surprisingly widespread feeling that the Beatles let the city down. 'They never came back, really, when they left in the Sixties; they never came back to raise Liverpool's profile,' grumbles Dave Holt, a former Cavern-goer, over a pint in a Mathew Street pub. 'Paul McCartney comes back occasionally to play – it seems he comes back when he needs a pay day.' This attitude is unfair. Paul had maintained a home on Merseyside all these years, visited frequently in a private capacity and, in backing Mark Featherstone-Witty's school, rescued the Inny from dereliction and brought new blood to the city, literally so in terms of the students who now came from around the country, and abroad, to study there, with corresponding social and economic benefits for Liverpool. LIPA also brought some welcome show business razzmatazz back to Merseyside, with Paul's personal and ongoing close association with LIPA helping persuade other celebrities to become patrons. Some commentators believe the opening of the institute helped begin a wider regeneration of the city. 'You had the Derek Hatton-era in Liverpool, which was pretty ghastly for the city, and everywhere was being run down, and it so happened that McCartney started to develop LIPA really before there was much hope in the city. It was one of the first things. And I think that gave other people hope, and things developed from there,' says local radio personality Spencer Leigh, referring to improvements that continued through 2008 when Liverpool became European Capital of Culture, with a vast amount of new building work and other enhancements to the city. And rich though Paul was, £3 million was not an insignificant amount of money to give away.

While Paul had been generous, he had not frittered money on LIPA, and most of the difficult conversations he'd had with Mark Featherstone-Witty were about finances. At times of crisis, such as the overspend on the roof, Paul's reaction tended to be expostulations of: 'You don't know what the fuck you're doing!' – which was the sort of thing he used to yell at Apple staff. While not pleasant, Paul's criticism was on target then as now, as Mark admits with laughter: 'There would always be the [reaction] from Paul, unless you're careful, "You don't know what the fuck you're doing," which of course would be partly true, unfortunately, because you don't do this, in one's lifetime, too often.' On Inauguration Day, though, with the refurbished auditorium filled with happy faces, all rancour was forgotten. Paul gave a passionate speech in which he talked about the tremendous start in life he'd received in this building (apparently forgetting that he had lost all interest in his own studies as a boy after music entered his life) ; now he hoped others would benefit. 'Obviously one of my feelings now is how proud my mum and dad would have been …' he said. Then he stopped, choked with emotion, thumped his lectern, and continued: 'But I won't go into that because I'll start crying.'

Any reference to Paul's parents was liable to tap a deep well of emotion in this highly sensitive and sentimental man, but this very public display of feeling was also to do with Paul's underlying concerns about Linda, who was now undergoing chemotherapy, despite the fact that the drugs she was taking had been tested on animals. This went against everything Linda believed in as an anti-vivisectionist. 'If a drug has got to be used on humans then legally it has to be finally tested on an animal,' Paul later acknowledged. 'This was difficult for Linda when she was undergoing treatment.'

Despite the feelings of sickness induced by the drugs, Linda continued to work the phones for Paul, as she had always done, calling Danny Fields and asking when he and his colleagues at the Rock 'n' Roll Hall of Fame were going to induct Paul as a solo artist; also calling Yoko to ask her, as a personal favour, if she would let Paul have his name before John's on 'Yesterday' when the second volume of the Beatles' *Anthology* CD series was released in March. The fact that Paul's most successful song was credited to Lennon & McCartney had always niggled with him; while it was well known that John had never thanked anyone for crediting him with that tune. John and Paul's joint authorship of the Beatles song book was, however, a principle upon which Lennon & McCartney royalties were divided, and Yoko was reluctant to grant a favour that might set a precedent. If they went through the catalogue deciding which were John's songs and which were Paul's it might become apparent that, more often than not, Paul's songs made more money. The credit on 'Yesterday' developed into 'a major issue', in Paul's words, concluding unhappily when Yoko told Linda she would never allow Paul to have his name before John's, a rebuff the McCartneys took hard, considering the fragile state of Linda's health when she asked the favour.

With Yoko and Paul again at daggers drawn, and George Harrison declining to collaborate with Paul on any more 'new' band songs, the brief *entente* in the Beatles War was at an end. Still, Paul remained on good terms with his minor ally Ritchie, with whom he had a melancholy new bond. The previous December, Ritchie's first wife Maureen had died of leukaemia at the age of 48, a death that touched Paul and Linda personally because of their own situation, because Mo was so young, and because she'd been an original member of the Beatles family, one of the first four girls alongside Cyn, Jane and Pattie. Mo was somebody Paul had been on holiday with, and seen constantly during the early days; she was also the mother of Ritchie's three children – Zak, Jason and Lee – who were like cousins to Paul's kids. He responded to her death by writing a moving song, 'Little Willow', encouraging Mo's children to be strong, rather as he had written 'Hey Jude' to buck up Julian Lennon after John abandoned his family. 'Little Willow' is a good and a touching tribute to Mo, whom Ritchie had remained close to after their divorce, and in May Ritchie came to Hog Hill Mill to record two new songs with Paul: the ballad 'Beautiful Night' and their first co-written song, 'Really Love You', both of which were produced by Jeff Lynne. These were powerful tunes, performed with gusto, Paul and Ritchie apparently able to forget their troubles in their music, while Paul's concerns for Linda seemed to bring a new sense of reflection to his lyrics.

Although Paul and Linda gave the impression publicly that they were confident of beating her cancer, Linda still wasn't well enough to be with Paul in June when the Queen visited LIPA. Shortly after this, Linda privately acknowledged how ill she was by making out her last will and testament. It was a simple matter. She left her entire estate in trust to Paul, who was appointed co-executor of the will along with John Eastman; the income from the trust was to be paid quarterly to Paul until his death, after which the trust would be shared equally between the couple's four children. Directing that her executors 'pay the expenses of my last illness and funeral', Linda signed the document at Hog Hill Mill on 4 July 1996, an appropriate date for a woman who had never relinquished her American citizenship. Also appropriately for a woman who'd made her life in the rock 'n' roll world, the witnesses were her husband's roadie and his studio engineer – John Hammel and Eddie Klein.

Publicly, the McCartneys maintained an optimistic 'we can beat this' façade, as composer David Matthews recalls: 'She never gave in … she was very brave. I think she believed she could overcome it. After all, she was living on all this very good food. That's supposed to be good for cancer.' Paul and David were working together now on *Standing Stone*, a symphonic tone poem of sorts (one with words) rooted in McCartney's interest in Celtic mythology, and intended as a centenary celebration for EMI. The starting point for the work was the enigmatic standing stone on the McCartneys' Scottish estate. Musing on what ancient hands had planted that slender but still massive finger of rock in the land had led Paul to paint a series of pictures and then, while jogging around the lanes in Sussex, he conjured up the beginning of a complementary epic poem, starting with the creation of Earth and a man who is, or believes himself to be, the first man, a character who comes to a new land where he meets a woman and erects a standing stone in gratitude for his survival; after which their peace is broken by invaders (as Kintyre was invaded by Vikings 1,000 years ago). Finally, the hero defeats the invaders using the cunning of Odysseus.

'Standing Stone' is a long (36 verses), densely woven and sophisticated poem unlike anything Paul had committed to paper before, making one wonder if it was all his own work. In fact, he did have some help with the editing of the poem. When the music of the same name was eventually released on CD, there was a discreet credit at the end of the liner notes: 'Standing Stone poem edited by Tom Pickard', with a similarly low-key acknowledgement when the poem appeared in the book, *Blackbird Singing*. Recommended to McCartney by their mutual friend Allen Ginsberg, Pickard had been invited to Blossom Farm to meet Paul at the end of 1995.

> Paul gave me a copy of his long poem, 'Standing Stone', and said that he was using it as a model for the musical piece of the same name. He thought the poem was too long and wanted help editing it. This seemed natural to me, as most of the poets that I know, including myself, get close colleagues to help them knock off the rough edges and tighten up loose lines and generally give it a polish. Not exactly a shoe-shine relationship ... maybe it required an occasional fellow cobbler's skill too.
>
> Over a month or so we went through every line together – mostly making them tighter, reversing order occasionally. He was an easy person to work with – completely without ego. He was happy to make changes where he saw the sense of it, and we pretty much agreed. Sometimes I'd suggest changes to a line but he would insist on keeping it, and that was a happy circumstance for me, picking up a few tips from a great songwriter. I mean we were approaching the thing from different perspectives, bringing two traditions together. He had already done that himself, writing it as a lyricist and a poet, and those traditions don't always sit well together – but I thought in that long poem he pulled it off admirably. But essentially, the epic was already written in full, by him alone and I just brought some editing, line-tightening skills to the table. Some of how I see poetry washed into it, pretty much like a musician might influence a piece in a session with a lick here and there ... the work is his.

This poem was not incorporated in the music of 'Standing Stone', but meant as a complement to and inspiration for the symphonic work. There would be a chorus, but the singers would be given simpler lines to sing. Nevertheless 'Standing Stone' was a project on 'the biggest possible scale', as David Matthews acknowledges, with 'huge pretensions'. The music itself was complicated, created over a long period of time with the help of a cabal of expert assistants. In addition to Matthews, the composers and arrangers John Fraser, John Harle and Steve Lodder all helped. Paul referred to the men as his Politburo. 'Again, I was trying to get him to do it, and again going through it for dynamics and phrasing which took *ages*,' says Matthews. 'It was very difficult to get him to cut anything. Sometimes I'd think it should be shorter in places, but he wouldn't agree. He had his own ideas.'

Paul and Linda returned to Kintyre that autumn with three of their children: Heather, approaching her 34th birthday; Stella, now 25; and 19-year-old James. Their neighbours Alice and Duncan McLean were retiring from High Ranachan Farm, and Paul and Linda wanted to buy the McLeans' 303 acres which, added to their existing landholding, would given them approximately 1,000 acres, roughly the same amount of land as they owned in Sussex and Arizona. As always, their motive was to preserve the landscape and its wildlife in a natural state – while also putting as much distance as possible between themselves and the public. The McCartneys went to visit the McLeans to tell them they were going to make an offer for the farm, which was accepted. Duncan McLean was happy to sell to Paul for the right price even though he knew McCartney wouldn't farm the land as he and his brother had done. The men had a drink on the deal, Duncan pouring out drams of Glenmorangie whisky, to Linda's apparent disapproval. 'I don't think she liked Paul to drink,' observes Mrs McLean. 'Linda was edging it away from him.' The women went into the kitchen to make tea. '[Heather] told us she had a little pottery business and she wanted to be independent of her mum and dad, and didn't want to be dependent on them for support.'

While Heather seemed fragile, Stella was as hearty and robust as Paul himself, whom she resembled strongly in personality and features, and was soon to be appointed Creative Director of the French fashion house Chloé. James was a quieter person who shared Dad's passion for music. When he took up the guitar, Paul advised his son to have formal lessons, to which the boy retorted: 'You didn't, Dad.' So a third generation James McCartney learned to play music by ear. Just before the trip to Scotland, Paul and James had recorded a song together, 'Heaven on a Sunday', James trading guitar licks with his father. A true family affair, Linda sang backing vocals. It was one of the last times she would record with Paul.

SIR PAUL AND LADY McCARTNEY

As Lee Eastman had predicted, the time came when Paul McCartney's considerable contribution to his country's cultural and economic life had to be recognised with more than an MBE. Paul and Linda's propensity for getting busted had probably delayed the receipt of more elevated honours, but it was now 16 years since the McCartneys' last arrest and, what with Paul's recent meeting with Prince Charles at St James' Palace, and his charitable work with LIPA and his local hospital in Rye, Paul's friends felt it was high time he received a KBE, elevating a Member of the Order of the British Empire to a knight of the realm.

Although Paul would always tell friends he didn't expect to be addressed as Sir Paul, as if he hadn't expected the honour, and didn't want to be seen to be swanking it, the knighthood was instigated by one of his closest associates, and supported by a campaign of friends. Having had a conversation with Paul's manager along the lines of 'Oh look who's got a knighthood now, while Paul is overlooked!', Mark Featherstone-Witty took action. Anyone can nominate friends and colleagues for honours by filling out a Cabinet Office nomination form. Mark did so, suggesting Paul would be a worthy recipient of a KBE. This was done apparently without Paul's express knowledge. Mark soon received a reply from the Cabinet Office. 'Some man rang back from the office that deals with these things, enquiring if I knew that Paul already had an award, his MBE. The implication, I suppose, was that this was enough. At that point I gave him a piece of my mind.' Mark also rallied support from friends and influential music industry figures, including Sir George Martin, who'd received his KBE the previous year. Their campaign was successful. News that Paul was to be knighted was announced in the New Year's honour's list, on 1 January 1997, the ceremony scheduled for March.

In the meantime, Sir George orchestrated 'Beautiful Night', one of the new songs Paul had recorded with Ritchie. Appropriately for a love song, the orchestration was overdubbed at Abbey Road Studios on Valentine's Day, part of which Paul spent at Cavendish Avenue with David Matthews working on *Standing Stone*, which Paul now wanted to hear. 'So he hired the London Symphony Orchestra so they could play it through,' laughs Matthews, amazed at such largesse. 'I don't think he quite realises how the rest of us have to put up with slightly less rehearsal time and so on. You know, he can afford to have absolutely everything he needs ...' The following week, on 11 March, Paul went to Buckingham Palace to be formally knighted by Her Majesty the Queen, watched by Mary, Stella and James. Lady McCartney, as Lin was now formally addressed, was too ill to attend, giving her husband instead a watch inscribed with the words, 'To Paul, my knight in shining armour'. Stella burst into tears during the ceremony, Mary saying afterwards: 'It was just like the end of a wonderful film with the Queen placing the sword on Dad's shoulders. I will never forget that moment.'*

Fourteen songs Sir Paul had been working on during his *Anthology* sabbatical were released in May as the album *Flaming Pie*, after John Lennon's humorous explanation of why the Beatles were so named: 'a man appeared on a flaming pie and said unto them, "From this day on you are Beatles with an A"'. The eponymous title song – again produced by Jeff Lynne – worked much better than the 'new' Beatles singles Lynne had produced for the *Anthology*, possessing a pleasingly fat sound. The words were good, too, as they were throughout this new LP, which came as a welcome change.

The proverb 'nice writes white' applies to Paul's career. Although ambitious, impatient and sometimes overbearing, Paul is essentially a decent man, a happily married family man for many years past. But domestic happiness does not tend to beget great art. Rather it engenders the bland; in Paul's case, prosaic and clichéd love songs. His albums typically featured one or two outstanding tunes, padded by filler, with a marked propensity for the sentimental, and though he agonised over some albums, many of his records had been put out before enough reflection and revision had taken place. *Flaming Pie* was different. The fact that the tracks had been written and recorded over a long period of time – the oldest, 'Calico Skies', dated back to 1991 – gave Paul a sense of perspective, allowing him to cut out weak material. Working on the *Anthology*, and talking about his life for his forthcoming biography, also caused Paul to reflect on the Beatles, and here were some of the best songs he'd written about the band and the wider

---

* Paul's knighthood was one of the first given to a pop star, predated only by Sir Cliff Richard (1995). These rock 'n' roll KBEs proved so popular with the public that HM's Government started handing them out almost like toffees. Elton John was knighted in 1998, then came Sir Mick Jagger (2003), even Sir Tom Jones (2005), but never Sir George Harrison or Sir Ringo Starr, which further set Paul apart from the boys.

Beatles family, including 'Flaming Pie', 'The World Tonight' and 'Little Willow'. Importantly, Paul McCartney sounded less cocksure, more like a man in his fifties should. There were love songs on the new record, but not 'silly love songs', more interesting ones like 'Somedays'; also songs about parenthood ('Young Boy'); while a melancholy sense of vanishing time imbued 'Heaven on a Sunday'. The collaborations with Ringo Starr and Steve Miller were joyous. The co-productions with Jeff Lynne also worked well, with Sir George Martin's orchestration lending a touch of class to the CD. There was in summary a sense of quality and substance to *Flaming Pie* that had been missing from Paul's albums for years, the material also having a touch of winter about it, as one expected from an artist reaching an age where loss and regret are as important as love and sex. Bob Dylan released such a wintry album in 1997, *Time out of Mind*. This was shortlisted along with *Flaming Pie* for Album of the Year at the Grammy Awards. Dylan won, deservedly, but *Flaming Pie* was a strong contender.

Moreover, *Flaming Pie* marks a turning point in Paul's mature career, after which his music generally becomes more interesting. In the years ahead he would sell less records, partly because of a sea change in the way the public consumes music, but the work he put out was often better than his more commercially successful albums of the Seventies and early Eighties. Certainly *Flaming Pie* is a finer record than *Wild Life* or *Venus and Mars*.

Paul also seemed less concerned now with being relentlessly commercial. As a case in point, he was working again with Youth on a second Fireman project, *Rushes*, recording enigmatic, trance-like ambient tracks which, though lacking conventional lyrics or melodies, are beautiful and moving. 'He just rang me up, he said: "I want to do some more Fireman. I'm really up for it, come down, and let's just do something new, and jam,"' remembers Youth.

So we did and I think, reading between the lines on that one, I didn't realise it at the time, but that was when Linda was very ill, and by the time we'd finished it she was dying, and for me it became very much a requiem for her … It certainly wasn't consciously discussed when we made it, but the emotion of it and the sadness and the melancholy, it definitely picked up on that. That was happening … It is a very sad [record].

From the sublime to the ridiculous: the Anita Howarth (*née* Cochrane) paternity case blew up again in May 1997 when one of her relatives gave newspapers details of the £5,000 pay-off Anita received from NEMS in 1964, an old story still capable of making front-page news in the British tabloids 33 years later (when the pay-off would have been worth £64,000 [or $97,920]). As a result, Anita and her son Philip, now a 33-year-old lighting technician, told their story to the *Daily Mail*. 'There was never any doubt in my mind that Paul was Philip's father,' Anita was quoted as saying, while her son described the paternity issue as an albatross around his neck, causing him to dislike Sir Paul and take comfort in drugs. He revealed that he'd developed a heroin habit as a young man, which led to petty crime. 'I had started stealing from everywhere, even from home. I had turned into a rather nasty character.' Anita then told Philip that Paul *wasn't* his father, thinking this would help him. It did for a while. Philip stopped using drugs. Mum joined the Jehovah's Witnesses. But when the story blew up again in 1997, Anita admitted to Philip she actually thought Paul was his father, but wasn't 100 per cent sure. The only way to know for certain was to take a DNA test, so they asked a solicitor to contact McCartney. The star didn't take the test, but Philip says he did, and so did another man whom Mum thought could be a contender, with the result – some years later – that this other man was proven to be Philip's father. Thus ended the four-decade farce of the Liverpool typist who claimed Paul fathered her child. Like the German barmaid story, it turned out to be completely untrue. Paul's only children were those he'd had with Linda, plus his adoptive daughter Heather.

That summer, the McCartneys checked into the Plaza Athénée Hotel in New York, so Linda could be treated by the renowned oncologist Larry Norton at the Memorial Sloan-Kettering Cancer Center. When she heard that Paul was in town, his most devoted New York fan Linda Aiello (*née* Magno) came by the Plaza Athénée with her friend, Toni Kraker, intending to give Paul gifts for his forthcoming 55th birthday. Linda Aiello was now a woman of 43, married to a New York cop, but part of her heart still belonged to Paul, whose signed photo from the *Give My Regards to Broad Street* publicity junket hung on her bedroom wall. Hotel staff warned Linda and Toni that it wasn't a good time to approach Sir Paul, but the women walked up to him anyhow as he rounded the corner. Paul reacted furiously, angry in a way the women had never seen before, refusing their gifts, saying they shouldn't be bothering him, and storming into the hotel. John Hammel then came out and explained: Paul and Linda had just been given some bad news. The girls later found out that Linda's cancer had spread to her right breast.

Suddenly, death was all around. The McCartneys were shocked when they heard in May 1997 that musician Jeff Buckley, son of Linda's Sixties' lover Tim, had drowned in the Mississippi River. The McCartneys had befriended Tim in recent years and were taken aback by his premature death, which followed the early demise of his father in 1975. Not long after this came news that George Harrison had throat cancer, which spread to his lungs. A lifelong smoker, his prognosis was not good. Then Derek Taylor, former Apple press officer, died at 63 of throat cancer. When Paul attended the annual Buddy Holly Week luncheon that September, without Linda, he appeared worn and tired, the grey showing through his thinning hair. Linda's appearance had also changed. This became evident when she felt able to accompany Paul to Paris in October to watch Stelly's first catwalk show for Chloé. Gone was Linda's long blonde hair. She had lost a good deal of it during chemotherapy, and had what was left cut short. Lin was determined to make the best of her trip, though, applauding and smiling enthusiastically during her daughter's show.

That autumn, Linda accompanied Paul to the London and New York premières of *Standing Stone*, at the Albert Hall and Carnegie Hall. Final preparations had been somewhat fraught, with Paul asking the composer Richard Rodney Bennett to re-orchestrate some of the work done with David Matthews. 'In the end he wanted a slightly richer sound,' says Matthews.

Richard is an absolute expert on producing the ultimate Hollywood sound, and Paul is really rather addicted to that. A lot of *Standing Stone* is like that, too, because [Richard] re-orchestrated the ends of the movements. They are very beautifully done. They are slightly in conflict with the rest of the piece, which is much more quirky. Suddenly the music sort of smoothes over and it becomes very, very sort of Hollywoodish – that's what Paul wanted.

There was also some to-ing and fro-ing over who would conduct the première performances, the original idea being to have fellow Liverpudlian Sir Simon Rattle conducting his City of Birmingham Symphony Orchestra. Rattle pulled out, apparently unsure about the piece. Another name conductor, the American Kent Nagano, was approached. 'Then he got cold feet, twice, and I had to ask him to stand down,' said Paul.

In the end, Lawrence Foster conducted the London Symphony Orchestra at the Royal Albert Hall on 14 October 1997, as he had in the recording studio. The huge theatre was packed on the night, Paul's presence lending a classical event the giddy atmosphere of a rock show, Sir Paul and Lady Linda holding hands as they took their seats, beaming like boyfriend and girlfriend, despite their careworn faces. Clearly Linda was proud for her husband, and Paul was delighted to share this moment with her, for ultimately the music the audience was about to hear revolved around their life together, and their love, as was indicated by the CD photography. The CD case and booklet were illustrated with Linda's photos of her horse Blankit beside their standing stone at High Park.

The audience applauded the entrance of the conductor, who bowed, turned to the orchestra and began the bold, energetic first movement about the creation of man, after which the piece followed the narrative of Paul's poem. The music was varied, incorporating characteristically catchy McCartney tunes, also some spare, modern music in the second movement, which adhered to Sir Paul's keyboard computer work, together with mistakes he'd made, liked and kept in; while Richard Rodney Bennett had indeed brought a lush, dramatic flair to the work. Inevitably, the piece built to an emotional climax, with the chorus singing a few simple but nonetheless powerful words Paul had written in praise of love:

Now
with all the time it seemed we had
whatever time I have to spare
will be with you
for ever more.

In the end, Paul's journey through life with Linda had led him to believe, as it says in the Bible, that life without love is meaningless, or as the Beatles sang so succinctly, 'All You Need is Love'. He'd been singing that theme his whole life. Now there was a strong sense in his writing, for *Standing Stone*, that he was addressing a lover whom he knew would soon pass beyond his touch.

Before the New York première in November, Linda spent time backstage at Carnegie Hall with Danny Fields, who introduced her to a friend of his who'd been a devoted McCartney fan in her youth, so much so that when Paul married Linda the girl wore mourning to school. 'So I brought her with me, now a woman, who had been a Paul worshipper [and introduced her to] Linda … I said, "This is Bonnie. She hates you for marrying Paul; she wore black when you got married."'

Lady Linda growled: 'If she still wants him, she can have him.'

The friends then talked until Paul appeared. 'Security people called him; it was time to go and they walked down the hallway at Carnegie Hall and she turned around and waved [goodbye].' It was the last time Danny ever saw Linda.

Paul and Linda then flew to Arizona to try alternative therapy. While they were at their ranch, Lin invited her ex-husband Mel See and his partner Beverly Wilk over for a barbecue. Although Mel's relationship with Paul and Lin had been difficult in the past, they had got along better in recent years, for Heather's sake, fragile as she was, and now they put their remaining differences behind them, spending a pleasant evening together on the porch, Paul cooking veggie burgers on the barbecue. 'They kind of made amends,' says Beverly. Linda was delighted when, after the sun went down, a family of javelina pigs came rooting around the porch after their titbits. She took pictures of the bold creatures. Mel and Linda and Paul parted on good terms, Paul giving Mel a painting he had made, titled *Holy Cow*. It was the last time Mel and Linda saw each other.

BEFORE THE DAWN

Paul and Lin came home to England for Christmas, spending the holidays with the children at Blossom Farm rather than on Merseyside. There was frost on the Sussex fields, the bare trees on the estate silhouetted against grey skies during the short mid-winter days. On 25 December Paul took Linda outside to see her present: a pair of Shetland ponies, festively named Shnoo and Tinsel, the animals' breath clouding in the winter air as they stood together patiently in the stables.

On Boxing Day Lin felt well enough to host a drinks party for friends and neighbours, including the now-elderly *Goon* star Spike Milligan and a young actor named Walter van Dijk, who had recently bought a cottage just outside the McCartney estate with his musician partner Anthony Marwood. Linda, who always took an interest in the local people, had extended a neighbourly invitation to Walter and Anthony. Chemotherapy had further altered Linda's appearance. 'She'd lost quite a bit of her hair,' reports Walter; 'there was just really sort of peach fuzz on her scalp.'

The Christmas party was well attended, many people gathering to talk in the kitchen. Walter was charmed to notice a Beatles poster stuck to the McCartney fridge. Paul's Fellowship of the Royal College of Music was framed on the wall. Walter congratulated Sir Paul on the fellowship. 'Yeah, it's kind of amazing for somebody who doesn't read a note of music,' Paul replied, adding sweetly: 'Nice fellow, though.' The food was vegetarian, naturally, and Lady McCartney felt well enough to urge guests who hadn't gone veggie to do so without delay, giving out inscribed copies of her cookbooks. She told those who said, apologetically, that they only ate fish that that wasn't good enough. 'Do you think fish don't experience pain when a hook goes into their mouth?' she asked, contorting her face. Paul spent some of the afternoon with Spike Milligan at the piano, writing a song. Then the old comedian – a family friend – announced he'd had enough. 'I'd like to wish you all a happy new year,' he said loudly, adding with characteristic curmudgeonliness: 'but I'll be glad to see the back of you.' Not long afterwards, Walter and Anthony said goodbye, too. 'We went into the sitting room, and [Linda] was sitting there with Stella and James and Mary – Stella was sort of sitting in between her legs – and she said, "Well, see you guys again next year!"'

Linda was putting on a brave face. In recent months she'd tried every possible treatment, consulting with the most eminent doctors in London and New York, undergoing ultra-strong doses of chemotherapy as well as a bone marrow transplant, all in an attempt to beat her cancer. She even gave up her lifelong habit of pot-smoking, though it was too late to make a difference. Linda was doomed, and she knew it. 'Look, that thing we talked about, that cancer business,' she said on the phone to Carla Lane, 'it's got a-hold of me.'

'Linda, darling, you don't know what's round the corner. They are working hard on it. Every day they come up with something. Let's have faith. One day somebody is going to say, "OK, I've cracked it." You're going to be here when that happens.'

'I don't think so,' replied her friend, a tough broad to the end, though still soppy over animals. One of Linda's final efforts on behalf of her fellow creatures was to spend £8,000 ($12,240) to liberate a pack of beagle pups bred for vivisection.

The reason for Linda's pessimism was that she had been told her liver was enlarged, indicating the cancer had spread to that vital organ. The situation was all but hopeless. Sir Paul and Lady Linda gathered themselves to travel to Paris to support Stella's second fashion show, then returned to Blossom Farm so Linda could attend to some final details. The cottage Heather was living in on the estate was transferred legally into her name, leaving Linda's vulnerable eldest child with a secure home; Linda helped her second daughter Mary plan her forthcoming wedding; and she and Paul went into Hog Hill Mill to record two of Linda's songs, 'Appaloosa', a childlike song of devotion to Blankit, the tone of which was quite a contrast to 'The Light Comes from Within', a furiously angry song about animal welfare littered with expletives. Linda spat out her contempt for those who'd mocked her as a simpleminded dreamer, lazy and thick, berating an imaginary male critic as a fucking no-one, a 'stupid dick'. Paul and James backed Lin on this shrill parting shot to the world, after which she went home and wrapped up gifts for family members and friends, making arrangements for the presents to be delivered after her death. She also made her goodbye calls.

'Hi, Honey!' she said brightly when she got Carla on the line, sounding so well, perhaps because of her medication.

'Hi, what are you doing?' asked Carla. Linda explained that she and Paul were getting ready to go to Arizona; it sounded as if their car was at the door. (Carla heard Paul in the background saying, 'Come on …')

'Now, listen, I'll be away for five days,' she said. 'Have you got any more chickens?'

'Of course, I've always got hundreds of them,' replied Carla, referring to the chickens at her animal sanctuary.

'When I come back, I want you to bring me some, OK? About seven.' Carla made a note of it. This sounded optimistic. After a pause, Linda let her mask slip, saying suddenly: 'I love you, Carla.' It was out of character for Linda to express herself so emotionally, and when Carla put the phone down she sat and thought about it. 'Now that hit me hard. She doesn't talk like that … I knew that something awful was about to happen.'

Sir Paul and Lady Linda flew to Tucson at the end of March, driving from the airport to their desert hideaway, turning right off East Redington Road, through their unmarked metal gate, and down a dusty track to their little tin-roof house by the wash. Neighbours in this lonesome desert community heard that the McCartneys were back, and that Linda was poorly, but nobody made a fuss. Mel See received word that Lin didn't want to see anybody except immediate family; the children were at the house with Paul. It was springtime in the desert, beautifully warm in contrast to the English winter, but not yet too hot. The wildlife was up and about, the javelinas rooting for the fruit of the prickly pear cacti, rattlesnakes slithering out from under rocks after their hibernation. The cottonwood trees down by the wash had shed their blossom of cotton ball buds across the trails; the saguaro were coming into bloom, big white flowers opening up in the spring sunshine. The really big cacti were already ancient when Linda was born, and they would stand here solemnly after she had gone. Paul and Linda rode out together while they could, enjoying the wilderness.

Around the end of the first week in April, Linda's liver began to fail. Doctors warned Paul that his wife only had days left. One doctor suggested he warn her that she was about to die. Paul chose not to, believing Lin wouldn't want to know. On the afternoon of Wednesday 15 April 1998, Paul and Linda went for a last desert ride. Paul had to put a hay bale down for Linda to step up on as she climbed carefully into her saddle. As they rode gently along the trails a rattlesnake crossed their path. The sun was setting as they arrived home, just before 7:00 p.m., smouldering red over distant Tucson, its last rays streaming through the sentinel cacti. The desert night has a timeless stillness, the stars very bright. When the sun rose on Thursday 16 April, Linda felt too unwell to get up and spent the day in her bed, a gentle breeze blowing through the house as the sun warmed the tin roof, and the red-tailed hawks wheeled overheard looking for prey. She slipped into a coma. Night again, the last night. The darkest hour comes before the dawn. The children told their mother they loved her. She became restless around 3:00 a.m. Paul got into bed with Linda and told her she was on Blankit; they were riding through the Sussex woods; 'the bluebells are all out, and the sky is clear blue'. By the time he'd finished the story his wife was dead.

RUN DEVIL RUN

IN MEMORIAM

Although she had spent her married life with Paul in England, Linda McCartney died as she was born, an American, and her funeral was a characteristically American affair. A few hours after her death, on the morning of Friday 17 April 1998, Linda's casket was driven down the desert road from Tanque Verde onto the freeway and into Tucson – past strip malls and apartment complexes – to the Bring Funeral Home, where a private service was held and her body cremated. Paul and the children then flew directly back to the UK with the ashes.

News of Linda's demise began to reach the media almost immediately, with journalists going first to Paul's press officer, Geoff Baker, who deliberately misinformed the callers that Linda had died 'on holiday in Santa Barbara', Santa Barbara being a codename used within MPL for when Sir Paul was in the USA privately. He had no particular connections to Santa Barbara. As Geoff knew they would, reporters descended upon Santa Barbara and began a wild goose chase for the family and a nonexistent Californian death certificate, the subterfuge giving the family time to get home and scatter Linda's ashes, which they did at Blossom Farm and High Park in Scotland, where many family pets are buried.

Linda's death was a major news story, partly because it came as a surprise to journalists, who had gained the impression she was successfully fighting her cancer. Friends were also taken aback. Carla Lane heard the news on the radio at Broadhurst Manor in West Sussex.

It was a shock, followed by another shock three days later when the postman delivered a posthumous gift from Linda of antique glass beads Carla had admired. 'I can't guess when she posted them or who posted them, I've no idea. But they came.' The children also received gifts from beyond the grave.

Paul invited Carla and Chrissie Hynde to Blossom Farm, where the women found the widower in a sorry condition, roaming around his estate looking at things Linda liked, talking constantly about her, exhausted. 'Paul was just *haggard*. I mean, he sat there like an old man, lost,' says Carla. 'He was shattered.' Another friend invited to the farm was the animator Geoff Dunbar, who'd recently suffered a loss. 'My mother died four days before Linda, so it was like a double hit. I spent a bit of time with Paul and he was racked with grief … He sobbed like a baby. So did I.'

Six weeks later, Paul gathered himself together to lead a memorial service for Linda at St Martin's-in-the-Fields on Trafalgar Square. Born into a Jewish family, Linda had lived her life without religion for the most part, invoking God only rarely, when she saw animals mistreated, for example, and *in extremis*. In death she would be honoured in two great Christian churches, in London then later in the month in New York. Paul attended personally to the details with the same professionalism he brought to his concert performances, selecting the music and briefing everybody who would be called upon to speak, sing or play an instrument. Rain was falling as he led his children into St Martin's on Monday 8 June, a large crowd of press and public gathered around the steps of the church. Though Linda had never been popular with the British press or public, her passing had occasioned expressions of respect and even affection, while the bereaved family were naturally to be pitied. Press photographers caught images of Stella leading a distraught Heather McCartney into church, the older sibling's face contorted with grief. The 700 mourners inside the church included, above and beyond Paul's relations, the first public coming together of the three surviving Beatles since Ritchie married in 1981. George Harrison was himself now fighting cancer. There was no Yoko. Other guests included MPL staff, musicians who had played with Paul on his records and on stage, and friends such as Brian Clarke, Dave Gilmour, Billy Joel, Sir Elton John, Carla Lane, Twiggy Lawson, Sir George and Lady Martin, Spike Milligan, Michael Parkinson, Sir David* and Lady Puttnam, Eric and Gloria Stewart and Pete Townshend.

When everybody was assembled, George and Ritchie sitting along-side the McCartneys, John McGeachy, a Campbeltown mechanic who'd played pipes on 'Mull of Kintyre', appeared on the balcony, clad in tartan, playing the tune of Wings' greatest hit, continuing to do so as he descended through the church and down into the crypt, the pipes reverberating through the building. This was Paul's idea. The Brodsky Quartet performed arrangements of hymns and songs, including 'The Lovely Linda'. Actress Joanna Lumley read the poem 'Death is Nothing'. LIPA students sang 'Blackbird', which had been Linda's favourite song of Paul's; Carla spoke about Linda's devotion to animals, and everybody sang 'Let It Be', after which Pete Townshend told what he intended to be a light-hearted story about Linda setting her cap at Paul in the Sixties. 'The story I told at the memorial was that Linda had once – quite tongue-in-cheek – told me she was going to marry "one of the Beatles",' explains Townshend, adding that Paul put him right after the service. 'Paul has never been angry with me over this, but did tell me after the memorial that he had pursued Linda, and she had never pursued him.' This was of course the opposite of what everybody else said.

In a highly emotional address, Sir Paul told the congregation: 'She was my girlfriend. I have lost my girlfriend and it is very sad. I still cannot believe it, but I have to because it is true.' As he spoke, Shnoo and Tinsel, the Shetland ponies Paul had given Lin for Christmas, were led into the church. Two weeks later, Paul presided over a similar memorial at the Riverside Church in New York, attended by the Eastmans and American friends such as Ralph Lauren and Paul Simon, but again no Yoko. She wasn't invited.

Paul was little seen in public during the following weeks. To distract himself, he did some light work, hiring the up-and-coming musician Nitin Sawhney to mix a drum and bass version of 'Fluid', one of the tracks from the forthcoming second Fireman album. Sawhney lived and worked at the time in one room in a house in South London. Paul came over and spent the evening, chatting with the younger man about his life and interests, including the work of the Indian writer Rabindranath

---

* The film-maker was knighted in 1995, elevated to the peerage as Lord Puttnam in 1997.

Tagore. 'In love all of life's contradictions dissolve and disappear' was a Tagore maxim Paul had quoted in the liner notes of the *Pipes of Peace* album. Sawhney reflected that, as a British Asian, he had the Beatles to thank for introducing him to the classical music of his ancestral homeland, via the Beatles' association with Ravi Shankar. Paul spoke to Nitin nonchalantly about 'the band' and 'John', knowing Sawhney would know immediately what he meant. He wore his legend lightly, helping the younger man relax.

> He immediately put me at ease by saying, "I used to live in a place like this years ago and I wrote a track in a room like this called 'Scrambled Eggs' and it went on to become 'Yesterday'. I went, 'Wow!' Then he played it on my guitar, which freaked me out as well.

Paul went away having made a new friend.

That July, Paul travelled to Liverpool to preside at the LIPA graduation ceremony, whereby he appeared on stage with Mark Featherstone-Witty to listen to speeches and present each graduating student with a commemorative pin, shaking the graduating men by the hand and kissing the women. He had committed to do this every year and was good to his word, deporting himself like a benevolent nineteenth-century mill owner. Behind the scenes, Featherstone-Witty found his Lead Patron a changed man, however. 'He had lost his greatest companion, and the meetings we had he was always in tears.'

Backstage at the graduation, Paul shared a beer with an old acquaintance named Joe Flannery, who'd booked the Beatles in association with Brian Epstein in the very early days. 'You know, Joe, Linda's there,' said Paul, patting his shoulder as if to indicate an angel sitting there. That same day, his old home, 20 Forthlin Road, was being opened by the National Trust, who had bought the house and returned the décor to how it looked when the McCartneys were in residence. It was a rare honour to have the National Trust turn one's childhood home into a museum, and Flannery asked Paul if he was going to attend the opening. No, he said. To his mind, it was his parents' rather than 'Paul McCartney's house', as it was being billed in the press, and this description of the house had clearly annoyed him. Also, while he'd driven past 20 Forthlin Road many times, he'd not been back inside since he left in the Sixties. He feared it would upset him.

That August, Paul returned to Long Island with Mary, Stella and James. This summer the annual family trip had a melancholy aspect in that Linda wasn't with them and, worse, Paul and the kids had to sign legal papers allowing Linda's will to proceed to probate. To avoid UK taxes, the will had been drawn up under the laws of New York, where Linda had been technically domiciled during her marriage, sporadically exercising her right to vote, maintaining her principal investment account with a Manhattan firm, while brother John handled her affairs at Eastman & Eastman. As a beneficiary of the trust, Heather McCartney's signature was also required on the papers, but she failed to accompany her adoptive father and siblings to the signing on 28 August. Reportedly, she had also arrived in Tucson a few minutes too late to say goodbye to her mother.

Long Island summers had been a feature of the McCartney Year since the mid-1970s and were a source of happy memories. Paul and Lin had watched the kids grow up with their American cousins on Lily Pond Lane, Paul amusing himself beachcombing, painting and sailing his Sunfish on Georgica Pond. They had been content to stay with the Eastmans for most of this time, only recently renting a house of their own. Now Paul bought a summer house in the area, to show he meant to maintain close relations with Linda's American family. One mile down the road from John Eastman's residence, in a part of East Hampton favoured by the super-rich, Paul typically bought a much more modest house in the less showy village of Amagansett. The property at Pintail Lane was tucked away in the woods, literally on the wrong side of the railroad tracks, without an ocean view; not where one would expect to find a great celebrity, yet in character with other homes he had acquired over the years.

The McCartney family appeared together in public in Sussex on Saturday 27 September when Mary McCartney married Alistair Donald, whom she'd met at school in Rye and who now worked in London as a film-maker. The service had been on hold for some time because of Linda's illness, but couldn't be postponed much longer because, like her mother when she married Paul, Mary was pregnant. Sir Paul walked his daughter down the aisle of the church of St Peter and St Paul in Peasmarsh, having driven her the short distance from Blossom Farm in a vintage Hispano-Suiza he'd owned since the Sixties. James McCartney turned up rock 'n' roll-style swinging a bottle of Jack Daniel's, which a church warden confiscated at the door.

The following month Paul released a posthumous collection of Linda's songs as the album *Wide Prairie*, a CD put together with love, but not one that did Lin's memory any favours. Rather, it reminded the listener of what a dud note Linda struck as a singer, the recordings shrill and amateurish despite Paul's presence. Linda's aggressive parting message to the world, 'The Light Comes from Within', had been written during her journeys to and from London for cancer treatment, when she was feeling crotchety. 'It was her answer to all the people who had ever put her down and that whole dumb male chauvinist attitude that to her had caused so much harm in our society,' explained Paul, who charged his song plugger Joe Reddington with getting this difficult record on air. When Joe told Paul that the BBC simply wouldn't play it, primarily because of the bad language, but that he'd persuaded the Corporation to put Linda's more attractive tune 'Seaside Woman' on its playlists instead, the angry star fired his plugger. 'He just threw a wobbler,' recalls Joe, 'said: "Get rid of him!" And that was it.' In truth, 'The Light Comes from Within' was a terrible song. Even when Linda covered a lovely old standard like 'Mister Sandman', as she did on *Wide Prairie*, she sounded coarse.

Far more impressive was the second Fireman album, *Rushes*, slipped out at the same time as *Wide Prairie*, and similarly ignored by the press and public. Ambient trance music was never destined for mass consumption, but *Rushes* is music that stirs the soul, showing a considerable development in McCartney's partnership with Youth. For the second track, named 'palo verde' after a tree native to Arizona, Paul incorporated recordings of Linda talking, and her horse galloping, snorting and whinnying in a ghostly 12-minute wash of sound. Paul's voice is heard assuring the spirit of his departed wife that he will love her 'always', the track concluding with six doleful glockenspiel notes, repeated like a death knell. This was unusual and inventive new music, in the same pioneering tradition as the tape loops of 'Tomorrow Never Knows' and the orchestral sections of 'A Day in the Life', growing on the listener the more often it is heard.

The death of Linda had hit all the family hard. James, the youngest, had been particularly close to Mum and was very upset, while Linda's eldest was bereft. Always something of a worry, Heather McCartney stayed at home much of the time after her mother died, unable to function normally. 'I could see no reason for living any more,' she told the

Sunday Times a year later, presenting herself as a jittery, insecure woman of 36 who'd never married or had children, living as a virtual recluse in her cottage on the edge of the Sussex estate with her Airedale dog and two cats. Some days she felt so wretched she couldn't even answer the telephone.

Living up to the McCartney name had long been a source of anxiety for Heather. She had tried to make her mark as a photographer, like Mum, then as a potter, seemingly soon wearying of both pastimes. Now, less than a year after Mum died, Heather attempted to launch herself as an interior designer, making a rare public appearance at a trade fair in Atlanta, Georgia, in January 1999. In Atlanta to show-case the Heather McCartney Housewares Collection – a range of cushions and other household knick-knacks – she brought Dad to help her face the press. 'I knew that if I felt overwhelmed, he would say: "We've got to go now – Bye," and he would get me out. He has always guided me like that. Protected me.' Sir Paul sat alongside his daughter as she spoke about her designs, which apparently owed a lot to the experience of going to Mexico with Mel See to meet the Hoichol Indians, not that she mentioned her natural father by name. She referred to Paul as her 'real daddy'. The next day, Paul and Heather flew to New York, where Heather belatedly signed the necessary probate documents, printing her name in childish, wobbly letters markedly different to her siblings' confident signatures.

One of Linda's dying wishes was that Paul should be inducted into the Rock 'n' Roll Hall of Fame in his own right, and this happened in March 1999 when Paul was carried in on a wave of sympathy for his loss. Stella McCartney attended the New York ceremony with her father wearing a white T-shirt printed with the words 'ABOUT FUCKING TIME!' The following month, on 3 April, Dad became a granddad when Mary Donald (*née* McCartney) gave birth to a son named Arthur. Sir Paul showed off his grandson at the Royal Albert Hall two weeks later during a rock concert in Linda's memory. 'He said, "Look, he was born between Easter and Passover, so that's perfect, because he's Jewish, because his grandmother is Jewish,"' reports Danny Field, who visited Paul's box and was surprised by what he heard the star say, because Linda had shown no interest in her Jewishness. 'Linda would never have said that.' Meanwhile, Chrissie Hynde confided in Danny that Paul had laid down the law to her about the line-up for the concert, wanting different acts. 'No one wants to be around him when he's not smiling,' a chastened Chrissie told Danny after a difficult meeting with the great man.

The curator, Wolfgang Suttner, also found Sir Paul in uncompromising mood as final preparations were made for the long-planned show of paintings at the Lÿz Art Forum in Siegen, Germany. Generally, Suttner had found Paul easy to deal with on the project. The musician agreed that the cost of the show shouldn't fall on the taxpayers of Westphalia, saying he would pay for the transportation and insurance of his pictures. Sir Paul was punctual for meetings and Suttner learned that McCartney's word was his bond. 'What Paul said happened. If Paul said, "I'm there," he was there. That was fantastic.' Reliability is often considered to be a characteristically German virtue and it is one that Paul appreciated. 'He told me once, "I love to be punctual, and you Germans are so efficient."' It also helped that Paul had a little of the language, actually less than one might think considering he studied German in school and spent part of his youth in Hamburg, but enough to be polite. 'He likes Germany … He told me it's his second best market in the world after the USA, and one of the best countries to tour.' Also, Germans didn't resent his wealth, as Paul sometimes felt the English did.

In the build-up to the art show, Suttner found how sensitive Sir Paul was to criticism. The curator had asked an academic, Professor Gundolf Winter, to look through Paul's pictures with a view to writing an essay for the catalogue, but Paul didn't like what the professor wrote. 'He said a lot of wonderful things about the pictures, but he also said Paul would never have a position in art history,' says Suttner. 'He's a good painter but not a worldwide [artist]. At that time he was not happy about this. He told us: "No, I don't want the show! … I won't come." He was a little bit pissed off.' At times like this, Paul forgot his invented persona as the humble, unknown English painter Paul Miller and reminded Wolfy that he was Sir Paul McCartney, former member of the Beatles! What's more, he was the Beatle responsible for the iconic jacket designs for *Sgt. Pepper*, the *White Album* and *Abbey Road*, so he knew a thing or two about art. Professor Winter's essay was quietly dropped from the catalogue, replaced with a more complimentary one by Christoph Tannert.

Having sent his artist friend Brian Clarke ahead to make sure everything was in *ordnung*, as the Germans say, Paul arrived in Siegen on the eve of his show, requesting last-minute changes just when Wolfy and his team were exhausted. 'He is never getting tired. He costs you a lot of strength.' A large number of press turned up for the opening the next day, 30 April 1999, Paul effortlessly charming the journalists, and posing patiently for the photographers. Then the doors opened to the public. Typically, a show at the Lÿz Art Forum attracted 4,000 people during its run. Approximately 45,000 people came to see Paul McCartney's paintings.

As to the quality of Paul's art, opinion was divided. The waspish British critic Brian Sewell was profoundly unimpressed:

> Paul McCartney's paintings are a self-indulgent impertinence so far from art that the art critic has no suitable words for them – they are, indeed, beneath criticism. They may have some private and personal value as therapy, but exposed to the public gaze they betray his arrogance and vanity … he is not a painter.

The less demanding viewer could find things to enjoy in the work of this enthusiastic amateur: a modest, dream-like quality at least. On the scale of rock star painters, of which they are many, Paul comes fractionally above Bob Dylan (who is very bad), but below Joni Mitchell, who is quite good.

RUN DEVIL RUN

Two months later, Sir Paul attended an awards show at the Dorchester Hotel in London, where he had once celebrated the release of *A Hard Day's Night* and, later in the Sixties, had an acrimonious business meeting with Allen Klein. This time he pitched up at the hotel with a host of celebrities to support the *Daily Mirror* newspaper's Pride of Britain Awards, whereby the paper recognised people who had 'made a difference' in various ways, including by acts of bravery. It was a coup to have lured Sir Paul out of mourning for the event. Little had been seen of him in public during the 13 months since Linda died. Paul was so inactive that MPL had just recorded a £368,979 annual loss ($564,537). He came to the Dorchester on 20 May 1999 primarily to remember Linda, by presenting an award in her name to a campaigning vegetarian friend of theirs, Juliet Gellatley.

Towards the end of the ceremony, Heather Mills strode on stage, a good-looking woman of 31, wearing an eye-catching, red, translucent top. With large, shapely breasts, a wide, inviting smile, and a flirtatious toss of her thick blonde hair, she was what Paul might once have termed 'a right little raver'. Speaking in a strong northern accent, Heather explained to the audience that she was at the Dorchester to introduce a friend of hers, student Helen Smith, who had shown fortitude in coping with the loss of both her legs, an arm and a hand due to septicaemia. Although it was not immediately obvious, Ms Mills was herself an amputee, wearing a prosthetic leg. A slight stiffness in her walk was the only sign of the disability.

'Who's that?' Paul asked Piers Morgan, Editor of the *Mirror*.

'That's Heather Mills,' replied the journalist, briefing Sir Paul on someone who was a minor celebrity in the tabloid world: the plucky model who'd lost a leg in a road accident and now raised money for charity.

'She's quite a girl, isn't she?'

Heather travelled to Cambodia after the Dorchester show. When she returned home she discovered that Sir Paul had telephoned and left a message for her: 'It's Paul McCartney here. I'd like to talk to you about the charity work.' He meant the Heather Mills Health Trust, an organisation Heather advertised in the back of her newly published autobiography, *Out on a Limb*. Although Heather did charitable work, and tended to talk casually about 'my charity', she hadn't yet registered the trust with the Charity Commission, as organisations with an income over £5,000 ($7,650) are obliged to do in England before they can properly call themselves a charity. Heather's organisation received a windfall 30 times this amount when, in August 1999, Paul invited the charity worker to his office and gave her a cheque for £150,000 (£229,500), which she gratefully accepted for the trust. But she didn't get around to registering the Trust as a charity for a further seven months.

As she left MPL that summer day, Heather noticed Sir Paul was admiring her backside. He hadn't looked with lust at a woman since Linda died. He felt guilty doing so, then told himself Linda wouldn't mind. Indeed, he convinced himself that Lin was sending him messages via the wildlife on the Sussex estate: '... there were strange metaphysical occurrences that seemed to mean something. Animal noises. Bird noises. You'd ask yourself a question under the stars

and, like, there'd be like an owl in the valley going *whoo-whoo-whoo*.'
In short, he had decided to date Heather Mills.

In contrast to her predecessors, Jane Asher and Linda Eastman, but
in common with Paul himself, Heather had been raised in the working-
class north of England. Born Heather Anne Mills on 12 January 1968 –
that is, between *Magical Mystery Tour* and the Beatles' *White Album*
– Heather was the middle child of John and Bernice Mills, with an older
brother named Shane and a younger sister, Fiona, to whom she was
close. Dad was a soldier, living in Aldershot when Heather was born,
and her life prior to meeting Paul was troubled, eventful and slightly
mysterious.

Family life started to fall apart in the mid-1970s when Mum was
involved in a car accident. During her convalescence, Heather and
Fiona were taken into care. Heather came to look back on the children's
home as preferable to life with her dad, whom she disliked intensely.
When Mum came out of hospital, the reunited family moved to a council estate near Washington, Tyne and Wear, where Heather claims Dad
hit Mum, and that she and another girl were abducted by a man who
kept them prisoners in his flat, fondled Heather and masturbated
himself, until the girls were rescued by police.* Mum then left home, to
live with an actor named Charles Stapley, leaving the children with their
father.

When she was ten, Heather was caught shoplifting. The police let
her off with a warning. Dad seemed unconcerned about her thieving,
but flew into rages if the house wasn't in order, lashing out at the kids.
Heather decided her father was a madman. Around the time she was
13, John Mills was imprisoned for fraud, with the result that the children
went to live with their mother and Charles Stapley in Clapham, South
London. Heather claims she ran away from this home at 14 to join the
fair on Clapham Common; she started sleeping rough under railway
arches, mixing with drug addicts, rent boys and prostitutes. Then she
got a Saturday job with a jeweller, from whom she stole. Heather was
arrested, taken to court and given a probationary sentence for theft. A
precocious teenager who dressed provocatively, Heather next strayed
into the fringes of the sex industry, finding employment around the age

---

* The friend disputed Heather's published account of these events in *Out on a Limb*,
and took legal action against Heather for identifying her in the book and falsifying
events. She won compensation.

of 16 in a Soho hostess club; that is, a red-light district bar where men are encouraged by semi-clad women to spend extortionate amounts on drink. She didn't work as a hostess herself. When she went for the interview she showed herself to be so naive, apparently, that the boss put her to work as a regular barmaid. Nonetheless, our heroine entered the seedy side of Soho, which exists alongside the smart offices of creative types like Paul McCartney, whose building was just around the corner on Soho Square.

Paul was promoting *Press to Play* when Heather met her first husband in a Soho bar named Bananas. Alfred Karmal, who went by the name Alfie, was ten years Heather's senior, a father of two going through a divorce. He took photos of Heather for her first modelling portfolio, which his sister shopped around town. Agents suggested the busty teenager might be suited to 'glamour' modelling, the sex industry euphemism for topless and soft porn shoots, though Alfie says he only found out later that Heather did such work. By Heather's account she progressed almost directly to being a more respectable 'swimsuit model'.

Two years passed. Alfie and Heather were living together in a semi-detached house in suburban Stanmore, Middlesex. Their relationship was tempestuous.

> One Friday she called me and said she'd been asked to go to Paris for some modelling … I didn't hear from her all weekend. I just wondered where the Hell she was. I was worried about her. And then she phoned up on Sunday night and said, 'I'm not coming back. Bye-bye.'

Heather writes in her memoir that at this stage in her adventures she became 'the face' of a large cosmetics firm, which brought her to live and work in France. 'I would have to live in Paris for twelve months with an option of another year if things went well. But the best thing about it was the money – I'd be paid £1,500 a day [$2,295] … It was the chance of a lifetime.' The firm was sufficiently substantial to accommodate Heather in a luxury Paris hotel. She was earning so much that she sent enough money home for Dad to buy himself a new BMW. Alfie has no idea how much if any of this story is true. 'It was difficult to believe anything she said, because I caught her out lying to me so often –

Where she was going, what she was doing …' Heather's frankly incredible French adventure came to a suitably improbable ending in December 1988 when, by her own account, the unnamed boss of her unidentified cosmetics firm fell so violently in love with his model that she fled France, catching a late-night ferry home to Dover. Heather telephoned Alfie to pick her up at the docks, thus resuming their relationship. 'She asked me to marry her about 50 times that same week.'

On the assurance that she would see a psychiatrist, to help her stop telling lies, so he says, Alfie agreed to marry Heather. Their wedding took place on 6 May 1989. They couple lived once more in Stanmore, then Hoddesdon, a commuter town in Hertfordshire. Heather suffered the first of two ectopic pregnancies, ran a small modelling agency for a while, and had cosmetic surgery on her breasts. Then she went to Yugoslavia for a ski holiday, had an affair with her ski instructor, Milos, came home briefly, then left Alfie once and for all in 1991. He recalls:

I came home from work and she's gone, packed all her cases, smashed the front door. A big pane of glass by the front door. She'd scraped all the wallpaper carrying her bags, getting out – took off. And that was that. I didn't know where she was. Her sister didn't know where she was. Nobody knew where she was … I found out she was in Yugoslavia, fucking around.

He also claims to have found out that Heather had driven the car he'd bought her to the nearest garage and sold it for cash. Alfie says Heather sold her rings, too. In her memoirs, Heather tells the story differently, writing that she told Alfie she was going to Yugoslavia to be with her ski instructor boyfriend. 'My marriage hadn't had a pretty ending. When I told him I was leaving, Alfie had been first shocked, then angry, then bitter,' she wrote in *Out on a Limb*. 'He'd told me that running away to Yugoslavia was just like running off to the fair when I was thirteen.' In any event, she left and Alfie filed for divorce.

Heather now found herself in the middle of a civil war in Yugoslavia, as the country began to fall apart with the collapse of communist hegemony in Eastern Europe. She became involved in aid work for war victims, developing a particular interest in people who had lost limbs in landmine explosions. On trips home to the UK, Heather raised money and resources for these people and resumed her modelling career, which became so successful, by her account, that she was able to buy a Saab convertible and a flat in the salubrious London suburb of Hampstead. Milos was history. One night at Stringfellow's nightclub, Heather met a well-paid bond dealer named Raffaele Mincione, with whom she began a new affair. Heather had already resolved to end this relationship when the couple set off for a walk in Kensington Gardens on Sunday 8 August 1993. As they crossed Kensington Road, walking towards the park, a passing police motorcycle collided with Heather, tearing off her left foot in the accident. Surgeons subsequently amputated all but six inches of the leg below the knee to create a clean stump. This was the turning point in Heather Mills's life.

For a single 25-year-old woman with little education who traded on her looks, losing a leg would appear to be an almost insurmountable calamity, and it seemed that way to Heather at first. The sight of her stump was shocking, and when Heather tried to go to the toilet on her own she fell over. She wept, asking 'Why me?', but then pulled herself together in a way that showed tremendous character. The tabloid press was eager to tell the tale of a sexy model turned plucky amputee, so Heather auctioned her story to journalists from her hospital bed. Apart from being photogenic, she proved a good talker, quite charismatic in her own way. After discharging herself from hospital, Heather started to appear regularly in the tabloids and on daytime television. The *Daily Star* gave her its Gold Star Award for courage; she met the Prime Minister, John Major, at Downing Street, a previously unimaginable situation for the shoplifter turned glamour model. As Charles Stapley observes, the attention Heather now received because of her accident made her a somebody, 'which she'd always wanted to be'.

Soon Heather was doing bits of broadcasting, and writing her autobiography. She courted publicity, talking to journalists about her charity work and her love life, which continued to be eventful. Raffaele was dumped, two more fiancés following, neither of whom she married. Heather now seemed obsessed with her celebrity, granting endless interviews to talk about herself and her causes. Likened by credulous journalists to fellow landmine campaigner Princess Diana, Heather became the subject of increasingly improbable articles: she was being nominated for a Nobel Prize; she planned to ski for Britain in the Paralympics; a Hollywood movie was to be made of her life; a career in politics beckoned. 'By my mid-forties I want to be Secretary of State for

Health,' she announced ridiculously in 1998. Then something almost as unlikely happened. Heather began to date the greatest living Englishman.

'THE MORE YOU MET HER, THE MORE YOU KNEW SHE WAS A NUTTER'

That July, Sir Paul McCartney attended a choral concert at Charterhouse School in Surrey to commemorate Linda's memory. Sir Paul, the recently knighted Sir Richard Rodney Bennett, David Matthews and Paul's old friend John Tavener were among nine composers who contributed choral works for A Garland for Linda. Paul's piece, *Nova*, has a distinctly religious feel, Paul asking in the libretto the question Christ asked on the cross: 'God where are you?' Paul concluded that God was everywhere, in nature, in every snowflake and blade of grass. Paul may have gone further in this spiritual direction, in his music and in his life, had he not been yanked out of his grief by his vivacious new girlfriend.

Heather Mills had only recently got engaged again, after a ten-day romance, to documentary film-maker Chris Terrill. The couple set 8 August 1999 as their wedding day. A week beforehand, Heather called it off, telling her fiancé she was going on holiday to Greece. In fact, she accompanied Sir Paul to America for his summer vacation in the Hamptons. When they returned to the UK, Paul and Heather were inseparable. They tucked themselves up in the Forecastle, a quaint hideaway cottage Paul owned in Rye, near the town's old church. Then, in October, they left the love nest to release a charity record, *Voice*, in which Heather delivered a monologue about limbless people while Paul played guitar and sang backing vocals. Heather proved herself to be as hopeless a musical partner as Linda had been. It was, though, typical of Paul to take on the interests of the women in his life. He had always done so.

Paul had also always been one of the most romantic of men. For Hallowe'en he arranged a tryst with Heather in a London hotel, filling their suite with Hallowe'en lanterns. Heather noticed Paul was so happy he was literally dancing down the street, like his hero Fred Astaire. A few days later, he invited Heather and her sister Fiona to Peasmarsh for a bonfire night party. Blossom Farm had become a shrine to Linda since her demise, with a memorial fountain tinkling outside the kitchen window where she and Paul had once fed Wirral the Squirrel. Heather couldn't decently come and stay here. So she and Fiona were accommodated in another property on the estate, a house named Beanacres. The *News of the World* broke the story of the romance after its photographers caught Heather leaving the property the next day. Clearly they had been tipped off.

Rejuvenated by his relationship with Heather, Paul picked up the reins of his career, releasing *Working Classical*, a CD that featured attractive arrangements of tunes Linda had inspired, 'My Love', 'Maybe I'm Amazed' and 'The Lovely Linda', played by the Loma Mar Quartet. He also returned to his roots, recording a new rock 'n' roll album, *Run Devil Run*, with guitarist mates Dave Gilmour and Mick Green. Ian Paice from Deep Purple played drums and Pete Wingfield keyboards. Recorded quickly over five days at Abbey Road Studios, *Run Devil Run* had the same attractive live sound as *CHOBA B CCCP* and *Unplugged*. Like those two records, the set list featured songs Paul had grown up listening to, most of them obscure, with a couple of newly written tracks including the title song, 'Run Devil Run', inspired by a voodoo remedy Paul had picked up in Atlanta to ward off evildoers, thieves and liars. To promote the CD, and help mark the end of the millennium, Paul decided to perform these rockers at the Cavern.

Music fans had come to appreciate what a grievous loss the destruction of the Cavern had been in 1973, with the result that a replica had been built nearby, opening for business in 1984. The new Cavern was on the same side of Mathew Street, but slightly deeper underground, with a recreated vaulted ceiling, and a second, larger stage area where various acts performed, including Beatles tribute bands of which there were now many. Sir Paul performed in this larger room with his *Run Devil Run* band on 14 December 1999, playing to 300 selected guests and millions watching on the Internet. A rather clinical, emotionless event was enlivened by a heckler yelling for 'Satisfaction'. Paul stopped, glanced up crossly and said: 'There's a little wag in the crowd – read my lips [then mouthed the words] Fuck Off!' Later he discovered the heckler was a member of his own family.

A few days later, Paul invited Heather to Rembrandt to help the McCartneys usher in the new millennium. It was at this Merseyside house party that Heather was introduced to Paul's children, 'a difficult situation for everybody,' she later admitted. The 'relies' also looked upon her askance. 'The first time she ever appeared was at Paul's house, New Year's Eve,' recalls Mike Robbins. 'I went in the kitchen for some reason. It's only a little kitchen there. Seated at a table in the kitchen, in white fur, and a white Cossack fur hat,* is this very glamorous-looking blonde who I'd never seen.' Mike extended his hand. She didn't shake it, and seemed to want to stay in the kitchen rather than join everybody else in the living room.

> I said to [my wife], 'Have you seen the bird?' She said, 'No.' I said, 'Go and have a look.' So [Bett] wandered into the kitchen, comes back a bit later and said, 'Oh, very strange young lady.' I said, 'One of Paul's brief bits of crumpet I presume.' And that was Heather – the first time we met her. And the more you met her, the more you knew she was a nutter. She was weird.

Paul clearly didn't think so. After the holidays, he took his children to Parrot Cay, a resort island in the British West Indies. The day the children left for home, Heather flew in to join her boyfriend. During a walk along the beach Paul told Heather that pirates once used the island and pirate relics could sometimes be found under the rocks. Coming to a likely stone, he suggested she turn it over. Heather did so, discovering that Paul had been out on the beach earlier and scratched a heart, with their names in it, in the sand underneath. 'I stood there shaking my head in disbelief. This man was too much.'

ANOTHER DEATH IN ARIZONA

For the past 15 years Mel See had lived with his partner Beverly Wilk on the outskirts of Tucson, Arizona. Recently, he'd begun seeing a new woman in Santa Fe. He seemed unable to choose between his two lovers. Feeling guilty, Mel became depressed, withdrawn and increasingly irrational. 'He kept saying, "I betrayed you,"' recalls Beverly. 'He was just really weird …' Mel was prescribed anti-depressants, but

---

* Surely fun fur. Paul and Heather were both fiercely anti-fur.

didn't like taking them, and became increasingly intense and strange. He read the Bible and his favourite Ernest Hemingway books obsessively and said peculiar things. Mel hit bottom on Saturday 18 March, 2000, pleading with Beverly not to leave him. Beverly said she wasn't going anywhere, though they slept in separate rooms. She woke in the night to find her boyfriend standing over her bed. 'I couldn't do it to you and Heather,' he told her.

'What's wrong, Mel?'

Beverly didn't get a sensible answer.

She got up in time to see Mel walking out of the house. 'I'm going down to the wash for a walk,' he said. When he didn't come back, Beverly went to look for him. She found Mel lying in a hollowed-out palo verde tree that he loved, having shot himself in the head like his hero Hemingway. Remarkably, Mel had chosen to take his life in exactly the same way, and at exactly the same age, as Hemingway: both men were days away from their 62nd birthdays when they blew their brains out. 'I looked and I saw him lying there,' said Beverly, 'and I just ran ...'

Mel had left a note of sorts in his office; a piece of scribble, with crossings out and addendums. It began: 'To Heather, executor, instructions for my cremation ...' Obviously realising this was too great a burden to put on his daughter, Mel had then struck out Heather's name and addressed the note instead to a male friend, informing him that he wanted his body to be cremated and his ashes scattered over his parents' grave. He asked for forgiveness. A phone call was made to John Eastman, who contacted Paul, who told Heather that her father had died. Mel's suicide placed an almost intolerable additional strain on an already fragile woman who, two years after losing her mother at 56, now lost her natural father at 61 in extremely distressing circumstances. More upset followed.

It is standard police procedure in Arizona to have a homicide unit investigate any violent death, a fact the British press got hold of and beat up into a story about Linda's first husband possibly being murdered, nonsense that was fuelled by irresponsible local gossip about who might have wanted Mel dead. Such rumours persist in Tucson, with one former neighbour claiming improbably that Mel's anthropology had been a cover for his real work for the CIA. This is almost certainly untrue, as was the homicide story. 'It didn't turn into a full-blown murder investigation,' says Lieutenant Deanna Coultas of the Pima County sheriff's office. 'I believe it was classified as a suicide.'

Although the main purpose of Mel's 'will' was to make sure his friends and family had his body cremated, he was buried on 27 March at the Evergreen Cemetery in Tucson. The marker reads:

JOSEPH MEL SEE
COMPANION MENTOR AND DAD
1938–2000

So ended the life of the man who may have been the Jojo of 'Get Back'. More significantly, it was an event from which Heather McCartney seemed unable to recover, becoming a virtual recluse thereafter. Her design businesses fell into desuetude, as did her pottery. A high wooden fence was erected around her Sussex cottage, where she became a hermit. 'The last time I met her [she] was in a dreadful state,' says neighbour Veronica Languish. 'Terrible thing, a girl like that, got everything to live for and nothing.'

BEHOLD MY HEART

The other Heather now took centre stage in Sir Paul's life, with stories emerging in the press that Heather Mills might not be an ideal girl-friend for the star. Her ex-husband Alfie Karmal made his position clear when he told the *Sunday People*: 'Marrying Heather was the biggest mistake of my life.' Other negative stories followed from different sources suggesting that during her time as a 'swimsuit model' in Paris Heather had actually kept rich Arabs company, including the arms dealer Adnan Khashoggi. Heather had been a 'party girl', said a fellow model, who claimed to have introduced Heather to a seamy world where pretty girls were rewarded with gifts and cash. It looked bad. A private investigator contacted Alfie, saying he worked for a client who needed to know whether certain things about Heather were true – such as who paid for her plastic surgery. Alfie concluded that the private eye was working for Sir Paul McCartney.

Despite these stories, Sir Paul chose to support Heather, making his support public when he walked onto the set of a cheesy TV show his girlfriend was appearing on, *Stars and Their Lives*, to affirm his love for Heather. Many onlookers and friends of Sir Paul wondered why the star invested such trust in a self-publicising minor celebrity with a dubious past. Paul's cousin Mike Robbins suggests the answer is sex. Although Paul had enjoyed a vigorous bachelorhood, he had been in a monogamous relationship for almost 30 years, and in that time friends and family observed that Paul had lost some of his worldliness. Then along came a busty blonde who may have had a certain expertise in the bedroom. 'I'm being crude now, [but he was] cock happy,' says Mike. 'And he confused [sex with love]. He couldn't tell the difference.'

Another way to look at Paul's relationship with Heather is to consider that, like John Lennon, McCartney had spent his adult life in a situation where almost everybody he met venerated him. Most people couldn't behave normally around a Beatle. John and Paul had chosen as their partners gutsy women who treated them as normal people. Yoko, Linda and Heather were all three a match for their dominant, wilful partners. And the senior Beatles were both of them a handful. John and Paul had become so famous, so rich and so powerful that they were inevitably slightly monstrous. They were only comfortable with equally monstrous women.

Other, normal people naturally struggled to see what Paul saw in Linda and particularly in Heather, whom almost nobody had a good word for. Paul's fans didn't like Heather any better than his 'relies' did. That autumn, a selection of Paul's paintings were shown at the Matthew Marks Gallery in New York. Linda Aiello and Toni Kraker showed up, greeting Heather brightly as she left the gallery. 'Hi Heather!' chirped the women. 'She gave us the look, you know, when somebody is saying to themselves "Get a life!"' says Linda.

> She put her nose in the air, she turned her face [away]. Two seconds later here he comes, Paul, bopping up. 'Hi girls!' thumbs up. 'How are you doing?' Now she sees that he knew us ... If I tell you how she changed – like a light switch. She just switched on ... smiled all of a sudden. But to me, *so fake*.

Yet Paul was besotted. Happy in bed, he found himself showered with money again when Neil Aspinall gathered together the 27 Beatles singles that had reached number one in the UK or USA on a CD titled

Beatles 1. Although many commentators figured Beatles fans already owned all these songs, and wouldn't buy the compilation, *Beatles 1* made number one in 34 countries, becoming, amazingly, the best-selling album of the decade in the USA. It seemed there was no end to the public's appetite for the Beatles. Flushed with his windfall, Paul took Heather to India for most of January 2001, arriving in Cochin on the Malabar Coast by private jet, then touring the country, staying in the most exquisite hotels. Paul delighted in arranging romantic surprises and treats for his girlfriend during their Indian holiday, including an overnight train journey to Jaipur on her 33rd birthday. As they lay in their stateroom, rolling through the night, Paul picked up his Gibson Backpacker acoustic and composed 'Riding Into Jaipur'.

The couple flew on to the USA. Paul took Heather shopping in Manhattan on Valentine's Day, then to the top of the Empire State Building where he wrote their names on the stonework. That evening, they danced in the Rainbow Room. Travelling west to LA, Paul was inspired to record almost a whole album of new music in two weeks, working with Rusty Anderson, a rangy Californian guitarist, powerhouse drummer Abe Laboriel Jr, and Gabe Dixon on keyboards. The American band created a nice sound, captured by producer David Kahne, but it was the lyrics that were most interesting. Although there were references to Paul's first marriage on *Driving Rain*, most of the songs seemed to be about his new relationship, revealing a man befuddled by love, with intimations of disagreements, rifts and doubts. Paul sang on 'Lonely Road' that he had tried to get over his new girl, but she had been tested and found true. He sounded vulnerable, making it plain in 'About You' that in the wake of Linda's death he felt he'd fallen into a slump as bad as that he suffered when the Beatles broke up. As Linda saved him then, Heather was pulling him out of his grief now. He was inordinately grateful, and terrified he would lose her, besotted and adoring. To top it all, there was 'Heather', a pretty tune with a lyric based on Edward Lear's *The Owl and the Pussycat*, with Paul and Heather sailing away into a dreamy world of magic and love. While he worked on this album, Paul rented a property on Heather Road, Beverly Hills. They liked their 'Heather House' so well he bought it. Back home, MPL loaned Heather £800,000 (£1.2m) to buy and fix up another house, Angel's Rest, part of a terrace of gorgeous, whitewashed houses on a private shingle beach near Hove in Sussex. Paul and Heather were often to be found walking hand in hand by the shore.

Like many a widower who plunges into a new relationship before he has finished grieving for his late wife, Paul's infatuation with Heather coexisted with deep feelings for Linda. There was a song titled 'Magic' on *Driving Rain* about the moment he first spoke to a girl who became his love. This wasn't about Heather, but Linda. In May Paul released a double CD retrospective, *Wingspan*, that charted the story of Wings, the cover art featuring Linda's hands making the Wings symbol. Paul sat for interviews conducted by his daughter Mary, and filmed by her husband Alistair, for an accompanying documentary, during which he spoke lovingly of that happy time in his life, 'having my best mate, my wife, to sing along with ...'

When a book of Paul's poems and lyrics was published, it was dedicated to Linda and the children. Introduced and edited by Adrian Mitchell, *Blackbird Singing* made an ambitious case for Paul as a poet, a singing poet in the tradition of Blake and Homer, Mitchell argued, in that most of the selected works were song lyrics. This was too strong. The best of Paul's Beatles songs, 'Penny Lane' for example, did have a poetic quality, but a modest one. Many of his post-Beatles songs looked bare as orphans on the page, without their music. 'Mull of Kintyre' just about worked as a poem, but Denny Laine says he wrote much of that. Of the work Paul had written as poetry *per se*, 'Ivan', 'Meditate' and 'Standing Stone' were among the better efforts in *Blackbird Singing*, though again Paul had help with the latter, and Adrian Mitchell acknowledged in his introduction that he 'made suggestions for small cuts or changes ...' to other poems in the book. As in the workshop of a great Renaissance painter, many talented men now toiled, with little credit, in the illustrious name of Sir Paul McCartney.

In the last months of Linda's life Paul had been offered a commission by Magdalen College, Oxford, to write a choral work for the college's new auditorium. Paul and Lin had paid a visit to the ancient university, and accepted the commission, which was prestigious but unpaid. Paul would bankroll the project. He started work shortly before Linda died. 'We thought, after Linda died, nothing was going to happen,' says Anthony Smith, then President of Magdalen, but Sir Paul came back to Oxford for All Souls' Night in November 1998, when Linda's name was read as part of the service, and resumed work on the commission shortly thereafter. Although Smith had originally suggested a relatively modest piece, reflecting the academic seasons, Paul began to think of a much grander composition to commemorate his love for Linda. He found his title on a flying visit to New York in May 2000, where he had gone at his friend Sir John Tavener's* invitation to narrate a poem as part of a Tavener concert at the church of St Ignatius Loyola. As he waited to speak, Paul noticed a statue of Christ, over which was inscribed Ecce Cor Meum. With his schoolboy Latin, Paul deduced that this meant 'Behold My Heart'.

Paul worked on *Ecce Cor Meum* with David Matthews through the summer of 2001, frequently travelling to Oxford to stay with Anthony Smith in the President's residence. When he wasn't working, Paul could slip over to the college bar where, refreshingly, the students were sophisticated enough not to ask for his autograph, but spoke to him in a normal, civilised way. He mixed easily with everybody on campus, from the choir boys he charmed with stories of his own failed career as a chorister ('If I'd been accepted by Liverpool [Anglican] Cathedral, there would have been no Beatles,' he told them) to the dons. Smith feared that some of his learned colleagues might condescend to Paul, but everybody was respectful of what the musician had achieved in his career, and indeed quietly thrilled to have him at Magdalen, female colleagues noticeably dressing up when Sir Paul came to dine. McCartney's ambition to compose complex classical works seemed to the academics a laudable desire to stretch himself. Says Smith, who found Sir Paul to have acquired gravitas as he neared 60:

> He has aspired to be something more as a person. He involves himself in great causes. He wants to do something for the world and as he feels himself growing bigger his musical work is developing at the same time and he no longer wants to write singles for teenagers as he did many decades ago. He wants to be a composer. He is that. How good and durable he is, the future will decide … He has now established himself as a public person in a way that commands respect, [and] I think he also has a sense of himself as a bit of a national monument.

* Knighted in 2000.

Heather Mills made a less favourable impression in Oxford, the charity worker showing little interest in Paul's classical projects, unless she had suggestions for changes, which she gave freely in the irritating manner of Yoko Ono. 'I think she felt she knew best about the music as well [as other things],' snorts Smith. 'I think she was trying to put Paul right quite a lot of the time, and I don't think he felt that was necessary.' There was a sense of the couple not being entirely at one, perhaps because Paul was working on a piece in praise of his past love, and while he and Ms Mills didn't row publicly, there were awkward silences at the President's house. Heather was often on the phone to do with her charitable works. 'I didn't get a strong sense that she was in love,' says Smith,

and then she left in the middle of the night once. She was always doing the counselling work on the phone with kids who were suffering from cancer and so on, and I think it was because of that she left very early on one day, because one of them had been phoning her or something … Her own life was very important to her.

Among Sir Paul's friends and associates the consensus was that Heather was trouble. Many worrying stories were swirling around about her. Eric Stewart was so concerned about what he heard that he wrote a letter to Paul:

She went to that charity show knowing she would meet him, and I do believe she said to somebody before that she was going to marry him, so I sent a letter warning him. I didn't get a reply, but as soon as they got together the people I knew at MPL, all these old friends, suddenly [seemed] to disappear, they got replaced. Suddenly I couldn't ring him there. I could ring him at home or at the studio, but there nobody would put you through to him. What's going on here? It was like he was trying to sweep out anybody who knew him and Linda together.

At least that was Eric's perception of what was going on at MPL. When Paul introduced Heather Mills to another old friend, Tony 'Measles' Bramwell, with whom he'd been reconciled since their 1978 spat, Bramwell immediately remembered Heather as a girl who used to hang around the London clubs. 'Heather looked at me in horror, knowing I'd been in the clubs when she was slapping around [looking for] a rich man.' Unwilling to spend time in Measles' company, Heather announced: 'There's nobody interesting here, I'm going shopping.' Paul followed her meekly, Bramwell concluding that Heather was every bit as horrible as he had always found Yoko Ono to be.

That summer Paul took Heather to Liverpool, where he was to preside over the annual LIPA graduation ceremony. Beforehand, he introduced his girlfriend to Mark Featherstone-Witty, who didn't like her any more than Bramwell or Smith. 'Normally, in a normal conversation, you meet somebody, "Tell me a little bit about yourself," and at some point in the conversation you expect the favour to be returned,' Featherstone-Witty observes. 'Two and a half hours later she was still talking. Ha Ha Ha! I've met self-centred people in my life, but I think she has to get the gold star; she has the Oscar for somebody who is self-centred.'

Yet Paul was smitten. After the ceremony, he drove Heather to the Lake District, checking into the Sharrow Bay Hotel on Ullswater where, one night before dinner, he dropped down on his knee and said: 'I love you, Heather. Will you marry me?' Paul presented his girlfriend with a sapphire and diamond engagement ring he'd bought in India in January. (The fact he'd waited six months before offering it to Heather tells its own story.) When the charity worker said she would marry him, the famous widower burst into tears.

THAT DIFFICULT SECOND MARRIAGE

THE CONCÉRT FOR NEW YORK

On the morning of 11 September 2001, Sir Paul McCartney and his fiancée Heather Mills were sitting in the first-class compartment of a commercial aeroplane at John F. Kennedy Airport, about to fly to London. As their aircraft taxied for take-off, the couple saw the familiar outline of Manhattan blemished by a pall of smoke rising from the World Trade Center. The captain asked everybody to remain calm as he found out what was happening. Passengers instinctively started calling family members on their cell phones. They were all still sitting there 17 minutes later when a second terrorist-guided aircraft slammed into the South Tower of the Trade Center, shortly after which came news of a third plane hitting the Pentagon and that, as a result, all commercial flights were grounded. When they had disembarked, Paul and Heather were driven back to Long Island where, like most people, the couple sat watching television coverage of these extraordinary events.

Paul and Heather had been in New York so that Heather could collect an award for her charity work. Since getting engaged to Sir Paul, she had become more prominent in public life on both sides of the Atlantic, giving the impression she expected to be taken notice of independently of her fiancé, though she wouldn't have received anything like as much attention if her name hadn't been linked with his. Linda had always been happy to be Paul's consort, never trying to overshadow him. With Heather there was the sense of a rival ego. Ever since she first sold her story to the British tabloids, she had revelled in media attention, albeit pretty second-rate stuff. Now she swaggered on an international stage.

In fact Heather soon bored of sitting at home with Paul in Amagansett and left him there to fulfil 'urgent charity commitments' in the UK.

When she returned to Long Island a few days later, Heather suggested to Paul that he 'do a charity concert' for 9/11. Paul wasn't immediately keen. His new album, *Driving Rain*, was due out and he didn't want to give the impression he was using the disaster to sell records. Heather told him not to be so silly. 'Write a song about freedom,' she suggested, picking a touchstone word used repeatedly by President George W. Bush in the aftermath of the terrorist attacks, his speeches implying a link with Saddam Hussein's regime in Iraq, which the US subsequently invaded. Many observers, Paul included, came to see this as a blunder, there being no proven link between 9/11 and Saddam's Iraq. 'The opportunity that was lost was that people felt a massive natural sympathy for the people of America, and the political moves that followed 9/11 wasted that opportunity,' he later remarked. 'It was like someone in the playground got hit, and didn't quite know who hit him, and he just decided to swipe out at the nearest person – and that turned out to be Iraq.' In the immediate aftermath of the attacks, however, empathising with the hurt suffered by the American people, Paul acceded to his fiancée's suggestion and set President Bush's rhetoric to music.

The song 'Freedom', co-written with Heather, was one of McCartney's most lumpen compositions, with a heavy-handed football chant of a tune and lyrics that read like the words culled from Republican bumper stickers:

> *This is my right, a right given by God*
> *To live a free life, to live in freedom*
>
> *Talkin' about freedom*
> *I'm talkin' 'bout freedom*
> *I will fight for the right*
> *To live in freedom*

Harvey Weinstein and the television company VH-1 were already planning a concert in aid of the firefighters and other emergency workers who had suffered and distinguished themselves during the attacks, with the Who committed to perform. Sir Paul was persuaded to abandon plans for his own 9/11 concert and join the VH-1 event. In doing so, he became the headliner, with some backstage bad feeling. 'I think the Who feel that they were in before Paul,' comments a VH-1 executive.

> The Who were the first people contacted, and they agreed to anchor it, and when other people heard the Who were in they started coming in. At the same time Paul was in town and [he] became the anchor and headliner of the Concert for New York, but as you might understand there was a certain amount of confusion among some of the other people who felt that, 'Gee, I committed before Paul did, how come it's become Paul's concert?' … It starts to get into a touchy area because different people's egos are involved.

Pete Townshend remembers events differently:

> When I was approached by Harvey Weinstein, Paul had already made a commitment I think – pressed by Heather Mills who was on a plane on the runway at Kennedy with him watching as the towers fell. He was simply unsure how the show was going to unfold. We did not commit to play on condition of being headliners or anchors. We just committed to do it … It may be of course that our MANAGEMENT [sic] were peeved that Paul should take over the anchor spot. But we would always defer to the Stones or the Beatles (Macca).

The show at Madison Square Garden on 20 October 2001 was a highly emotional event featuring appearances by actors, sports stars and political figures, including New York's Mayor Rudolph Giuliani. Roughly half the acts were British, with David Bowie, Eric Clapton, Jagger and Richards, Sir Elton John and the Who all performing before Sir Paul took the stage in an FDNY T-shirt. Starting with 'I'm Down', he went on to perform two songs from his new album including the single 'From a Lover to a Friend', before closing with 'Yesterday', 'Freedom' and 'Let It Be', the finale being a foot-stomping reprise of 'Freedom', which was released as a single. The show, which raised millions for charity, naturally overshadowed the release of *Driving Rain*, a weak album that made little impact on the charts. Likewise, 'Freedom' just scraped into *Billboard*'s Hot 100.

The momentous events of 9/11 also overshadowed the last days of George Harrison, who, having survived a knife attack by a maniac intruder at Friar Park in 1999, was in the US receiving treatment for cancer. His situation was terminal. Paul visited his old friend at Staten Island University Hospital in November. Theirs had always been a difficult relationship, from the Quarry Men until a year ago when the *Anthology* book was published. George had worked in the past with Genesis, a small British publishing house, to produce expensive, leather-bound limited editions of his book, *I Me Mine*, and his friend Derek Taylor's memoir, *Fifty Years Adrift*. George had told the Apple board he wanted the *Anthology* book to come out initially in a similar, leather-bound edition. Paul was aghast. 'Paul objected because he was vegetarian,' reports George's confidant Neil Innes. 'So George was muttering about that. [The relationship] had got a bit strained towards the end with silly things.' All bickering was now put to one side. Sitting by the hospital bed of his childhood friend, and colleague in one of the great musical adventures of the twentieth century, Paul took George's hand in his and stroked it tenderly. As he left the hospital, he reflected that he'd never touched George like that before in all the years they'd known each other.

It was with fast-fading George in mind, and the loss of Linda, that Paul prepared for the first performances of his choral work *Ecce Cor Meum*. Beforehand, Paul and Heather stayed again in Oxford as guests of Magdalen President Anthony Smith, who found he liked Ms Mills no more now that she was Sir Paul's fiancée.

> You know when a woman loves a man she's with, and there was no love there. Everyone could see it. Everyone around [them]. You could just see it, you could *feel* it, and he didn't, or he had convinced himself that, because he was a good man, which he is, an extremely morally motivated person, in all things, I think, he felt he *ought* to love her. That's my theory.

The first performance of *Ecce Cor Meum* was held in the new college chapel, then before a larger audience at the Sheldonian Theatre. The piece was demanding and under-rehearsed, which Paul's collaborator David Matthews found surprising in light of the fact that the normally punctilious Paul had previously made as much time and money available as was necessary to ensure his classical works came off well. Perhaps he was distracted by his new love. In any event, Paul got up on stage to excuse *Ecce Cor Meum* as a work in progress. He would make changes before bringing it before an audience again.

Three weeks later, on 29 November 2001, George Harrison died aged 58. Paul received the news in a late-night telephone call from Olivia Harrison, who had her husband cremated in a private ceremony in California. The death was a momentous loss, the third Beatle to have left the stage before his time (counting Stuart Sutcliffe), and Paul seemed determined not to fumble his public reaction as he had when John died almost 21 years ago. Arranging to meet the press in the lane outside his Sussex estate, he spoke to reporters of how George was his childhood friend, a brave, beautiful, funny man whose music would live forever, revealing nothing of their difficult personal relationship. 'I love him, like he's my brother,' he said mournfully as the crows cawed to each other in the trees.

BACK ON THE ROAD

In the new year, Paul took Heather back to India, where he bought her more jewellery, one of many ways in which he showed generosity towards his fiancée. He also advanced her £150,000 ($229,500) to decorate her new seaside home near Hove, writing off the original £800,000 home loan as a gift, and gave Heather a joint Coutts credit card – a useful accoutrement as they set out together on tour.

Initially planned as a spring tour of 20 North American cities, the so-called *Driving USA* tour grew into a 14-month round-the-world odyssey with a sense that Paul was seeking to demonstrate to his fiancée what a big star he was. Though this may seem unnecessary to anybody with the slightest interest in popular culture, Heather professed herself largely ignorant of Paul's history, claiming not to know that classic songs that came on the radio – 'Back in the USSR', for example – were by the Beatles. Her favourite group was the Australian heavy rock act AC/DC.

Paul's new road band featured the Americans Rusty Anderson and Abe Laboriel Jr from the *Driving Rain* sessions; he also rehired Englishman Paul 'Wix' Wickens who'd played keyboards on tour and on record with McCartney between 1989 and '93. As an old hand, Wix told the Americans how exciting it would be to play with Paul on stage, 'the right voice singing these songs, and you're all part of it'. The last member to join the band was Californian Brian Ray, who would play guitar and bass (when Paul took up a different instrument). The musicians performed their first gig together when Paul sang 'Freedom' at Super Bowl XXXVI in New Orleans in February 2002, an event that also served to commemorate 9/11, the tour proper starting two months later in Oakland, California.

Having associated himself so closely with 9/11, Sir Paul continued to wrap himself in the American flag during his progress across the United States in 2002, literally waving the Stars and Stripes on stage in Oakland, while subtly encouraging stories about his shows 'healing' America as the Beatles were seen to do in the Sixties after the assassination of President Kennedy. While he chose his words carefully – 'there is a sort of healing thing going on again, and I'm proud to be part of that ... we didn't set out to do that with this tour, but we're here at the right time ...' – such sentiments could appear opportunistic.

Sir Paul's journey across the USA was almost regal, in the style of a man who really was the king of pop, whatever Michael Jackson claimed. The routine was that Sir Paul and his fiancée arrived at the venue mid-afternoon in a black, presidential-style limousine, flanked by police outriders, the star letting his window down slightly to wave to the fans waiting on the rampway, with their cameras and old LPs, wailing 'Paul! Paul!' in the faint hope of an autograph. He then played a lengthy sound check before retiring to his private backstage area, cordoned off and personalised with an Indian theme – drapes, cushions and scented candles. Before the show, Paul received VIP guests here, did press interviews, and ate a vegetarian repast prepared by the nine-strong kitchen staff, who were briefed to serve 'nothing with a face', which included caviar. Fortunately, Heather was also vegetarian. Everybody else on tour was obliged to be vegetarian so long as they expected to eat at Paul's expense.

As the doors opened and the punters swarmed into the arena, Paul selected his stage clothes from two racks of trousers, shirts and jackets, and began his final, pre-show ritual. First he drank a cup of tea, then he went into one the vast backstage bathrooms, a corner of which had been prepared for his ablutions, which included inhaling warm water to clear his airways. Next he collected his band – Abe, Brian, Rusty and Wix – who stiffened to attention when 'the boss' entered their room. They sang warm-up songs together, Paul enjoying a comical chorus of 'Hey Hey We're the Monkees'; he then accepted a ritual

Strepsil throat lozenge from John Hammel, whom he gave a high five in return, sucked the sweet for a few moments, took it out and placed it on a speaker cabinet, the same speaker every night. Paul is a man of routine. He would then peek out at the audience, turning back from the curtain with a pantomime look of terror as if to say: 'THERE'S TOO MANY PEOPLE OUT THERE – I CAN'T GO ON!' Finally, he went into a huddle with his band, asking God for a good show. Despite all the demands on His time, God usually obliged.

On the other side of the curtain, the audience were being entertained by a pageant of actors in colourful costume – Indian god, Magritte man with umbrella, clowns and acrobats – who paraded down the aisles to ambient music, including snatches of *Rushes*, then mounted the stage in a Cirque du Soleil-style tableau. Just before the audience became too restless – 'This is all very well, but when's the darn show gonna begin?' – McCartney stepped on stage to a roar of excited recognition. He stood there for a moment accepting the love as his band took their places, then struck up 'Hello Goodbye' from 1967, when the world was fab and nobody dreamed of terrorists crashing planes into skyscrapers. The 15,000 or so people in the audience – a wide range of ages these days from mothers with their babies to the elderly – visibly relaxed as the music smoothed their cares. As guitarist Brian Ray observed, the concert-goers seemed to grow younger before his eyes.

Ever since his watershed tour of 1989/90, Paul had increased the Beatles content of his live show. Back in 1989 he played about 14 Beatles songs each night, slightly less than half the concert. Thirteen years later he played approximately 23 Beatles songs as part of a longer, 36-number set, with an all-Beatles encore. Tried and tested solo and Wings material such as 'Live and Let Die' filled out the middle of the programme, together with one or two recent numbers. Each night Paul spoke to the audience about his fiancée as an introduction to 'Your Loving Flame'. Other numbers now assumed a memorial purpose. Paul played 'My Love' for Linda, something that seemingly irritated Heather. During a solo acoustic set, Paul introduced 'Here Today' as a song he'd written 'after my dear friend John passed away'. He then exchanged his Martin guitar for a ukulele, telling the audience how, when he used to go round to George Harrison's house, the ukuleles would come out after dinner, his friend being a George Formby fan.

'I said to him, "I do a little song on ukulele." I played it for him and I'll do it for you tonight as a tribute to George.' Paul proceeded to perform George's most lovely song, 'Something', accompanying himself on ukulele, a very touching moment indeed, introduced in such a way that audiences might be forgiven for thinking this was the one and only night Paul had paid this musical tribute to his friend. In fact, once he realised how well it worked, Paul gave his ukulele 'Something', with a virtually verbatim prologue, every night. It became as much a fixture of his show as the audience response section of 'Hey Jude' and the explosions in 'Live and Let Die'.

Despite the routine, the concerts were entertaining and moving, the spectacle enhanced by huge display screens, as big as those in Times Square, a montage of colours and themed images, pictures of Beatle-mania accompanying 'I Saw Her Standing There' for example. At the end of this particular song Paul had an alarming habit of tossing his famous Höfner violin bass to John Hammel, whose other duties included ensuring the boss's guitars had new strings for every show, standing guard while he briefly but warmly greeted his VIP visitors backstage, and pouring a celebratory glass of Dom Pérignon for Paul and Heather on the bus afterwards.

In pictures taken by Paul's official tour photographer, Bill Bernstein, Paul and Heather presented the image of happiness on tour, but away from the cameras there were ugly scenes between the couple. In mid-May, the *Driving USA* tour reached Florida, Paul and Heather checking into the Turnberry Isle Resort and Club in Miami. On Saturday 18 May, Paul played the second of two shows at the National Car Rental Center in Fort Lauderdale, returning to the Miami hotel with Heather after-wards. This was the end of the first part of his tour and naturally an opportunity to party. In the early hours of the following morning, hotel guests awoke to hear Paul and Heather having a blazing row. Paul was heard shouting: 'I don't want to marry you. The wedding's off!' Heath-er's engagement ring was then apparently flung – by an unknown hand – from their hotel window. Told that a valuable ring had 'fallen' from Sir Paul's suite, hotel staff spent a good part of the following day searching for it, hiring metal detectors to help them do the job. The ring was even-tually found and returned to Sir Paul, who was by this time back in England, where he had gone to help celebrate his monarch's Golden Jubilee.

To mark Queen Elizabeth II's 50 years on the throne a unique pop concert was staged on 3 June 2002* inside the usually private grounds of Buckingham Palace. The bill included a roll-call of British rock stars – rock music being one of Britain's more successful post-war industries – headed naturally by Sir Paul. It was good to see such a quintessentially English artist at the centre of such a very British event, especially after Paul had wrapped himself in the American flag on tour in the USA, the star playing Beatles songs on his Magic Piano in the grounds of Buckingham Palace, the music relayed to a million people outside the garden walls on what was a beautiful, soft summer's evening in the capital. At the end of the show, Paul played a cheeky reprise of 'Her Majesty', the bonus ditty that concluded *Abbey Road*, daring to flirt with a monarch who was 43 when he made that album, and was now a grandmother of 76. At the end of the show, when the Queen came on stage to join Sir Paul and the other artists, McCartney suggested to Her Majesty that they might hold a show like this in her back garden every year, to which she replied tartly that she didn't think so.

Apart from coming home to play for his Queen, this summer break in Sir Paul's tour schedule gave Paul and Heather an opportunity to get married. For they had patched up their relationship after that quarrel in Miami. In acknowledgement of the musician's Irish ancestry, the wedding was held in County Monaghan, the land of Paul's maternal ancestors. The Mohins had been poor farmers, so poor Grandfather Mohin left Ireland to make his living on the mainland. Two generations later, his grandson returned as one of the richest stars in show business, so rich he hired a castle for his big day, booking himself and his guests into Castle Leslie, an hour south of Belfast. The whole affair was meant to be secret, but the castle's octogenarian owner Sir John Leslie let the cat out of the bag a week in advance when he told journalists: 'It's next Tuesday, but it's top secret.' The world's press then stood at the gates of Castle Leslie and watched enormous supplies of food, booze, sound equipment, fireworks and flowers trucked onto the estate.

Paul's Liverpool family were summoned to Heathrow Airport, where they were put on a chartered plane to Ireland. Brother Mike was to be best man again. Ringo Starr led the list of celebrity friends, who also

---

* The Queen's Coronation was held in 1953, but she actually became Queen the previous year when her father George VI died, making 2002 the Golden Jubilee.

included Dave Gilmour, Chrissie Hynde, Twiggy Lawson, Sir George Martin and Nitin Sawhney. Once again, Yoko Ono was notably absent. Heather's aged father John Mills wasn't invited either. While Paul's daughters Mary and Stella attended, there was no sight of Heather and James, both of whom were understood to be against Dad's second marriage.

The ceremony itself was to be held in St Salvator's Church on the Leslie estate at 4:30 p.m. Tuesday 11 June. The guests assembled inside the seventeenth-century church, where they waited, and waited, press helicopters thudding overhead as photographers took aerial pictures, Sir Paul pacing up and down nervously, a sprig of lavender from Dad's bush at Rembrandt in his button-hole for luck. He needed it. Brother Mike was present and correct, unlike when Paul married Lin, but the bride-to-be was missing. 'We were all sitting in the church for an hour, our bums on the hard seats, packed; where are they?' recalls cousin Mike Robbins. 'We're an hour waiting for her, waiting to come down the [aisle].' Finally the music started. 'Thank Christ for that! By then we are talking to each other. Everybody is standing up and talking in this little church, talking to people you've never met before.' Some say Heather had been delayed putting on her wedding dress, others that she and Paul had had a last-minute row. In any event it was with a sense of relief that the couple emerged from the church as husband and wife to be showered with confetti.

The reception was lavish. 'A huge marquee was erected to give a vast dinner for 300 guests served on gold plates, which the guests were told to keep as souvenirs,' reports Sir John Leslie. The food had an Indian theme, the wines rare and expensive vintages. The dinner proved too rich for some. Notes Mike Robbins, whose enjoyment of the big day was further tempered by suspicions about the bride:

You couldn't get anything decent to eat. It was *magnificent*. There were Indian maidens in saris giving you little bhaji things, [but] I hate bloody foreign food. I thought, *Hasn't anybody got a sausage roll or a pork pie?* But, oh, it was magnificent. The flowers! It cost bloody millions, must have done. And by then we knew, the family knew, my family are not dopey, we knew this was a wrong'un.

Paul gave a hilarious wedding speech, causing his guests to cry with laughter. 'I don't recall any of it, but I remember thinking, God, he's a sharp cookie,' says Nitin Sawhney. 'He's very, very funny. And he will say things with absolutely no fear, [which] makes people very funny.' Then everybody adjourned to the second marquee, where there was a band and dancing, at the end of which Sir Paul and Lady McCartney boarded Paul's motor boat the *Barnaby Rudge*, which he'd had brought over from Rye and bedecked with flowers. A colossal fireworks display erupted as the married couple chugged away down the lake cheered by their relatives and friends.

Six years hence, when this union ended in a divorce court, telling personal details emerged about the build-up to the wedding, including the fact that Paul continued to wear Linda's ring until the day itself, then exchanged it for a new ring; and that he and Heather used contraception until their wedding night. In other words, he didn't seem sure he was doing the right thing until the last minute. Then he made the mistake of his life.

HER MAJESTY'S A PRETTY NICE GIRL

Sir Paul's performance at Buckingham Palace was another step in an evolving relationship with his monarch. It started in a sense when Paul won a prize for a schoolboy essay about her Coronation. Playing before members of the Royal Family at the Royal Variety Show ten years later was a landmark in the Beatles' story, two years after which the Queen bestowed MBEs upon the fab four, unprecedented for pop stars at the time. Over subsequent years, Paul had been presented to the Royal Family many times, been invited to dinners, performed at St James' Palace, received a personal donation from the Queen for LIPA, then welcomed her to his school, after which he'd been knighted and asked to headline her Golden Jubilee concert. His easy manner with his monarch showed how well acquainted they now were.

That July, the Queen paid an official visit to Liverpool, taking the time to call in on the Walker Art Gallery where Paul was showing his paintings. 'I had to mind him on the day the Queen came,' recalls Liverpudlian journalist Gillian Reynolds, who was active in raising money for the city's museums. 'It's a bit like minding the Pope. Everybody wanted to touch the hem of his garment.' Gillian was struck as others have been by Paul's easy, conversational manner with the Queen. Whereas almost everybody was obsequious and flustered in Her Majesty's presence, Paul remained relaxed with a woman he had clearly got to know quite well over the past four decades.

> It was really strange because he was so cheery and chatty with the Queen. He said, 'Oh, Your Majesty, you're a keen photographer, we'd love to show some of your work here in the Walker.' It took my breath away … She gave him this very roguish look and she said, 'I bet you would!' … She was really quite flirtatious with him – acknowledging a somewhat closer relationship than one might expect.

After a summer break, Paul resumed his North American tour, renamed the Back in the US tour, travelling with Heather, who was entitled to call herself Lady McCartney since their wedding but tended to style herself Heather Mills McCartney. She took the opportunity of being in America to promote a revised version of her autobiography, retitled *A Single Step*, from which had been excised the more lurid details of her affair with Milos the Yugoslav ski instructor, with new pages added that gave a surprisingly candid insight into her relationship with Sir Paul. In the book, Heather revealed intimate details of their courtship as well as making it plain how much she disapproved of his smoking marijuana. Interviewed by the broadcaster Barbara Walters on TV, Heather made further complaints about hubby. 'I am married to the most famous person in the world and that is very unfortunate for me,' she said, making it clear she didn't like her charity work being overshadowed by Paul. Indeed, she seemed to find her husband generally annoying. 'This is a man who has had his own way his entire life,' she told Walters. 'When you become famous at 19, it is sometimes hard to listen to other people's opinions.'

Then came the first in a series of alleged marital arguments. According to court documents later leaked to the press (we shall come to the how and why later), when Paul's tour reached Los Angeles that autumn Heather complained to her husband about the Barbara Walters interview, in which the host had tackled her on some of the less flattering stories emerging about her early life. Paul apparently dismissed Heather's concerns, saying she was in a mood. Heather decided he was drunk. The row allegedly escalated when they got back to their LA home. According to Heather's account later set down in legalese: 'The Petitioner [Sir Paul] grabbed the Respondent [Heather] by the neck and pushed her over a coffee table. He then went outside, and in his drunken state he fell down a hill, cutting his arm (which remains scarred to this day).'

This alleged incident occurred shortly before a break in the tour. Heather stayed in the US, appearing on *Larry King Live*. Her experience with Barbara Walters had not put her off American chat shows. Indeed, she appeared repeatedly on *Larry King* in the months to come, usually to talk about her charity work, though she increasingly found herself facing tough questions about her past. Larry was as likely as Barbara to put her on the spot. 'Did you ever have to prostitute yourself?' King asked Heather directly on 1 November 2002.

'No, never!'

On the day of this broadcast, on the other side of the Atlantic, the people of Campbeltown were commemorating the life of Paul's first wife with the opening of a memorial garden in the wee toon. After Linda's death, local people contacted Paul to ask if he might help them open an art gallery in his wife's name, with a permanent display of her photographs. Paul's vet, Alastair Cousin, went to see the musician in London about it and gained the impression Paul was all for the gallery, that is until Heather Mills came on the scene. 'It was put very much down the list of priorities as far as he was concerned ... So I'm afraid that really never happened, which was a big disappointment.' Instead, the town created a memorial garden, the centrepiece of which is an amateurish bronze of Linda, sculpted by Paul's cousin Jane Robbins.

Sir Paul didn't attend the opening, and was rarely seen in Kintyre these days. Heather didn't seem to care for a place so heavily loaded with memories of her husband's first marriage. And the star himself was back on the road, playing shows in Mexico, then Japan. In November 2002 a new double live album appeared, *Back in the US* (marketed as *Back in the World* outside the United States). Its chief point of interest was that Paul unilaterally reversed the Lennon-McCartney credits on the Beatles songs featured – all songs Paul had written alone, or with limited help from John – to 'composed by Paul McCartney and John Lennon'. Yoko was not impressed. Even Ringo was quoted as saying it was 'underhand'. Still, the lone two surviving Beatles appeared together on stage at the Royal Albert Hall in November to honour George Harrison, a year and a day since his death. In a long, perfectly paced tribute show – featuring many old friends, from 82-year-old Ravi Shankar to Eric Clapton – Paul played 'Something' on the ukulele, with Ritchie, Eric and the house band coming in halfway through, which proved an even more effective arrangement than Paul's solo version. In future, he'd do the song this way. 'I was choked with emotion at the Concert for George when he sang "Something",' comments Ravi Shankar. 'It is amazing to see how much he [still] loves to perform and sing.'

Paul now set out on the European leg of what was becoming a world tour. '[It was] as if we were listening to the best Beatles' tribute band in the world,' wrote Ray Connolly perspicaciously in his *Daily Mail* review of the first night in Paris. A few days later, in his Barcelona dressing room, Sir Paul gave to the *Daily Mirror* what now reads as an ironic comment on his second marriage: 'Heather said to me this morning, "I don't think of you as rich, you know."' Only rich enough to give Heather a cash gift of £250,000 in December ($382,500), after which he set up a £360,000-a-year allowance for his wife ($550,800), paid quarterly. As the tour progressed, more unflattering stories began to emerge about Heather at home in England where, in early May, Channel 4 broadcast an investigation, *Heather Mills: The Real Mrs McCartney*, which contrasted her account of her life in print with what people who knew her remembered. There appeared to be gaps between the story and the truth.

A childhood girlfriend disputed details in Heather's memoirs about the two of them being held prisoner by a paedophile in Tyne and Wear. She sued Heather on the grounds that the model's memoir had identified her without permission, and falsified the events themselves, and won compensation. Charles Stapley, effectively Heather's stepfather, likewise disputed Heather's published story of running away from him and her mother to join the fair on Clapham Common. 'When she disappeared at the weekends, and she was still at school, she did go and sleep in the back of a truck with a chap who worked on the dodgems, but that was just at weekends,' he said, describing Heather as a 'damaged personality'. The Clapham jeweller who'd employed Heather as a teenager alleged that she stole far more from him than she had admitted to in her books, including gold chains worth £25,000 ($38,250). 'She virtually plundered the shop,' asserted Jim Guy. Most damaging was the testimony of two women associates of Adnan Khashoggi who spoke of Heather enjoying the high life with wealthy Arabs in London and Paris at the time she claimed to be working as a model for a French cosmetics firm. Ros Ashley, who said she met Heather in Khashoggi's London hotel, and allegedly groomed her for success in this twilight world, said her friend's ambition was to 'meet a wealthy man [who] would be able to give her a good lifestyle and a little bit of prestige and status'. It seemed she had been looked after by a Lebanese business-man for a time, but had excelled herself in marrying Sir Paul.

In May 2003, McCartney's world tour reached Rome, the star playing two prestige shows at the Colosseum, a relatively small acoustic show inside the ancient amphitheatre on 10 May, followed by a free rock concert for half a million people outside the stadium the following day. This was the biggest show of Paul's career to date. Heather was again upset about stories in the press, it would later be alleged, and again Paul seemed indifferent to her concerns. 'An argument ensued in the bathroom during which [Sir Paul] became angry and pushed [Heather] into the bath', according to the divorce papers later leaked to the press. The couple apparently argued over Heather's decision not to accom-pany her husband to an after-show party, choosing to have dinner with her sister Fiona instead. Sir Paul allegedly withdrew his security people 'in a fit of pique', leaving Heather unprotected among a mob of fans.

Ten days later, Paul played the AOL Stadium in Hamburg, introduc-ing Heather to his old St Pauli friends Horst Fascher and Astrid Kirch-herr, who in common with so many of Paul's associates didn't warm to his second wife. Astrid felt Heather had taken advantage of Paul's vulnerability. 'He was so protected by Linda, and surrounded with her love and care, that he was like an unborn baby towards women, and [Heather] just could roll him around her fingers,' she remarks. 'Then being handicapped and good-looking, he probably felt sorry [for] this woman with one leg. [But] she turned out a bitch.' Few people were able to be so candid to Paul's face of course. His children had told him what they thought of Heather, but he'd rejected their counsel. There was increasingly an element of the Emperor's New Clothes about this marriage.

Away from Paul's hearing, Heather was a figure of ridicule, some of it cruel. It wasn't her fault she'd lost a leg, and indeed she had coped bravely with her disability, but being a monopod seemed funny to some.

Sick jokes went round pubs and offices, as they had when Paul married Linda. 'What do you call a dog with Wings?' people had asked in the 1970s.

The punch line was: 'Linda McCartney'.

Now they asked: 'What's got three legs and lives on a farm?'

'Paul McCartney and Heather Mills.'

Sir Paul didn't hear any of this. He lived in a world where everybody told him how great he was and every year brought new levels of achievement. He was reaching a stage in his career where it wasn't enough just to play huge, sold-out shows. His tours had to include special event concerts, such as giving that first pop concert at the Colosseum. For years Paul had wanted to play behind the Iron Curtain, too. He had grown up in a Cold War world, whereby the USSR in particular was perceived as an impenetrable, sinister place, so he found the idea of playing in Red Square enticing. In post-glasnost Russia, Paul was given his chance.

Before the Moscow show, Paul and Heather were granted an audience in the Kremlin with President Vladimir Putin. The McCartneys told the President they were campaigning against landmines, a subject he deflected deftly. When Putin said he probably wouldn't be attending the concert itself, Paul treated the Russian leader to a private performance of 'Let It Be'. In the event the President did come to the show in Red Square on 24 May 2003. Never had there been a better place to sing 'Back in the USSR', with its ironic Cold War lyrics.

The world tour ended with another big open-air concert at the King's Dock in Liverpool on 1 June 2003 (Paul played the same venue in 1990), after which the star took Heather to Long Island, where she'd already upset the locals. Paul was a familiar and popular figure in the Hamptons. Storeowners and restaurateurs had known him and his family for years, and appreciated the unostentatious way Paul conducted himself on holiday. One of his favourite haunts was the Amagansett pizzeria, Felice's Restaurant, run by an Italian family who had also known and loved Linda. They couldn't stand Heather. 'I don't want to talk about her!' says restaurateur Alda Lupo Stipanoe, throwing up her hands in dismay when Heather's name is mentioned. 'Nothing like the first wife. The first wife was a lady.' Staff in the town library likewise found the new Lady McCartney impossible. 'He is very charming. She was a complete bitch – rude, sense of importance, everything he isn't,' comments one librarian. Amagansett is where the next alleged domestic row occurred, according to the divorce papers. Heather had made her disapproval of marijuana clear, yet pot-smoking was an old habit with her husband. The allegation is this: 'In Long Island in August 2003, [Heather] asked [Sir Paul] if he had been smoking marijuana. He became very angry, yelled at her, grabbed her neck and started choking her.'

Despite apparently being at each other's throats, the couple returned to the UK to attend Stella McCartney's 30 August wedding, on the Isle of Bute, to publisher Alasdhair Willis. Then they flew back down to Sussex. Like most of Paul's homes, the Sussex estate was imbued with Linda's memory. Since Lin's death, Paul had hardly used Blossom Farm. The house they built in the 1980s was left as a shrine to his late wife. When he and Heather visited the estate, they stayed on Woodlands Farm, an adjacent property he'd acquired in 1989. As the name suggests, this new part of the estate included extensive woodland, in which was a large man-made lake. Paul had commissioned a pavilion and lodge to be built on the lakeside, the pavilion being a glass-fronted structure from which he could observe the wildlife, while the lodge was a substantial two-storey log cabin in which Sir Paul intended to live with Heather and their baby for, having suffered one miscarriage, Heather was pregnant again with their child. The Cabin, as he and Heather named the lakeside lodge, was under construction and was due to be finished in 2004.

While Paul and Heather were on the estate in September 2003 they had another in their series of alleged domestic rows, this time during dinner, according to the *News of the World* newspaper, which reported that the cleaner came in the next day to find a mark on the wall over the chair in which Paul sat, indicating that a bottle of tomato ketchup had been hurled at the star. Food was all over the place, with crockery, glasses and lamps broken. There was no reference to this incident, which would have been a story against Heather, in the leaked divorce papers.

All of which may help explain why Sir Paul was in such a foul mood when he went walkabout in London in the early hours of Friday 19 September 2003. Having dined in Soho with John Hammel and his PR man Geoff Baker, Paul decided he wanted to take a look at the American illusionist David Blaine, who was staging a fast in a Perspex box suspended next to Tower Bridge. This stunt had attracted widespread ridicule, Londoners coming by to heckle Blaine for doing something so asinine. When Sir Paul rolled up at Tower Bridge at 1:00 a.m., Geoff Baker hailed a press photographer, Kevin Wheal, who was watching the stunt for the *Evening Standard*. 'Oi mate!' Baker called out. 'Macca's over here. Do you want to come and get a picture?' Baker urged the photographer to be quick, intending to introduce him to Paul first and ask if he would pose for a picture, which he would normally; 'he likes the press, you know, to an extent'. Unfortunately, Wheal started running at the star, as Geoff recalls. 'I thought, Oh fuck it! It was the running that caused the freak out.'

McCartney told the snapper he didn't want to be photographed. 'Listen mate, I've come to see this stupid cunt,' Sir Paul said, indicating David Blaine and pushing Wheal away; 'you're not going to take a picture of me tonight – Fuck off, I'm a pedestrian on a private visit.' Wheal says it was evident McCartney had been drinking.

A member of the public came up and asked if he could shake Paul's hand. 'Fuck off,' replied McCartney. He then told Baker he was fired and ordered his driver to take him home to St John's Wood.

The next day's papers were full of this delicious story, which combined the ongoing comedy of Blaine's stupid stunt with the novelty of a foul-mouthed Sir Paul McCartney f-ing and blinding in public when he was apparently the worse for drink. A police officer at the scene was quoted as saying: 'Mr McCartney came down here rather drunk [and] was very abusive.' Kevin Wheal made a complaint of common assault, which came to nothing, and Geoff Baker was reinstated as Paul's PR man. Baker strenuously denies claims that Paul was drunk. 'It was me that was drunk,' he says, loyally taking the blame for this most unfortunate, out-of-character incident.

Paul spent much of the next month lying low in his house on Cavendish Avenue, occasionally escorting his pregnant wife across the road for a walk in Regent's Park. Heather was then admitted to the nearby Hospital of St John and St Elizabeth where, on 28 October 2003, she gave birth to a baby girl they named Beatrice Milly, the first name in honour of Heather's late mother, the second after one of Paul's aunts. The star was a father again at 61, and caught in an increasingly difficult second marriage.

WHEN PAUL WAS SIXTY-FOUR

IN WHICH THE HAPPY COUPLE MOVE INTO THEIR NEW HOME

Paul and Heather began family life with baby Bea in the Cabin, their new lodge house in the Sussex woods, after the builders finished work in February 2004. Essentially, Sir Paul was seeking to recreate the snug family life he'd enjoyed with Linda when they came down from London to live in Waterfall, his original arboreal cottage on the other side of the estate. The two homes were strikingly similar, but this was not a comparable marriage.

The union was not *yet* an unremitting Hell. The couple had their good days, and could even appear very happy together, as when Paul invited Dave Gilmour and Nitin Sawhney to dinner. Nitin liked what he had seen of Heather so far, though he noted that, despite being half her husband's age, she lacked Paul's *joie de vivre*. 'She seemed quite jaded in comparison to him. He seemed [like] somebody who was a young person in an older body – he's very boyish.' Before dinner, Paul took his guests out to a shed in the woods where he kept drinks, and mixed cocktails. Heather came down from the Cabin and joined them, telling the men how Paul had swept her off her feet when they met. She cooked and served a vegetarian meal, and then they all jammed around the piano – Heather playing sax, an instrument she had a passing acquaintance with. Husband and wife seemed *en rapport* that evening, and Paul did everything he could to keep Heather happy in the days ahead.

That Christmas, Sir Paul had given his wife a second £250,000 cash gift, meaning he'd given her £500,000 ($765,000) in the space of 12 months. She used the money to buy a £450,000 ($688,500) apartment at Thames Reach, a new apartment complex on the River Thames at Hammersmith. This was in addition to the beach house Paul had bought for her on the south coast, and his own homes in Sussex, Merseyside, London, Scotland and the United States, giving the couple the run of at least 13 properties.* Paul also used his contacts to get Heather a star guest to interview when she filled in as presenter on *Larry King Live* in April 2004. At Paul's request, Paul Newman agreed to be quizzed by Heather, who made a poor job of the interview in the opinion of critics. Despite this flop, Heather remained ambitious to establish herself as a media personality in the United States, which was in itself a significant cause of disagreement in the marriage. While Paul was happy to visit the USA regularly, he wanted to continue to live in the UK, and to bring Bea up in England, as he had raised his older children. He didn't want Bea's mother abroad for too much of the year.

In reply, Heather grumbled that Paul expected her to accompany him everywhere *he* went, according to divorce papers leaked to the press. It was alleged in the documents that Heather had other complaints, such as her claim that Paul didn't want her to breastfeed Beatrice, telling his wife 'they are my breasts' and 'I don't want a mouthful of breast milk'. Heather breastfed her baby for six weeks until Paul supposedly wore her down, after which she gave up, feeling 'miserable and demoralised'. Heather was still having surgical procedures done because of her 1993 accident, and she was allegedly unhappy about having to defer one such operation to accommodate Paul's holiday plans. She also wearied of Paul's request that she cook for them every night, like his mum and Linda had done. According to the divorce papers, Paul apparently expected Heather to play the established role of a traditional housewife/mother, even when she was hobbling around with a broken pelvic plate (as she was at Christmas). The list of alleged complaints grew longer: she liked to get up early, but he slept late, and he wanted her beside him when he woke. She wanted to use a bedpan in the night, because she found getting to the bathroom difficult; he 'objected vociferously, saying that it would be like being in "an old woman's home"'.

---

* There are three main residences on the Sussex estate, plus other houses that stand empty or are used by staff, in addition to nearby properties at Hog Hill, Rye and Hove; with other homes in London, Merseyside, Scotland, New York City, Long Island, Arizona and Los Angeles.

Heather was also at loggerheads with Paul's pot-smoking PR man, Geoff Baker, a rare survivor of the Paul and Linda era (as Eric Stewart noted, Paul had let many of the old staff go since Heather had come on the scene). Heather and Geoff were like cat and dog, barely on speaking terms by the time Paul's entourage squelched onto Worthy Farm in Somerset on Saturday 26 June 2004 to headline the Glastonbury Festival.

Sir Paul had heard from his friends what a great gig Glastonbury was – one of the largest and most famous music festivals in the world, as well as a delightfully eccentric event – so he told his office to contact the festival's farmer-founder Michael Eavis in 2003 asking if he could accommodate Macca at Glastonbury that year. When Eavis reported that the headline Saturday night slot was already taken by Radiohead, it was arranged that Paul would bring his show to Glastonbury's Pyramid Stage in 2004 instead. 'He brought all the trimmings with him, he had all the gas lights … so much production. We were quite overwhelmed at the amount of energy that his people put into that show,' says Eavis, who felt a personal connection to Paul as a man in his 60s who'd grown up with the Beatles' music and who, like Paul, had recently lost a wife to cancer.

The Glastonbury Festival attracted 150,000 people over the weekend of 25–27 June 2004, the main arena packed for the headline show on Saturday night, a vast and muddy medieval army of an audience waving banners and flags under driving rain as Sir Paul began his set. Glastonbury is, of course, near Stonehenge, with numerous other ancient and supposedly mystical sites in the area, which captured the interest of a star who'd always had a weakness for mumbo-jumbo.* 'Standing in the conference of key stones we are buzzing,' Paul told his audience excitedly, apparently feeling the magick. Clearly exhilarated, he proceeded to give one of the best shows of his life, two and a half hours of music complete with his greatest hits and choicest Beatles anecdotes. American audiences loved it when Paul talked to them from the stage about the Beatles, but Macca had always been viewed with more scepticism at home. 'Boring!' shouted irreverent young hecklers as Paul rattled on about the 1960s, which was of less interest to these scamps than what they might be doing in the 2060s. There were also sarcastic requests

* Ley lines, tarot, astrology and transcendental meditation have all held his interest.

for 'Rupert and the Frog Song'. Turning a deaf ear, Sir Paul continued to deliver a powerhouse set. Even the cheekiest urchins in the crowd were singing along to 'Hey Jude' by the end.

When Paul came off stage, he asked to see Michael Eavis. 'Normally they are so drained afterwards that they don't want to see anybody, so I didn't expect him to be chatty and friendly and everything, but he was so excited, he was so thrilled, he was weeping tears of joy. It was such a good show,' says the impresario-farmer. 'The pair of us we just hugged each other for a bit. It was lovely.' The men also spoke of having lost their wives to cancer, but then Eavis – a gentle, lovable fellow – saw Heather looking daggers at them from across the room and sensed she wanted him to leave. 'She was a bit edgy.'

Geoff Baker didn't survive the Heather era. He left Sir Paul's employ three months after Glastonbury, with an unusually harsh testimonial from the boss. Reacting to a suggestion in the press that Heather was behind Baker's sacking, Paul said in a statement: 'The actual truth, which I had been trying to spare him the embarrassment of going public with, was that he had gradually been getting more and more unstable over the past few years.' The David Blaine incident had apparently been a turning point.

> I was trying to keep out of sight of a small crowd of photographers when to my horror I saw Geoff pointing me out to the paparazzi who then ran towards me in a feeding frenzy ... just another example of his crazy behaviour. After that I tried to let him down gently, but it was my decision alone to let him go as I didn't want that kind of instability around me.

After 15 years of loyal service, Baker took his sacking remarkably well. 'He was pissed off, wasn't he? He was having a go at me. I can't lie and say I wasn't drinking too much, because I was.' Baker remained touchingly loyal to his old boss after his dismissal, never saying a bad word about him. Heather was another matter. Baker had grown to loathe the woman, as so many had.

When Linda McCartney read hurtful things about herself in the press, she wisely chose to turn the other cheek, expressing her frustration only at the very end of her life in 'The Light Comes from Within'. She would have made it far worse had she moaned. This is the mistake

Heather now made. She was increasingly and obviously irked by the negative press she received in Britain, which grew increasingly hostile as a consensus developed that she was a shrill, devious, self-publicising harridan into whose clutches a great man had tragically fallen. When Heather was informed in advance that the *Sunday Times* would be running a story in which it was observed that losing a leg was the best thing that ever happened to Heather, she allegedly implored Paul to intervene. He was scheduled to play at the forthcoming Super Bowl, his second appearance at the event in three years. Rupert Murdoch's Fox network broadcast the Super Bowl and Murdoch owned the *Sunday Times*. According to divorce papers, Heather suggested Paul tell Murdoch he wouldn't play the show unless the press baron pulled the *Times* story. Paul refused. Yet he did register dismay at the article in a defence of Heather on her website, writing that the press were 'wildly wrong' about his wife, and denying stories about her manipulating him. Contrary to reports, she hadn't made him have plastic surgery; nor made him dye his hair; he'd been doing that for years; she wasn't behind the sacking of Baker; and she wasn't at loggerheads with his children. 'The media sometimes suggests a rift between my kids and Heather, but in fact we get on great …' Which was not what others said.

After appearing at Live 8 in the summer of 2005, Paul took his band back on the road in September with a string of US arena shows. To warm the audience up before each concert, a montage of images were shown on the enormous display screens alongside the stage, telling the story of Paul's life in pictures, his marriage to Linda passed over quickly, followed by abundant images of his winsome second wife. Paul had a new album to plug, *Chaos and Creation in the Backyard*, another of his occasional one-man-band records, made in London and Los Angeles with the British producer Nigel Goodrich, who'd made his name with Radiohead. Being Paul's producer was frequently a poisoned chalice, as we have seen, and this collaboration got off to a typically difficult start when Goodrich dared urge Sir Paul to try harder. 'Fuck off, Nigel!' replied the star, who walked out of the studio. He decided to persevere with Goodrich nonetheless, and having a strong character behind the glass helped Paul create a good album. Standout tracks include 'Jenny Wren' and 'Promise to You Girl', in which Paul refers to sweeping away the dead leaves of his past. Most intriguing were the words to 'Riding to Vanity Fair', in which Paul sang about someone who'd used him on their journey to Vanity Fair, the fictional town of the depraved and the dishonest in Bunyan's *Pilgrim's Progress*, which Paul had a copy of as a boy. *Vanity Fair* is also a satirical novel by Thackeray, of course, featuring 'the odious little adventuress' Becky Sharp, a scheming minx with a resemblance to Heather Mills, though Paul surely wasn't thinking of his wife in that way. He wouldn't say who he had in mind for the song.

The album cracked the top ten in Britain and the US, where Paul was spending a lot of time, partly to appease his wife. After decades in which he had used hotels when he came to New York, Paul now had his own Manhattan apartment, in a townhouse on West 54th Street, between Fifth Avenue and Sixth Avenue, next door to the offices of Eastman & Eastman and across the street from the Museum of Modern Art. The townhouse accommodated MPL Communications, the American arm of Sir Paul's now very large publishing company. The star had the upper storeys converted into a penthouse apartment for himself and Heather, who made it clear that she also had her eye on space downstairs as a private office. Paul told his wife 'he did not want her to have an office in the same building', according to the leaked divorce papers. Even though Heather argued that the idea made sense, in that she could work the phones while Bea was taking her nap, Paul wouldn't relent. Instead, he 'reluctantly agreed to provide her with alternative office space in the city'. Heather told Paul that the new office – a 20-minute walk away – was too far and too small, further complaining of being chased by paparazzi when she went to have a look. When she refused to use it, Paul called her an 'ungrateful bitch', a remark that particularly upset Heather, because his staff overheard.

Some readers might think Paul was speaking the plain truth in calling his wife ungrateful, considering everything he'd done for her. For a man who'd always lived relatively modestly, he was exceptionally generous to his second wife. On top of the large cash gifts, the £360,000-a-year allowance, the joint credit card, the beach house, the London flat at Thames Reach and the New York office, during 2005 he gave Heather jewellery worth £264,000 ($403,920). Yet, like Oliver Twist, Heather always wanted more. In November she emailed Paul Winn, Paul's accountant at MPL in London, asking Winn to pay £480,000 ($734,400) into her NatWest Bank account so she could clear a £480,000 mortgage on her Thames Reach property. She asked for the money twice, but did not receive it for the very good reason there was no mortgage on the flat – a situation later characterised in court as verging on the fraudulent.

Paul was seen to slip into St John's Wood Church in December 2005 and sit alone in quiet contemplation. This church had special memories for him, as the place he and Linda had their 1969 wedding blessed. Church workers who were putting up the Christmas decorations when Paul came in also noted that it was around the time of the 25th anniversary of John Lennon's murder. What a lot had happened to Paul since that awful day, and what a mess he now found himself in.

WHEN YOU'RE IN HELL, KEEP GOING

When it seemed things could hardly get worse for Sir Paul and Lady McCartney, it emerged that their new Cabin and its pavilion had been constructed on the Sussex estate without planning permission. When this surprising oversight was noticed, and Paul applied for retrospective permission, Rother District Council turned him down. Paul now faced the prospect of having to demolish the home he had built for his new family, or launch a planning battle to retain the buildings. Unlikely though it was that he would win such a contest, he chose the latter course of action, employing experts to prepare a case that relied partly on their client's need for 'privacy and security', arguing that it was important that his residence 'is isolated and completely screened from public view and intervention. The Estate Lodge [Cabin] and associated Pavilion satisfy these requirements completely.'

While this retrospective application proceeded, Paul and Heather campaigned in Canada against the annual seal cull, which they added to a list of causes that included being pro-veggie, anti-poverty and anti-landmines. These predictably safe and worthy issues gave Heather endless reason to expound on television and in print to the degree that she and Paul started to appear more than a little tiresome, the antithesis of the tradition of the rich undertaking their good works discreetly. And there was now a whiff of bullshit about the McCartneys. While they appeared together as a united, loving couple, posing with a cuddly seal pup in Canada in March 2006, they were on the brink of separation. Just before the final break-up, Heather tried *again* to extract cash from MPL to clear what she now claimed were four loans on the Thames

Reach property, totalling £450,000 ($688,500). On 1 March 2006, the accountant Paul Winn informed Heather that he would not pay her the money 'without proof that the loans exist ...' Heather could not provide such proof because there was no mortgage.

Seven weeks after Paul Winn knocked back this latest request for money, Paul asked Heather to accompany him on a trip, according to the leaked divorce papers. She had recently had 'revision surgery' on her left leg. The papers alleged that Paul failed to make adequate provision for his wife in the circumstances. She was apparently obliged to 'crawl on her hands and knees up the aeroplane steps'. Three days later, on Tuesday 25 April 2006, the couple reportedly had a particularly bad domestic row which ended with Sir Paul allegedly pouring the remainder of a bottle of red wine over Heather. He then 'threw what remained in his wine glass at the Respondent', as the story went in legal papers. 'The Petitioner [Sir Paul] then reached to grab [Heather's] wine glass and broke the bowl of the glass from the stem. He then lunged at the Respondent with the broken, sharp stem of the wine glass, which cut and pierced the Respondent's arm just below the elbow, and it began to bleed profusely. He proceeded to manhandle the Respondent, flung her into her wheelchair and wheeled it outside, screaming at her to apologise for "winding him up".'

The following evening, despite Heather asking Paul to stay with her in the Cabin because she felt unable to cope with Beatrice alone, Sir Paul allegedly stalked off into the woods. She telephoned him, according to the leaked divorce papers, begging him to come back. '[Sir Paul] mocked her pleas, mimicking the voice of a nagging spouse, and refused to return.' When McCartney did return from his walk, he seemed the worse for drink.

[Heather] pulled him, staggering, towards the ground-floor bathroom, undressed him, ran the bath and helped him into it. She then phoned the Petitioner's psychiatrist for advice and he told her not to attempt to move him (she might otherwise 'do herself an injury'), to get a duvet and two pillows, to empty the bath of water, cover him, and leave him there. The Respondent thereupon dragged herself upstairs, on her hands and knees ... and brought back down the duvet and pillows. She found that [Paul] had vomited on himself. She rinsed him off, and (worried that he might choke if he vomited again in the night, unattended), she got him out of the bath, dried him, and dragged him upstairs to bed …

The sun rose on Thursday 27 April, the last full day of Paul and Heather's life together. Believing Paul would be too hung over to help, according to the leaked divorce papers, Heather called a babysitter to get Beatrice ready for nursery, then drove to the school. When Heather returned to the Cabin, Paul was up, trying to make a joke of what had happened the night before. That evening Sir Paul drank 'very little (a half bottle of wine)' and went to bed. The allegations continue:

> The following day, Friday 28 April 2006, the Petitioner went to London, but said he would be back in time to help the Respondent put Beatrice to bed. He did not arrive back at her bedtime, even though he knew the Respondent could not cope on her own … At 10:00 p.m. [Sir Paul] returned home staggering drunk and slurring his words, demanding his dinner. The Respondent stated that it was on the stove but that she would not be cooking for him again, as he had no respect for her. The Petitioner called her 'a nag' and went to bed. That evening the Respondent realised the marriage had irretrievably broken down and left, crawling on her hands and knees whilst dragging her wheelchair, crutches and basic personal possessions to the car.

They separated the following day, after less than four years of married life.

The McCartneys announced their separation a month later, blaming the media largely: 'Our parting is amicable and both of us still care about each other very much but have found it increasingly difficult to maintain a normal relationship with the constant intrusion into our private lives …' Heather sold her Thames Reach property and bought a barn conversion not far from the Peasmarsh estate, accompanied almost constantly by her sister Fiona and a male personal trainer. Sir Paul sought solace with his grown-up children, spending time with Stella and her husband at their country house in Worcestershire. Stelly was now a wealthy and famous woman in her own right, head of the eponymous Stella McCartney fashion house, with boutique stores in London and abroad.

Now it was clear that Sir Paul's ill-starred marriage had failed, the popular British press, for whom Sir Paul had always been a pet, began to publish the harshest and most sensational stories about his estranged wife. LADY MACCA HARD CORE PORN SHAME screamed the front page of the *Sun* on 5 June 2006. Its journalists had laid their hands on a German sex manual from 1988, *Die Freuden der Liebe* (*The Joys of Love*), in which Heather was pictured nude and semi-nude, simulating sex acts with an equally bare male model. The picture set, shot in London around the time of Heather's supposed stint as a cosmetics model in France, was presented as a sex manual, but a manual without any words, leading the *Sun* to describe the images as pure pornography, thereby labelling Heather a 'former porn star'. Heather's lawyers disputed the picture set was pornography, describing the book as 'a lover's guide', which became a moot point when even more explicit pictures of Heather emerged, including classic top-shelf images of the model with her legs splayed apart.

The *News of the World* then published HEATHER THE £5K HOOKER, alleging that during the time Heather had supposedly been a legitimate model in Paris she had actually been working in London and elsewhere as a whore. Unlike the nudey pictures, there was no empirical evidence Heather had taken part in group sex with Arabs for £5,000 ($7,650), as the *News of the World* alleged. It was all down to the word of denizens of this shadowy world. Heather threatened to sue, but no action came to trial. Sir Paul's friends said he was oblivious to Heather's past, if indeed the hooker story was true, but even if she had been a prostitute, would he really have been so shocked? Paul had knocked about with working girls in Hamburg.

Such was the sorry state of Paul's affairs as he reached 64. A lifetime ago, 'When I'm Sixty-Four' had been one the first tunes McCartney composed at Forthlin Road, putting lyrics to the song in his twenties when the Beatles recorded *Sgt. Pepper's Lonely Hearts Club Band*. Precociously, he had projected himself decades into the future, envisaging life as a grey-haired old man sitting by the fire with his wife. If they scrimped and saved, perhaps they could afford a summer holiday in the Isle of Wight, cheered by visits from their grandkids Vera, Chuck and Dave. Now he'd reached this fabled age, the reality was rather different. Paul's hair might indeed be grey, but he'd dyed out the traces; the wife he expected to live with into old age was gone, so was his second wife, and theirs had not been a life of sitting by the fire. As to scrimping and saving, Sir Paul had so much money, and so many assets, he didn't have a clear idea how much he was worth. With a divorce settlement looming, he had to hire the accountants Ernst & Young to find out how rich he actually was.

Paul did have three grandchildren, though: Arthur, Elliot and Miller. The first two were Mary's boys, aged seven and three respectively, the third was Stelly's 16-month-old son. In the weeks leading up to Grand-dad's landmark birthday, Mary and Stella marshalled everybody at Abbey Road Studios to record a family rendition of 'When I'm Sixty-Four' as a surprise gift. Sir Paul was out of the country when they made the recording. He was in Las Vegas, where Cirque du Soleil was hold-ing a dress rehearsal for *Love*, a new Beatles-themed show that neces-sitated a coming together between Paul and Yoko, who hadn't been on the best of terms in recent years. They seemed OK now. When Paul returned home from Vegas, the family, including little Bea, greeted him in Sussex with a rousing chorus of 'When I'm Sixty-Four' and gave him their special recording.

A month later, Paul filed for divorce from Heather on the grounds of her unreasonable behaviour. Heather replied that *he* had been the unreasonable one, and she would contest the action. Paul had the locks changed at 7 Cavendish Avenue and the press were on hand to photo-graph the moment when Heather tried in vain to open the front gate, eventually sending a man over the top to open it from within, where-upon Paul's staff called the police. All good fun. On 11 August, Paul's lawyers offered the other side a quickie divorce based on 'cross-decrees' (his complaint and her reply), without getting into a long debate about who was in the wrong. Heather's lawyers rejected this, with a draft 'Answer and Cross-Petition' – that is, Heather's allegations about Paul's behaviour during their marriage. The damaging document was couched in 'very strong terms indeed', in the words of the divorce judge, and was leaked to the press. Before that leak, however, came another important stage in the proceedings: Ernst & Young reported on what Sir Paul was worth.

Speculation about how rich Paul McCartney was had been a journal-istic parlour game for years. By common agreement, Sir Paul was the wealthiest Beatle, possibly the richest rock star in the world. Most recently, the *Sunday Times* had estimated his wealth at £825 million, easily making him a dollar billionaire. The true size of Sir Paul's wealth was less than this figure (which erroneously gave Paul the direct benefit of Linda's estate). He was still an exceedingly wealthy man, though, the owner of 'vast – I repeat vast – wealth' as the divorce judge remarked breathlessly. Sir Paul's net wealth added up to approximately £387 million ($592m), concluded the accountants, making him the richest rock star in Britain and one of the wealthiest entertainers in the world. There is little doubt the figure is accurate (as much as such audits can be with fluctuating share prices, property values and currency exchanges). Ernst & Young had access to all Sir Paul's financial records, including his extensive publishing interests and shares in Apple Corps and other companies through which Beatles money still flowed.

In detail, Sir Paul's business assets came to approximately £241 million ($369m). In addition he owned property worth £33.9 million ($51.8m), investments of £34.3 million ($52.4m), and another £15.1 million ($23.1m) in various bank accounts (interestingly, he kept £6,000 [$9,180] in ready cash, to pay the milkman perhaps). Valuables, including original artwork by de Kooning, Magritte, Matisse, Picasso and Renoir, were worth another £32.2 million ($49.26m), with £36 million ($55m) tucked away in pension funds. In a statement, Paul said that most of this wealth had been accumulated prior to his marriage, though he had added £39 million to his fortune during the marriage (or $59.6m). In that time he had been generous to not only his wife, but also her family, lending Fiona Mills £421,000 ($644,130) to buy a house, and buying another Mills relative a £193,000 property ($295,290). All these figures were as yet confidential, as the details of divorces usually remain. This was to be a highly unusual divorce, however, both in its bitterness and in how much information emerged into the public domain.

The first watershed of information came a month after the Ernst & Young report was delivered confidentially to the interested parties when, at lunchtime on 17 October 2006, a fax machine at the Press Association emitted 9 of 13 pages of Heather's 'Answer and Cross-Petition'. As we have seen, Heather is identified in the document as 'the Respondent', replying to a case brought by 'the Petitioner' (Paul). Included were all the allegations we have already read of cruelty and mistreatment, starting with the night in 2002 when Sir Paul allegedly got drunk and pushed Heather over a coffee table, to the events of April 2006. In addition, the document alleged: 'The Petitioner has been physically violent towards the Respondent.' He had behaved in a 'vindictive, punitive manner' to his wife and, 'In breach of his promises to the Respondent made when she agreed to marry him, the Petitioner continued to use illegal drugs, and to consume alcohol to excess, throughout the marriage ...' This fax was a windfall for the press, many newspapers printing the document verbatim, with reporters wondering who had been so kind as to send them the gift. It had been faxed anonymously. The fax was traced to a newsagent's shop in London's Drury Lane, the proprietor of which said a woman sent it. Heather Mills denied she was behind the leak, and began defamation proceedings against the *Daily Mail* and the *Sun* when these papers gave their readers that impression. In their defence, the publishers asserted Heather *had* been behind the leak, in order to damage Sir Paul's reputation, and furthermore the allegations were lies. Again Heather's action for defamation never came to trial.

Sir Paul's lawyers verified the papers were genuine, by issuing a statement saying the star would like to respond, but the appropriate place to do so was in the divorce court. 'Our client will be defending these allegations rigorously and appropriately.' Behind the scenes, lawyers prepared a counter-claim against Heather in which they not only accused her of leaking the documents, but also of leaking details of private phone calls between Paul and his daughter Stella which had got into the press, while further alleging that during the marriage Sir Paul had been subject to 'verbal abuse, extreme jealousy, false accusations of violence, and that throughout the marriage the wife had shown a consistent inability to tell the truth'.

It was the allegation that Paul had got drunk and pushed Heather around, ultimately stabbing her with a broken glass, that was most astonishing. Could Paul truly be such a termagant husband? Paul enjoyed a drink, with some evidence that he drank immoderately on occasion. The reader will recall Linda pushing Paul's whisky glass away when the McCartneys visited their Kintyre neighbours in 1996. Others tell similar stories. 'I saw when he got drunk and I saw when [Linda] would sort of clear the house because he was on the verge of getting drunk,' says Danny Fields. There had been stand-up rows with girlfriends, Francie Schwartz implying in her memoirs that Paul was sometimes a little rough back in the Sixties. Yet friends were outraged by suggestions Paul was an abusive drunk. Eric Stewart, who had written to warn Paul about Heather before they married – and received no reply

– now wrote offering himself as a character witness in the divorce. Eric explains why he wrote to Paul:

> She's saying he's a drunk, he's abusive. He's not. Not in that way. He might be abusive verbally with people – he won't suffer fools – but he's not abusive physically to anybody. I said, 'I will speak for you in court and I will say what I knew about her setting you up.' And I did get a reply that time and he said, 'Thanks for all that. if I need you I'll let you know.'

It was a bleak time. On 21 October 2006, Paul's old friend Brian Brolly, who'd helped him set up MPL, died of a heart attack. A week later, Beatrice McCartney's third birthday degenerated into an ugly scene when press came to an open-air play centre where Paul and Heather had taken the child as a treat, resulting in a fracas with photographers.

Unable to stop the flood of ugly stories, Sir Paul adopted a policy of dignified silence, pressing on with his work as Heather became ever more excitable and vociferous. Her popularity plummeted accordingly, reaching its nadir when she became the butt of a TV presenter's joke. Presenting an awards show in London, Jonathan Ross described Heather as such a 'fucking liar [I] wouldn't be surprised if we found out she's actually got two legs'.

BEHOLD MY (BROKEN) HEART

Nine years since the President of Magdalen College invited Sir Paul to write a modest choral work for the new college auditorium – and two years since the try-outs in Oxford – Sir Paul premièred the final version of *Ecce Cor Meum* at the Royal Albert Hall. Commissioned during Linda's last months, the music had been in the works so long that Paul had been widowed, remarried and separated in the meantime.

Arranged in four movements, with a melancholy orchestral interlude written in the immediate aftermath of Linda's death, *Ecce Cor Meum* was in many ways a typical example of McCartney music: there were lovely tunes, beautifully played and orchestrated, yet the result was uneven, bland in places, overwrought at the end, while the libretto struck the critic from the *Independent* as 'sententious'. A bit of a mess really, reflecting the fact that *Ecce*, like his other classical works, was the result of hired hands trying to express what they thought Paul wanted to hear. Yet the crowd at the Albert Hall – many of whom were Beatles fans who just wanted to see Sir Paul close up – gave the work an enthusiastic reception, and urged him to his feet at the end to say a few words, which he did with his usual confidence and grace, acknowledging the support of friends and family in the audience.

There was in fact further personal discord behind the scenes. Although the extended McCartney family was close, Paul's wealth had long created dissent in the clan. As we have seen, Paul had been very generous over the years with his family, helping relatives buy homes, lending money and in some instances putting 'relies' on the McCartney Pension so they didn't need to work. Still some weren't satisfied. When one relative was reminded by Paul's accountant around the time of *Ecce Cor Meum* that a loan Paul had made, to help the relative buy their home, had not been repaid, the relation apparently retorted: 'Fuck him, he's got enough money and I don't need to fuckin' pay him back.'

Several relatives were invited to the première of *Ecce Cor Meum*, Paul's Uncle Mike and his Aunt Bett Robbins being among those who accepted tickets, with Paul's PA Holly Dearden booking the now-elderly couple into a first-class London hotel, where a butler greeted them with vintage champagne. As they enjoyed Paul's hospitality, the Robbins discovered that not all the 'relies' were so pleased with their arrangements. Word had got about that Aunt Joan had been chauffeur-driven all the way from the Wirral to the show, in light of the fact she was in her 80s, leading to younger family members asking MPL to lay on door-to-door cars for them, too. 'They wanted not only [a] free hotel, they wanted free cars from Liverpool and back again – because Joan Mac had a car,' says Mike, who was told by Holly Dearden that one relation slammed the phone down on her when informed a car wasn't available, telling the PA angrily: 'I don't want to talk to the monkey, I want to talk to the organ grinder.' As a result, some of Paul's nearest and dearest were not at *Ecce Cor Meum*.

All of a sudden it wasn't as much fun being Paul McCartney. That winter Sir Paul abandoned his planning battle to keep the Cabin, agreeing to tear the wooden house down. There was slim consolation in the fact the council said he could keep the pavilion. A routine medical examination also revealed that Paul had a 'minor heart irregularity'. It turned out to be nothing much to worry about, thankfully, unlike the news from Heather's lawyers, three days before Christmas, that she wanted £50 million ($76.5m) as her divorce settlement. Just what you wanted to hear before the holidays. In the new year, Paul counter-offered with a more reasonable £16.5 million ($25.2m), which together with assets Heather had accrued during their marriage meant she would walk away with about £20 million ($30.6m). She turned this offer down as insufficient. Paul also filed an affidavit that revealed how much he had wanted their marriage to work. 'I believed it was for life,' he said, sadly.

THE EVER-PRESENT PAST

WHEN LOVE GOES WRONG

Heather Mills didn't believe Sir Paul was only worth £387 million ($592m). He'd told his wife he was twice as rich, as her barrister informed the judge during a preliminary divorce hearing. Mr Justice Sir Hugh Bennett, a near contemporary of Sir Paul's, having been born in 1943, and a fellow knight of the realm, asked for updated estimates of the star's assets as a result, but the difference didn't prove significant.

Heather claimed to be short of cash so, while the divorce was thrashed out, Sir Paul agreed to pay his wife an interim sum of £5.5 million ($8.4m), which would give her enough to live on and buy a house. She chose a large, secluded property at Robertsbridge, 13 miles from Peasmarsh. This way they could both have access to Bea, and take turns ferrying her to a local preparatory school. Unlike Paul's older children, Bea would be educated privately.

As his second marriage drew to an expensive conclusion, Sir Paul severed another important connection. He had signed with EMI as a young Beatle, and released all his subsequent UK records with the company, but the star now decided the old firm wasn't up to the challenge of marketing his new album, *Memory Almost Full*. Like most major record labels, EMI was suffering in the age of digital downloads, with several of its biggest acts voicing dissatisfaction with their sales figures, on top of which the company had recently been taken over by a private equity firm. Paul began talking to Hear Music, a new company co-founded by the Starbucks chain, whose executives impressed Sir Paul partly by promising that, if he signed with them, *Memory Almost*

Full would be on sale not only in the company's coffee shops in the West but in 400 Starbucks in China, one of the few territories he hadn't yet conquered.

With the exception of the lovesick *Driving Rain*, Paul's rock albums had been getting more interesting lately, and *Memory Almost Full* turned out to be a particularly good listen, opening with the party pop of 'Dance Tonight' then plunging into more introspective territory. After young love, soured love has inspired more good songs than any other human experience. Bob and Sara Dylan's problems in the 1970s led to Dylan making his supreme album *Blood on the Tracks*, for example. While *Memory Almost Full* wasn't that strong, it followed in the same tradition. Paul expresses bitter-sweet thanks to a lover whom one presumes is Heather in 'Gratitude', acknowledging that she'd done him wrong, but he couldn't hate her for it. Meanwhile 'You Tell Me' found Paul exploring memories of Linda, the focus of the song given away by the reference to a red cardinal, a bird native to the Arizona desert. Other songs looked back to the Beatles, Paul's 'ever-present past'. Once, he'd tried to ignore his history. Now he dealt with it squarely. The lovely 'That Was Me' presents a musical slide show of his early life, from scout camp to sweating cobwebs on stage at the Cavern as the Beatles worked their way up and out of Liverpool and onto TV. 'That was me!' Paul yelped, as if surprised to realise the glossy young man on the *Ed Sullivan Show* was the sexagenarian singing now.

There are no better lyrics on *Memory Almost Full* than in 'The End of the End' in which the star faces down death itself. Composed at Cavendish Avenue on Dad's old NEMS piano, the lyric is original, poetic and true in way that had eluded Paul for much of his career, with simple and pleasing rhymes that remain in the mind, the second verse of the song being especially elegant:

> *On the day that I die I'd like jokes to be told,*
> *And stories of old to be rolled out like carpets*
> *that children have played on,*
> *And laid on while listening to stories of old.*

Yet Paul wasn't ready to stop. That autumn he was seen with a new girlfriend, a dark, pencil-thin American named Nancy Shevell. Almost a quarter of a century Paul's junior, Nancy was the daughter of a New Jersey trucking magnate, Myron 'Mike' Shevell, who'd led a colourful life. A fraud investigation caused Shevell's companies to go bankrupt in the 1970s, after which he took over New England Motor Freight (NEMF), a small firm located in Elizabeth, New Jersey, *Sopranos* territory, building the company up into a huge concern with a $400 million turnover (£261m), facing accusations of racketeering in the process.

Nancy Shevell was involved in this family firm. She joined NEMF in 1983 after graduating from Arizona State, the same university Linda attended. The following year, Nancy married law student Bruce Blakeman, who became prominent in the political life of New Jersey. In 1988, when Nancy Shevell was a Vice President of NEMF, the US government sued the trucking firm, with other defendants, for colluding with the Mafia. The chief defendant in the case was the head of the Genovese crime family, Vincent 'Chin' Gigante, whom Mike Shevell allegedly conspired with in hiring labour. In bringing the court action, the government sought, in part, to stop Nancy's father 'endeavoring to obtain the assistance of organised crime figures regarding any labor relations matters'. Shevell entered a 'Consent Decree' by which he agreed to restore union members 'who had been deprived of work as a result of the sweetheart arrangement' and promised not to get involved in labour negotiations again. NEMF kept on trucking.

Apart from helping run the family firm, Nancy and her husband raised a son named Arlen, maintaining homes in New York and the Hamptons, where they first became friendly with Paul and Linda. The Blakemans were still married, though separated, when Nancy began seeing Sir Paul in October 2007. In many ways, Nancy was a similar woman to Linda: she was American, Jewish, the moneyed daughter of a tough, self-made man. She had also suffered a bout with breast cancer and, again like Linda, was a denizen of New York and Long Island. Nancy's Manhattan apartment was a 10-minute walk from the building where Linda used to live on the Upper East Side. In romancing Nancy, Paul was retracing his past.

The couple were first photographed together on a beach in the Hamptons in the autumn of 2007. When he got home to London, Paul went to see Nitin Sawhney, who'd developed a successful career since they first worked together. Sawhney had invited his superstar friend to contribute to his new album, *London Undersound*. The musicians had talked about Paul doing a song about his experiences with the paparazzi during his relationship with Heather Mills, but Paul was more exercised now about the photographers who had caught him with Nancy. 'He came in feeling quite passionate and saying, "I'm amazed they managed to take a picture of me. I didn't think they were around. I really didn't expect that,"' recalls Sawhney. 'In one way he was quite admiring of it. He kind of laughed it off. But you could see it wasn't something he felt that comfortable with either.' These sentiments went into 'My Soul', in which Paul spoke and sang about photographers stealing the soul. Sawhney chose not to improve Paul's vocal digitally, allowing the star to sound his age. 'Some people have said *Oh he sounds a bit old!* I think, well, good. He's not a young bloke.'

Paul's reaction to the paparazzi was mild compared to that of his estranged wife, who allowed herself to be endlessly wound up by the media. On the morning of 31 October, Heather invited herself onto the morning television show *GMTV* to rant about the British press, going 'right over the top' in the words of the divorce judge. Heather began by replying to the most damaging stories that had been published about her in recent months, her alleged past as a porn model and prostitute, stating that she had never made a secret of being a 'glamour model'. As a teenager she aspired to be a celebrity topless model, like Maria Whittaker. 'That was the thing to be in the Eighties.' She had written about topless modelling in her memoirs. 'Paul knew about my glamour-modelling.' Because of the photo-shoot she'd done for *Die Freuden Der Liebe*, the press now portrayed her, in her words, as a 'hard core porn queen'. Her face expressed incredulity, as if she'd never seen the pictures of herself with her legs open.

Becoming increasingly worked up, she reminded television viewers of the very worst the papers had written: 'They've called me a whore, a gold-digger, a fantasist, a liar, the most unbelievably hurtful things, and I've stayed quiet for my daughter, but we've had death threats. I've been close to suicide. So upset about this,' she said, apparently overcome with emotion, though it looked like she was pretending to cry. 'I've had worse press than a paedophile, or a murderer,' she wailed, 'and I've done nothing but charity for 20 years.'

Heather compared the way photographers treated her to the experience of the late Princess of Wales. 'What did the paparazzi do to Diana? They chased her and they killed her,' she stated, in an extravagant and inaccurate analogy.* Heather then referred to her recent appearance on the American TV show, *Dancing with the Stars*. 'The only respite I got [from the media] was going to America and I did *Dancing with the Stars*, because our charity was so damaged and we needed the money. I was the only person on the show that gave the money to the charity ...' (The impression was that she had given *all* the money to charity. When the divorce judge came to study the paperwork he found Heather had been paid $200,000 [then worth about £110,000] from which she donated £50,000 to the vegetarian group Viva! – which, by the by, wasn't a registered charity at the time.)

Turning to her divorce case, Heather hinted darkly that she was the victim of a conspiracy. 'There is so much fear from a certain party of the truth coming out that lots of things have been put out and done,' she said mysteriously, repeating that she'd had death threats. 'That means my daughter's life is at risk, because she's with me all the time.' Despite the millions Paul had given her, Heather claimed she had to borrow money to hire bodyguards. 'A certain part of the tabloid media created such a hate campaign against me, they put my life and my daughter's life at risk. And that's why I considered killing myself,' she said, welling up again, 'because I thought if I'm dead, she's safe, and she can be with her father, and that is the truth. That's the truth.'

Heather was ridiculed for this TV appearance, which apart from being a hysterical display seemingly contravened a legal agreement that she wouldn't talk about the case in public. As a result, Heather's relationship with her legal advisors broke down and she began representing herself in the case. Her outburst was also in marked contrast to the dignified silence maintained by Sir Paul. A hint of what he was feeling came when he said, in reply to a question about the divorce: 'As Winston Churchill once said, "If you're going through Hell, keep going!"' But he said no more.

* As the official inquiry into her death found, Princess Diana was killed in a car accident at the hands of a speeding chauffeur who had exceeded the legal drink-drive limit.

INTO THE LAND OF MAKE-BELIEVE

The gothic towers of the Royal Courts of Justice were cloaked in London fog as Sir Paul McCartney was driven down the Strand on Monday 11 February 2008, day one of a week of hearings during which his divorce would be settled. Seeing the press photographers erecting their ladders outside the main entrance of the High Court, which looks like a cross between a medieval church and an English public school as imagined by J.K. Rowling, Sir Paul ordered his driver to take him round the back way. He was familiar with the building. It is where he came in 1971 to sue his fellow Beatles.

Heather was already inside, a sharp-faced blonde in a pink blouse, black skirt and black boots, her false leg clumping on the flagstones as she strode down the corridor to Court 34. Having parted company with her lawyers, the famous charity worker was representing herself with the help of three 'McKenzie friends', a system whereby litigants in person are able to have people in court to advise them. In Heather's case these were her sister Fiona, a solicitor advocate named David Rosen, and an American attorney Michael Shilub. In contrast, Sir Paul was represented by two of the most expensive and formidable lawyers in the land, Nicholas Mostyn QC and solicitor Fiona Shackleton.

A surprisingly slight figure in person, Sir Paul entered the corridor with a bouncy step, wearing a pinstripe suit, white shirt and tie, a scarf round his neck, non-leather shoes on his feet with thick, moulded soles. At 65, the grey was showing again at the roots of his tinted hair, which had been arranged to disguise where he was thinning, while his sagging jowls carried a trace of winter tan. He was nevertheless still handsome and affable. He wished the ladies and gentlemen of the press a friendly 'good morning', holding the door open for Ms Shackleton as they made their way into the ornate, wood-panelled courtroom, from which the press were excluded.

Inside Court 34, Heather asked Justice Bennett for a £125 million settlement ($191.2m). She said this vast sum would enable her to support herself and Bea in the style they had become accustomed to, allowing her to buy a new London home (in the £10 million [$15 m] price range), a $4.5 million (£3m) New York apartment and an office in Brighton, giving her a total of seven residences, all of which had to be staffed, naturally. The balance of the divorce payment would be invested to generate an income of £3.25 million a year ($4.97m), on which she expected to be able to get by.

Paul's barristers argued in reply that Heather should leave the marriage with total assets of no more than £15 million ($22.9m), on top of which Sir Paul would pay for Beatrice's nanny, education and security. Heather addressed the judge personally, relating details of Paul's alleged assault on her with a wine glass in April 2006, also claiming her husband had colluded with the press in a hate campaign against her. The arguments went on all week. On Friday, a Beatles fan managed to approach Sir Paul in the corridor outside the courtroom with a copy of the *White Album* for signature. Paul refused. When the fan told Heather, she remarked mischievously: 'That's a pity. You are the sort of person who made him what he is today.'

When the couple failed to agree a settlement within the week, Justice Bennett retired to formulate his own judgment. As Sir Paul waited, he consoled Nancy Shevell, whose unmarried 50-year-old brother Jon, a fellow executive with the family trucking firm, had been found dead of an overdose at the Beverly Hills Hotel.

Justice Bennett emailed his draft judgment to Paul and Heather, who were called back to the High Court on Monday 17 March 2008 for the conclusion of their case. Paul was in a good mood when he came to court that morning, burbling to himself – 'bup-bup-bup!' – as he mounted the steps to Court 34. A more subdued Heather followed, dressed for the big day in a curious harlequin trouser suit of many colours.

Behind the 'No Admittance' sign, Justice Bennett read his 58-page judgment aloud to the McCartneys. The headline result was that Sir Paul should pay Lady McCartney a lump sum of £16.5 million ($25.2m), meaning that, with the wealth she had acquired during their marriage, the charity worker would walk away with cash and assets worth £24.3 million ($37.1m), which was £100 million less than she'd asked for, and roughly what Paul had offered her two years ago. In addition, Paul would pay approximately £35,000 a year ($53,000) for Beatrice's nanny and education. As much as anybody who has to go to court to end their marriage can be said to be victorious, Paul was.

With Sir Paul's agreement, and in order to quash press speculation about a case that had already generated acres of newsprint, with many wild allegations, the judge intended to do something very unusual. He wanted to publish his judgment in full on the court website, so the press and public could read the true facts of the matter. Normally, the terms of a divorce remain confidential. Although Heather had been pre-warned about this, the fact that intimate details of her case were about to become common knowledge took her aback. She asked for personal details about her and Beatrice to be redacted. Some were, but she still wasn't happy, and in the dramatic final moments of the case the angry charity worker tipped a jug of water over Fiona Shackleton's head.

Heather emerged into the public corridor to announce to the press that she would speak to them outside. 'We've got to do this in front of the TV cameras!' she said, leading the pack away down the corridor towards the Strand.

Sir Paul emerged from the courtroom minutes later with Ms Shackleton, her hair plastered down on her head like a dog that's been put under a garden hose. Asked what the outcome of the case was, Paul said: 'You will see – it will all be revealed!' Indeed, the press were being given a printed summary of the judgment as his wife began her speech at the Strand gate of the High Court, surrounded by a large crowd of reporters, photographers and cameramen. In talking about the case, as she proceeded to do at length, Heather contravened a court order.

'First of all, I just want to say I'm so glad it's over,' she said over the sound of passing traffic and the rustle of cameras, proclaiming herself happy with the £16.5 million settlement. It was as good as could be expected considering she wasn't represented by a barrister (entirely her own fault). 'Obviously the court do not want a litigant in person to do well … so when they write the judgment up, they're never going to try and make it look in my favour.' She was angry that the full judgment was going to be made public, and would be appealing against this. 'I wanted to keep the judgment private. Paul has just said he wants it public, that's the only reason I'm talking. He's always wanted it public because he wants to look like he's this generous Sir Paul.'

Away from the cameras, just inside the door of the Royal Courts of Justice, Heather's sister Fiona told journalists that all the negative headlines about Heather in recent times had been orchestrated by Paul. 'I can't believe a man can be that low,' she sniped, adding poison-ously in case anybody had forgotten the history that had taken place in this very building: 'He sued his three best friends, remember.'

Heather's appeal was unsuccessful, and the next day Justice Bennett's judgment was published in full, giving the public unprecedented detail not only of the divorce but of Sir Paul's personal life. The star had effectively sanctioned the court to tell the world what he was worth, where he lived and what security he had. The rationale, perhaps, was that the document showed him to be an honest man, while Justice Bennett came to highly critical conclusions about Heather Mills McCartney. His words made fascinating reading.

'The wife is a strong willed and determined personality. She has shown great fortitude in the face of, and overcoming her disability,' His Lordship wrote at the start of his judgment, adding that Heather was 'a kindly person ... devoted to her charitable causes' and that she had conducted her own case with 'steely, yet courteous determination'. That was the best he could say about her.

> The husband's evidence was, in my judgment, balanced. He expressed himself moderately though at times with justifiable irritation, if not anger. He was consistent, accurate and honest. But I regret to have to say I cannot say the same about the wife's evidence. Having watched and listened to her give evidence, having studied the documents, and having given in her favour every allowance for the enormous strain she must have been under (and in conducting her own case) I am driven to the conclusion that much of her evidence, both written and oral, was not just inconsistent and inaccurate but also less than candid. Overall she was a less than impressive witness.

This was damning, and the subsequent details proved very revealing.

During the case, Heather argued that she was 'wealthy and financially independent in her own right' before she met Paul, claiming to have been a millionairess since 1999. She earned approximately £200,000 a year ($306,000) as a model, and up to £25,000 an hour ($38,250) as a celebrity speaker. If Heather persuaded the judge she was already a woman of means she could expect a higher settlement. But the judge decided Heather's claims of being rich in her own right were 'wholly exaggerated' and lacking corroboration. 'During the hearing she was asked repeatedly to produce bank statements ... No bank statements were ever produced.' Her tax returns showed her annual earnings were in the more modest range of £11,500 to £112,000

($17,595–$171,360) prior to her marriage. Also, there was no paperwork to support her assertion that she gave the rest of her income to charity.

The judge referred to Paul's marriage to Linda McCartney:

Repeatedly in his evidence the husband described how even during his relationship with the wife [Heather] in 1999 to 2002 he was grieving for Linda. I have no doubt the husband found the wife very attractive. But equally I have no doubt that he was still very emotionally tied to Linda. It is not without significance that until the husband married the wife he wore the wedding ring given to him by Linda. Upon being married to the wife he removed it and it was replaced by a ring given to him by the wife. The wife for her part must have felt rather swept off her feet by a man as famous as the husband. I think this may well have warped her perception leading her to indulge in make-belief.

To that end, the judge rejected Heather's claims that she and Paul had lived together as man and wife since March 2000, accepting Sir Paul was correct in saying they only started cohabiting on their wedding night in June 2002, when they also stopped using contraception.

As Paul had made clear, there was 'considerable volatility in their relationship' leading up to the big day at Castle Leslie. 'There were good times, there were bad times,' noted the judge, 'and the relationship always left in the husband's mind a question whether he and the wife were going to be ultimately right for each other.'

Justice Bennett described Heather's claim that Paul had bought the house in Beverly Hills as a gift for her as 'wishful thinking'. She claimed to have passed up business opportunities for his sake. 'I would have made millions,' Heather told the judge extravagantly during the case, saying her husband held her back. Yet tax returns showed Heather earned more during her marriage than before it and, far from hindering her career, Paul had arranged for her to interview Paul Newman on *Larry King Live*. Heather alleged that Paul frustrated her charitable activities, and failed to make good with his promised donations. On the contrary, the judge found that Paul introduced Heather to the animal welfare organisations she now associated herself with, notably Viva!, while his sister-in-law Jody Eastman introduced Heather to the Adopt-

A-Minefield organisation, to which Paul had given an astounding £3.4 million ($5.2m) during their marriage.

Heather had taken credit for 'counselling' Paul after his bereavement and said she had helped him get on better with his children, particularly his adoptive daughter Heather (of whom almost nothing was seen these days). She also helped him write songs, encouraged him to tour, and helped with set design and stage-lighting. 'I was his full-time wife, mother, lover, confidante, business partner and psychologist,' she had told the court. Paul agreed that Heather helped him over Linda's death, but denied she encouraged him to get back on the road. 'He firmly said that she contributed nothing to the tours,' reported Justice Bennett.

> Her presence on his tours came about because she loved the husband, enjoyed being there and because she thoroughly enjoyed the media and public attention. I am prepared to accept that her presence was emotionally supportive to him but to suggest that in some way she was his 'business partner' is, I am sorry to have to say, make-belief.

Her claim to have been Paul's psychologist was 'typical of her make-belief'.

Sir Paul was an immensely rich man before he met Heather and the judge noted that he'd grown richer during the marriage, through touring rather than record sales. He quoted Sir Paul on the records he had made during the marriage – including *Driving Rain*, *Standing Stone* and *Chaos and Creation in the Backyard* – saying that though they had been critically acclaimed, the work 'has not yet been profitable'. The judge saw no evidence to corroborate Heather's claim that her husband was twice as rich as he said he was. As to Heather's own assets, they were principally due to her husband's generosity. Justice Bennett listed the numerous gifts and loans Sir Paul had given his wife, and addressed the repeated requests Heather had made to MPL for £450,000 ($688,500) to clear a nonexistent mortgage on her Thames Reach apartment. 'Mr Mostyn put to her that that was a fraudulent attempt to extract money from the husband,' the judge noted.

In my judgment it is unnecessary to go so far as to characterise what the wife attempted as fraudulent. However, it is not an episode that does her any credit whatsoever. Either she knew or must have known that there were no loans on Thames Reach, yet she tried to suggest that there were and thereby obtain monies by underhand means. Her attempts when cross-examined to suggest that she may have got in a muddle and confused this property with others, to my mind, had a hollow ring. In the light of the husband's generosity towards her, as I have set out, I find the wife's behaviour distinctly distasteful ... it damages her overall credibility.

Heather now possessed cash and property totalling £7.8 million ($11.9m), mostly thanks to Paul. She was spending at a rapid rate, though, having blown £3.7 million ($5.6m) during a recent 15-month period – including £184,463 ($282,228) on private planes and helicopters – and she apparently expected to continue living the high life. By her calculation, she would spend £499,000 a year on holidays ($763,470); £125,000 on clothes ($191,250); £30,000 a year ($45,900) on equestrian activities (even though she did not ride, as the judge noted); and £39,000 a year ($59,670) on wine (even though she hardly drank). Bennett was scathing: 'Although she strongly denied it her case boils down to the syndrome of "me, too".'

Heather was greatly concerned about her personal security, telling the court she'd received death threats, and claiming Sir Paul was behind stories about her leaked to the press, which compromised her security. As a result, she claimed to have spent £349,862 ($535,288) on security men, and expected to spend £542,000 a year ($829,260) to provide her and Bea with round-the-clock protection in future. Despite being asked repeatedly by the judge, she failed to produce 'one single invoice or receipt' to substantiate these expenses, while Heather's fortress mentality contrasted to what Paul told the court about his own security.

Aside from when he was on tour, Sir Paul said he'd never felt the need for full-time security people, not until Heather insisted on it. He acquiesced to her request, but had reverted to his freewheeling ways since their separation. He had no full-time bodyguards in Sussex, relying on estate workers to keep their eyes open for intruders. 'The only person with me on a permanent basis is my PA, John Hammel.' John did not stay with him at night, however, and he and Linda had brought up their kids largely without protection.

> It is not healthy for a child to have security 24/7. It sets them apart from their peers and makes them an object of curiosity and, at times, ridicule. Such children live in gilded cages. I do not want this for Beatrice. I am rarely photographed with Beatrice. She needs as normal an upbringing as possible, and surrounding her with round-the-clock security is not the way to achieve this.

Paul added that Heather's attitude to the press was contradictory: she courted attention, yet complained about what the papers published. The judge noted that Heather had been 'her own worst enemy' at times.

Heather had attempted to bring allegations about Paul's conduct into the divorce case; that is, the lurid allegations leaked to the press in October 2006. 'The conduct complained of by the wife can be summarised as follows,' recapped the judge.

> Prior to their separation at the end of April 2006 the husband treated the wife abusively and/or violently culminating in the unhappy events of 25 April 2006 ... He abused alcohol and drugs. He was possessive and jealous. He failed to protect the wife from the attention of the media. He was insensitive to her disability. Furthermore, it is alleged that post-separation the husband manipulated and colluded with the press against the wife and has failed to enforce confidentiality by his friends and associates. The wife blames the husband for the leaking to the media of her Answer and Cross-Petition which alleges in strong terms unreasonable behaviour by the husband against her. The husband has failed to provide her with a sufficient degree of security from the media and generally he has behaved badly.

In reply, Sir Paul's QC told the court about Heather's conduct *after* the separation. 'First, it is said on 25 June 2006 the wife illegally bugged the husband's telephone, in particular a call between him and his daughter Stella in which Stella made very unflattering comments about the wife,' the judge summarised. 'It is further said the wife subsequently leaked the intercepted material to the press so as to discredit him.' (This had seemingly led to a *Sunday Mirror* story, 'The Maccagate Tapes').

Second, on 17 October 2006 the wife, or someone acting on her behalf, leaked to the media some or all of the contents of her Answer and Cross-Petition which contained untrue and distorted allegations against the husband in order to discredit him. Third, the wife has failed to abide by court orders re[garding] confidentiality. On 31 October 2007 and 1 November 2007 the wife gave several interviews to UK and US television stations in which she made many false statements about the husband and these proceedings in order to discredit him. Individually and collectively these actions, it is said, represent a deliberate attempt by the wife to ruin the husband's reputation.

Somebody leaked Heather's Answer and Cross-Petition to the press.

Both the wife and the husband accuse each other of doing it. The wife says that the husband did it in order to capitalise on his good press and to blacken the wife's name for making such unfounded allegations. The husband says the wife did it in order to blacken his reputation.

The judge chose not to decide who was lying.

In his closing comments, Justice Bennett said that if an applicant came before him with an excessive claim, which they failed to back up with logical arguments, then they had themselves to blame if they failed to get what they wanted. 'This case is a paradigm example of an applicant failing to put a rational and logical case and thus failing to assist the court in its quasi-inquisitorial role to reach a fair result.' He ordered that neither Paul nor Heather disclose further details to the media. Even Heather learned to be bound by this order and, unable to say anything of substance about her husband, and with plenty of money to spend, she faded into the semi-obscurity from whence she had come, occasionally popping up on TV, and employing a succession of public relations consultants, who found themselves hard-pressed to improve her image. One spent much of his time trying to turn Heather's Wikipedia entry to her favour.

BACK TO THE BEGINNING

Many of Paul's associates had died prematurely, several worn down by the rigours of the rock 'n' roll lifestyle. Brian, John, Linda and George had all passed away before their time, along with a host of supporting players in the epic story of Paul's life. Now Neil Aspinall, the backroom boy who had as much claim as anyone to being the 'fifth Beatle', was dying of cancer in New York. Paul went to see him, as he had George, thanked Nell, as the boys always called their friend fondly, for all he had done for the band, discreetly paid his medical bills, and mourned his passing when he died in March 2008 at the age of 66.

Neither Paul nor Ringo attended Neil's funeral in his adoptive home town of Twickenham, just outside London. 'We went to Neil's house for the reception afterwards and Yoko said to me, "Where is Paul and Ringo?" And I said, "I don't know. You should know better than I do where they are'," says Peter Brown, who attended the service along with Olivia Harrison, Sir George Martin and Mary and James McCartney.

> Paul was represented through his children, but he and Ringo were not there. Now whether they thought it was more discreet for them not to go ... but it wasn't as if there was going to be a million paparazzi or anything. So I don't know what happened that day.

Sir Paul spent a good part of the spring on holiday with Nancy Shevell, his *decree nisi* coming through in May, at the end of which he returned to Liverpool to help his home town celebrate its year as European Capital of Culture. In recent times Liverpool had been perceived not so much as a place to go to enrich one's mind as a scruffy, declining seaport beset with social and economic problems. So the Capital of Culture accolade – a European Union initiative to boost investment in designated cities – was a welcome fillip to Merseyside. A huge amount of money was being invested in building works, including a new shopping arcade opposite the docks, part of which had some time since been restored and given World Heritage status, with the city hosting an impressive series of cultural events in 2008 ranging from art shows to symphony concerts. Art with a capital A was all very well, but for millions Liverpool was the Beatles, and the city's year as Capital of

Culture would ring hollow without a Beatle or two in attendance. They got both.

Ringo Starr, now in his 68th year, opened Liverpool's celebratory year by playing drums on the roof of St George's Hall in the city centre on 8 January 2008, and proclaiming improbably that he might return from tax exile in Monte Carlo to live on Merseyside. When Ringo subsequently told Jonathan Ross on TV that he couldn't think of a single thing about Liverpool he actually missed, and had only said he might come back to please the crowd, Liverpudlians were outraged. Many had long thought Ringo thick, and this seemed to prove it. Ringo's head was cut off a topiary likeness of the band in Allerton, while cabbies told visitors to the city that if 'that twat' ever came back to Merseyside he'd be pelted with eggs.

The centrepiece of the year of culture was the Liverpool Sound concert on Sunday 1 June at Anfield, iconic home of Liverpool Football Club. The event was headlined, naturally, by the other, more important ex-Beatle, the one who, drugs and women aside, rarely put a foot wrong. Sir Paul McCartney arrived on Merseyside a few days in advance of the show, spending part of Saturday driving around the city with his major-domo John Hammel, son James and daughter Beatrice, a lively little kid now coming up for five. In contrast to Paul's older children, Bea was being brought up by her mum in an atmosphere of conspicuous wealth. This tour of Liverpool was intended to show her the normal world Daddy came from.

Stopping at 72 Western Avenue, Speke, Paul led Bea up the garden path to the door of his old corpy house. 'This is where Daddy used to live,' he told the child, as they posed for a souvenir picture outside what was now a run-down terrace. As they did so, the man next door popped his head over the wall. 'All right, Macca!' James 'Brickhead' Gillat, a tattooed joiner, hailed the superstar.

'All right, la,' rejoined McCartney pleasantly. 'Is there anybody in?'

Sir Paul rang the bell of number 72 to introduce himself to the current occupants, Paddy and Lyn Kearney. He hoped they didn't mind him taking a souvenir picture on the doorstep. The Kearneys and Brickhead were charmed by Paul, who still seemed connected to ordinary people. 'He never walked away from us, never turned his back on us,' says Brickhead admiringly after the great man left.

When Paul cruised by Forthlin Road with John, James and Bea, he decided not to go up to the door, wary of the tourists who arrived every few minutes to stand outside this much better-known address, taking pictures and pulling off bits of the hedge as keepsakes. Visitors on the National Trust tour were admitted in small groups by the live-in custodian John Halliday, who calculates he'd shown 70,000 people around Paul's old house in the ten years it had been open to the public. One of John's ambitions was to give Paul himself the tour, and now here was his chance. 'I glanced out of the corner of me eye. He wasn't driving; he was in the front passenger seat – I thought, *that's Paul!* He gives me the thumbs up. I thought he'd come in, but he drove past.'

National Trust ticketholders were taken to Mendips before Forthlin Road, Aunt Mimi's old home, also now managed by the charity. The two houses were included in the same £15 tour. This particular afternoon, Mendips was closed for a private visit from Yoko Ono and her son Sean. A well-preserved little woman of 75, with clever, sparkling eyes, and a daringly low *décolletage*, Yoko attended a host of events in the city that weekend, including a rare coming together of most of the surviving members of the Beatles family at LIPA the following afternoon.

As her contribution to the festivities, and to raise money for LIPA, Stella McCartney staged a lunchtime fashion show at the Institute on Sunday 1 June. Sir Paul showed up with son James, taking a seat in the front row of the Paul McCartney Auditorium alongside Yoko Ono and Olivia Harrison. Paul kissed the widows and chatted with Yoko as if they'd never been anything but best friends. Watching them, one was reminded of a royal court, all eyes upon the heads of state, attended in turn by their lords and ladies. In the court of the Beatles, the followers included Paul's brother Mike (his show business career as Mike McGear a distant memory), Sir George Martin, snowy-haired and almost stone deaf at 82, the rotund figure of the elderly court artist Sir Peter Blake, and LIPA chief Mark Featherstone-Witty. Every king needs a servant, and John Hammel hovered nearby, quick to tell the press photographers they'd taken enough pictures. Sir Paul welcomed the PR opportunity of a happy snap with Yoko – it made the front pages of the nationals the next day – but he didn't want pictures of himself with Beatrice, who was being minded by Mike McCartney a few rows back, a pretty little girl dressed head to foot in pink.

When John Hammel had shooed the snappers away, Bea stood on her chair and loudly asked Daddy for an ice cream. Sir Paul turned, acknowledged Bea's presence with an affectionate, fatherly expression, upon which she ran to him, climbed into his lap and chattered away for a few minutes before going back to sit with Uncle Mike for the start of the show.

Stella McCartney strode onto the stage – a perky, ginger-haired woman of 36 – to acknowledge her family links to Liverpool. 'I've got about 50,000 relatives in this city,' she said, upon which Sir Paul shouted: 'Three cheers for Stella!' The audience did as it was told. During the ensuing catwalk parade, Paul and his son sat with fuzzy looks on their faces watching the leggy beauties model Stella's latest creations, Paul taking the occasional picture on his mobile phone as if lining up dates for later. Bea returned with a balloon, scrambled into Daddy's lap, then fell asleep with her thumb in her mouth. 'I thought, fantastic, he's got a great relationship with her,' notes Mark Featherstone-Witty.

Liverpool was overcast that evening as 36,000 people streamed towards Anfield for the concert, most of the ticketholders local people, though others had come from around the world to see Sir Paul play his home town. The fact he was playing at Anfield was special: the McCartneys had lived briefly round the corner at 10 Sunbury Road, and a home town show always has that bit of extra emotion. After the support acts, the Kaiser Chiefs and Zutons, two of whose members had attended LIPA, the comedian Peter Kay appeared on stage to a warm reception. 'It's my job to introduce the star turn tonight, ladies and gentlemen,' said Kay, who is hugely popular in the north.

He's a local lad who's done very well for himself in the old music game. He's played with some amazing people over the years: Stevie Wonder, Rupert the Bear [big laugh] and the Beatles! [huge cheer] ... In conjunction with Liverpool County Council [boos and hisses], BBC Radio Merseyside [cheers] and Heatwave Sun Bed Centre, Norris Green [laughs], it is my duty to reveal Britain has got talent, ladies and gentleman, and his name is Sir Paul Mildred McCARTNEEEEEY!

Strolling on stage in a silver suit, Paul opened with 'Hippy Hippy Shake', taking his audience back to the Cavern. Next came 'Jet', the audience punching the air with the repeated exclamations of 'Jet!', singing along to the verses in the style of a football crowd at a home fixture. 'Liverpool! I love ya!' exclaimed Paul at the end of the number, and who would doubt him? In recent years he'd spent more time in the city than at any stage since the early Sixties, becoming almost a familiar figure in the streets again. Stories of the star strolling about town – popping into Lewis's to buy a tie one day – were legion. 'I was born just down the road from here, Walton Hospital, Rice Lane,' he reminded his audience, 'and I lived in Sunbury Road.' Sitting in the Lower Centenary Stand, Brenda Rothwell turned to the person sitting beside her and said excitedly: 'I live next door!' After 'Got to Get You into My Life' Paul held up his Höfner bass and cried: 'OK, let's hear it for Speke! For Garston! ...' Local people cheered their suburb.

Paul sang 'My Love' for Linda, whose picture appeared on the huge screens (all images of Heather excised). The audience applauded everything the star said, his every joke and story, and sang along heartily to almost every song, the ukulele tribute to George Harrison raising the crowd to a collective roar when Paul sang his friend's sweetly questioning lyric, meant originally for George's first wife, Pattie Boyd, but having a universal resonance: 'You're asking me will my love grow/I don't know, I don't know'. The words echoed around the stadium as a football chant, tears pricking the eyes of performer and fans. Olivia was watching. Yoko was beside her. She appeared to approve Paul's performance of 'Give Peace a Chance', as a tribute to her late husband. Paul signed off with 'I Saw Her Standing There', setting middle-aged Liverpudlians jiving in the aisles, round ladies of pensionable age recreating the dance steps of their youth, touching their ample bosoms and sending out their love with the palms of their hands as Paul sang of his heart going *boom*.

With a detonation of fireworks, the home town celebration of the greatest pop band ever was over. In the club's trophy room, Sir Paul greeted the selected friends, celebrity guests and relatives who'd been gathered to meet him briefly after the show, going down the line shaking hands and exchanging friendly words with everyone. 'Even though I've known him all these years, I'm still in awe of the fact he's a Beatle,' says Sam Leach, a promoter from the early days who was among the guests. 'If I call him Sir Paul, he laughs.' Outside, the rest of the audience shuffled away down the narrow, red-brick streets of Anfield, chanting with drowsy happiness, 'Liverpool! Liverpool!'

FURTHER ON DOWN THE ROAD

The musician's life is on the road, and for an artist who loves to perform, tours are a pleasure, an opportunity to cast the happy spell of music over an audience and bask in their appreciation. 'I think it's basically magic,' Paul has said. 'There is such a thing as magic, and the Beatles were magic.'

Later that summer Paul indulged himself, and offset the cost of his recent divorce, with massive one-off shows in Kiev and Quebec (the latter to celebrate the province's 400th birthday). *En route* to Canada, he joined Billy Joel on stage at Shea Stadium for the final concert at that famous venue before it was demolished to make way for a new home for the New York Mets. Afterwards, he got his old Ford Bronco out of his Amagansett garage, took Chuck Berry's tip and motored west with Nancy Shevell on Route 66, via Chicago, St Louis, Flagstaff, Arizona (not forgetting Winona), 2,000 miles and more to LA. Everyday folks found themselves bumping into Sir Paul and his girlfriend at gas stations and diners along the way, the couple apparently happy together and happy to pose for pictures. It was a road trip he'd always wanted to make.

That autumn saw the release of a welcome third Fireman album, the records Paul made with Youth being among the most interesting of his later career. *Electric Arguments* was more song-based than their previous projects, with proper lyrics that seemed to criticise an ex-love – references to betrayal, lies and a woman who went looking for a pay daddy ('Highway') – without identifying Heather. Paul was always careful that way. Although a more mainstream offering than *Rushes*, the record was still too different for Macca traditionalists. 'I don't like this *Electric Arguments*,' says New Yorker Linda Aiello, who otherwise lives in a state of McCartney devotion. 'It's not him, because it really isn't him. It's the Fireman … I can't get into it.'

In the spring of 2009 Paul appeared on stage at Radio City Music Hall in New York with Ringo Starr, in support of Transcendental Meditation, one of the dopier Sixties' crazes, but something the men had carried with them into old age. More North American shows followed. Having helped mark the closure of Shea Stadium, Paul played three sell-outs at the new home of the New York Mets, Citi Fields, promoted with an appearance on David Letterman's *Late Show* at the Ed Sullivan Theater where the Beatles first electrified America. Paul performed a special homecoming set from the marquee, later releasing a live CD of the New York concerts, *Good Evening New York City*. Excluding the Radio City benefit, Paul played a dozen shows across the USA in the year, grossing almost $41 million (£26.7m). Together with the other concerts he'd given recently, the divorce was paid for.

Two old foes died that summer, first Michael Jackson in suspicious circumstances aged 50, never having given Paul a pay rise on Northern Songs, part of which Jackson had sold to Sony to help fund his excessive lifestyle, putting the songs beyond Paul's grasp. It seemed he would never get them back now. Paul insisted in his tribute that he and Jackson had never really fallen out, despite all his grousing. Ten days later, almost unnoticed amidst the Jackson news, a true enemy, Allen Klein, died aged 77. As old friends and foes alike dropped away, McCartney rolled on, looking spry for a man approaching 70, popping over to Paris with Nancy to attend Stella's latest fashion show, casting a paternal eye over son James as he recorded his first album at Hog Hill Mill, while Dad worked on a guitar concerto and oversaw the endless exploitation of the Beatles' back catalogue, being the driving force behind the *Beatles Rock Band* video game, released in the autumn of 2009, around the same time as a complete digital reissue of the Beatles' studio albums. Although almost everybody already had all this music, and the box sets cost almost $300 (£196), they sold strongly, helping make the Beatles the second best-selling act of the decade in America, just behind Eminem, a remarkable achievement for a group that split 39 years ago.

Always busy, Paul recorded a song for a new Robert De Niro picture, *Everybody's Fine*, and had a movie of his own in the works – the animated film about Wirral the Squirrel he and Linda had decided on years back based on stories he used to tell the kids. To introduce the character to the public, Paul and Geoff Dunbar created in the first instance an illustrated children's book, *High in the Clouds*, the plot of which harked back to the death of Mary McCartney – a trauma Paul still spoke of as if he were an orphaned child. 'That association [is] very, very strong in *High in the Clouds*,' says Dunbar. 'For us in our childhoods, Mum was this great thing.' In the book, Wirral loses his mother, as Paul had, after which the creature goes off into the world to find adventure, music and love with a cute little red squirrel named Wilhamina. At the end, the two characters stand together, looking at the stars. 'If only Mum was with us,' says Wirral.

'She is,' replied Wilhamina, clutching his paw.

This little story expresses much of Paul's own life: a sentimental man formed by his childhood experiences in Liverpool, from whence he had gone searching for love in a musical world. (For Wilhamina read Linda.) Now his squirrel story was to be made into a 3D Hollywood film. Hopefully it would be ready in time for Bea to appreciate, before she began to realise the enormity of who Daddy was.

THE ROAD GOES EVER ON

On a frosty night in December 2009, with Christmas in the air, Sir Paul McCartney opened his latest tour – a European tour – in Hamburg, second city of his musical genesis. It was way back in 1960 that Paul first drove here with the boys, in Allan Williams's overloaded van, to play the Indra. A lifetime later, Paul flew back by private jet to play the Color Line Arena, five subway stops from the Reeperbahn, declining an invitation to meet the city's mayor, and keeping his fans waiting as he played a late sound check and ate his customary vegetarian pre-show supper. Although the animal rights group PETA, which McCartney had long been associated with, had stalls at the Hamburg show, distributing Eat No Meat literature, the intense animal activism of Linda's day was gone. Once upon a time the McCartneys screened fierce anti-vivisection films before their shows, and banned meat products from gigs. Tonight, fans munched *schinkenwurst* at the concessions, while those who'd purchased €319 ($440) VIP ticket packages tucked into gourmet meats in the Platinum bar.

Germans are a punctual people, so when the advertised start time came and went, and they were obliged to wait a further 80 minutes for the show to begin, they became disgruntled, slow-clapping, booing and hissing the unseen star. Finally, Sir Paul stepped up on the stage –

dressed in the dark suit, white shirt and braces he favoured these days for live performances – greeting his audience with a supremely confident shrug as if to say: 'What's up?' Eleven thousand grumpy Germans were immediately pacified, then brought to their feet by the upbeat sound of 'Magical Mystery Tour', Paul as ever following Uncle Mike's advice to him and John at the Fox and Hounds, Caversham. 'A good act is shaped like a W,' Mike had told the boys. You had to start on a high.

The sound quality was poor in Hamburg, as it invariably is in sports arenas, reedy at the top and boomy at the bottom, Paul's vocals echoing off the back rows – these seats being so far from the stage that he put his hands to his eyes, peered down the hall and asked the people down there if they were all right – and his voice sounded thin at first, like an old man's. But as he warmed up his voice strengthened, the band complementing and covering for the star while never presuming to upstage him.

'Danke schön! Guten tag, Hamburg,' said Paul, venturing a little schoolboy German, soon reverting to English. 'It really is interesting to be back here in Hamburg.'

'What about a trip to the Reeperbahn?' asked a fan in front.

'Hmmm.' Paul considered it. *'Not tonight.'*

He spoke about when the Beatles first came to town, 'when we were children', and how they had met up with other 'slightly older children', name-checking old friends in the audience. In the first few rows sat Horst Fascher, Astrid Kirchherr and Klaus Voormann, little old people wrapped up warm on a cold December night. Indeed, the audience was mostly comprised of the late middle-aged, chubby, affluent and grey, glancing occasionally at their watches to make sure they didn't get home too late. Although of an age with these pensioners, and despite his skin hanging down like the jowls of an old dog, Paul looked younger than them all, thanks principally to the art of his hairdresser. Apart from being dyed chestnut brown, his hair was so lustrous and thick these days one wondered if he was wearing a wig.

Taking off his jacket, and rolling up his sleeves, Sir Paul also looked more than ever like a nineteenth-century mill owner. This was not a young artist who needed the audience's approval. He was here because he enjoyed playing music and revisiting the past, and those lucky enough to have a ticket were fortunate to share the moment with him. Between songs he regaled us all with stories from the old days, like the night his mate Jimi (Jimi Hendrix, that is) played 'Sgt. Pepper' at the Saville Theatre, and asked Eric (Clapton, you know) to come up and tune his guitar. Everybody, audience and band included, listened attentively to an elder telling tales of a vanished age. Linda was never far from Paul's mind. As he played 'The Long and Winding Road', photos Linda had taken of their Arizona ranch, including the desert trail they rode just before she died, were shown on the screens. 'Here Today' was performed 'für meinen freund, John ... Are you listening?' Paul asked suddenly, glancing up at the roof as if to find his friend's ghost sitting in the rafters. 'Something' was done again on the ukulele for George, while pictures of the other departed Beatle were shown. Paul held his arms up to the last picture, a huge blow-up of a young smiling George, murmuring 'Georgie! Georgie!' in salute. When Paul turned back, his face was wet with tears.

With both John and George gone, and Ritchie always of lesser importance, it had fallen to Paul to carry the Beatles torch. Along with the sadness, there was a sense that he felt liberated by the fact John and George weren't around to snipe at him any more. He could say and play whatever he liked now, including putting two Beatles numbers in his set for the first time, 'And I Love Her' and 'Ob-La-Di, Ob-La-Da', both of which went down a storm with the Germans even if John had mocked the latter as 'granny music'.

After 'Yesterday' and 'Helter Skelter', Paul informed his audience that it was time for him to go home. The Hamburgers, who'd booed two hours previously, groaned. 'It's time for you to go home, too,' Paul reminded them; it was almost midnight. He thanked his band and his crew. 'But most of all, tonight, we want to thank *you*,' he said, before playing 'Sgt. Pepper's Lonely Hearts Club Band', segueing into 'The End', pictures of a sun going down on the screens as Paul sang the sublime last lines about the love you take being equal to the love you make, after which everybody exhaled a happy *Ahhhhh*.

'Yeah, yeah, yeah, yeah.'

As one fan remarked, 'the best music – *ever*'.

'Danke schön, Hamburg. We'll see you next time!'

ACKNOWLEDGEMENTS

With this book I set out to write a better-balanced, more detailed and more comprehensive life of Paul McCartney than has previously been achieved. I did not have an agenda to find fault with Sir Paul, nor did I seek to glorify his career glibly. Rather I have tried to tell the epic story of his life truthfully and fairly as I have found the facts to be from studying him closely, as an entomologist might put another kind of beetle under the microscope.

As a foundation for my work I travelled extensively, visiting the places that feature in Sir Paul's life, collecting documentary material (family records, real estate, financial and legal papers), and conducting interviews with approximately 220 people, including his friends, neighbours, family members and fellow musicians. I also read everything in print about the musician and his close associates, and I would like to acknowledge the published sources I found most helpful.

More books have been written about the Beatles, probably, than any act in show business. Hunter Davies's *The Beatles*, first published in 1968, retains its interest, as does Philip Norman's 1981 history *Shout!* It is, however, the reference books by Mark Lewisohn that stand apart for the author's fastidious attention to detail, with his *The Complete Beatles Chronicle* (1992) being the Bible of Beatles reference. Despite the fact that it glosses over or misses out important parts of the Beatles' story, the Beatles' *Anthology* – by which I mean the documentary series and the companion book published in 2000 – is also an invaluable record of the band members' thoughts and recollections. Regarding magazines and fanzines, I turned repeatedly to *Melody Maker* in the UK and *Rolling Stone* in the USA, while Paul McCartney's own *Club Sandwich* was a useful resource.

Several previous full-length biographies have been written of Sir Paul. Aside from Barry Miles's very good 1997 book *Paul McCartney: Many Years from Now*, none are of much note, and despite its undoubted strengths, not least as a record of the artist's views on every aspect of the Beatles' story, *Many Years from Now* is mostly a book about the Sixties. It is also a partisan book, written in close conjunction with and indeed vetted by its subject. Working without Sir Paul's cooperation, I have striven to create a more impartial biography that is also broader in scope, taking equal account of the artist's time in the Beatles and his life during the decades that have followed. For this reason *Fab* is divided into two halves, with the second part of the book telling the story of his adventures since 1970.

I am grateful to the following people for giving me information: Jane Abbott (formerly Brainsby), Linda Aiello (*née* Magno), John Aldridge, Carlos Alomar, Lord (Jeffrey) Archer, the late Al Aronowitz, Anthony Bailey, Geoff Baker, Marty Balin, Christine Barnwell, Tony Barrow, Bob Bass, Sid Bernstein, Roag Best, Douglas Binder, Jamie Black, Kate Black, Tony 'Measles' Bramwell, Geoffrey Brand, Al Brodax, Peter Brown, Yolanda Byrne (*née* Ventre), Ian Campbell, Howie and Sheila Casey, Clem Cattini, Natalie Clark, Maureen Cleave, John Coates, Mary and Rory Colville, Bob Cote, Alastair Cousin, Rosemary Crouch, Carl Davis, Rod Davis, Len Deighton, Prince Stanislas Klossowski 'Stash' de Rola, Ken Dodd, Joe Dolce, Barbara Doran (*née* Eves), John Duff Lowe, Geoff Dunbar, Michael Eavis, Dudley Edwards, Ron Ellis, Royston Ellis, Geoff Emerick, Eldon Erwin, Bernie Evans, Horst Fascher, Mark Featherstone-Witty, Brenda Fenton, Iris Fenton (*née* Caldwell), John Fenton, Danny Fields, Bill Flanagan, Joe Flannery, Herbie Flowers, Ray Fooks, Bruce Forsyth, Frank Foy, Steve Gadd, Johnny Gentle, James 'Brickhead' Gillat, Brian Gregg, Brian Griffiths, Adrian and Evelyn Grumi, Jim Guercio, Rosi Haitmann (later Sheridan), John Halliday, Colin Hanton, Ian Harris, Bill Harry, Billy Hatton, Jann Haworth, Peter Hodgson, Derek Holgate, Steve Holley, John 'Hoppy' Hopkins, Philip Howarth, Erika Hübers (*née* Wohlers), Edward Hunter, Frank Ifield, Neil Innes, Ian James, Glyn Johns, Mickey Jones, Laurence Juber, Susan Justice (*née* Aldridge), Alfie Karmal, Norman Kauffman, John Kay, Paddy and Lyn

Kearney, Gibson Kemp, Astrid Kirchherr, Barbara Knight (*née* Wilson), Marijke Koger-Dunham, Al Kooper, Jonathan Kress, Bettina Krischbin (*née* Hübers), Denny Laine, Carla Lane, Veronica and Bob Languish, Sam Leach, Sir John Leslie, Sir Michael Lindsay-Hogg, Andrew Loog Oldham, Graham Lowe, Barbara Lyon (*née* Lunt), Doug Mackenzie, E. Rex Makin, Imelda Marcos, Gerry Marsden, Lilian Marshall, Salvatore 'Pico' Martens, David Mason, David Matthews, the late Victor Maymudes, Joan McCartney, Henry McCullough, Jim 'the Rock' McGeachy (Senior) and his son Jimmy, John McGeachy, Robbie McIntosh, Ian McKerral, George McMillan, Barry Miles, Fiona Mills, Elliot Mintz, Maria Mohin, Paul Morrisey, Billy Morton, Brian Moses, Kate Muir, Len Murray, Bill and Maggie Nelson, Mike Nesmith, Dr Roy Newsome, Ann Nicholson (*née* Ventre), Steve Nieve, Frieda Norris (*née* Kelly), Steve Norris, Ray O'Brien, Boston O'Donohue, Richard Ogden, Hugh Padgham, Dick Page, Major Peter Parkes, Eryl Parry, Graham Partington, Tom Pickard, Charlie Piggott, Ian Pillans, Simon Posthuma, Claude 'Curly' Putman Jr, Lord (David) Puttnam, Joe Reddington, Ruth Reeves (*née* Lallemann), Gillian Reynolds, Mike Robbins, Brenda Rothwell, Willy Russell, Lord St Germans, Sir Jimmy Savile, Nitin Sawhney, Helga Schultz, Denny Seiwell, Brian Sewell, Ravi Shankar, Gene Shaw, Tony Sheridan, Jane Shevell, Don Short, Anthony Smith, Murial Smith, Sir James Douglas Spooner, Philip Sprayregen, Alvin Stardust, Eric and Gloria Stewart, Alda Lupo Stipanoe (and family), Hamish Stuart, Pauline Sutcliffe, Wolfgang Suttner, Sir John Tavener, Marga and Ted 'Kingsize' Taylor, Peter Tomkins, Pete Townshend, Isabel Turnbull, Walter van Dijk (and his mother Jeann), Janet Vaughan, Peter Vogl, Lisa Voice, Jürgen Vollmer, David Waite, Edie Warren, Donald Warren-Knott, Peter Webb, Nat Weiss, Kevin Wheal, Andy White, Gaz Wilcox, Beverly Wilk, Allan Williams, June Woolley, David Young, Youth and Debra and Sherry Zeller.

Thank you additionally to the following individuals and organisations for help and advice: Abbey Road Studios; Rebecca Chapman at the British Society of Songwriters, Composers and Authors (BASCA); Lt Deanna Coultas of the Tucson, AZ, police; Caroline Cowie at the National Union of Teachers (NUT); Geoff Garvey for Sussex research; Matthew Davis for translating in Hamburg, and Harald Mau for being our Hamburg guide; Dr Bob Hieronimus for *Yellow Submarine* help; Spencer Leigh at BBC Radio Merseyside; Ken McNab for Scottish connections; Pete Norman for Heather Mills and the Old Liobians for Liverpool Institute information. Particular thanks to Kevin Roach and Andy Simons at Liverpool Record Office; also to Richard Farnell at Liverpool City Council; Edda and Heidi at the Hans Tasiemka Archives; and the staff of the British Film Institute, the Barbican and Guildhall libraries, the British Library/British Newspaper Library, and New York Public Library. Thank you also to my editors, Natalie Jerome at Harper-Collins in London; Ben Schafer at Da Capo in New York and Tim Rostron at Doubleday Canada; to Nick Fawcett and Helen Hawksfield who worked on the copy-editing of *Fab*; and to my agents Kate Lee at ICM in New York and Gordon Wise at Curtis Brown, London.

SOURCE NOTES

Some shorthand forms are used in these notes. Paul McCartney and other key characters are referred to firstly by their full name, then by initials. So Paul McCartney becomes PM, John Lennon JL, etc.

When referring to the Beatles' *Anthology*, I indicate in parenthesis whether I mean the documentary, book or CDs (and their liner notes).

Justice Bennett's March 2008 High Court judgment in the divorce of Sir Paul and Heather Mills McCartney is 'the Bennett judgment'.

The Times is the [London] *Times*.

1: A LIVERPOOL FAMILY

Paul McCartney (PM) quote – 'They may not look much …' – *Sunday Times magazine* (9 June 1991).

Liverpool history: I consulted *Liverpool 800* (Belchem) and *Liverpool* (Sharples). Thanks also to Richard Farnell at Liverpool City Council.

McCartney-Mohin family history: author's discussions with relatives including John Aldridge, Ian Harris, Susan Justice (*née* Aldridge), Joan McCartney (quoted), Maria Mohin and Mike Robbins (quoted); the 1911 Census; records of birth, death and marriages; *Up the Beatles Family Tree* (Humphrey-Smith *et al.*); *Thank U Very*

Much (Mike McCartney) and *The McCartneys: In the Town Where They Were Born* (Roach).

All Mike Robbins quotes to the author.

Jim played 'until his teeth gave out': PM in the *Anthology* (book).

Jim meets Mary: *The McCartneys: In the Town Where They Were Born* (Roach).

Air raids: the booklet *Air Raids on Liverpool*, Liverpool Record Office.

Parents marry: marriage certificate.

Sectarian problems: *Liverpool 800* (Belchem).

Ringo Starr (RS) quoted from the *Anthology* (book).

PM born: birth certificate.

PM baptised: church records at Liverpool Record Office.

Mike McCartney's birth: birth certificate.

Relations with brother: author's interviews.

Speke history: *The Illustrated History of Liverpool's Suburbs* (Lewis). Thanks also to former Joseph Williams pupils Barbara Doran (*née* Eves), Marjorie Knight (*née* Wilson) and Barbara Lyon (*née* Lunt).

Inspiration for 'Mother Nature's Son': *Paul McCartney: Many Years from Now* (Miles).

Mary resigns job: *The McCartneys: In the Town Where They Were Born* (Roach).

Thanks to the current resident of 12 Ardwick Rd, Liverpool, who did not wish to be named.

Jim McCartney's phrase 'Put it there': *Club Sandwich* # 52.

Will Stapleton story: thanks firstly to a McCartney relative who wishes to be anonymous (includes recalled dialogue). The story of the SS *Apapa* is substantiated by reports in the *Liverpool Evening News* (11, 12 and 14 Oct. 1949; also 3 Nov. 1949); *The Times* (12 Oct. 1949); and the *Manchester Guardian* (12 Oct./24 Nov. 1949). I also consulted family records to establish the link between Stapleton and Edie McCartney. Many thanks to Kevin Roach at Liverpool Record office for helping me find related press reports.

Will at Scargreen Avenue: *Kelly's* Street Directories.

McCartneys get their TV: *Thank U Very Much* (McCartney).

Coronation prize: Liverpool Record Office; and the original essay.

The Liverpool Institute: thanks to old boys Bernie Evans, John Duff Lowe, Ian James (quoted), Billy Morton and Steve Norris (quoted). The author visited the school and consulted the admissions register and other documents. Thanks also to the Liobians.

Arthur Askey: *Liverpool 800* (Belchem). Thanks also to Peter Hodgson.

PM on his schooldays: documentary film *Echoes* (MPL, 2004).

Macca nickname bestowed: *Thank U Very Much* (Mike McCartney). In this book, PM's brother spells the nickname 'Maca', but it is commonly expressed as Macca.

Neil 'Nell' Aspinall: Liverpool Institute admissions; *Fifty Years Adrift* (Taylor).

PM meets George Harrison (GH): *I Me Mine* (Harrison); GH quoted from the *Anthology* (book).

Description of 20 Forthlin Road: author's visit to what is now a National Trust property, the accompanying guide book, author's discussions with the caretaker John Halliday and neighbours.

Mary McCartney quote – 'Nothing, love' – *Thank U Very Much* (Mike McCartney).

Death of Mary McCartney: thanks to Mike Robbins and Joan McCartney (both quoted); also death certificate.

2: JOHN

PM hears his father cry: *Anthology* (book).

Swapped his trumpet: PM on the *South Bank Show* (Jan. 1978). Also a 1964 interview with *Beat Instrumental*, reprinted in *The Beatles Book* (Feb. 2001).

Skiffle/learns guitar/2006 auction of guitar: author's interview with Ian James (quoted).

Attends Donegan concert at Liverpool Empire: PM in *Paul McCartney: Many Years from Now* (Miles) and *Liverpool Evening Express* (5 Nov. 1956).

First record bought: the *Anthology* (book).

Billy Morton quoted from author's interview.

First song written: *Club Sandwich* # 41.

John Lennon (JL) background: author's interviews; *John Lennon: The Life* (Norman) [including Mimi's affair and quote about Elvis]; *Up the Beatles' Family Tree* (Humphrey-Smith *et al.*); author's visit to Mendips; also the National Trust booklet about the house, from which I quote Aunt Mimi, 'John, your little friend's here.'

Daily Howl extract: the *Anthology* (documentary).

The Quarry Men: author's interviews with Rod Davis (quoted), John Duff Lowe and Colin Hanton (quoted). Background: *The Quarrymen* (Davies) and the *Anthology* (book).

Scout camp: *Thank U Very Much* (McCartney).

Butlin's: author's interview with Mike Robbins.

Early girlfriends: thanks to Marjorie Knight (*née* Wilson) and Ann Nicholson (*née* Ventre [quoted exchange with PM]).

Sex: Ian James interview; and *Paul McCartney: Many Years from Now* (Miles).

Bill Harry quoted from author's interview.

Tony 'Measles' Bramwell quoted from author's interview.

John Duff Lowe quoted from author's interview.

Conversation between PM and JL about poster: recalled by Colin Hanton to author.

Making the shellac disc: author's interviews; PM quoted from *Anthology* (book and liner notes to CD Vol. 1).

Death of Julia Lennon: *John Lennon Encyclopaedia* (Harry); and the *Anthology* (book).

PM writes 'When I'm Sixty-Four': quoted from the *Anthology* (book).

Hanton quits band: author's interview (quoted).

GH leaves school: *I Me Mine* (Harrison).

The Casbah: author's visit and *Beatle!* (Best [also Best background]).

PM meets Dot Rhone: Rhone to the *Daily Mail* (11 Oct. 1997).

Stuart Sutcliffe: *The Stuart Sutcliffe Retrospective* (University of Liverpool, 2009); author's discussion with Pauline Sutcliffe and her book *The Beatles' Shadow*.

Paul's 1959 art prize: Liverpool Record Office; and PM's comments in *Paul McCartney: Paintings*.

Trip to Caversham: author's interview with Mike Robbins (quotes).

Allan Williams: author's interview (quotes). Also interview with Howie Casey. Background reading: *The Man Who Gave the Beatles Away* (Williams).

Band name: author's interviews including Royston Ellis and Bill Harry (both quoted). Thanks also to Ellis for his unpublished memoirs (used with permission), and to Spencer Leigh. PM attributes the final spelling of Beatles to JL in the *Anthology* (book) and elsewhere.

JL on the origins of the Beatles name: *Being a Short Diversion of the Dubious Origins of Beatles* (Lennon), published in *Mersey Beat* (6–20 July 1961).

Johnny Gentle tour: author's interview with Gentle (quoted).

Tommy Moore's girlfriend – 'You can piss off!' – *The Complete Beatles Chronicle* (Lewisohn).

PM on Janice the Stripper: *Mersey Beat* (6 Sept. 1962).

Bruno Koschmider meeting: author's interview with Williams, who says Koschmider was crippled in a fall. Klaus Voormann writes in his book *Hamburg Days* that Koschmider's leg was shot off. Thanks also to Howie Casey and Horst Fascher.

PM's exams: *Paul McCartney: Many Years from Now* (Miles) and *Shout!* (Norman).

Leaving Liverpool: author's interviews. Also *John* (Lennon); *McCartney* (Flippo) and *Shout!* (Norman).

3: HAMBURG

Hamburg: author's visit and local interviews.

Details of 1943 RAF bombing are from *Churchill: A Life* by Martin Gilbert (London: Pimlico, 2000).

PM – 'but with strip clubs' – *Mersey Beat* (20 Sept. 1962).

Horst Fascher meets the Beatles: author's interviews (quoted).

The Indra: author's local enquiries and interviews with Howie Casey, Horst Fascher, Ruth Lallemann (later Reeves) and Rosi Haitmann (later Sheridan), both of whom are quoted. Background reading includes *The Complete Beatles Chronicle* (Lewisohn).

Details of Bambi Kino accommodation: *Hamburg Days* (Kirchherr).

Meeting the Exis: author's interviews with Astrid Kirchherr and Jürgen Vollmer (both quoted from the author's interviews, except where indicated). Background reading: *The Beatles in Hamburg* (Vollmer) and *Hamburg Days* (Kirchherr and Voormann).

Kirchherr – 'I thought it was like …' – her book *Hamburg Days*.

Dialogue about Paul's hair: *The Beatles in Hamburg* (Vollmer).

Ruth Lallemann and Rosi Sheridan quoted from author's interviews.

PM – 'We were kids let off the leash …' – the *Anthology* (documentary).

GH is quoted on losing his virginity from the *Anthology* (book), and Pete Best from his memoir, *Beatle!*

Erika Wohlers quoted from author's correspondence.

Tony Sheridan quoted from author's interview.

The fire: Paul's interviews (various) and his contemporaneous letter reproduced in the *Anthology* (book).

Returning home: *Thank U Very Much* (McCartney) in which is reproduced a letter from Massey & Coggins showing

PM was paid to 8 March 1961. Other little jobs: author's interviews; Miles refers to the post office job in his book *In the Sixties*.

Allan Williams quoted from author's interview.

The Cavern: author's interviews with Tony Bramwell, Frieda Kelly and Ray O'Brien (all quoted). Also Willy Russell. Background reading: *The Cavern* (Leigh).

Williams's regrets: *The Man Who Gave the Beatles Away* (Williams).

PM breaks guitar: a 1964 interview with *Beat Instrumental*, reprinted in *The Beatles Book* (Feb. 2001).

PM's altercation with Stu: dialogue from *The Beatles' Shadow* (Sutcliffe). Ruth Reeves and Tony Sheridan quoted from author's interviews.

GH on fighting Stu: *Fifty Years Adrift* (Taylor).

'My Bonnie' makes number 32 in Germany: *Hit Bilanz* (Hamburg: Taurus Press, 1990).

Gerry Marsden quoted from author's interview.

The trip to Paris: author's interview with Jürgen Vollmer.

Brian Epstein (BE): background: author's interviews with E. Rex Makin (quoted) and others. Background: *Brian Epstein* (Coleman), including Queenie Epstein quote.

BE – 'I was one of those ...' – *A Cellarful of Noise* (Epstein), and BE's exchanges with GH and PM.

Allan Williams and E. Rex Makin quoted from author's interviews.

PM's comment – 'I hope ...' – *Brian Epstein* (Coleman).

4: LONDON

The contract: the agreement, eventually signed by BE and dated 1 Oct. 1962, was reproduced in the press prior to auction in 2008.

'Greatest recording organisation ...': EMI publicity material reproduced in *The Complete Beatles Recording Sessions* (Lewisohn).

EMI history: www.emi.com; also *The Incredible Music Machine* (Lowe); and the Royal Warrant Holders' Association.

Tony Barrow link and all Barrow quotes: author's interview.

Aldershot gig: Sam Leach to author; also his book *The Rocking City*.

Decca audition: Barrow interview; *The Complete Beatles Chronicle* (Lewisohn) and the *Anthology* (CD Vol. 1 liner notes).

BE quoted from his memoir *A Cellarful of Noise* and *The Beatles Book* (May 1992).

Mother sighed: *I Should Have Known Better* (Ellis).

George Martin (GM) personality and background: author's meeting with; his memoir *All You Need is Ears* and interview with *Melody Maker* (21 Aug. 1962). GM quoted from last two.

Stuart Sutcliffe's demise: author's interviews with Astrid Kirchherr (quoted) and Pauline Sutcliffe, who is quoted from *The Beatles' Shadow*; also the *Stuart Sutcliffe Retrospective* (University of Liverpool, 2009) and *Hamburg Days* (Kirchherr).

PM – 'My mother died when I was 14 ...' – *Shout!* (Norman).

Astrid Kirchherr quoted from author's interview.

At the Star-Club: author's background reading and interviews with, among others, Horst Fascher and Kingsize Taylor (quoted).

GM offers a contract: *The Complete Beatles Chronicle* (Lewisohn).

Meeting GM: *All You Need is Ears* (Martin [quoted]).

The slow version of 'Love Me Do' can be heard on the *Anthology* (CD Vol. 1).

GM's comment on Pete Best – 'almost sullen' – in interview for the DVD release of *A Hard Day's Night* (Special Features).

PM's comment on GM taking them aside: the *Anthology* (book).

Bob Wooler on Best: *Mersey Beat* (31 Aug. 1961).

Fan club: author's interview with Frieda Kelly.

Trip to Manchester: Bobbie Brown's letter reproduced in *The Complete Beatles Chronicle* (Lewisohn).

Bill Harry quoted from author's interview.

Dot Rhone is quoted from the *Daily Mail* (11 Oct. 1997) and *The Beatles* (Spitz).

Paul had VD: author's interviews with Peter Brown, Horst Fascher and E. Rex Makin (quoted).

Dialogue between BE and Pete Best: *Beatle!* (Best).

PM's call and comment about saving money: *Shout!* (Norman).

Neil Aspinall's affair with Mona Best/birth of Roag: thanks to Roag Best (quoted).

Suicide attempt: *Beatle!* (Best).

Ringo Starr (RS) background: author's interviews; the *Anthology* (book); *The Encyclopaedia of Beatles People* (Harry) and *Ringo Starr: Straight Man or Joke?* (Clayton ['it was like joining ...']).

RS – 'I can read, but ...' – the *Anthology* (book).

Mick Jagger quote: induction speech at the Rock 'n' Roll Hall of Fame 1988.

Tony Barrow quoted from author's interview.

GM and Richards quote: *The Complete Beatles Recording Sessions* (Lewisohn).

Recording 'Love Me Do': author's interview with Andy White (quoted).

Rhone on 'PS I Love You': *Daily Mail* (11 Oct. 1997).

PM's Lifeline: thanks to Frieda Kelly (quoted).

Iris Caldwell on PM and recalled dialogue: quoted from author's interview.

First car: PM to the *Daily Mail* (24 Nov. 1984).

All Frank Ifield quotes to author. Background: *I Remember Me* (Ifield). NB: Ifield doesn't remember the Liverpool Empire story the same way as Iris, but notes, laughing, that 'they might have had a guilty conscience'.

Gerry Marsden quote to author.

GM – 'You've Just made ...' – *The Complete Beatles Recording Sessions* (Lewisohn).

Ruth Lallemann quoted from author's interview.

Mal Evans background: the *Anthology* (documentary).

Broken windscreen: *The Complete Beatles Chronicle* (Lewisohn).

Beatle sandwich: the *Anthology* (book).

Break-up with Iris: quoted from author's interview.

5: THE MANIA

Recording the first album: *All You Need is Ears* (Martin) and *The Complete Beatles Chronicle* (Lewisohn).

Dick James deal: sources include Ray Coleman's books *Brian Epstein* and *McCartney Yesterday & Today*; also *Shout!* (Norman) and the *Guardian* (13 Feb. 1965).

PM on the James deal: *Paul McCartney: Many Years from Now* (Miles).

PM on the moment he knew he'd made it: interviewed by David Frost (26 May 1986), reported in *Club Sandwich* # 41.

PM meets Jane Asher: *Radio Times* (2 May 1963) and her 9 Oct. 1965 *TV Times* interview.

JL quote from *Mr Confidential* (Hutchins). PM told Hunter Davies for *The Beatles* that he had thought Jane a 'rave London bird'. Thanks also to Alvin Stardust.

The Ashers at Wimpole Street: author's interviews with Tony Barrow (quoted), Barry Miles and Lord St Germans. Background reading: articles about Asher in the *TV Times* (9 and 30 Oct. 1965); *Who's Who* and *Paul McCartney: Many Years from Now*.

Background on Dr Asher: author's interview with Miles and the *Sunday Express* (19 April 1964), reporting his disappearance.

Dr Asher's suicide: death certificate (in which the cause of death is given as 'Killed himself')

Wimpole street literary associations: *Flush* (Woolf); *A Reader's Guide to Writer's London* (Cunningham) and Lord St Germans.

Speeding conviction: *Liverpool Echo*, 26 Aug, 1963, with thanks to Peter Hodgson and Kevin Roach at Liverpool Record Office.

21st party at the Epsteins': author's interviews with Billy Hatton and E. Rex Makin (both quoted); *Brian Epstein* (Coleman) and *John Lennon: The Life* (Norman). Also Barrow to author (quoted).

Mike McCartney goes into show business: his memoir, *Thank U Very Much* and author's interview with a family member. Tony Bramwell quoted from author's interview.

Tenerife holiday: Klaus Voormann in the Special Features DVD interviews of *A Hard Day's Night*.

Pete Shotton on Lennon's holiday with BE: *The Quarrymen* (Davies).

PM on John's sexuality: *Brian Epstein* (Coleman).

Gordon Millings quoted from the Special Features DVD interviews of *A Hard Day's Night*.

PM meets Denny Laine: author's interview with Laine.

Final shows at the Cavern: author's interviews with Frieda Kelly and Willy Russell (both quoted).

PM on writing 'She Loves You': *Paul McCartney: Many Years from Now* (Miles). GM reaction to song from the Special Features section of the DVD of *A Hard Day's Night*.

Trip to Greece and RS quote: the *Anthology* (book).

Green Street Flat: *The Beatles' London* (Lewisohn).

Lennon-McCartney songs covered by others: *Club Sandwich* # 74. PM quoted from *The Complete Beatles Recording Sessions* (Lewisohn).

Meeting Andrew Loog Oldham (and background): author's interview with Loog Oldham and his book *Stoned*. NB: Various versions of this story have appeared in print, including PM saying he and JL bumped into Jagger and Richards when they passed by in a cab in Charing Cross Road. Loog Oldham's account is the most complete. Charlie Watts quoted from *According to the Rolling Stones*; Bill Wyman quoted from his book *Stone Alone*; Glyn Johns quoted from author's interview.

Derek Taylor's early interest in the Beatles: *Fifty Years Adrift* (Taylor).

The Beatles on *Sunday Night at the London Palladium*: author's interview with Bruce Forsyth (quoted); Godfrey Winn quoted from the *Sketch* (14 Oct. 1963); also *Daily Mirror* of the same date.

William Mann's article: *The Times* (27 Dec. 1963).Beatlemania: the first use of the term in the British press appears to be as a headline to Vincent Mulchrone's *Daily Mail* feature on 21 Oct. 1963, after which it was widely used by all newspapers.

Regarding Ed Sullivan seeing the Beatles at Heathrow, New York promoter Sid Bernstein told the author: 'Sullivan said, "Who are these Beatles?" He thought it was an animal act.' Sullivan is quoted from *The Beatles Off the Record* (Badman).

The Royal Variety Show: author's interview with Don Short (quoted); *Daily Mirror* (5 and 6 Nov. 1963); and *Daily Express* (5 Nov. 1963).

PM moves into Wimpole Street and his life there: author's interview with Miles, and his book *Paul McCartney: Many Years from Now*; also *The Beatles' London* (Lewisohn). Bramwell quoted from author's interview.

JL on writing in the basement: to *Playboy*, collected in *The Beatles Off the Record* (Badman).

Ken Dodd quoted from discussion with author.

Lunch with Sir Joseph Lockwood: *The Complete Beatles Recording Sessions* (Lewisohn).

£2,000 a week: as reported contemporaneously in the *Daily Sketch* (14 Oct. 1963).

Oxfam: author's interview with Lord Archer (quoted).

Wimbledon fan convention: author's interview with Frieda Kelly. Neil Aspinall quoted from the *Anthology* (book).

6: AMERICA

The 1963 *Beatles Christmas Record*: the recording.

Christmas show: *The Complete Beatles Chronicle* (Lewisohn). Thanks to Liverpool broadcaster Spencer Leigh, who pointed out that girls were screaming for Gerry and the Pacemakers when he saw them on the same bill as the Beatles.

Paris shows: author's interview with Mickey Jones (quoted). Thanks also to Jürgen Vollmer.

Jim and Mike McCartney visit: *Thank U Very Much* (McCartney).

GM quoted from his book *All You Need is Ears*.

PM on 'I Want to Hold Your Hand' going to number one in the US quoted from the *Anthology* (book).

RS's comment on the plane to New York: *The Beatles: A Diary* (Miles).

Alan Livingston quoted from *All You Need is Ears* (Martin).

Blackpool rock litigation: *Daily Telegraph* (14 Dec. 1963).

Licensing deal: author's interviews with John Fenton and Lord St Germans (both quoted).

DJ announcement: *America's Century* (Daniel, ed.) and *The Beatles* (Davies).

Capitol Records spent money: the figure most often given is $50,000. In the *Anthology* (documentary) GH mentions $70,000.

Capitol PR campaign: *The Capitol Albums Vol. 1* liner notes.

Arrival in New York: documentary footage; press reports and author's interview with Sid Bernstein (quoted).

The 'turning point': BE in *A Cellarful of Noise*.

BE at the Plaza Hotel: *I Should Have Known Better* (Ellis). The story of BE being photographed is described by Ross Benson in *Paul McCartney: Behind the Myth*. Thanks also to John Fenton (quoted).

PM – 'We came out of nowhere ...' – the *Anthology* (book).

Train to Washington: Maylses brothers' film *The Beatles: The First Visit* (Apple Corps, 1990); article by Al Aronowitz: *Saturday Evening Post* (21 March 1964).

PM asked by David English on train about illegitimate child, and PM's quoted reply: *Paul McCartney: Behind the Myth* (Benson).

Erika Hübers (*née* Wohlers) is quoted from correspondence with the author. Also correspondence and interviews with her daughter.

A Hard Day's Night chapter subheading taken from the marquee of the London Pavilion. Also the DVD of the film, with its Special Features interviews, featuring GM interview (quoted).

Ringoism: *The Complete Beatles Chronicle* (Lewisohn).

First use of grotty and fab: *Oxford English Dictionary*. NB: PM uses 'fab' in a letter dated 9 May 1962 (*Thank U Very Much*);

and in *Mersey Beat* (20 Sept. 1962). Thanks also to Tony Barrow.

Richard Lester quoted from the DVD release of *A Hard Day's Night* (Special Features).

Europe, Hong Kong and Australia: press including the *Saturday Evening Post* (15 Aug. 1964 [blood vessel]); *Fifty Years Adrift* (Taylor); the *Anthology* (documentary) and *The Complete Beatles Chronicle* (Lewisohn).

At the Dorchester and dialogue and quotation: *Thank U Very Much* (McCartney); also *At the Apple's Core* (O'Dell). John Lennon reunited with his father: *John Lennon: The Life* (Norman).

Mike McCartney on the 'covenant': his book *Thank U Very Much*.

McCartney Pension: author's interviews.

Liverpool première: author's interviews including Frank Foy (quoted); TV footage of the homecoming and press reports including *Mersey Beat* (16 July 1964); *Daily Mirror* (11 July 1964), and the *Saturday Evening Post* (15 Aug. 1964).

Anita Cochrane's story: author's interviews with Tony Barrow, Peter Brown and Anita's half-brother Ian Pillans (all quoted); Anita's interviews with the *Daily Mail* (31 May-2 June 1997) and family records, including her birth certificate which reveals the inconsistency of dates. I also referred to Anita's interview with the *Daily Star* (1 Feb. 1983).

No father's name on Philip Cochrane's birth certificate: birth certificate.

The poem is reproduced from the *Daily Mail* (10 May 1997).

Derek Taylor wrote about the paternity claim in his book *Fifty Years Adrift* (quoted).

1964 North American tour hysteria: the *Anthology* (book) including GM quote; *The Beatles Book* and press reports including the *Daily Sketch* (20 Aug. 1964).

Peggy Lipton quoted from her book, *Breathing Out*.

Meeting Dylan: I drew on conversations conducted with Al Aronowitz and Victor Maymudes (both deceased) for my book *Down the Highway: The Life of Bob Dylan*; also Aronowitz's article *Let's 'ave a Larf* (The Blacklisted Journalist, 1995). The BE quote is from *Fifty Years*

Adrift (Taylor). PM's 'There are seven Levels': *Paul McCartney: Many Years from Now* (Miles).

7: YESTERDAY

Home moves: author's enquiries and *The Beatles' London* (Lewisohn).

Peter and Gordon success: *Guinness Book of British Hit Singles* (Roberts, ed.)

Jim McCartney – 'I'd usually …' – *The Beatles* (Davies).

PM's purchase of Rembrandt: author's enquiries and interviews, including an employee who didn't wish to be named.

Jim meets his second wife: author's interview with Mike Robbins (quoted and recalled dialogue).

Jim's proposal: Angela McCartney is quoted from her interview with the *Sun* (6 July 1981). Marriage: marriage certificate.

JL on songwriting: the *Anthology* (book).

Beatles for Sale: GM quoted from *The Complete Beatles Recording Sessions* (Lewisohn); PM quoted from the *Anthology* (book) on 'Eight Days a Week'.

Eric Clapton quoted from his autobiography.

Jimmy Savile quoted from author's interview.

'Ticket to Ride': author's interview with Mike Robbins (quoted).

Studio chatter: the *Anthology* (CD Vol. 2).

Taxation: HM Treasury.

Northern Songs flotation: articles in the *Guardian* (13 Feb. 1965; 6 Jan. 1966) and the *Economist* (20 Feb. 1965). Also *Paul McCartney: Many Years from Now* (Miles).

Harold Wilson's speech: *White Heat* (Sandbrook).

Aunts knock through: Joan McCartney and Mike Robbins to author.

'nutty': … *up front* (Spinetti).

Shooting *Help!* in the Bahamas for tax reasons: various including *I Should Have Known Better* (Ellis).

Pot-smoking during *Help!*: the *Anthology* (documentary); also Richard Lester's comments in the DVD re-release of *Help!*

John's compliment: PM quoted from *Playboy* interview (Dec. 1984).

'Swinging City': *Time* (15 April 1966).

Lord St Germans quoted from author's interviews.

PM learns he is a millionaire: *Paul McCartney: Many Years from Now* (Miles).

Purchase of 7 Cavendish Avenue: author's local enquiries and interviews, with particular thanks to neighbours and local residents including Mrs Fenton, Mrs Evelyn Grumi and family, John Kay and Peter Vogl.

Tony Barrow quoted from author's interview.

PM – 'possibly the smash of the century' – the *Anthology* (book).

Writing of 'Yesterday': I referred to *Yesterday and Today* (Coleman), including PM's quote, 'I just fell …', GH's comment, the Alma Cogan evening and Bruce Welch's villa.

GM on arranging 'Yesterday': his book *All You Need is Ears*.

PM on meeting Terry Doran: *Paul McCartney: Many Years from Now* (Miles).

First LSD trip: based on GH's comments (quoted) in the *Anthology* (book) and author's interview with Gibson Kemp. Also *Wonderful Today* (Boyd). PM quoted from the *Anthology* (documentary).

Leslie Halliwell on *Help!*: *Halliwell's Film Guide*.

Blackpool Night Out: TV footage. Thanks also to Tony Barrow.

Shea Stadium: the documentary *The Beatles at Shea Stadium* (NEMS Enterprises, 1965); author's interviews with Barrow and Bernstein (quoted exchange with BE) and Barrow's book *John, Paul, George, Ringo & Me* from which I quote 'to create a momentary display …'

Stones present: *Stone Alone* (Wyman).

LA vacation: Don Sort quoted from author's interview; Peggy Lipton is quoted from *Breathing Out* (Lipton).

PM's birthday gift to Jane: *TV Times* (9 Oct. 1965). Four in a bed: author's interview with Mike Robbins (quoted).

Meeting Elvis: Chris Hutchins's report for the *NME* (3 Sept. 1963): the *Anthology* (book [PM quoted]); and *Careless Love* (Guralnick).

JL's remark about meeting Elvis: author's interview with Tony Barrow.

8: FIRST FINALE

Meeting the Queen and receiving their MBEs: PM and GH quoted from the *Anthology* (book). Soldiers sent medals back: *Shout!* (Norman). PM's relationship with the Queen: author's interviews.

JL's reason for returning his MBE: his 1969 telegram to HRH.

RS – 'I'm not really into ...' – *Postcards from the Boys* (Starr).

JL claimed the Beatles smoked a joint in Buckingham Palace, contradicted by GH in the *Anthology* (book).

GM goes freelance: *All You Need is Ears* (Martin).

'Plastic soul' comment: the *Anthology* (CD liner notes Vol. 2).

PM on who wrote what: *Paul McCartney: Many Years from Now* (Miles).

'We Can Work it Out': thanks to Spencer Leigh for his thoughts.

Janet Vaughan on 'Michelle': author's interview (quoted).

PM on 'I'm Looking Through You' and his open relationship with Jane Asher: his comments in *The Beatles* (Davies) and *Paul McCartney: Many Years from Now* (Miles).

Jane Asher declines to speak: correspondence with the author.

Jann Haworth on Paul and Jane: author's interview (quoted).

PM to Barry Miles: *Paul McCartney: Many Years from Now* (Miles). Also PM on 'You Won't See Me' and 'I'm Looking Through You'.

Miles on his friendship with PM, and the avant-garde connections: quoted from author's interview. Thanks also to Jann Haworth.

Attends Luciano Berio lecture: *Daily Mail* (25 Feb. 1966). Quotes from *In the Sixties* (Miles).

Maggie McGivern relationship: her interview with the *Daily Mail* (12 April 1997).

PM acquires Martha: *Punch* (23 Nov. 1966).

Paul's aristocratic friends: author's interviews including Dudley Edwards.

Tara Browne background: author's interviews and profiles written upon his death.

Sale of Lenmac: I rely on Ray Coleman's book *Yesterday and Today*.

PM on 'For No One': *Paul McCartney: Many Years from Now* (Miles).

Gibson Kemp quoted from author's interview.

PM on composing 'Eleanor Rigby': the *South Bank Show* (Jan. 1978).

Bernard Herrmann influence: GM to *Melody Maker* (28 Aug. 1971).

Michael Lindsay-Hogg quoted from author's interviews.

Jane Asher on the Cold War: *Saga* (Oct. 2007).

Len Deighton quoted from correspondence with the author.

Peter Brown on the paternity claims: quoted from author's interview.

Erica Hübers quoted from correspondence with author.

Marijuana on tour: Peter Brown's book *The Love You Make*.

Manila concerts: Imelda Marcos is quoted from an interview with the author. I also referred to my interviews with Tony Barrow and Peter Brown and their memoirs. (BE's conversation is from Brown's *The Love You Make*.)

Maureen Cleave's interview with PM, *Evening Standard* (25 March 1966); author's correspondence with Cleave (quoted); and reference to her 4 March 1966 interview with JL (quoted). Reaction to JL's 'Jesus' interview: *Evening News* (5 Aug. 1966); the *Anthology* (documentary).

Peter Brown on PM's fear of assassination: author's interview (quoted).

Chicago Press conference: *The Beatles Off the Record* (Badman).

Unsold tickets at Shea Stadium in 1966: author's interview with Sid Bernstein.

Linda McCartney (LM) in the press box: *Sixties* (Linda McCartney). NB: LM seemed unsure which Shea Stadium show she attended. In *Sixties* she writes that she saw the Beatles at the stadium in '65 *and* '66. In seems more likely LM only attended the second show, if she sat in the press box. She'd just started taking photographs professionally that year.

Riot at Dodger Stadium: *The Complete Beatles Chronicle* (Lewisohn).

BE in LA: author's interviews with Peter Brown and Nat Weiss (quoted). Additional background: *Brian Epstein* (Coleman).

Candlestick Park: audio recording of the show; author's interviews with Barrow and Marty Balin (quoted).

9: LINDA

Ravi Shankar quoted from correspondence with the author.

PM's trip to France and quote: *Paul McCartney: Many Years from Now* (Miles) including the quote, 'It made me remember why we all wanted to get famous.'

Dylan on fame: *Down the Highway* (Sounes).

PM on *The Family Way*: the *Anthology* (book). GM quoted from his book *All You Need is Ears*.

Jane Asher goes to America: press cuttings including *London Life* (1 Oct. 1966) and PM to the *Daily Sketch* (14 Jan. 1967) in which he talks about *Cathy Come Home*.

Tony Bramwell quoted from author's interview.

Recording 'Penny Lane': author's interview with David Mason (quoted).

PM's involvement with BEV: author's interview with Douglas Binder and Dudley Edwards (both quoted).

Cavendish décor: author's interviews and Dudley Edwards (quoted) and Miles.

Nico visits: author's interview with Dudley Edwards. Thanks also to Paul Morrisey.

PM's motorbike accident: the *Anthology* (book).

Recording *Sgt. Pepper*: author's interviews; *The Complete Beatles Recording Sessions* (Lewisohn).

JL inspired by Tara Browne's death to write 'A Day in the Life': *John Lennon: The Life* (Norman), for example. No connection between Browne and 'Day in the Life': PM in his book *Paul McCartney: Paintings*.

Douglas Binder quoted from author's interview.

Old boys from the Inny interpret 'A Day in the Life': author's interview with Steve Norris.

Correspondence with Stockhausen: author's interview with Sir John Tavener.

Alban Berg quote from *The Rest is Noise* (Ross).

GM on the orchestral climax: *Melody Maker* (28 Aug. 1971).

Mike Nesmith quoted from correspondence with author.

Carnival of Light: author's interview with Dudley Edwards (quoted).

Encounter with Joe Orton: his *Diaries*.

GM's 'biggest mistake': *The Beatles Book* (Nov. 1994).

Creating the *Sgt. Pepper* cover: author's interview with Jann Haworth (quoted).

San Francisco visit: author's interview with Marty Balin (quoted).

PM reunited with Jane in Colorado: *The Beatles: A Diary* (Miles).

Brian Wilson abandons *Smile*: *Heroes and Villains* (Gaines).

Magical Mystery Tour chart: the original pie chart drawing reproduced in *The Complete Beatles Chronicle* (Lewisohn).

PM quote – 'a crazy roly-poly Sixties' film' – the *Anthology* (documentary).

Redlands bust: Marianne Faithfull's memoir *Faithfull* and Bill Wyman's *Stone Alone*.

PM's friendship with Prince Stash: author's interview with Stash (quoted).

PM meets Linda Eastman, later McCartney (LM): author's interviews with Tony Bramwell, Peter Brown and Dudley Edwards (all quoted).

LM – 'I was impressed …' – *Paul McCartney: Many Years from Now* (Miles).

LM background: author's interviews with Marty Balin, Peter Brown, Danny Fields, Al Kooper and Nat Weiss. Also vital records and court documents. For Eastman family history I am indebted to Danny Fields and his book *Linda McCartney: The Biography*, supplemented by my interviews with Sid Bernstein and Linda's half-brother Philip Sprayregen (both quoted).

Mel See background: author's interviews with his common-law wife Beverly Wilk, and Arizona friends Jonathan Kress (quoted) and Debra and Sherry Zeller.

Heather's date of birth: birth record.

LM takes up photography: *Club Sandwich* # 64.

LM – 'I was the only photographer …' and 'My father used to …' – *Linda's Pictures* (McCartney).

Danny Fields and Nat Weiss quoted from author's interviews.

Sgt. Pepper party: author's interviews with Peter Brown (quoted) and Sir Jimmy Savile. Also *Linda's Pictures* and *Sixties* (McCartney).

LM's fling with Prince Stash: author's interview with Prince Stash (quoted).

10: HELLO, GOODBYE

Yellow Submarine: author's interviews with Al Brodax, John Coates (both quoted) and Norman Kauffman.

BE quotes/weekend party: *Fifty Years Adrift* (Taylor).

PM and Jane Asher reunited: *Daily Express* (30 May 1967).

Dudley Edwards quoted from author's interview.

Ned Rorem on *Sgt. Pepper*: *Time* (22 Sept. 1967).

Sir Joseph Lockwood quoted from the *Sunday Times* (14 May 1967).

US record sales: Recording Industry Association of America (RIAA).

JL on *Sgt. Pepper*: *Lennon Remembers* (Wenner).

PM's purchase of High Park: author's interviews and local enquiries in Kintyre with particular thanks to Jamie and Katie Black (quoted and recalled dialogue), Rory and Mary Colville, Alice and Duncan McLean, and Jimmy McGeachy (father and son).

Inspiration for 'The Long and Winding Road': PM interviewed for *Club Sandwich* # 41. Also the *Daily Express* (15 June 1967).

'Christ, it's a Beatle!': recalled by Rory Colville in an interview with the author.

PM meets the Campbeltown Pipe Band: author's interview with Jim McGeachy Snr (quoted).

PM's LSD confession: *People* (18 June 1967).

Use of cocaine and heroin: *Paul McCartney: Many Years from Now* (Miles).

Drug busts: author's interviews with John Hopkins, Prince Stanislas de Rola and others. Background reading: *Faithfull* (Marianne Faithfull); *Symphony for the Devil* (Norman); *Old Gods Almost Dead* (Davis) and *In the Sixties* (Miles).

GH on PM's LSD confession: the *Anthology* (book).

Aunt Ginny and the spliff: author's interview with Mike Robbins (quoted).

'Come Back Milly!': videotape of *Our World*.

GM's difficult week: his book *All You Need is Ears*. Thanks also to David Mason.

Apple School: *Fifty Years Adrift* (Taylor). Also author's interview with Janet Vaughan.

Simon Posthuma and Marijke Koger are quoted from the author's interviews and correspondence, except 'It is wrong …' which is from *Rolling Stone* (9 Nov. 1967).

Magic Alex: author's interviews with associates and background reading.

Maharishi background: his *Daily Telegraph* obituary (7 Feb. 2008).

Trip to Bangor: press reports including the *Sunday Times* (27 Aug. 1967).

Cynthia Lennon quoted from her book, *John*.

BE's decline and death: author's interviews with Peter Brown (quoted), E. Rex Makin and Nat Weiss (quoted).

BE on PM: *A Cellarful of Noise* (Epstein).

'mincing along' quote: author's interview with Ron Ellis, who knew the band in the early days.

PM on his friendship with Robert Fraser: *Paul McCartney: Many Years from Now* (Miles).

Rolling Stones' advance: *Symphony for the Devil* (Norman).

Epstein's death: author's interview with Peter Brown except 'Paul was shocked and saddened …', which is from *The Love You Make* (Brown). Also press coverage of the Beatles' reactions.

11: PAUL TAKES CHARGE

BE's death reported: *Daily Mirror* (28 Aug. 1967).

E. Rex Makin on BE's death: quoted from author's interview.

Aftermath of BE's death: author's interview with Peter Brown (quoted).

Peter Theobald on *Magical Mystery Tour* quoted from *Look of London* (20 Jan. 1968). Also PM quote to Theobald.

Magical Mystery Tour background: author's interviews and background reading including the *Anthology* (book) and *The Complete Beatles Chronicle* (Lewisohn).

Catherine Osborne quoted from the *Daily Express* (4 Sept. 1967).

Raymond Revue Bar scene: author's interview with Neil Innes (JL comment recalled by).

Hunter Davies quoted from his feature for the *Sunday Times* (24 Dec. 1967).

Jamie Black quoted from author's interview.

Jane Asher on how PM had changed: *The Beatles* (Davies).

Dudley Edwards swaps a statue of Shiva for Jane's Ford: author's interview (quoted).

Arguments at Rembrandt: Angela McCartney to the *Sun* (7 July 1981).

PM and Jane Asher on their relationship: *The Beatles* (Davies).

PM on the reception for *Magical Mystery Tour*: *Daily Mirror* (28 Dec. 1967).

GH – 'the world famous ...' – the *Anthology* (book).

PM on the bridge: *Life* (18 March 1968).

PM on his discussion with GH in Rishikesh and the scene there: the *Anthology* (book); also *At the Apple's Core* (O'Dell) and *Wonderful Today* (Boyd).

Apple Records: author's interviews with Sir John Tavener (quoted) and others.

PM on 'Come and Get it': the *Anthology* (book).

Mary Hopkin recording: PM is quoted from an Apple press release reproduced in *Fifty Years Adrift*. The author also referred to Hopkin's 1992 interview with *Goldmine* and a May 2009 interview for BBC Radio 4's *Front Row*.

Trip to New York: author's interviews and background reading including *At the Apple's Core* (O'Dell).

PM to New York press: *The Beatles Off the Record* (Badman).

PM meets LM in New York: LM quoted from her book, *Sixties*; Nat Weiss quoted from author's interview.

Yoko Ono (YO) background: *John Lennon: The Life* (Norman), including JL quote; *John* (Cynthia Lennon), including Cynthia Lennon's quote; and *The John Lennon Encyclopaedia* (Harry).

YO goes first to PM: *Paul McCartney: Many Years from Now* (Miles).

12: WEIRD VIBES

White Album demo session: *The Complete Beatles Recording Sessions* (Lewisohn).

Opening of Apple Tailoring: Apple Press Office Timeline in *Fifty Years Adrift* (Taylor).

Tony Bramwell quoted from author's interview.

PM's reaction to Yoko joining the recording sessions and Yoko quote: *Here, There and Everywhere* (Emerick).

Xenophobic and sexist remarks: *The Love You Make* (Brown).

Mike McCartney's wedding: author's interview with Tony Barrow (quoted), *Thank U Very Much* (McCartney) and *The Beatles Unseen* (Hayward).

PM's affair with Francie Schwartz, her quotes and recalled dialogue: *Body Count* (Schwartz). Also author's interview with Tony Bramwell (quoted), Barry Miles and others.

PM on 'Blackbird': *Paul McCartney: Many Years from Now* (Miles).

PM in LA: author's interview with Tony Bramwell, quotes and recalled dialogue, except 'We were all conscious ...' which is from the *Mail on Sunday* (14 March 1999).

Peggy Lipton is quoted from her book *Breathing Out*.

LM – 'dirty weekend' – *Wingspan* documentary (MPL, 2001).

Recording *Thingumybob*: author's interviews with Roy Newsome and Geoffrey Brand (quoted).

Arguments in the studio, including
dialogue between JL and PM, 'granny
music shit' and row with GM: *Here,
There and Everywhere* (Emerick).

GM indiscretion: *I Should Have Known
Better* (Ellis).

Chris Thomas on first working with PM:
Sound on Sound (Dec. 1995).

Culmination of Schwartz affair, dialogue
and aftermath: *Body Count* (Schwartz).
NB: Maggie McGivern makes it plain in
her interview with the *Daily Mail* (12
April 1997) that she was also seeing PM
at this time, though it is not clear
whether she is the woman whose home
he visited the night he was with
Schwartz.

Jane Asher's appearance on Simon Dee's
show: *Sunday Mirror* (21 July 1968).

Tony Bramwell and Jann Haworth
reaction quoted from author's
interviews.

JL and YO come to stay: *John Lennon: The
Life* (Norman) and *Body Count*
(Schwartz).

Ending of Schwartz affair: her book *Body
Count*. Miles made it clear in an
interview with the author that PM had
asked her to leave before.

Tony Barrow on the Asher break-up:
interview with author.

PM visits Cynthia: *John* (Cynthia Lennon)
including quotation.

PM on 'Hey Jude': *Paul McCartney: Many
Years from Now* (Miles).

PM on the Apple Shop closure: *Shout!*
(Norman).

'Hey Jude' graffiti: *The Beatles: A Diary*
(Miles) and *The Beatles Book* (Dec.
2001).

Filming 'Hey Jude' promo: author's
interview with Michael Lindsay-Hogg
(quoted).

Sending out the Apple discs: *The Longest
Cocktail Party* (DiLello).

The Queen to Sir Joseph Lockwood, and
his reaction to the *Two Virgins* sleeve:
Shout! (Norman).

Bad vibes/RS leaving the band: the
Anthology (book).

RS quote: *Postcards from the Boys* (Starr).

Several chicks at Cavendish: *Paul
McCartney: Many Years from Now*
(Miles).

LM gets the call: *Linda McCartney* (Fields).

Marty Balin quoted from author's
interview.

LM on her decision to come to London:
Paul McCartney: Many Years from Now
(Miles).

13: WEDDING BELLS

JL drug bust: *John Lennon: The Life*
(Norman).

Peter Brown quoted from author's
interview.

PM on being in New York quoted from
Paul McCartney: Many Years from Now
(Miles); also *Wingspan* (MPL, 2001).

Philip Sprayregen and Danny Fields
quoted from author's interviews.

PM on Heather at infants school: *Paul
McCartney: Many Years from Now*
(Miles).

Heather McCartney on her childhood:
Sunday Times (28 Nov. 1999).

Life at High Park: an interview with the
McCartneys in the *Evening Standard* (22
April 1971); *Melody Maker* (20 Nov. 1971);
and *Sixties* (Linda McCartney).

LM stops using the Pill: *Paul McCartney:
Many Years from Now* (Miles).

LM – 'You know, I could make you ...' –
recalled by PM in the *Wingspan*
documentary (MPL, 2001).

Richard Hamilton background and
quotes: *Remake/Remodel* (Bracewell).

White Album sales: RIAA.

PM produces 'I am the Urban Spaceman':
author's interview with Neil Innes
(quoted).

PM visits Hunter Davies: *The Beatles*
(Davies).

Philip Sprayregen quoted from author's
interview.

David Jacobs dies: *Guardian* (20 Dec.
1968).

Hell's Angels for Xmas: *The Longest
Cocktail Party* (DiLello), including GH
quote and lead stripped from the roof.

JL's Christmas recording: *The Love You
Make* (Brown).

Glyn Johns on *Get Back*: author's interview
(quoted).

What JL said to GM about an 'honest
album': the *Anthology* (book).

Michael Lindsay-Hogg quoted from
author's interviews.

'Two of Us' about PM and LM: PM in
Wingspan (MPL, 2001).
Band dialogue from the movie Let It Be.
GH 'bringing home bad vibes': Wonderful
Today (Boyd).
PM assumed JL was joking about hiring
Clapton: the Anthology (book).
Magic Alex's useless studio: Fifty Years
Adrift (Taylor); All You Need is Ears
(Martin); and author's interview with
Glyn Johns (quoted).
Origins of 'Let it Be' and 'The Long and
Winding Road': Paul McCartney: Many
Years from Now (Miles).
Origins of 'Get Back': Revolution in the
Head (MacDonald).
Beverly Wilk on Mel See quoted from
author's interview.
JL to Ray Coleman: The Lives of John
Lennon (Goldman).
Allen Klein background: author's
interviews and Philip Norman's books
Symphony for the Devil and Shout!
Peter Brown quotes: author's interview.
Derek Taylor's boozy press room and
Brown's lunches: Fifty Years Adrift
(Taylor).
Beatles dialogue about the concert:
recorded conversation from the Let It Be
sessions.
Michael Lindsay-Hogg on the rooftop
concert: author's interview (quoted).
Glyn Johns on his version of Let It Be:
quoted from author's interviews.
PM's marriage to Linda Eastman:
marriage certificate; author's
interviews, news footage and
contemporaneous reports in The Times
and Daily Mirror (both 13 March 1960
[LM quoted from the Mirror]).
Mike McCartney best man: Thank U Very
Much (McCartney).
PM on the pre-marital row: Woman (1 Dec.
1984).
Jill and hairdresser and the Apple
Scruffs/'The Eyes and Ears of the
World': Waiting for the Beatles
(Bedford).
GH's drug bust: The Longest Cocktail Party
(DiLello) and The Beatles (Spitz).
LM gave the impression she was an
Eastman-Kodak: Danny Fields has her
saying so in his biography to impress
people during her early photographic
assignments.

John and Yoko marry: Les Anthony's
interview with the News of the World (4
June 1972) and John Lennon: The Life
(Norman).
'Wedding Bells Are Breaking Up that Old
Gang of Mine': PM has often cited this
song, which the Beatles sang in the
early days, as an analogy for why the
Beatles came adrift: in the Anthology
(book) for instance.

14: CREATIVE DIFFERENCES

Tony Bramwell and Peter Brown on the
problems at Apple: quoted from
author's interviews.
What Klein said to John Eastman and
'Proceedings got off to …': The Love You
Make (Brown). Also the letter that
annoyed the Epsteins.
Clive Epstein sues the Beatles: Daily
Express (24 June 1969).
ATV move: Yesterday and Today (Coleman).
PM quotes – 'We're a big act!' and 'I said,
"It's Friday night …' – the Anthology
(documentary).
Glyn Johns on the row with Klein: quoted
from author's interview.
PM records with Steve Miller: author's
interview with Johns; Miller quoted
from Paul McCartney Now and Then
(Barrow and Bextor).
PM's anonymous postcards to Taylor, and
PM's comment to staff, 'Don't forget,
you're not very good …': Fifty Years
Adrift (Taylor).
Apple sackings and resignations:
author's interviews with Tony
Bramwell, Peter Brown and Barry Miles
(quoted).
Alistair Taylor quoted from The Beatles
(Spitz). Background reading: The Love
You Make (Brown) and Shout! (Norman).
Dr Asher's suicide: his death certificate.
LM to RS – 'Oh, they've got you, too' –
Shout! (Norman).
Recording 'Give Peace a Chance': The
Complete Beatles Chronicle (Lewisohn).
GM on being asked to produce the
Beatles again: the Anthology (book).
JL's car accident: The Longest Cocktail
Party (DiLello) and John Lennon: The Life
(Norman).

Dekker poem: *The Oxford Book of English Verse* (Ricks, ed.).

Emerick on Yoko and her conversation with PM: his book *Here, There and Everywhere*.

Michael Lindsay-Hogg quoted from author's interview on the rough cut of *Let It Be*.

Origins of 'Polythene Pam': author's interview with Royston Ellis (quoted) and his unpublished memoirs by permission.

Scruffs climb through the bathroom window and dialogue: *Waiting for the Beatles* (Bedford).

Miles on the break-ins: author's interview (quoted).

Abbey Road name change: Abbey Road Studios.

Mary McCartney born: birth cert., *Daily Mirror* (29 Aug. 1969), and PM interview with the *Daily Mail* (19 Oct. 1998).

JL tells PM he's leaving the group: reconstructed from JL's comments to *Rolling Stone*, collected in *Lennon Remembers* (Wenner).

PM comments in the *Anthology* (documentary) that the Beatles always played 'good'.

Paul is Dead (1966): author's interview with Tony Barrow (quoted). 1969 recurrence of story: *Life* (4 Nov 1969 [including PM quotes]). Also *The Longest Cocktail Party* (DiLello) and Terence Spencer's remarks in *Paul McCartney: A Life* (Carlin).

Tony Bramwell on the break-up of the band: author's interview (quoted).

PM's 'breakdown' interview: *Wingspan* (MPL, 2001).

Linda's concern: author's interviews with Danny Fields, and background sources.

PM screams at RS: RS's affidavit to the High Court, 24 Feb. 1971.

The *McCartney* LP Q&A: quoted from the Q&A.

Establishment of McCartney Productions: Companies House records.

'Paul is Quitting the Beatles': *Daily Mirror* (10 April 1970); also author's interview with Don Short. Brown reaction: author's interview (quoted).

15: 'HE'S NOT A BEATLE ANY MORE!'

Paul McCartney's memo to Klein: reproduce in the *Anthology* (book).

Glyn Johns quoted from author's interview.

Melody Maker review of *McCartney* (18 April 1970). PM's retort published: 2 May 1970.

Michael Lindsay-Hogg quoted from author's interview. He is also the source for George Harrison blocking the release of a DVD of *Let It Be*.

Phil Spector quoted from the BBC *Arena* documentary broadcast 25 Oct. 2008.

Rupert: PM's interview with the *Evening Standard* (22 April 1970). Also *Fifty Years Adrift* (Taylor).

Denny Seiwell background and the making of *Ram*: author's interview with Seiwell (quoted).

Linda Aiello (*née* Magno) quoted from author's interview.

PM's fear of kidnapping: author's interview with Mike Robbins (quoted).

LM – 'He's not a Beatle any more!' – recalled by Linda Aiello in author's interview.

Ram recording dates (different to those published elsewhere) are based on Monique Seiwell's diaries.

PM told a reporter around this time – 'I think the other three are the most honest, sincere men I have ever met ...' – *Evening Standard*, 21 April 1970.

PM on his decision to take the Beatles to court: *Reveille* (24 April 1971).

PM – 'I single-handedly saved ...' – *Paul McCartney: Many Years from Now* (Miles).

Worst moment of life: *Rolling Stone* (3 May 2007).

Writ issued and court proceedings: as reported contemporaneously in the press.

JL to *Rolling Stone: Lennon Remembers* (Wenner).

PM's response to reading JL's interview: *Rolling Stone* (31 Jan. 1974).

High Court evidence including quotes: contemporaneous court reports.

Recording in LA: author's interview with Jim Guercio (quoted) and Denny Seiwell.

PM wins at the High Court: *Daily Telegraph* (12 March 1971).

Sir James Douglas Spooner quoted from author's interview.

PM attends Mick Jagger's wedding: author's interview with Duncan and Alice McLean (quoted throughout).

Girls in the woods: author's interview with Rory Colville (quoted). PM quoted from the *Sun* (2 July 1971).

PM expands his Scottish farm: author's interviews with neighbouring farmers, and estate records.

PM on his wife writing with him: *Reveille* (1 May 1971).

Sued by Northern Songs: *Evening Standard* (23 July 1971).

Thrillington project: author's interviews with Clem Cattini (quoted) and Herbie Flowers.

Album quote – 'Born in Coventry Cathedral …' – is from the liner notes of the 1995 CD re-release of *Thrillington*.

PM adopts Heather See: adoption certificate. PM is quoted on bringing up Heather from his interview with the *Evening Standard* (22 April 1970).

Americans come to Kintyre: author's interview with Denny Seiwell (quoted).

Lessons with Mrs Matthews: author's interview with Evelyn Grumi (quoted).

GM on Paul and Linda's musical partnership: *Melody Maker* (4 Sept. 1971).

PM – 'comforting' – *Wingspan* (MPL, 2001).

Denny Laine background and quotes: author's interview.

Stella McCartney born: birth certificate. Birth and naming of the band: PM in *Wingspan* and *Daily Express* (9 Feb. 1997). Thanks also to Denny Seiwell.

16: THE NEW BAND

Recording *Wild Life*: author's interviews with Denny Laine and Denny Seiwell (both quoted).

JL and Phil Spector in conversation: *Melody Maker* (6 Nov. 1971).

Wings launch party: *Melody Maker* (13 Nov. 1971).

PM speaks about the Beatles and responds to 'How Do You Sleep?':

Melody Maker (20 Nov. 1971). JL's open letter to PM: *Melody Maker* (4 Dec. 1971).

Trouble with Cavendish neighbours: the dispute with Mrs Griswold was documented in the *Sunday People* (21 Jan. 1972). Also author's interview with former neighbour Evelyn Grumi.

Henry McCullough joins Wings: author's interview with Laine and McCullough (both quoted).

PM on LM being 'absolute rubbish' on keyboards: *South Bank Show* (Jan. 1978).

'Give Ireland Back to the Irish': author's interviews and press coverage. PM's comments from contemporaneous TV news footage.

University tour: author's interviews with McCullough and Seiwell and contemporaneous press coverage in *Melody Maker* (various). Also *Newsweek* (29 Oct. 1973); *Daily Express* (9 Feb. 1977); *The Best of the Beatles Book* (Dean) and *Club Sandwich* # 40.

Sun ad: the *Sun* (21 Feb. 1972).

LM's analysis of Irish problem: *Melody Maker* (26 Feb. 1972).

Reader's letter: *Melody Maker* (4 March 1972).

Stelly nickname: PM to *Daily Telegraph* (10 March 2001).

'Mary Had a Little Lamb': author's interview with Laine (quoted). Also *Club Sandwich* # 64 (the *Basil Brush Show*).

Wings Over Europe tour: author's interviews with Laine, McCullough and Seiwell (quoted). Also press coverage.

Denny Laine meets Jo Jo Patrie: author's interview with Laine except quote about groupies, which is from his 1 Feb. 1984 interview with the *Sun*.

Smoking dope on Wings Over Europe tour: author's interviews with McCullough and Seiwell; and Denny Laine's *Sun* interview (1 Feb. 1984).

Gothenburg bust: author's interviews with McCullough and Seiwell (quoted) and press reports.

Scottish bust: author's interview with PM's lawyer Len Murray (quoted) and contemporaneous press reports including the *Evening News* (8 March 1973 [PM's quotes]).

Conversation between PM and McCullough and his quotes: author's interview with McCullough.

Making *Red Rose Speedway*: author's interviews with Glyn Johns and Denny Seiwell (both quoted).

James Paul McCartney: footage of the ATV show.

Recording 'Live and Let Die': *All You Need is Ears* (Martin).

17: IN THE HEART OF THE COUNTRY

Wings' 1973 UK tour: author's interviews with band members and press coverage.

Changes to Liverpool: *Liverpool 800* (Belchem) and *Liverpool* (Sharples).

Closure of the Cavern: *The Cavern* (Leigh [includes PM quote]).

Purchase of Waterfall: author's local enquiries and interviews; land and property records.

Purchase of Nor Va Jak Music: PM quoted from *Playboy* (Dec. 1984); *Club Sandwich* # 21 and 39; and the *Evening Standard* (15 Feb. 1973). Thanks also to Lilian Marshall.

Lamborghini: *Evening News* (13 Dec. 1972).

LM's necklace: *Cosmopolitan* (Jan. 1973).

McCullough and Seiwell leave Wings: author's interviews (quoted); thanks also to Denny and Monique Seiwell for consulting their diaries.

Duncan McLean and Denny Laine quoted from author's interviews.

Henry McCullough quoted from author's interview.

PM's dialogue – 'What the Hell's going on?' – reported by Denny Laine in his interview with the author.

Making *Band on the Run*: author's interview with Laine; liner notes and supplementary interview material for the 25th anniversary edition of the album; *Club Sandwich* # 68; and *Here, There and Everywhere* (Emerick [from which the engineer is quoted]).

Uncle Will Stapleton: see notes to Chapter 1.

The McCartneys in Kintyre: author's interviews with the Black family, Rory Colville (quoted) and their vet Alastair Cousin (quoted).

US visa problems: PM to *Newsweek* (29 Oct. 1973).

JL's visa problems and his Lost Weekend: *John Lennon: The Life* (Norman) and *The Lives of John Lennon* (Goldman).

LM and May Pang friends: author's interview with Sid Bernstein.

PM on his advice to JL: *Q* magazine (Oct. 1986).

Tennessee working holiday: author's interview with Curly Putman Jr and *Club Sandwich* # 71.

New line-up of Wings: author's interview with Howie Casey and Denny Laine (both quoted).

PM quoted on his father's song: *Standing Stone* liner notes.

John, Paul, George, Ringo ... & Bert: author's interview with Willy Russell (quoted).

Beatles partnership dissolved: *Daily Telegraph* (10 Jan. 1975).

Making *Venus and Mars*: author's interview with Denny Laine (quoted).

Prince Stash on the Mother's Pride commercial: author's interview.

Laine on McCulloch: author's interview (quoted).

PM on Linda *vis-à-vis* Billy Preston: *Sunday Times* magazine (April 1976).

LA bust: press reports and author's interview with Peter Brown (quoted).

Blair Sabol on Linda McCartney: the *Village Voice* (14 April 1975).

GH's problems: *Wonderful Today* (Boyd) and *The Beatles After the Break-Up* (Badman).

McCartneys visit the Dakota Christmas 1975: Bob Gruen quoted from *Linda McCartney* (Fields).

Mal Evans' death: the *Anthology* (book), *Paul McCartney: Many Years from Now* (Miles) and an article about Evans's diaries by Mark Edmonds published online at http://lifeofthebeatles.blogspot.com.

Jim McCartney's last days: author's interviews with family members and neighbours including Doug Mackenzie (quoted).

Ruth McCartney's allegations are from interviews with the *Mail on Sunday* (3 Dec. 2006) and *Sunday* magazine (14 Aug. 1988), from which her mother Angie McCartney is quoted.

Death of Jim McCartney: death certificate.

Mike McCartney on PM's failure to attend their father's funeral: *Thank U Very Much* (McCartney).

Denny Laine and Mike Robbins quoted from author's interviews.

Deteriorating relationship between PM and his stepmother is documented in newspaper interviews Angie and Ruth have given over the years, including Angie McCartney's *Sun* series 'The Mean Side of Paul McCartney' (6–8 July 1981) and Ruth McCartney's interview with *Sunday* magazine (14 Aug. 1988) in which she says that Jim's allowance was stopped after he died.

MPL Communications and new offices: Companies house and Land Register records.

18: THE GOOD LIFE

Last meetings with John Lennon (JL): author's interview with Elliot Mintz (quoted); *The Beatles After the Break-Up* (Badman), from which JL's comments (to *Playboy* magazine) are quoted. Also *Live from New York* (Shales and Miller) and *John Lennon: The Life* (Norman).

Wings Over America tour: author's interview with Howie Casey and Denny Laine (both quoted); *Club Sandwich* # 2 and 3 (Hammel background); the concert film *Rockshow*; PM's April 1976 interview with the *Sunday Times* magazine and *Time* (31 May 1976).

LM buys Lucky Spot: *Club Sandwich* # 63.

First Buddy Holly Week luncheon: *Club Sandwich* # 1, 21 and 59.

The McCartney Year: author's interviews, including a member of PM's staff who wishes to remain anonymous, and Howie Casey, Adrian Grumi, Mike Robbins and Denny Seiwell.

Venice show: *Club Sandwich* # 1 and the *Daily Express* (27 Sept. 1976).

Income: MPL company records.

PM on his earnings: the *Daily Express*, 11 Feb. 1977.

Purchase and establishment of office at 1 Soho Square/MPL staffing: author's local enquires and interviews. Thanks to Howie Casey, Lilian Marshall, Richard Ogden and Barry Miles.

Launch of *Club Sandwich*: back issues, including # 10 (Sue Cavanaugh profile) and # 79 (Bert Danher profile).

Sale of 3 Savile Row: *Fifty Years Adrift* (Taylor).

7 Cavendish Avenue in the 1970s: author's interview with neighbours Brenda Fenton, Evelyn Grumi and her son Adrian (both quoted); also Joe Reddington; and the *Sunday Mirror* (23 May 1976).

Improvements to Waterfall: author's local enquiries and interviews including Veronica Languish (quoted) and planning records. Denny Laine quoted from author's interview.

Paulditz: *Sunday Mirror* (undated).

Purchase of Bill Black's bass: *Club Sandwich* # 1.

'Boil Crisis': *The Unknown Paul McCartney* (Peel).

Recording *London Town*: author's interviews and *Club Sandwich* # 2, 3 and 6.

US Rangers: *Linda McCartney* (Fields).

PM on his row with the captain of the *El Toro*: *Club Sandwich* # 26.

Denny Laine on writing 'Mull of Kintyre': author's interview (quoted).

Recording with the Campbeltown Pipe Band: author's interviews with pipe band members Ian Campbell, Jimmy McGeachy (father and son), John McGeachy and Ian McKerral.

Jimmy McCulloch leaves Wings: *Blackbird* (Giuliano).

Joe English leaves Wings: *The Paul McCartney Encyclopaedia* (Harry).

James McCartney born: birth certificate. Also 23 Sept. 1977 press release.

Success of 'Mull of Kintyre': author's interviews, press coverage and PM's commentary on the *McCartney Years* DVD (MPL, 2007).

Tony Bramwell falls out with PM over *London Town*: author's interview (quoted).

The Rutles: author's interview with Neil Innes (quoted).

Annie première: *Club Sandwich* # 8.

New deal with CBS/EMI: the *Observer* (24 June 1979).

Third and final version of Wings: author's interviews with band members Steve Holley, Laurence Juber and Denny Laine (all quoted).

Recording *Back to the Egg*: author's
interviews with Holley, Juber and Laine.
The author also referred to his interview
with Chris Thomas for the book
Seventies.

Movie project: author's interview with
Willy Russell (quoted).

Rockestra session: author's interviews;
Club Sandwich # 12 and 44. Keith
Moon's demise, including Annette
Walter-Lax quote ('bucket of pills'), is
from *Dear Boy: The Life of Keith Moon*
(Fletcher).

Black Dyke Band: author's interview with
Major Peter Parkes.

Frank Music sweetener: *Paul McCartney*
(Benson).

PM on his good fortune: the *Observer* (24
June 1979).

19: GO TO JAIL

Heather McCartney problems: author's
interviews and background reading
including PM's comments in *Paul
McCartney: Many Years from Now* (Miles)
and the *Daily Mail* (12 June 1980).

The move to Sussex: author's interviews
with Rosemary Crouch, Veronica
Languish, Barry Miles and Ray Fooks
(quoted).

LM quoted on the vegetarian epiphany
from the 1989 World Tour book;
Laurence Juber quoted from author's
interview.

Purchase of Lower Gate Farm/Blossom
Farm: Land Registry and local council
planning records.

Eric Clapton's wedding party: Boyd's and
Clapton's autobiographies and *Eric
Clapton* (Schumacher).

GH's affair with Maureen Starkey:
Wonderful Today (Boyd).

Jimmy McCulloch dies: *Knocking on
Heaven's Door* (Talevski).

Still planning a *Band on the Run* movie:
author's interviews with Lord Puttnam
and Willy Russell (quoted).

GH hated school: *I Me Mine* (Harrison).

Royal Court shows: author's interviews
including Howie Casey (quoted).

PM on playing Beatles songs: quoted
from the *Evening Standard* (26 Nov.
1979).

Steve Holley quoted on the Christmas
shows, and throughout the chapter,
from author's interview.

Glasgow Apollo Show: author's interviews
with Wings and pipe band members
including Ian Campbell (quoted).

The Concerts for Kampuchea: author's
interviews with Wings members
(quoted). PM on Julian Lennon's failure
to show: *Club Sandwich* # 37/38.

Japanese bust: author's interviews with
musicians Howie Casey, Steve Holley,
Laurence Juber and Denny Laine (all
quoted).

Philp Sprayregen quoted from author's
interview.

Fear of rape: PM to *Playboy* (Dec. 1984).

Donald Warren-Knott quoted throughout
from author's interview.

LM quote – 'the only one …' – *Woman's
Own* (26 July 1980). Also 'You take
drugs, don't you?'

PM in Holland quoted from *Sunday Mirror*
(21 Jan. 1980).

BL Parker quoted from *Daily Telegraph* (26
Jan. 1980).

I also referred to PM's interview with the
Sunday Times (18 May 1980); the *Sunday
Times* (Nov. 1984); *The Beatles After the
Break-Up* (Badman); and *McCartney:
The Biography* (Flippo), re Kenneth
Lambert. Conspiracy theory: *The Lives
of John Lennon* (Goldman).

Making *McCartney II*: the author referred
to PM's explanations of the songs in
Club Sandwich # 19; also the *Sunday
Times* (18 May 1980).

Laine and Holley tour: *Club Sandwich* # 22.

PM on the revived *Rupert* project: *Daily
Express* (7 Nov. 1980); also author's
interview with animator Geoff Dunbar
(quoted).

PM's wedding present to Howie and
Sheila Casey: author's interview with
the Caseys (quoted).

Hot Hitz and Kold Kutz: author's interviews
with Holley and Juber.

Hübers story breaks: *Sunday People* (30
Nov. 1980). Also author's interviews and
correspondence with mother and
daughter.

JL death/PM reaction: author's interview
with Denny Laine and Joe Reddington
(both quoted). Background reading:
Fifty Years Adrift (Taylor); *Paul*

McCartney: Many Years from Now (Miles); John Lennon: The Life (Norman). Also author's interviews with Al Kooper who spent the day after the assassination working in the studio with GH at Friar Park.

LM – 'I could tell …' – quoted from Linda McCartney (Fields).

PM's 'it's a drag' reaction quoted verbatim from his TV interview outside AIR Studios.

20: INTO THE EIGHTIES

Cremation and mourning of JL: author's interviews and The Lives of John Lennon (Goldman).

Bill Harry quoted from author's interview.

Working with Eric Stewart: author's interview with Stewart (quoted throughout).

Recording in Montserrat: author's interviews with Steve Gadd (quoted) and Denny Laine. Also All You Need is Ears (Martin) and Club Sandwich # 24.

Dylan buys bullet-proof vest: Down the Highway (Sounes).

Run-in with photographers: Daily Express (19 Feb. 1981). No comment from PM was published.

'Take it Away' had been intended for RS' album: Ringo Starr: Straight Man or Joker? (Clayton).

PM on recording with Stevie Wonder: The McCartney Years (MPL Communications, 2007).

RS' wedding and reception: Club Sandwich # 24; Ringo Starr: Straight Man or Joker? (Clayton).

Denny Laine leaves Wings: author's interview and Club Sandwich # 24.

PM's criticism of Michael McCartney and Derek Taylor: Fifty Years Adrift (Taylor).

PM's quoted account of other conversations at the reception: The Beatles (Davies).

Angie McCartney's story: the Sun (6–8 July 1981).

Row over the birth certificate and PM quote: Sunday Mirror (5 Nov. 1995).

Purchase of the shellac disc: author's interview with John Duff Lowe

(quoted). Thanks also to Colin Hanton. PM quoted from the Anthology (book).

PM's new house at Blossom Farm: planning applications.

1981 riots: Chronicle of the 20th Century (Crystal, ed.). Paul's reaction: Club Sandwich # 72.

Lew Grade sells Northern Songs: McCartney Yesterday & Today (Coleman); The Times (4 Jan. 1982 [PM quote]) and the Sunday Times (22 Aug. 1982).

PM on Michael Jackson calling: Harper's (Nov. 1984).

Working with Jackson: author's interview with Joe Reddington (recalled dialogue between PM and Jackson re: horse riding); McCartney Yesterday & Today (Coleman); and PM's interview with Rolling Stone (5 Nov. 1987 [recalled conversation with Jackson re initial phone call]).

Reunion with Peggy Lipton: Breathing Out (Lipton).

Heather's teenage years: Evening Standard (20 Nov. 1981), her interview with the Sunday Times (28 Nov. 1999 [Heather quoted]); Club Sandwich # 25; PM in his 1989 tour booklet (on Heather dating Billy Idol); author's interviews with Tony Bramwell (quoted), Steve Gadd, Evelyn Grumi and the Languish family of Peasmarsh.

Riding accident: author's interviews; PM quoted from the Daily Mail (11 May 1982).

PM takes up jogging and painting: quoted from interview with the Sunday Express (4 May 1997); also Paul McCartney Paintings (McCartney).

PM commissions Rupert and the Frog Song: author's interview with Geoff Dunbar (quoted).

Making Give My Regards to Broad Street: author's interviews with Lord Puttnam, Willy Russell and Peter Webb (all quoted). Also Eric Stewart. PM's interviews in connection with the picture including the Sunday Times magazine (4 Nov. 1984) and Sunday magazine (30 Sept. 1984). Background reading and the quote 'a musical fantasy drama …': Club Sandwich # 28.

Financing: author's interviews and MPL company records.

21: TRIVIAL PURSUITS

Anita Howarth (née Cochrane): press coverage in the *Sun* (28 Jan. 1983) and other papers; author's interview with Peter Brown. Anita Howarth is quoted from the *Daily Star* (1 Feb. 1983).

McCartneys burn *The Love You Make*: interviewed in *Playboy* (Dec. 1984).

Hübers case: press coverage and author's correspondence with Bettina Hübers and her mother Erika.

PM loses at High Court: *Daily Mail* (15 Feb. 1983).

Jo Jo Laine story: *Sunday People* (17 April 1983).

PM blanks Jo Jo: author's discussion with her son Boston O'Donohue.

PM talks about Heather McCartney's punk phase: in the *Sunday Times*, for example, 16 May 1980.

The McCartneys buy their Arizona ranch: author's local research, Pima County real estate records and interviews with neighbours including Bob Bass and Erwin Eldon (both quoted).

PM – 'not that good with words' – *Club Sandwich* # 26.

Lord Puttnam on PM: quoted from author's interview.

Hübers loses paternity case: quoted from author's interview.

Barbados bust: author's interview with Eric and Gloria Stewart (quoted, and recalled dialogue).

PM talks about his drug use: *Daily Star* (19 Jan. 1984).

THE PIPES OF POT: *Daily Star* (18 Jan. 1984).

LM quoted from the *Guardian* report of her UK court appearance (5 Jan. 1984).

Denny Laine's story: the *Sun* (31 Jan.–3 Feb. 1984).

Final preparations and release of *Give My Regards to Broad Street*: author's interview with Peter Webb (quoted).

Hog Hill Mill: property records and author's interviews with neighbours and those who have visited the studio.

Reunited with Ann Ventre: author's interview.

Death of Meatloaf drummer: author's interview with his Cavendish Avenue landlady Lisa Voice; also *Knocking on Heaven's Door* (Talevski).

Release of *Broad Street*: author's interviews with Spencer Leigh, Eric Stewart and Peter Webb (all quoted). Review: *Daily Mail* (30 Nov. 1984).

The necessary fifth draft: PM quoted in his 1989–90 *Paul McCartney World Tour* booklet.

Rupert and the Frog Song: author's interview with Geoff Dunbar (quoted).

Ivor Novello Awards: BASCA.

Making *Press to Play*: author's interviews with Carlos Alomar, Hugh Padgham and Eric Stewart (all quoted).

Brian Moses on school dispute: quoted from author's interview. I also referred to Moses' letter to the *Teacher* (24 May 1985) and the *Daily Mirror* (6 June 1985), from which I quote: 'I had always admired him ...'

Live Aid: video tape of the show; *Is That It?* (Geldof), from which I quote Bob Geldof's letter to PM; PM's comments in *Club Sandwich* # 41 and the *Independent* (14 Dec. 1990).

PM's and GH's phone row: PM to *Sunday Express* (28 Oct. 1984).

Michael Jackson buys ATV Music: the *Guardian* (16 Aug. 1985).

Hugh Padgham quoted from author's interview.

'Press to Play' video: *Club Sandwich* # 80.

Eric Stewart quoted from author's interview.

22: THE NEXT BEST THING

PM hires Richard Ogden: thanks to Richard Ogden. Also *Club Sandwich* # 45.

LM to the Duke of Edinburgh: PM in *Hello!* (15 Aug. 1998).

LM's friendship with Carla Lane: author's interviews with Carla Lane (quoted throughout [also recalled dialogue between LM and Chrissie Hynde]).

LM's horses: author's interviews and the documentary *Appaloosa*, an MPL production broadcast on BBC2 (July 1994).

Ferdinand the bullock: *Club Sandwich* # 73.

Bob Languish quoted from author's interview.

James McCartney speaks at school about vegetarianism: Ray Fooks to author.

Animals rights songs: Carla Lane and the CD *Wide Prairie*.

LM's cookbook: I referred to quote from *Linda McCartney's Home Cooking*, and my discussion with Richard Ogden.

Making *CHOBA B CCCP*: thanks to Richard Ogden; also *Club Sandwich #* 49 and 'How the Beatles Rocked the Kremlin', a BBC *Storyville* documentary broadcast 7 Sept. 2009.

Fan club members given tickets for TV shows: *Club Sandwich #* 46. *Last Resort*: author's interview with Steve Nieve (quoted).

Aunt Ginny dies: death certificate.

Mike Robbins quoted from author's interview.

Christmas presents: author's interview with Joe Reddington (quoted).

Elvis Costello on working with PM: the *Independent* (18 June 1992).

New band: author's interview with Robbie McIntosh and Hamish Stuart (quoted). Also *Club Sandwich #* 50.

Wix – 'almost a veggie' – *Club Sandwich #* 53.

Band pay: author's interview with McIntosh.

PM's continued hurt about Denny Laine interview: author's interviews with band members.

The Beatles inducted into the Rock 'n' Roll Hall of Fame: author's interview with Danny Fields (quoted); *McCartney: The Biography* (Flippo); PM interview with *Rolling Stone*, (15 June 1989) and www.rockhall.com.

Founding LIPA: author's interview with Mark Featherstone-Witty (quoted [including 'a right bastard']); his books *Optimistic, Even Then* and *LIPA in Pictures: The First Ten Years*; and *Club Sandwich #* 60. Thanks also to Richard Ogden.

1989–90 world tour: author's first-hand experience and interviews with tour members including Geoff Baker, Robbie McIntosh, Richard Ogden and Hamish Stuart (quoted). Also the tour booklet (PM quoted from).

Collaboration with Barry Miles: author's interviews with Miles.

Heather McCartney's problems: author's enquiries in Arizona, including interview with Beverly Wilk (quoted). Press reports in the *Sunday Mirror* (12 Nov. 1989) and *Daily Express* (13 Nov. 1989) and Heather's comments to the *Sunday Times* (28 Nov. 1999), *Daily Telegraph* (4 Feb. 1999) and *The Times* (7 Aug. 1997 [quoted]).

Pottery connections in Rye: author's local enquiries.

Visa deal: Richard Ogden and *Rolling Stone* (8 Feb. 1990).

Ian James reunited with PM: author's interview with James (quoted).

Knebworth show: the bootleg.

World tour statistics: *Club Sandwich #* 55/56.

23: MUSIC IS MUSIC

Appearing in *Bread*: author's interview with Carla Lane.

PM's dialogue with Carl Davis, and Davis on authorship: *Sunday Times magazine* (9 June 1991).

The Liverpool Oratorio: *Club Sandwich #* 58 and the MPL documentary *Ghosts of the Past* (PM quoted). Thanks also to Carl Davis.

Walked out of *La Bohème*: *Paul McCartney: Many Years from Now* (Miles).

Ray Connolly interview: *Club Sandwich #* 12.

Schuller quotation from *The Rest is Noise* (Ross).

Collaborating with Miles: author's interview with Miles (quoted).

Making 'Pipes of Peace' video: *Club Sandwich #* 32.

MTV Unplugged: author's interviews with Robbie McIntosh and Hamish Stuart (quoted). Also discussions with Richard Ogden; and the recording of the show.

Sales of *Linda McCartney's Home Cooking*: *Sunday Mirror* magazine (14 April 1991).

On LM's frozen food: Alastair Cousin, Carla Lane and Mike Robbins (all quoted from author's interviews).

Traces of meat found: *Linda McCartney* (Fields); and LM to *OK!* (6 March 1998).

'Noratorio': PM to the *Sunday Times* (9 June 1991).

PM meets Michael Portillo MP: *Optimistic, Even Then* (Featherstone-Witty).

Oratorio reviewed: *Independent on Sunday* (20 June 1991).

Lee Eastman dies: *New York Times* obituary (2 Aug. 1991) and author's interview with Philip Sprayregen.

Rolls Royce gift: PM to *Harper's* (Nov. 1984).

MPL song catalogue: *Playboy* (Dec. 1984), and *Club Sandwich* # 80.

Writes 'Calico Skies': *Flaming Pie* liner notes.

Mark Featherstone-Witty on John Eastman and PM's impatience in Nov. 1991: *Optimistic, Even Then.*

LIPA fundraising: author's interview with Mark Featherstone-Witty (quoted); his book *Optimistic, Even Then* and *Club Sandwich* # 64.

The author saw a copy of PM's correspondence with Prince Charles. Featherstone-Witty says the Prince didn't donate.

George Harrison and LIPA: author's correspondence with Mark Featherstone-Witty.

Donald Warren-Knott quoted from author's interview.

Details of Mark Featherstone-Witty's relationship with PM, fundraising figures and 'gay' conversation with Richard Ogden, are from *Optimistic, Even Then* and author's discussions with Richard Ogden and Featherstone-Witty (both quoted).

Danny Fields quoted from author's interview.

Making *Off the Ground*: author's interviews with McIntosh (quoted) and Stuart; also *Club Sandwich* # 64 and 65.

The Fireman project: author's interview with Youth (quoted).

Grundig deal: author's interview with Mark Featherstone-Witty and *Optimistic, Even Then*. Also the LIPA ticket and backstage meetings with PM.

1993 US ticket sales: *The Paul McCartney Encyclopaedia* (Harry).

Richard Ogden leaves MPL: author's discussion with Ogden. PM on the decision to extend 1993 tour: *Club Sandwich* # 69.

Ivan Vaughan dies: death certificate; author's interview with his widow Janet (quoted).

'Ivan' is published in the book *Blackbird Singing*.

James McCartney surfing drama: the *Sun* (14 Sept. 1993).

MPL turnover: company records.

PM – 'I'm off to be a Beatle now' – author's interview with Hamish Stuart.

24: A THREE-QUARTERS REUNION

Neil Aspinall quoted from the *Daily Telegraph* (18 Nov.1995).

Anthology background: the *Anthology* Special Features DVD; *Barefaced Lies and Boogie-Woogie Boasts* (Holland); *Club Sandwich* # 72; *Beatles Unlimited* magazine # 124 (*Barnaby Rudge*); and *Sound on Sound* (Dec. 1995).

GH's financial problems: author's interviews; *George Harrison* (Clayson); *The Beatles Book* (March 1995). 'My Sweet Lord' court case: *All Things Must Pass* (Shapiro) and *The Encyclopaedia of Beatles People* (Harry). GH bails out *Life of Brian*: *Seventies* (Sounes).

PM – 'serious money' – off-the-record interview.

GH – 'the most ancient …' – *Anthology* (Special Features DVD).

PM's induction speech at the Rock 'n' Roll Hall of Fame: *Club Sandwich* # 69.

Campaign to induct PM: author's interview with Danny Fields (quoted), and his book *Linda McCartney*.

Recording 'Free as a Bird': the *Anthology* (Special Features DVD and CD Vol. 1 liner notes); and *Club Sandwich* # 72 and 76 (PM quoted).

GH on 'Free as a Bird': the *Anthology* (documentary).

Geoff Emerick quoted from discussion with the author.

George Martin quoted from *Sound on Sound* (Dec. 1995).

PM quoted on watching the footage and the choice of tracks on the *Anthology* (CD Vol. 1); *Club Sandwich* # 76.

Bob Smeaton quoted from *The Beatles Book* (Dec. 1995).

PM quoted on compiling the CD: *Club Sandwich* # 76.

PM's painting: *Paul McCartney: Paintings* and author's interview with Wolfgang Suttner (quoted).

LIPA progress: author's interview with Mark Featherstone-Witty (quoted), except 'He went on to …' which is from his book *Optimistic, Even Then.*

PM helps Horst Fascher: quoted from author's interview.

PM helps his local hospital and other charitable work: thanks to Ann Hostler at Rye Health Care Ltd. Also the *Independent on Sunday* (16 July 1999).

'Real Love'/Harrison's dissent: author's interviews and PM's comments to the *Sunday Express Boulevard* magazine (4 May 1997).

Third song: *The Beatles Book* (March 1996).

Recording new songs with Steve Miller and others: *Flaming Pie* liner notes.

Working with David Matthews: author's interview and correspondence with Matthews (quoted). Also *Independent on Sunday* (5 Oct. 1997).

PM performs at St James' Palace: *Club Sandwich* # 74.

PM works with Ginsberg and asks for help with 'Standing Stone': author's correspondence with Tom Pickard.

The Hodgsons' find: author's interviews with Peter Hodgson (quoted).

Heather McCartney Designs: company records.

Stella McCartney graduates: *Independent* magazine (28 Oct. 1995); *Stella May Day*: *The Unknown Paul McCartney* (Peel).

James McCartney's car accident: *Daily Mail* (4 May 1995); and *The Beatles Book* (June 1995).

Barry Miles quoted from author's interview.

Pete Best makes money at last: author's interviews.

GH – 'It sounds like them now …' – the *Anthology* (documentary).

The *Anthology* release: author's interviews; *The Beatles Book* (various editions); George Martin quoted from *Sound on Sound* (Dec. 1995); and author's interview with Hodgson.

MPL turnover: company records.

25: PASSING THROUGH THE DREAM OF LOVE

LM has cancer: PM's interview with the *Daily Mail* (17 Oct. 1998); *Garland for Linda* liner notes; author's interviews with Danny Fields and Carla Lane (quoted), and LM's death certificate.

LIPA cost: author's interview with Mark Featherstone-Witty, and his books.

What PM has and hasn't done for Liverpool: Dave Holt and Spencer Leigh quoted from author's interviews.

LIPA Inauguration: author's interview with Mark Featherstone-Witty and his book *LIPA the First Ten Years* (PM quoted).

Chemotherapy: *Daily Mirror* (23 Oct. 1998).

LM tries to get PM nominated: Danny Fields to author.

PM on his and LM's attempt to reverse the credit on 'Yesterday' for the *Anthology*: *Rolling Stone* (6 Dec. 2001).

Maureen Starkey dies: *The Beatles* (Davies [updated)]

LM's will: the document, dated 4 July 1996, filed in the Surrogate Court of New York (File # 179-99).

Standing Stone: author's interview and correspondence with David Matthews and Tom Pickard (both quoted); also *Paul McCartney: Paintings*.

PM buys High Ranachan Farm: author's interview with Alice and Duncan McLean (quoted).

James McCartney records 'Heaven on a Sunday' with parents: *Flaming Pie* liner notes; and PM's interview with the *Sunday Express Boulevard* magazine (4 May 1997 [James McCartney quote]).

Knighthood: author's interview with Featherstone-Witty (quoted).

PM revealed the watch inscription at LM's London memorial, the *Sun* (9 June 1998).

Mary McCartney quoted from the *Daily Express* (12 March 1997).

Rushes: author's interview with Youth (quoted).

Conclusion of the Anita Cochrane story: newspaper coverage including mother and son's interviews with the *Daily Mail* (31 May and 2 June 1997); author's discussion with Philip Howarth; also interview with relative Ian Pillans.

LM treated by Larry Norton: Danny Fields interview.

Confrontation at Plaza Athénée: author's interview with Linda Aiello (quoted).

Cancer spreads: PM interview with *Daily Mail* (17 Oct. 1998).

McCartneys upset by the death of Tim Buckley: author's interview with Danny Fields.

GH cancer: *All Things Must Pass* (Shapiro), and *Knocking on Heaven's Door* (Talevski).

Associates die: author's interviews; *The Beatles* (Davies [updated]) and *Knocking on Heaven's Door* (Talevski).

PM's appearance at 1997 Buddy Holly Week: *Club Sandwich* # 83.

Last-minute changes to *Standing Stone*: David Matthews quoted from author's interview; PM on Kent Nagano from his interview with the *Independent on Sunday* (5 Oct. 1997).

Danny Fields's last meeting with LM: author's interview (also subsequent quotes).

Barbecue in Arizona: author's interview with Beverly Wilk (quoted). Christmas at Blossom Farm: details that emerged during LM's London memorial service, *Daily Mail* (9 June 1998); and author's interview with Walter van Dijk (quoted).

LM quit smoking marijuana: PM to Chrissie Hynde in *USA Weekend* (30 Oct. 1998).

Final discussions with Carla Lane/ recalled dialogue: author's interview.

Rescued puppies: the *Daily Mail* (4 Oct. 1997).

PM transfers property to Heather's name: property records.

Final recording sessions: *Wide Prairie* liner notes.

LM's last days and death: death certificate; author's local enquiries in Arizona, press reports including PM's interview with the *Daily Mail* (17 Oct. 1998).

PM's last words to LM: his statement released at her death (21 April 1998); also *Beatles Unlimited* # 141.

26: RUN DEVIL RUN

LM's funeral: Arizona death certificate and author's local enquires.

Geoff Baker dissembles: press cuttings and author's discussions with Baker.

Carla Lane and Geoff Dunbar quoted from author's interviews.

In extremis: PM on *Breakfast with Frost* (7 Dec. 1997, reprinted in *The Beatles Book* [Jan. 1998]), saying his wife's illness made them 'talk to God, or It, a little more often'.

London and New York memorials: press coverage and author's interviews and correspondence with mourners including Carla Lane, Danny Fields, John McGeachy, Lord Puttnam, Eric Stewart and Pete Townshend (quoted on his speech).

Works with Nitin Sawhney: author's interview with Sawhney (quoted).

Attends LIPA graduation: author's interviews with Mark Featherstone-Witty and Joe Flannery (both quoted).

Heather McCartney's signature missing: court documents. That she arrived in Tucson too late to say goodbye to her mother was reported in the *Sunday Times* (26 April 1998).

PM buys Amagansett property: author's local enquiries; also Justice Bennett's March 2008 High Court judgment in the McCartney divorce (hereafter referred to as the Bennett judgment).

James McCartney at sister Mary's wedding: author's interview with church warden Walter Piggott.

PM on 'The Light Comes from Within': *Wide Prairie* liner notes.

PM fires Reddington: author's interview with Reddington (quoted).

Effect of LM's death on Heather and James McCartney: author's interviews including Beverly Wilk (Heather) and friends and neighbours in Sussex (James).

Heather McCartney launches household range: quoted from the *Daily Telegraph* (4 Feb. 1999) and her 1999 Atlanta press conference (*The Paul McCartney Encyclopaedia*).

Heather said she felt life wasn't worth living: quoted in the *Sunday Times* (28 Nov. 1999).

Signatures on probate documents: LM's will, Surrogate Court, New York, File # 179-99.

Arthur Donald born: birth certificate.

Danny Fields quoted from author's interview (includes comment by Hynde to Fields).

German exhibition: author's interview with Wolfgang Suttner. Also *Paul McCartney: Paintings*.

Brian Sewell quoted from correspondence with the author.

PM meets Heather Mills (HM): her revised memoir, *A Single Step*, and coverage of the Pride of Britain Awards in *OK!* magazine (11 June 1999).

PM's dialogue with Piers Morgan is quoted from his book, *The Insider*.

The Heather Mills Health Trust: *Out on a Limb*; www.charity-commission.gov.uk, and charity commission documentation; HM's 17 Nov. 1999 interview with Pete Norman for *People* magazine in which she talks of 'the/my charity' prior to its registration. Thanks also to Sarah Nelson at the Charity Commission.

PM on animal noises: *Rolling Stone* (6 Dec. 2001).

HM's background story: primarily based on her book *Out on a Limb*; also author's interviews with Alfie Karmal (quoted), and the 2003 Channel 4 documentary *Heather Mills: The Real Mrs McCartney*, from which Charles Stapley is quoted.

HM is likened to Princess Diana: *OK!* (9 Feb. 1997); Paralympics: *Hello!* (22 July 1995): Nobel nomination: HM interview with Pete Norman, 1999; film of her life/ministerial ambition: *Daily Mail* (17 Jan. 1998).

Garland for Linda: liner notes of the *Garland for Linda* CD, and author's interviews and correspondence with David Matthews and Sir John Tavener.

PM's developing relationship with HM is based primarily on the Bennett judgment (unless otherwise indicated).

Engagement to Terrill: *The [Daily] Mirror* (5 July 1999). HM jilts Terrill: various press reports including *News of the World* (7 Nov. 1999).

HM goes to Long Island with PM: Bennett judgment.

Hallowe'en tryst: described by HM in *A Single Step*.

Bonfire night: *News of the World* (7 Nov. 1999).

Fountain: author's interview with Carla Lane.

Cavern show: *Live at the Cavern Club* DVD (MPL, 2000) and *The Cavern* (Leigh).

Christmas and New Year with PM: *A Single Step* (HM quote); and author's interview with Mike Robbins (quoted).

Parrot Cay: *A Single Step* and Bennett judgment.

Mel See's decline, death and burial: author's interviews with Jonathan Kress, Beverly Wilk (quoted) and the Zeller family; Mel See's will; and records of the Evergreen Mortuary and Cemetery, Tucson, AZ. Thanks also to Lt Deanna Coultas of the Pima County Sheriff's Office in Arizona (quoted).

Veronica Languish is quoted from author's interview.

Alfie Karmal tells his story: *Sunday People* (9 April 2000).

HM a 'party girl': Ros Ashley in the *Mail on Sunday* (23 April 2000).

Mike Robbins quoted from author's interview.

Linda Aiello quoted from author's interview.

Indian trip: Bennett judgment. Also thanks to Pete Norman.

Recording *Driving Rain*: liner notes.

'Heather House' and purchase of Angel's Rest: Bennett judgment.

PM on working with Linda: *Wingspan* documentary (MPL, 2001).

Adrian Mitchell quoted from his introduction to *Blackbird Singing* (McCartney).

Working on *Ecce Cor Meum*: author's interview with David Matthews and Anthony Smith (quoted).

Anthony Smith, Eric Stewart, Tony Bramwell and Mark Featherstone-Witty on HM: all quoted from author's interviews.

Proposal and engagement: HM describes in *A Single Step*; also the Bennett judgment. Thanks to Pete Norman.

27: THAT DIFFICULT SECOND MARRIAGE

PM witnesses 9/11: *A Single Step* (Mills) and PM's interview with *Rolling Stone* (3 May 2007).

'Urgent charity commitments' and HM to PM: *A Single Step*.

HM helped write 'Freedom': *Each One Believing*.

Concert for New York: *A Single Step* (Mills); footage of the show, and author's interview with a VH-1 executive who did not wish to be named. Thanks also to Pete Townshend (quoted from correspondence with author).

Decline and death of GH: author's interview with Neil Innes (quoted); GH's death certificate; *A Single Step* (Mills).

First performance of *Ecce Cor Meum*: author's interviews with David Matthews and Anthony Smith (quoted).

PM's reaction to death of GH: videotape of his meeting with the press.

Financial generosity with HM: Bennett judgment.

HM's ignorance of Beatles songs: PM to *Reader's Digest* (Nov. 2001).

Tour routine: *Each One Believing*; *Back in the USA* DVD (PM and Wix quoted, and Brian Ray observation).

PM was reported saying Heather walked out of show rehearsals when he played 'a song I wrote for Linda': *Mail on Sunday* (5 Nov. 2006).

Defenestrated ring: *News of the World* (2 June 2002).

Golden Jubilee concert: television coverage.

PM marries HM: marriage certificate, press coverage, author's correspondence with Sir John Leslie (quoted); and author's interviews with guests Geoff Baker, Mike Robbins and Nitin Sawhney (last two quoted).

Details emerged about PM's behaviour leading up to the wedding day: Bennett judgment.

Walker Art Gallery: author's interview with Gillian Reynolds (quoted).

Heather Mills McCartney to Barbara Walters: *Sunday Express* (2 Oct. 2002). Also Walters on *the View* (25 April 2007).

LA row: quotes are from HM's response to PM's divorce petition, leaked to the press in Oct. 2006 and widely reported.

HM to Larry King: BBC News online (1 Nov. 2002).

Kintyre memorial: author's interview with Alastair Cousin (quoted). Thanks also to former town councillor George McMillan.

Song credits on *Back in the US*: liner notes.

RS quote: the *Sun* (12 Jan. 2008).

Concert for George: DVD of the show (Oops Publishing Ltd, 2003); and author's interviews with Neil Innes and Ravi Shankar (quoted).

Ray Connolly review: *Daily Mail* (28 March 2003).

PM to *Daily Mirror* – 'Heather said to me ...': edition of 7 April 2003.

Money given to HM and miscarriage: Bennett judgment.

Channel 4 documentary: *Heather Mills: The Real Mrs McCartney* (broadcast 7 May 2003).

Rome row: quotes are from HM's response to PM's divorce petition, leaked to the press in Oct. 2006 and widely reported.

Astrid Kirchherr on HM: quoted from author's interview.

Stella McCartney's opposition to HM: author's interviews and press reports.

Red Square show: *Each One Believing* (PM quoted).

Amagansett folk on Heather Mills: author's interviews with Alda Lupo Stipanoe and a library worker who didn't wish to be named (both quoted).

Long Island row: the quote is from HM's response to PM's divorce petition, leaked to the press in Oct. 2006 and widely reported.

Living at Woodlands Farm: author's local interviews.

Construction of the pavilion and lodge/ Cabin: planning records and Bennett judgment.

Ketchup fight: *News of the World* (22 Oct. 2006).

David Blaine incident: author's interviews with Geoff Baker and Kevin Wheal (both quoted); and coverage in the *Daily Mirror* and *Sun* (20 Sept. 2003).

Birth of Beatrice McCartney: birth certificate.

28: WHEN PAUL WAS SIXTY-FOUR

The Cabin is finished/PM's generosity to wife: Bennett judgment.

Dinner party: author's interview with Nitin Sawhney (quoted).

Thirteen homes: Bennett judgment and author's enquiries in the UK and USA.

Larry King Live booking: Bennett judgment.

HM's complaints: quoted from HM's response to PM's divorce petition, leaked to the press.

Glastonbury Festival: author's interview with Michael Eavis (quoted); film of the show (PM quoted) and BBC News Online coverage.

PM's interest in ley lines, etc.: his comments on stage at Glastonbury; interviews and author's correspondence with Geoff Baker (astrology).

Heather and Baker not talking/Baker fired: author's discussion with Baker (quoted); also Mail on Sunday (12 Sept. 2004).

HM and the Sunday Times article: HM's response to PM's divorce petition, leaked to the press.

PM on Baker: his 2005 statement at www.heathermillsmccartney.com. Also PM's defence of his wife.

PM tells Nigel Goodrich to 'fuck off': Rolling Stone (20 Oct. 2005).

PM had The Pilgrim's Progress as a child: New Yorker (4 June 2007). Refusal to say who he had in mind for 'Riding to Vanity Fair': Observer Music Monthly (Sept. 2005).

New York building/row: New York public records and Bennett judgment.

Money and gifts given by PM to wife and her requests to Paul Winn for money to clear a nonexistent mortgage: Bennett judgment, in which Justice Bennett revealed that Sir Paul's QC had 'put to [Heather in court] that that was a fraudulent attempt to extract money from the husband …' The Judge decided it didn't go as far as fraud. 'However, it is not an episode that does her any credit whatsoever.' See also Chapter 29.

PM at St John's Wood Church: thanks to church worker Christine Barnwell.

Planning application: Rother District Council.

Posing with seals: Hello! (14 March 2006).

HM asks MPL again for money: Bennett judgment.

Events leading up to separation: HM's response to PM's divorce petition, leaked to the press.

Separation date/purchase of Pandora's Barn: Bennett judgment.

Separation statement: BBC News online (17 May 2006).

PORN SHAME story: the Sun (5 June 2006).

£5K HOOKER story: the News of the World (11 June 2006).

Love: All Together Now documentary (2008).

PM turns 64: Sunday Mirror (18 June 2006) and PM's interview with The Times (14 Dec. 2007).

PM files for divorce, etc: Bennett judgment.

HM locked out of Cavendish: Evening Standard (8 Aug. 2006).

Justice Bennett quoted on 'very strong terms' from his High Court judgment.

Ernst & Young audit: Bennett judgment.

Leaking of the cross-petition, contents and aftermath: Evening Standard and Daily Mail (18 Oct. 2006); Press Gazette (27 Oct. 2006); The Times (24 Oct. 2006) and the Sunday Times (5 Nov. 2006). Also Bennett judgment.

Defamation action never came to trial: Heather Mills McCartney vs. News Group, Queen's Bench, # HQ06X03218 (stayed).

PM's lawyers respond: the Sun (19 Oct. 2006).

Danny Fields and Eric Stewart quoted from author's interview.

Brian Brolly dies: death certificate.

Beatrice McCartney's third birthday: News of the World and Mail on Sunday reports (29 Oct. 2006).

Jonathan Ross quip: Daily Mail (31 Oct. 2006).

Première of Ecce Cor Meum: DVD of the première; author's interview with Anthony Smith. Independent review by Michael Church (4 Nov. 2006).

Family trouble: author's interviews.

Mike Robbins quoted from author's interview.

Christmas/new year divorce negotiations: Bennett judgment.

29: THE EVER-PRESENT PAST

McCartney divorce: Bennett judgment.

PM leaves EMI: *The Times* (15 Dec. 2007) and the *New Yorker* (4 June 2007).

Writes 'The End of the End': *Interview* (July 2007).

US Government vs. Vincente Gigante, Myron Shevell and others: Case # 88-4396 (thanks to the US Dept of Labor). The author also referred to www.nemf.com, Bruce Blakeman's law firm site, www.abramslaw.com, and spoke with Myron Shevell's ex-wife Jane.

Nitin Sawhney quoted from author's interview.

HM on *GMTV*; video tape of 31 Oct. 2007 show.

HM's donation to Viva!: Bennett judgment. The organisation's lack of charitable status at the time was confirmed by Tony Wardle of Viva!

PM quote – 'As Winston Churchill once ...' – the *Radio Times* (Oct. 2007).

At the Royal Courts of Justice: author's notes and the Bennett judgment.

Fan asks PM for autograph at High Court: *Daily Telegraph* (16 Feb. 2008).

Death of Jon Shevell: death certificate.

Final hearings in the McCartney divorce: author's notes and Bennett judgment.

HM statement on the High Court steps: author's notes.

Maccagate story: the *Sunday Mirror* (4 Nov. 2007).

Fiona Mills at court to author (quoted).

Wikipedia manipulation: author's

interview with a Mills employee who wished to speak off the record.

Neil Aspinall dies: AP obituary (24 March 2008) and author's interview with Peter Brown (quoted).

RS comments on Jonathan Ross show and reaction: *Liverpool Echo* (21 Jan. 2008).

Cabbie to author.

PM's June 2008 tour of Liverpool: author's notes and interviews including 'Brickhead' John Halliday (both quoted).

YO at Mendips/LIPA fashion show (May 2008): author's notes. Mark Featherstone-Witty quoted from author's interview.

Liverpool Sound concert: author's notes and interviews with fellow attendees including Joe Flannery, Sam Leach and Brenda Rothwell (last two quoted).

PM – 'I think it's basically magic ...' – *Rolling Stone* (3 May 2007).

Third Fireman album: author's interview with Youth and Linda Aiello (quoted).

US ticket grosses: *Los Angeles Times* (31 Dec. 2009).

PM on Michael Jackson's death: www. paulmccartney.com.

PM in Paris: *Evening Standard* (5 Oct. 2009).

Guitar Concerto: *New Yorker* (4 June 2007).

PM the driving force behind Beatles Rock Band: Yoko Ono to the [*Daily*] *Telegraph magazine* (19 Sept. 2009).

Biggest acts of decade: the *Guardian* (9 Dec. 2010).

High in the Clouds: the book and author's interview with Geoff Dunbar (quoted).

Hamburg show: author's notes.

BIBLIOGRAPHY

Arnason, HH. *A History of Modern Art*. London: Thames & Hudson, 1988.

Badman, Keith. *The Beatles Off the Record*. London: Omnibus Press, 2000.

Barrow, Tony. *John, Paul, George, Ringo and Me*. London: André Deutsch, 2006.

Barrow, Tony and Robin Bextor (Julian Newby, ed.). *Paul McCartney: Now and Then*. London: Carlton Publishing, 2004.

[The] Beatles. *Anthology.* London: Cassell, 2000.

Bedford, Carol. *Waiting for the Beatles: An Apple Scruff's Story*. Poole (UK): Blandford Press, 1984.

Belchem, John, ed. *Liverpool 800: Culture Character & History*. Liverpool: Liverpool University Press, 2006.

Benson, Ross. *Paul McCartney Behind the Myth*. London: Gollancz, 1993.

Best, Pete and Patrick Doncaster. *Beatle! The Pete Best Story*. London: Plexus, 1985.

Brown, Peter and Steven Gaines. *The Love You Make*. New York: Putnam, 2002.

Boyd, Pattie with Penny Junor. *Wonderful Today*. London: Hodder Headline, 2007.

Bracewell, Michael. *Re-make/Re-model: Art, Pop, Fashion and the Making of Roxy Music 1953–1972*. London: Faber & Faber, 2007.

Bramwell, Tony with Rosemary Kingsland. *Magical Mystery Tours: My Life with the Beatles*. London: Robson Books, 2005.

Carlin, Peter Ames. *Paul McCartney: A Life*. London: Robson Books, 2009.

Clapton, Eric. *Eric Clapton: The Autobiography*. London: Arrow Books, 2008.

Clayson, Alan. *George Harrison*. London: Sanctuary, 2001.

Clayson, Alan. *Ringo Starr: Straight Man or Joker?* London: Sidgwick & Jackson, 1991.

Coleman, Ray. *Brian Epstein: The Man Who Made the Beatles*. London: Viking, 1989.

Coleman, Ray. *McCartney Yesterday & Today*. London: Boxtree, 1995.

Crick, Michael. *Jeffrey Archer: Stranger than Fiction*. London: Hamish Hamilton, 1995.

Cunningham, Ian. *A Reader's Guide to Writers' London*. London: Prion Books, 2001.

Davies, Hunter. *The Beatles*. London: Jonathan Cape, 1985 (revised edn).

Davies, Hunter. *The Quarrymen*. London: Omnibus, 2001.

Davis, Stephen. *Old Gods Almost Dead: The 40-Year Odyssey of the Rolling Stones*. London: Aurum, 2006.

Dean, Johnny, ed. *The Best of the Beatles Book*. London: Beat Publications, 2005.

DiLello, Richard. *The Longest Cocktail Party*. London: Charisma Books, 1973.

Draper, Robert. *The Rolling Stone Story*. Edinburgh: Mainstream, 1990.

Ellis, Geoffrey. *I Should Have Known Better: A Life in Pop Management*. London: Thorogood, 2004.

Emerick, Geoff with Howard Massey. *Here, There and Everywhere: My Life Recording the Music of the Beatles*. New York: Gotham Books, 2007.

Epstein, Brian. *A Cellarful of Noise*. London: New English Library, 1965.

Esslin, Martin. *The Theatre of the Absurd*. London: Methuen, 2001.

Faithfull, Marianne with David Dalton. *Faithfull*. London: Penguin Books, 1995.

Featherstone-Witty, Mark. *LIPA in Pictures: The First Ten Years*. Liverpool: LIPA Press, 2006.

Featherstone-Witty, Mark. *Optimistic, Even Then: The Creation of Two Performing Arts Institutes*. London: SPA Press, 2001.

Fields, Danny. *Linda McCartney: The Biography*. London: Little, Brown, 2000.

Fletcher, Tony. *Dear Boy: The Life of Keith Moon*. London: Omnibus Press, 1999.

Flippo, Chet. *McCartney: The Biography*. London: Sidgwick & Jackson, 1988.

Gaines, Steven. *Heroes and Villains: The True Story of the Beach Boys*. London: Macmillan, 1986.

Geldof, Bob. *Is That It?* Harmondsworth (UK): Penguin, 1986.

Gentle, Johnny and Ian Forsyth. *Johnny Gentle & The Beatles: First Ever Tour*. Runcorn (UK): Merseyrock Publications, 1998.

Giuliano, Geoffrey. *Blackbird: The Unauthorized Biography of Paul McCartney*. London: Smith Gryphon, 1991.

Goldman, Albert. *The Lives of John Lennon*. London: Bantam, 1988.

Guralnick, Peter. *Careless Love: The Unmaking of Elvis Presley*. London: Little, Brown, 1999.

Harrison, George. *I Me Mine*. London: Phoenix, 2004 (1st edn 1980).

Harry, Bill. *The Encyclopedia of Beatles People*. London: Blandford, 1997.

Harry, Bill. *The John Lennon Encyclopedia*. London: Virgin, 2000.

Harry, Bill. *Mersey Beat: The Beginnings of the Beatles*. London: Omnibus Press, 1977.

Harry, Bill. *The Paul McCartney Encyclopedia*. London: Virgin, 2002.

Hayward, Mark. *The Beatles Unseen*. London: Weidenfeld & Nicolson, 2005.

Holland, Jools. *Barefaced Lies and Boogie-Woogie Boasts*. London: Penguin, 2007.

Humphrey-Smith, Cecil R. with Michael H. Heenan and Jenifer Mount. *Up the Beatles' Family Tree*. Canterbury (UK): Achievements Ltd, 1966.

Ifield, Frank with Pauline Halford. *I Remember Me: The First 25 Years*. Hertford (UK): Kempton Marks, 2005.

Kirchherr, Astrid and Klaus Voormann (compiled by Ulf Krüger). *Hamburg Days*. Guildford (UK): Genesis, 1999.

Krüger, Ulf. *Beatles Guide Hamburg*. Hamburg: Europa Verlag, 2001.

Leach, Sam. *The Rocking City*. Gwyneddd (UK): Pharoah Press, 1999.

Leigh, Spencer. *The Cavern: The Most Famous Club in the World*. London: SAF, 2006.

Lennon, Cynthia. *John*. London: Hodder & Stoughton, 2005.

Lewis, David. *The Illustrated History of Liverpool's Suburbs*. Derby (UK): Breedon Books, 2003.

Lewisohn, Mark. *The Beatles' London*. London: Portico, 1998 (revised edn).

Lewisohn, Mark. *The Complete Beatles Chronicle*. London: Hamlyn, 2000.

Lewisohn, Mark. *The Complete Beatles Recording Sessions*. London: Hamlyn, 1989.

Lipton, Peggy with David and Coco Dalton. *Breathing Out*. New York: St Martin's Press, 2005.

Loewenstein, Dora and Philip Dodd, eds. *According to the Rolling Stones*. London: Phoenix, 2003.

Loog Oldham, Andrew. *Stoned*. London: Secker & Warburg, 2000.

Lowe, Jacques, ed. *The Incredible Music Machine*. London: Quartet Books, 1982.

MacDonald, Ian. *Revolution in the Head: The Beatles' Records and the Sixties*. London: Pimlico, 1995.

Marks, J. *Rock and Other Four Letter Words*. New York: Bantam, 1968.

Martin, George. *All You Need is Ears*. New York: St Martin's Press, 1979.

McCartney, Linda. *Linda's Pictures*. London: Pavilion, 1976.

McCartney, Linda and Peter Cox. *Linda McCartney's Home Cooking*. London: Bloomsbury, 1989.

McCartney, Linda. *Sixties: Portrait of an Era*. London: Pyramid Books, 1992.

McCartney, Mike. *Remember*. London: Merehurst, 1992.

McCartney, Mike. *Thank U Very Much: Mike McCartney's Family Album*. St Albans (UK): Granada, 1982.

McCartney, Paul. *Blackbird Singing: Paul McCartney, Poems and Lyrics 1965–1999*. London: Faber & Faber, 2001.

McCartney, Paul, Geoff Dunbar and Philip Ardagh. *High in the Clouds*. London: Faber & Faber, 2003.

McNab, Ken. *The Beatles in Scotland*. Edinburgh: Polygon, 2008.

Miles, Barry. *The Beatles: A Diary*. London: Omnibus Press, 2007.

Miles, Barry. *In the Sixties*. London: Jonathan Cape, 2002.

Miles, Barry. *Paul McCartney: Many Years from Now*. London: Vintage, 1998.

Mills, Heather with Pamela Cockerill. *Out on a Limb*. London: Little, Brown, 1995.

Mills McCartney, Heather with Pamela Cockerill. *A Single Step*. New York: Warner Books, 2002.

Morgan, Piers. *The Insider*. London: Ebury Press, 2005.

MPL Communications Ltd. *Each One Believing: Paul McCartney On Stage, Off Stage and Backstage*. San Francisco: Chronicle Books, 2004.

Norman, Philip. *John Lennon: The Life*. London: HarperCollins, 2008.

Norman, Philip. *Shout! The True Story of the Beatles*. London: Elm Tree Books, 1981.

Norman, Philip. *Symphony for the Devil: The Rolling Stones Story*. New York: Linden Press, 1984.

O'Dell, Denis with Bob Neaverson. *At the Apple's Core: The Beatles from the Inside*. London: Peter Owen, 2002.

Orton, Joe, John Lahr, ed. *The Orton Diaries*. London: Methuen, 1986.

Peel, Ian. *The Unknown Paul McCartney: McCartney and the Avant-garde*. Richmond (UK): Reynolds & Hearn, 2002.

Ricks, Christopher, ed. *The Oxford Book of English Verse*. Oxford: Oxford University Press, 1999.

Roach, Kevin. *The McCartneys: In the Town Where They Were Born*. Liverpool: Trinity Mirror, 2009.

Roberts, David, ed. *Guinness World Records [Book of] British Hit Singles*. London: Guinness World Records, 2002.

Ross, Alex. *The Rest is Noise: Listening to the Twentieth Century*. London: Fourth Estate, 2008.

Ross, Robert. *Monty Python Encyclopedia*. London: Batsford, 2001.

Salewicz, Chris. *McCartney*. London: Futura, 1987.

Sandbrook, Dominic. *White Heat: A History of Britain in the Swinging Sixties*. London: Little, Brown, 2006.

Sandford, Christopher. *McCartney*. London: Century, 2006.

Schumacher, Michael. *Eric Clapton*. London: Sphere, 1998.

Schwartz, Francie. *Body Count*. San Francisco: Straight Arrow Books, 1972.

Shales, Tom with James Andrew Miller. *Live from New York*. Boston: Black Bay Books, 2002.

Shankar, Ravi. *My Life, My Music*. London: Jonathan Cape, 1969.

Shapiro, Marc. *All Things Must Pass: The Life of George Harrison*. London: Virgin, 2002.

Sharples, Joseph. *Liverpool*. New Haven (US): Yale University Press, 2004.

Sounes, Howard. *Down the Highway: The Life of Bob Dylan*. New York: Grove, 2001.

Sounes, Howard. *Seventies: The Sights, Sounds and Ideas of a Brilliant Decade*. London: Simon & Schuster, 2006.

Spinetti, Victor with Peter Rankin ... *up front*. London: Portico, 2008.

Spitz, Bob. *The Beatles: The Biography*. New York: Little, Brown, 2005.

Starr, Ringo. *Postcards from the Boys*. London: Cassell Illustrated, 2005.

Strong, Martin C. *The Great Rock Discography*. Edinburgh: Canongate, 1999.

Sutcliffe, Pauline and Douglas Thompson. *The Beatles' Shadow: Stuart Sutcliffe and his Lonely Hearts Club Band*. London: Pan, 2002.

Talevski, Nick. *Knocking on Heaven's Door*. London: Omnibus Press, 2006.

Taylor, Derek. *Fifty Years Adrift*. Guildford (UK): Genesis, 1984.

Thackeray, W.M. *Vanity Fair*. New York: Everyman, 1908 (st edn 1848).

Tremlett, George. *The Paul McCartney Story*. London: Futura, 1975.

Vollmer, Jürgen. *The Beatles in Hamburg.* München (Germany): Schirmer/Mosel, 2004.

Vollmer, Jürgen. *From Hamburg to Hollywood.* Guildford (UK): Genesis, 1997.

Whitburn, Joel, ed. *The Billboard Book of Top 40 Hits.* New York: Billboard, 1996.

Williams, Allan and William Marshall. *The Man Who Gave the Beatles Away.* London: Elm Tree Books, 1975.

Woolf, Virginia. *Flush.* London: Persephone, 2005 (1st edn 1933).

Wyman, Bill with Ray Coleman. *Stone Alone: The Story of a Rock 'n' Roll Band.* London: Viking, 1990.

INDEX

'Children Children' 342

children's songs 143–4, 179, 397
  see also 'Rupert and the Frog Song';
    'We All Stand Together'; 'Yellow
    Submarine'

Chloé 469, 474

CHOBA B CCCP 412, 415, 496

A Chorus Line 348

Chris (Scruff) 246, 259

Christianity, John Lennon's
  comments on 152–4, 175

Christians, the 442

'The Christmas Song' 433

Cincinnati 110

Citi Fields 560

City of Birmingham Symphony
  Orchestra 475

Civil Rights 213

Civil, Alan 144

Clapton, Eric 118, 238, 261, 263, 302,
  320, 351, 430, 447, 449, 508, 519,
  537, 563

Clarke, Brian 420, 482, 488

Clarke, Stanley 373

Clarkson, Lana 272

Clash, the 345

classical music see Ecce Cor Meum;
  Liverpool Oratorio; McCartney,
  Paul

Cleave, Maureen 152–3, 175

Cliff Richard and the Shadows 67

Cliveden House 124

Cloud Nine 451

Club Sandwich 333, 412, 452

Coates, John 179

Coburn, James 313

cocaine 171, 177, 184, 320, 393, 447

Cochran, Eddie 19, 30, 86

Cochrane (later Howarth), Anita (and
  Philip) 107–9, 387, 473

Cochrane, Ian 108

Cochrane, Violet 107

Cogan, Alma 125

'Cold Turkey' 135

Coldwater Canyon 318, 319

Coleman, Ray 124, 241–2, 427

Collins, Phil 399, 404

Colman, Sid 57–8

Color Line Arena, the 561

Colosseum 521

Columbia Record label 55, 68

Colville, Rory 281–2

Colvilles, the 314

'Come and Get it' 204

'Come Go With Me' 22, 449

'Come On' (Chuck Berry) 86

'Come Together' 261, 458–9

'Coming Up' 354, 363

'Commonwealth Song' 240

computer-generated sheet music 459

Concerts for Kampuchea 354–5

Connolly, Ray 427, 519

Conteh, John 313

'The Continuing Story of Bungalow
  Bill' 209

'Cook of the House' 327

cookbooks, Linda's 410–11, 419, 430,
  477, 537

Cooke, Sam 242

Cooper, Michael 169

Corbett, Harry H. 124

'Coronation Day' (essay) 12, 516

Costello, Elvis 414–15, 437, 458

Coultas, Lieutenant Deanna 498

Country Dances (Benjamin Britten)
  427

'Country Hams' 316

County Monaghan 4, 514

Cousin, Alastair 314, 430, 518

Coutt's 114, 307, 510, 529

Cow Palace, San Francisco 109

'Cow' 410

Cox, Maureen see Starkey, Maureen
  (Mo) (née Cox)

Cox, Tony and Kyoka 207

Cream 449

'Crippled Inside' 290

Crossroads 318

Crowder, Alan 'the Crowd' Crowder
  333, 337, 356, 413

'Crying in the Chapel' (Elvis Presley)
  133

PICTURE CREDITS